D0747355

John Wesley's Sermons

An Anthology

San Diego Christian College
2100 Greenfield Drive
El Cajon, CA 92019

252
W513j

John Wesley's Sermons

An Anthology

Edited by

Albert C. Outler

&

Richard P. Heitzenrater

ABINGDON PRESS
NASHVILLE

JOHN WESLEY'S SERMONS: AN ANTHOLOGY

Compilation and Preface Copyright © 1991 by Abingdon Press.
Sermon texts reprinted from *The Works of John Wesley*, Volumes 1–4: *Sermons I–IV*, Copyright © 1984, 1985, 1986, 1987 by Abingdon Press.

All rights reserved.
No part of this book may be reproduced or transmitted in any form or by any means, electronic or mechanical, including photocopying and recording, or by any information storage or retrieval system, excerpt as may be expressly permitted by the 1976 Copyright Act or in writing from the publisher. Requests for permission should be addressed in writing to Abingdon Press, 201 Eighth Avenue, South, Nashville, TN 37203, U.S.A..

Library of Congress Cataloging-in-Publication Data

Wesley, John, 1703–1791
[Sermons. Selections]
John Wesley's Sermons: An Anthology / edited by Albert C. Outler and Richard P. Heitzenrater
p. cm.
"Originally published in 'The Works of John Wesley,' volumes 1–4: Sermons I-IV (Nashville: Abingdon Press. 1984–1987)"—T.p. verso
ISBN 0-687-20495-X (alk. paper)
1. Methodist Church—Sermons. 2. Sermons, English. I. Outler, Albert C., 1908–1989. II. Heitzenrater, Richard P., 1939- . III. Title
BX8333.W418S39 1991 91-23773
252'.07–dc20 CIP

00 01 02 03 04 — 10 9

Printed in the United States of America on acid-free paper

Cover illustration, from a ceramic of John Wesley by Josiah Wedgewood, reproduced by permission of the Methodist Archives and History Committee, England

To Carla Outler

CONTENTS

PREFACE

In his *Journal* in 1757, John Wesley made the comment, 'I do indeed *live* by preaching.' He had long before recognized, 'My tongue is a devoted thing.' Preaching was a primary means by which the Good News was spread in the Methodist Revival. But Wesley also recognized that written sermons, in published form, provided an excellent medium for nurture and reflection among his people. He began to publish sermons (many of them never preached as such) in 1746 with an eye toward helping the reader 'see in the clearest manner what those doctrines are which I embrace and teach as the essentials of true religion.'

Wesley stated in his Preface to the collection (*Sermons on Several Occasions*) that the three volumes of sermons, published in 1746, 1748, and 1750, contained 'the substance of what I have been preaching for between eight and nine years last past'. Most of the works were newly written or re-written, except for the first four sermons in volume one, which had been preached before the university at Oxford in 1738 or later (one of which was actually Charles's). His earlier sermons, some of them already published separately but most of them unpublished, were omitted from that first collected edition, since his own perception at the time was that he had not been an 'altogether' Christian before 1737–38.

In 1760, Wesley published yet another volume of *Sermons on Several Occasions* (though not numbered '4') to bring the total number of sermons in the four volumes to forty-three. A decade later, when he decided to publish his collected *Works*, he began the series with four volumes of sermons that included ten additional sermons that he had written and/or preached since 1760.

In the 1770s and 1780s, Wesley wrote more new sermons than he had previously published. Many of these he printed (in two instalments each) in his *Arminian Magazine*, begun in 1778. These were then published in volumes 5–8 of yet another collected edition of *Sermons of Several Occasions* (1787–88), bringing the total in that collection to about a hundred sermons. After Wesley's death, George Story published a ninth volume to include the *Magazine* sermons after 1788. The whole body of Wesley's sermons is composed of 151 published works and unpublished manuscripts.

This volume presents a selection of fifty sermons from the Bicentennial Edition of *The Works of John Wesley* (1980–84). Albert C. Outler, editor of the *Sermons* unit, had for some time considered also producing a supplemental one-volume collection of Wesley's 'best' sermons. Professor Outler felt that the recent tendency to focus only on forty-four 'standard' sermons (pre-1763) had overlooked Wesley's own comment that some additional later sermons represented his 'maturest' thoughts. For Wesley, Outler says, 'the project remained open-ended,' as seen in his continuing to publish new sermons written during the last twenty-five years of his life.

A week before his death, Professor Outler suggested a list of sermons for such a volume, choosing a broad range of topics that spread across Wesley's lifetime. Many of these Outler saw as 'landmark' sermons, though by accident of timing (and decisions of the British Methodist Conference in the twentieth century) they had not generally been considered 'standard' sermons. Outler's list was subsequently enhanced by the addition of a few sermons suggested by persons who teach doctrinal and historical studies in the church and the academy.

For years, Outler struggled with the question of how to order the sermons in the larger project, torn between three approaches: the basic ordering of the last Wesley collection (somewhat arbitrary, though partly chronological, partly theological); a new ordering by theological outline; or a new ordering by chronological sequence. The latter was his first impulse, in order to exhibit Wesley's thought 'in its successive stages of development.' Such an ordering, he felt, would highlight the question of constancy and change in Wesley's theology. On the one hand, it would demonstrate the continuity of some basic ideas from his Oxford period onward; on the other hand, it would 'shatter most of the conventional views' of the constancy of his theological course after 1738. In the end, Outler decided to order the 151 sermons in the *Works* project in a manner following Wesley's own publications. For this one-volume anthology, however, he suggested a chronological sequence, following his initial impulse.

The sermons selected for this volume, therefore, represent the heart of Wesley's theology, expressed in a variety of ways throughout his lifetime. The Board of Directors of the Wesley Works Editorial Project had long considered the possibility of producing selections from the various units of the larger collection. In paperback and focused on the Wesley text, such individual volumes would provide a less expensive alternative for home or classroom study of major Wesley documents. For more detailed research, the scholarly apparatus and the more comprehensive collection of texts is still invaluable and available in the larger edition. This anthology was approved by the Board in 1990 as a work supplementary to the Bicentennial Edition being produced by the Wesley Works Editorial Project.

The text of the sermons here presented was initially produced by the textual editor of the *Works* project, Professor Frank Baker, and is virtually the same as in the larger edition. For the most part based on the first editions, these texts represent the collation of all known editions published in Wesley's lifetime. The spelling, capitalization, and punctuation have been modernized in most instances, but no attempt has been made to change the characteristic syntax of his eighteenth-century style.

The introductions to each sermon in this volume are for the most part distilled from those of Professor Outler in the larger work. A few revisions have been made in the light of subsequent research. In the introductions, titles of sermons that were first published separately are given in italics; titles of other sermons are given in quotation marks.

The modern editorial footnotes to the sermons themselves have been removed, but Wesley's annotations have been retained. Most of the Wesleyan notes are simple citations of selected biblical quotations and have been returned to their original parenthetical position in the body of the text. A few citations have been silently corrected or extended to minimize the use of editorial brackets. The meaning of the Greek, Hebrew, and Latin words or phrases that Wesley occasionally used is normally clear in context. Translations of the Latin quotations that might otherwise be obscure have been provided.

It is hoped that the more widespread availability and study of these materials will enhance the broader appreciation of Wesley's thought in our own day and contribute to a better understanding of the Wesleyan heritage.

Richard P. Heitzenrater
Southern Methodist University
Dallas, Texas

THE IMAGE OF GOD

Sermon 141 – 1730

AN INTRODUCTORY COMMENT

This is John Wesley's first 'university sermon', preached in St. Mary's, the university church at Oxford, on November 15, 1730. It is a lively sermon that deals with the prime issue of Christian anthropology: the original design of human nature considered in the light of the crucial biblical metaphor of 'the image of God' and in the face of the tragic consequences of the Fall.

The argument is ordered into three stages: first, the original perfections of the *imago Dei* in Adam and Eve; second, the fall and defacement of that image; and third, the mystery of grace and the promise of the image's restoration. It is, therefore, an important statement of Wesley's early basic understanding of the 'way of salvation'.

The idea of Adam's perfections, the tradition of 'original righteousness', was a commonplace at the time and had come to Wesley through the Cambridge Platonists and John Norris. One might wonder why a creature so perfect should ever have fallen from his paradisiacal state. Wesley's answer was that God had designed the virtue of obedience as the precondition to all the others, and when this virtue was tested by an arbitrary command and Adam disobeyed, all his other perfections fell away into ruin. Thereafter, human nature has been, in effect, an inversion of its original design, in intellect, will, and affections.

One of the more interesting 'asides' in this sermon is Wesley's description of the physiological effects of Adam's eating of the forbidden fruit. His discussion amounts to a speculative account of a correlation between bad nutrition and the onset and course of arteriosclerosis–a hypothesis far enough beyond its own time that modern medicine is still in process of drawing it out.

Wesley never published this sermon. The manuscript, probably the 'fair copy' that he used in the pulpit, is in the Colman Miscellany in the Methodist Archives, Manchester. His diary indicates that he had composed the sermon during the five days, October 27–31, 1730. In the following three years, he also preached this sermon in Stanton, two churches in London, and another church in Oxford.

The Image of God

So God created man in his own image.
Genesis 1:27

[1.] A truth that does so much honour to human nature, that gives so advantageous an account of it as this, could not fail, one would think, of being well entertained by all to whom that nature belonged. And accordingly some there have been in all ages who gladly received and firmly retained it; who asserted, not only that man was sprung from God, but that he was his likeness from whom he sprung; that the image of his divine Parent was still visible upon him, who had transfused as much of himself into this his picture as the materials on which he drew would allow.

[2.] But to this it has constantly been opposed: if man was made in the image of God, whence flow those numberless imperfections that stain and dishonour his nature? Why is his body exposed to sickness and pain, and at last to a total dissolution? Why is his soul still more disgraced and deformed by ignorance and error, by unruly passions, and what is worse than all, as it contains them all, by vice? A fine picture—this ignorant, wretched, guilty creature—of a wise, happy, and holy Creator!

[3.] I am ashamed to say there are [those] of our age and nation who greedily close with this old objection, and eagerly maintain that they were not made in the image of the living God, but of the beasts that perish; who heartily contend that it was not the divine but the brutal likeness in which they were created, and earnestly assert 'that they themselves are beasts' in a more literal sense than ever Solomon meant it. These consequently reject with scorn the account God has given of man, and affirm it to be contrary to reason and [to the account] itself, as well as it is to their practice.

[4.] The substance of his account is this: 'God created man upright; in the image of God created he him; but man found out to himself many inventions.' Abusing the liberty wherewith he was endowed, he rebelled against his Creator, and wilfully changed the image of the incorruptible God into sin, misery, and corruption. Yet his merciful, though rejected, Creator would not forsake even the depraved work of his own hands, but provided for him, and offered to him a means of being 'renewed after the image of him that created him'.

[5.] That it may appear whether this account of man is contrary to itself and reason or no, I shall endeavour to show the parts of it more distinctly, by inquiring: I, how man was made in the image of God; II, how he lost that image; and III, how he may recover it.

I. Man was originally made in the image of God.

1. First with regard to his understanding. He was endued, after the likeness of his Maker, with a power of distinguishing truth from falsehood; either by a simple view wherein he made the nearest approach to that all-seeing Nature, or by comparing one thing with another (a manner of knowledge perhaps peculiar to himself) and often inferring farther truths from these preceding comparisons.

(1) And in several properties of it, as well as in the faculty itself, man at first resembled God. His understanding was just; everything appeared to him according to its real nature. It never was betrayed into any mistake; whatever he perceived, he perceived as it was. He thought not at all of many things, but he thought wrong of none. (2) And as it was just, it was likewise clear. Truth and evidence went hand in hand; as nothing appeared in a false light, so neither in a glimmering one. Light and darkness there were, but no twilight; whenever the shades of ignorance withdrew, in that moment the broader day appeared, the full blaze of knowledge shined. He was equally a stranger to error and doubt; either he saw not at all, or he saw plainly. (3) And hence arose that other excellence of his understanding: being just and clear, it was swift in its motion. Nothing was then as quick as thought but that which alone is capable of it—spirit. How far anything of which we have any conception must fall short of expressing its swiftness will be readily seen by all who observe but one instance of it in our first father: in how short a space he 'gave names to all cattle, and to the fowls of the air, and to every beast of the field'. And names not arbitrarily imposed, but expressive of their inward natures. (4) Sufficiently showing thereby not only the swiftness, but likewise the greatness of his understanding. For how extensive a view must he have had who could command so vast a prospect! What a comprehension was that, to take in at once almost an infinity of objects! Such doubtless it was that the visible creation would soon have been too small for its capacity.

2. And yet even this just, this clear, this swift, this comprehensive understanding was the least part of that image of God wherein man was originally made. Far greater and nobler was his second endowment, namely, a will equally perfect. It could not but be perfect while it followed the dictates of such an understanding. His affections were rational, even, and regular—if we may be allowed to say 'affections', for properly speaking he had but one: man was what God is, Love. Love filled the whole expansion of his soul; it possessed him without a rival. Every movement of his heart was love: it knew no other fervour. Love was his vital heat; it was the genial warmth that animated his whole frame. And the flame of it was continually streaming forth, directly to him from whom it came, and by reflection to all sensitive natures, inasmuch as they too were

his offspring; but especially to those superior beings who bore not only the superscription, but likewise the image of their Creator.

3. What made his image yet plainer in his human offspring was, thirdly, the liberty he originally enjoyed; the perfect freedom implanted in his nature, and interwoven with all its parts. Man was made with an entire indifference, either to keep or change his first estate: it was left to himself what he would do; his own choice was to determine him in all things. The balance did not incline to one side or the other unless by his own deed. His Creator would not, and no creature besides himself could, weigh down either scale. So that, in this sense, he was the sole lord and sovereign judge of his own actions.

4. The result of all these–an unerring understanding, an uncorrupt will, and perfect freedom–gave the last stroke to the image of God in man, by crowning all these with happiness. Then indeed to live was to enjoy, when every faculty was in its perfection, amidst abundance of objects which infinite wisdom had purposely suited to it, when man's understanding was satisfied with truth, as his will was with good; when he was at full liberty to enjoy either the Creator or the creation; to indulge in rivers of pleasure, ever new, ever pure from any mixture of pain.

II. How it was this wise, virtuous, happy creature was deprived of these perfections, how man lost the image of God, we are, secondly, to inquire. And the plain answer is this: the liberty of man necessarily required that he should have some trial; else he would have had no choice whether he would stand or no, that is, no liberty at all. In order to this necessary trial God said unto him, 'Of every tree of the garden thou mayst freely eat, but of the tree of the knowledge of good and evil, thou shalt not eat of it.' To secure him from transgressing this sole command, as far as could be done without destroying his liberty, the consequence was laid before him: 'In the day that thou eatest thereof thou shalt surely die.' Yet man did eat of it, and the consequence accordingly was death on him and all his descendants, and preparatory to death, sickness and pain, and folly and vice and slavery.

And 'tis easy to observe by what regular steps all these would succeed each other, if God did not miraculously prevent it, but suffer nature to take its course. But we should observe, first, that man even at his creation was a compound of matter and spirit; and that it was ordained by the original law that during this vital union neither part of the compound should act at all but together with its companion; that the dependence of each upon the other should be inviolably maintained; that even the operations of the soul should so far depend upon the body as to be exerted in a more or less perfect manner, as this was more or less aptly disposed.

This being observed, we may easily conceive how the forbidden fruit might work all those effects which are implied in the word 'death', as being introductory to, and paving the way for it. Which particulars of the following account are founded on Scripture and consequently certain, and which are built on conjecture and therefore proposed only as probable, it will not be hard to distinguish.

1. Its first effect must have been on his body, which, being before prepared for immortality, had no seeds of corruption within itself and adopted none from without. All its original particles were incorruptible, and therefore the additional ones taken in, being for pleasure rather than use, cannot be supposed ever to have cleaved to its native substance, ever to have adhered to any part of it, as none needed any reparation. By this means both the juices contained must have been still of the same consistence, and the vessels containing them have kept the same spring, and remained ever clear and open.

On the contrary, the fruit of that tree alone of whose deadly nature he was forewarned seems to have contained a juice, the particles of which were apt to cleave to whatever they touched. Some of these, being received into the human body, might adhere to the inner coats of the finer vessels; to which again other particles that before floated loose in the blood, continually joining, would naturally lay a foundation for numberless disorders in all parts of the machine. For death in particular; since, more foreign matter cleaving to the former every day, the solid parts of the body would every day lose something of their spring, and so be less able to contribute their necessary assistance to the circulation of the fluids. The smaller channels would gradually fill up, especially those that lie near the extremities, where the current, by reason of its distance from the fountain, was always more slow and languid. The whole tide, as the force that threw it forward abated, must [also] have abated its swiftness in proportion, till at length that force utterly failing, it ceased to move, and rested in death.

Indeed had Adam taken the antidote as well as the poison, had he again put forth his hand, and taken of the fruit of the Tree of Life, nothing of this could have followed. 'Tis sure this would have made him live for ever, naturally speaking, notwithstanding he had eaten death. 'Tis likely it would have done so by its thin, abstersive nature, particularly fitted to counteract the other, to wipe off its particles, wheresoever adhering, and so restore the eater to immortality.

However this be, thus much is certain: the moment wherein that fruit was tasted, the sentence of death passed on that body, which before was impassive and immortal. And this immortal having put on mortality, the next stroke fell on its companion: the soul felt a like change through all her powers, except only that she could not die. The instrument being now quite untuned, she could no longer make the same harmony: 'the corruptible body pressed down the soul', with which it soared so high during its incorruption.

2. His understanding first found the want of suitable organs; its notions were just no longer. It mistook falsehood for truth, and truth for falsehood.

Error succeeded and increased ignorance. And no wonder, when it was no longer clear; when it not only saw through a glass, but darkly too, that glass being now grown thick and dull, having lost great part of its transparency. And hence it was that doubt perplexed it as well as error, that it could neither rest in knowledge nor ignorance. Through clouds like these its most laborious steps could win but little ground. With its clearness went its swiftness too; confusion and slowness came together. Instead of being able to find out the natures of ten thousand creatures almost in a moment, it became unable to trace out fully the nature of any one in many years. Nay, unable (so was the largeness of its capacity impaired, as well as the swiftness of its progress) with that apprehension for which the visible world was before but a scanty prospect, to take in at one view all the properties of any single creature therein.

3. How much the will suffered when its guide was thus blinded we may easily comprehend. Instead of the glorious one that possessed it whole *before,* it was *now* seized by legions of vile affections. Grief and anger and hatred and fear and shame, at once rushed in upon it; the whole train of earthly, sensual, and devilish passions fastened on and tore it in pieces. Nay, love itself, that ray of the Godhead, that balm of life, now became a torment. Its light being gone, it wandered about seeking rest and finding none; till at length, equally unable to subsist without any and to feel out its proper object, it reclined itself upon the painted trifles, the gilded poison of earthly enjoyments.

4. Indeed, what else could the human mind do when it had no freedom left? Liberty went away with virtue; instead of an indulgent master it was under a merciless tyrant. The subject of virtue became the slave of vice. It was not willingly that the creature obeyed vanity; the rule was now perforce; the sceptre of gold was changed into a rod of iron. Before, the bands of love indeed drew him toward heaven; yet if he would, he could stoop down to earth. But now, he was so chained down to earth he could not so much as lift up his eyes toward heaven.

5. The consequence of his being enslaved to a depraved understanding and a corrupted will could be no other than the reverse of that happiness which flowed from them when in their perfection. Then were the days of man evil as well as few; then, when both his faculties were decayed, and bitterness poured on their earthly objects, and heavenly ones withdrawn, the mortal, foolish, vicious, enslaved creature was delivered over to his [un]sought-for misery.

How such a creature as this, as every fair inquirer finds by experience himself to be, could come from the hands of the good God, has been the just wonder of all ages. And let the infidel look to it; let him surmount the difficulty if he can upon any scheme beside the Christian. Upon this indeed it is no difficulty at all; all is rational, plain, and easy, while we observe, on the one hand, that not the good God but man himself made man what he is now; on the other, how he may recover what he wilfully lost, which is the subject of our third inquiry.

III. Who indeed shall recover us from the body of this death? Who shall restore our native immortality? We answer with the Apostle, 'I thank God, Jesus Christ our Lord!' 'As in Adam all died, so in Christ shall all be made alive'—all who accept of the means which he hath prepared, who walk by the rules which he hath given them. All these shall by dying conquer the first death, and shall never taste the second. The seeds of spiritual death they shall gradually expel, before this earthly tabernacle is dissolved, that this too, when it has been taken down and thoroughly purged, may be rebuilt 'eternal in the heavens'.

1. The first step to this glorious change is humility, a knowledge of ourselves, a just sense of our condition: which the evil spirit himself, either overruled by or mimicking the true God, recommended on the front of his temple in those celebrated words, 'Know Thyself,' which a better prophet than he recommends to all those who would 'be transformed by the renewing of their minds'—'I say unto every man—not to think of himself more highly than he ought to think.'

'Tis almost needless to remark how conducive this is to the attainment of all other knowledge; or, in other words, how conducive it is to the improvement of the understanding. An erroneous opinion of ourselves naturally leads us into numberless errors; whereas to those who know their own folly (beside the natural advantage of it) the Lord of nature 'giveth the spirit of wisdom, and enlightens the eyes of their understanding, after the likeness in which they were created' (Eph. 1:17–18; [Col. 3:10]).

2. The understanding, thus enlightened by humility, immediately directs us to reform our will by charity. To root out of our souls all unmanly passions, and to give place to them, no, not an hour; to put away all malice, uncleanness, intemperance, 'all bitterness, wrath, and evil-speaking'; to collect the scattered beams of that affection which is truly human, truly divine, and fix them on that Sovereign Good 'in whom we live, move, and have our being'; for his sake, lastly, and after his example, to be 'kind one to another, tender-hearted, forgiving one another, even as God, for Christ's sake, hath forgiven us' (Eph. 4:32).

3. Thus it is that the 'law of the Spirit of life makes us free from the law of sin and death'; thus it restores us, first to knowledge, and then to virtue, and freedom, and happiness. Thus are we 'delivered from the bondage of corruption into the glorious liberty of the sons of God'; into that liberty which not only implies the absence of all pain, unless what is necessary to future pleasure, but such a measure of present happiness as is a fit introduction to that which flows at God's right hand for evermore!

[IV.1.] One thing I would observe from what has been said—how extremely pitiable their condition is who are insensible of their innate disease, or refuse the only cure of it. 'Tis true, even those who are not invested with authority (such doubtless 'bear not the sword in vain') are apt to look upon these as the proper objects of anger, and not of compassion. Yet our Lord, when he beheld even that city which had killed the servants, and was about to murder the son, of its master, wept over it, and suffered all other passions to melt down into commiseration. Yet those whom we are often tempted to behold with passions of quite another nature, 'who are alienated from the image of God through the ignorance that is in them', are by our confession not more guilty than these, and little less unhappy. They are always sick, often in pain; destruction and unhappiness are in their ways; the way of peace have they not known, 'an evil disease cleaves to them'; their inward parts are very misery. Their understanding is darkened; clouds of ignorance and error are ever before their eyes, 'because the God of this world hath blinded their hearts', and infinitely increased its native corruption. Their love is fixed on mean, perishing, unsatisfying objects, and the frequent anguish that must flow from such a choice is sharpened by innumerable restless passions, that tear asunder their helpless prey. God help him who is a slave to such masters! Man cannot; he can only pity him! He can only, when he seeth such a one dragging his chain, and possibly talking loud of his own freedom, plunging through the flames of a fever into those that never shall be quenched, and perhaps dreaming he is in perfect health, recommend [him] to that All-sufficient Mercy to which all things are possible!

2. Yes, one step farther he may, he ought to go: he ought to acknowledge the riches of that mercy shown to himself, and indeed to all of us who have our education in a truly Christian country; who have all the opportunities of obtaining a better mind which the art of man and the wisdom of God can give; of obtaining this knowledge—knowledge, the basis of whatsoever things are pure, whatsoever things are honourable or lovely—[which] is held out to us with no sparing hand; we are suffered, courted, pressed to enjoy it. Others are glad if they can snatch a few drops from the rivulets that flow hence: we lie at the fountain-head of these living waters, and command all their various streams. The attainment of knowledge is the pleasure of many; of us, 'tis the business too. Our business it is to know in particular that we are all originally foolish and vicious, and that there is no truth in our whole religion more absolutely necessary to be known than this. Because if man be not naturally corrupt, then all religion, Jewish and Christian, is vain, seeing it is all built on this—all method[s] of cure presupposing the disease. We can scarce avoid knowing how slight all objections against this fundamental truth must be while there is even this one argument for it: if man be naturally mortal, then he is naturally sinful; seeing one cause must work both sin and death. The seeds of

Why?

natural being likewise the seeds of moral corruption, must undermine our understanding as well as our life, and the affections with the understanding. We are almost forced to know both the necessity and the divine efficacy of our religion; to see that if man be naturally corrupt, then Christianity is of God; seeing there is no other religion, as 'there is no other God which can deliver after this sort' from that corruption. We, lastly, have daily opportunities of knowing, if Christianity be of God, then of how glorious a privilege are they thought worthy who persuade others to accept of its benefits. Seeing when the author of it 'cometh in the clouds of heaven', and 'those that slept in the dust of the earth shall awake,' they who have saved others from sin and its attendant death 'shall shine as the brightness of the firmament'; they who have reprinted the image of God on many souls 'as the stars for ever'!

Now unto God the Father, God the Son, and God the Holy Ghost, be ascribed all honour and praise, now and for ever.

THE CIRCUMCISION OF THE HEART

Sermon 17 – 1733

AN INTRODUCTORY COMMENT

This sermon is one of Wesley's most careful and complete statements of his doctrine of holiness. It is an updated version of a sermon written fifteen years earlier for delivery in St. Mary's, Oxford, on January 1, 1733, the Feast of the Circumcision of Christ. As Wesley began to plan this sermon, the project was complicated by the appearance of a derogatory letter in *Fog's Weekly Journal*, Saturday, December 9, about 'this Sect called Methodists'. The obvious effect of such defamation was the arousal of popular curiosity, which assured him of a larger audience than he might have expected otherwise. But such a degree of public interest also made the occasion more crucial for Wesley and helps to explain the uncommon carefulness of his preparations. He spent close to thirty hours writing a first draft and then took nearly as long to consult with others about its further refinement. This sermon helped to establish Wesley as a man of note in the university who would preach six university sermons in the next two-and-one-half years.

This work contains Wesley's most distinctive doctrine: Christian perfection understood as perfect love of God and neighbour, rooted in a radical faith in Christ's revelation of that love and its power. It was his first public statement of this doctrine, and one which he continued to regard as a landmark. The earliest of the sermons published in his four-volume collection, it is carefully placed at the beginning of volume two (1748).

This work demonstrates that the basic elements of Wesley's soteriology (with the exception of the Moravian emphases on 'faith alone' and on assurance) were already in place at Oxford in the early 1730s. Original sin is there (though more as a disease than an obliterated *imago Dei*) and so also is the *non posse non peccare* (I.3). Christ's atonement is affirmed as the sole ground of our redemption, and he can add (I.7, in 1748) a personal confession in the language of his Aldersgate experience without disturbing the rhetoric or sense in any noticeable way. He spells out the theme of the Christian's participation in God as the essence of Christian existence. The means to this single end are also delineated–not faith alone, but humility (i.e., repentance), faith, hope, and love. 'The Circumcision of the Heart' may profitably be paired with 'Justification by Faith' (1746) as two halves of the same gospel and as twin foundation stones in Wesley's theology as a whole.

The Circumcision of the Heart

Circumcision is that of the heart,
in the spirit and not in the letter.
Romans 2:29

1. 'Tis the melancholy remark of an excellent man that 'he who now preaches the most essential duties of Christianity runs the hazard of being esteemed by a great part of his hearers "a setter forth of new doctrines".' Most men have so *lived away* the substance of that religion, the profession whereof they still retain, that no sooner are any of those truths proposed which difference the Spirit of Christ from the spirit of the world than they cry out, 'Thou bringest strange things to our ears; we would know what these things mean'—though he is only preaching to them 'Jesus, and the resurrection', with the necessary consequence of it. If Christ be risen, ye ought then to die unto the world, and to live wholly unto God.

2. A hard saying this to the 'natural man' who is alive unto the world, and dead unto God, and one that he will not readily be persuaded to receive as the truth of God, unless it be so qualified in the interpretation as to have neither use nor significancy left. He 'receiveth not the' words 'of the Spirit of God', taken in their plain and obvious meaning. 'They are foolishness unto him; neither' indeed 'can he know them, because they are spiritually discerned': they are perceivable only by that spiritual sense which in him was never yet awakened, for want of which he must reject as idle fancies of men what are both the 'wisdom' and the 'power of God'.

3. That 'circumcision is that of the heart, in the spirit, and not in the letter', that the distinguishing mark of a true follower of Christ, of one who is in a state of acceptance with God, is not either outward circumcision or baptism, or any other outward form, but a right state of soul—a mind and spirit renewed after the image of him that created it—is one of those important truths that can only be 'spiritually discerned'. And this the Apostle himself intimates in the next words: 'Whose praise is not of men, but of God.' As if he had said, 'Expect not, whoever thou art who thus followest thy great Master, that the world, the men who follow him not, will say, "Well done, good and faithful servant!" Know that the "circumcision of the heart", the seal of thy calling, is "foolishness with the world". Be content to wait for thy applause till the day of thy Lord's appearing. In that day shalt thou "have praise of God" in the great assembly of men and angels.'

I design, first, particularly to inquire wherein this circumcision of the heart consists; and secondly to mention some reflections that naturally arise from such an inquiry.

I.1. I am first to inquire wherein that circumcision of the heart consists which will receive the praise of God. In general we may observe it is that habitual disposition of soul which in the Sacred Writings is termed 'holiness', and which directly implies the being cleansed from sin, 'from all filthiness both of flesh and spirit', and by consequence the being endued with those virtues which were also in Christ Jesus, the being so 'renewed in the image of our mind' as to be 'perfect, as our Father in heaven is perfect'.

2. To be more particular, circumcision of heart implies humility, faith, hope, and charity. Humility, a right judgment of ourselves, cleanses our minds from those high conceits of our own perfections, from the undue opinions of our own abilities and attainments which are the genuine fruit of a corrupted nature. This entirely cuts off that vain thought, 'I am rich, and wise, and have need of nothing'; and convinces us that we are by nature 'wretched, and poor, and miserable, and blind, and naked'. It convinces us that in our best estate we are of ourselves all sin and vanity; that confusion, and ignorance, and error, reign over our understanding; that unreasonable, earthly, sensual, devilish passions usurp authority over our will: in a word, that there is no whole part in our soul, that all the foundations of our nature are out of course.

3. At the same time we are convinced that we are not sufficient of ourselves to help ourselves; that without the Spirit of God we can do nothing but add sin to sin; that it is he alone 'who worketh in us' by his almighty power, either 'to will or do' that which is good—it being as impossible for us even to think a good thought without the supernatural assistance of his Spirit as to create ourselves, or to renew our whole souls in righteousness and true holiness.

4. A sure effect of our having formed this right judgment of the sinfulness and helplessness of our nature is a disregard of that 'honour which cometh of man' which is usually paid to some supposed excellency in us. He who knows himself neither desires nor values the applause which he knows he deserves not. It is therefore 'a very small thing with him to be judged by man's judgment'. He has all reason to think, by comparing what it has said either for or against him with what he feels in his own breast, that the world, as well as the god of this world, was 'a liar from the beginning'. And even as to those who are not of the world, though he would choose (if it were the will of God) that they should account of him as of one desirous to be found a faithful steward of his Lord's goods, if haply this might be a means of enabling him to be of more use to his fellow-servants, yet as this is the one end of his wishing for their approbation, so he does not at all rest upon it. For he is assured that whatever God wills he can never want instruments to perform; since he is able,

even of these stones, to raise up servants to do his pleasure.

5. This is that lowliness of mind which they have learned of Christ who follow his example and tread in his steps. And this knowledge of their disease, whereby they are more and more cleansed from one part of it, pride and vanity, disposes them to embrace with a willing mind the second thing implied in 'circumcision of heart'—that faith which alone is able to make them whole, which is the one medicine given under heaven to heal their sickness.

6. The best guide of the blind, the surest light of them that are in darkness, the most perfect instructor of the foolish, is faith. But it must be such a faith as is 'mighty through God, to the pulling down of strongholds', to the overturning all the prejudices of corrupt reason, all the false maxims revered among men, all evil customs and habits, all that 'wisdom of the world' which 'is foolishness with God'; as 'casteth down imaginations' (reasonings) 'and every high thing that exalteth itself against the knowledge of God, and bringeth into captivity every thought to the obedience of Christ'.

7. 'All things are possible to him that' thus 'believeth': 'the eyes of his understanding being enlightened,' he *sees* what is his calling, even to 'glorify God, who hath bought him with' so high 'a price, in his body and in his spirit, which now are God's' by redemption, as well as by creation. He feels what is 'the exceeding greatness of his power' who, as he raised up Christ from the dead, so is able to quicken us—'dead in sin'—'by his Spirit which dwelleth in us'. 'This is the victory which overcometh the world, even our faith': that faith which is not only an unshaken assent to all that God hath revealed in Scripture, and in particular to those important truths, 'Jesus Christ came into the world to save sinners'; he 'bare our sins in his own body on the tree'; 'he is the propitiation for our sins; and not for ours only, but also for the sins of the whole world';* but likewise the revelation of Christ in our hearts: a divine evidence or conviction of his love, his free, unmerited love to me a sinner; a sure confidence in his pardoning mercy, wrought in us by the Holy Ghost—a confidence whereby every true believer is enabled to bear witness, 'I know that my Redeemer liveth'; that *I* 'have an advocate with the Father', that 'Jesus Christ the righteous is' *my* Lord, and 'the propitiation for *my* sins.' I know he 'hath loved *me*, and given himself for *me*'. He 'hath reconciled *me*, even *me* to God'; and *I* 'have redemption through his blood, even the forgiveness of sins'.

8. Such a faith as this cannot fail to show evidently the power of him that inspires it, by delivering his children from the yoke of sin, and 'purging their consciences from dead works'; by strengthening them so that they are no longer constrained to 'obey sin in the desires thereof'; but instead of 'yielding their members unto' it, 'as instruments of unrighteousness', they now 'yield' themselves entirely 'unto God, as those that are alive from the dead'.

* N.B. The following part of this paragraph is now added [in 1748] to the sermon formerly preached [in 1733].

9. Those who are thus by faith 'born of God' have also 'strong consolation through hope'. This is the next thing which the 'circumcision of the heart' implies—even the testimony of their own spirit with the Spirit which witnesses in their hearts, that they are the children of God. Indeed it is the same Spirit who works in them that clear and cheerful confidence that their heart is upright toward God; that good assurance that they now do, through his grace, the things which are acceptable in his sight; that they are now in the path which leadeth to life, and shall, by the mercy of God, endure therein to the end. It is he who giveth them a lively expectation of receiving all good things at God's hand—a joyous prospect of that 'crown of glory' which is 'reserved in heaven' for them. By this anchor a Christian is kept steady in the midst of the waves of this troublesome world, and preserved from striking upon either of those fatal rocks, presumption or despair. He is neither discouraged by the misconceived severity of his Lord, nor does he 'despise the richness of his goodness'. He neither apprehends the difficulties of the race set before him to be greater than he has strength to conquer, nor expects them to be so little as to yield him the conquest till he has put forth all his strength. The experience he already has in the Christian warfare, as it assures him his 'labour is not in vain' if 'whatever his hand findeth to do, he doth it with his might,' so it forbids his entertaining so vain a thought as that he can otherwise gain any advantage, as that any virtue can be shown, any praise attained, by 'faint hearts and feeble hands'—or indeed by any but those who pursue the same course with the great Apostle of the Gentiles: 'I (says he) so run, not as uncertainly; so fight I, not as one that beateth the air. But I keep under my body, and bring it into subjection; lest by any means when I have preached to others, I myself should be a castaway.'

10. By the same discipline is every good soldier of Christ to 'inure himself to endure hardships'. Confirmed and strengthened by this, he will be able not only to renounce 'the works of darkness', but every appetite, too, and every affection which is not subject to the law of God. For 'everyone', saith St. John, 'who hath this hope purifieth himself, even as he is pure.' It is his daily care, by the grace of God in Christ, and through the blood of the covenant, to purge the inmost recesses of his soul from the lusts that before possessed and defiled it: from uncleanness, and envy, and malice, and wrath, from every passion and temper that is 'after the flesh', that either springs from or cherishes his native corruption; as well knowing that he whose very 'body is the temple of God' ought to admit into it nothing common or unclean; and that 'holiness becometh' that 'house for ever' where the Spirit of holiness vouchsafes to dwell.

11. Yet lackest thou one thing, whosoever thou art, that to a deep humility and a steadfast faith hast joined a lively hope, and thereby in a good measure cleansed thy heart from its inbred pollution. If thou wilt be perfect, add to all these charity: add love, and thou hast the 'circumcision of the heart'. 'Love is

the fulfilling of the law,' 'the end of the commandment'. Very excellent things are spoken of love; it is the essence, the spirit, the life of all virtue. It is not only the first and great command, but it is all the commandments in one. Whatsoever things are just, whatsoever things are pure, whatsoever things are amiable or honourable; if there be any virtue, if there be any praise, they are all comprised in this one word—love. In this is perfection and glory and happiness. The royal law of heaven and earth is this, 'Thou shalt love the Lord thy God with all thy heart, and with all thy soul, and with all thy mind, and with all thy strength.'

12. Not that this forbids us to love anything besides God: it implies that we 'love our brother also'. Nor yet does it forbid us (as some have strangely imagined) to take pleasure in anything but God. To suppose this is to suppose the fountain of holiness is directly the author of sin, since he has inseparably annexed pleasure to the use of those creatures which are necessary to sustain the life he has given us. This therefore can never be the meaning of his command. What the real sense of it is both our blessed Lord and his apostles tell us too frequently and too plainly to be misunderstood. They all with one mouth bear witness that the true meaning of those several declarations—'The Lord thy God is one Lord; thou shalt have no other gods but me,' 'Thou shalt love the Lord thy God with all thy strength,' 'Thou shalt cleave unto him'; 'The desire of thy soul shall be to his name'—is no other than this. The one perfect good shall be your ultimate end. One thing shall ye desire for its own sake—the fruition of him that is all in all. One happiness shall ye propose to your souls, even an union with him that made them, the having 'fellowship with the Father and the Son', the being 'joined to the Lord in one Spirit'. One design ye are to pursue to the end of time—the enjoyment of God in time and in eternity. Desire other things so far as they tend to this. Love the creature—as it leads to the Creator. But in every step you take be this the glorious point that terminates your view. Let every affection, and thought, and word, and work, be subordinate to this. Whatever ye desire or fear, whatever ye seek or shun, whatever ye think, speak, or do, be it in order to your happiness in God, the sole end as well as source of your being.

13. Have no end, no ultimate end, but God. Thus our Lord: 'One thing is needful.' And if thine eye be singly fixed on this one thing, 'thy whole body shall be full of light.' Thus St. Paul: 'This one thing I do; I press toward the mark, for the prize of the high calling in Christ Jesus.' Thus St. James: 'Cleanse your hands, ye sinners, and purify your hearts, ye double-minded.' Thus St. John: 'Love not the world, neither the things that are in the world. For all that is in the world, the lust of the flesh, the lust of the eye, and the pride of life, is not of the Father, but is of the world.' The seeking happiness in what gratifies either the desire of the flesh, by agreeably striking upon the outward senses; the desire of the eye, of the imagination, by its novelty, greatness, or beauty;

or the pride of life, whether by pomp, grandeur, power, or the usual consequence of them, applause and admiration: 'is not of the Father'—cometh not from, neither is approved by, the Father of spirits—'but of the world'—it is the distinguishing mark of those who will not have him reign over them.

II.1. Thus have I particularly inquired what that 'circumcision of the heart' is which will obtain the praise of God. I am in the second place to mention some reflections that naturally arise from such an inquiry, as a plain rule whereby every man may judge himself whether he be of the world or of God.

And, first, it is clear from what has been said that no man has a title to the praise of God unless his heart is circumcised by humility, unless he is little, and base, and vile in his own eyes; unless he is deeply convinced of that inbred 'corruption of his nature, whereby he is very far gone from original righteousness', being prone to all evil, averse to all good, corrupt and abominable; having a 'carnal mind', which 'is enmity against God, and is not subject to the Law of God, nor indeed can be'; unless he continually feels in his inmost soul that without the Spirit of God resting upon him he can neither think, nor desire, nor speak, nor act, anything good or well-pleasing in his sight.

No man, I say, has a title to the praise of God till he feels his want of God: nor indeed till he seeketh that 'honour, which cometh of God only', and neither desires nor pursues that which cometh of man, unless so far only as it tends to this.

2. Another truth which naturally follows from what has been said is that none shall obtain the honour that cometh of God unless his heart be circumcised by faith, even a 'faith of the operation of God'; unless, refusing to be any longer led by his senses, appetites, or passions, or even by that blind leader of the blind, so idolized by the world, natural reason, he lives and 'walks by faith', directs every step as 'seeing him that is invisible', 'looks not at the things that are seen, which are temporal, but at the things that are not seen, which are eternal'; and governs all his desires, designs, and thoughts, all his actions and conversations, as one who is entered in within the veil, where Jesus sits at the right hand of God.

3. It were to be wished that they were better acquainted with this faith who employ much of their time and pains in laying another foundation, in grounding religion on 'the eternal *fitness* of things', on 'the intrinsic *excellence* of virtue', and the *beauty* of actions flowing from it—on the *reasons*, as they term them, of good and evil, and the *relations* of beings to each other. Either these accounts of the grounds of Christian duty coincide with the scriptural or not. If they do, why are well-meaning men perplexed, and drawn from the weightier matters of the law by a cloud of terms whereby the easiest truths are explained into obscurity? If they are not, then it behoves them to consider who is the author of this new doctrine, whether he is likely to be 'an angel from

heaven' who 'preacheth another gospel' than that of Christ Jesus—though if he were, God, not we, hath pronounced his sentence: 'Let him be accursed!'

4. Our gospel, as it knows no other foundation of good works than faith, or of faith than Christ, so it clearly informs us we are not his disciples while we either deny him to be the author or his Spirit to be the inspirer and perfecter both of our faith and works. 'If any man have not the Spirit of Christ, he is none of his.' He alone can quicken those who are dead unto God, can breathe into them the breath of Christian life, and so prevent, accompany, and follow them with his grace as to bring their good desires to good effect. And 'as many as are thus led by the Spirit of God, they are the sons of God.' This is God's short and plain account of true religion and virtue; and 'other foundation can no man lay.'

5. From what has been said we may, thirdly, learn that none is truly 'led by the Spirit' unless that 'Spirit bear witness with his spirit, that he is a child of God'; unless he see the prize and the crown before him, and 'rejoice in hope of the glory of God': so greatly have they erred who have taught that in serving God we ought not to have a view to our own happiness. Nay, but we are often and expressly taught of God to have 'respect unto the recompense of reward', to balance the toil with the 'joy set before us', these 'light afflictions' with that 'exceeding weight of glory'. Yea, we are 'aliens to the covenant of promise', we are 'without God in the world', until God of 'his abundant mercy hath begotten us again unto a living hope' of the 'inheritance incorruptible, undefiled, and that fadeth not away'.

6. But if these things are so, 'tis high time for those persons to deal faithfully with their own souls—who are so far from finding in themselves this joyful assurance, that they fulfil the terms and shall obtain the promises of that covenant, as to quarrel with the covenant itself, and blaspheme the terms of it, to complain they are too severe, and that no man ever did or shall live up to them! What is this but to reproach God, as if he were an hard master requiring of his servants more than he enables them to perform; as if he had mocked the helpless works of his hands by binding them to impossibilities, by commanding them to overcome where neither their own strength nor his grace was sufficient for them?

7. These blasphemers might almost persuade those to imagine themselves guiltless who, in the contrary extreme, hope to fulfil the commands of God without taking any pains at all. Vain hope! that a child of Adam should ever expect to see the kingdom of Christ and of God without striving, without '*agonizing*' first 'to enter in at the strait gate'! That one who was 'conceived and born in sin', and whose 'inward parts are very wickedness', should once entertain a thought of being 'purified as his Lord is pure' unless he 'tread in his steps', and 'take up his cross daily'; unless he 'cut off the right hand', and 'pluck out the right eye and cast it from him'; that he should ever dream of

shaking off his old opinions, passions, tempers, of being 'sanctified throughout in spirit, soul, and body', without a constant and continued course of general self-denial!

8. What less than this can we possibly infer from the above cited words of St. Paul, who, 'living in "infirmities, in reproaches, in necessities, in persecutions, in distresses" for Christ's sake, who being full of "signs, and wonders, and mighty deeds", who having been "caught up into the third heaven", yet reckoned' (as a late author strongly expresses it) that 'all his virtues' would be 'insecure, and' even 'his salvation in danger, without this constant self-denial. "So run I", says he, "not as uncertainly; so fight I, not as one that beateth the air." By which he plainly teaches us that he who does not thus run, who does not thus' deny himself daily, does 'run uncertainly, and fighteth to as little purpose as he that "beateth the air".'

9. To as little purpose does he talk of 'fighting the fight of faith', as vainly hope to attain the crown of incorruption (as we may, lastly, infer from the preceding observations), whose heart is not circumcised by love. Cutting off both the lust of the flesh, the lust of the eye, the pride of life, engaging the whole man, body, soul, spirit, in the ardent pursuit of that one object, is so essential to a child of God that 'without it whosoever liveth is counted dead before him.' 'Though I speak with the tongues of men and angels, and have not love, I am as sounding brass, or a tinkling cymbal. Though I have the gift of prophecy, and understand all mysteries, and all knowledge, and though I have all faith so as to remove mountains, and have not love, I am nothing. Nay, though I give all my goods to feed the poor, and my body to be burned, and have not love, it profiteth me nothing.'

10. Here then is the sum of the perfect law: this is the true 'circumcision of the heart'. Let the spirit return to God that gave it, with the whole train of its affections. 'Unto the place from whence all the rivers came, thither' let them flow again. Other sacrifices from us he would not; but the living sacrifice of the heart he hath chosen. Let it be continually offered up to God through Christ, in flames of holy love. And let no creature be suffered to share with him: for he is a jealous God. His throne will he not divide with another: he will reign without a rival. Be no design, no desire admitted there but what has him for its ultimate object. This is the way wherein those children of God once walked, who being dead still speak to us: 'Desire not to live but to praise his name; let all your thoughts, words, and works tend to his glory. Set your heart firm on him, and on other things only as they are in and from him.' 'Let your soul be filled with so entire a love of him that you may love nothing but for his sake.' 'Have a pure intention of heart, a steadfast regard to his glory in all your actions.' 'Fix your eye upon the blessed hope of your calling, and make all the things of the world minister unto it.' For then, and not till then, is that 'mind in us which was also in Christ Jesus', when in every motion of our

heart, in every word of our tongue in every work of our hands, we 'pursue nothing but in relation to him, and in subordination to his pleasure'; when we, too, neither think, nor speak, nor act, to fulfil our 'own will, but the will of him that sent us'; when whether we 'eat, or drink, or whatever we do, we do all to the glory of God'.

THE ONE THING NEEDFUL

Sermon 146 – 1734

AN INTRODUCTORY COMMENT

Wesley's diary suggests that he had written this sermon in May 1734. Both the text, Luke 10:42, and the theme of salvation as the restoration of the defaced image of God continued to preoccupy Wesley thereafter. There are at least fifty references to his having preached on Luke 10:42 in the following fifty-seven years. It is, therefore, interesting that John left this sermon unpublished. It survived only in Charles Wesley's hand in a volume of sermons that Charles had copied from his brother's manuscripts. There is also, on the page previous to this sermon, a listing of the ten places (including St. Mary's, Oxford) where John had already preached it in the years 1734–36. Charles records his also having preached it in Boston (New England) and in and around London during the years 1736–38.

What is especially notable, theologically, is Wesley's interpretation of Luke's phrase, 'the one thing needful', as signifying 'the renewal of our fallen nature'. He would have known Jeremy Taylor's famous essay, *Unum Necessarium* (1655), but there 'the one thing needful' was 'the practice of true repentance'. Other commentators provided a series of other options, but not this idea of restoration. Later, in his *Explanatory Notes*, Wesley would echo Matthew Poole's view (from his *Annotations*) that this phrase referred to 'the care of the soul with reference to eternity'.

The young Wesley, however, had turned back to the Christian-Platonic vision of the *imago Dei*—created, defaced, restored—as the essence of human nature. He goes so far as to talk of the recovery of 'the image wherein we were formed' in terms of regaining 'an angelical nature'. This theme of participation in the divine life had come to him through Malebranche, John Norris, and William Law. In none of those sources, however, was this doctrine linked to the text in Luke 10:42. The result is that here we have an early allegorical venture pressed further than was Wesley's wont. It is the earliest exposition that we have of an idea that will be thereafter woven into the textures of his mature doctrines of the 'way of salvation' as the chief agendum of Christian living.

The One Thing Needful

One thing is needful.
Luke 10:42

1. Could we suppose an intelligent being, entirely a stranger to the state of this world and its inhabitants, to take a view of their various enterprises and employments, and thence conjecture the end of their existence, he would surely conclude that these creatures were designed to be busied about many things. While he observed not only the infinite difference of the ends which different men were pursuing, but how vast a multitude of objects were successively pursued by almost every different person, he might fairly infer that for all these things were the sons of men placed upon the earth, even to gratify their several desires with sensual pleasure, or riches, or honour, or power.

2. How surprised then would he be to hear their Creator declare to all, without distinction, 'One thing is needful!' But how much more when he knew that this one thing needful for men, their one business, the one end of their existence, was none of all those things which men were troubled about, none of all those ends they were pursuing, none of all those businesses wherein they were so deeply engaged, which filled their hearts and employed their hands. Nay, that it was an end not only distinct from but contrary to them all—as contrary as light and darkness, heaven and hell, the kingdom of God and that of Satan!

3. The only thought he could form in their favour must be, that they had a surplusage of time at their command; that they therefore trifled a few hours, because they were assured of thousands of years wherein to work. But how beyond measure would he be amazed when he heard farther that these were creatures of a day; that as they yesterday arose out of the dust, so tomorrow they were to sink into it again; that the time they had for their great work was but a span long, a moment; and yet that they had no manner of assurance of not being snatched away in the midst of this moment, or indeed at the very beginning of it! When he saw that all men were placed on a narrow, weak, tottering bridge, whereof either end was swallowed up in eternity; that the waves and storms which went over it were continually bearing away one after another, in an hour when they looked not for it; and that they who yet stood, knew not but they should plunge into the great gulf the very next instant, but well knew that if they fell before they had finished their work they were lost, destroyed, undone—for ever: how would all utterance, nay, all thought, be lost!

How would he express, how would he conceive the senselessness, the madness, of those creatures who, being in such a situation, could think of anything else, could talk of anything else, could do anything besides, could find time for any other design, or care, but that of ensuring the one thing needful!

4. It cannot, therefore, be an improper employment for us, first, to observe what this one thing needful is; and, secondly, to consider a few of the numberless reasons that prove this to be the one thing needful.

[I.] 1. We may observe what this one thing is, in which, 'tis true, many things are comprised—as are all the works of our callings, all that properly belong to our several stations in the world, insomuch that whoever neglects any of these so far neglects the one thing needful. And this indeed can no otherwise be pursued than by performing all the works of our calling, but performing them in such a manner as in and by every one to advance our great work.

2. Now this great work, this one thing needful, is the renewal of our fallen nature. In the image of God was man made, but a little lower than the angels. His nature was perfect, angelical, divine. He was an incorruptible picture of the God of glory. He bore his stamp on every part of his soul; the brightness of his Creator shone mightily upon him. But sin hath now effaced the image of God. He is no longer nearly allied to angels. He is sunk lower than the very beasts of the field. His soul is not only earthly and sensual, but devilish. Thus is the mighty fallen! The glory is departed from him! His brightness is swallowed up in utter darkness!

3. From the glorious liberty wherein he was made he is fallen into the basest bondage. The devil, whose slave he now is, to work his will, hath him so fast in prison that he cannot get forth. He hath bound him with a thousand chains, the heavy chains of his own vile affections. For every inordinate appetite, every unholy passion, as it is the express image of the god of this world, so it is the most galling yoke, the most grievous chain, that can bind a free-born spirit. And with these is every child of Adam, everyone that is born into this world, so loaded that he cannot lift up an eye, a thought to heaven; that his whole soul cleaveth unto the dust!

4. But these chains of darkness under which we groan do not only hold us in on every side, but they are within us, too; they enter into our soul; they pierce through its inmost substance. Vile affections are not only so many chains, but likewise so many diseases. Our nature is distempered, as well as enslaved; the whole head is faint, and the whole heart sick. Our body, soul, and spirit, are infected, overspread, consumed, with the most fatal leprosy. We are all over, within and without, in the eye of God, full of diseases, and wounds, and putrifying sores. Every one of our brutal passions and diabolical tempers, every kind of sensuality, pride, selfishness, is one of those deadly wounds, of

those loathsome sores, full of corruption, and of all uncleanness.

5. To recover our first estate, from which we are thus fallen, is the one thing now needful—to re-exchange the image of Satan for the image of God, bondage for freedom, sickness for health. Our one great business is to rase out of our souls the likeness of our destroyer, and to be born again, to be formed anew after the likeness of our Creator. It is our one concern to shake off this servile yoke and to regain our native freedom; to throw off every chain, every passion and desire that does not suit an angelical nature. The one work we have to do is to return from the gates of death to perfect soundness; to have our diseases cured, our wounds healed, and our uncleanness done away.

II.1. Let us in the second place consider a few of the numberless reasons which prove that this is the one thing needful; so needful that this alone is to be had in view, and pursued at all times and in all places; not indeed by neglecting our temporal affairs, but by making them all minister unto it; by so conducting them all, that every step therein may be a step to this higher end.

2. Now, that the recovery of the image of God, of this glorious liberty, of this perfect soundness, is the one thing needful upon earth, appears first from hence, that the enjoyment of them was the one end of our creation. For to this end was man created, to love God; and to this end alone, even to love the Lord his God with all his heart, and soul, and mind, and strength. But love is the very image of God: it is the brightness of his glory. By love man is not only made like God, but in some sense one with him. 'If any man love God, God loveth him, and cometh to him, and maketh his abode with him.' He 'dwelleth in God, and God in him'; and 'he that is thus joined to the Lord is one spirit.' Love is perfect freedom. As there is no fear, or pain, so there is no constraint in love. Whoever acts from this principle alone, he doth whatsoever he will. All his thoughts move freely; they follow the bent of his own mind, they run after the beloved object. All his words flow easy and unconstrained; for it is the abundance of the heart that dictates. All his actions are the result of pure choice: the thing he would, that he does, and that only. Love is the health of the soul, the full exertion of all its powers, the perfection of all its faculties. Therefore, since the enjoyment of these was the one end of our creation, the recovering of them is the one thing now needful.

3. May not the same truth appear, secondly, from hence, that this was the one end of our redemption; of all our blessed Lord did and suffered for us; of his incarnation, his life, his death? All these miracles of love were wrought with no other view than to restore us to health and freedom. Thus himself testifies of the end of his coming into the world: 'The Spirit of the Lord is upon me; he hath sent me to heal the broken-hearted, to preach deliverance to the captives'; or, as the prophet expresses it, 'to preach good tidings to the meek, to bind up the broken-hearted, to proclaim liberty to the captives, and

the opening of the prison to them that are bound'. For this only he lived, that he might heal every disease, every spiritual sickness of our nature. For this only he died, that he might deliver those who were all their lifetime subject to bondage. And it was in pursuance of the very same design that he gave us his merciful law. The end of his commandment, too, was only our health, liberty, perfection, or, to say all in one word, charity. All the parts of it centre in this one point, our renewal in the love of God; either enjoining what is necessary for our recovery thereof, or forbidding what is obstructive of it. Therefore this, being the one end of our redemption as well as our creation, is the one thing needful for us upon earth.

4. This is the one thing needful, thirdly, because it is the one end of all God's providential dispensations. Pleasure and pain, health and sickness, riches and poverty, honour and dishonour, friends and enemies, are all bestowed by his unerring wisdom and goodness with a view to this one thing. The will of God, in allotting us our several portions of all these, is solely our sanctification; our recovery from that vile bondage, the love of his creatures, to the free love of our Creator. All his providences, be they mild or severe, point at no other end than this. They are all designed either to wean us from what is not, or to unite us to what is worthy our affection. Are they pleasing? Then they are designed to lift up our hearts to the Parent of all good. Are they painful? Then they are means of rooting out those passions that forcibly withhold us from him. So that all lead that same way, either directly or indirectly, either by gratitude or mortification. For to those that have ears to hear, every loss, especially of what was nearest and dearest to them, speaks as clearly as if it were an articulate voice from heaven, 'Little children, keep yourselves from idols.' Every pain cries aloud, 'Love not the world, neither the things of the world.' And every pleasure says, with a still small voice, 'Thou shalt love the Lord thy God with all thy heart.'

5. To the same end are all the internal dispensations of God, all the influences of his Holy Spirit. Whether he gives us joy or sorrow of heart, whether he inspires us with vigour and cheerfulness, or permits us to sink into numbness of soul, into dryness and heaviness, 'tis all with the same view, viz., to restore us to health, to liberty, to holiness. These are all designed to heal those inbred diseases of our nature, self-love, and the love of the world. They are all given together with the daily bread of his external dispensations, to enable us to turn that into proper nourishment, and so recover his love, the health of our souls. Therefore the renewal of our nature in this love being not only the one end of our creation and our redemption, but likewise of all the providences of God over us, and all the operations of his Spirit in us, must be, as the eternal wisdom of God hath declared, the one thing needful.

[III.] Exh[ortation.] 1. How great reason is there, then, even in the Christian world, to resume the Apostle's exhortation, 'Awake, thou that sleepest, and arise from the dead!' Hath not Christ given thee light? Why then sittest thou still in the shadow of death? What slumber is this which hangs on thy temples? Knowest thou not that only one thing is needful? What then are all these? Why hath any but that the least place in thy thoughts, the least share in thy affections? Is the entertainment of the senses the one thing needful? Or the gratifying the imagination with uncommon, or great, or beautiful objects? Our Lord saith not so. Saith he then that the one thing is to acquire a fortune, or to increase that thou hast already? I tell you, Nay: these may be the thoughts of those that dream, but they cannot [be those] of waking men. Is it to obtain honour, power, reputation, or (as the phrase is) to get preferment? Is the one thing to gain a large share in that fairest of the fruits of earth, learning? No. Though any of these may sometimes be conducive to, none of them is, the one thing needful. That is simply to escape out of the snare of the devil, to regain an angelical nature; to recover the image wherein we were formed; to be like the Most High. This, this alone, is the one end of our abode here; for this alone are we placed on the earth; for this alone did the Son of God pour out his blood; for this alone doth his Holy Spirit watch over us. One thing we have to do, to press towards this mark of the prize of our high calling; to emerge out of chains, diseases, death, into liberty, health, and life immortal!

2. Let us well observe, that our Lord doth not call this our main concern, our great business, the chief thing needful, but the *one* thing—all others being either parts of this or quite foreign to the end of life. On this then let us fix our single view, our pure unmixed intention; regarding nothing at all, small or great, but as it stands referred to this. We must use many means; but let us ever remember we have but one end. For as while our eye is single our whole body will be full of light, so, should it ever cease to be single, in that moment our whole body would be full of darkness.

3. Be we then continually jealous over our souls, that there be no mixture in our intention. Be it our one view in all our thoughts, and words, and works, to be partakers of the divine nature, to regain the highest measure we can of that faith which works by love, and makes us become one spirit with God. I say, the highest measure we can; for who will plead for any abatement of health, liberty, life, and glory? Let us then labour to be made perfectly whole, to burst every bond in sunder; to attain the fullest conquest over this body of death, the most entire renovation of our nature; knowing this, that when the Son of man shall send forth his angels to cast the double-minded into outer darkness, then shall the single of heart receive the one thing they sought, and shine forth as the sun in the kingdom of their Father!

Now to God the Father, God the Son, and God the Holy Ghost, be ascribed all honour and glory, adoration and worship, both now and for ever. Amen.

SALVATION BY FAITH

Sermon 1 – 1738

AN INTRODUCTORY COMMENT

This sermon is the first of four that Wesley prefixed to his first volume of collected sermons as proof of the consistency of his new preaching, whether before the University of Oxford or to the masses in Moorfields. Those four sermons also mark out the successive stages of his alienation from the university as he made the radical shift in his commitment to the Revival as his new vocation.

As an Oxford tutor, Wesley was subject to occasional appointment as preacher in the university services on Sundays and saints' days, which 'all doctors, masters, graduates, and scholars' were obliged to attend. Even though this obligation was often honoured in the breach, such occasions were still splendid sounding boards for preachers with earnest messages. John Wesley preached nine university sermons between November 1730 and September 1735, far more than the usual rotation would have required. This frequency suggests that Wesley was more widely appreciated at Oxford as a preacher than the popular stereotypes have suggested or, perhaps, that Wesley was more willing than others to serve in this capacity, and took their turns if called upon.

The university officials asked Wesley to preach again in Oxford on the Festival of St. Barnabas, June 11, 1738, soon after his return from Georgia. During the previous months, Wesley had undergone the radical change of heart and mind that culminated on May 24, 1738, about which his Oxford colleagues would have known little. Meanwhile, he had already tested his 'new gospel' ('salvation by faith alone') in several churches in and near London, invariably stirring up controversy, which resulted in his being banned from those pulpits.

He could not have expected a sympathetic hearing at Oxford. 'Salvation by Faith' was, however, the first public occasion after his 'Aldersgate' experience for a positive evangelical manifesto. It is worth noting that its Moravian substance is qualified by echoes from the Book of Homilies, as in the claim that salvation involved a power not to commit sin. There is also an obvious Anglican nuance in the definition of saving faith presented here.

Salvation by Faith

By grace ye are saved through faith.
Ephesians 2:8

1. All the blessings which God hath bestowed upon man are of his mere grace, bounty, or favour: his free, undeserved favour, favour altogether undeserved, man having no claim to the least of his mercies. It was free grace that 'formed man of the dust of the ground, and breathed into him a living soul', and stamped on that soul the image of God, and 'put all things under his feet'. The same free grace continues to us, at this day, life, and breath, and all things. For there is nothing we are, or have, or do, which can deserve the least thing at God's hand. 'All our works thou, O God, hast wrought in us.' These therefore are so many more instances of free mercy: and whatever righteousness may be found in man, this also is the gift of God.

2. Wherewithal then shall a sinful man atone for any the least of his sins? With his own works? No. Were they ever so many or holy, they are not his own, but God's. But indeed they are all unholy and sinful themselves, so that every one of them needs a fresh atonement. Only corrupt fruit grows on a corrupt tree. And his heart is altogether corrupt and abominable, being 'come short of the glory of God', the glorious righteousness at first impressed on his soul, after the image of his great Creator. Therefore having nothing, neither righteousness nor works, to plead, his 'mouth is utterly stopped before God'.

3. If then sinful man find favour with God, it is 'grace upon grace' (χάριν ἀντι χάριτος). If God vouchsafe still to pour fresh blessings upon us—yea, the greatest of all blessings, salvation—what can we say to these things but 'Thanks be unto God for his unspeakable gift!' And thus it is. Herein 'God commendeth his love toward us, in that, while we were yet sinners, Christ died' to save us. 'By grace', then, 'are ye saved through faith.' Grace is the source, faith the condition, of salvation.

Now, that we fall not short of the grace of God, it concerns us carefully to inquire:

I. What faith it is through which we are saved.
II. What is the salvation which is through faith.
III. How we may answer some objections.

I. What faith it is through which we are saved.

1. And, first, it is not barely the faith of a heathen. Now God requireth of

a heathen to believe 'that God is, and that he is a rewarder of them that diligently seek him'; and that he is to be sought by 'glorifying him as God by giving him thanks for all things', and by a careful practice of moral virtue, of justice, mercy, and truth, toward their fellow-creatures. A Greek or Roman, therefore, yea, a Scythian or Indian, was without excuse if he did not believe thus much: the being and attributes of God, a future state of reward and punishment, and the obligatory nature of moral virtue. For this is barely the faith of a heathen.

2. Nor, secondly, is it the faith of a devil, though this goes much farther than that of a heathen. For the devil believes, not only that there is a wise and powerful God, gracious to reward and just to punish, but also that Jesus is the Son of God, the Christ, the Saviour of the world. So we find him declaring in express terms: 'I know thee who thou art, the Holy One of God' (Luke 4:34). Nor can we doubt but that unhappy spirit believes all those words which came out of the mouth of the Holy One; yea, and whatsoever else was written by those holy men of old, of two of whom he was compelled to give that glorious testimony, 'These men are the servants of the most high God, who show unto you the way of salvation.' Thus much then the great enemy of God and man believes, and trembles in believing, that 'God was made manifest in the flesh'; that he will 'tread all enemies under his feet'; and that 'all Scripture was given by inspiration of God.' Thus far goeth the faith of a devil.

3. Thirdly, the faith through which we are saved, in that sense of the word which will hereafter be explained, is not barely that which the apostles themselves had while Christ was yet upon earth; though they so believed on him as to 'leave all and follow him'; although they had then power to work miracles, 'to heal all manner of sickness, and all manner of disease'; yea, they had then 'power and authority over all devils': and which is beyond all this, were sent by their Master to 'preach the kingdom of God'. Yet after their return from doing all these mighty works their Lord himself terms them, 'a faithless generation'. He tells them 'they could not cast out a devil, because of their unbelief.' And when long after, supposing they had some already, they said unto him, 'Increase our faith,' he tells them plainly that of this faith they had none at all, no, not as a grain of mustard seed: 'The Lord said, If ye had faith as a grain of mustard seed, ye might say unto this sycamine tree, Be thou plucked up by the roots, and be thou planted in the sea; and it should obey you.'

4. What faith is it then through which we are saved? It may be answered: first, in general, it is a faith in Christ—Christ, and God through Christ, are the proper object of it. Herein therefore it is sufficiently, absolutely, distinguished from the faith either of ancient or modern heathens. And from the faith of a devil it is fully distinguished by this—it is not barely a speculative, rational thing, a cold, lifeless assent, a train of ideas in the head; but also a

disposition of the heart. For thus saith the Scripture, 'With the heart man believeth unto righteousness.' And, 'If thou shalt confess with thy mouth the Lord Jesus, and shalt believe with thy *heart* that God hath raised him from the dead, thou shalt be saved.'

5. And herein does it differ from that faith which the apostles themselves had while our Lord was on earth, that it acknowledges the necessity and merit of his death, and the power of his resurrection. It acknowledges his death as the only sufficient means of redeeming man from death eternal, and his resurrection as the restoration of us all to life and immortality; inasmuch as he 'was delivered for our sins, and rose again for our justification'. Christian faith is then not only an assent to the whole gospel of Christ, but also a full reliance on the blood of Christ, a trust in the merits of his life, death, and resurrection; a recumbency upon him as our atonement and our life, as *given for us*, and *living in us*. It is a sure confidence which a man hath in God, that through the merits of Christ *his* sins are forgiven, and *he* reconciled to the favour of God; and in consequence hereof a closing with him and cleaving to him as our 'wisdom, righteousness, sanctification, and redemption' or, in one word, our salvation.

II. What salvation it is which is through this faith is the second thing to be considered.

1. And, first, whatsoever else it imply, it is a present salvation. It is something attainable, yea, actually attained on earth, by those who are partakers of this faith. For thus saith the Apostle to the believers at Ephesus, and in them to the believers of all ages, not, 'Ye *shall be*' (though that also is true), but 'Ye *are* saved through faith.'

2. Ye are saved (to comprise all in one word) from sin. This is the salvation which is through faith. This is that great salvation foretold by the angel before God brought his first-begotten into the world: 'Thou shalt call his name Jesus, for he shall save his people from their sins.' And neither here nor in other parts of Holy Writ is there any limitation or restriction. All his people, or as it is elsewhere expressed, all that believe in him, he will save from all their sins: from original and actual, past and present sin, of the flesh and of the spirit. Through faith that is in him they are saved both from the guilt and from the power of it.

3. First, from the guilt of all past sin. For whereas 'all the world is guilty before God'; insomuch that should he 'be extreme to mark what is done amiss, there is none that could abide it'; and whereas 'by the law is only the knowledge of sin', but no deliverance from it, so that 'by fulfilling the deeds of the law no flesh can be justified in his sight'; now 'the righteousness of God, which is by faith of Jesus Christ', 'is manifested unto all that believe'. Now they are 'justified freely by his grace through the redemption that is in Jesus Christ. Him God

hath set forth to be a propitiation through faith in his blood, to declare his righteousness for (or by) the remission of the sins that are past.' Now hath Christ 'taken away the curse of the law, being made a curse for us'. He hath 'blotted out the handwriting that was against us, taking it out of the way, nailing it to his cross'. 'There is therefore no condemnation now to them which believe in Christ Jesus.'

4. And being saved from guilt, they are saved from fear. Not indeed from a filial fear of offending, but from all servile fear, from that 'fear which hath torment', from fear of punishment, from fear of the wrath of God, whom they now no longer regard as a severe master, but as an indulgent Father. 'They have not received again the spirit of bondage, but the Spirit of adoption, whereby they cry, Abba, Father: the Spirit itself also bearing witness with their spirit, that they are the children of God.' They are also saved from the fear, though not from the possibility, of falling away from the grace of God, and coming short of the great and precious promises. They are 'sealed with the Holy Spirit of promise, which is the earnest of their inheritance'. Thus have they 'peace with God through our Lord Jesus Christ. . . . They rejoice in hope of the glory of God. . . . And the love of God is shed abroad in their hearts through the Holy Ghost which is given unto them.' And hereby they are 'persuaded' (though perhaps not all at all times, nor with the same fullness of persuasion) 'that neither death, nor life, nor things present, nor things to come, nor height, nor depth, nor any other creature, shall be able to separate them from the love of God, which is in Christ Jesus our Lord.'

5. Again, through this faith they are saved from the power of sin as well as from the guilt of it. So the Apostle declares, 'Ye know that he was manifested to take away our sins, and in him is no sin. Whosoever abideth in him sinneth not' (1 John 3:5–6). Again, 'Little children, let no man deceive you. . . . He that committeth sin is of the devil.' 'Whosoever believeth is born of God.' And, 'Whosoever is born of God doth not commit sin; for his seed remaineth in him: and he cannot sin, because he is born of God.' Once more, 'We know that whosoever is born of God sinneth not; but he that is begotten of God keepeth himself, and that wicked one toucheth him not' (1 John 5:18).

6. He that is by faith born of God sinneth not (1) by any habitual sin, for all habitual sin is sin reigning; but sin cannot reign in any that believeth. Nor (2) by any wilful sin; for his will, while he abideth in the faith, is utterly set against all sin, and abhorreth it as deadly poison. Nor (3) by any sinful desire; for he continually desireth the holy and perfect will of God; and any unholy desire he by the grace of God stifleth in the birth. Nor (4) doth he sin by infirmities, whether in act, word, or thought; for his infirmities have no concurrence of his will; and without this they are not properly sins. Thus, 'He that is born of God doth not commit sin.' And though he cannot say he *hath not sinned*, yet now '*he sinneth not*'.

7. This then is the salvation which is through faith, even in the present world: a salvation from sin and the consequences of sin, both often expressed in the word 'justification', which, taken in the largest sense, implies a deliverance from guilt and punishment, by the atonement of Christ actually applied to the soul of the sinner now believing on him, and a deliverance from the power of sin, through Christ 'formed in his heart'. So that he who is thus justified or saved by faith is indeed 'born again'. He is 'born again of the Spirit' unto a new 'life which is hid with Christ in God'. And as a 'newborn babe he gladly receives the ἄδολον, the sincere milk of the word, and grows thereby'; 'going on in the might of the Lord his God', 'from faith to faith', 'from grace to grace', 'until at length he comes unto a perfect man, unto the measure of the stature of the fullness of Christ'.

III. The first usual objection to this is,

1. That to preach salvation or justification by faith only is to preach against holiness and good works. To which a short answer might be given: it would be so if we spake, as some do, of a faith which was separate from these. But we speak of a faith which is not so, but necessarily productive of all good works and all holiness.

2. But it may be of use to consider it more at large: especially since it is no new objection, but as old as St. Paul's time, for even then it was asked, 'Do we not make void the law through faith?' We answer, first, all who preach not faith do manifestly make void the law, either directly and grossly, by limitations and comments that eat out all the spirit of the text; or indirectly, by not pointing out the only means whereby it is possible to perform it. Whereas, secondly, 'We establish the law', both by showing its full extent and spiritual meaning, and by calling all to that living way whereby 'the righteousness of the law may be fulfilled in them'. These, while they trust in the blood of Christ alone, use all the ordinances which he hath appointed, do all the 'good works which he had before prepared that they should walk therein', and enjoy and manifest all holy and heavenly tempers, even the same 'mind that was in Christ Jesus'.

3. But does not preaching this faith lead men into pride? We answer, accidentally it may. Therefore ought every believer to be earnestly cautioned (in the words of the great Apostle): 'Because of unbelief the first branches were broken off, and thou standest by faith. Be not high-minded, but fear. If God spared not the natural branches, take heed lest he spare not thee. Behold therefore the goodness and severity of God: on them which fell, severity; but toward thee, goodness, if thou continue in his goodness: otherwise thou also shalt be cut off.' And while he continues therein, he will remember those words of St. Paul, foreseeing and answering this very objection: 'Where is boasting, then? It is excluded. By what law? Of works? Nay; but by the law of faith' (Rom. 3:27). If a man were justified by his works, he would have whereof to glory.

But there is no glorying for him 'that worketh not, but believeth on him that justifieth the ungodly' (Rom. 4:5). To the same effect are the words both preceding and following the text: 'God, who is rich in mercy, . . . even when we were dead in sins, hath quickened us together with Christ (by grace ye are saved), . . . that he might show the exceeding riches of his grace in his kindness toward us through Christ Jesus. For by grace ye are saved through faith: and that not of yourselves' (Eph. 2:4–5, 7–8). Of yourselves cometh neither your faith nor your salvation. 'It is the gift of God,' the free, undeserved gift—the faith through which ye are saved, as well as the salvation which he of his own good pleasure, his mere favour, annexes thereto. That ye believe is one instance of his grace; that believing, ye are saved, another. 'Not of works, lest any man should boast.' For all our works, all our righteousness, which were before our believing, merited nothing of God but condemnation, so far were they from deserving faith, which therefore, whenever given, is not 'of works'. Neither is salvation of the works we do when we believe. For 'it is' then 'God that worketh in us'. And, therefore, that he giveth us a reward for what he himself worketh only commendeth the riches of his mercy, but leaveth us nothing whereof to glory.

4. However, may not the speaking thus of the mercy of God, as saving or justifying freely by faith only, encourage men in sin? Indeed it may and will; many will 'continue in sin, that grace may abound'. But their blood is upon their own head. The goodness of God ought to lead them to repentance, and so it will those who are sincere of heart. When they know there is yet forgiveness with him, they will cry aloud that he would blot out their sins also through faith which is in Jesus. And if they earnestly cry and faint not, if they seek him in all the means he hath appointed, if they refuse to be comforted till he come, he 'will come, and will not tarry'. And he can do much work in a short time. Many are the examples in the Acts of the Apostles of God's working this faith in men's hearts as quick as lightning falling from heaven. So in the same hour that Paul and Silas began to preach the jailer *repented, believed,* and *was baptized*—as were three thousand by St. Peter on the day of Pentecost, who all repented and believed at his first preaching. And, blessed be God, there are now many living proofs that he is still thus 'mighty to save'.

5. Yet to the same truth, placed in another view, a quite contrary objection is made: 'If a man cannot be saved by all that he can do, this will drive men to despair.' True, to despair of being saved by their own works, their own merits or righteousness. And so it ought; for none can trust in the merits of Christ till he has utterly renounced his own. He that 'goeth about to establish his own righteousness' cannot receive the righteousness of God. The righteousness which is of faith cannot be given him while he trusteth in that which is of the law.

6. But this, it is said, is an uncomfortable doctrine. The devil spoke like

himself, that is, without either truth or shame, when he dared to suggest to men that it is such. 'Tis the only comfortable one, 'tis 'very full of comfort', to all self-destroyed, self-condemned sinners. That 'whosoever believeth on him shall not be ashamed'; that 'the same Lord over all is rich unto all that call upon him'—here is comfort, high as heaven, stronger than death! What! Mercy for all? For Zaccheus, a public robber? For Mary Magdalene, a common harlot? Methinks I hear one say, 'Then I, even I, may hope for mercy!' And so thou mayst, thou afflicted one, whom none hath comforted! God will not cast out thy prayer. Nay, perhaps he may say the next hour, 'Be of good cheer, thy sins are forgiven thee'; so forgiven that they shall reign over thee no more; yea, and that 'the Holy Spirit shall bear witness with thy spirit that thou art a child of God.' O glad tidings! Tidings of great joy, which are sent unto all people. 'Ho, everyone that thirsteth, come ye to the waters; come ye and buy without money, and without price.' Whatsoever your sins be, 'though red, like crimson', though 'more than the hairs of your head', 'return ye unto the Lord, and he will have mercy upon you, and to our God, for he will abundantly pardon.'

7. When no more objections occur, then we are simply told that salvation by faith only ought not to be preached as the first doctrine, or at least not to be preached to all. But what saith the Holy Ghost? 'Other foundation can no man lay than that which is laid, even Jesus Christ.' So, then, 'that whosoever believeth on him shall be saved' is and must be the foundation of all our preaching; that is, must be preached first. 'Well, but not to all.' To whom then are we not to preach it? Whom shall we except? The poor? Nay, they have a peculiar right to have the gospel preached unto them. The unlearned? No. God hath revealed these things unto unlearned and ignorant men from the beginning. The young? By no means. 'Suffer these' in any wise 'to come unto Christ, and forbid them not.' The sinners? Least of all. He 'came not to call the righteous, but sinners to repentance'. Why then, if any, we are to except the rich, the learned, the reputable, the moral men. And 'tis true, they too often except themselves from hearing; yet we must speak the words of our Lord. For thus the tenor of our commission runs: 'Go and preach the gospel to every creature.' If any man wrest it or any part of it to his destruction, he must bear his own burden. But still, 'as the Lord liveth, whatsoever the Lord saith unto us, that we will speak.'

8. At this time more especially will we speak, that 'by grace ye are saved through faith': because never was the maintaining this doctrine more seasonable than it is at this day. Nothing but this can effectually prevent the increase of the Romish delusion among us. 'Tis endless to attack one by one all the errors of that Church. But salvation by faith strikes at the root, and all fall at once where this is established. It was this doctrine (which our Church justly calls 'the strong rock and foundation of the Christian religion') that first drove popery out of these kingdoms, and 'tis this alone can keep it out. Nothing but

this can give a check to that immorality which hath overspread the land as a flood. Can you empty the great deep drop by drop? Then you may reform us by dissuasives from particular vices. But let 'the righteousness which is of God by faith' be brought in, and so shall its proud waves be stayed. Nothing but this can stop the mouths of those who 'glory in their shame', 'and openly deny the Lord that bought them'. They can talk as sublimely of the law as he that hath it written by God in his heart. To hear them speak on this head might incline one to think they were not far from the kingdom of God. But take them out of the law into the gospel; begin with the righteousness of faith, with 'Christ, the end of the law to everyone that believeth', and those who but now appeared almost if not altogether Christians stand confessed the sons of perdition, as far from life and salvation (God be merciful unto them!) as the depth of hell from the height of heaven.

9. For this reason the adversary so rages whenever 'salvation by faith' is declared to the world. For this reason did he stir up earth and hell to destroy those who first preached it. And for the same reason, knowing that faith alone could overturn the foundations of his kingdom, did he call forth all his forces, and employ all his arts of lies and calumny, to affright that glorious champion of the Lord of Hosts, Martin Luther, from reviving it. Nor can we wonder thereat. For as that man of God observes, 'How would it enrage a proud strong man armed to be stopped and set at nought by a little child, coming against him with a reed in his hand!'—especially when he knew that little child would surely overthrow him and tread him under foot. 'Even so, Lord Jesus!' Thus hath thy strength been ever 'made perfect in weakness'! Go forth then, thou little child that believest in him, and his 'right hand shall teach thee terrible things'! Though thou art helpless and weak as an infant of days, the strong man shall not be able to stand before thee. Thou shalt prevail over him, and subdue him, and overthrow him, and trample him under thy feet. Thou shalt march on under the great Captain of thy salvation, 'conquering and to conquer', until all thine enemies are destroyed, and 'death is swallowed up in victory'.

Now thanks be to God which giveth us the victory through our Lord Jesus Christ, to whom, with the Father and the Holy Ghost, be blessing and glory, and wisdom, and thanksgiving, and honour, and power, and might, for ever and ever. Amen.

FREE GRACE

Sermon 110 – 1739

AN INTRODUCTORY COMMENT

This sermon is the signal of a major schism in the ranks of English evangelicals, marked by a personal breach between John Wesley and George Whitefield that was never more than partially healed. Wesley herein totally rejected predestination in all its Calvinist versions, with the predictable result that terms for further doctrinal dialogue between the 'Calvinists' and 'Arminians' were sharply constricted.

Whitefield and Wesley had been active allies in the mid-1730s, and Whitefield had opened Wesley's way into the Revival in 1739. Whitefield, an exciting preacher who was Wesley's junior by ten years, took for granted that the doctrine of justification by faith stood or fell with the presupposition of irresistible grace. Wesley had preached against predestination within weeks of the launching of the Revival, believing that this kind of preaching was a necessary corollary of preaching universal redemption by faith. On April 26, 1739, he drew lots about restricting his attack on predestination but received the lot, 'preach and print'; consequently he published this sermon. It went through at least ten pamphlet editions during his lifetime but was not included in his collected *Sermons*. In his collected *Works*, Wesley inserted it among his controversial writings.

In 1765, Wesley claimed that on the point of justification, he had never differed 'from [Mr. Calvin] an hair's breadth'. It would seem that he had forgotten the charges levied here in *Free Grace*. If Wesley came later to share and commend a truly 'catholic spirit', *Free Grace* is a useful illustration of Wesley's temper and methods as a polemicist, despite the irenic tone of his prefatory note to the reader:

> Nothing but the strongest conviction, not only that what is here advanced is 'the truth as it is in Jesus', but also that I am indispensably obliged to declare this truth to all the world, could have induced me openly to oppose the sentiments of those whom I highly esteem for their works' sake: at whose feet may I be found in the day of the Lord Jesus!
>
> Should any believe it his duty to reply hereto, I have only one request to make: let whatsoever you do be done in charity, in love, and in the spirit of meekness. Let your very disputing show that you have 'put on, as the elect of God, bowels of mercies, gentleness, long-suffering': that even according to this time it may be said, 'See how these Christians love one another.'

Free Grace

He that spared not his own Son, but delivered him up for us all, how shall he not with him also freely give us all things?
Romans 8:32

1. How freely does God love the world! While we were yet sinners, 'Christ died for the ungodly.' While we were 'dead in sin', God 'spared not his own Son, but delivered him up for us all.' And how 'freely with him' does he 'give us all things'! Verily, free grace is all in all!

2. The grace or love of God, whence cometh our salvation, is free in all, and free for all.

3. First, it is free in all to whom it is given. It does not depend on any power or merit in man; no, not in any degree, neither in whole, nor in part. It does not in any wise depend either on the good works or righteousness of the receiver; not on anything he has done, or anything he is. It does not depend on his endeavours. It does not depend on his good tempers, or good desires, or good purposes and intentions; for all these flow from the free grace of God. They are the streams only, not the fountain. They are the fruits of free grace, and not the root. They are not the cause, but the effects of it. Whatsoever good is in man, or is done by man, God is the author and doer of it. Thus is his grace free in all, that is, no way depending on any power or merit in man, but on God alone, who freely gave us his own Son, and 'with him freely giveth us all things'.

4. But is it free for all, as well as in all? To this some have answered: 'No: it is free only for those whom God hath ordained to life, and they are but a little flock. The greater part of mankind God hath ordained to death; and it is not free for them. Them God hateth, and therefore before they were born decreed they should die eternally. And this he absolutely decreed; because so was his good pleasure, because it was his sovereign will. Accordingly, they are born for this: to be destroyed body and soul in hell. And they grow up under the irrevocable curse of God, without any possibility of redemption. For what grace God gives he gives only for this: to increase, not prevent, their damnation.'

5. This is that decree of predestination. But methinks I hear one say: 'This is not the predestination which I hold. I hold only "the election of grace". What I believe is no more than this, that God, before the foundation of the world, did elect a certain number of men to be justified, sanctified, and

glorified. Now all these will be saved, and none else. For the rest of mankind God leaves to themselves: so they follow the imaginations of their own hearts, which are only evil continually, and, waxing worse and worse, are at length justly punished with everlasting destruction.'

6. Is this all the predestination which you hold? Consider; perhaps this is not all. Do not you believe 'God ordained them to this very thing'? If so, you believe the whole decree; you hold predestination in the full sense, which has been above described. But it may be you think you do not. Do not you then believe God hardens the hearts of them that perish? Do not you believe he (literally) hardened Pharaoh's heart, and that for this end he raised him up (or created him)? Why, this amounts to just the same thing. If you believe Pharaoh, or any one man upon the earth, was created for this end–to be damned–you hold all that has been said of predestination. And there is no need you should add that God seconds his decree, which is supposed unchangeable and irresistible, by hardening the hearts of those vessels of wrath whom that decree had before fitted for destruction.

7. Well, but it may be you do not believe even this. You do not hold any decree of reprobation. You do not think God decrees any man to be damned, nor hardens, irresistibly fits him for damnation. You only say, 'God eternally decreed that, all being dead in sin, he would say to some of the dry bones, "Live", and to others he would not; that consequently these should be made alive, and those abide in death–these should glorify God by their salvation, and those by their destruction.'

8. Is not this what you mean by 'the election of grace'? If it be, I would ask one or two questions. Are any who are not thus elected, saved? Or were any, from the foundation of the world? Is it possible any man should be saved unless he be thus elected? If you say 'No', you are but where you was. You are not got one hair's breadth further. You still believe that in consequence of an unchangeable, irresistible decree of God the greater part of mankind abide in death, without any possibility of redemption: inasmuch as none *can* save them but God, and he *will not* save them. You believe *he hath absolutely decreed not to save them*; and what is this but decreeing to damn them? It is, in effect, neither more nor less; it comes to the same thing. For if you are dead, and altogether unable to make yourself alive; then if God has absolutely decreed he will make others only alive, and not you, he hath absolutely decreed your everlasting death–you are absolutely consigned to damnation. So then, though you use softer words than some, you mean the selfsame thing. And God's decree concerning the election of grace, according to your own account of it, amounts to neither more nor less than what others call, 'God's decree of reprobation'.

9. Call it therefore by whatever name you please–'election', 'preterition', 'predestination', or 'reprobation'–it comes in the end to the same thing. The

sense of all is plainly this: 'By virtue of an eternal, unchangeable, irresistible decree of God, one part of mankind are infallibly saved, and the rest infallibly damned; it being impossible that any of the former should be damned, or that any of the latter should be saved.'

10. But if this be so, then is all preaching vain. It is needless to them that are elected. For they, whether with preaching or without, will infallibly be saved. Therefore the end of preaching, 'to save souls', is void with regard to them. And it is useless to them that are not elected. For they cannot possibly be saved. They, whether with preaching or without, will infallibly be damned. The end of preaching is therefore void with regard to them likewise. So that in either case, our preaching is vain, as your hearing is also vain.

11. This then is a plain proof that the doctrine of predestination is not a doctrine of God, because it makes void the ordinance of God, and God is not divided against himself. A second is that it directly tends to destroy that holiness which is the end of all the ordinances of God. I do not say, 'None who hold it are holy' (for God is of tender mercy to those who are unavoidably entangled in errors of any kind), but that the doctrine itself—that every man is either elected or not elected from eternity, and that the one must inevitably be saved, and the other inevitably damned—has a manifest tendency to destroy holiness in general, for it wholly takes away those first motives to follow after it, so frequently proposed in Scripture: the hope of future reward and fear of punishment, the hope of heaven and fear of hell. That 'these shall go away into everlasting punishment, and those into life eternal' is no motive to him to struggle for life who believes his lot is cast already: it is not reasonable for him so to do if he thinks he is unalterably adjudged either to life or death. You will say, 'But he knows not whether it is life or death.' What then? This helps not the matter. For if a sick man knows that he must unavoidably die or unavoidably recover, though he knows not which, it is not reasonable for him to take any physic at all. He might justly say (and so I have heard some speak, both in bodily sickness and in spiritual), 'If I am ordained to life, I shall live; if to death, I shall die. So I need not trouble myself about it.' So directly does this doctrine tend to shut the very gate of holiness in general, to hinder unholy men from ever approaching thereto, or striving to enter in thereat.

12. As directly does this doctrine tend to destroy several particular branches of holiness. Such are meekness and love: love, I mean, of our enemies, of the evil and unthankful. I say not that none who hold it have meekness and love (for as is the power of God, so is his mercy), but that it naturally tends to inspire or increase a sharpness or eagerness of temper which is quite contrary to the meekness of Christ—as then especially appears, when they are opposed on this head. And it as naturally inspires contempt or coldness toward those whom we suppose outcasts from God. 'Oh, (but you say) I suppose no particular man a reprobate.' You mean, you would not, if you could help it.

You can't help sometimes applying your general doctrine to particular persons. The enemy of souls will apply it for you. You know how often he has done so. But you 'rejected the thought with abhorrence'. True; as soon as you could. But how did it sour and sharpen your spirit in the meantime! You well know it was not the spirit of love which you then felt towards that poor sinner, whom you supposed or suspected, whether you would or no, to have been hated of God from eternity.

13. Thirdly, this doctrine tends to destroy the comfort of religion, the happiness of Christianity. This is evident as to all those who believe themselves to be reprobated, or who only suspect or fear it. All the great and precious promises are lost to them. They afford them no ray of comfort. 'For they are not the elect of God; therefore they have neither lot nor portion in them.' This is an effectual bar to their finding any comfort or happiness, even in that religion whose 'ways' were designed to be 'ways of pleasantness, and all her paths peace'.

14. And as to you who believe yourselves the elect of God, what is your happiness? I hope, not a notion, a speculative belief, a bare opinion of any kind; but a feeling possession of God in your heart, wrought in you by the Holy Ghost; or, 'the witness of God's Spirit with your spirit, that you are a child of God'. This, otherwise termed 'the full assurance of faith', is the true ground of a Christian's happiness. And it does indeed imply a full assurance that all your past sins are forgiven, and that you are *now* a child of God. But it does not necessarily imply a full assurance of our future perseverance. I do not say, 'This is never joined to it,' but that it is not necessarily implied therein; for many have the one who have not the other.

15. Now, this witness of the Spirit experience shows to be much obstructed by this doctrine; and not only in those who, believing themselves reprobated, by this belief thrust it far from them, but even in them that have 'tasted of that good gift', who yet have soon lost it again, and fallen back into doubts, and fears, and darkness—'horrible darkness that might be felt'. And I appeal to any of you who hold this doctrine to say, between God and your own hearts, whether you have not often a return of doubts and fears concerning your election or perseverance? If you ask, 'Who has not?' I answer, 'Very few of those that hold this doctrine.' But many, very many of those that hold it not, in all parts of the earth; many of those who know and feel they are in Christ today, and 'take no thought for the morrow'; who 'abide in him' by faith from hour to hour, or rather from moment to moment. Many of these have enjoyed the uninterrupted witness of his Spirit, the continual light of his countenance, from the moment wherein they first believed, for many months or years to this day.

16. That assurance of faith which these enjoy excludes all doubt and fear. It excludes all kind of doubt and fear concerning their future perseverance;

though it is not properly (as was said before) an assurance of what is future, but only of what *now* is. And this needs not for its support a speculative belief that whoever is once ordained to live, must live. For it is wrought from hour to hour by the mighty power of God, 'by the Holy Ghost which is given unto them'. And therefore that doctrine is not of God, because it tends to obstruct, if not destroy, this great work of the Holy Ghost, whence flows the chief comfort of religion, the happiness of Christianity.

17. Again, how uncomfortable a thought is this, that thousands and millions of men, without any preceding offence or fault of theirs, were unchangeably doomed to everlasting burnings! How peculiarly uncomfortable must it be to those who have put on Christ! To those who being filled with 'bowels of mercy, tenderness, and compassion', could even 'wish themselves accursed for their brethren's sake'.

18. Fourthly, this uncomfortable doctrine directly tends to destroy our zeal for good works. And this it does, first, as it naturally tends (according to what was observed before) to destroy our love to the greater part of mankind, namely, the evil and unthankful. For whatever lessens our love must so far lessen our desire to do them good. This it does, secondly, as it cuts off one of the strongest motives to all acts of bodily mercy, such as feeding the hungry, clothing the naked, and the like, viz., the hope of saving their souls from death. For what avails it to relieve their temporal wants who are just dropping into eternal fire? 'Well; but run and snatch them as brands out of the fire.' Nay, this you suppose impossible. They were appointed thereunto, you say, from eternity, before they had done either good or evil. You believe it is the will of God they should die. And 'who hath resisted his will?' But you say you 'do not know whether these are elected or not.' What then? If you know they are one or the other, that they are either elected or not elected, all your labour is void and vain. In either case your advice, reproof, or exhortation, is as needless and useless as our preaching. It is needless to them that are elected; for they will infallibly be saved without it. It is useless to them that are not elected; for with or without it they will infallibly be damned. Therefore you cannot, consistently with your principles, take any pains about their salvation. Consequently those principles directly tend to destroy your zeal for good works—for all good works, but particularly for the greatest of all, the saving of souls from death.

19. But, fifthly, this doctrine not only tends to destroy Christian holiness, happiness, and good works, but hath also a direct and manifest tendency to overthrow the whole Christian revelation. The point which the wisest of the modern unbelievers most industriously labour to prove is that the Christian revelation is not necessary. They well know, could they once show this, the conclusion would be too plain to be denied. 'If it be not necessary, it is not true.' Now this fundamental point you give up. For supposing that eternal, unchangeable decree, one part of mankind must be saved, though the

Christian revelation were not in being, and the other part of mankind must be damned, notwithstanding that revelation. And what would an infidel desire more? You allow him all he asks. In making the gospel thus unnecessary to all sorts of men you give up the whole Christian cause. 'O tell it not in Gath! Publish it not in the streets of Askelon! Lest the daughters of the uncircumcised rejoice, lest the sons of unbelief triumph!'

20. And as this doctrine manifestly and directly tends to overthrow the whole Christian revelation, so it does the same thing, by plain consequence, in making that revelation contradict itself. For it is grounded on such an interpretation of some texts (more or fewer it matters not) as flatly contradicts all the other texts, and indeed the whole scope and tenor of Scripture. For instance: the asserters of this doctrine interpret that text of Scripture, 'Jacob have I loved, but Esau have I hated,' as implying that God in a literal sense hated Esau and all the reprobated from eternity. Now what can possibly be a more flat contradiction than this, not only to the whole scope and tenor of Scripture, but also to all those particular texts which expressly declare, 'God is love'? Again, they infer from that text, 'I will have mercy on whom I will have mercy' (Rom. 9:15), that God is love only to some men, viz., the elect, and that he hath mercy for those only: flatly contrary to which is the whole tenor of Scripture, as is that express declaration in particular, 'The Lord is loving unto *every* man, and his mercy is over *all* his works' (Ps. 145:9). Again, they infer from that and the like texts, 'It is not of him that willeth, neither of him that runneth, but of God that showeth mercy,' that he showeth mercy only to those to whom he had respect from all eternity. 'Nay, but who replieth against God' now? You now contradict the whole oracles of God, which declare throughout, 'God is no respecter of persons' (Acts 10:34); 'There is no respect of persons with him' (Rom. 2:11). Again, from that text, 'The children being not yet born, neither having done good or evil, that the purpose of God according to election might stand, not of works, but of him that calleth, it was said unto her (unto Rebecca), The elder shall serve the younger'—you infer that our being predestinated or elect no way depends on the foreknowledge of God. Flatly contrary to this are all the Scriptures; and those in particular, 'elect according to the foreknowledge of God' (1 Pet. 1:2), [and] 'Whom he did foreknow, he also did predestinate' (Rom. 8:29).

21. And, 'The same Lord over all is rich in mercy to all that call upon him' (Rom. 10:12). But you say, 'No: he is such only to those for whom Christ died. And those are not all, but only a few, "whom God hath chosen out of the world"; for he died not for all, but only for those who were "chosen in him before the foundation of the world"' (Eph. 1:4). Flatly contrary to your interpretation of these Scriptures also is the whole tenor of the New Testament; as are in particular those texts: 'Destroy not him with thy meat for whom Christ died' (Rom. 14:15)—a clear proof that Christ died, not only for those that are

saved, but also for them that perish; He is 'the Saviour of the world' (John 4:42); He is 'the Lamb of God, that taketh away the sins of the world' (John 1:29); 'He is the propitiation, not for our sins only, but also for the sins of the whole world' (1 John 2:2); 'He (the living God) is the Saviour of all men' (1 Tim. 4:10); 'He gave himself a ransom for all' (1 Tim. 2:6); 'He tasted death for every man' (Heb. 2:9).

22. If you ask, 'Why then are not all men saved?' the whole law and the testimony answer: first, not because of any decree of God, not because it is his pleasure they should die. For, 'as I live, saith the Lord God, I have no pleasure in the death of him that dieth' (Ezek. 18:32). Whatever be the cause of their perishing it cannot be his will, if the oracles of God are true; for they declare, 'He is not willing that any should perish, but that all should come to repentance' (2 Pet. 3:9). He 'willeth that all men should be saved'. And they, secondly, declare what is the cause why all men are not saved: namely, that they will not be saved. So our Lord expressly: 'They will not come unto me that they may have life' (John 5:40); 'The power of the Lord is present to heal them,' but they will not be healed. They 'reject the counsel', the merciful counsel 'of God against themselves', as did their stiff-necked forefathers. And therefore are they without excuse, because God would save them, but they will not be saved. This is the condemnation, 'How often would I have gathered you together, and ye would not' (Matt. 23:37).

23. Thus manifestly does this doctrine tend to overthrow the whole Christian revelation, by making it contradict itself; by giving such an interpretation of some texts as flatly contradicts all the other texts, and indeed the whole scope and tenor of Scripture—an abundant proof that it is not of God. But neither is this all. For, seventhly, it is a doctrine full of blasphemy; of such blasphemy as I should dread to mention but that the honour of our gracious God and the cause of his truth will not suffer me to be silent. In the cause of God, then, and from a sincere concern for the glory of his great name, I will mention a few of the horrible blasphemies contained in this horrible doctrine. But first, I must warn every one of you that hears, as ye will answer it at the great day, not to charge me (as some have done) with blaspheming because I mention the blasphemy of others. And the more you are grieved with them that do thus blaspheme, see that ye 'confirm your love towards them' the more, and that your heart's desire and continual prayer to God be, 'Father, forgive them; for they know not what they do.'

24. This premised, let it be observed that this doctrine represents our Blessed Lord—'Jesus Christ the righteous', 'the only-begotten Son of the Father, full of grace and truth'—as an hypocrite, a deceiver of the people, a man void of common sincerity. For it cannot be denied that he everywhere speaks *as if he was* willing that all men should be saved. Therefore, to say *he was not* willing that all men should be saved is to represent him as a mere hypocrite and

dissembler. It can't be denied that the gracious words which came out of his mouth are full of invitations to all sinners. To say, then, he did not *intend* to save all sinners is to represent him as a gross deceiver of the people. You cannot deny that he says, 'Come unto me, all ye that are weary and heavy laden.' If then you say he calls those that cannot come, those whom he knows to be unable to come, those whom he can make able to come but will not, how is it possible to describe greater insincerity? You represent him as mocking his helpless creatures by offering what he never intends to give. You describe him as saying one thing and meaning another; as pretending the love which he had not. Him 'in whose mouth was no guile' you make full of deceit, void of common sincerity. Then especially, when, drawing nigh the city, 'he wept over it', and said, 'O Jerusalem, Jerusalem, thou that killest the prophets, and stonest them that are sent unto thee, how often would I have gathered thy children together . . . and *ye would not*' (ἠθέλησα . . . καὶ οὐκ ἠθελήσατε). Now if you say, 'They would', but 'he would not,' you represent him (which who could hear?) as weeping crocodile's tears, weeping over the prey which himself had doomed to destruction.

25. Such blasphemy this, as one would think might make the ears of a Christian tingle. But there is yet more behind; for just as it honours the Son, so doth this doctrine honour the Father. It destroys all his attributes at once. It overturns both his justice, mercy, and truth. Yea, it represents the most Holy God as worse than the devil; as both more false, more cruel, and more unjust. More false; because the devil, liar as he is, hath never said he 'willeth all men to be saved'. More unjust; because the devil cannot, if he would, be guilty of such injustice as you ascribe to God when you say that God condemned millions of souls to everlasting fire prepared for the devil and his angels for continuing in sin, which for want of that grace *he will not* give them, they cannot avoid. And more cruel; because that unhappy spirit 'seeketh rest and findeth none'; so that his own restless misery is a kind of temptation to him to tempt others. But God 'resteth in his high and holy place'; so that to suppose him of his own mere motion, of his pure will and pleasure, happy as he is, to doom his creatures, whether they will or no, to endless misery, is to impute such cruelty to him as we cannot impute even to the great enemy of God and man. It is to represent the most high God (he that hath ears to hear, let him hear!) as more cruel, false, and unjust than the devil.

26. This is the blasphemy clearly contained in 'the horrible decree' of predestination. And here I fix my foot. On this I join issue with every asserter of it. You represent God as worse than the devil—more false, more cruel, more unjust. But you say you will 'prove it by Scripture'. Hold! What will you prove by Scripture? That God is worse than the devil? It cannot be. Whatever that Scripture proves, it never can prove this. Whatever its true meaning be, this cannot be its true meaning. Do you ask, 'What is its true meaning, then?' If I

say, 'I know not,' you have gained nothing. For there are many Scriptures the true sense whereof neither you nor I shall know till death is swallowed up in victory. But this I know, better it were to say it had no sense at all than to say it had such a sense as this. It cannot mean, whatever it mean besides, that the God of truth is a liar. Let it mean what it will, it cannot mean that the Judge of all the world is unjust. No Scripture can mean that God is not love, or that his mercy is not over all his works. That is, whatever it prove beside, no Scripture can prove predestination.

27. This is the blasphemy for which (however I love the persons who assert it) I abhor the doctrine of predestination: a doctrine upon the supposition of which, if one could possibly suppose it for a moment (call it election, reprobation, or what you please, for all comes to the same thing) one might say to our adversary the devil: 'Thou fool, why dost thou roar about any longer? Thy lying in wait for souls is as needless and useless as our preaching. Hearest thou not that God hath taken thy work out of thy hands? And that he doth it much more effectually? Thou, with all thy principalities and powers, canst only so assault that we may resist thee; but he can irresistibly destroy both body and soul in hell! Thou canst only entice; but his unchangeable decree to leave thousands of souls in death compels them to continue in sin till they drop into everlasting burnings. Thou temptest; he forceth us to be damned; for we cannot resist his will. Thou fool, why goest thou about any longer seeking whom thou mayest devour? Hearest thou not that God is the devouring lion, the destroyer of souls, the murderer of men? Moloch caused only children to pass through the fire, and that fire was soon quenched; or, the corruptible body being consumed, its torment was at an end. But God, thou art told, by his eternal decree, fixed before they had done good or evil, causes not only "children of a span long" but the parents also to pass through the fire of hell—that "fire which never shall be quenched"; and the body which is cast thereinto, being now incorruptible and immortal, will be ever consuming, and never consumed, but "the smoke of their torment", because it is God's good pleasure, "ascendeth up for ever and ever".'

28. O how would the enemy of God and man rejoice to hear these things were so! How would he cry aloud and spare not! How would he lift up his voice and say: 'To your tents, O Israel! Flee from the face of this God, or ye shall utterly perish. But whither will ye flee? Into heaven? He is there. Down to hell? He is there also. Ye cannot flee from an omnipresent, almighty tyrant. And whether ye flee or stay, I call heaven his throne, and earth his footstool to witness against you, ye shall perish, ye shall die eternally. Sing, O hell, and rejoice ye that are under the earth! For God, even the mighty God, hath spoken, and devoted to death thousands of souls, from the rising up of the sun unto the going down thereof. Here, O death, is thy sting! They shall not, cannot escape; for the mouth of the Lord hath spoken it. Here, O grave, is thy victory!

Nations yet unborn, or ever they have done good or evil, are doomed never to see the light of life, but thou shalt gnaw upon them for ever and ever. Let all those morning stars sing together who fell with Lucifer, son of the morning. Let all the sons of hell shout for joy! For the decree is past, and who shall disannul it?'

29. Yea, the decree is past. And so it was before the foundation of the world. But what decree? Even this: '"I will set before" the sons of men "life and death, blessing and cursing"; and the soul that chooseth life shall live, as the soul that chooseth death shall die.' This decree, whereby 'whom God did foreknow, he did predestinate,' was indeed from everlasting. This, whereby all who suffer Christ to make them alive are 'elect, according to the foreknowledge of God', now 'standeth fast, even as the moon, and as the faithful witness in heaven'. And when heaven and earth shall pass away, yet this shall not pass away; for it is as unchangeable and eternal as is the being of God that gave it. This decree yields the strongest encouragement to abound in all good works, and in all holiness; and it is a well-spring of joy, of happiness also, to our great and endless comfort. This is worthy of God. It is every way consistent with all the perfections of his nature. It gives us the noblest view both of his justice, mercy, and truth. To this agrees the whole scope of the Christian revelation, as well as all the parts thereof. To this Moses and all the prophets bear witness, and our blessed Lord and all his apostles. Thus Moses, in the name of his Lord: 'I call heaven and earth to record against you this day, that I have set before you life and death, blessing and cursing; therefore choose life, that thou and thy seed may live.' Thus Ezekiel (to cite one prophet for all): 'The soul that sinneth, it shall die. The son shall not bear (eternally) the iniquity of the father. The righteousness of the righteous shall be upon him, and the wickedness of the wicked shall be upon him' (Ezek. 18:20). Thus our blessed Lord: 'If any man thirst, let him come to me and drink' (John 7:37). Thus his great Apostle, St. Paul: 'God commandeth all men everywhere to repent' (Acts 17:30). 'All men, everywhere'—every man in every place, without any exception, either of place or person. Thus St. James: 'If any of you lack wisdom, let him ask of God, who giveth to all men liberally and upbraideth not, and it shall be given him' (Jas. 1:5). Thus St. Peter: 'The Lord is . . . not willing that any should perish, but that all should come to repentance' (2 Pet. 3:9). And thus St. John: 'If any man sin, we have an advocate with the Father, . . . and he is the propitiation for our sins; and not for ours only, but for the sins of the whole world' (1 John 2:1–2).

30. O hear ye this, ye that forget God! Ye cannot charge your death upon him. 'Have I any pleasure at all that the wicked should die, saith the Lord God? Repent, and turn from all your transgressions; so iniquity shall not be your ruin. Cast away from you all your transgressions, whereby ye have transgressed; . . . for why will ye die, O house of Israel? For I have no pleasure in the death

of him that dieth, saith the Lord God. Wherefore turn yourselves, and live ye' (Ezek. 18:23, etc.). 'As I live, saith the Lord God, I have no pleasure in the death of the wicked, . . . Turn ye, turn ye from your evil ways; for why will ye die, O house of Israel?' (Ezek. 33:11).

THE ALMOST CHRISTIAN

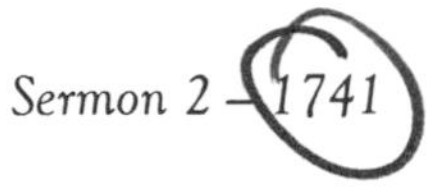

AN INTRODUCTORY COMMENT

When Wesley's turn as university preacher came round in 1741, the Revival was in full swing, and Wesley had found in its leadership an alternative career. He had not only begun to shift his loyalties from Oxford to his own Societies, but he had also become one of the university's harsher critics. John Gambold advised him that he would face a hostile audience, but Wesley was in no mood to mollify them. Indeed, Wesley was aware of the mounting tension. On June 28 he had preached at Charles Square, London, to a large congregation on 'Almost thou persuadest me to be a Christian' (cf. Acts 26:28). This was the sermon that, revised and with a new 'application', he delivered at Oxford on the feast day of St. James the Apostle, July 25.

Wesley's theme in this sermon—the radical difference between nominal and real Christianity—was already a familiar one in Puritan preaching. It was, indeed, already conventional to shift from the text's plain reference (Agrippa's being almost persuaded to become a Christian) to a discussion of nominal Christianity. Wesley draws out the distinctions between two types of Christians, the high-minded hypocrite (the 'almost' Christian) and his new conception of the 'altogether' Christian, openly expressing doubt that there are many of the latter in Oxford. Wesley's Methodist readers would have clearly perceived that their leader had affronted the Anglican establishment in one of its citadels and had survived.

Wesley's description of the 'almost' Christian expands upon one of his favourite biblical images: those having 'the form of godliness, but denying the power thereof' (2 Tim. 3:5). He describes at some length the sincere person who avoids evil, does good, and uses the means of grace—a trilogy here deprecated but soon to become fixed as the outline of the *General Rules* for the people called Methodists. The 'altogether' Christian, however, is one who has the 'faith that worketh by love', love of God and love of neighbour. Although Wesley later wavered in this evaluation of the 'almost' Christian (see especially 'The More Excellent Way'), his view of the true Christian was consistently tied to a theology of grace through faith and grounded in an ethic of love.

Wesley published this sermon in London shortly after its delivery in Oxford; it was reprinted at least twenty-five times during his lifetime and was the second piece in every edition of his collected *Sermons*.

The Almost Christian

Almost thou persuadest me to be a Christian.
Acts 26:28

And many there are who go thus far: ever since the Christian religion was in the world there have been many in every age and nation who were 'almost persuaded to be Christians'. But seeing it avails nothing before God to go *only thus far*, it highly imports us to consider,

First, what is implied in being *almost*,

Secondly, what in being *altogether* a Christian.

I.1. Now in the being 'almost a Christian' is implied, first, heathen honesty. No one, I suppose, will make any question of this, especially since by heathen honesty here I mean, not that which is recommended in the writings of their philosophers only, but such as the common heathens expected of one another, and many of them actually practised. By the rules of this they were taught that they ought not to be unjust; not to take away their neighbour's goods, either by robbery or theft; not to oppress the poor, neither to use extortion toward any; not to cheat or overreach either the poor or rich in whatsoever commerce they had with them; to defraud no man of his right, and if it were possible to owe no man anything.

2. Again, the common heathens allowed that some regard was to be paid to truth as well as to justice. And accordingly they not only had him in abomination who was forsworn, who called God to witness to a lie, but him also who was known to be a slanderer of his neighbour, who falsely accused any man. And indeed little better did they esteem wilful liars of any sort, accounting them the disgrace of humankind, and the pests of society.

3. Yet again, there was a sort of love and assistance which they expected one from another. They expected whatever assistance anyone could give another without prejudice to himself. And this they extended, not only to those little offices of humanity which are performed without any expense or labour, but likewise to the feeding the hungry if they had food to spare, the clothing the naked with their own superfluous raiment, and in general the giving to any that needed such things as they needed not themselves. Thus far (in the lowest account of it) heathen honesty went, the first thing implied in the being 'almost a Christian'.

4. A second thing implied in the being 'almost a Christian' is the having a form of godliness, of that godliness which is prescribed in the gospel of

Christ–the having the *outside* of a real Christian. Accordingly the 'almost Christian' does nothing which the gospel forbids. He taketh not the name of God in vain, he blesseth and curseth not, he sweareth not at all, but his communication is 'Yea, yea,' 'nay, nay.' He profanes not the day of the Lord, nor suffers it to be profaned, even by the stranger that is within his gates. He not only avoids all actual adultery, fornication, and uncleanness, but every word or look that either directly or indirectly tends thereto: nay, and all idle words, abstaining both from all detraction, backbiting, talebearing, evil-speaking, and from 'all foolish talking and jesting' (εὐτραπελία), a kind of virtue in the heathen moralist's account. Briefly, from all conversation that is not 'good to the use of edifying', and that consequently 'grieves the Holy Spirit of God, whereby we are sealed to the day of redemption'.

5. He abstains from 'wine wherein is excess', from revellings and gluttony. He avoids, as much as in him lies, all strife and contention, continually endeavouring to live peaceably with all men. And if he suffer wrong, he avengeth not himself, neither returns evil for evil. He is no railer, no brawler, no scoffer, either at the faults or infirmities of his neighbour. He does not willingly wrong, hurt, or grieve any man; but in all things acts and speaks by that plain rule, 'Whatsoever thou wouldst not he should do unto thee, that do not thou to another.'

6. And in doing good he does not confine himself to cheap and easy offices of kindness, but labours and suffers for the profit of many, that by all means he may help some. In spite of toil or pain, 'whatsoever his hand findeth to do, he doth it with his might,' whether it be for his friends or for his enemies, for the evil or for the good. For, being 'not slothful in' this or in any 'business', 'as he hath opportunity he doth good', all manner of good, 'to all men', and to their souls as well as their bodies. He reproves the wicked, instructs the ignorant, confirms the wavering, quickens the good, and comforts the afflicted. He labours to awaken those that sleep, to lead those whom God hath already awakened to the fountain opened for sin and for uncleanness, that they may wash therein and be clean; and to stir up those who are saved through faith to adorn the gospel of Christ in all things.

7. He that hath the form of godliness uses also the means of grace; yea, all of them, and at all opportunities. He constantly frequents the house of God; and that not as the manner of some is, who come into the presence of the Most High either loaded with gold and costly apparel, or in all the gaudy vanity of dress, and either by their unseasonable civilities to each other or the impertinent gaiety of their behaviour disclaim all pretensions to the form as well as to the power of godliness. Would to God there were none, even among ourselves, who fall under the same condemnation: who come into his house, it may be, gazing about, or with all the signs of the most listless, careless indifference, though sometimes they may *seem* to use a prayer to God for his

blessing on what they are entering upon; who during that awful service are either asleep or reclined in the most convenient posture for it; or, as though they supposed God was asleep, talking with one another, or looking round, as utterly void of employment. Neither let these be accused of the form of godliness. No: he who has even this behaves with seriousness and attention in every part of that solemn service. More especially when he approaches the table of the Lord it is not with a light or careless behaviour, but with an air, gesture, and deportment which speaks nothing else but 'God be merciful to me, a sinner!'

8. To this if we add the constant use of family prayer by those who are masters of families, and the setting times apart for private addresses to God, with a daily seriousness of behaviour—he who uniformly practises this outward religion has the form of godliness. There needs but one thing more in order to his being 'almost a Christian', and that is, sincerity.

9. By sincerity I mean a real, inward principle of religion from whence these outward actions flow. And indeed if we have not this we have not heathen honesty; no, not so much of it as will answer the demand of a heathen, Epicurean poet. Even this poor wretch, in his sober intervals, is able to testify:

Oderunt peccare boni virtutis amore;
*Oderunt peccare mali formidine poenae.**

So that if a man only abstains from doing evil in order to avoid punishment,

*Non pasces in cruce corvos***

saith the pagan—there, 'thou hast thy reward'. But even he will not allow such a harmless man as this to be so much as a *good heathen.* If then any man from the same motive (viz. to avoid punishment, to avoid the loss of his friends, or his gain, or his reputation) should not only abstain from doing evil but also do ever so much good—yea, and use all the means of grace—yet we could not with any propriety say, this man is even 'almost a Christian'. If he has no better principle in his heart he is only a hypocrite altogether.

10. Sincerity therefore is necessarily implied in the being 'almost a Christian': a real design to serve God, a hearty desire to do his will. It is necessarily implied that a man have a sincere view of pleasing God in all things: in all his conversation, in all his actions; in all he does or leaves undone. This design, if any man be 'almost a Christian', runs through the whole tenor of his life. This is the moving principle both in his doing good, his abstaining from evil, and his using the ordinances of God.

11. But here it will probably be inquired, Is it possible that any man living

* ['Good men avoid sin from the love of virtue; wicked men avoid sin from the fear of punishment,' cf. Horace, *Epistles*, I.xvi.52–53.]

** ['Thou shalt not be hanged,' Horace, *Epistles*, I.xvi.48.]

should go so far as this and nevertheless be *only* 'almost a Christian'? What more than this can be implied in the being 'a Christian altogether'? I answer, first, that it is possible to go thus far, and yet be but 'almost a Christian', I learn not only from the oracles of God, but also from the sure testimony of experience.

12. Brethren, 'great is my boldness toward you in this behalf.' And 'forgive me this wrong' if I declare my own folly upon the housetop, for yours and the gospel's sake. Suffer me then to speak freely of myself, even as of another man. I am content to be abased so ye may be exalted, and to be yet more vile for the glory of my Lord.

13. I did go thus far for many years, as many of this place can testify: using diligence to eschew all evil, and to have a conscience void of offence; redeeming the time, buying up every opportunity of doing all good to all men; constantly and carefully using all the public and all the private means of grace; endeavouring after a steady seriousness of behaviour at all times and in all places. And God is my record, before whom I stand, doing all this in sincerity; having a real design to serve God, a hearty desire to do his will in all things, to please him who had called me to 'fight the good fight', and to 'lay hold of eternal life'. Yet my own conscience beareth me witness in the Holy Ghost that all this time I was but 'almost a Christian'.

II. If it be inquired, 'What more than this is implied in the being "altogether a Christian"?' I answer:

1. First, the love of God. For thus saith his Word: 'Thou shalt love the Lord thy God with all thy heart, and with all thy soul, and with all thy mind, and with all thy strength.' Such a love of God is this as engrosses the whole heart, as takes up all the affections, as fills the entire capacity of the soul, and employs the utmost extent of all its faculties. He that thus loves the Lord his God, his spirit continually 'rejoiceth in God his Saviour'. 'His delight is in the Lord,' *his* Lord and his all, to whom 'in everything he giveth thanks'. All *his* 'desire is unto God, and to the remembrance of his name'. His heart is ever crying out, 'Whom have I in heaven but thee? and there is none upon earth that I desire beside thee.' Indeed, what can he desire beside God? Not the world, or the things of the world. For he is 'crucified to the world, and the world crucified to him'. He is crucified to the desire of the flesh, the desire of the eye, and the pride of life. Yea, he is dead to pride of every kind: for love 'is not puffed up', but he that dwelling in love 'dwelleth in God, and God in him', is less than nothing in his own eyes.

2. The second thing implied in the being 'altogether a Christian' is the love of our neighbour. For thus said our Lord in the following words: 'Thou shalt love thy neighbour as thyself.' If any man ask, 'Who is my neighbour?' we reply, 'Every man in the world; every child of his who is "the Father of the

spirits of all flesh".' Nor may we in any wise except our enemies, or the enemies of God and their own souls. But every Christian loveth these also as himself; yea, 'as Christ loved us'. He that would more fully understand what manner of love this is may consider St. Paul's description of it. It is 'long-suffering and kind. It envieth not. It is not rash or hasty in judging. It is not puffed up,' but maketh him that loves, the least, the servant of all. Love 'doth not behave itself unseemly', but 'becometh all things to all men'. She 'seeketh not her own', but only the good of others, that they may be saved. Love 'is not provoked'. It casteth out wrath, which he who hath is wanting in love. It 'thinketh no evil'. It 'rejoiceth not in iniquity, but rejoiceth in the truth'. It 'covereth all things, believeth all things, hopeth all things, endureth all things'.

3. There is yet one thing more that may be separately considered, though it cannot actually be separate from the preceding, which is implied in the being 'altogether a Christian', and that is the ground of all, even faith. Very excellent things are spoken of this throughout the oracles of God. 'Everyone', saith the beloved disciple, 'that believeth, is born of God.' 'To as many as received him gave he power to become the sons of God, even to them that believe on his name.' And, 'This is the victory that overcometh the world, even our faith.' Yea, our Lord himself declares, 'He that believeth in the Son hath everlasting life'; and 'cometh not into condemnation, but is passed from death unto life'.

4. But here let no man deceive his own soul. It is diligently to be noted, the 'faith which bringeth not forth repentance' and love, and all good works, is not that 'right living faith' which is here spoken of, 'but a dead and devilish one. . . . For even the devils believe that Christ was born of a virgin, that he wrought all kind of miracles, declaring himself very God; that for our sakes he suffered a most painful death, to redeem us from death everlasting; that he rose again the third day; that he ascended into heaven and sitteth at the right hand of the Father, and at the end of the world shall come again to judge both the quick and the dead. These articles of our faith the devils believe, and so they believe all that is written in the Old and New Testament. And yet for all this faith, they be but devils. They remain still in their damnable estate, lacking the very true Christian faith.'*

5. 'The right and true Christian faith is' (to go on in the words of our own Church) 'not only to believe that Holy Scripture and the articles of our faith are true, but also to have a sure trust and confidence to be saved from everlasting damnation by Christ'—it is a 'sure trust and confidence' which a man hath in God 'that by the merits of Christ his sins *are* forgiven, and he reconciled to the favour of God'—'whereof doth follow a loving heart to obey his commandments.'

6. Now whosoever has this faith which 'purifies the heart', by the power of God who dwelleth therein, from pride, anger, desire, 'from all

* Homily on the Salvation of Man [Pt. III].

unrighteousness', 'from all filthiness of flesh and spirit'; which fills it with love stronger than death both to God and to all mankind—love that doth the works of God, glorying to spend and to be spent for all men, and that endureth with joy, not only the reproach of Christ, the being mocked, despised, and hated of all men, but whatsoever the wisdom of God permits the malice of men or devils to inflict; whosoever has this faith, thus 'working by love', is not *almost* only, but *altogether* a Christian.

7. But who are the living witnesses of these things? I beseech you, brethren, as in the presence of that God before whom 'hell and destruction are without a covering: how much more the hearts of the children of men!'—that each of you would ask his own heart, 'Am I of that number? Do I so far practise justice, mercy, and truth, as even the rules of heathen honesty require? If so, have I the very *outside* of a Christian? The form of godliness? Do I abstain from evil, from whatsoever is forbidden in the written Word of God? Do I, whatever good my hand findeth to do, do it with my might? Do I seriously use all the ordinances of God at all opportunities? And is all this done with a sincere design and desire to please God in all things?'

8. Are not many of you conscious that you never came thus far? That you have not been even 'almost a Christian'? That you have not come up to the standard of heathen honesty? At least, not to the form of Christian godliness? Much less hath God seen sincerity in you, a real design of pleasing him in all things. You never so much as intended to devote all your words and works, your business, studies, diversions to his glory. You never even designed or desired that whatsoever you did should be done 'in the name of the Lord Jesus', and as such should be a 'spiritual sacrifice, acceptable to God through Christ.'

9. But supposing you had, do good designs and good desires make a Christian? By no means, unless they are brought to good effect. 'Hell is paved', saith one, 'with good intentions.' The great question of all, then, still remains. Is the love of God shed abroad in your heart? Can you cry out, 'My God and my all'? Do you desire nothing but him? Are you happy in God? Is he your glory, your delight, your crown of rejoicing? And is this commandment written in your heart, 'that he who loveth God love his brother also'? Do you then love your neighbour as yourself? Do you love every man, even your enemies, even the enemies of God, as your own soul? As Christ loved you? Yea, dost thou believe that Christ loved *thee*, and gave himself for thee? Hast thou faith in his blood? Believest thou the Lamb of God hath taken away *thy* sins, and cast them as a stone into the depth of the sea? That he hath blotted out the handwriting that was against *thee*, taking it out of the way, nailing it to his cross? Hast *thou* indeed redemption through his blood, even the remission of *thy* sins? And doth his Spirit bear witness with *thy* spirit, that thou art a child of God?

10. The God and Father of our Lord Jesus Christ, who now standeth in

the midst of us, knoweth that if any man die without this faith and this love, good it were for him that he had never been born. Awake, then, thou that sleepest, and call upon thy God: call in the day when he may be found. Let him not rest till he 'make his goodness to pass before thee, till he proclaim unto thee the name of the Lord'—'the Lord, the Lord God, merciful and gracious, long-suffering, and abundant in goodness and truth; keeping mercy for thousands, forgiving iniquity, and transgression, and sin.' Let no man persuade thee by vain words to rest short of this prize of thy high calling. But cry unto him day and night who 'while we were without strength died for the ungodly', until thou knowest in whom thou hast believed, and canst say, 'My Lord and my God.' Remember 'always to pray and not to faint', till thou also canst lift up thy hand unto heaven and declare to him that liveth for ever and ever, 'Lord, thou knowest all things; thou knowest that I love thee.'

11. May we all thus experience what it is to be not almost only, but altogether Christians! Being justified freely by his grace, through the redemption that is in Jesus, knowing we have peace with God through Jesus Christ, rejoicing in hope of the glory of God, and having the love of God shed abroad in our hearts by the Holy Ghost given unto us!

CHRISTIAN PERFECTION

Sermon 40 – 1741

AN INTRODUCTORY COMMENT

For Wesley, salvation was the total restoration of the deformed image of God in us, and its fullness was the recovery of our negative power not to sin and our positive power to love God supremely. Wesley chose to call that furthest reach of grace in sanctification and its triumphs in this life 'Christian Perfection', a position that he had stated earlier in 'The Circumcision of the Heart' (1733). Just as justification and regeneration are thresholds for the Christian life in earnest ('what God does for us'), so also sanctification is 'what God does in us', fulfilling the human potential according to his primal design. Few Christians had ever denied some such prospect after death; few, in the West at least, had ever envisioned it as a realistic possibility in this life. Thus, Wesley's encouragement to his people to 'go on to perfection' and to 'expect to be made perfect in love in this life' aroused lively fears that this teaching would foster more of the self-righteous perfectionism already made objectionable by earlier pietists.

This fear was in the background of Bishop Edmund Gibson's interview with Wesley in the latter end of the year 1740. When Wesley told him 'without any disguise or reserve' what he meant by perfection, the bishop suggested that he 'publish it to all the world'. John proceeded to write and publish this sermon in 1741, appending his brother Charles's poem, 'The Promise of Sanctification'. There is no record of Wesley actually preaching this sermon, and there is no other record of his use of Phil. 3:12 as a sermon text.

Wesley maintained that he had no difficulty in harmonizing 'Christian perfection' with his later emphases on 'faith alone' and 'assurance'. Many Protestants were bound to see in the Wesleyan doctrine, despite all its formal disclaimers, a bald advertisement of spiritual pride and implicit works-righteousness. Even the Methodists, working from their own unexamined Latin traditions of forensic righteousness, tended to interpret 'perfection' in terms of a perfected spiritual elitism and so misunderstood Wesley and the early Eastern traditions of *teleos* as a never ending aspiration for all of love's perfecting fullness. Thus, 'Christian Perfection' came to be the most distinctive and also the most widely misunderstood of all Wesley's doctrines. He continued to teach it, however, as the farthest horizon of his vision of Christian existence, an idea with radical implications for personal ethics and for social transformation as well.

Christian Perfection

Not as though I had already attained, either were already perfect.
Philippians 3:12

1. There is scarce any expression in Holy Writ which has given more offence than this. The word 'perfect' is what many cannot bear. The very sound of it is an abomination to them. And whosoever 'preaches perfection' (as the phrase is), i.e. asserts that it is attainable in this life, runs great hazard of being accounted by them worse than a heathen man or a publican.

2. And hence some have advised, wholly to lay aside the use of those expressions, 'because they have given so great offence'. But are they not found in the oracles of God? If so, by what authority can any messenger of God lay them aside, even though all men should be offended? We have not so learned Christ; neither may we thus give place to the devil. Whatsoever God hath spoken, that will we speak, whether men will hear or whether they will forbear: knowing that then alone can any minister of Christ be 'pure from the blood of all men', when he hath 'not shunned to declare unto them all the counsel of God'.

3. We may not therefore lay these expressions aside, seeing they are the words of God, and not of man. But we may and ought to explain the meaning of them, that those who are sincere of heart may not err to the right hand or to the left from the mark of the prize of their high calling. And this is the more needful to be done because in the verse already repeated the Apostle speaks of himself as not perfect: 'Not', saith he, 'as though I were already perfect.' And yet immediately after, in the fifteenth verse, he speaks of himself, yea and many others, as perfect. 'Let us', saith he, 'as many as be perfect, be thus minded.'

4. In order therefore to remove the difficulty arising from this seeming contradiction, as well as to give light to them who are pressing forward to the mark, and that those who are lame be not turned out of the way, I shall endeavour to show,

First, in what sense Christians are *not*, and

Secondly, in what sense they *are*, perfect.

I. 1. In the first place I shall endeavour to show in what sense Christians are *not perfect*. And both from experience and Scripture it appears, first, that they are not perfect in knowledge: they are not *so* perfect in this life as to be free from ignorance. They know, it may be, in common with other men, many things relating to the present world; and they know, with regard to the world to come, the general truths which God hath revealed. They know likewise (what 'the natural man receiveth not', for these things 'are spiritually discerned') 'what manner of love it is wherewith the Father hath loved them, that they should be called the sons of God'. They know 'the mighty working of his Spirit' in their hearts, and the wisdom of his providence directing all their paths, and causing all things to work together for their good. Yea, they know in every circumstance of life what the Lord requireth of them, and how 'to keep a conscience void of offence both toward God and toward man'.

2. But innumerable are the things which they know not. 'Touching the Almighty himself', 'they cannot search him out to perfection.' 'Lo, these are but a part of his ways; but the thunder of his power who can understand?' They cannot understand, I will not say, how 'there are three that bear record in heaven, the Father, the Son, and the Holy Spirit, and these three are one'; or how the eternal Son of God 'took upon himself the form of a servant'; but not any one attribute, not any one circumstance of the divine nature. Neither is it for them 'to know the times and seasons' when God will work his great works upon the earth; no, not even those which he hath in part revealed, by his servants the prophets, since the world began. Much less do they know when God, having 'accomplished the number of his elect, will hasten his kingdom'; when 'the heavens shall pass away with a great noise, and the elements shall melt with fervent heat.'

3. They know not the reasons even of many of his present dispensations with the sons of men; but are constrained to rest here, though 'clouds and darkness are round about him, righteousness and judgment are the habitation of his seat.' Yea, often with regard to his dealings with themselves doth their Lord say unto them, 'What I do, thou knowest not now; but thou shalt know hereafter.' And how little do they know of what is ever before them, of even the visible works of his hands! How 'he spreadeth the north over the empty place, and hangeth the earth upon nothing.' How he unites all the parts of this vast machine by a secret chain which cannot be broken. So great is the ignorance, so very little the knowledge of even the best of men.

4. No one then is so perfect in this life as to be free from ignorance. Nor, secondly, from mistake, which indeed is almost an unavoidable consequence of it; seeing those who 'know but in part' are ever liable to err touching the things which they know not. 'Tis true the children of God do not mistake as to the things essential to salvation. They do not 'put darkness for light, or light for darkness', neither 'seek death in the error of their life'. For they are 'taught of God', and the way which he teaches them, the way of holiness, is so plain that 'the wayfaring man, though a fool, need not err therein.' But in things unessential to salvation they do err, and that frequently. The best and wisest of men are frequently mistaken even with regard to facts; believing those things

not to have been which really were, or those to have been done which were not. Or suppose they are not mistaken as to the fact itself, they may be with regard to its circumstances; believing them, or many of them, to have been quite different from what in truth they were. And hence cannot but arise many farther mistakes. Hence they may believe either past or present actions which were or are evil to be good; and such as were or are good to be evil. Hence also they may judge not according to truth with regard to the characters of men; and that not only by supposing good men to be better, or wicked men to be worse, than they are, but by believing them to have been or to be good men who were or are very wicked; or perhaps those to have been or to be wicked men who were or are holy and unreprovable.

5. Nay, with regard to the Holy Scriptures themselves, as careful as they are to avoid it, the best of men are liable to mistake, and do mistake day by day; especially with respect to those parts thereof which less immediately relate to practice. Hence even the children of God are not agreed as to the interpretation of many places in Holy Writ; nor is their difference of opinion any proof that they are not the children of God on either side. But it is a proof that we are no more to expect any living man to be *infallible* than to be *omniscient.*

6. If it be objected to what has been observed under this and the preceding head that St. John speaking to his brethren in the faith says, 'Ye have an unction from the Holy One, and know all things' (1 John 2:20), the answer is plain—'Ye know all things that are needful for your soul's health.' That the Apostle never designed to extend this farther, that he could not speak it in an absolute sense, is clear first from hence: that otherwise he would describe the disciple as 'above his Master'; seeing Christ himself, as man, knew not all things. 'Of that hour', saith he, 'knoweth no man, no, not the Son, but the Father only.' It is clear, secondly, from the Apostle's own words that follow: 'These things have I written unto you concerning them that deceive you,' as well as from his frequently repeated caution, 'Let no man deceive you,' which had been altogether needless had not those very persons who had that unction from the Holy One been liable not to ignorance only but to mistake also.

7. Even Christians therefore are not *so* perfect as to be free either from ignorance or error. We may, thirdly, add: nor from infirmities. Only let us take care to understand this word aright. Let us not give that soft title to known sins, as the manner of some is. So, one man tells us, 'Every man has his infirmity, and mine is drunkenness.' Another has the infirmity of uncleanness; another of taking God's holy name in vain; and yet another has the infirmity of calling his brother, 'Thou fool,' or returning 'railing for railing'. It is plain that all you who thus speak, if ye repent not, shall with your infirmities go quick into hell. But I mean hereby not only those which are properly termed 'bodily infirmities', but all those inward or outward imperfections which are not of a moral nature. Such are weakness or slowness of understanding,

dullness or confusedness of apprehension, incoherency of thought, irregular quickness or heaviness of imagination. Such (to mention no more of this kind) is the want of a ready or of a retentive memory. Such in another kind are those which are commonly in some measure consequent upon these: namely slowness of speech, impropriety of language, ungracefulness of pronunciation—to which one might add a thousand nameless defects either in conversation or behaviour. These are the infirmities which are found in the best of men in a larger or smaller proportion. And from these none can hope to be perfectly freed till the spirit returns to God that gave it.

8. Nor can we expect till then to be wholly free from temptation. Such perfection belongeth not to this life. It is true, there are those who, being given up to work all uncleanness with greediness, scarce perceive the temptations which they resist not, and so seem to be without temptation. There are also many whom the wise enemy of souls, seeing [them] to be fast asleep in the dead form of godliness, will not tempt to gross sin, lest they should awake before they drop into everlasting burnings. I know there are also children of God who, being now 'justified freely', having found 'redemption in the blood of Christ', for the present feel no temptation. God hath said to their enemies, 'Touch not mine anointed, and do my children no harm.' And for this season, it may be for weeks or months, he causeth them to 'ride on high places'; he beareth them as on eagles' wings, above all the fiery darts of the wicked one. But this state will not last always, as we may learn from that single consideration that the Son of God himself, in the days of his flesh, was tempted even to the end of his life. Therefore so let his servant expect to be; for 'it is enough that he be as his Master.'

9. Christian perfection therefore does not imply (as some men seem to have imagined) an exemption either from ignorance or mistake, or infirmities or temptations. Indeed, it is only another term for holiness. They are two names for the same thing. Thus everyone that is perfect is holy, and everyone that is holy is, in the Scripture sense, perfect. Yet we may, lastly, observe that neither in this respect is there any absolute perfection on earth. There is no 'perfection of degrees', as it is termed; none which does not admit of a continual increase. So that how much soever any man hath attained, or in how high a degree soever he is perfect, he hath still need to 'grow in grace', and daily to advance in the knowledge and love of God his Saviour.

II.1. In what sense then are Christians perfect? This is what I shall endeavour, in the second place, to show. But it should be premised that there are several stages in Christian life as well as in natural: some of the children of God being but new-born babes, others having attained to more maturity. And accordingly St. John, in his first Epistle (1 John 2:12, etc.), applies himself severally to those he terms little children, those he styles young men, and those whom he entitles fathers. 'I write unto you, little children', saith the Apostle, 'because your sins are forgiven you'; because thus far ye have attained, being 'justified freely', you 'have peace with God, through Jesus Christ'. 'I write unto you, young men, because ye have overcome the wicked one'; or (as he afterwards adds) 'because ye are strong, and the word of God abideth in you.' Ye have quenched the fiery darts of the wicked one, the doubts and fears wherewith he disturbed your first peace, and the witness of God that your sins are forgiven now 'abideth in your heart'. 'I write unto you, fathers, because ye have known him that is from the beginning.' Ye have known both the Father and the Son and the Spirit of Christ in your inmost soul. Ye are 'perfect men, being grown up to the measure of the stature of the fullness of Christ'.

2. It is of these chiefly I speak in the latter part of this discourse; for these only are properly Christians. But even babes in Christ are in such a sense perfect, or 'born of God' (an expression taken also in divers senses) as, first, not to commit sin. If any doubt of this privilege of the sons of God, the question is not to be decided by abstract reasonings, which may be drawn out into an endless length, and leave the point just as it was before. Neither is it to be determined by the experience of this or that particular person. Many may suppose they do not commit sin when they do, but this proves nothing either way. 'To the law and to the testimony' we appeal. 'Let God be true, and every man a liar.' By his Word will we abide, and that alone. Hereby we ought to be judged.

3. Now the Word of God plainly declares that even those who are justified, who are born again in the lowest sense, do not 'continue in sin'; that they cannot 'live any longer therein' (Rom. 6:1, 2); that they are 'planted together in the likeness of the death of Christ' (Rom. 6:5); that their 'old man is crucified with him, the body of sin being destroyed, so that thenceforth they do not serve sin'; that 'being dead with Christ, they are freed from sin' (Rom. 6:6,7); that they are 'dead unto sin', and 'alive unto God' (Rom. 6:11); that 'sin hath not dominion over them', who are 'not under the law, but under grace'; but that these, 'being made free from sin, are become the servants of righteousness' (Rom. 6:15, 18).

4. The very least which can be implied in these words is that the persons spoken of therein, namely all real Christians or believers in Christ, are made free from outward sin. And the same freedom which St. Paul here expresses in such variety of phrases St. Peter expresses in that one: 'He that hath suffered in the flesh hath ceased from sin; that he no longer should live . . . to the desires of men, but to the will of God' (1 Pet. 4:1–2). For this 'ceasing from sin', if it be interpreted in the lowest sense, as regarding only the outward behaviour, must denote the ceasing from the outward act, from any outward transgression of the law.

5. But most express are the well-known words of St. John in the third chapter

of his first Epistle (verse eight, etc.): 'He that committeth sin is of the devil; for the devil sinneth from the beginning. For this purpose the Son of God was manifested, that he might destroy the works of the devil. Whosoever is born of God doth not commit sin; for his seed remaineth in him, and he cannot sin, because he is born of God.' And those in the fifth, verse eighteen: 'We know that whosoever is born of God sinneth not. But he that is begotten of God keepeth himself, and that wicked one toucheth him not.'

6. Indeed it is said this means only, he sinneth not *wilfully; or he doth not commit sin habitually*; or, *not as other men do*; or, *not as he did before*. But by whom is this said? By St. John? No. There is no such word in the text, nor in the whole chapter, nor in all this Epistle, nor in any part of his writings whatsoever. Why, then, the best way to answer a bold assertion is simply to deny it. And if any man can prove it from the Word of God, let him bring forth his strong reasons.

7. And a sort of reason there is which has been frequently brought to support these strange assertions, drawn from the examples recorded in the Word of God: 'What!', say they, 'did not Abraham himself commit sin, prevaricating and denying his wife? Did not Moses commit sin when he provoked God "at the waters of strife"? Nay, to produce one for all, did not even David, "the man after God's own heart", commit sin in the matter of Uriah the Hittite, even murder and adultery?' It is most sure he did. All this is true. But what is it you would infer from hence? It may be granted, first, that David, in the general course of his life, was one of the holiest men among the Jews. And, secondly, that the holiest men among the Jews *did sometimes commit sin*. But if you would hence infer that *all Christians do, and must commit sin, as long as they live*, this consequence we utterly deny. It will never follow from those premises.

8. Those who argue thus seem never to have considered that declaration of our Lord: 'Verily I say unto you, among them that are born of women there hath not risen a greater than John the Baptist. Notwithstanding, he that is least in the kingdom of heaven is greater than he' (Matt. 11:11). I fear indeed there are some who have imagined 'the kingdom of heaven' here to mean the kingdom of glory. As if the Son of God had just discovered to us that the least glorified saint in heaven is greater than any man upon earth! To mention this is sufficiently to refute it. There can therefore no doubt be made but 'the kingdom of heaven' here (as in the following verse, where it is said to be 'taken by force') or, 'the kingdom of God', as St. Luke expresses it, is that kingdom of God on earth whereunto all true believers in Christ, all real Christians, belong. In these words then our Lord declares two things. First, that before his coming in the flesh among all the children of men, there had not been one greater than John the Baptist; whence it evidently follows that neither Abraham, David, nor any Jew was greater than John. Our Lord, secondly, declares that he which is least in the kingdom of God (in that kingdom which he came

to set up on earth, and which 'the violent' now began 'to take by force') is greater than he. The plain consequence is, the least of these who have now Christ for their King is greater than Abraham or David or any Jew ever was. None of them was ever greater than John. But the least of these is greater than he. Not 'a greater prophet' (as some have interpreted the word), for this is palpably false in fact, but greater in the grace of God and the knowledge of our Lord Jesus Christ. Therefore we cannot measure the privileges of real Christians by those formerly given to the Jews. 'Their ministration' (or dispensation) we allow 'was glorious'; but ours 'exceeds in glory'. So that whosoever would bring down the Christian dispensation to the Jewish standard, whosoever gleans up the examples of weakness recorded in the law and the prophets, and thence infers that they who have 'put on Christ' are endued with no greater strength, doth 'greatly err, neither knowing the Scriptures nor the power of God'.

9. 'But are there not assertions in Scripture which prove the same thing, if it cannot be inferred from those examples? Does not the Scripture say expressly, "Even a just man sinneth seven times a day"?' I answer, No. The Scripture says no such thing. There is no such text in all the Bible. That which seems to be intended is the sixteenth verse of the twenty-fourth chapter of the Proverbs, the words of which are these: 'A just man falleth seven times, and riseth up again.' But this is quite another thing. For, first, the words 'a day' are not in the text. So that if a just man falls seven times in his life it is as much as is affirmed here. Secondly, here is no mention of 'falling into sin' at all: what is here mentioned is 'falling into temporal affliction'. This plainly appears from the verse before, the words of which are these: 'Lay not wait, O wicked man, against the dwelling of the righteous; spoil not his resting place.' It follows, 'For a just man falleth seven times, and riseth up again: but the wicked shall fall into mischief.' As if he had said, 'God will deliver him out of his trouble. But when thou fallest, there shall be none to deliver thee.'

10. But, however, in other places, continue the objectors, Solomon does assert plainly, 'There is no man that sinneth not' (1 Kgs. 8:46; 2 Chron. 6:36); yea, 'there is not a just man upon earth that doth good, and sinneth not' (Eccles. 7:20). I answer: Without doubt, thus it was in the days of Solomon. Yea, thus it was from Adam to Moses, from Moses to Solomon, and from Solomon to Christ. There was *then* no man that sinned not. Even from the day that sin entered into the world there was not a just man upon earth that did good and sinned not, *until* the Son of God was manifested 'to take away our sins'. It is unquestionably true that 'the heir, as long as he is a child, differeth nothing from a servant.' And that 'even so' they (all the holy men of old who were under the Jewish dispensation) 'were', during that infant state of the church, 'in bondage under the elements of the world. But when the fullness of the time was come, God sent forth his Son, made under the law,

to redeem them that were under the law, that they might receive the adoption of sons'; that they might receive that 'grace which is now made manifest by the appearing of our Saviour, Jesus Christ, who hath abolished death, and brought life and immortality to light through the gospel' (2 Tim. 1:10). Now therefore they 'are no more servants, but sons'. So that, whatsoever was the case of those under the law, we may safely affirm with St. John that since the gospel was given, 'He that is born of God sinneth not.'

11. It is of great importance to observe, and that more carefully than is commonly done, the wide difference there is between the Jewish and the Christian dispensation, and that ground of it which the same Apostle assigns in the seventh chapter of his Gospel, verse thirty-eight, etc. After he had there related those words of our blessed Lord, 'He that believeth on me, as the Scripture hath said, out of his belly shall flow rivers of living water,' he immediately subjoins, 'This spake he of the Spirit,' οὗ ἔμελλον λαμβάνειν οἱ πιστεύοντες εἰς αὐτόν, 'which they who should believe on him were afterwards to receive. For the Holy Ghost was not yet given, because that Jesus was not yet glorified.' Now the Apostle cannot mean here (as some have taught) that the miracle-working power of the Holy Ghost was not yet given. For this was given: our Lord had given it to all his apostles when he first sent them forth to preach the gospel. He then gave them 'power over unclean spirits to cast them out', power to 'heal the sick', yea, to 'raise the dead'. But the Holy Ghost was not yet given in his sanctifying graces, as he was after Jesus was glorified. It was then when 'he ascended up on high, and led captivity captive', that he 'received those gifts for men, yea, even for the rebellious, that the Lord God might dwell among them.' And 'when the day of Pentecost was fully come', then first it was that they who 'waited for the promise of the Father' were made more than conquerors over sin by the Holy Ghost given unto them.

12. That this great salvation from sin was not given till Jesus was glorified St. Peter also plainly testifies, where speaking of his 'brethren in the flesh' as now 'receiving the end of their faith, the salvation of their souls', he adds: 'Of which salvation the prophets have inquired and searched diligently, who prophesied of the grace (i.e. the gracious dispensation) that should come unto you; searching what, or what manner of time, the Spirit of Christ which was in them did signify, when it testified beforehand the sufferings of Christ and the glory (the glorious salvation) that should follow. Unto whom it was revealed that not unto themselves, but unto us they did minister the things which are now reported unto you by them that have preached the gospel unto you with the Holy Ghost sent down from heaven' (viz., at the day of Pentecost, and so unto all generations, into the hearts of all true believers). On this ground, even 'the grace which was brought unto them by the revelation of Jesus Christ', the Apostle might well build that strong exhortation, 'Wherefore, girding up the loins of your mind, . . . as he which hath called you is holy, so be ye holy in

all manner of conversation' (1 Pet. 1:9,10, etc.).

13. Those who have duly considered these things must allow that the privileges of Christians are in no wise to be measured by what the Old Testament records concerning those who were under the Jewish dispensation, seeing the fullness of times is now come, the Holy Ghost is now given, the great salvation of God is brought unto men by the revelation of Jesus Christ. The kingdom of heaven is now set up on earth; concerning which the Spirit of God declared of old (so far is David from being the pattern or standard of Christian perfection), 'He that is feeble among them at that day, shall be as David; and the house of David shall be as God, as the angel of the Lord before them' (Zech. 12:8).

14. If therefore you would prove that the Apostle's words, 'He that is born of God sinneth not,' are not to be understood according to their plain, natural, obvious meaning, it is from the New Testament you are to bring your proofs; else you will fight as one that beateth the air. And the first of these which is usually brought is taken from the examples recorded in the New Testament. 'The Apostles themselves (it is said) committed sin; nay the greatest of them, Peter and Paul: St. Paul by his sharp contention with Barnabas, and St. Peter by his dissimulation at Antioch.' Well; suppose both Peter and Paul did then commit sin. What is it you would infer from hence? That *all the other apostles* committed sin sometimes? There is no shadow of proof in this. Or would you thence infer that *all the other Christians* of the apostolic age committed sin? Worse and worse. This is such an inference as one would imagine a man in his senses could never have thought of. Or will you argue thus?—'If two of the apostles did once commit sin, then *all other Christians, in all ages,* do, and will commit sin as long as they live.' Alas, my brother! a child of common understanding would be ashamed of such reasoning as this. Least of all can you with any colour of argument infer that any man *must* commit sin at all. No; God forbid we should thus speak. No necessity of sinning was laid upon *them.* The grace of God was surely sufficient for them. And it *is* sufficient for *us* at this day. With the temptation which fell on *them* that *was* a way to escape, as there *is* to every soul of man in every temptation; so that whosoever is tempted to any sin *need* not yield; for no man is tempted above that he is able to bear.

15. 'But St. Paul besought the Lord thrice, and yet he could not escape from his temptation.' Let us consider his own words literally translated: 'There was given to me a thorn, to the flesh, an angel or messenger of Satan, to buffet me. Touching this I besought the Lord thrice, that it (or he) might depart from me. And he said unto me, My grace is sufficient for thee: for my strength is made perfect in weakness. Most gladly therefore will I rather glory in these my weaknesses, that the strength of Christ may rest upon me. Therefore I take pleasure in weaknesses . . . ; for when I am weak, then am I strong.'

16. As this Scripture is one of the strongholds of the patrons of sin, it may be proper to weigh it thoroughly. Let it be observed then, first, it does by no means appear that this thorn, whatsoever it was, occasioned St. Paul to commit sin, much less laid him under any necessity of doing so. Therefore from hence it can never be proved that any Christian *must* commit sin. Secondly, the ancient Fathers inform us it was bodily pain: 'a violent headache', saith Tertullian (*De Pudicitia*, [§13]), to which both Chrysostom and St. Jerome agree. St. Cyprian expresses it a little more generally, in those terms, 'many and grievous torments of the flesh and of the body' ('Carnis et corporis multa ac gravia tormenta', *De Mortalitate*). Thirdly, to this exactly agree the Apostle's own words, 'A thorn to the flesh to smite, beat, or buffet me. . . . My strength is made perfect in weakness'—which same word occurs no less than four times in these two verses only. But, fourthly, whatsoever it was, it could not be either inward or outward sin. It could no more be inward stirrings than outward expressions of pride, anger, or lust. This is manifest beyond all possible exception from the words that immediately follow: 'Most gladly will I glory in these my weaknesses, that the strength of Christ rested upon me.' What! Did he glory in pride, in anger, in lust? Was it through these 'weaknesses' that the strength of Christ rested upon him? He goes on: 'Therefore I take pleasure in weaknesses; for when I am weak, then am I strong'; i.e. when I am weak *in body*, then am I strong *in spirit*. But will any man dare to say, When I am weak by pride or lust, then am I strong in spirit? I call you all to record this day, who find the strength of Christ resting upon you, can *you* glory in anger, or pride, or lust? Can *you* take pleasure in *these* infirmities? Do *these* weaknesses make you strong? Would you not leap into hell, were it possible, to escape them? Even by yourselves, then, judge whether the Apostle could glory and take pleasure in them! Let it be, lastly, observed, that this thorn was given to St. Paul 'above fourteen years' before he wrote this Epistle, which itself was wrote several years before he finished his course. So that he had after this a long course to run, many battles to fight, many victories to gain, and great increase to receive in all the gifts of God and the knowledge of Jesus Christ. Therefore from any spiritual weakness (if such it had been) which he *at that time* felt, we could by no means infer that he was never made strong, that Paul the aged, the father in Christ, still laboured under the same weaknesses; that he was in no higher state till the day of his death. From all which it appears that this instance of St. Paul is quite foreign to the question, and does in no wise clash with the assertion of St. John, 'He that is born of God sinneth not.'

17. 'But does not St. James directly contradict this? His words are, "In many things we offend all" (Jas. 3:2). And is not *offending* the same as *committing sin?*' In this place I allow it is. I allow *the persons here spoken of* did commit sin; yea, that they *all* committed *many* sins. But who are 'the persons here spoken of'? Why, those 'many masters' or 'teachers' whom God had not sent (probably

the same 'vain men' who taught that 'faith without works' which is so sharply reproved in the preceding chapter); not the Apostle himself, nor any real Christian. That in the word 'we' (used by a figure of speech common in all other as well as the inspired writings) the Apostle could not possibly include himself or any other true believer appears evidently, first, from the use of the same word in the ninth verse: 'Therewith (saith he) bless *we* God and therewith curse *we* men. Out of the same mouth proceedeth blessing and cursing.' True; but not out of the mouth of the Apostle, nor of anyone who is in Christ a new creature. Secondly, from the verse immediately preceding the text, and manifestly connected with it: 'My brethren, be not many masters (or teachers), knowing that *we* shall receive the greater condemnation: for in many things *we* offend all.' 'We'! Who? Not the apostles, not true believers; but they who know they should 'receive the greater condemnation' because of those many offences. But this could not be spoke of the Apostle himself, or of any who trod in his steps, seeing 'there is no condemnation for them who walk not after the flesh, but after the Spirit.' Nay, thirdly, the very verse itself proves that 'we offend all' cannot be spoken either of all men, or of all Christians; for in it there immediately follows the mention of a man who 'offends not', as the 'we' first mentioned did; from whom therefore he is professedly contradistinguished, and pronounced 'a perfect man'.

18. So clearly does St. James explain himself and fix the meaning of his own words. Yet, lest anyone should still remain in doubt, St. John, writing many years after St. James, puts the matter entirely out of dispute by the express declarations above recited. But here a fresh difficulty may arise. How shall we reconcile St. John with himself? In one place he declares, 'Whosoever is born of God doth not commit sin.' And again, 'We know that he which is born of God sinneth not.' And yet in another he saith, 'If we say that we have no sin, we deceive ourselves, and the truth is not in us.' And again, 'If we say that we have not sinned we make him a liar, and his word is not in us.'

19. As great a difficulty as this may at first appear, it vanishes away if we observe, first, that the tenth verse fixes the sense of the eighth: 'If we say we have no sin' in the former being explained by, 'If we say we have not sinned' in the latter verse. Secondly, that the point under present consideration is not whether we *have or have not sinned heretofore*, and neither of these verses asserts that we *do sin, or commit sin* now. Thirdly, that the ninth verse explains both the eighth and tenth: 'If we confess our sins, he is faithful and just to forgive us our sins, and to cleanse us from all unrighteousness.' As if he had said, 'I have before affirmed, "The blood of Jesus Christ cleanseth us from all sin." But let no man say, I need it not; I have no sin to be cleansed from. If we say "that we have no sin", "that we have not sinned", we deceive ourselves, and make God a liar. But if we confess our sins, he is faithful and just, not only to forgive our sins, but also to cleanse us from all unrighteousness, that we

may go and sin no more.'

20. St. John therefore is well consistent with himself, as well as with the other holy writers; as will yet more evidently appear if we place all his assertions touching this matter in one view. He declares, first, 'The blood of Jesus Christ cleanseth us from all sin.' Secondly, 'No man can say I have not sinned, I have no sin to be cleansed from.' Thirdly, 'But God is ready both to forgive our past sins and to save us from them for the time to come.' Fourthly, 'These things I write unto you', saith the Apostle, 'that ye may not sin: but if any man should sin', or 'have sinned' (as the word might be rendered) he need not continue in sin, seeing 'we have an advocate with the Father, Jesus Christ the righteous.' Thus far all is clear. But lest any doubt should remain in a point of so vast importance the Apostle resumes this subject in the third chapter, and largely explains his own meaning. 'Little children', saith he, 'let no man deceive you' (as though I had given any encouragement to those that continue in sin); 'he that doth righteousness is righteous, even as he is righteous. He that committeth sin is of the devil; for the devil sinneth from the beginning. For this purpose the Son of God was manifested, that he might destroy the works of the devil. Whosoever is born of God doth not commit sin; for his seed remaineth in him, and he cannot sin, because he is born of God. In this the children of God are manifest, and the children of the devil' (1 John 3:7–10). Here the point, which till then might possibly have admitted of some doubt in weak minds, is purposely settled by the last of the inspired writers, and decided in the clearest manner. In conformity therefore both to the doctrine of St. John, and to the whole tenor of the New Testament, we fix this conclusion: 'A Christian is so far perfect as not to commit sin.'

21. This is the glorious privilege of every Christian; yea, though he be but 'a babe in Christ'. But it is only of those who 'are strong in the Lord', and 'have overcome the wicked one', or rather of those who 'have known him that is from the beginning', that it can be affirmed they are in such a sense perfect as, secondly, to be freed from evil thoughts and evil tempers. First, from evil or sinful thoughts. But here let it be observed that thoughts concerning evil are not always evil thoughts; that a thought concerning sin and a sinful thought are widely different. A man, for instance, may think of a murder which another has committed, and yet this is no evil or sinful thought. So our blessed Lord himself doubtless thought of or understood the thing spoken by the devil when he said, 'All this will I give thee if thou wilt fall down and worship me.' Yet had he no evil or sinful thought, nor indeed was capable of having any. And even hence it follows that neither have real Christians; for 'everyone that is perfect is as his master' (Luke 6:40). Therefore, if he was free from evil or sinful thoughts, so are they likewise.

22. And indeed, whence should evil thoughts proceed in the servant who is 'as his master'? 'Out of the heart of man (if at all) proceed evil thoughts'

(Mark 7:21). If therefore his heart be no longer evil, then evil thoughts can no longer proceed out of it. If the tree were corrupt, so would be the fruit. But the tree is good. The fruit therefore is good also (Matt. 12:33). Our Lord himself bearing witness: 'Every good tree bringeth forth good fruit. A good tree cannot bring forth evil fruit, as a corrupt tree cannot bring forth good fruit' (Matt. 7:17–18).

23. The same happy privilege of real Christians St. Paul asserts from his own experience: 'The weapons of our warfare', saith he, 'are not carnal, but mighty through God to the pulling down of strongholds; casting down imaginations' (or 'reasonings' rather, for so the word λογισμούς signifies: all the reasonings of pride and unbelief against the declarations, promises, or gifts of God) 'and every high thing that exalteth itself against the knowledge of God; and bringing into captivity every thought to the obedience of Christ' (2 Cor. 10:4, etc.).

24. And as Christians indeed are freed from evil thoughts, so are they, secondly, from evil tempers. This is evident from the above-mentioned declaration of our Lord himself: 'The disciple is not above his master; but everyone that is perfect shall be as his master.' He had been delivering just before some of the sublimest doctrines of Christianity, and some of the most grievous to flesh and blood: 'I say unto you, love your enemies, do good to them which hate you: and unto him that smiteth thee on the one cheek, offer also the other.' Now these he well knew the world would not receive, and therefore immediately adds, 'Can the blind lead the blind? Will they not both fall into the ditch?' As if he had said, 'Do not confer with flesh and blood touching these things, with men void of spiritual discernment, the eyes of whose understanding God hath not opened, lest they and you perish together.' In the next verse he removes the two grand objections with which these wise fools meet us at every turn: 'these things are too grievous to be borne,' or, 'they are too high to be attained,' saying, 'The disciple is not above his master.' Therefore if I have suffered be content to tread in my steps. And doubt ye not then but I will fulfil my word: 'For everyone that is perfect shall be as his master.' But his Master was free from all sinful tempers. So therefore is his disciple, even every real Christian.

25. Every one of these can say with St. Paul, 'I am crucified with Christ: nevertheless I live; yet not I, but Christ liveth in me'—words that manifestly describe a deliverance from inward as well as from outward sin. This is expressed both negatively, 'I live not'—my evil nature, the body of sin, is destroyed—and positively, 'Christ liveth in me'—and therefore all that is holy, and just, and good. Indeed both these, 'Christ liveth in me,' and 'I live not,' are inseparably connected; for 'what communion hath light with darkness' or 'Christ with Belial?'

26. He therefore who liveth in true believers hath 'purified their hearts by

faith', insomuch that 'everyone that hath Christ in him, the hope of glory', 'purifieth himself even as he is pure' (1 John 3:3). He is purified from pride; for Christ was lowly of heart. He is pure from self-will or desire; for Christ desired only to do the will of his Father, and to finish his work. And he is pure from anger, in the common sense of the word; for Christ was meek and gentle, patient and long-suffering. I say, 'in the common sense of the word'; for all anger is not evil. We read of our Lord himself that he once 'looked round with anger' (Mark 3:5). But with what kind of anger? The next word shows, συλλυπούμενος, being *at the same time* 'grieved for the hardness of their hearts'. So then he was *angry at the sin*, and in the same moment *grieved for the sinners*; angry or displeased *at the offence*, but sorry *for the offenders*. With anger, yea, hatred, he looked upon *the thing*; with grief and love upon the *persons*. Go thou that art perfect, and do likewise. 'Be thus angry, and *thou* sinnest not': feeling a displacency at every offence against God, but only love and tender compassion to the offender.

27. Thus doth Jesus 'save his people from their sins': and not only from outward sins, but also from the sins of their hearts; from evil thoughts and from evil tempers. 'True', say some, 'we shall thus be saved from our sins, but not till death; not in this world.' But how are we to reconcile this with the express words of St. John? 'Herein is our love made perfect, that we may have boldness in the day of judgment: because as he is, so are we *in this world*' (1 John 4:17). The Apostle here beyond all contradiction speaks of himself and other living Christians, of whom (as though he had foreseen this very evasion, and set himself to overturn it from the foundation) he flatly affirms that not only at or after death but 'in this world' they are as their Master.

28. Exactly agreeable to this are his words in the first chapter of this Epistle: 'God is light, and in him is no darkness at all. If we walk in the light, as he is in the light, we have fellowship one with another, and the blood of Jesus Christ his Son cleanseth us from all sin.' And again, 'If we confess our sins, he is faithful and just to forgive us our sins, and to cleanse us from all unrighteousness' (1 John 1:5, etc.). Now it is evident the Apostle here also speaks of a deliverance wrought 'in this world'. For he saith not, 'the blood of Christ will cleanse' (at the hour of death, or in the day of judgment) but it 'cleanseth (at the time present) us (living Christians) from all sin.' And it is equally evident that if *any sin* remain we are not cleansed from *all sin*: if *any* unrighteousness remain in the soul it is not cleansed from *all* unrighteousness. Neither let any sinner against his own soul say that this relates to justification only, or the cleansing us from the guilt of sin. First, because this is confounding together what the Apostle clearly distinguishes, who mentions first, 'to forgive us our sins', and then 'to cleanse us from all unrighteousness'. Secondly, because this is asserting justification by works in the strongest sense possible. It is making all inward as well as outward holiness necessarily previous to justification. For

if the cleansing here spoken of is no other than the cleansing us from the guilt of sin, then we are not cleansed from guilt; i.e. are not justified, unless on condition of 'walking in the light, as he is in the light'. It remains, then, that Christians are saved in this world from all sin, from all unrighteousness; that they are now in such a sense perfect as not to commit sin, and to be freed from evil thoughts and evil tempers.

29. Thus hath the Lord fulfilled the things he spake by his holy prophets, which have been since the world began: by Moses in particular, saying, 'I will circumcise thine heart, and the heart of thy seed, to love the Lord thy God with all thy heart, and with all thy soul' (Deut. 30:6); by David, crying out, 'Create in me a clean heart, and renew a right spirit within me'; and most remarkably by Ezekiel, in those words: 'Then will I sprinkle clean water upon you, and ye shall be clean; from all *your* filthiness, and from *all* your idols will I cleanse you. A new heart also will I give you, and a new spirit will I put within you, and cause you to walk in my statutes, and ye shall keep my judgments, and do them. . . . Ye shall be my people, and I will be your God. I will also save you from all your uncleannesses. . . . Thus saith the Lord your God, In the day that I shall have cleansed you from all your iniquities . . . the heathen shall know that I the Lord build the ruined places; . . . I the Lord have spoken it, . . . and I will do it' (Ezek. 36:25, etc.).

30. 'Having therefore these promises, dearly beloved', both in the law and in the prophets, and having the prophetic word confirmed unto us in the gospel by our blessed Lord and his apostles, 'let us cleanse ourselves from all filthiness of flesh and spirit, perfecting holiness in the fear of God.' 'Let us fear lest' so many promises 'being made us of entering into his rest' (which he that hath entered into 'is ceased from his own works') 'any of us should come short of it.' 'This one thing let us do: forgetting those things which are behind, and reaching forth unto those things which are before, let us press toward the mark for the prize of the high calling of God in Christ Jesus'; crying unto him day and night till we also are 'delivered from the bondage of corruption into the glorious liberty of the sons of God.'

'AWAKE, THOU THAT SLEEPEST'

Sermon 3 – 1742

AN INTRODUCTORY COMMENT

Charles Wesley's evangelical conversion had preceded his brother's by three days. The following year, in July 1739, Charles preached a sermon on justification before the university at Christ Church 'with great boldness'. In June 1740 he had spent a week in Oxford 'preaching repentance' but discovered that 'learned Gallio cared for none of these things', comparing the indifference of the Roman consul in Acts 18:17 with that of the university. He came up for appointment as university preacher in St. Mary's on April 4, 1742, his first and last occasion for preaching there.

Charles's message, with a barrage of invidious questions for its climax, most likely would have aroused some resentment in his auditory, though Thomas Salmon (a historian who was in the audience) reported that his accusations fell largely on deaf ears. In any case, this sermon would have persuaded any Methodist reader of Charles's wholehearted identification with his brother's cause and theirs. This sermon is then a lively evangelical statement, giving Charles's personal identification with the Revival, and his valedictory to Oxford.

Charles interprets the sleep mentioned in the text as signifying 'the natural state of man': 'that deep sleep of the soul into which the sin of Adam hath cast all who spring from his loins'. Bereft of spiritual senses, the sleeper is called by God to know his true state and repent. Charles does not shy away from the doctrines of assurance or perceptible inspiration, reiterating a theme typical of early Wesleyan preaching: it is not possible to have received the Spirit of Christ and not know it. Before the decade was out, the Wesleys would retreat from the stark either/or implications of this stance, but would continue to hold that the indwelling of the Spirit is the commonly expected privilege of all believers.

The title of this sermon as published was *A Sermon preached on Sunday, April 4, 1742, before the University of Oxford. By Charles Wesley, M.A., Student of Christ Church.* The drop-title prefixed to the individual editions of the sermon was simply 'Ephes. v.14'; some variant of this heading continued in all subsequent editions until 1795, when its present title appeared for the first time.

'Awake, Thou That Sleepest'

Awake, thou that sleepest, and arise from the dead,
and Christ shall give thee light.
Ephesians 5:14

In discoursing on these words I shall, with the help of God,

First, describe the sleepers to whom they are spoken;

Secondly, enforce the exhortation, 'Awake thou that sleepest, and arise from the dead'; and,

Thirdly, explain the promise made to such as do awake and arise—'Christ shall give thee light.'

I.1. And first, as to the sleepers here spoken to. By sleep is signified the natural state of man: that deep sleep of the soul into which the sin of Adam hath cast all who spring from his loins; that supineness, indolence, and stupidity, that insensibility of his real condition, wherein every man comes into the world, and continues till the voice of God awakes him.

2. Now 'they that sleep, sleep in the night.' The state of nature is a state of utter darkness, a state wherein 'darkness covers the earth, and gross darkness the people.' The poor unawakened sinner, how much knowledge soever he may have as to other things, has no knowledge of himself. In this respect 'he knoweth nothing yet as he ought to know.' He knows not that he is a fallen spirit, whose only business in the present world is to recover from his fall, to regain that image of God wherein he was created. He sees *no necessity* for 'the one thing needful', even that inward universal change, that 'birth from above' (figured out by baptism) which is the beginning of that total renovation, that sanctification of spirit, soul, and body, 'without which no man shall see the Lord'.

3. Full of all diseases as he is, he fancies himself in perfect health. Fast bound in misery and iron, he dreams that he is happy and at liberty. He says, 'Peace, peace,' while the devil as 'a strong man armed' is in full possession of his soul. He sleeps on still, and takes his rest, though hell is moved from beneath to meet him; though the pit, from whence there is no return, hath opened its mouth to swallow him up. A fire is kindled around him, yet he knoweth it not; yea, it burns him, yet he lays it not to heart.

4. By one who sleeps we are therefore to understand (and would to God we might all understand it!) a sinner satisfied in his sins, contented to remain

in his fallen state, to live and die without the image of God; one who is ignorant both of his disease and of the only remedy for it; one who never was warned, or never regarded the warning voice of God 'to flee from the wrath to come'; one that never yet saw he was in danger of hell-fire, or cried out in the earnestness of his soul, 'What must I do to be saved?'

5. If this sleeper be not outwardly vicious, his sleep is usually the deepest of all: whether he be of the Laodicean spirit, 'neither cold nor hot', but a quiet, rational, inoffensive, good-natured professor of the religion of his fathers; or whether he be zealous and orthodox, and 'after the most straitest sect of our religion lives a Pharisee'; that is, according to the scriptural account, one that *justifies himself*, one that labours 'to establish his own righteousness' as the ground of his acceptance with God.

6. This is he who 'having a form of godliness, denies the power thereof'; yea, and probably reviles it, wheresoever it is found, as mere extravagance and delusion. Meanwhile the wretched self-deceiver thanks God that he 'is not as other men are, adulterers, unjust, extortioners'. No, he doth no wrong to any man. He 'fasts twice in the week', uses all the means of grace, is constant at church and sacrament; yea, and 'gives tithes of all that he has', does all the good that he can. 'Touching the righteousness of the law', he is 'blameless': he wants nothing of godliness but the power; nothing of religion but the spirit; nothing of Christianity but the truth and the life.

7. But know ye not that however highly esteemed among men such a Christian as this may be, he is an abomination in the sight of God, and an heir of every woe which the Son of God yesterday, today, and for ever denounces against 'scribes and Pharisees, hypocrites'? He hath 'made clean the outside of the cup and the platter', but within is full of all filthiness. 'An evil disease cleaveth' still 'unto him,' so that 'his inward parts are very wickedness'. Our Lord fitly compares him to a 'painted sepulchre', which 'appears beautiful without', but nevertheless is 'full of dead men's bones and of all uncleanness'. The bones indeed are no longer dry; 'the sinews and flesh are come up upon them, and the skin covers them above: but there is no breath in them,' no Spirit of the living God. And 'if any man have not the Spirit of Christ, he is none of his.' 'Ye are Christ's', 'if so be that the Spirit of God dwell in you.' But if not, God knoweth that ye abide in death, even until now.

8. This is another character of the sleeper here spoken to. He abides in death, though he knows it not. He is dead unto God, 'dead in trespasses and sins'. 'For to be carnally minded is death.' Even as it is written, 'By one man sin entered into the world, and death by sin; and so death passed upon all men'—not only temporal death, but likewise spiritual and eternal. 'In the day thou eatest (said God to Adam) thou shalt surely die.' Not bodily (unless as he then became mortal) but spiritually: thou shalt lose the life of thy soul; thou shalt die to God, shalt be separated from him, thy essential life and happiness.

9. Thus first was dissolved the vital union of our soul with God, insomuch that 'in the midst of' natural 'life we are' now 'in' spiritual 'death'. And herein we remain till the Second Adam becomes a quickening spirit to us, till he raises the dead, the dead in sin, in pleasure, riches, or honours. But before any dead soul can live, he 'hears (hearkens to) the voice of the Son of God': he is made sensible of his lost estate, and receives the sentence of death in himself. He knows himself to be 'dead while he liveth', dead to God and all the things of God; having no more power to perform the actions of a living Christian than a dead body to perform the functions of a living man.

10. And most certain it is that one dead in sin has not 'senses exercised to discern' spiritual 'good and evil'. 'Having eyes, he sees not; he hath ears, and hears not.' He doth not 'taste and see that the Lord is gracious'. He 'hath not seen God at any time', nor 'heard his voice', nor 'handled the Word of life'. In vain is the name of Jesus 'like ointment poured forth', and 'all his garments smell of myrrh, aloes, and cassia'. The soul that sleepeth in death hath no perception of any objects of this kind. His heart is 'past feeling', and understandeth none of these things.

11. And hence, having no spiritual senses, no inlets of spiritual knowledge, the natural man receiveth not the things of the Spirit of God; nay, he is so far from receiving them that whatsoever is spiritually discerned is mere foolishness unto him. He is not content with being utterly ignorant of spiritual things, but he denies the very existence of them. And spiritual sensation itself is to him the foolishness of folly. 'How', saith he, 'can these things be?' How can any man *know* that he is alive to God? Even as you know that your body is now alive. Faith is the life of the soul: and if ye have this life abiding in you, ye want no marks to evidence it *to yourself*, but that ἔλεγχος Πνεύματος, that divine consciousness, that 'witness of God', which is more and greater than ten thousand human witnesses.

12. If he doth not now bear witness with thy spirit that thou art a child of God, O that he might convince thee, thou poor unawakened sinner, by his demonstration and power, that thou art a child of the devil! O that as I prophesy there might now be 'a noise and a shaking', and may 'the bones come together, bone to his bone'. Then 'come from the four winds, O breath, and breathe on these slain that they may live!' And do not ye harden your hearts and resist the Holy Ghost, who even now is come to 'convince you of sin', 'because you believe not on the name of the only-begotten Son of God'.

II.1. Wherefore, 'Awake, thou that sleepest, and arise from the dead.' God calleth thee now by my mouth; and bids thee know thyself, thou fallen spirit, thy true state and only concern below: 'What meanest thou, O sleeper? Arise! Call upon thy God, if so be thy God will think upon thee, that thou perish not.' A mighty tempest is stirred up round about thee, and thou art sinking into the depths of perdition, the gulf of God's judgments. If thou wouldst escape them, cast thyself into them. 'Judge thyself', and thou shalt 'not be judged of the Lord.'

2. Awake, awake! Stand up this moment, lest thou 'drink at the Lord's hand the cup of his fury'. Stir up thyself 'to lay hold on the Lord', 'the Lord thy righteousness, mighty to save!' 'Shake thyself from the dust.' At least, let the earthquake of God's threatenings shake thee. Awake and cry out with the trembling jailer, 'What must I do to be saved?' And never rest till thou believest on the Lord Jesus, with a faith which is his gift, by the operation of his Spirit.

3. If I speak to any one of you more than to another it is to thee who thinkest thyself unconcerned in this exhortation. 'I have a message from God unto thee.' In his name I 'warn *thee* to flee from the wrath to come'. Thou unholy soul, see thy picture in condemned Peter, lying in the dark dungeon between the soldiers, bound with two chains, the keepers before the door keeping the prison. The night is far spent, the morning is at hand when thou art to be brought forth to execution. And in these dreadful circumstances thou art fast asleep; thou art fast asleep in the devil's arms, on the brink of the pit, in the jaws of everlasting destruction.

4. O may 'the angel of the Lord come upon thee, and the light shine into thy prison'! And mayst thou feel the stroke of an almighty hand raising thee with, 'Arise up quickly, gird thyself, and bind on thy sandals, cast thy garment about thee, and follow me.'

5. Awake, thou everlasting spirit, out of thy dream of worldly happiness. Did not God create thee for himself? Then thou canst not rest till thou restest in him. Return, thou wanderer. Fly back to thy ark. 'This is not thy home.' Think not of building tabernacles here. Thou art but 'a stranger, a sojourner upon earth'; a creature of a day, but just launching out into an unchangeable state. Make haste; eternity is at hand. Eternity depends on this moment: an eternity of happiness, or an eternity of misery!

6. In what state is thy soul? Was God, while I am yet speaking, to require it of thee, art thou ready to meet death and judgment? Canst thou stand in his sight, 'who is of purer eyes than to behold iniquity'? Art thou 'meet to be partaker of the inheritance of the saints in light'? Hast thou 'fought a good fight and kept the faith'? Hast thou secured 'the one thing needful'? Hast thou recovered the image of God, even 'righteousness and true holiness'? Hast thou 'put off the old man and put on the new'? Art thou 'clothed upon with Christ'?

7. Hast thou oil in thy lamp? Grace in thy heart? Dost thou 'love the Lord thy God with all thy heart, and with all thy mind, and with all thy soul, and with all thy strength'? Is 'that mind in thee which was also in Christ Jesus'? Art thou a Christian indeed? That is, a new creature? Are 'old things passed away, and all things become new'?

8. Art thou 'partaker of the divine nature'? 'Knowest thou not that Christ

is in thee, except thou be reprobate?' Knowest thou that 'God dwelleth in thee, and thou in God, by his Spirit which he hath given thee'? Knowest thou not that 'thy body is a temple of the Holy Ghost, which thou hast of God'? Hast thou 'the witness in thyself', 'the earnest of thine inheritance'? Art thou 'sealed by that Spirit of promise unto the day of redemption'? 'Hast thou received the Holy Ghost?' Or dost thou start at the question, not knowing whether there be any Holy Ghost?

9. If it offends thee, be thou assured that thou neither art a Christian nor desirest to be one. Nay, thy 'very prayer is turned into sin'; and thou hast solemnly mocked God this very day by praying for 'the inspiration of his Holy Spirit', when thou didst not believe there was any such thing to be received.

10. Yet on the authority of God's Word and our own Church I must repeat the question, 'Hast thou received the Holy Ghost?' If thou hast not thou art not yet a Christian; for a Christian is a man that is 'anointed with the Holy Ghost and with power'. Thou art not yet made a partaker of pure religion and undefiled. Dost thou know what religion is? That it is a participation of the divine nature, the life of God in the soul of man: 'Christ formed in the heart', 'Christ in thee, the hope of glory'; happiness and holiness; heaven begun upon earth; 'a kingdom of God within thee', 'not meat and drink', no outward thing, 'but righteousness, and peace, and joy in the Holy Ghost'; an everlasting kingdom brought into thy soul, a 'peace of God that passeth all understanding'; a 'joy unspeakable and full of glory'?

11. Knowest thou that 'in Jesus Christ neither circumcision availeth anything, nor uncircumcision; but faith that worketh by love'; but a new creation? Seest thou the necessity of that inward change, that spiritual birth, that life from the dead, that holiness? And art thou thoroughly convinced that 'without it no man shall see the Lord'? Art thou labouring after it? 'Giving all diligence to make thy calling and election sure'? 'Working out thy salvation with fear and trembling'? 'Agonizing to enter in at the strait gate'? Art thou *in earnest* about thy soul? And canst thou tell the Searcher of hearts, 'Thou, O God, art the thing that I long for!' 'Lord, thou knowest all things! Thou knowest that I *would* love thee!'

12. Thou hopest to be saved. But what reason hast thou to give of the hope that is in thee? Is it because thou hast done no harm? Or because thou hast done much good? Or because thou art not like other men, but wise, or learned, or honest, and morally good? Esteemed of men, and of a fair reputation? Alas, all this will never bring thee to God. It is in his account lighter than vanity. Dost thou 'know Jesus Christ whom he hath sent'? Hath he taught thee that 'by grace we are saved through faith? And that not of ourselves: it is the gift of God; not of works, lest any man should boast'? Hast thou received the faithful saying as the whole foundation of thy hope, that 'Jesus Christ came into the world to save sinners'? Hast thou learned what that meaneth, 'I came not to

call the righteous, but sinners to repentance'? 'I am not sent but to the lost sheep'? Art thou (he that heareth, let him understand!) lost, dead, *damned already?* Dost thou know thy deserts? Dost thou feel thy wants? Art thou 'poor in spirit'? Mourning for God and refusing to be comforted? Is the prodigal 'come to himself', and well content to be therefore thought 'beside himself' by those who are still feeding upon the husks which he hath left? Art thou willing to 'live godly in Christ Jesus'? And dost thou therefore 'suffer persecution'? Do 'men say all manner of evil against thee falsely, for the Son of man's sake'?

13. O that in all these questions ye may hear the voice that wakes the dead, and feel that hammer of the Word which 'breaketh the rock in pieces'! 'If ye will hear his voice today, while it is called today, harden not your hearts.' Now 'awake, thou that sleepest' in spiritual death, that thou sleep not in death eternal! Feel thy lost estate, and 'arise from the dead.' Leave thine old companions in sin and death. Follow thou Jesus, and 'let the dead bury their dead.' 'Save thyself from this untoward generation.' 'Come out from among them, and be thou separate, and touch not the unclean thing; and the Lord shall receive thee.' 'Christ shall give thee light.'

III.1. This promise I come, lastly, to explain. And how encouraging a consideration is this, that whosoever thou art who obeyest his call, thou canst not seek his face in vain. If thou even now 'awakest and arisest from the dead', he hath bound himself to 'give thee light'. 'The Lord shall give thee grace and glory'; the light of his grace here, and the light of his glory when thou receivest the 'crown that fadeth not away.' 'Thy light shall break forth as the morning,' and thy darkness be as the noonday. 'God, who commanded the light to shine out of darkness', shall 'shine in thy heart, to give the knowledge of the glory of God in the face of Jesus Christ.' 'On them that fear the Lord shall the Sun of righteousness arise with healing in his wings.' And 'in that day it shall be said unto thee', 'Arise, shine; for thy light is come, and the glory of the Lord is risen upon thee.' For Christ shall reveal himself in thee. And he is 'the true light'.

2. God is light, and will give himself to every awakened sinner that waiteth for him. And thou shalt then be a temple of the living God, and Christ shall 'dwell in thy heart by faith'. And, 'being rooted and grounded in love', thou shalt 'be able to comprehend with all saints what is the breadth, and length, and depth, and height' of that 'love of Christ which passeth knowledge, that thou mayest be filled with all the fullness of God.'

3. Ye see your calling, brethren. We are called to be 'an habitation of God through his Spirit'; and through his Spirit dwelling in us 'to be saints' here, 'and partakers of the inheritance of the saints in light'. So 'exceeding great are the promises which are given unto us', actually given unto us who believe. For

by faith 'we receive, not the spirit of the world, but the Spirit which is of God'—the sum of all the promises—'that we may know the things that are freely given to us of God.'

4. The Spirit of Christ is that great gift of God which at sundry times and in divers manners he hath promised to man, and hath fully bestowed since the time that Christ was glorified. Those promises before made to the fathers he hath thus fulfilled: 'I will put my Spirit within you, and cause you to walk in my statutes' (Ezek. 36:27). 'I will pour water upon him that is thirsty, and floods upon the dry ground: I will pour my Spirit upon thy seed, and my blessing upon thine offspring' (Isa. 44:3).

5. Ye may all be living witnesses of these things, of remission of sins, and the gift of the Holy Ghost. 'If thou canst believe, all things are possible to him that believeth.' 'Who among you is there that feareth the Lord', and yet 'walketh on in darkness, and hath no light?' I ask thee in the name of Jesus, believest thou that 'his arm is not shortened at all'? That he is still 'mighty to save'? That he is 'the same yesterday, today, and for ever'? That 'he hath *now* power on earth to forgive sins'? 'Son, be of good cheer; thy sins are forgiven.' God, for Christ's sake, hath forgiven thee. Receive this, 'not as the word of man; but as it is, indeed, the word of God'; and thou art 'justified freely through faith'. Thou shalt be sanctified also through faith which is in Jesus, and shalt set to thy seal, even thine, 'that God hath given unto us eternal life, and this life is in his Son'.

6. Men and brethren, let me freely speak unto you, and 'suffer ye the word of exhortation', even from one the least esteemed in the church. Your conscience beareth you witness in the Holy Ghost that these things are so, 'if so be ye have tasted that the Lord is gracious'. 'This is eternal life, to know the only true God, and Jesus Christ whom he hath sent.' This experimental knowledge, and this alone, is true Christianity. He is a Christian who hath received the Spirit of Christ. He is not a Christian who hath not received him. Neither is it possible to have received him and not know it. For 'at that day' (when he cometh, saith the Lord) 'ye shall know that I am in my Father, and you in me, and I in you' (John 14:20). This is that 'Spirit of truth, whom the world cannot receive, because it seeth him not, neither knoweth him. But ye know him; for he dwelleth with you, and shall be in you.'

7. The world cannot receive him, but utterly rejecteth the promise of the Father, contradicting and blaspheming. But every spirit which confesseth not this is not of God. Yea, 'this is that spirit of antichrist, whereof ye have heard that it should come into the world; and even now it is in the world.' He is antichrist whosoever denies the inspiration of the Holy Ghost, or that the indwelling Spirit of God is the common privilege of all believers, the blessing of the gospel, the unspeakable gift, the universal promise, the criterion of a real Christian.

8. It nothing helps them to say, 'We do not deny the *assistance* of God's Spirit, but only this *inspiration*, this "receiving the Holy Ghost" and being *sensible* of it. It is only this *feeling* of the Spirit, this being *moved* by the Spirit, or *filled* with it, which we deny to have any place in sound religion.' But in 'only' denying this you deny the whole Scriptures, the whole truth and promise and testimony of God.

9. Our own excellent Church knows nothing of this devilish distinction; but speaks plainly of 'feeling the Spirit of Christ' (Article 17); of being 'moved by the Holy Ghost' (Office of consecrating Priests [i.e., Deacons]), and knowing and 'feeling there is no other name than that of Jesus whereby we can receive any salvation' (Visitation of the Sick). She teaches us also to pray for the 'inspiration of the Holy Spirit' (Collect before the Holy Communion), yea, that we may be 'filled with the Holy Ghost' (Order of Confirmation). Nay, and every presbyter of hers professes to 'receive the Holy Ghost by the imposition of hands'. Therefore to deny any of these is in effect to renounce the Church of England, as well as the whole Christian revelation.

10. But 'the wisdom of God' was always 'foolishness with men'. No marvel, then, that the great mystery of the gospel should be now also 'hid from the wise and prudent', as well as in the days of old; that it should be almost universally denied, ridiculed, and exploded as mere frenzy, and all who dare avow it still branded with the names of madmen and enthusiasts. This is that 'falling away' which was to come—that general apostasy of all orders and degrees of men which we even now find to have overspread the earth. 'Run to and fro in the streets of Jerusalem, and see if you can find a man,' a man that loveth the Lord his God with all his heart, and serveth him with all his strength. How does our own land mourn (that we look no farther) under the overflowings of ungodliness! What villainies of every kind are committed day by day; yea, too often with impunity by those who sin with a high hand, and glory in their shame! Who can reckon up the oaths, curses, profaneness, blasphemies; the lying, slandering, evil speaking; the sabbath-breaking, gluttony, drunkenness, revenge; the whoredoms, adulteries, and various uncleanness; the frauds, injustice, oppression, extortion, which overspread our land as a flood?

11. And even among those who have kept themselves pure from those grosser abominations, how much anger and pride, how much sloth and idleness, how much softness and effeminacy, how much luxury and self-indulgence, how much covetousness and ambition, how much thirst of praise, how much love of the world, how much fear of man is to be found! Meanwhile, how little of true religion! For where is he that loveth either God or his neighbour, as he hath given us commandment? On the one hand are those who have not so much as the form of godliness; on the other, those who have the form only: there stands the open, there the painted sepulchre. So that, in very deed, whosoever were earnestly to behold any public gathering together

of the people (I fear those in our churches are not to be excepted) might easily perceive 'that the one part were Sadducees, and the other Pharisees': the one having almost as little concern about religion as if there were 'no resurrection, neither angel nor spirit'; and the other making it a mere lifeless form, a dull round of external performances without either true faith, or the love of God, or joy in the Holy Ghost.

12. Would to God I could except us of this place. 'Brethren, my heart's desire and prayer to God for you is that ye may be saved' from this overflowing of ungodliness, and that here may its proud waves be stayed! But is it so indeed? God knoweth, yea, and our own conscience, it is not. We have not kept ourselves pure. Corrupt are we also and abominable; and few are there that understand any more, few that worship God in spirit and in truth. We too are 'a generation that set not our hearts aright, and whose spirit cleaveth not steadfastly unto God'. He hath appointed us indeed to be 'the salt of the earth. But if the salt have lost its savour, it is thenceforth good for nothing but to be cast out, and to be trodden under foot of men.'

13. And 'shall I not visit for these things? saith the Lord. Shall not my soul be avenged on such a nation as this?' Yea, we know not how soon he may say to the sword, 'Sword, go through this land!' He hath given us long space to repent. He lets us alone this year also. But he warns and awakens us by thunder. His judgments are abroad in the earth. And we have all reason to expect that heaviest of all, even 'that he should come unto us quickly, and remove our candlestick out of its place, except we repent and do the first works'; unless we return to the principles of the Reformation, the truth and simplicity of the gospel. Perhaps we are now resisting the last effort of divine grace to save us. Perhaps we have well-nigh 'filled up the measure of our iniquities' by rejecting the counsel of God against ourselves, and casting out his messengers.

14. O God, 'in the midst of wrath remember mercy'! Be glorified in our reformation, not in our destruction. Let us 'hear the rod, and him that appointed it'. Now that 'thy judgments are abroad in the earth', let 'the inhabitants of the world learn righteousness'.

15. My brethren, it is high time for us to awake out of sleep; before 'the great trumpet of the Lord be blown', and our land become a field of blood. O may we speedily see the things that make for our peace, before they are hid from our eyes! 'Turn thou us, O good Lord, and let thine anger cease from us.' 'O Lord, look down from heaven, behold and visit this vine', and cause us to know the time of our visitation. 'Help us, O God of our salvation, for the glory of thy name; O deliver us, and be merciful to our sins, for thy name's sake.' 'And so will we not go back from thee: O let us live, and we shall call upon thy name. Turn us again, O Lord God of hosts, show the light of thy countenance, and we shall be whole.'

'Now unto him that is able to do exceeding abundantly above all that we can ask or think, according to the power that worketh in us, unto him be glory in the church by Christ Jesus throughout all ages, world without end. Amen.'

SCRIPTURAL CHRISTIANITY

Sermon 4 – 1744

AN INTRODUCTORY COMMENT

Wesley's turn as university preacher came up yet again for August 24, 1744, the Feast of St. Bartholomew, commemorating the Great Ejectment of the Nonconformists in England in 1662, in which both of Wesley's grandfathers had suffered. In the meantime, the Revival was gaining momentum: the first 'conference' of Methodist preachers had been held, and the Methodists had faced the anger of the English mobs. Although the University could not refuse Wesley his turn, one might have expected a substitute. But Wesley apparently decided not to avoid the situation, and the stage was set for a confrontation.

The first three parts of Wesley's sermon constitute (1) his positive conception of the 'way of salvation', (2) an interesting missiological perspective, and (3) an early statement of his eschatological ideas. The sum of these parts is evangelical and Anglican. In the fourth part judgment is passed, with scant charity, that Oxford's hypocrisies are an intolerable offence to God and a general hindrance to the Christian mission. This sermon was an evangelical proclamation; it was also an act of defiance.

Wesley's sermon became the talk of the town. The Vice-Chancellor requested to see his notes, which could have been censured. The university officials, however, decided rather to punish him by 'a mortifying neglect'. Methodists, then and later, could see no proper warrant for anyone to have taken offence at such a sermon that simply preached the gospel. John Wesley himself was straightforward in his reaction: 'I am now clear of the blood of these men. I have fully delivered my own soul.' His Methodist readers would have recognized the heroic stature of their leader who had preached 'plain truth' to academic people to their face and at the cost of rejection by them.

Wesley published this sermon shortly after its delivery, prefaced with a signed note to the reader (dated October 20, 1744) that was also included in the several pamphlet reprints but not in his collected *Sermons:*

> It was not my design when I wrote ever to print the latter part of the following sermon. But the false and scurrilous accounts of it which have been published almost in every corner of the nation constrain me to publish the whole, just as it was preached, that men of reason may judge for themselves.

Scriptural Christianity

And they were all filled with the Holy Ghost.
Acts 4:31

1. The same expression occurs in the second chapter, where we read, 'When the day of Pentecost was fully come, they were all' (the apostles, with the women, and the mother of Jesus, and his brethren) 'with one accord in one place. And suddenly there came a sound from heaven, as of a rushing mighty wind. . . . And there appeared unto them cloven tongues, like as of fire, and it sat upon each of them. And they were all filled with the Holy Ghost' (Acts 2:1–4). One immediate effect whereof was, they 'began to speak with other tongues' (Acts 2:4), insomuch that both the 'Parthians, Medes, Elamites', and the other strangers who 'came together' 'when this was noised abroad', 'heard them speak' in their several 'tongues, the wonderful works of God' (Acts 2:9, 11).

2. In this chapter we read that when the apostles and brethren had been praying and praising God, 'the place was shaken where they were assembled together, and they were all filled with the Holy Ghost' (Acts 4:31). Not that we find any visible appearance here, such as had been in the former instance: nor are we informed that the *extraordinary* gifts of the Holy Ghost were then given to all or any of them, such as 'the gifts of healing, of working other miracles, of prophecy, of discerning spirits', the speaking with 'divers kinds of tongues', and 'the interpretation of tongues' (1 Cor. 12:9–10).

3. Whether these gifts of the Holy Ghost were designed to remain in the church throughout all ages, and whether or not they will be restored at the nearer approach of the 'restitution of all things', are questions which it is not needful to decide. But it is needful to observe this, that even in the infancy of the church God divided them with a sparing hand. 'Were all' even then 'prophets?' Were 'all workers of miracles? Had all the gifts of healing? Did all speak with tongues?' No, in no wise. Perhaps not one in a thousand. Probably none but the teachers in the church, and only some of them (1 Cor. 12:28–30). It was therefore for a more excellent purpose than this that 'they were all filled with the Holy Ghost.'

4. It was to give them (what none can deny to be essential to all Christians in all ages) 'the mind which was in Christ', those holy 'fruits of the Spirit' which whosoever hath not 'is none of his'; to fill them with 'love, joy, peace, long-suffering, gentleness, goodness'; to endue them with 'faith' (perhaps it might be rendered 'fidelity'), with 'meekness and temperance'; to enable them

to 'crucify the flesh with its affections and lusts' (Gal. 5:22–24), its passions and desires; and, in consequence of that *inward change*, to fulfil all *outward* righteousness, 'to walk as Christ also walked', in the 'work of faith, the patience of hope, the labour of love' (1 Thess. 1:3).

5. Without busying ourselves then in curious, needless inquiries touching those *extraordinary* gifts of the Spirit, let us take a nearer view of these his *ordinary* fruits, which we are assured will remain throughout all ages: of that great work of God among the children of men which we are used to express by one word, 'Christianity'; not as it implies a set of opinions, a system of doctrines, but as it refers to men's hearts and lives. And this Christianity it may be useful to consider under three distinct views:

I. As beginning to exist in individuals.
II. As spreading from one to another.
III. As covering the earth.

I design to close these considerations with a plain practical application.

I. And first, let us consider Christianity in its rise, as beginning to exist in individuals.

[1.] Suppose then one of those who heard the Apostle Peter preaching 'repentance and remission of sins' was 'pricked to the heart', was convinced of sin, repented, and then 'believed in Jesus'. By this 'faith of the operation of God', which was the very 'substance', or subsistence, 'of things hoped for', the demonstrative 'evidence of invisible things' (Heb. 11:1), he instantly 'received the Spirit of adoption, whereby he (now) cried Abba, Father' (Rom. 8:15). Now first it was that he could 'call Jesus Lord, by the Holy Ghost' (1 Cor. 12:3), 'the Spirit itself bearing witness with his spirit that he was a child of God' (Rom. 8:16). Now it was that he could truly say, 'I live not, but Christ liveth in me; and the life which I now live in the flesh I live by faith in the Son of God, who loved me and gave himself for me' (Gal. 2:20).

2. This then was the very essence of his faith, a divine ἔλεγχος (evidence or conviction) of the love of God the Father, through the Son of his love, to him a sinner, now 'accepted in the beloved'. And 'being justified by faith, he had peace with God' (Rom. 5:1), yea, 'the peace of God ruling in his heart'; a peace 'which, passing all understanding' (πάντα νοῦν, all barely rational conception), 'kept his heart and mind' from all doubt and fear, through the 'knowledge of him in whom he had believed'. He could not therefore 'be afraid of any evil tidings'; for his 'heart stood fast, believing in the Lord'. He feared not what man could do unto him, knowing 'the very hairs of his head were all numbered'. He feared not all the powers of darkness, whom God was daily 'bruising under his feet'. Least of all was he afraid to die; nay, he 'desired to depart and be with Christ' (Phil. 1:23); who 'through death had destroyed him that had the power of death, even the devil, and delivered them who through

fear of death were all their lifetime', till then, 'subject to bondage' (Heb. 2:14–15).

3. 'His soul' therefore 'magnified the Lord, and his spirit rejoiced in God his Saviour.' He rejoiced in him 'with joy unspeakable', who 'had reconciled him to God, even the Father'; 'in whom he had redemption through his blood, the forgiveness of sins.' He rejoiced in that 'witness of God's Spirit with his spirit that he was a child of God'; and more abundantly 'in hope of the glory of God'; in hope of the glorious image of God, the full 'renewal of his soul in righteousness and true holiness'; and in hope of that 'crown of glory', that 'inheritance incorruptible, undefiled, and that fadeth not away'.

4. 'The love of God' was also 'shed abroad in his heart by the Holy Ghost which was given unto him' (Rom. 5:5). 'Because he was a son, God had sent forth the Spirit of his Son into his heart, crying Abba, Father!' (Gal. 4:6). And that filial love of God was continually increased by the 'witness he had in himself' (1 John 5:10) of God's pardoning love to him, by 'beholding what manner of love it was which the Father had bestowed upon him, that he should be called a child of God' (1 John 3:1). So that God was the desire of his eyes, and the joy of his heart; his portion in time and in eternity.

5. He that thus 'loved God' could not but 'love his brother also'; and 'not in word only, but in deed and in truth'. 'If God', said he, 'so loved us, we ought also to love one another' (1 John 4:11); yea, every soul of man, as the 'mercy' of God 'is over all his works' (Ps. 145:9). Agreeably hereto, the affection of this lover of God embraced all mankind for his sake; not excepting those whom he had never seen in the flesh, or those of whom he knew nothing more than that they were 'the offspring of God', for whose souls his Son had died; not excepting the *evil* and *unthankful*, and least of all his enemies, those who 'hated, or persecuted, or despitefully used' him for his Master's sake. These had a peculiar place both in his heart and his prayers. He loved them 'even as Christ loved us'.

6. And 'love is not puffed up' (1 Cor. 13:4). It abases to the dust every soul wherein it dwells. Accordingly he was 'lowly of heart', little and mean and vile in his own eyes. He neither sought nor received the 'praise of men', 'but that which cometh of God only'. He was meek and long-suffering, gentle to all, and easy to be entreated. Faithfulness and truth never forsook him; they were 'bound about his neck, and wrote on the table of his heart'. By the same Spirit he was enabled to be 'temperate in all things', 'refraining his soul even as a weaned child'. He was 'crucified to the world, and the world crucified to him'—superior to 'the desire of the flesh, the desire of the eye, and the pride of life.' By the same almighty love was he saved both from passion and pride, from lust and vanity, from ambition and covetousness, and from every temper which was not in Christ.

7. It may be easily believed, he who had this love in his heart would 'work

no evil to his neighbour'. It was impossible for him knowingly and designedly to do harm to any man. He was at the greatest distance from cruelty and wrong, from any unjust or unkind action. With the same care did he 'set a watch before his mouth, and keep the door of his lips', lest he should offend in tongue either against justice, or against mercy or truth. He 'put away all lying', falsehood, and fraud; 'neither was guile found in his mouth'. He 'spake evil of no man'; nor did an unkind word ever come out of his lips.

8. And as he was deeply sensible of the truth of that word, 'without me ye can do nothing', and consequently of the need he had to be 'watered' of God 'every moment'; so he 'continued daily' in all the ordinances of God, the stated channels of his grace to man: 'in the apostles' doctrine' or teaching, receiving that food of the soul with all readiness of heart; 'in the breaking of bread', which he found to be 'the communion of the body of Christ'; and 'in the prayers' and praises offered up by the great congregation. And thus he daily 'grew in grace', increasing in strength, in the knowledge and love of God.

9. But it did not satisfy him barely to abstain from doing evil. His soul was athirst to do good. The language of his heart continually was, 'My Father worketh hitherto, and I work.' My Lord 'went about doing good'; and shall not I 'tread in his steps'? 'As he had opportunity', therefore, if he could do no good of a higher kind, he fed the hungry, clothed the naked, helped the fatherless or stranger, visited and assisted them that were sick or in prison. He 'gave all his goods to feed the poor'. He rejoiced to labour or to suffer for them; and whereinsoever he might profit another, there especially to 'deny himself'. He counted nothing too dear to part with for them, as well remembering the word of his Lord, 'Inasmuch as ye have done it unto one of the least of these my brethren, ye have done it unto me' (Matt. 25:40).

10. Such was Christianity in its rise. Such was a Christian in ancient days. Such was every one of those who, 'when they heard' the threatenings of 'the chief priests and elders', 'lifted up their voice to God with one accord, . . . and were all filled with the Holy Ghost. . . . The multitude of them that believed were of one heart and of one soul' (so did the love of him in whom they had believed constrain them to love one another). 'Neither said any of them that ought of the things which he possessed was his own; but they had all things common.' So fully were they crucified to the world and the world crucified to them. 'And they continued steadfastly . . .' 'with one accord . . .' 'in the apostles' doctrine, and in the breaking of bread, and in prayers.' 'And great grace was upon them all; neither was there any among them that lacked: for as many as were possessors of lands or houses sold them, and brought the prices of the things that were sold, and laid them down at the apostles' feet; and distribution was made unto every man according as he had need' (Acts 4:31–5).

II.1. Let us take a view, in the second place, of this Christianity as spreading from one to another, and so gradually making its way into the world. For such was the will of God concerning it, who 'did not light a candle to put it under a bushel, but that it might give light to all that were in the house'. And this our Lord had declared to his first disciples, 'Ye are the salt of the earth, . . . the light of the world,' at the same time that he gave that general command, 'Let your light so shine before men that they may see your good works, and glorify your Father which is in heaven' (Matt. 5:13–16).

2. And, indeed, supposing a few of these lovers of mankind to see 'the whole world lying in wickedness', can we believe they would be unconcerned at the sight? At the misery of those for whom their Lord died? Would not their bowels yearn over them, and their hearts 'melt away for very trouble'? Could they then stand idle all the day long? Even were there no command from him whom they loved? Rather, would they not labour, by all possible means, to 'pluck some of these brands out of the burning'? Undoubtedly they would: they would spare no pains to bring back whomsoever they could of those poor 'sheep that had gone astray' 'to the great Shepherd and Bishop of their souls' (1 Pet. 2:25).

3. So the Christians of old did. They laboured, having opportunity, to 'do good unto all men' (Gal. 6:10), warning them to 'flee from the wrath to come'; now, now, to 'escape the damnation of hell'. They declared, 'The times of ignorance God winked at; but now he calleth all men everywhere to repent' (Acts 17:30). They cried aloud, 'Turn ye, turn ye from your evil ways'; 'so iniquity shall not be your ruin' (Ezek. 18:30). They 'reasoned' with them 'of temperance and righteousness', or justice, of the virtues opposite to their reigning sins, and 'of judgment to come' (Acts 24:25), of the wrath of God which would surely be executed on evil-doers in that day when he should judge the world.

4. They endeavoured herein to speak to every man severally as he had need. To the careless, to those who lay unconcerned in darkness and in the shadow of death, they thundered, 'Awake, thou that sleepest; . . . arise from the dead, and Christ shall give thee light.' But to those who were already awakened out of sleep, and groaning under a sense of the wrath of God, their language was, 'We have an advocate with the Father; . . . he is the propitiation for our sins.' Meantime those who had believed they 'provoked to love and to good works'; to 'patient continuance in well-doing'; and to 'abound more and more' in that 'holiness, without which no man can see the Lord' (Heb. 12:14).

5. And their labour was not in vain in the Lord. His 'word ran and was glorified'. It 'grew mightily and prevailed'. But so much the more did offences prevail also. The world in general were offended, 'because they testified of it that the works thereof were evil' (John 7:7). The men of pleasure were offended, not only because these men were 'made', as it were, 'to reprove their thoughts' ('He professeth', said they, 'to have the knowledge of God; he calleth himself

the child of the Lord'; 'his life is not like other men's; his ways are of another fashion; he abstaineth from our ways, as from filthiness; he maketh his boast that God is his Father'; Wisd. 2:13–16), but much more because so many of their companions were taken away and would no more 'run with them to the same excess of riot' (1 Pet. 4:4). The men of reputation were offended, because as the gospel spread they declined in the esteem of the people; and because many no longer dared to 'give them flattering titles', or to pay man the homage due to God only. The men of trade called one another together and said, 'Sirs, ye know that by this craft we have our wealth. But ye see and hear that these men have persuaded and turned away much people; . . . so that this our craft is in danger to be set at nought (Acts 19:25–27). Above all the men of religion, so called—the men of *outside* religion, 'the saints of the world'—were offended, and ready at every opportunity to cry out, 'Men of Israel, help!' (Acts 21:28). 'We have found these men pestilent fellows, movers of sedition throughout the world' (Acts 24:5). 'These are the men that teach all men everywhere against the people and against the law' (Acts 21:28).

6. Thus it was that the heavens grew black with clouds, and the storm gathered amain. For the more Christianity spread, 'the more hurt was done', in the account of those who received it not; and the number increased of those who were more and more enraged at these 'men who (thus) turned the world upside down' (Acts 17:6); insomuch that they more and more cried out, 'Away with such fellows from the earth; it is not fit that they should live'; yea, and sincerely believed that 'whosoever' should 'kill them would do God service'.

7. Meanwhile they did not fail to 'cast out their name as evil' (Luke 6:22); so that this 'sect was everywhere spoken against' (Acts 28:22). 'Men said all manner of evil of them', even as had been done of 'the prophets that were before them' (Matt. 5:11,12). And whatever any would affirm, others would believe; so that offences grew as the stars of heaven for multitude. And hence arose, at the time foreordained of the Father, persecution in all its forms. Some, for a season, suffered only shame and reproach; some, 'the spoiling of their goods' (Heb. 10:34); some 'had trial of mocking and scourging'; some 'of bonds and imprisonment' (Heb. 11:36); and others 'resisted unto blood'.

8. Now it was that the pillars of hell were shaken, and the kingdom of God spread more and more. Sinners were everywhere 'turned from darkness to light, and from the power of Satan unto God'. He gave his children 'such a mouth, and such wisdom, as all their adversaries could not resist'. And their lives were of equal force with their words. But above all, their sufferings spake to all the world. They 'approved themselves' the servants of God 'in afflictions, in necessities, in distresses; in stripes, in imprisonments, in tumults, in labours' (2 Cor. 6:4–5); 'in perils in the sea, in perils in the wilderness; in weariness and painfulness, in hunger and thirst, in cold and nakedness'. And when, having 'fought the good fight', they were 'led as . . . sheep to the

slaughter', and 'offered upon the sacrifice and service of their faith', then the blood of each found a voice, and the heathen owned, 'He being dead, yet speaketh.'

9. Thus did Christianity spread itself in the earth. But how soon did the tares appear with the wheat! And 'the mystery of iniquity' work as well as 'the mystery of godliness'! How soon did Satan find a seat, even 'in the temple of God'! Till 'the woman fled into the wilderness', and 'the faithful were (again) minished from the children of men.' Here we tread a beaten path: the still increasing corruptions of the succeeding generations have been largely described from time to time, by those witnesses God raised up, to show that he had 'built his church upon a rock, and the gates of hell should not' wholly 'prevail against her' (Matt. 16:18).

III.1. But shall we not see greater things than these? Yea, greater than have been yet from the beginning of the world? Can Satan cause the truth of God to fail? Or his promises to be of none effect? If not, the time will come when Christianity will prevail over all, and cover the earth. Let us stand a little, and survey (the third thing which was proposed) this strange sight, a *Christian world*. 'Of this the prophets of old inquired and searched diligently': of this 'the Spirit which was in them testified' (1 Pet. 1:10,11, etc.): 'It shall come to pass in the last days, that the mountain of the Lord's house shall be established in the top of the mountains, and shall be exalted above the hills, and all nations shall flow unto it. . . . And they shall beat their swords into ploughshares, and their spears into pruning-hooks. Nation shall not lift up sword against nation; neither shall they learn war any more' (Isa. 2:2,4). 'In that day there shall be a root of Jesse, which shall stand for an ensign of the people. To it shall the Gentiles seek, and his rest shall be glorious. And it shall come to pass in that day, that the Lord shall set his hand again to recover the remnant of his people; . . . and he shall set up an ensign for the nations, and shall assemble the outcasts of Israel, and gather together the dispersed of Judah, from the four corners of the earth' (Isa. 11:10–12). 'The wolf shall (then) dwell with the lamb, and the leopard shall lie down with the kid; and the calf, and the young lion, and the fatling together; and a little child shall lead them. . . . They shall not hurt nor destroy (saith the Lord) in all my holy mountain: for the earth shall be full of the knowledge of the Lord, as the waters cover the sea' (Isa. 11:6,9).

2. To the same effect are the words of the great Apostle, which it is evident have never yet been fulfilled: 'Hath God cast away his people? God forbid. . . . But through their fall, salvation is come to the Gentiles. And if the diminishing of them be the riches of the Gentiles, how much more their fullness? . . . For I would not, brethren, that ye should be ignorant of this mystery; . . . that blindness in part is happened to Israel, until the fullness of the Gentiles be

come in: and so all Israel shall be saved' (Rom. 11:1, 11-12, 25-6).

3. Suppose now the fullness of time to be come, and the prophecies to be accomplished—what a prospect is this! All is 'peace, quietness, and assurance forever'. Here is no din of arms, no 'confused noise', no 'garments rolled in blood'. 'Destructions are come to a perpetual end': wars are ceased from the earth. Neither is there any intestine jar remaining: no brother rising up against brother; no country or city divided against itself, and tearing out its own bowels. Civil discord is at an end for evermore, and none is left either to destroy or hurt his neighbour. Here is no oppression to 'make (even) the wise man mad'; no extortion to 'grind the face of the poor'; no robbery or wrong; no rapine or injustice; for all are 'content with such things as they possess'. Thus 'righteousness and peace have kissed each other' (Ps. 85:10); they have 'taken root and filled the land'; righteousness flourishing out of the earth, and 'peace looking down from heaven'.

4. And with righteousness or justice, mercy is also found. The earth is no longer 'full of cruel habitations'. 'The Lord hath destroyed both the bloodthirsty' and malicious, the envious and revengeful man. Were there any provocation, there is none that now knoweth to 'return evil for evil': but indeed there is none doth evil, no not one; for all are 'harmless as doves'; and being 'filled with peace and joy in believing', and united in one body, by one Spirit, they all 'love as brethren'; they are all 'of one heart, and of one soul, neither saith any of them that ought of the things which he possesseth is his own'. There is none among them that lacketh; for every man loveth his neighbour as himself. And all walk by one rule: 'Whatever ye would that men should do unto you, even so do unto them.'

5. It follows that no unkind word can ever be heard among them—no 'strife of tongues', no contention of any kind, no railing, or evil speaking—but everyone 'opens his mouth with wisdom, and in his tongue there is the law of kindness'. Equally incapable are they of fraud or guile: their 'love is without dissimulation'; their words are always the just expression of their thoughts, opening a window into their breast, that whosoever desires may look into their hearts and see that only love and God are there.

6. Thus, where 'the Lord God omnipotent taketh to himself his mighty power, and reigneth', doth he 'subdue all things to himself', cause every heart to overflow with love, and fill every mouth with praise. 'Happy are the people that are in such a case; yea, blessed are the people who have the Lord for their God' (Ps. 144:15). 'Arise, shine (saith the Lord), for thy light is come, and the glory of the Lord is risen upon thee. . . . Thou hast known that I the Lord am thy Saviour and thy Redeemer, the mighty God of Jacob. . . . I have made thy officers peace, and thy exactors righteousness. Violence shall no more be heard in thy land, wasting nor destruction within thy borders; but thou shalt call thy walls "Salvation", and thy gates "Praise". . . . Thy people are all righteous; they

shall inherit the land for ever, the branch of my planting, the work of my hands, that I may be glorified' (Isa. 60:1, 16–18, 21). 'The sun shall no more be thy light by day; neither for brightness shall the moon give light unto thee: but the Lord shall be unto thee an everlasting light, and thy God thy glory' (Isa. 60:19).

IV. Having thus briefly considered Christianity as beginning, as going on, and as covering the earth, it remains only that I should close the whole with a plain practical application.

1. And first I would ask, Where does this Christianity now exist? Where, I pray, do the Christians live? Which is the country, the inhabitants whereof are 'all (thus) filled with the Holy Ghost'? Are all 'of one heart and of one soul'? Cannot suffer one among them to 'lack anything', but continually give 'to every man as he hath need'? Who one and all have the love of God filling their hearts, and constraining them to love their neighbour as themselves? Who have all 'put on bowels of mercies, humbleness of mind, gentleness, long-suffering'? Who offend not in any kind, either by word or deed, against justice, mercy, or truth, but in every point do unto all men as they would these should do unto them? With what propriety can we term any a Christian country which does not answer this description? Why then, let us confess we have never yet seen a Christian country upon earth.

2. I beseech you, brethren, by the mercies of God, if ye do account *me* a madman or a fool, yet 'as a fool bear with me.' It is utterly needful that someone should use great plainness of speech toward you. It is more especially needful at *this* time; for who knoweth but it is the *last*? Who knoweth how soon the righteous judge may say, 'I will no more be entreated for this people'? 'Though Noah, Daniel, and Job, were in this land, they should but deliver their own souls.' And who will use this plainness if I do not? Therefore I, even I, will speak. And I adjure you, by the living God, that ye steel not your breasts against receiving a blessing at *my* hands. Do not say in your heart, *Non persuadebis, etiamsi persuaseris*; or, in other words, Lord, thou shalt not 'send by whom thou wilt send'! Let me rather perish in my blood than be saved by this man!

3. 'Brethren, I am persuaded better things of you, though I thus speak.' Let me ask you, then, in tender love, and in the spirit of meekness, Is this city a *Christian* city? Is Christianity, *scriptural* Christianity, found here? Are we, considered as a community of men, so 'filled with the Holy Ghost' as to enjoy in our hearts, and show forth in our lives, the genuine fruits of that Spirit? Are all the magistrates, all heads and governors of colleges and halls, and their respective societies (not to speak of the inhabitants of the town), 'of one heart and of one soul'? Is 'the love of God shed abroad in our hearts'? Are our tempers the same that were in him? And are our lives agreeable thereto? Are we 'holy as he which hath called us is holy, in all manner of conversation'?

4. I entreat you to observe that here are no *peculiar notions* now under consideration; that the question moved is not concerning *doubtful opinions* of one kind or another; but concerning the undoubted, fundamental branches (if there be any such) of our *common Christianity*. And for the decision thereof I appeal to your own conscience, guided by the Word of God. He therefore that is not condemned by his own heart, let him go free.

5. In the fear, then, and in the presence of the great God before whom both you and I shall shortly appear, I pray you that are in authority over us, whom I reverence for your office' sake, to consider (and not after the manner of dissemblers with God), are you 'filled with the Holy Ghost'? Are ye lively portraitures of him whom ye are appointed to represent among men? 'I have said, Ye are gods,' ye magistrates and rulers; ye are by office so nearly allied to the God of heaven! In your several stations and degrees ye are to show forth unto us 'the Lord our Governor'. Are all the thoughts of your hearts, all your tempers and desires, suitable to your high calling? Are all your words like unto those which come out of the mouth of God? Is there in all your actions dignity and love? A greatness which words cannot express, which can flow only from an heart full of God—and yet consistent with the character of 'man that is a worm, and the son of man that is a worm'!

6. Ye venerable men who are more especially called to form the tender minds of youth, to dispel thence the shades of ignorance and error, and train them up to be wise unto salvation, are you 'filled with the Holy Ghost'? With all those 'fruits of the Spirit' which your important office so indispensably requires? Is your heart whole with God? Full of love and zeal to set up his kingdom on earth? Do you continually remind those under your care that the one rational end of all our studies is to know, love, and serve 'the only true God, and Jesus Christ whom he hath sent'? Do you inculcate upon them day by day that 'love alone never faileth'? Whereas, 'whether there be tongues, they shall fail', or philosophical 'knowledge, it shall vanish away'; and that without love all learning is but splendid ignorance, pompous folly, vexation of spirit. Has all you teach an actual tendency to the love of God, and of all mankind for his sake? Have you an eye to this end in whatever you prescribe touching the kind, the manner, and the measure of their studies; desiring and labouring that wherever the lot of these young soldiers of Christ is cast they may be so many 'burning and shining lights', 'adorning the gospel of Christ in all things'? And permit me to ask, Do you put forth all your strength in the vast work you have undertaken? Do you labour herein with all your might? Exerting every faculty of your soul? Using every talent which God hath lent you, and that to the uttermost of your power?

7. Let it not be said that I speak here as if all under your care were intended to be clergymen. Not so; I only speak as if they were all intended to be Christians. But what example is set them by us who enjoy the beneficence of

our forefathers; by fellows, students, scholars; more especially those who are of some rank and eminence? Do ye, brethren, abound in the fruits of the Spirit, in lowliness of mind, in self-denial and mortification, in seriousness and composure of spirit, in patience, meekness, sobriety, temperance, and in unwearied, restless endeavours to do good in every kind unto all men, to relieve their outward wants, and to bring their souls to the true knowledge and love of God? Is this the general character of fellows of colleges? I fear it is not. Rather, have not pride and haughtiness of spirit, impatience and peevishness, sloth and indolence, gluttony and sensuality, and even a proverbial uselessness, been objected to us, *perhaps* not always by our enemies, nor *wholly* without ground? O that God would roll away this reproach from us, that the very memory of it might perish for ever!

8. Many of us are more immediately consecrated to God, called to 'minister in holy things'. Are we then patterns to the rest, 'in word, in conversation, in charity; in spirit, in faith, in purity'? (1 Tim. 4:12). Is there written on our forehead and on our heart, 'Holiness to the Lord'? From what motives did we enter upon this office? Was it indeed with a single eye 'to serve God, trusting that we were inwardly moved by the Holy Ghost to take upon us this ministration, for the promoting of his glory, and the edifying of his people'? And have we 'clearly determined, by God's grace, to give ourselves wholly to this office? Do we forsake and set aside, as much as in us lies, all worldly cares and studies? Do we apply ourselves wholly to this one thing, and draw all our cares and studies this way'? Are we 'apt to teach'? Are we 'taught of God', that we may be able to teach others also? Do we know God? Do we know Jesus Christ? Hath God 'revealed his Son in us'? And hath he 'made us able ministers of the new covenant'? Where then are 'the seals of our apostleship'? Who that 'were dead in trespasses and sins' have been quickened by our word? Have we a burning zeal to save souls from death, so that for their sake we often forget even to eat our bread? Do we speak plain, 'by manifestation of the truth commending ourselves to every man's conscience in the sight of God'? (2 Cor. 4:2). Are we dead to the world and the things of the world, 'laying up all our treasure in heaven'? 'Do we lord it over God's heritage'? Or are we the least, the 'servants of all'? When we bear the reproach of Christ, does it sit heavy upon us, or do we rejoice therein? When we are 'smitten on the one cheek', do we resent it? Are we impatient of affronts? Or do we 'turn the other also'; 'not resisting the evil', but 'overcoming evil with good'? Have we a bitter zeal, inciting us to strive sharply and passionately with them 'that are out of the way'? Or is our zeal the flame of love? So as to direct all our words with sweetness, lowliness, and meekness of wisdom?

9. Once more: what shall we say concerning the youth of this place? Have *you* either the form or the power of Christian godliness? Are you humble, teachable, advisable; or stubborn, self-willed, heady, and high-minded? Are you

obedient to your superiors as to parents; or do you despise those to whom you owe the tenderest reverence? Are you diligent in your easy business, pursuing your studies with all your strength? Do you 'redeem the time', crowding as much work into every day as it can contain? Rather, are ye not conscious to yourselves that you waste away day after day, either in reading what has no tendency to Christianity, or in gaming, or in—you know not what? Are you better managers of your fortune than of your time? Do you, out of principle, take care to 'owe no man anything'? Do you 'remember the sabbath day to keep it holy'; to spend it in the more immediate worship of God? When you are in his house do you consider that God is there? Do you behave 'as seeing him that is invisible'? Do you know how to 'possess your bodies in sanctification and honour'? Are not drunkenness and uncleanness found among you? Yea, are there not of you who 'glory in their shame'? Do not many of you 'take the name of God in vain', perhaps habitually, without either remorse or fear? Yea, are there not a multitude of you that are forsworn? I fear, a swiftly increasing multitude. Be not surprised, brethren: before God and this congregation I own myself to have been of that number; solemnly swearing to 'observe all those customs' which I then knew nothing of, 'and those statutes' which I did not so much as read over, either then, or for some years after. What is perjury, if this is not? But if it be, O what a weight of sin, yea, sin of no common dye, lieth upon us! And doth not 'the Most High regard it'?

10. May it not be one of the consequences of this that so many of you are a generation of *triflers*; triflers with God, with one another, and with your own souls? For how few of you spend, from one week to another, a single hour in private prayer? How few have any thought of God in the general tenor of your conversation? Who of you is in any degree acquainted with the work of his Spirit? His supernatural work in the souls of men? Can you bear, unless now and then in a church, any talk of the Holy Ghost? Would you not take it for granted if one began such a conversation that it was either 'hypocrisy' or 'enthusiasm'? In the name of the Lord God Almighty I ask, What religion are *you* of? Even the talk of Christianity ye cannot, will not, bear! O my brethren! What a Christian city is this? 'It is time for thee, Lord, to lay to thine hand!'

11. For indeed what probability—what possibility rather (speaking after the manner of men)—is there that Christianity, scriptural Christianity, should be again the religion of this place? That all orders of men among us should speak and live as men 'filled with the Holy Ghost'? By whom should this Christianity be restored? By those of you that are in authority? Are you convinced then that this is scriptural Christianity? Are you desirous it should be restored? And do ye not count your fortune, liberty, life, dear unto yourselves, so ye may be instrumental in the restoring it? But suppose ye have this desire, who hath any power proportioned to the effect? Perhaps some of you have made a few faint attempts, but with how small success! Shall Christianity then be restored by

young, unknown, inconsiderable men? I know not whether ye yourselves could suffer it. Would not some of you cry out, 'Young man, in so doing thou reproachest us!' But there is no danger of your being put to the proof, so hath 'iniquity overspread us like a flood'. Whom then shall God send? The famine, the pestilence (the last messengers of God to a guilty land), or the sword? 'The armies of the' Romish 'aliens', to reform us into our first love? Nay, rather 'let us fall into thy hand, O Lord, and let us not fall into the hand of man.'

Lord, save, or we perish! Take us out of the mire, that we sink not! O help us against these enemies! For vain is the help of man. Unto thee all things are possible. According to the greatness of thy power, preserve thou those that are appointed to die. And preserve us in the manner that seemest thee good; not as we will, but as thou wilt!

JUSTIFICATION BY FAITH

Sermon 5 – 1746

AN INTRODUCTORY COMMENT

There is no mistaking the threatening tone and spirit of Wesley's university sermons in the late 1730s and 1740s; they measure his move from pious don to itinerant evangelist. In 'Justification by Faith', however, we come to his first fully positive exposition of his new soteriology—faith alone. Wesley's claim to William Law in 1738 that he had never heard of the doctrine of *sola fide* is scarcely credible, since a wide-ranging controversy on this very point had been raging in the Church of England between Puritans and Anglicans since the latter half of the sixteenth century. In 1739 Wesley extracted and published Robert Barnes's *Treatise on Justification by Faith Only, According to the Doctrine of the Eleventh Article of the Church of England*; he had long known the Articles (specifically IX–XIV) and the Homilies (specifically the first five of 1547). What is credible is that his preoccupations with holy living and the means of grace had obscured the priority of justifying faith as antecedent to, and the ground of, 'the faith that works by love'. Now he is prepared to explain how Christ's mediation and advocacy effect the pardon of a repentant sinner. Although some sections (esp. III.3 and IV.6) give evidence that this essay was addressed to the theological community, the basic explanation is plain enough for 'plain people'—justification is pardon from both the guilt and power of sin, made possible by faith, the only necessary condition of justification. Just as clear is his ordering of repentance, justification, and sanctification: 'no works done before justification are good,' a typically strong statement by Wesley at this time, though it overlooks the value of 'works meet for repentance', which he will soon begin to accent. Another favourite Wesleyan theme seen here is the linkage between God's design for humanity (happiness) and God's demand upon it (holiness).

The first record in the *Journal* of an oral sermon on justification from Rom. 4:5 is for May 28, 1738, at the chapel in Long Acre, London. He seems to have preached from this text at least eight more times before June 8, 1742, when he preached on justification at Epworth (probably from his father's tombstone). This written sermon was first published in the first volume of his collected *Sermons on Several Occasions* (1746). Although found in every edition of his collected sermons, it was never reprinted separately. It stands as the earliest full summary of the basic form of Wesley's mature soteriology.

Justification by Faith

To him that worketh not, but believeth on him that justifieth the ungodly, his faith is counted to him for righteousness.
Romans 4:5

1. How a sinner may be justified before God, the Lord and Judge of all, is a question of no common importance to every child of man. It contains the foundation of all our hope, inasmuch as while we are at enmity with God there can be no true peace, no solid joy, either in time or in eternity. What peace can there be while our own heart condemns us? And much more he that 'is greater than our heart, and knoweth all things'? What solid joy, either in this world or that to come, while 'the wrath of God abideth on us'?

2. And yet how little hath this important question been understood! What confused notions have many had concerning it! Indeed not only confused, but often utterly false, contrary to the truth as light to darkness; notions absolutely inconsistent with the oracles of God, and with the whole analogy of faith. And hence, erring concerning the very foundation, they could not possibly build thereon; at least, not 'gold, silver, or precious stones', which would endure when 'tried as by fire', but only 'hay and stubble', neither acceptable to God nor profitable to man.

3. In order to do justice, as far as in me lies, to the vast importance of the subject, to save those that seek the truth in sincerity from 'vain jangling' and 'strife of words', to clear the confusedness of thought into which so many have already been led thereby, and to give them true and just conceptions of this great mystery of godliness, I shall endeavour to show,

First, what is the general ground of this whole doctrine of justification;
Secondly, what justification is;
Thirdly, who they are that are justified; and,
Fourthly, on what terms they are justified.

I. I am first to show what is the general ground of this whole doctrine of justification.

1. In the image of God was man made; holy as he that created him is holy, merciful as the author of all is merciful, perfect as his Father in heaven is perfect. As God is love, so man dwelling in love dwelt in God, and God in him. God made him to be 'an image of his own eternity', an incorruptible

picture of the God of glory. He was accordingly pure, as God is pure, from every spot of sin. He knew not evil in any kind or degree, but was inwardly and outwardly sinless and undefiled. He 'loved the Lord his God with all his heart, and with all his mind, and soul, and strength'.

2. To man thus upright and perfect God gave a perfect law, to which he required full and perfect obedience. He required full obedience in every point, and this to be performed without any intermission from the moment man became a living soul till the time of his trial should be ended. No allowance was made for any falling short. As, indeed, there was no need of any, man being altogether equal to the task assigned, and thoroughly furnished for every good word and work.

3. To the entire law of love which was written in his heart (against which, perhaps, he could not sin directly) it seemed good to the sovereign wisdom of God to superadd one positive law: 'Thou shalt not eat of the fruit of the tree that groweth in the midst of the garden'; annexing that penalty thereto, 'In the day thou eatest thereof, thou shalt surely die.'

4. Such then was the state of man in paradise. By the free, unmerited love of God he was holy and happy; he knew, loved, enjoyed God, which is (in substance) life everlasting. And in this life of love he was to continue for ever if he continued to obey God in all things. But if he disobeyed him in any he was to forfeit all. 'In that day (said God) thou shalt surely die.'

5. Man did disobey God; he 'ate of the tree of which God commanded him, saying, Thou shalt not eat of it.' And in that day he was condemned by the righteous judgment of God. Then also the sentence whereof he was warned before began to take place upon him. For the moment he tasted that fruit he died. His soul died, was separated from God; separate from whom the soul has no more life than the body has when separate from the soul. His body likewise became corruptible and mortal, so that death then took hold on this also. And being already dead in spirit, dead to God, dead in sin, he hastened on to death everlasting, to the destruction both of body and soul in the fire never to be quenched.

6. Thus 'by one man sin entered into the world, and death by sin. And so death passed upon all men,' as being contained in him who was the common father and representative of us all. Thus 'through the offence of one' all are dead, dead to God, dead in sin, dwelling in a corruptible, mortal body, shortly to be dissolved, and under the sentence of death eternal. For as 'by one man's disobedience all were made sinners', so by that offence of one 'judgment came upon all men to condemnation' (Rom. 5:12, etc.).

7. In this state we were, even all mankind, when 'God so loved the world that he gave his only begotten Son, to the end we might not perish but have everlasting life.' In the fullness of time he was made man, another common head of mankind, a second general parent and representative of the whole

human race. And as such it was that 'he bore our griefs', the Lord 'laying upon him the iniquities of us all'. Then 'was he wounded for our transgressions, and bruised for our iniquities.' 'He made his soul an offering for sin.' He poured out his blood for the transgressors. He 'bare our sins in his own body on the tree', that 'by his stripes we might be healed'. And 'by that one oblation of himself once offered' he 'hath redeemed me and all mankind'; having thereby 'made a full, perfect, and sufficient sacrifice and satisfaction for the sins of the whole world'.

8. In consideration of this, that the Son of God hath 'tasted death for every man', God hath now 'reconciled the world to himself, not imputing to them their former trespasses'. And thus, 'as by the offence of one judgment came upon all men to condemnation, even so by the righteousness of one the free gift came upon all men unto justification.' So that for the sake of his well-beloved Son, of what he hath done and suffered for us, God now vouchsafes on one only condition (which himself also enables us to perform) both to remit the punishment due to our sins, to reinstate us in his favour, and to restore our dead souls to spiritual life, as the earnest of life eternal.

9. This therefore is the general ground of the whole doctrine of justification. By the sin of the first Adam, who was not only the father but likewise the representative of us all, we all 'fell short of the favour of God', we all became 'children of wrath'; or, as the Apostle expresses it, 'Judgment came upon all men to condemnation.' Even so by the sacrifice for sin made by the second Adam, as the representative of us all, God is so far reconciled to all the world that he hath given them a new covenant. The plain condition whereof being once fulfilled, 'there is no more condemnation for us', but we are 'justified freely by his grace through the redemption that is in Jesus Christ'.

II.1. But what is it to be 'justified'? What is 'justification'? This was the second thing which I proposed to show. And it is evident from what has been already observed that it is not the being made actually just and righteous. This is *sanctification*; which is indeed in some degree the immediate *fruit* of justification, but nevertheless is a distinct gift of God, and of a totally different nature. The one implies what God *does for us* through his Son; the other what he *works in us* by his Spirit. So that although some rare instances may be found wherein the term 'justified' or 'justification' is used in so wide a sense as to include sanctification also, yet in general use they are sufficiently distinguished from each other both by St. Paul and the other inspired writers.

2. Neither is that far-fetched conceit that justification is the clearing us from accusation, particularly that of Satan, easily provable from any clear text of Holy Writ. In the whole scriptural account of this matter, as above laid down, neither that accuser nor his accusation appears to be at all taken in. It cannot indeed be denied that he is the 'accuser of men', emphatically so called. But it does

in no wise appear that the great Apostle hath any reference to this, more or less, in all that he hath written touching justification either to the Romans or the Galatians.

3. It is also far easier to take for granted than to prove from any clear Scripture testimony that justification is the clearing us from the accusation brought against us by *the law*. At least, if this forced, unnatural way of speaking mean either more or less than this, that whereas we have transgressed the law of God and thereby deserved the damnation of hell, God does not inflict on those who are justified the punishment which they had deserved.

4. Least of all does justification imply that God is *deceived* in those whom he justifies; that he thinks them to be what in fact they are not, that he accounts them to be otherwise than they are. It does by no means imply that God judges concerning us contrary to the real nature of things, that he esteems us better than we really are, or believes us righteous when we are unrighteous. Surely no. The judgment of the all-wise God is always according to truth. Neither can it ever consist with his unerring wisdom to think that I am innocent, to judge that I am righteous or holy, because another is so. He can no more in this manner confound me with Christ than with David or Abraham. Let any man to whom God hath given understanding weigh this without prejudice, and he cannot but perceive that such a notion of justification is neither reconcilable to reason nor Scripture.

5. The plain scriptural notion of justification is pardon, the forgiveness of sins. It is that act of God the Father whereby, for the sake of the propitiation made by the blood of his Son, he 'showeth forth his righteousness (or mercy) by the remission of the sins that are past'. This is the easy, natural account of it given by St. Paul throughout his whole Epistle. So he explains it himself, more particularly in this and in the following chapter. Thus in the next verses but one to the text, 'Blessed are they (saith he) whose iniquities are forgiven, and whose sins are covered. Blessed is the man to whom the Lord will not impute sin.' To him that is justified or forgiven God 'will not impute sin' to his condemnation. He will not condemn him on that account either in this world or in that which is to come. His sins, all his past sins, in thought, word, and deed, 'are covered', are blotted out; shall not be remembered or mentioned against him, any more than if they had not been. God will not inflict on that sinner what he deserved to suffer, because the Son of his love hath suffered for him. And from the time we are 'accepted through the Beloved', 'reconciled to God through his blood', he loves and blesses and watches over us for good, even as if we had never sinned.

Indeed the Apostle in one place seems to extend the meaning of the word much farther, where he says: 'Not the hearers of the law, but the doers of the law shall be justified.' Here he appears to refer our justification to the sentence of the great day. And so our Lord himself unquestionably doth when he says,

'By thy words thou shalt be justified'; proving thereby that 'for every idle word men shall speak they shall give an account in the day of judgment.' But perhaps we can hardly produce another instance of St. Paul's using the word in that distant sense. In the general tenor of his writings it is evident he doth not; and least of all in the text before us, which undeniably speaks, not of those who have already 'finished their course', but of those who are now just setting out, just beginning 'to run the race which is set before them'.

III.1. But this is the third thing which was to be considered, namely, who are they that are justified? And the Apostle tells us expressly, the ungodly: he, that is, God, 'justifieth the ungodly'; the ungodly of every kind and degree, and none but the ungodly. As 'they that are righteous need no repentance,' so they need no forgiveness. It is only sinners that have any occasion for pardon: it is sin alone which admits of being forgiven. Forgiveness therefore has an immediate reference to sin and (in this respect) to nothing else. It is our 'unrighteousness' to which the pardoning God is 'merciful'; it is our 'iniquity' which he 'remembereth no more'.

2. This seems not to be at all considered by those who so vehemently contend that man must be sanctified, that is, holy, before he can be justified; especially by such of them as affirm that universal holiness or obedience must precede justification (unless they mean that justification at the last day which is wholly out of the present question); so far from it, that the very supposition is not only flatly impossible (for where there is no love of God there is no holiness, and there is no love of God but from a sense of his loving us) but also grossly, intrinsically absurd, contradictory to itself. For it is not a *saint* but a *sinner* that is *forgiven*, and under the notion of a sinner. God *justifieth* not the godly, but the *ungodly*; not those that are holy already, but the unholy. Upon what condition he doth this will be considered quickly; but whatever it is, it cannot be holiness. To assert this is to say the Lamb of God takes away only those sins which were taken away before.

3. Does then the good Shepherd seek and save only those that are found already? No. He seeks and saves that which is lost. He pardons those who need his pardoning mercy. He saves from the guilt of sin (and at the same time from the power) sinners of every kind, of every degree: men who till then were altogether ungodly; in whom the love of the Father was not; and consequently in whom dwelt no good thing, no good or truly Christian temper, but all such as were evil and abominable–pride, anger, love of the world, the genuine fruits of that 'carnal mind which is enmity against God'.

4. These 'who are sick', the 'burden of whose sins is intolerable', are they that 'need a physician'; these who are guilty, who groan under the wrath of God, are they that need a pardon. These who are 'condemned already', not only by God but also by their own conscience, as by a thousand witnesses, of

all their ungodliness, both in thought, and word, and work, cry aloud for him that 'justifieth the ungodly' 'through the redemption that is in Jesus'—'the ungodly and him that worketh not', that worketh not before he is justified anything that is good, that is truly virtuous or holy, but only evil continually. For his heart is necessarily, essentially evil, till the love of God is shed abroad therein. And while the tree is corrupt so are the fruits, 'for an evil tree cannot bring forth good fruit'.

5. If it be objected, 'Nay, but a man, before he is justified, may feed the hungry, or clothe the naked; and these are good works,' the answer is easy. He *may* do these, even before he is justified. And these are in one sense 'good works'; they are 'good and profitable to men'. But it does not follow that they are, strictly speaking, good in themselves, or good in the sight of God. All truly 'good works' (to use the words of our Church) 'follow after justification', and they are therefore 'good and acceptable to God in Christ', because they 'spring out of a true and living faith'. By a parity of reason all 'works done before justification are not good', in the Christian sense, 'forasmuch as they spring not of faith in Jesus Christ' (though from some kind of faith in God they may spring), 'yea, rather for that they are not done as God hath willed and commanded them to be done, we doubt not' (how strange soever it may appear to some) 'but they have the nature of sin.'

6. Perhaps those who doubt of this have not duly considered the weighty reason which is here assigned why no works done before justification can be truly and properly good. The argument runs thus:

No works are good which are not done as God hath willed and commanded them to be done:

But no works done before justification are done as God hath willed and commanded them to be done:

Therefore no works done before justification are good.

The first proposition is self-evident. And the second, that no works done before justification are done as God hath willed and commanded them to be done, will appear equally plain and undeniable if we only consider God hath willed and commanded that 'all our works should be done in charity' (ἐν ἀγάπῃ), in love, in that love to God which produces love to all mankind. But none of our works can be done in this love while the love of the Father (of God as our Father) is not in us. And this love cannot be in us till we receive the 'Spirit of adoption, crying in our hearts, Abba, Father'. If therefore God doth not 'justify the ungodly', and him that (in this sense) 'worketh not', then hath Christ died in vain; then, notwithstanding his death, can no flesh living be justified.

IV.1. But on what terms then is he justified who is altogether 'ungodly', and till that time 'worketh not'? On one alone, which is faith. He 'believeth in him that justifieth the ungodly', and 'he that believeth is not condemned';

yea, he 'is passed from death unto life'. For 'the righteousness (or mercy) of God is by faith of Jesus Christ unto all and upon all them that believe; . . . whom God hath set forth to be a propitiation through faith in his blood', that 'he might be just, and (consistently with his justice) the justifier of him which believeth in Jesus. . . . Therefore we conclude that a man is justified by faith without the deeds of the law'—without previous obedience to the moral law, which indeed he could not till now perform. That it is the moral law, and that alone, which is here intended, appears evidently from the words that follow: 'Do we then make void the law through faith? God forbid! Yea, we establish the law.' What law do we establish by faith? Not the ritual law; not the ceremonial law of Moses. In no wise; but the great, unchangeable law of love, the holy love of God and of our neighbour.

2. Faith in general is a divine, supernatural ἔλεγχος, 'evidence' or conviction 'of things not seen', not discoverable by our bodily senses as being either past, future, or spiritual. Justifying faith implies, not only a divine evidence or conviction that 'God was in Christ, reconciling the world unto himself', but a sure trust and confidence that Christ died for *my* sins, that he loved *me*, and gave himself for *me*. And at what time soever a sinner thus believes, be it in early childhood, in the strength of his years, or when he is old and hoary-haired, God justifieth that ungodly one; God for the sake of his Son pardoneth and absolveth him who had in him till then no good thing. Repentance indeed God had given him before. But that repentance was neither more nor less than a deep sense of the want of all good, and the presence of all evil. And whatever good he hath or doth from that hour when he first believes in God through Christ, faith does not *find* but *bring*. This is the fruit of faith. First the tree is good, and then the fruit is good also.

3. I cannot describe the nature of this faith better than in the words of our own Church: 'The only instrument of salvation' (whereof justification is one branch) 'is faith: that is a sure trust and confidence that God both hath and will forgive our sins, that he hath accepted us again into his favour, for the merits of Christ's death and Passion. . . . But here we must take heed that we do not halt with God through an inconstant, wavering faith. Peter coming to Christ upon the water, because he fainted in faith, was in danger of drowning. So we, if we begin to waver or doubt, it is to be feared that we should sink as Peter did, not into the water but into the bottomless pit of hell-fire' (Second Sermon on the Passion [*Homilies*]).

Therefore have 'a sure and constant faith, not only that the death of Christ is available for all the world, but that he hath made a full and sufficient sacrifice for *thee*, a perfect cleansing of *thy* sins, so that thou mayst say with the Apostle, he loved *thee*, and gave himself for *thee*. For this is to make Christ *thine own*, and to apply his merits unto *thyself* (Sermon on the Sacrament, First Part [*Homilies*]).

4. By affirming that this faith is the term or *condition* of justification I mean, first, that there is no justification without it. 'He that believeth not is condemned already'; and so long as he believeth not that condemnation cannot be removed, 'but the wrath of God abideth on him'. As 'there is no other name given under heaven than that of Jesus of Nazareth,' no other merit whereby a condemned sinner can ever be saved from the guilt of sin; so there is no other way of obtaining a share in his merit than 'by faith in his name'. So that as long as we are without this faith we are 'strangers to the covenant of promise', we are 'aliens from the commonwealth of Israel', and 'without God in the world'. Whatsoever virtues (so called) a man may have—I speak of those unto whom the gospel is preached; 'for what have I to do to judge them that are without?'—whatsoever good works (so accounted) he may do, it profiteth not: he is still a 'child of wrath', still under the curse, till he believes in Jesus.

5. Faith therefore is the *necessary* condition of justification. Yea, and the *only necessary* condition thereof. This is the second point carefully to be observed: that the very moment God giveth faith (for 'it is the gift of God') to the 'ungodly', 'that worketh not', that 'faith is counted to him for righteousness'. He hath no righteousness at all antecedent to this, not so much as negative righteousness or innocence. But 'faith is imputed to him for righteousness' the very moment that he believeth. Not that God (as was observed before) thinketh him to be what he is not. But as 'he made Christ to be sin for us' (that is, treated him as a sinner, punished him for our sins), so he counteth us righteous from the time we believe in him (that is, he doth not punish us for our sins, yea, treats us as though we were guiltless and righteous).

6. Surely the difficulty of assenting to this proposition, that faith is the *only condition* of justification, must arise from not understanding it. We mean thereby thus much: that it is the only thing without which none is justified, the only thing that is immediately, indispensably, absolutely requisite in order to pardon. As on the one hand, though a man should have everything else, without faith, yet he cannot be justified; so on the other, though he be supposed to want everything else, yet if he hath faith he cannot but be justified. For suppose a sinner of any kind or degree, in a full sense of his total ungodliness, of his utter inability to think, speak, or do good, and his absolute meetness for hell-fire—suppose, I say, this sinner, helpless and hopeless, casts himself wholly on the mercy of God in Christ (which indeed he cannot do but by the grace of God)—who can doubt but he is forgiven in that moment? Who will affirm that any more is *indispensably required* before that sinner can be justified?

Now if there ever was one such instance from the beginning of the world (and have there not been, and are there not ten thousand times ten thousand?) it plainly follows that faith is, in the above sense, the sole condition of justification.

7. It does not become poor, guilty, sinful worms, who receive whatsoever blessings they enjoy (from the least drop of water that cools our tongue to the immense riches of glory in eternity) of grace, of mere favour, and not of debt, to ask of God the reasons of his conduct. It is not meet for us to call him in question 'who giveth account to none of his ways'; to demand, 'Why didst thou make faith the condition, the only condition of justification? Wherefore didst thou decree, "He that believeth", and he only, "shall be saved"?' This is the very point on which St. Paul so strongly insists in the ninth chapter of this Epistle, viz., that the terms of pardon and acceptance must depend, not on us, but 'on him that calleth us'; that there is no 'unrighteousness with God' in fixing his own terms, not according to ours, but his own good pleasure: who may justly say, 'I will have mercy on whom I will have mercy,' namely, on him who believeth in Jesus. 'So then it is not of him that willeth, nor of him that runneth', to choose the condition on which he shall find acceptance, 'but of God that showeth mercy,' that accepteth none at all but of his own free love, his unmerited goodness. 'Therefore hath he mercy on whom he will have mercy,' viz., on those who believe on the Son of his love; 'and whom he will', that is, those who believe not, 'he hardeneth'—leaves at last to the hardness of their hearts.

8. One reason, however, we may humbly conceive, of God's fixing this condition of justification—'If thou believest in the Lord Jesus Christ thou shalt be saved'—was to 'hide pride from man'. Pride had already destroyed the very angels of God, had cast down a 'third part of the stars of heaven'. It was likewise in great measure owing to this, when the tempter said, 'Ye shall be as gods,' that Adam fell from his own steadfastness and brought sin and death into the world. It was therefore an instance of wisdom worthy of God to appoint such a condition of reconciliation for him and all his posterity as might effectually humble, might abase them to the dust. And such is faith. It is peculiarly fitted for this end. For he that cometh unto God by this faith must fix his eye singly on his own wickedness, on his guilt and helplessness, without having the least regard to any supposed good in himself, to any virtue or righteousness whatsoever. He must come as a *mere sinner* inwardly and outwardly, self-destroyed and self-condemned, bringing nothing to God but ungodliness only, pleading nothing of his own but sin and misery. Thus it is, and thus alone, when his 'mouth is stopped', and he stands utterly 'guilty before God', that he can 'look unto Jesus' as the whole and sole 'propitiation for his sins'. Thus only can he be 'found in him' and receive the 'righteousness which is of God by faith'.

9. Thou ungodly one who hearest or readest these words, thou vile, helpless, miserable sinner, I charge thee before God, the judge of all, go straight unto him with all thy ungodliness. Take heed thou destroy not thy own soul by pleading thy righteousness, more or less. Go as altogether ungodly, guilty, lost,

destroyed, deserving and dropping into hell, and thou shalt then find favour in his sight, and know that he justifieth the ungodly. As such thou shalt be brought unto the 'blood of sprinkling' as an undone, helpless, damned sinner. Thus 'look unto Jesus'! There is 'the Lamb of God, who taketh away *thy* sins'! Plead thou no works, no righteousness of thine own; no humility, contrition, sincerity! In no wise. That were, in very deed, to deny the Lord that bought thee. No. Plead thou singly the blood of the covenant, the ransom paid for thy proud, stubborn, sinful soul. Who art thou that now seest and feelest both thine inward and outward ungodliness? Thou art the man! I want thee for my Lord. I challenge *thee* for a child of God by faith. The Lord hath need of thee. Thou who feelest thou art just fit for hell art just fit to advance his glory: the glory of his free grace, justifying the ungodly and him that worketh not. O come quickly. Believe in the Lord Jesus; and *thou*, even *thou*, art reconciled to God.

THE WAY TO THE KINGDOM

Sermon 7 – 1746

AN INTRODUCTORY COMMENT

This sermon has a double text. The second one (Rom. 14:17) is invoked informally in the first paragraph and reminds us of Wesley's first 'tombstone sermon' at Epworth, June 6, 1742: 'I stood near the east end of the church, upon my father's tombstone, and cried, "The Kingdom of heaven is not meats and drinks, but righteousness, and peace, and joy in the Holy Ghost."' That sermon was never published but probably has its residues here. He preached from that text eighteen times in the half-decade 1739–43, and twelve times thereafter (the last in 1791).

The formal text here is Mark 1:15, a favourite of Wesley's in his oral preaching (191 times between 1742 and 1790). The result of these two texts here, however, is a single sermon with an integrated, cumulative argument that progresses from a negative comment on what true religion is not (viz., correct praxis and doctrine) to a positive definition of what it is (viz., love of God and neighbour, empowered by grace). This discussion allows him to mention one of his consistent themes, that true religion does not consist in orthodoxy (which he defines as 'right opinions'), and to reiterate his dual emphasis on 'holiness and happiness'. These points lead into an exhortation to repentance and belief that includes another summary statement about repentance as true self-knowledge and authentic contrition. Belief is never 'bare assent' but rather an assenting trust, the first-fruits of which are reconciliation and peace. Wesley then calls the reader to persevere in the face of critics who are armed with 'the wisdom of the world'. The conclusion is a celebration of Christian joy in the Holy Ghost.

It is worth comparing this sermon with Wesley's later sermon on the same text, *The Repentance of Believers* (1767), which makes a rather different point: the Christian's progress in sanctification does not preclude repentance. Indeed, since repentance means self-knowledge, the farther Christians are along their way to sanctification, the more sensitive they are to their shortfalls in faith, hope, and love.

This sermon, first published in volume one of Wesley's collected *Sermons* (1746), was included in the later collections as well, and in at least three separate pamphlet editions during the 1780s.

The Way to the Kingdom

The kingdom of God is at hand: repent ye, and believe the gospel.
Mark 1:15

These words naturally lead us to consider, first, the nature of true religion, here termed by our Lord 'the kingdom of God', which, saith he, 'is at hand'; and secondly, the way thereto, which he points out in those words, 'Repent ye, and believe the gospel.'

I.1. We are, first, to consider the nature of true religion, here termed by our Lord 'the kingdom of God'. The same expression the great Apostle uses in his Epistle to the Romans, where he likewise explains his Lord's words, saying, 'The kingdom of God is not meat and drink; but righteousness, and peace, and joy in the Holy Ghost' (Rom. 14:17).

2. 'The kingdom of God', or true religion, 'is not meat and drink.' It is well known that not only the unconverted Jews, but great numbers of those who had received the faith of Christ, were notwithstanding 'zealous of the law' (Acts 21:20), even the ceremonial law of Moses. Whatsoever therefore they found written therein, either concerning meat and drink offerings, or the distinction between clean and unclean meats, they not only observed themselves, but vehemently pressed the same even on those 'among the Gentiles' (or heathens) 'who were turned to God'. Yea, to such a degree that some of them taught, wheresoever they came among them, 'Except ye be circumcised, and keep the law' (the whole ritual law), 'ye cannot be saved' (Acts 15:1, 24).

3. In opposition to these the Apostle declares, both here and in many other places, that true religion does not consist in *meat* and *drink*, or in any ritual observances; nor indeed in any outward thing whatever, in anything exterior to the heart; but whole substance thereof lying in 'righteousness, peace, and joy in the Holy Ghost'.

4. Not in any *outward thing*, such as *forms* or *ceremonies*, even of the most excellent kind. Supposing these to be ever so decent and significant, ever so expressive of inward things; supposing them ever so helpful, not only to the vulgar, whose thought reaches little farther than their sight, but even to men of understanding, men of strong capacities, as doubtless they may sometimes be; yea, supposing them, as in the case of the Jews, to be appointed by God himself; yet even during the period of time wherein that appointment remains in force, true religion does not principally consist therein—nay, strictly speak-

ing, not at all. How much more must this hold concerning such rites and forms as are only of human appointment! The religion of Christ rises infinitely higher and lies immensely deeper than all these. These are good in their place; just so far as they are in fact subservient to true religion. And it were superstition to object against them while they are applied only as occasional helps to human weakness. But let no man carry them farther. Let no man dream that they have any intrinsic work; or that religion cannot subsist without them. This were to make them an abomination to the Lord.

5. The nature of religion is so far from consisting in these, in forms of worship, or rites and ceremonies, that it does not properly consist in any outward actions of what kind so ever. It is true a man cannot have any religion who is guilty of vicious, immoral actions; or who does to others what he would not they should do to him if he were in the same circumstance. And it is also true that he can have no real religion who 'knows to do good, and doth it not'. Yet may a man both abstain from outward evil, and do good, and still have no religion. Yea, two persons may do the same outward work—suppose, feeding the hungry, or clothing the naked—and in the meantime one of these may be truly religious and the other have no religion at all; for the one may act from the love of God, and the other from the love of praise. So manifest it is that although true religion naturally leads to every good word and work, yet the real nature thereof lies deeper still, even in 'the hidden man of the heart'.

6. I say of the *heart*. For neither does religion consist in *orthodoxy* or *right opinions*; which, although they are not properly outward things, are not in the heart, but the understanding. A man may be orthodox in every point; he may not only espouse right opinions, but zealously defend them against all opposers; he may think justly concerning the incarnation of our Lord, concerning the ever blessed Trinity, and every other doctrine contained in the oracles of God. He may assent to all the three creeds—that called the Apostles', the Nicene, and the Athanasian—and yet 'tis possible he may have no religion at all, no more than a Jew, Turk, or pagan. He may be almost as orthodox as the devil (though indeed not altogether; for every man errs in something, whereas we can't well conceive him to hold any erroneous opinion) and may all the while be as great a stranger as he to the religion of the heart.

7. This alone is religion, truly so called: this alone is in the sight of God of great price. The Apostle sums it all up in three particulars—'righteousness, and peace, and joy in the Holy Ghost'. And first, *righteousness*. We cannot be at a loss concerning this if we remember the words of our Lord describing the two grand branches thereof, on which 'hang all the law and the prophets': 'Thou shalt love the Lord thy God with all thy heart, and with all thy mind, and with all thy soul, and with all thy strength. This is the first and great commandment' (Mark 12:30), the first and great branch of Christian righteousness. Thou shalt delight thyself in the Lord thy God; thou shalt seek and find all happiness in

him. He shall be 'thy shield, and thy exceeding great reward', in time and in eternity. All thy bones shall say, 'Whom have I in heaven but thee? And there is none upon earth that I desire beside thee!' Thou shalt hear and fulfil his word who saith, 'My son, give me thy heart.' And having given him thy heart, thy inmost soul, to reign there without a rival, thou mayest well cry out in the fullness of thy heart, 'I will love thee, O Lord, my strength. The Lord is my strong rock and my defence: my Saviour, my God, and my might, in whom I will trust; my buckler, the horn also of my salvation, and my refuge.'

8. And the second commandment is like unto this; the second great branch of Christian righteousness is closely and inseparably connected therewith, even 'Thou shalt love thy neighbour as thyself.' 'Thou shalt love'—thou shalt embrace with the most tender goodwill, the most earnest and cordial affection, the most inflamed desires of preventing or removing all evil and of procuring for him every possible good—'thy neighbour'; that is, not only thy friend, thy kinsman, or thy acquaintance; not only the virtuous, the friendly, him that loves thee, that prevents or returns thy kindness; but every child of man, every human creature, every soul which God hath made: not excepting him whom thou never hast seen in the flesh, whom thou knowest not either by face or name; not excepting him whom that knowest to be evil and unthankful, him that still despitefully uses and persecutes thee. Him thou shalt 'love as thyself'; with the same invariable thirst after his happiness in every kind, the same unwearied care to screen him from whatever might grieve or hurt either his soul or body.

9. Now is not this love 'the fulfilling of the law'? The sum of all Christian righteousness? Of all inward righteousness; for it necessarily implies 'bowels of mercies, humbleness of mind' (seeing 'love is not puffed up'), 'gentleness, meekness, long-suffering' (for love 'is not provoked', but 'believeth, hopeth, endureth all things'): and of all outward righteousness, for 'love worketh no evil to his neighbour', either by word or deed. It cannot willingly either hurt or grieve anyone. And it is zealous of good works. Every lover of mankind, as he hath opportunity, 'doth good unto all men', being ('without partiality and without hypocrisy') 'full of mercy and good fruits'.

10. But true religion, or a heart right toward God and man, implies happiness as well as holiness. For it is not only righteousness, but also 'peace and joy in the Holy Ghost'. What peace? 'The peace of God', which God only can give, and the world cannot take away; the peace 'which passeth all understanding', all (barely) rational conception; being a supernatural sensation, a divine taste of 'the powers of the world to come'; such as the natural man knoweth not, how wise soever in the things of this world; nor, indeed, can he know it in his present state, 'because it is spiritually discerned'. It is a peace that banishes all doubt, all painful uncertainty, the Spirit of God 'bearing witness with the spirit' of a Christian that he is 'a child of God'. And it banishes

fear, all such fear as hath torment; the fear of the wrath of God, the fear of hell, the fear of the devil, and in particular, the fear of death; he that hath the peace of God 'desiring' (if it were the will of God) 'to depart and to be with Christ'.

11. With this peace of God, wherever it is fixed in the soul, there is also 'joy in the Holy Ghost'; joy wrought in the heart by the Holy Ghost, by the ever-blessed Spirit of God. He it is that worketh in us that calm, humble rejoicing in God, through Christ Jesus, 'by whom we have now received the atonement', καταλλαγήν, the reconciliation with God; and that enables us boldly to confirm the truth of the royal Psalmist's declaration, 'Blessed is the man' (or rather, 'happy,' אשרי היש) 'whose unrighteousness is forgiven, and whose sin is covered.' He it is that inspires the Christian soul with that even, solid joy which arises from the testimony of the Spirit that he is a child of God; and that gives him to 'rejoice with joy unspeakable', 'in hope of the glory of God'—hope both of the glorious image of God, which is in part and shall be fully 'revealed in him', and of that crown of glory which fadeth not away, reserved in heaven for him.

12. This holiness and happiness, joined in one, are sometimes styled in the inspired writings, 'the kingdom of God' (as by our Lord in the text), and sometimes, 'the kingdom of heaven'. It is termed 'the kingdom of God' because it is the immediate fruit of God's reigning in the soul. So soon as ever he takes unto himself his mighty power, and sets up his throne in our hearts, they are instantly filled with this 'righteousness, and peace, and joy in the Holy Ghost'. It is called 'the kingdom of heaven' because it is (in a degree) heaven opened in the soul. For whosoever they are that experience this, they can aver before angels and men,

Everlasting life is won:
Glory is on earth begun;

according to the constant tenor of Scripture, which everywhere bears record, 'God hath given unto us eternal life, and this life is in his Son. He that hath the Son' (reigning in his heart) 'hath life,' even life everlasting (1 John 5:11–12). For 'this is life eternal, to know thee, the only true God, and Jesus Christ, whom thou hast sent . . .' (John 17:3). And they to whom this is given may confidently address God, though they were in the midst of a fiery furnace,

Thee . . . , Lord, safe-shielded by thy power,
Thee, Son of God, Jehovah, we adore,

In form of man descending to appear:
To thee be ceaseless hallelujahs given.

Praise, as in heaven thy throne, we offer here;
For where thy presence is displayed, is heaven.

13. And this 'kingdom of God', or of heaven, 'is at hand'. As these words were originally spoken they implied that 'the time' was then 'fulfilled', God being made 'manifest in the flesh', when he would set up his kingdom among men, and reign in the hearts of his people. And is not the time now fulfilled? For 'Lo (saith he), I am with you always', you who preach remission of sins in my name, 'even unto the end of the world' (Matt. 28:20). Wheresoever therefore the gospel of Christ is preached, this his 'kingdom is nigh at hand'. It is not far from every one of you. Ye may this hour enter thereinto, if so be ye hearken to his voice, 'Repent ye, and believe the gospel.'

II.1. This is the way: walk ye in it. And first, repent, that is, know yourselves. This is the first repentance, previous to faith, even conviction, or self-knowledge. Awake, then, thou that sleepest. Know thyself to be a sinner, and what manner of sinner thou art. Know that corruption of thy inmost nature, whereby thou are very far gone from original righteousness, whereby 'the flesh lusteth' always 'contrary to the Spirit', through that 'carnal mind which is enmity against God', which 'is not subject to the law of God, neither indeed can be'. Know that thou art corrupted in every power, in every faculty of thy soul, that thou art totally corrupted in every one of these, all the foundations being out of course. The eyes of thine understanding are darkened, so that they cannot discern God or the things of God. The clouds of ignorance and error rest upon thee, and cover thee with the shadow of death. Thou knowest nothing yet as thou oughtest to know, neither God, nor the world, nor thyself. Thy will is no longer the will of God, but is utterly perverse and distorted, averse from all good, from all which God loves, and prone to all evil, to every abomination which God hateth. Thy affections are alienated from God, and scattered abroad over the earth. All thy passions, both thy desires and aversions, thy joys and sorrows, thy hopes and fears, are out of frame, are either undue in their degree, or placed on undue objects. So that there is no soundness in thy soul, but 'from the crown of the head to the sole of the foot' (to use the strong expression of the prophet) there are only 'wounds, and bruises,and putrefying sores'.

2. Such is the inbred corruption of thy heart, of thy very inmost nature. And what manner of branches canst thou expect to grow from such an evil root? Hence springs unbelief, ever departing from the living God; saying, 'Who is the Lord that I should serve him?' 'Tush! Thou, God, carest not for it.' Hence independence, affecting to be like the Most High; hence pride, in all its forms, teaching thee to say, 'I am rich, and increased in goods, and have need of nothing.' From this evil fountain flow forth the bitter streams of vanity, thirst of praise, ambition, covetousness, the lust of the flesh, the lust of the eye,

and the pride of life. From this arise anger, hatred, malice, revenge, envy, jealousy, evil surmisings; from this, all the foolish and hurtful lusts that now 'pierce thee through with many sorrows', and if not timely prevented will at length 'drown thy soul in everlasting perdition'.

3. And what fruits can grow on such branches as these? Only such as are bitter and evil continually. Of pride cometh contention, vain boasting, seeking and receiving praise of men, and so robbing God of that glory which he cannot give unto another. Of the lust of the flesh come gluttony or drunkenness, luxury or sensuality, fornication, uncleanness, variously defiling that body which was designed for a temple of the Holy Ghost: of unbelief, every evil word and work. But the time would fail, shouldst thou reckon up all; all the idle words thou hast spoken, provoking the Most High, grieving the Holy One of Israel; all the evil works thou hast done, either wholly evil in themselves, or at least not done to the glory of God. For thy actual sins are more than thou art able to express, more than the hairs of thy head. Who can number the sands of the sea, or the drops of rain, or thy iniquities?

4. And knowest thou not that 'the wages of sin is death'—death not only temporal, but eternal. 'The soul that sinneth, it shall die'; for the mouth of the Lord hath spoken it. It shall die the second death. This is the sentence, to 'be punished' with never-ending death, 'with everlasting destruction from the presence of the Lord, and from the glory of his power'. Knowest thou not that every sinner ἔνοχος ἔστι τῇ γεέννῃ τοῦ πυρός, not properly is 'in danger of hell-fire'—that expression is far too weak—but rather, 'is under the sentence of hell-fire'; doomed already, just dragging to execution? Thou art guilty of everlasting death. It is the just reward of thy inward and outward wickedness. It is just that the sentence should now take place. Dost thou see, dost thou feel this? Art thou thoroughly convinced that thou deservest God's wrath and everlasting damnation? Would God do thee any wrong if he now commanded the earth to open up and swallow thee up? If thou wert now to go down quick into the pit, into the fire that never shall be quenched? If God hath given thee truly to repent, thou hast a deep sense that these things are so; and that it is of his mere mercy thou art not consumed, swept away from the face of the earth.

5. And what wilt thou do to appease the wrath of God, to atone for all thy sins, and to escape the punishment thou hast so justly deserved? Alas, thou canst do nothing; nothing that will in any wise make amends to God for one evil work or word or thought. If thou couldst now do all things well, if from this very hour, till thy soul should return to God, thou couldst perform perfect, uninterrupted obedience, even this would not atone for what is past. The not increasing thy debt would not discharge it. It would still remain as great as ever. Yea, the present and future obedience of all the men upon earth, and all the angels in heaven, would never make satisfaction to the justice of God for

one single sin. How vain then was the thought of atoning for thy own sins by anything thou couldst do! It costeth far more to redeem one soul than all mankind is able to pay. So that were there no other help for a guilty sinner, without doubt he must have perished everlastingly.

6. But suppose perfect obedience for the time to come could atone for the sins that are past, this would profit thee nothing; for thou art not able to perform it; no, not in any one point. Begin now. Make the trial. Shake off that outward sin that so easily besetteth thee. Thou canst not. How then wilt thou change thy life from all evil to all good? Indeed, it is impossible to be done, unless first thy heart be changed. For so long as the tree remains evil, it cannot bring forth good fruit. But art thou able to change thy own heart from all sin to all holiness? To quicken a soul that is dead in sin? Dead to God and alive only to the world? No more than thou art able to quicken a dead body, to raise to life him that lieth in the grave. Yea, thou art not able to quicken thy soul in any degree, no more than to give any degree of life to the dead body. Thou canst do nothing, more or less, in this matter; thou art utterly without strength. To be deeply sensible of this, how helpless thou art, as well as how guilty and how sinful, this is that 'repentance not to be repented of' which is the forerunner of the kingdom of God.

7. If to this lively conviction of thy inward and outward sins, of thy utter guiltiness and helplessness, there be added suitable affections—sorrow of heart for having despised thy own mercies; remorse and self-condemnation, having the mouth stopped, shame to lift up thine eyes to heaven; fear of the wrath of God abiding on thee, of his curse hanging over thy head, and of the fiery indignation ready to devour those who forget God and obey not our Lord Jesus Christ; earnest desire to escape from that indignation, to cease from evil and learn to do well—then I say unto thee, in the name of the Lord, 'Thou art not far from the kingdom of God.' One step more and thou shalt enter in. Thou dost 'repent'. Now, 'believe the gospel'.

8. 'The gospel' (that is, good tidings, good news for guilty, helpless sinners) in the largest sense of the word means the whole revelation made to men by Jesus Christ; and sometimes the whole account of what our Lord did and suffered while he tabernacled among men. The substance of all is, 'Jesus Christ came into the world to save sinners'; or, 'God so loved the world that he gave his only begotten Son, to the end we might not perish, but have everlasting life'; or, 'He was bruised for our transgressions, he was wounded for our iniquities; the chastisement of our peace was upon him, and with his stripes we are healed.'

9. Believe this, and the kingdom of God is thine. By faith thou attainest the promise: 'He pardoneth and absolveth all that truly repent and unfeignedly believe his holy gospel.' As soon as ever God hath spoken to thy heart, 'Be of good cheer, thy sins are forgiven thee,' his kingdom comes; thou hast

righteousness, and peace, and joy in the Holy Ghost.

10. Only beware thou do not deceive thy own soul with regard to the nature of this faith. It is not (as some have fondly conceived) a bare assent to the truth of the Bible, of the articles of our creed, or of all that is contained in the Old and New Testament. The devils believe this, as well as I or thou; and yet they are devils still. But it is, over and above this, a sure trust in the mercy of God through Christ Jesus. It is a confidence in a pardoning God. It is a divine evidence or conviction that 'God was in Christ, reconciling the world to himself, not imputing to them their former trespasses'; and in particular that the Son of God hath loved *me* and given himself for *me*; and that I, even I, am now reconciled to God by the blood of the cross.

11. Dost thou thus believe? Then the peace of God is in thy heart, and sorrow and sighing flee away. Thou art no longer in doubt of the love of God; it is clear as the noonday sun. Thou criest out, 'My song shall be always of the loving-kindness of the Lord: with my mouth will I ever be telling of thy truth, from one generation to another.' Thou art no longer afraid of hell, or death, or him that had once the power of death, the devil: no, nor painfully afraid of God himself; only thou hast a tender, filial fear of offending him. Dost thou believe? Then thy 'soul doth magnify the Lord,and thy spirit rejoiceth in God thy Saviour'. Thou rejoicest in that thou hast 'redemption through his blood, even the forgiveness of sins'. Thou rejoicest in that 'Spirit of adoption which crieth in thy heart, Abba, Father!' Thou rejoicest in a 'hope full of immortality'; in reaching forth unto the 'mark of the prize of thy high calling'; in an earnest expectation of all the good things which God hath prepared for them that love him.

12. Dost thou now believe? Then 'the love of God is' now 'shed abroad in thy heart.' Thou lovest him, because he first loved us. And because thou lovest God, thou lovest thy brother also. And being filled with 'love, peace, joy', thou art also filled with 'long-suffering, gentleness, fidelity, goodness, meekness, temperance', and all the other fruits of the same Spirit–in a word, with whatever dispositions are holy, are heavenly or divine. For while thou 'beholdest with open (uncovered) face' (the veil now being taken away) 'the glory of the Lord', his glorious love, and the glorious image wherein thou wast created, thou art 'changed into the same image, from glory to glory, by the Spirit of the Lord'.

13. This repentance, this faith, this peace, joy, love; this change from glory to glory, is what the wisdom of the world has voted to be madness, mere enthusiasm, utter distraction. But thou, O man of God, regard them not: be thou moved by none of these things. Thou knowest in whom thou hast believed. See that no man take thy crown. Whereunto thou has already attained, hold fast, and follow, till thou attain all the great and precious promises. And thou who has not yet known him, let not vain men make thee

ashamed of the gospel of Christ. Be thou in nothing terrified by those who speak evil of the things which they know not. God will soon turn thy heaviness into joy. O let not thy hands hang down. Yet a little longer, and he will take away thy fears, and give thee the spirit of a sound mind. 'He is nigh that justifieth': 'Who is he that condemneth? It is Christ that died; yea, rather, that rose again; who is even now at the right hand of God, making intercession for thee.' Now cast thyself on the Lamb of God, with all thy sins, how many soever they be; and 'an entrance shall *now* be ministered unto *thee* into the kingdom of our Lord and Saviour Jesus Christ'!

THE SPIRIT OF BONDAGE AND OF ADOPTION

Sermon 9 – 1746

AN INTRODUCTORY COMMENT

In this sermon Wesley returns to the theme of 'faith alone', now in the context of a borrowed typology about the three states of man: natural, legal, and evangelical (a scheme that presupposes man's original state as that of innocence). His classical source for such a scheme is St. Augustine; his modern source here would have been Thomas Boston. Wesley's interest in such typologies may be seen as early as 1734, when he talked with the Oxford Methodists about the 'three different states of man: natural, Jewish (or fearful), and evangelical–the two last only, salvable'.

At this point in the development of his soteriology after 1738, the term 'natural' was understood by John Wesley (as it had been by Charles in '*Awake, Thou That Sleepest*') as a condition of moral anomie. Later (in 'On Working Out Our Own Salvation'), he would revise his view and assert that 'there is no man that is in a state of mere nature, no man, unless he has quenched the Spirit, that is wholly void of the [prevenient] grace of God.' Also, sin is not relativized here as it is in some earlier sermons (as deliberate violations of known laws of God); rather, 'it extends to every temper, desire, thought, and motion of the heart.'

Wesley's main concern, however, is with the contrast between the harrowed conscience and spiritual despair of those who in their legal state have been awakened (but continue as guilt-ridden, despite their best efforts) and the peace, joy, and good conscience of those who have heard the gospel and are assured of God's justifying grace. Thus, this sermon is Wesley's interpretation of the contrast delineated in Romans 7 and 8, with Romans 7 taken as a description of despair in the legal state and Romans 8 as St. Paul's celebration of evangelical grace. The sermon concludes with an invitation to those living under the Law to accept God's proffered pardon and to 'rejoice and love like the angels of God'.

It is worth noting that this sermon and four of the five other sermons that follow after the bloc of 'university sermons' have their texts from Romans. This coincidence is not accidental, for these are the sermons in which Wesley has distilled the essence of his gospel of justification. He had already preached from Romans 8:15 thirteen times in the early years of the Revival (1739-43). He seems to have neglected it thereafter.

This sermon appeared in all the collected editions of Wesley's *Sermons* beginning in 1746. It was reprinted separately in Dublin in 1747.

The Spirit of Bondage and of Adoption

Ye have not received the spirit of bondage again unto fear; but ye have received the Spirit of adoption, whereby we cry, Abba, Father.
Romans 8:15

1. St. Paul here speaks to those who are the children of God by faith. Ye, saith he, who are indeed his children, have drunk into his Spirit. 'Ye have not received the spirit of bondage again unto fear'; but 'because ye are sons, God hath sent forth the Spirit of his Son into your hearts.' 'Ye have received the Spirit of adoption, whereby we cry, Abba, Father.'

2. The spirit of bondage and fear is widely distant from this loving Spirit of adoption. Those who are influenced only by slavish fear cannot be termed the sons of God. Yet some of them may be styled his servants, and 'are not far from the kingdom of heaven'.

3. But it is to be feared the bulk of mankind, yea, of what is called 'the Christian world', have not attained even this; but are still afar off, 'neither is God in all their thoughts.' A few names may be found of those who love God; a few more there are that fear him. But the greater part have neither the fear of God before their eyes, nor the love of God in their hearts.

4. Perhaps most of you, who by the mercy of God now partake of a better spirit, may remember the time when ye were as they, when ye were under the same condemnation. But at first ye knew it not, though ye were wallowing daily in your sins and in your blood; till in due time ye 'received the spirit of fear' (ye *received*; for this also is the gift of God); and afterwards fear vanished away, and the spirit of love filled your hearts.

5. One who is in the first state of mind, without fear or love, is in Scripture termed 'a natural man'. One who is under the spirit of bondage and fear is sometimes said to be 'under the law' (although that expression more frequently signifies one who is under the Jewish dispensation, who thinks himself obliged to observe all the rites and ceremonies of the Jewish law). But one who has exchanged the spirit of fear for the spirit of love is properly said to be 'under grace'.

Now because it highly imports us to know what spirit we are of, I shall endeavour to point out distinctly, first, the state of a 'natural man'; secondly, that of one who is 'under the law'; and thirdly, of one who is 'under grace'.

I.1. And, first, the state of a 'natural man'. This the Scripture represents as a state of sleep. The voice of God to him is, 'Awake, thou that sleepest.' For his soul is in a deep sleep. His spiritual senses are not awake; they discern neither spiritual good nor evil. The eyes of his understanding are closed; they are sealed together, and see not. Clouds and darkness continually rest upon them; for he lies in the valley of the shadow of death. Hence, having no inlets for the knowledge of spiritual things, all the avenues of his soul being shut up, he is in gross, stupid ignorance of whatever he is most concerned to know. He is utterly ignorant of God, knowing nothing concerning him as he ought to know. He is totally a stranger to the law of God, as to its true, inward, spiritual meaning. He has no conception of that evangelical holiness without which no man shall see the Lord; nor of the happiness which they only find whose 'life is hid with Christ in God'.

2. And for this very reason, because he is fast *asleep*, he is in some sense at *rest*. Because he is *blind*, he is also *secure*: he saith, 'Tush, . . . there shall no harm happen unto me.' The darkness which covers him on every side keeps him in a kind of peace—so far as peace can consist with the works of the devil, and with an earthly, devilish mind. He *sees* not that he stands on the edge of the pit; therefore he *fears* it not. He cannot tremble at the danger he does not know. He has not understanding enough to fear. Why is it that he is in no dread of God? Because he is totally ignorant of him: if not 'saying in his heart, There is no God', or that he 'sitteth on the circle of the heavens', 'and humbleth' not 'himself to behold the things' which are done on earth; yet satisfying himself as well, to all Epicurean intents and purposes, by saying, 'God is merciful'; confounding and swallowing up at once in that unwieldy idea of mercy all his holiness and essential hatred of sin, all his justice, wisdom, and truth. He is in no dread of the vengeance denounced against those who obey not the blessed law of God, because he understands it not. He imagines the main point is to *do thus*, to be *outwardly* blameless—and sees not that it extends to every temper, desire, thought, motion of the heart. Or he fancies that the obligation hereto is ceased, that Christ came to 'destroy the law and the prophets', to save his people *in*, not *from* their sins, to bring them to heaven without holiness; notwithstanding his own words, 'Not one jot or tittle of the law shall pass away till all things are fulfilled,' and, 'Not everyone that saith unto me, Lord, Lord, shall enter into the kingdom of heaven; but he that doth the will of my Father which is in heaven.'

3. He is secure, because he is utterly ignorant of himself. Hence he talks of 'repenting by and by'; he does not indeed exactly know when; but some time or other before he dies—taking it for granted that this is quite in his own power. For what should hinder his doing it if he will? If he does but once set a resolution, no fear but he will make it good.

4. But this ignorance never so strongly glares as in those who are termed 'men of learning'. If a natural man be one of these, he can talk at large of his

rational faculties, of the freedom of his will and the absolute necessity of such freedom in order to constitute man a moral agent. He reads and argues, and proves to a demonstration that every man may do as he will, may dispose his own heart to evil or good as it seems best in his own eyes. Thus the god of this world spreads a double veil of blindness over his heart, lest by any means 'the light of the glorious gospel of Christ should shine' upon it.

5. From the same ignorance of himself and God there may sometimes arise in the natural man a kind of joy in congratulating himself upon his own wisdom and goodness. And what the world calls joy he may often possess. He may have pleasure in various kinds, either in gratifying the desires of the flesh, or the desire of the eye, or the pride of life—particularly if he has large possessions, if he enjoy an affluent fortune. Then he may 'clothe himself in purple and fine linen, and fare sumptuously every day'. And *so long as* he thus *doth well unto himself*, 'men will' doubtless 'speak good of'' him. They will say he is a happy man; for indeed this is the sum of worldly happiness—to dress, and visit, and talk, and eat, and drink, and rise up to play.

6. It is not surprising if one in such circumstances as these, dosed with the opiates of flattery and sin, should imagine, among his other waking dreams, that he walks in great *liberty*. How easily may he persuade himself that he is at liberty from all 'vulgar errors' and from the 'prejudice' of education, judging exactly right, and keeping clear of all extremes. 'I am free (may he say) from all the *enthusiasm* of weak and narrow souls; from *superstition*, the disease of fools and cowards, always righteous overmuch; and from *bigotry*, continually incident to those who have not a free and generous way of thinking.' And too sure it is that he is altogether free from the 'wisdom which cometh from above', from holiness, from the religion of the heart, from the whole mind which was in Christ.

7. For all this time he is the servant of sin. He commits sin, more or less, day by day. Yet he is not troubled; he 'is in no bondage' (as some speak), he feels no condemnation. He contents himself (even though he should profess to believe that the Christian revelation is of God) with: 'Man is frail. We are all weak. Every man has his infirmity.' Perhaps he quotes Scripture: 'Why, does not Solomon say, "The righteous man falls into sin seven times a day"? And doubtless they are all hypocrites or enthusiasts who pretend to be better than their neighbours.' If at any time a serious thought fix upon him, he stifles it as soon as possible with, 'Why should I fear, since God is merciful, and Christ died for sinners?' Thus he remains a willing servant of sin, content with the bondage of corruption; inwardly and outwardly unholy, and satisfied therewith; not only not conquering sin, but not striving to conquer, particularly that sin which doth so easily beset him.

8. Such is the state of every 'natural man'; whether he be a gross, scandalous transgressor, or a more reputable and decent sinner, having the form though

not the power of godliness. But how can such an one be 'convinced of sin'? How is he brought to *repent?* To be 'under the law'? To receive the 'spirit of bondage unto fear'? This is the point which is next to be considered.

II.1. By some awful providence, or by his Word applied with the demonstration of his Spirit, God touches the heart of him that lay asleep in darkness and in the shadow of death. He is terribly shaken out of his sleep, and awakes into a consciousness of his danger. Perhaps in a moment, perhaps by degrees, the eyes of his understanding are opened, and now first (the veil being in part removed) discern the real state he is in. Horrid light breaks in upon his soul; such light as may be conceived to gleam from the bottomless pit, from the lowest deep, from a lake of fire burning with brimstone. He at last sees the loving, the merciful God is also 'a consuming fire'; that he is a just God and a terrible, rendering to every man according to his works, entering into judgment with the ungodly for every idle word, yea, and for the imaginations of the heart. He now clearly perceives that the great and holy God is 'of purer eyes than to behold iniquity'; that he is an avenger of everyone who rebelleth against him, and repayeth the wicked to his face; and that 'it is a fearful thing to fall into the hands of the living God.'

2. The inward, spiritual meaning of the law of God now begins to glare upon him. He perceives the 'commandment is exceeding broad', and 'there is nothing hid from the light thereof.' He is convinced that every part of it relates not barely to outward sin or obedience, but to what passes in the secret recesses of the soul, which no eye but God's can penetrate. If he now hears, 'Thou shalt not kill,' God speaks in thunder, 'He that hateth his brother is a murderer'; he that saith unto his brother, " 'Thou fool," is obnoxious to hellfire.' If the law say, 'Thou shalt not commit adultery,' the voice of the Lord sounds in his ears, 'He that looketh on a woman to lust after her hath committed adultery with her already in his heart.' And thus in every point he feels the Word of God 'quick and powerful, sharper than a two-edged sword'. It pierces 'even to the dividing asunder of his soul and spirit, his joints and marrow'. And so much the more because he is conscious *to himself* of having neglected so great salvation; of having 'trodden under foot the Son of God' who would have saved him from his sins, and 'counted the blood of the covenant an unholy', a common, unsanctifying 'thing'.

3. And as he knows 'all things are naked and opened unto the eyes of him with whom we have to do,' so he sees himself naked, stripped of all the fig-leaves which he had sewed together, of all his poor pretences to religion or virtue, and his wretched excuses for sinning against God. He now sees himself like the ancient sacrifices, τετραχηλισμένον, 'cleft in sunder', as it were, from the neck downward, so that all within him stands confessed. His heart is bare, and he sees it is all sin, 'deceitful above all things, desperately wicked'; that it

is altogether corrupt and abominable, more than it is possible for tongue to express; that there dwelleth there no good thing, but unrighteousness and ungodliness only; every motion thereof, every temper and thought, being only evil continually.

4. And he not only sees, but feels in himself, by an emotion of soul which he cannot describe, that for the sins of his heart, were his life without blame (which yet it is not, and cannot be; seeing 'an evil tree cannot bring forth good fruit'), he deserves to be cast into 'the fire that never shall be quenched'. He feels that 'the wages', the just reward, 'of sin', of his sin above all, 'is death'; even the second death, the death which dieth not, the destruction of body and soul in hell.

5. Here ends his pleasing dream, his delusive rest, his false peace, his vain security. His joy now vanishes as a cloud; pleasures once loved delight no more. They pall upon the taste; he loathes the nauseous sweet; he is weary to bear them. The shadows of happiness flee away, and sink into oblivion; so that he is stripped of all, and wanders to and fro seeking rest, but finding none.

6. The fumes of those opiates being now dispelled, he feels the anguish of a wounded spirit. He finds that sin let loose upon the soul (whether it be pride, anger, or evil desire; whether self-will, malice, envy, revenge, or any other) is perfect misery. He feels sorrow of heart for the blessings he has lost, and the curse which is come upon him; remorse for having thus destroyed himself, and despised his own mercies; fear, from a lively sense of the wrath of God, and of the consequences of his wrath; of the punishment which he has justly deserved, and which he sees hanging over his head; fear of death, as being to him the gate of hell, the entrance of death eternal; fear of the devil, the executioner of the wrath and righteous vengeance of God; fear of men, who if they were able to kill his body, would thereby plunge both body and soul into hell; fear, sometimes arising to such a height that the poor, sinful, guilty soul is terrified with everything, with nothing, with shades, with a leaf shaken of the wind. Yea, sometimes it may even border upon distraction, making a man 'drunken, though not with wine', suspending the exercise of the memory, of the understanding, of all the natural faculties. Sometimes it may approach to the very brink of despair; so that he who trembles at the name of death may yet be ready to plunge into it every moment, to 'choose strangling rather than life'. Well may such a man 'roar', like him of old, 'for the very disquietness of his heart'. Well may he cry out, 'The spirit of a man may sustain his infirmities; but a wounded spirit who can bear?'

7. Now he truly desires to break loose from sin, and begins to struggle with it. But though he strive with all his might he cannot conquer; sin is mightier than he. He would fain escape; but he is so fast in prison that he cannot get forth. He resolves against sin, but yet sins on; he sees the snare, and abhors–and runs into it. So much does his boasted reason avail–only to

enhance his guilt, and increase his misery! Such is the freedom of his will–free only to evil; free to 'drink in iniquity like water'; to wander farther and farther from the living God, and do more 'despite to the Spirit of grace'!

8. The more he strives, wishes, labours to be free, the more does he feel his chains, the grievous chains of sin, wherewith Satan binds and 'leads him captive at his will'. His servant he is, though he repine ever so much; though he rebel, he cannot prevail. He is still in bondage and fear by reason of sin: generally of some outward sin, to which he is peculiarly disposed either by nature, custom, or outward circumstances; but always of some inward sin, some evil temper or unholy affection. And the more he frets against it, the more it prevails; he may bite, but cannot break his chain. Thus he toils without end, repenting and sinning, and repenting and sinning again, till at length the poor sinful, helpless wretch is even at his wit's end, and can barely groan, 'O wretched man that I am, who shall deliver me from the body of this death?'

9. This whole struggle of one who is 'under the law', under the 'spirit of fear and bondage', is beautifully described by the Apostle in the foregoing chapter, speaking in the person of an awakened man. 'I (saith he) was alive without the law once.' I had much life, wisdom, strength, and virtue–so I thought. 'But when the commandment came, sin revived, and I died' (Rom. 7:9). When the commandment, in its spiritual meaning, came to my heart with the power of God my inbred sin was stirred up, fretted, inflamed, and all my virtue died away. 'And the commandment, which was ordained to life, I found to be unto death. For sin, taking occasion by the commandment, deceived me, and by it slew me' (Rom. 7:10–11). It came upon me unawares, slew all my hopes, and plainly showed, in the midst of life I was in death. 'Wherefore the law is holy, and the commandment holy, and just, and good' (Rom. 7:12): I no longer lay the blame on this, but on the corruption of my own heart. I acknowledge that 'the law is spiritual; but I am carnal, sold under sin' (Rom. 7:14). I now see both the spiritual nature of the law, and my own carnal devilish heart, 'sold under sin', totally enslaved (like slaves bought with money, who were absolutely at their master's disposal). 'For that which I do, I allow not; for what I would, I do not; but what I hate, that I do' (Rom. 7:15). Such is the bondage under which I groan; such the tyranny of my hard master. 'To will is present with me, but how to perform that which is good I find not. For the good that I would I do not; but the evil which I would not, that I do' (Rom. 7:18–19). 'I find a law', an inward constraining power, 'that when I would do good, evil is present with me. For I delight in' (or consent to) 'the law of God, after the inward man' (Rom. 7:21–22). (In my mind: so the Apostle explains himself in the words that immediately follow; and so ὁ ἔσω ἄνθρωπος, 'the inward man', is understood in all other Greek writers.) 'But I see another law in my members', another constraining power, 'warring against the law of my mind', or inward man, 'and bringing me into captivity to the law', or power,

'of sin' (Rom. 7:23), dragging me as it were at my conqueror's chariot-wheels into the very thing which my soul abhors. 'O wretched man that I am, who shall deliver me from the body of this death!' (Rom. 7:24). Who shall deliver me from this helpless, dying life; from this bondage of sin and misery! Till this is done, 'I myself' (or rather, 'that I', αὐτὸς ἐγώ, *that man* I am now personating) 'with the mind', or inward man, 'serve the law of God'; my mind, my conscience, is on God's side: 'but with the flesh', with my body, 'the law of sin' (Rom. 7:25), being hurried away by a force I cannot resist.

10. How lively a portraiture is this of one 'under the law'! One who feels the burden he cannot shake off; who pants after liberty, power, and love, but is in fear and bondage still! Until the time that God answers the wretched man crying out, 'Who shall deliver me' from this bondage of sin, from this body of death?—'The grace of God, through Jesus Christ thy Lord.'

III.1. Then it is that this miserable bondage ends, and he is no more 'under the law, but under grace'. This state we are thirdly to consider; the state of one who has found 'grace', or favour in the sight of God, even the Father, and who has the 'grace', or power of the Holy Ghost, reigning in his heart; who has received, in the language of the Apostle, 'the Spirit of adoption, whereby he now cries, Abba, Father'.

2. 'He cried unto the Lord in his trouble, and God delivers him out of his distress.' His eyes are opened in quite another manner than before, even to see a loving, gracious God. While he is calling, 'I beseech thee show me thy glory,' he hears a voice in his inmost soul, 'I will make all my goodness pass before thee, and I will proclaim the name of the Lord; I will be gracious to whom I will be gracious, and I will show mercy to whom I will show mercy.' And it is not long before 'the Lord descends in the cloud, and proclaims the name of the Lord.' Then he sees (but not with eyes of flesh and blood) 'The Lord, the Lord God; merciful and gracious, long-suffering, and abundant in goodness and truth; keeping mercy for thousands, and forgiving iniquities and transgression and sin.'

3. Heavenly, healing light now breaks in upon his soul. He 'looks on him whom he had pierced', and 'God, who out of darkness commanded light to shine, shineth in *his* heart.' He sees 'the light of the glorious love of God, in the face of Jesus Christ'. He hath a divine 'evidence of things not seen' by sense, even of 'the deep things of God'; more particularly of the love of God, of his pardoning love to him that believes in Jesus. Overpowered with the sight, his whole soul cries out, 'My Lord, and my God!' For he sees all his iniquities laid on him who 'bare them in his own body on the tree'; he beholds the Lamb of God taking away his sins. How clearly now does he discern 'that God was in Christ, reconciling the world unto himself; . . . making him sin for us, who knew no sin, that we might be made the righteousness of God

through him!' And that he himself is reconciled to God by that blood of the covenant!

4. Here end both the guilt and power of sin. He can now say, 'I am crucified with Christ. Nevertheless I live; yet not I, but Christ liveth in me. And the life which I now live in the flesh', even in this mortal body, 'I live by faith in the Son of God, who loved me and gave himself for me.' Here end remorse and sorrow of heart, and the anguish of a wounded spirit. 'God turneth his heaviness into joy.' He 'made sore', and now 'his hands bind up'. Here ends also that bondage unto fear; for 'his heart standeth fast, believing in the Lord.' He cannot fear any longer the wrath of God; for he knows it is now turned away from him, and looks upon him no more as an angry judge, but as a loving Father. He cannot fear the devil, knowing he has 'no power, except it be given him from above'. He fears not hell, being an heir of the kingdom of heaven. Consequently, he has no fear of death, by reason whereof he was in time past for so many years 'subject to bondage'. Rather, knowing that 'if the earthly house of this tabernacle be dissolved, he hath a building of God, a house not made with hands, eternal in the heavens, he groaneth earnestly, desiring to be clothed upon with that house which is from heaven.' He groans to shake off this house of earth, that 'mortality may be swallowed up of life'; knowing that 'God hath wrought him for the selfsame thing; who hath also given him the earnest of his Spirit.'

5. And 'where the Spirit of the Lord is, there is liberty'; liberty not only from guilt and fear, but from sin, from that heaviest of all yokes, that basest of all bondage. His labour is not now in vain. The snare is broken, and he is delivered. He not only strives, but likewise prevails; he not only fights, but conquers also. 'Henceforth he doth not serve sin (Rom. 6:6). He is dead unto sin and alive unto God. . . . Sin doth not now reign, even in his mortal body', nor doth he 'obey it in the desires thereof'. He does not 'yield his members as instruments of unrighteousness unto sin, but as instruments of righteousness unto God'. For 'being now made free from sin, he is become the servant of righteousness'.

6. Thus 'having peace with God, through our Lord Jesus Christ', 'rejoicing in hope of the glory of God', and having power over all sin, over every evil desire and temper, and word and work, he is a living witness of the 'glorious liberty of the sons of God': all of whom, being partakers of 'like precious faith', bear record with one voice, 'We have received the Spirit of adoption, whereby we cry, Abba, Father!'

7. It is this Spirit which continually 'worketh in them, both to will and to do of his good pleasure', It is he that sheds the love of God abroad in their hearts, and the love of all mankind; thereby purifying their hearts from the love of the world, from the lust of the flesh, the lust of the eye, and the pride of life. It is by him they are delivered from anger and pride, from all vile and

inordinate affections. In consequence, they are delivered from evil words and works, from all unholiness of conversation; doing no evil to any child of man, and being zealous of all good works.

8. To sum up all. The 'natural man' neither fears nor loves God; one 'under the law' fears, one 'under grace' loves him. The first has no light in the things of God, but walks in utter darkness. The second sees the painful light of hell; the third, the joyous light of heaven. He that sleeps in death has a false peace. He that is awakened has no peace at all. He that believes has true peace, the peace of God, filling and ruling his heart. The heathen, baptized or unbaptized, hath a fancied liberty, which is indeed licentiousness; the Jew (or one under the Jewish dispensation) is in heavy, grievous bondage; the Christian enjoys the true glorious liberty of the sons of God. An unawakened child of the devil sins willingly; one that is awakened sins unwillingly; a child of God 'sinneth not, but keepeth himself, and the wicked one toucheth him not'. To conclude: the natural man neither conquers nor fights; the man under the law fights with sin, but cannot conquer; the man under grace fights and conquers, yea is 'more than conqueror, through him that loveth him'.

IV.1. From this plain account of the threefold state of man—the 'natural', the 'legal', and the 'evangelical'—it appears that it is not sufficient to divide mankind into sincere and insincere. A man may be sincere in any of these states; not only when he has the 'Spirit of adoption', but while he has the 'spirit of bondage unto fear'. Yea, while he has neither this fear, nor love. For undoubtedly there may be sincere heathens as well as sincere Jews or Christians. This circumstance, then, does by no means prove that a man is in a state of acceptance with God.

'Examine yourselves', therefore, not only whether ye are sincere, but 'whether ye be in the faith.' Examine narrowly; for it imports you much. What is the ruling principle in your soul? Is it the love of God? Is it the fear of God? Or is it neither one nor the other? Is it not rather the love of the world? The love of pleasure? Or gain? Of ease; or reputation? If so, you are not come so far as a Jew. You are but a *heathen* still. Have you heaven in your heart? Have you the Spirit of adoption, ever crying, 'Abba, Father'? Or do you cry unto God as 'out of the belly of hell', overwhelmed with sorrow and fear? Or are you a stranger to this whole affair, and cannot imagine what I mean? Heathen, pull off the mask. Thou hast never put on Christ. Stand barefaced. Look up to heaven; and own before him that liveth for ever and ever, thou hast no part either among the sons or servants of God.

Whosoever thou art, dost thou commit sin, or dost thou not? If thou dost, is it willingly, or unwillingly? In either case God hath told thee whose thou art—'He that committeth sin is of the devil.' If thou committest it willingly thou art his faithful servant. He will not fail to reward thy labour. If unwillingly, still thou art his servant. God deliver thee out of his hands!

Art thou daily fighting against all sin; and daily more than conqueror? I acknowledge thee for a child of God. O stand fast in thy glorious liberty. Art thou fighting, but not conquering; striving for the mastery, but not able to attain? Then thou art not yet a believer in Christ. But follow on; and thou shalt know the Lord. Art thou not fighting at all, but leading an easy, indolent, fashionable life? O how hast thou dared to name the name of Christ! Only to make it a reproach among the heathen? Awake, thou sleeper! Call upon thy God, before the deep swallow thee up.

2. Perhaps one reason why so many think of themselves more highly than they ought to think, why they do not discern what state they are in, is because these several states of soul are often mingled together, and in some measure meet in one and the same person. Thus experience shows that the legal state, or state of fear, is frequently mixed with the natural; for few men are so fast asleep in sin but they are sometimes more or less awakened. As the Spirit of God does not 'wait for the call of man', so at some times he *will* be heard. He puts them in fear, so that for a season at least the heathen 'know themselves to be but men'. They feel the burden of sin, and earnestly desire to flee from the wrath to come. But not long. They seldom suffer the arrows of conviction to go deep into their souls; but quickly stifle the grace of God, and return to their wallowing in the mire.

In like manner the evangelical state, or state of love, is frequently mixed with the legal. For few of those who have the spirit of bondage and fear remain always without hope. The wise and gracious God rarely suffers this; for he remembereth that we are but dust. And he willeth not that 'the flesh should fail before him, or the spirit which he hath made'. Therefore, at such times as he seeth good he gives a dawning of light unto them that sit in darkness. He causes a part of his goodness to pass before them, and shows he is a 'God that heareth the prayer'. They see the promise which is by faith in Christ Jesus, though it be yet afar off; and hereby they are encouraged to 'run with patience the race which is set before them'.

3. Another reason why many deceive themselves is because they do not consider how far a man may go and yet be in a natural, or at best a legal state. A man may be of a compassionate and a benevolent temper; he may be affable, courteous, generous, friendly; he may have some degree of meekness, patience, temperance, and of many other moral virtues; he may feel many desires of shaking off all vice, and attaining higher degrees of virtue; he may abstain from much evil—perhaps from all that is grossly contrary to justice, mercy, or truth; he may do much good, may feed the hungry, clothe the naked, relieve the widow and fatherless; he may attend public worship, use prayer in private, read many books of devotion—and yet for all this he may be a mere natural man, knowing neither himself nor God; equally a stranger to the spirit of fear and

to that of love; having neither repented nor believed the gospel.

But suppose there were added to all this a deep conviction of sin, with much fear of the wrath of God; vehement desires to cast off every sin, and to fulfil all righteousness; frequent rejoicing in hope, and touches of love often glancing upon the soul: yet neither do these prove a man to be 'under grace', to have true, living, Christian faith, unless the Spirit of adoption abide in his heart, unless he can continually cry, 'Abba, Father!'

4. Beware, then, thou who art called by the name of Christ, that thou come not short of the mark of thy high calling. Beware thou rest not, either in a natural state, with too many that are accounted 'good Christians', or in a legal state, wherein those who are 'highly esteemed of men' are generally content to live and die. Nay, but God hath prepared better things for thee, if thou follow on till thou attain. Thou art not called to fear and tremble, like devils, but to rejoice and love, like the angels of God. 'Thou shalt love the Lord thy God with all thy heart, and with all thy soul, and with all thy mind, and with all thy strength.' Thou shalt 'rejoice evermore.' Thou shalt 'pray without ceasing.' Thou shalt 'in everything give thanks.' Thou shalt do the will of God 'on earth, as it is done in heaven'. O 'prove' thou 'what is that good and acceptable and perfect will of God.' Now 'present' thyself 'a living sacrifice, holy, acceptable to God.' 'Whereunto thou hast already attained', 'hold fast', by 'reaching forth unto those things which are before'; until 'the God of peace . . . make thee perfect in every good work, working in thee that which is well-pleasing in his sight, through Jesus Christ, to whom be glory for ever and ever! Amen!'

THE WITNESS OF THE SPIRIT

DISCOURSE I

Sermon 10 – 1746

AN INTRODUCTORY COMMENT

While there is no record that this sermon was ever preached in this form, it represents a central concern of Wesley's theology–the ground and character of Christian assurance. This doctrine was also a bone of contention with his critics. In *A Farther Appeal* (1745), Wesley had entered the lists against men like Edmund Gibson (Bishop of London), Thomas Herring (Archbishop of York), and Richard Smalbroke (Bishop of Lichfield and Coventry), all of whom had understood Wesley's doctrines of assurance and of religious intuition as 'enthusiasm'. Presently, he would be denounced by George Lavington (Bishop of Exeter) in *The Enthusiasm of Methodists and Papists Compared* (1749). It was therefore important in 1746, as Wesley prepared this sermon for his collection of *Sermons on Several Occasions*, to summarize the issues and to clarify his own position as simply and directly as possible.

It was clear enough that Wesley's theory of religious knowledge was frankly intuitionist in some ways, but that approach had been all too easily misconstrued as a one-sided subjectivism. Thus, he had to clarify his distinction between the ways in which assurance might be felt ('the witness of our own spirit') and the objective ground of any such experience (the prior and direct 'witness of the Holy Spirit'). The controversy was as old as second-century Montanism at least, and Wesley's balanced stress on an objective witness and a subjective one was not new. The question at issue between 'enthusiasts' and 'rationalists' was whether believers' consciousness of justification and reconciliation was an inference from their religious and moral feelings, or whether those feelings, if valid, were first prompted by a free and direct testimony of the Spirit to one's being a child of God. Characteristically, Wesley opts for a both/and solution, stressing the believers' own consciousness of God's favour but even more strongly the priority of the Spirit's prevenient and direct witness as the necessary precondition of any feelings of assurance. That this point is the crucial one for Wesley would appear from the fact that he repeats the same basic argument for it in a second discourse (with the same title) over twenty years later.

The Witness of the Spirit
Discourse I

The Spirit itself beareth witness with our spirit, that we are the children of God.
Romans 8:16

1. How many vain men, not understanding what they speak, neither whereof they affirmed, have wrested this Scripture to the great loss if not the destruction of their souls! How many have mistaken the voice of their own imagination for this 'witness of the Spirit' of God, and thence idly presumed they were the children of God while they were doing the works of the devil! These are truly and properly *enthusiasts*; and, indeed, in the worst sense of the word. But with what difficulty are they convinced thereof, especially if they have drank deep into that spirit of error! All endeavours to bring them to the knowledge of themselves they will then account 'fighting against God'. And that vehemence and impetuosity of spirit which they call 'contending earnestly for the faith' sets them so far above all the usual methods of conviction that we may well say, 'With men it is impossible.'

2. Who can then be surprised if many reasonable men, seeing the dreadful effects of this delusion, and labouring to keep at the utmost distance from it, should sometimes lean toward another extreme? If they are not forward to believe any who speak of having this witness concerning which others have so grievously erred; if they are almost ready to set all down for 'enthusiasts' who use the expressions which have been so terribly abused? Yea, if they should question whether the witness or testimony here spoken of be the privilege of *ordinary* Christians, and not rather one of those *extraordinary* gifts which they suppose belonged only to the apostolic age?

3. But is there any necessity laid upon us of running either into one extreme or the other? May we not steer a middle course? Keep a sufficient distance from that spirit of error and enthusiasm without denying the gift of God and giving up the great privilege of his children? Surely we may. In order thereto, let us consider, in the presence and fear of God,

First: What is this 'witness (or testimony) of our spirit'? What is the 'testimony of God's Spirit'? And how does he 'bear witness with our spirit that we are the children of God'?

Secondly: How is this joint testimony of God's Spirit and our own clearly and solidly distinguished from the presumption of a natural mind, and from the delusion of the devil?

I.1. Let us first consider, what is the 'witness' or 'testimony of our spirit'? But here I cannot but desire all those who are for swallowing up the testimony of the Spirit of God in the rational testimony of our own spirit to observe that in this text the Apostle is so far from speaking of the testimony of our own spirit *only*, that it may be questioned whether he speaks of it *at all*—whether he does not speak *only* of the testimony of God's Spirit. It does not appear but the original text may fairly be understood thus. The Apostle had just said, in the preceding verse, 'Ye have received the Spirit of adoption, whereby we cry, Abba, Father,' and immediately subjoins, Αὐτὸ τὸ πνεῦμα (some copies read τὸ αὐτὸ πνεῦμα) συμμαρτυρεῖ τῷ πνεύματι ἡμῶν, ὅτι ἐσμὲν τέκνα θεοῦ; which may be translated, 'The same Spirit beareth witness to our spirit that we are the children of God' (the preposition *σύν* only denoting that he witnesses this *at the same time* that he enables us to cry, 'Abba, Father!'). But I contend not; seeing so many other texts, with the experience of all real Christians, sufficiently evince that there is in every believer both the testimony of God's Spirit, and the testimony of his own, that he is a child of God.

2. With regard to the latter, the foundation thereof is laid in those numerous texts of Scripture which describe the marks of the children of God; and that so plain that he which runneth may read them. These are also collected together, and placed in the strongest light, by many both ancient and modern writers. If any need farther light he may receive it by attending on the ministry of God's Word, by meditating thereon before God in secret, and by conversing with those who have the knowledge of his ways. And by the reason or understanding that God has given him—which religion was designed not to extinguish, but to perfect, according to that [word] of the Apostle, 'Brethren, be not children in understanding; in malice (or wickedness) be ye children; but in understanding be ye men' (1 Cor. 14:20). Every man applying those scriptural marks to himself may know whether he is a child of God. Thus if he know, first, 'As many as are led by the Spirit of God' into all holy tempers and actions, 'they are the sons of God' (for which he has the infallible assurance of Holy Writ); secondly, I am thus 'led by the Spirit of God'—he will easily conclude, 'Therefore I am a "son of God".'

3. Agreeable to this are all those plain declarations of St. John in his First Epistle, 'Hereby we know that we do know him, if we keep his commandments' (1 John 2:3). 'Whoso keepeth his word, in him verily is the love of God perfected; hereby know we that we are in him' (1 John 2:5)—that we are indeed the children of God. 'If ye know that he is righteous, ye know that everyone that doth righteousness is born of him' (1 John 2:29). 'We know that we have passed from death unto life, because we love the brethren' (1 John 3:14). 'Hereby we know that we are of the truth, and shall assure our hearts before him'; namely, because we 'love' one another not 'in word, neither in tongue; but in deed and in truth' (1 John 3:18). 'Hereby know we that we dwell in

him, . . . because he hath given us of his (loving) Spirit' (1 John 4:13). And, 'Hereby we know that he abideth in us, by the (obedient) spirit which he hath given us' (1 John 3:24).

4. It is highly probable there never were any children of God, from the beginning of the world unto this day, who were farther advanced in the grace of God and the knowledge of our Lord Jesus Christ than the Apostle John at the time when he wrote these words, and the 'fathers in Christ' to whom he wrote. Notwithstanding which, it is evident both the Apostle himself and all those pillars in God's temple were very far from despising these marks of their being the children of God; and that they applied them to their own souls for the confirmation of their faith. Yet all this is no other than rational evidence: the 'witness of our spirit', our reason or understanding. It all resolves into this: those who have these marks, they are the children of God. But we have these marks: therefore we are children of God.

5. But how does it appear that we have these marks? This is a question which still remains. How does it appear that we do love God and our neighbour? And that we keep his commandments? Observe that the meaning of the question is, How does it appear to *ourselves*—not to *others*. I would ask him then that proposes this question, How does it appear to you that you are alive? And that you are now in ease and not in pain? Are you not immediately conscious of it? By the same immediate consciousness you will know if your soul is alive to God; if you are saved from the pain of proud wrath, and have the ease of a meek and quiet spirit. By the same means you cannot but perceive if you love, rejoice, and delight in God. By the same you must be directly assured if you love your neighbour as yourself; if you are kindly affectioned to all mankind, and full of gentleness and longsuffering. And with regard to the outward mark of the children of God, which is (according to St. John) the keeping his commandments, you undoubtedly know in your own breast if, by the grace of God, it belongs to you. Your conscience informs you from day to day if you do not take the name of God within your lips unless with seriousness and devotion, with reverence and godly fear; if you remember the sabbath day to keep it holy; if you honour your father and mother; if you do to all as you would they should do unto you; if you possess your body in sanctification and honour; and if, whether you eat or drink, you are temperate therein, and do all to the glory of God.

6. Now this is properly the 'testimony of our own spirit', even the testimony of our conscience, that God hath given us to be holy of heart, and holy in outward conversation. It is a consciousness of our having received, in and by the Spirit of adoption, the tempers mentioned in the Word of God as belonging to his adopted children; even a loving heart toward God and toward all mankind, hanging with childlike confidence on God our Father, desiring nothing but him, casting all our care upon him, and embracing every child of

man with earnest, tender affection, so as to be ready to lay down our life for our brother, as Christ laid down his life for us—a consciousness that we are inwardly conformed by the Spirit of God to the image of his Son, and that we walk before him in justice, mercy, and truth; doing the things which are pleasing in his sight.

7. But what is that testimony of God's Spirit which is superadded to and conjoined with this? How does he 'bear witness with our spirit that we are the children of God'? It is hard to find words in the language of men to explain 'the deep things of God'. Indeed there are none that will adequately express what the children of God experience. But perhaps one might say (desiring any who are taught of God to correct, to soften or strengthen the expression), the testimony of the Spirit is an inward impression on the soul, whereby the Spirit of God directly 'witnesses to my spirit that I am a child of God'; that Jesus Christ hath loved me, and given himself for me; that all my sins are blotted out, and I, even I, am reconciled to God.

8. That this 'testimony of the Spirit of God' must needs, in the very nature of things, be antecedent to the 'testimony of our own spirit' may appear from this single consideration: we must be holy of heart and holy in life before we can be conscious that we are so, before we can have 'the testimony of our spirit' that we are inwardly and outwardly holy. But we must love God before we can be holy at all; this being the root of all holiness. Now we cannot love God till we know he loves us: 'We love him, because he first loved us.' And we cannot know his pardoning love to us till his Spirit witnesses it to our spirit. Since therefore this 'testimony of his Spirit' must precede the love of God and all holiness, of consequence it must precede our inward consciousness thereof, or the 'testimony of our spirit' concerning them.

9. Then, and not till then—when the Spirit of God beareth that witness to our spirit, 'God hath loved thee and given his own Son to be the propitiation for thy sins'; 'the Son of God hath loved thee, and hath washed thee from thy sins in his blood'—'we love God, because he first loved us,' and for his sake we 'love our brother also'. And of this we cannot but be conscious to ourselves: we 'know the things that are freely given to us of God'; we know that we love God and keep his commandments; and hereby also 'we know that we are of God.' This is that testimony of our own spirit which, so long as we continue to love God and keep his commandments, continues joined with the testimony of God's Spirit, 'that we are the children of God'.

10. Not that I would by any means be understood by anything which has been spoken concerning it to exclude the operation of the Spirit of God, even from the 'testimony of our own spirit'. In no wise. It is he that not only worketh in us every manner of thing that is good, but also shines upon his own work, and clearly shows what he has wrought. Accordingly this is spoken of by St. Paul as one great end of our receiving the Spirit, 'that we may know the things

which are freely given to us of God'; that he may strengthen the testimony of our conscience touching our 'simplicity and godly sincerity', and give us to discern in a fuller and stronger light that we now do the things which please him.

11. Should it still be inquired, 'How does the Spirit of God "bear witness with our spirit that we are the children of God" so as to exclude all doubt, and evince the reality of our sonship?'–the answer is clear from what has been observed above. And, first, as to the witness of our spirit: the soul as intimately and evidently perceives when it loves, delights, and rejoices in God, as when it loves and delights in anything on earth; and it can no more doubt whether it loves, delights, and rejoices, or no, than whether it exists, or no. If therefore this be just reasoning:

He that now loves God–that delights and rejoices in him with an humble joy, an holy delight, and an obedient love–is a child of God;

But I thus love, delight, and rejoice in God;

Therefore I am a child of God;

then a Christian can in no wise doubt of his being a child of God. Of the former proposition he has as full an assurance as he has that the Scriptures are of God. And of his thus loving God he has an inward proof, which is nothing short of self-evidence. Thus the 'testimony of our own spirit' is with the most intimate conviction manifested to our hearts; in such a manner as beyond all reasonable doubt to evince the reality of our sonship.

12. The *manner* how the divine testimony is manifested to the heart I do not take upon me to explain. 'Such knowledge is too wonderful and excellent for me; I cannot attain unto it.' 'The wind bloweth; and I hear the sound thereof'; but I cannot 'tell how it cometh, or whither it goeth'. As no one knoweth the things of a man save the spirit of a man that is in him, so the *manner* of the things of God knoweth no one save the Spirit of God. But the fact we know: namely, that the Spirit of God does give a believer such a testimony of his adoption that while it is present to the soul he can no more doubt the reality of his sonship than he can doubt of the shining of the sun while he stands in the full blaze of his beams.

II.1. How this joint testimony of God's Spirit and our spirit may be clearly and solidly distinguished from the presumption of a natural mind, and from the delusion of the devil, is the next thing to be considered. And it highly imports all who desire the salvation of God to consider it with the deepest attention, as they would not deceive their own souls. An error in this is generally observed to have the most fatal consequences; the rather, because he that errs seldom discovers his mistake till it is too late to remedy it.

2. And, first, How is this testimony to be distinguished from the presumption of a natural mind? It is certain, one who was never convinced of sin is

always ready to flatter himself, and to think of himself, especially in spiritual things, more highly than he ought to think. And hence it is in no wise strange if one who is vainly puffed up by his fleshly mind, when he hears of this privilege of true Christians, among whom he undoubtedly ranks himself, should soon work himself up into a persuasion that he is already possessed thereof. Such instances now abound in the world, and have abounded in all ages. How then may the real testimony of the Spirit with our spirit be distinguished from this damning presumption?

3. I answer, the Holy Scriptures abound with marks whereby the one may be distinguished from the other. They describe in the plainest manner the circumstances which go before, which accompany, and which follow, the true, genuine testimony of the Spirit of God with the spirit of a believer. Whoever carefully weighs and attends to these will not need to put darkness for light. He will perceive so wide a difference with respect to all these, between the real and the pretended witness of the Spirit, that there will be no danger—I might say, no possibility—of confounding the one with the other.

4. By these, one who vainly presumes on the gift of God might surely know, if he really desired it, that he hath been hitherto 'given up to a strong delusion' and suffered to 'believe a lie'. For the Scriptures lay down those clear, obvious marks as preceding, accompanying, and following that gift, which a little reflection would convince him, beyond all doubt, were never found in his soul. For instance, the Scripture describes repentance, or conviction of sin, as constantly going before this witness of pardon. So, 'Repent; for the kingdom of heaven is at hand' (Matt. 3:2). 'Repent ye, and believe the Gospel' (Mark 1:15). 'Repent, and be baptized every one of you . . . for the remission of sins' (Acts 2:38). 'Repent ye therefore, and be converted, that your sins may be blotted out' (Acts 3:19). In conformity whereto our Church also continually places repentance before pardon or the witness of it: 'He pardoneth and absolveth all them that truly repent and unfeignedly believe his holy gospel.' 'Almighty God . . . hath promised forgiveness of sins to all them who with hearty repentance and true faith turn unto him.' But he is a stranger even to this repentance. He hath never known 'a broken and a contrite heart'. 'The remembrance of his sins' was never 'grievous unto' him, nor 'the burden of them intolerable'. In repeating those words he never meant what he said; he merely paid a compliment to God. And were it only from the want of this previous work of God he hath too great reason to believe that he hath grasped a mere shadow, and never yet known the real privilege of the sons of God.

5. Again, the Scriptures describe the being born of God, which must precede the witness that we are his children, as a vast and mighty change, a change 'from darkness to light', as well as 'from the power of Satan unto God'; as a 'passing from death unto life', a resurrection from the dead. Thus the Apostle to the Ephesians: 'You hath he quickened, who were dead in trespasses and

sins' (Eph. 2:1). And again, 'When we were dead in sins, he hath quickened us together with Christ; . . . and hath raised us up together, and made us sit together in heavenly places in Christ Jesus' (Eph. 2:5, 6). But what knoweth he concerning whom we now speak of any such change as this? He is altogether unacquainted with this whole matter. This is a language which he does not understand. He tells you he always was a Christian. He knows no time when he had need of such a change. By this also, if he give himself leave to think, may he know that he is not born of the Spirit; that he has never yet known God, but has mistaken the voice of nature for the voice of God.

6. But waiving the consideration of whatever he has or has not experienced in time past, by the present marks may we easily distinguish a child of God from a presumptuous self-deceiver. The Scriptures describe that joy in the Lord which accompanies the witness of his Spirit as an humble joy, a joy that abases to the dust; that makes a pardoned sinner cry out, 'I am vile! What am I or my father's house?—Now mine eye seeth thee I abhor myself in dust and ashes!' And wherever lowliness is, there is meekness, patience, gentleness, long-suffering. There is a soft, yielding spirit, a mildness and sweetness, a tenderness of soul which words cannot express. But do these fruits attend that *supposed* testimony of the Spirit in a presumptuous man? Just the reverse. The more confident he is of the favour of God, the more is he lifted up. The more does he exalt himself, the more haughty and assuming is his whole behaviour. The stronger witness he imagines himself to have, the more overbearing is he to all around him, the more incapable of receiving any reproof, the more impatient of contradiction. Instead of being more meek, and gentle, and teachable, more 'swift to hear, and slow to speak', he is more slow to hear and swift to speak, more unready to learn of anyone, more fiery and vehement in his temper, and eager in his conversation. Yea, perhaps, there will sometimes appear a kind of fierceness in his air, his manner of speaking, his whole deportment, as if he were just going to take the matter out of God's hands, and himself to 'devour the adversaries'.

7. Once more: the Scriptures teach, 'This is the love of God' (the sure mark thereof) 'that we keep his commandments' (1 John 5:3). And our Lord himself saith, 'He that keepeth my commandments, he it is that loveth me' (John 14:21). Love rejoices to obey, to do in every point whatever is acceptable to the Beloved. A true lover of God hastens to do his will on earth as it is done in heaven. But is this the character of the presumptuous pretender to the love of God? Nay, but his love gives him a liberty to disobey, to break, not keep, the commandments of God. Perhaps when he was in fear of the wrath of God he did labour to do his will. But now, looking on himself as 'not under the law', he thinks he is no longer obliged to observe it. He is therefore less zealous of good works, less careful to abstain from evil, less watchful over his own heart, less jealous over his tongue. He is less earnest to deny himself, and to take up

his cross daily. In a word, the whole form of his life is changed since he has fancied himself to be 'at liberty'. He is no longer 'exercising himself unto godliness': 'wrestling not only with flesh and blood, but with principalities and powers', 'enduring hardships', 'agonizing to enter in at the strait gate'. No; he has found an easier way to heaven: a broad, smooth, flowery path, in which he can say to his soul, 'Soul, take thy ease; eat, drink, and be merry.' It follows with undeniable evidence that he has not the true testimony of his own spirit. He cannot be conscious of having those marks which he hath not, that lowliness, meekness, and obedience. Nor yet can the Spirit of the God of truth bear witness to a lie; or testify that he is a child of God when he is manifestly a child of the devil.

8. Discover thyself, thou poor self-deceiver! Thou who art confident of being a child of God; thou who sayest, 'I have the witness in myself,' and therefore defiest all thy enemies. Thou art weighed in the balance and found wanting, even in the balance of the sanctuary. The Word of the Lord hath tried thy soul, and proved thee to be reprobate silver. Thou art not lowly of heart; therefore thou hast not received the Spirit of Jesus unto this day. Thou art not gentle and meek; therefore thy joy is nothing worth: it is not joy in the Lord. Thou dost not keep his commandments; therefore thou lovest him not, neither art thou partaker of the Holy Ghost. It is consequently as certain and as evident as the oracles of God can make it, his Spirit doth not bear witness with thy spirit that thou art a child of God. O cry unto him, that the scales may fall off thine eyes; that thou mayst know thyself as thou art known; that thou mayst receive the sentence of death in thyself, till thou hear the voice that raises the dead, saying, 'Be of good cheer; thy sins are forgiven; thy faith hath made thee whole.'

9. 'But how may one who has the real witness in himself distinguish it from presumption?' How, I pray, do you distinguish day from night? How do you distinguish light from darkness? Or the light of a star, or glimmering taper, from the light of the noonday sun? Is there not an inherent, obvious, essential difference between the one and the other? And do you not immediately and directly perceive that difference, provided your senses are rightly disposed? In like manner, there is an inherent, essential difference between spiritual light and spiritual darkness; and between the light wherewith the sun of righteousness shines upon our heart, and that glimmering light which arises only from 'sparks of our own kindling'. And this difference also is immediately and directly perceived, if our spiritual senses are rightly disposed.

10. To require a more minute and philosophical account of the *manner* whereby we distinguish these, and of the *criteria* or intrinsic marks whereby we know the voice of God, is to make a demand which can never be answered; no, not by one who has the deepest knowledge of God. Suppose, when Paul answered before Agrippa, the wise Roman had said: 'Thou talkest of hearing

the voice of the Son of God. How dost thou know it was his voice? By what *criteria*, what intrinsic marks, dost thou know the voice of God? Explain to me the *manner* of distinguishing this from a human or angelic voice.' Can you believe the Apostle himself would have once attempted to answer so idle a demand? And yet doubtless the moment he heard that voice he knew it was the voice of God. But *how* he knew this who is able to explain? Perhaps neither man nor angel.

11. To come yet closer: suppose God were now to speak to any soul, 'Thy sins are forgiven thee.' He must be willing that soul should know his voice; otherwise he would speak in vain. And he is able to effect this, for whenever he wills, to do is present with him. And he does effect it. That soul is absolutely assured, 'This voice is the voice of God.' But yet he who hath that witness in himself cannot explain it to one who hath not. Nor indeed is it to be expected that he should. Were there any natural medium to prove, or natural method to explain the things of God to unexperienced men, then the natural man might discern and know the things of the Spirit of God. But this is utterly contrary to the assertion of the Apostle that 'he cannot know them, because they are spiritually discerned'; even by spiritual senses which the natural man hath not.

12. 'But how shall I know that my spiritual senses are rightly disposed?' This also is a question of vast importance; for if a man mistake in this he may run on in endless error and delusion. 'And how am I assured that this is not my case; and that I do not mistake the voice of the Spirit?' Even by the 'testimony of your own spirit'; by 'the answer of a good conscience toward God'. By the fruits which he hath wrought in your spirit you shall know the 'testimony of the Spirit of God'. Hereby you shall know that you are in no delusion; that you have not deceived your own soul. The immediate fruits of the Spirit ruling in the heart are 'love, joy, peace'; 'bowels of mercies, humbleness of mind, meekness, gentleness, long-suffering'. And the outward fruits are the doing good to all men, the doing no evil to any, and the walking in the light—a zealous, uniform obedience to all the commandments of God.

13. By the same fruits shall you distinguish this voice of God from any delusion of the devil. That proud spirit cannot humble thee before God. He neither can nor would soften thy heart and melt it first into earnest mourning after God and then into filial love. It is not the adversary of God and man that enables thee to love thy neighbour; or to put on meekness, gentleness, patience, temperance, and the whole armour of God. He is not divided against himself, or a destroyer of sin, his own work. No; it is none but the Son of God who cometh to 'destroy the works of the devil'. As surely therefore as holiness is of God, and as sin is the work of the devil, so surely the witness thou hast in thyself is not of Satan, but of God.

14. Well then mayst thou say, 'Thanks be unto God for his unspeakable

gift!' Thanks be unto God who giveth me to 'know in whom I have believed'; who 'hath sent forth the Spirit of his Son into my heart, crying Abba, Father', and even now 'bearing witness with my spirit that I am a child of God'! And see that not only thy lips, but thy life show forth his praise. He hath sealed thee for his own; 'glorify him then in thy body and thy spirit which are' his. Beloved, if thou 'hast this hope in thyself, purify thyself as he is pure'. While thou 'beholdest what manner of love the Father hath given thee, that thou shouldst be called a child of God', 'cleanse thyself from all filthiness of flesh and Spirit, perfecting holiness in the fear of God'; and let all thy thoughts, words, and works be a spiritual sacrifice, holy, acceptable to God through Christ Jesus!

THE MEANS OF GRACE

Sermon 16 – 1746

AN INTRODUCTORY COMMENT

This sermon carries us back to Wesley's earlier conflicts with the Moravians and other 'quietists' about the role and function of 'ordinances' in general and their relation to the spontaneous experience of 'assurance' in particular. The fourth Extract of his *Journal* (1739–41) is a circumstantial account of his rift with the Moravians, and this question of ordinances is a crucial issue in that dispute. Wesley preached from Malachi 3 six times (including June 1741) but never recorded any use of this specific verse as a text. This sermon was published in all collections of his sermons from the first (1746) and was reprinted separately at least five times during his lifetime.

What is clear is that a sizeable group of Methodists in 1746 still continued to regard all 'outward observances' as superfluous, or even harmful, in their spiritual life. Considering themselves to be true evangelicals, they understood their conversions and 'baptisms of the Spirit' as having superseded their water baptisms, the Eucharist, and all other sacramental acts (or 'ordinances' as they preferred to call them). It is these Methodist 'quietists' who are the primary audience for this sermon. Wesley's purpose is to enforce upon them the validity, and even the necessity, of 'the means of grace' as taught and administered in the Church of England.

The upshot of this controversy had been Wesley's abandonment of the Fetter Lane society, his forming of the new society in Upper Moorfields at the Foundery, and his constant advocacy thereafter of an equal emphasis upon 'conversion' and 'assurance', on the one hand, and a faithful, expectant usage of all the means of grace, on the other. The result is a sort of 'high-church' evangelicalism—a rare combination, then and since. But how to appropriate this tradition for people whose sacramental sense had atrophied and whose spontaneous experiences of grace were so much more vivid than their usual experiences of its ordinances and means? How to make clear the difference between the proper use and possible abuse of such means or to suggest how strenuous a 'waiting upon the Lord' can and should be in the Christian life? These are the tasks attempted in this 'discourse'.

The Means of Grace

Ye are gone away from mine ordinances, and have not kept them.
Malachi 3:7

[I].1. But are there any 'ordinances' now, since life and immortality were brought to light by the gospel? Are there, under the Christian dispensation, any 'means' ordained of God as the usual channels of his grace? This question could never have been proposed in the apostolical church unless by one who openly avowed himself to be a heathen, the whole body of Christians being agreed that Christ had ordained certain outward means for conveying his grace into the souls of men. Their constant practice set this beyond all dispute; for so long as 'all that believed were together, and had all things common' (Acts 2:44), 'they continued steadfastly in the teaching of the apostles, and in the breaking of bread, and in prayers'(Acts 2:42).

2. But in process of time, when 'the love of many waxed cold,' some began to mistake the *means* for the *end*, and to place religion rather in doing those outward works than in a heart renewed after the image of God. They forgot that 'the end of' every 'commandment is love, out of a pure heart, with faith unfeigned': the loving the Lord their God with all their heart, and their neighbour as themselves; and the being purified from pride, anger, and evil desire, by a 'faith of the operation of God'. Others seemed to imagine that though religion did not principally consist in these outward means, yet there was something in them wherewith God was well-pleased, something that would still make them acceptable in his sight, though they were not exact in the weightier matters of the law, in justice, mercy, and the love of God.

3. It is evident, in those who abused them thus, they did not conduce to the end for which they were ordained. Rather, the things which should have been for their health were to them an occasion of falling. They were so far from receiving any blessing therein, that they only drew down a curse upon their head; so far from growing more heavenly in heart and life, that they were twofold more the children of hell than before. Others clearly perceiving that these means did not convey the grace of God to those children of the devil, began from this particular case to draw a general conclusion, 'that they were not means of conveying the grace of God.'

4. Yet the number of those who *abused* the ordinances of God was far greater than of those who *despised* them, till certain men arose, not only of great understanding (sometimes joined with considerable learning), but who like-

wise appeared to be men of love, experimentally acquainted with true, inward religion. Some of these were burning and shining lights, persons famous in their generations, and such as had well deserved of the church of Christ for standing in the gap against the overflowings of ungodliness.

It cannot be supposed that these holy and venerable men intended any more at first than to show that outward religion is nothing worth without the religion of the heart; that 'God is a Spirit, and they who worship him must worship him in spirit and truth'; that, therefore, external worship is lost labour without a heart devoted to God; that the outward ordinances of God then profit much when they advance inward holiness, but when they advance it not are unprofitable and void, are lighter than vanity; yea, that when they are used, as it were, *in the place* of this, they are an utter abomination to the Lord.

5. Yet is it not strange if some of these, being strongly convinced of that horrid profanation of the ordinances of God which had spread itself over the whole church, and wellnigh driven true religion out of the world, in their fervent zeal for the glory of God and the recovery of souls from that fatal delusion, spake as if outward religion were *absolutely nothing*, as if it had *no* place in the religion of Christ. It is not surprising at all if they should not always have expressed themselves with sufficient caution; so that unwary hearers might believe they condemned all outward means as altogether unprofitable, and as not designed of God to be the ordinary channels of conveying his grace into the souls of men.

Nay, it is not impossible some of these holy men did at length themselves fall into this opinion: in particular those who, not by choice, but by the providence of God, were cut off from all these ordinances—perhaps wandering up and down, having no certain abiding-place, or dwelling in dens and caves of the earth. These, experiencing the grace of God in themselves, though they were deprived of all outward means, might infer that the same grace would be given to them who of set purpose abstained from them.

6. And experience shows how easily this notion spreads, and insinuates itself into the minds of men: especially of those who are thoroughly awakened out of the sleep of death, and begin to feel the weight of their sins a burden too heavy to be borne. These are usually impatient of their present state, and trying every way to escape from it. They are always ready to catch at any new thing, any new proposal of ease or happiness. They have probably tried most outward means, and found no ease in them—it may be, more and more of remorse and fear and sorrow and condemnation. It is easy, therefore, to persuade these that it is better for them to abstain from all those means. They are already weary of striving (as it seems) in vain, of labouring in the fire; and are therefore glad of any pretence to cast aside that wherein their soul had no pleasure; to give over the painful strife, and sink down into an indolent inactivity.

II.1. In the following discourse I propose to examine at large whether there are any means of grace.

By 'means of grace' I understand outward signs, words, or actions ordained of God, and appointed for this end—to be the *ordinary* channels whereby he might convey to men preventing, justifying, or sanctifying grace.

I use this expression, 'means of grace', because I know none better, and because it has been generally used in the Christian church for many ages: in particular by our own church, which directs us to bless God both for the 'means of grace and hope of glory'; and teaches us that a sacrament is 'an outward sign of inward *grace*, and a *means* whereby we receive the same'.

The chief of these means are prayer, whether in secret or with the great congregation; searching the Scriptures (which implies reading, hearing, and meditating thereon) and receiving the Lord's Supper, eating bread and drinking wine in remembrance of him; and these we believe to be ordained of God as the ordinary channels of conveying his grace to the souls of men.

2. But we allow that the whole value of the means depends on their actual subservience to the end of religion; that consequently all these means, when separate from the end, are less than nothing, and vanity; that if they do not actually conduce to the knowledge and love of God they are not acceptable in his sight; yea, rather, they are an abomination before him; a stink in his nostrils; he is weary to bear them—above all if they are used as a kind of 'commutation' for the religion they were designed to subserve. It is not easy to find words for the enormous folly and wickedness of thus turning God's arms against himself, of keeping Christianity out of the heart by those very means which were ordained for the bringing it in.

3. We allow likewise that all outward means whatever, if separate from the Spirit of God, cannot profit at all, cannot conduce in any degree either to the knowledge or love of God. Without controversy, the help that is done upon earth, he doth it himself. It is he alone who, by his own almighty power, worketh in us what is pleasing in his sight. And all outward things, unless he work in them and by them, are mere weak and beggarly elements. Whosoever therefore imagines there is any intrinsic *power* in any means whatsoever does greatly err, not knowing the Scriptures, neither the power of God. We know that there is no inherent power in the words that are spoken in prayer, in the letter of Scripture read, the sound thereof heard, or the bread and wine received in the Lord's Supper; but that it is God alone who is the giver of every good gift, the author of all grace; that the whole power is of him, whereby through any of these there is any blessing conveyed to our soul. We know likewise that he is able to give the same grace, though there were no means on the face of the earth. In this sense we may affirm that with regard to God there is no such thing as means, seeing he is equally able to work whatsoever pleaseth him by

any or by none at all.

4. We allow farther that the use of all means whatever will never atone for one sin; that it is the blood of Christ alone whereby any sinner can be reconciled to God; there being no other propitiation for our sins, no other fountain for sin and uncleanness. Every believer in Christ is deeply convinced that there is no *merit* but in him; that there is no *merit* in any of his own works; not in uttering the prayer, or searching the Scripture, or hearing the Word of God, or eating of that bread and drinking of that cup; so that if no more be intended by the expression some have used, 'Christ is the only means of grace,' than this–that he is the only *meritorious cause* of it–it cannot be gainsaid by any who know the grace of God.

5. Yet once more. We allow (though it is a melancholy truth) that a large proportion of those who are called Christians do to this day abuse the means of grace to the destruction of their souls. This is doubtless the case with all those who rest content in the form of godliness without the power. Either they fondly presume they are Christians already, because they do thus and thus, although Christ was never yet revealed in their hearts, nor the love of God shed abroad therein: or else they suppose they shall infallibly be so, barely because they use these means; idly dreaming (though perhaps hardly conscious thereof) either that there is some kind of *power* therein whereby sooner or later (they know not when) they shall certainly be made holy; or that there is a sort of *merit* in using them, which will surely move God to give them holiness or accept them without it.

6. So little do they understand that great foundation of the whole Christian building, 'By grace ye are saved.' Ye are saved from your sins, from the guilt and power thereof, ye are restored to the favour and image of God, not for any works, merits, or deservings of yours, but by the free *grace*, the mere mercy of God through the merits of his well-beloved Son. Ye are thus saved, not by any power, wisdom, or strength which is in you or in any other creature, but merely through the grace or power of the Holy Ghost, which worketh all in all.

7. But the main question remains. We know this salvation is the gift and the work of God. But how (may one say, who is convinced he hath it not) may I attain thereto? If you say, 'Believe, and thou shalt be saved,' he answers, 'True; but how shall I believe?' You reply, 'Wait upon God.' 'Well. But how am I to wait? In the means of grace, or out of them? Am I to wait for the grace of God which bringeth salvation by using these means, or by laying them aside?'

8. It cannot possibly be conceived that the Word of God should give no direction in so important a point; or that the Son of God who came down from heaven for us men and for our salvation should have left us undetermined with regard to a question wherein our salvation is so nearly concerned.

And in fact he hath not left us undetermined; he hath shown us the way wherein we should go. We have only to consult the oracles of God, to inquire what is written there. And if we simply abide by their decision, there can no possible doubt remain.

III.1. According to this, according to the decision of Holy Writ, all who desire the grace of God are to wait for it in the means which he hath ordained; in using, not in laying them aside.

And first, all who desire the grace of God are to wait for it in the way of *prayer*. This is the express direction of our Lord himself. In his Sermon upon the Mount, after explaining at large wherein religion consists, and describing the main branches of it, he adds: 'Ask, and it shall be given you; seek, and ye shall find; knock, and it shall be opened unto you. For everyone that asketh, receiveth; and he that seeketh, findeth; and to him that knocketh, it shall be opened' (Matt. 7:7–8). Here we are in the plainest manner directed to ask in order to, or as a *means* of, receiving; to seek in order to find the grace of God, the pearl of great price; and to knock, to continue asking and seeking, if we would enter into his kingdom.

2. That no doubt might remain our Lord labours this point in a more peculiar manner. He appeals to every man's own heart: 'What man is there of you, who, if his son ask bread, will give him a stone? Or if he ask a fish, will he give him a serpent? If ye then, being evil, know how to give good gifts unto your children, how much more shall your Father which is in heaven'—the Father of angels and men, the Father of the spirits of all flesh—'give good things to them that ask him?' (Matt. 7:9–11). Or, as he expresses himself on another occasion, including all good things in one, 'How much more shall your heavenly Father give the Holy Spirit to them that ask him?' (Luke 11:13). It should be particularly observed here that the persons directed to ask had not then received the Holy Spirit. Nevertheless our Lord directs them to use this means, and promises that it should be effectual; that upon asking they should receive the Holy Spirit from him whose mercy is over all his works.

3. The absolute necessity of using this means if we would receive any gift from God yet farther appears from that remarkable passage which immediately precedes these words: 'And he said unto them' (whom he had just been teaching how to pray) 'which of you shall have a friend, and shall go unto him at midnight, and shall say unto him, Friend, lend me three loaves; . . . and he from within shall answer, Trouble me not. . . . I cannot rise and give thee: I say unto you, though he will not rise and give him, because he is his friend, yet because of his importunity he will rise, and give him as many as he needeth. And I say unto you, ask and it shall be given you' (Luke 11:5, 7–9). 'Though he will not give him because he is his friend, yet because of his importunity he will rise and give him as many as he needeth.' How could our blessed Lord more plainly declare that we may receive of God by this means, by importunately asking, what otherwise we should not receive at all!

4. 'He spake also another parable to this end, that men ought always to pray, and not to faint,' till through this means they should receive of God whatsoever petition they asked of him: 'There was in a city a judge which feared not God, neither regarded man. And there was a widow in that city, and she came unto him, saying, Avenge me of my adversary. And he would not for a while; but afterward he said within himself, Though I fear not God, nor regard man, yet because this widow troubleth me I will avenge her, lest by her continual coming she weary me' (Luke 18:1–5). The application of this our Lord himself hath made. 'Hear what the unjust judge saith!' Because she continues to ask, because she will take no denial, therefore I will avenge her. 'And shall not God avenge his own elect which cry day and night unto him? I tell you he will avenge them speedily'—if they 'pray and faint not'.

5. A direction equally full and express to wait for the blessings of God in private prayer, together with a positive promise that by this means we shall obtain the request of our lips, he hath given us in those well-known words: 'Enter into thy closet; and when thou hast shut thy door, pray to thy Father which is in secret; and thy Father which seeth in secret shall reward thee openly' (Matt. 6:6).

6. If it be possible for any direction to be more clear, it is that which God hath given us by the Apostle with regard to prayer of every kind, public and private, and the blessing annexed thereto. 'If any of you lack wisdom, let him ask of God, that giveth to all men liberally' (if they ask; otherwise 'ye have not, because ye ask not', Jas. 4:2), 'and upbraideth not, and it shall be given him' (Jas. 1:5).

If it be objected, 'But this is no direction to unbelievers, to them who know not the pardoning grace of God; for the Apostle adds, "But let him ask in faith"; otherwise, "let him not think that he shall receive anything of the Lord."' I answer, the meaning of the word 'faith' in this place is fixed by the Apostle himself (as if it were on purpose to obviate this objection) in the words immediately following: 'Let him ask in faith, nothing wavering,' nothing *doubting*, μηδὲν διακρινόμενος—not doubting God heareth his prayer, and will fulfil the desire of his heart.

The gross, blasphemous absurdity of supposing 'faith' in this place to be taken in the full Christian meaning appears hence: it is supposing the Holy Ghost to direct a man who knows he has not this faith (which is here termed 'wisdom') to ask it of God, with a positive promise that 'it shall be given him'; and then immediately to subjoin that it shall not be given him unless he have it before he asks for it! But who can bear such a supposition? From this Scripture, therefore, as well as those cited above, we must infer that all who desire the grace of God are to wait for it in the way of prayer.

7. Secondly, all who desire the grace of God are to wait for it in 'searching the Scriptures'. Our Lord's direction with regard to the use of this means is

likewise plain and clear. 'Search the Scriptures', saith he to the unbelieving Jews, 'for they testify of me' (John 5:39). And for this very end did he direct them to search the Scriptures, that they might *believe in him.*

The objection that this is not a command, but only an assertion that they did 'search the Scriptures', is shamelessly false. I desire those who urge it to let us know how a command can be more clearly expressed than in those terms, Ἐρευνᾶτε τὰς γραφάς. It is as peremptory as so many words can make it.

And what a blessing from God attends the use of this means appears from what is recorded concerning the Bereans, who, after hearing St. Paul, 'searched the Scriptures daily, whether those things were so. Therefore many of them believed'—found the grace of God in the way which he had ordained (Acts 17:11–12).

It is probable, indeed, that in some of those who had 'received the word with all readiness of mind', 'faith came (as the same Apostle speaks) by hearing,' and was only confirmed by *reading* the Scriptures. But it was observed above that under the general term of 'searching the Scriptures' both hearing, reading, and meditating are contained.

8. And that this is a means whereby God not only gives, but also confirms and increases true wisdom, we learn from the words of St. Paul to Timothy: 'From a child thou hast known the Holy Scriptures, which are able to make thee wise unto salvation, through faith which is in Christ Jesus' (2 Tim. 3:15). The same truth (namely, that this is the great means God has ordained for conveying his manifold grace to man) is delivered, in the fullest manner that can be conceived, in the words which immediately follow: 'All Scripture is given by inspiration of God' (consequently, all Scripture is infallibly true), 'and is profitable for doctrine, for reproof, for correction, for instruction in righteousness'; to the end 'that the man of God may be perfect, thoroughly furnished unto all good works' (2 Tim. 3:16–17).

9. It should be observed that this is spoken primarily and directly of the Scriptures which Timothy had 'known from a child'; which must have been those of the Old Testament, for the New was not then wrote. How far then was St. Paul (though he was 'not a whit behind the very chief of the apostles', nor therefore, I presume, behind any man now upon earth) from making light of the Old Testament! Behold this, lest ye one day 'wonder and perish', ye who make so small account of one half of the oracles of God! Yea, and that half of which the Holy Ghost expressly declares that it is 'profitable', as a means ordained of God for this very thing, 'for doctrine, for reproof, for correction, for instruction in righteousness': to the end [that] 'the man of God may be perfect, thoroughly furnished unto all good works'.

10. Nor is this profitable only for the men of God, for those who walk already in the light of his countenance, but also for those who are yet in

darkness, seeking him whom they know not. Thus St. Peter: 'We have also a more sure word of prophecy'—literally, 'And we have the prophetic word more sure' (καὶ ἔχομεν βεβαιότερον τὸν προφητικὸν λόγον), confirmed by our being 'eye-witnesses of his majesty', and 'hearing the voice which came from the excellent glory'—'unto which (prophetic word; so he styles the Holy Scriptures) ye do well that ye take heed, as unto a light that shineth in a dark place, until the day dawn, and the day-star arise in your hearts' (2 Pet. 1:19). Let all, therefore, who desire that day to dawn upon their hearts, wait for it in 'searching the Scriptures'.

11. Thirdly, all who desire an increase of the grace of God are to wait for it in partaking of the Lord's Supper. For this also is a direction himself hath given: 'The same night in which he was betrayed, he took bread, and brake it, and said, Take, eat; this is my body' (that is, the sacred sign of my body). 'This do in remembrance of me. Likewise he took the cup, saying, This cup is the New Testament' (or covenant) 'in my blood' (the sacred sign of that covenant): 'this do ye . . . in remembrance of me. For as often as ye eat this bread and drink this cup, ye do show forth the Lord's death till he come' (1 Cor. 11:23-26)—ye openly exhibit the same by these visible signs, before God, and angels, and men; ye manifest your solemn remembrance of his death, till he cometh in the clouds of heaven.

Only 'let a man (first) examine himself,' whether he understand the nature and design of this holy institution, and whether he really desire to be himself made conformable to the death of Christ; 'and so (nothing doubting) let him eat of that bread and drink of that cup' (1 Cor. 11:28).

Here then the direction first given by our Lord is expressly repeated by the Apostle: 'Let him eat,' 'let him drink' (ἐσθιέτω, πινέτω—both in the imperative mood); words not implying a bare permission only, but a clear explicit command; a command to all those either who already are filled with peace and joy in believing, or who can truly say, 'The remembrance of our sins is grievous unto us; the burden of them is intolerable.'

12. And that this is also an ordinary stated means of receiving the grace of God is evident from those words of the Apostle which occur in the preceding chapter: 'The cup of blessing which we bless, is it not the communion (or communication) of the blood of Christ? The bread which we break, is it not the communion of the body of Christ?' (1 Cor. 10:16). Is not the eating of that bread, and the drinking of that cup, the outward, visible means whereby God conveys into our souls all that spiritual grace, that righteousness, and peace, and joy in the Holy Ghost, which were purchased by the body of Christ once broken and the blood of Christ once shed for us? Let all, therefore, who truly desire the grace of God, eat of that bread and drink of that cup.

IV.1. But as plainly as God hath pointed out the way wherein he will be inquired after, innumerable are the objections which men wise in their own eyes have from time to time raised against it. It may be needful to consider a few of these; not because they are of weight in themselves, but because they have so often been used, especially of late years, to turn the lame out of the way; yea, to trouble and subvert those who did run well, till Satan appeared as an angel of light.

The first and chief of these is, 'You cannot use these means (as you call them) without *trusting* in them.' I pray, where is this written? I expect you should show me plain Scripture for your assertion; otherwise I dare not receive it, because I am not convinced that you are wiser than God.

If it really had been as you assert, it is certain Christ must have known it. And if he had known it, he would surely have warned us; he would have revealed it long ago. Therefore, because he has not, because there is no tittle of this in the whole revelation of Jesus Christ, I am as fully assured your assertion is false as that this revelation is of God.

'However, leave them off for a short time to see whether you trusted in them or no.' So I am to disobey God in order to know whether I trust in obeying him! And do you avow this advice? Do you deliberately teach to 'do evil, that good may come'? O tremble at the sentence of God against such teachers! Their 'damnation is just'.

'Nay, if you are troubled when you leave them off, it is plain you trusted in them.' By no means. If I am troubled when I wilfully disobey God, it is plain his Spirit is still striving with me. But if I am not troubled at wilful sin, it is plain I am given up to a reprobate mind.

But what do you mean by '*trusting* in them'? Looking for the blessing of God therein? Believing that if I wait in this way I shall attain what otherwise I should not? So I do. And so I will, God being my helper, even to my life's end. By the grace of God I will *thus* trust in them till the day of my death; that is, I will believe that whatever God hath promised he is faithful also to perform. And seeing he hath promised to bless me in this way, I *trust* it shall be according to his Word.

2. It has been, secondly, objected, 'This is seeking salvation by works.' Do you know the meaning of the expression you use? What is 'seeking salvation by works'? In the writings of St. Paul it means either seeking to be saved by observing the ritual works of the Mosaic law, or expecting salvation for the sake of our own works, by the merit of our own righteousness. But how is either of these implied in my waiting in the way God has ordained, and expecting that he will meet me there because he has promised so to do?

I do expect that he will fulfil his Word, that he will meet and bless me in this way. Yet not for the sake of any works which I have done, nor for the merit of my righteousness; but merely through the merits and sufferings and love of his Son, in whom he is always well-pleased.

3. It has been vehemently objected, thirdly, that Christ is the only means of grace. I answer, this is mere playing upon words. Explain your term, and the objection vanishes away. When we say, 'Prayer is a means of grace,' we understand a channel through which the grace of God is conveyed. When you say, 'Christ is the means of grace,' you understand the sole price and purchaser of it; or, that 'no man cometh unto the Father, but through him.' And who denies it? But this is utterly wide of the question.

4. But does not the Scripture (it has been objected, fourthly) direct us to *wait* for salvation? Does not David say, 'My soul waiteth upon God; for of him cometh my salvation'? And does not Isaiah teach us the same thing, saying, 'O Lord, we have waited for thee'? All this cannot be denied. Seeing it is the gift of God, we are undoubtedly to *wait* on him for salvation. But how shall we wait? If God himself has appointed a way, can you find a better way of waiting for him? But that he hath appointed a way hath been shown at large, and also what that way is. The very words of the Prophet which you cite put this out of the question. For the whole sentence runs thus: 'In the way of thy judgments' (or ordinances), 'O Lord, have we waited for thee' (Isa. 26:8). And in the very same way did David wait, as his own words abundantly testify: 'I have waited for thy saving health, O Lord, and have kept thy law.' 'Teach me, O Lord, the way of thy statutes, and I shall keep it unto the end.'

5. 'Yea', say some, 'but God has appointed another way—"Stand still and see the salvation of God."'

Let us examine the Scriptures to which you refer. The first of them, with the context, runs thus: 'And when Pharaoh drew nigh, the children of Israel lifted up their eyes . . . , and they were sore afraid. And they said unto Moses, Because there were no graves in Egypt, hast thou taken us away to die in the wilderness? And Moses said unto the people, Fear ye not: stand still, and see the salvation of the Lord. And the Lord said unto Moses, Speak unto the children of Israel that they go forward. But lift thou up thy rod, and stretch out thine hand over the sea, and divide it. And the children of Israel shall go on dry ground through the midst of the sea' (Exod. 14:10-11, 13, 15-16).

This was the 'salvation' of God which they 'stood still' to see—by 'marching forward' with all their might!

The other passage wherein this expression occurs stands thus:

> There came some that told Jehoshaphat, saying, There cometh a great multitude against thee, from beyond the sea. And Jehoshaphat feared, and set himself to seek the Lord, and proclaimed a fast throughout all Judah. And Judah gathered themselves together to ask help of the Lord; even out of all the cities they came to seek the Lord. And Jehoshaphat stood in the congregation, in the house of the Lord. . . . Then upon Jahaziel came the Spirit of the Lord. . . . And he said, . . . Be not dismayed by reason of this great multitude. . . . Tomorrow go ye down against them; ye shall not need to fight in this battle. Set yourselves: stand

> ye still, and see the salvation of the Lord. . . . And they rose early in the morning and went forth. And when they began to sing and to praise, the Lord set ambushments against the children of Moab, Ammon, and Mount Seir, . . . and everyone helped to destroy another (2 Chron. 20:2–5, 14–17, 20, 22–23).

Such was the salvation which the children of Judah saw. But how does all this prove that we ought not to wait for the grace of God in the means which he hath ordained?

6. I shall mention but one objection more, which indeed does not properly belong to this head. Nevertheless, because it has been so frequently urged, I may not wholly pass it by.

'Does not St. Paul say, "If ye be dead with Christ, why are ye subject to *ordinances?*" (Col. 2:20). Therefore a Christian, one that is "dead with Christ", need not use the ordinances any more.'

So you say, 'If I am a Christian I am not subject to the ordinances of Christ!' Surely, by the absurdity of this you must see at the first glance that the ordinances here mentioned cannot be the ordinances of Christ! That they must needs be the Jewish ordinances, to which it is certain a Christian is no longer subject.

And the same undeniably appears from the words immediately following, 'Touch not, taste not, handle not'—all evidently referring to the ancient ordinances of the Jewish law.

So that this objection is the weakest of all. And in spite of all, that great truth must stand unshaken: that all who desire the grace of God are to wait for it in the means which he hath ordained.

V.1. But this being allowed—that all who desire the grace of God are to wait for it in the means he hath ordained—it may still be inquired how those means should be used, both as to the *order* and the *manner* of using them.

With regard to the former, we may observe there is a kind of order wherein God himself is generally pleased to use these means in bringing a sinner to salvation. A stupid, senseless wretch is going on in his own way, not having God in all his thoughts, when God comes upon him unawares, perhaps by an awakening sermon or conversation, perhaps by some awful providence; or it may be an immediate stroke of his convincing Spirit, without any outward means at all. Having now a desire to flee from the wrath to come, he purposely goes to *hear* how it may be done. If he finds a preacher who speaks to the heart, he is amazed, and begins 'searching the Scriptures', whether these things are so. The more he *hears* and *reads*, the more convinced he is; and the more he *meditates* thereon day and night. Perhaps he finds some other book which explains and enforces what he has heard and read in Scripture. And by all these means the arrows of conviction sink deeper into his soul. He begins also to *talk* of the things of God, which are ever uppermost in his thoughts; yea, and to talk with God, to *pray* to him, although through fear and shame he scarce knows what to say. But whether he can speak or no, he cannot but pray, were it only in 'groans which cannot be uttered'. Yet being in doubt whether 'the high and lofty One that inhabiteth eternity' will regard such a sinner as him, he wants to pray with those who know God, with the faithful 'in the great congregation'. But here he observes others go up to 'the table of the Lord'. He considers, Christ has said, 'Do this.' How is it that I do not? I am too great a sinner. I am not fit. I am not worthy. After struggling with these scruples a while, he breaks through. And thus he continues in God's way–in hearing, reading, meditating, praying, and partaking of the Lord's Supper–till God, in the manner that pleases him, speaks to his heart, 'Thy faith hath saved thee; go in peace.'

2. By observing this order of God we may learn what means to recommend to any particular soul. If any of these will reach a stupid, careless sinner, it is probably *hearing* or *conversation*. To such therefore we might recommend these, if he has ever any thought about salvation. To one who begins to feel the weight of his sins, not only hearing the Word of God but *reading* it too, and perhaps other *serious books*, may be a means of deeper conviction. May you not advise him also to *meditate* on what he reads, that it may have its full force upon his heart? Yea, and to *speak* thereof, and not be ashamed, particularly among those who walk in the same path. When trouble and heaviness take hold upon him, should you not then earnestly exhort him to pour out his soul before God? 'Always to pray and not to faint'? And when he feels the worthlessness of his own prayers, are you not to work together with God and remind him of going up into 'the house of the Lord', and praying with all them that fear him? But if he does this, the *dying word* of his Lord will soon be brought to his remembrance: a plain intimation that this is the time when we should second the motions of the blessed Spirit. And thus may we lead him step by step through all the means which God has ordained; not according to our own will, but just as the providence and the Spirit of God go before and open the way.

3. Yet as we find no command in Holy Writ for any particular order to be observed herein, so neither do the providence and the Spirit of God adhere to any, without variation: but the means into which different men are led, and in which they find the blessing of God, are varied, transposed, and combined together a thousand different ways. Yet still our wisdom is to follow the leadings of his providence and his Spirit; to be guided herein (more especially as to the means wherein we ourselves seek the grace of God) partly by his outward providence, giving us the opportunity of using sometimes one means, sometimes another; partly by our experience, which it is whereby his free Spirit is pleased most to work in our heart. And in the meantime the sure and general rule for all who groan for the salvation of God is this–whenever opportunity

serves, use all the means which God has ordained. For who knows in which God will meet thee with the grace that bringeth salvation?

4. As to the *manner* of using them, whereon indeed it wholly depends whether they should convey any grace at all to the user, it behoves us, first, always to retain a lively sense that God is above all means. Have a care therefore of limiting the Almighty. He doth whatsoever and whensoever it pleaseth him. He can convey his grace, either in or out of any of the means which he hath appointed. Perhaps he will. 'Who hath known the mind of the Lord? Or who hath been his counsellor?' Look then every moment for his appearing! Be it at the hour you are employed in his ordinances; or before, or after that hour; or when you are hindered therefrom—he is not hindered. He is always ready; always able, always willing to save. 'It is the Lord, let him do what seemeth him good!'

Secondly, *before* you use any means let it be deeply impressed on your soul: There is no *power* in this. It is in itself a poor, dead, empty thing: separate from God, it is a dry leaf, a shadow. Neither is there any *merit* in my using this, nothing intrinsically pleasing to God, nothing whereby I deserve any favour at his hands, no, not a drop of water to cool my tongue. But because God bids, therefore I do; because he directs me to wait in this way, therefore here I wait for his free mercy, whereof cometh my salvation.

Settle this in your heart, that the *opus operatum*, the mere work done, profiteth nothing; that there is no *power* to save but in the Spirit of God, no *merit* but in the blood of Christ; that consequently even what God ordains conveys no grace to the soul if you trust not in him alone. On the other hand, he that does truly trust in him cannot fall short of the grace of God, even though he were cut off from every outward ordinance, though he were shut up in the centre of the earth.

Thirdly, in using all means, seek God alone. In and through every outward thing look singly to the *power* of his Spirit and the *merits* of his Son. Beware you do not stick in the *work* itself; if you do, it is all lost labour. Nothing short of God can satisfy your soul. Therefore eye him in all, through all, and above all.

Remember also to use all means *as means*; as ordained, not for their own sake, but in order to the renewal of your soul in righteousness and true holiness. If therefore they actually tend to this, well; but if not, they are dung and dross.

Lastly, after you have used any of these, take care how you value yourself thereon; how you congratulate yourself as having done some great thing. This is turning all into poison. Think, 'If God was not there, what does this avail? Have I not been adding sin to sin? How long, O Lord! Save, or I perish! O lay not this sin to my charge!' If God was there, if his love flowed into your heart, you have forgot, as it were, the outward work. You see, you know, you feel, God is all in all. Be abased. Sink down before him. Give him all the praise. Let God 'in all things be glorified through Christ Jesus'. Let 'all your bones cry out', 'My song shall be always of the loving-kindness of the Lord: With my mouth will I ever be telling of thy truth, from one generation to another!'

THE MARKS OF THE NEW BIRTH

Sermon 18 – 1748

AN INTRODUCTORY COMMENT

In this sermon (as also later in 'The New Birth'), Wesley wrestles with an unresolved dilemma. He had been brought up to take baptismal regeneration for granted. John seems always to have believed that something happens in baptism (even infant baptism) that validates its propriety and necessity as the sacrament of Christian initiation. He rejected the logic of 'believer's baptism', which always presupposes 'conversion' before baptism.

Even so, his own experience and the dramatic conversions in the Revival had forced on him a recognition of yet another sort of regeneration, more nearly correlated with justification and assurance than with water baptism. While admitting that regeneration and its fruits are the full expectation of baptism, he pointedly asks the reader to turn away from the question of his condition at baptism and to ask 'whether at this hour you are a child of God or no'. Having been baptized in the past does not necessarily make one a child of God at present.

Thus, somewhat as he had explained 'the circumcision of the heart' as a personal transformation following baptism, so now he was in search of a doctrine of regeneration that would take seriously the realities of evangelical conversions and yet not repudiate his own sacramental traditions. Whether he ever fully succeeded is an open question.

Just as the 'circumcision of the heart' involves 'humility, faith, hope, and charity', so also 'the marks of the New Birth' are 'faith, hope, and love'. In expounding this Christian commonplace, however, Wesley comes to his crucial assertion that the regenerate believer receives real power (or 'the privilege') not to commit sin and so to enjoy unanxious peace in heart and mind. Here Wesley comes as close as he ever will to an unnuanced notion of the Christian life as sinless; he even goes on to denounce those who try to qualify this concept with the claim that the regenerate 'do not commit sin habitually'. In this sermon, then, Wesley lays out an important premise of his unfolding vision of Christian existence.

Wesley preached from John 3:8 as early as June 10, 1739, and frequently thereafter (thirteen times in all until December 1757). This written sermon, first published in volume two of his collected *Sermons* in 1748, was included in all subsequent collections during his lifetime.

The Marks of the New Birth

So is everyone that is born of the Spirit.
John 3:8

1. How is everyone that is 'born of the Spirit'? That is, 'born again', 'born of God'? What is meant by the being 'born again'? The being 'born of God'? Or, being 'born of the Spirit'? What is implied in the being a 'son' or a 'child of God'? Or, having the 'Spirit of adoption'? That these privileges, by the free mercy of God, are ordinarily annexed to baptism (which is thence termed by our Lord in the preceding verse the being 'born of water and of the Spirit') we know; but we would know what these privileges are. What is 'the new birth'?

2. Perhaps it is not needful to give a definition of this, seeing the Scripture gives none. But as the question is of the deepest concern to every child of man (since 'except a man be born again', 'born of the Spirit', he 'cannot see the kingdom of God'), I propose to lay down the marks of it in the plainest manner, just as I find them laid down in Scripture.

I.1. The first of these (and the foundation of all the rest) is faith. So St. Paul, 'Ye are all the children of God by faith in Christ Jesus' (Gal. 3:26). So St. John, 'To them gave he power' (ἐξουσίαν, right, or privilege, it might rather be translated) 'to become the sons of God, even to them that believe on his name: which were born', when they believed, ('not of blood, nor of the will of the flesh', not by natural generation, 'nor of the will of man', like those children adopted by men, in whom no inward change is thereby wrought, 'but) of God' (John 1:12-13). And again in his General Epistle, 'Whosoever believeth that Jesus is the Christ is born of God' (1 John 5:1).

2. But it is not a barely notional or speculative faith that is here spoken of by the apostles. It is not a bare assent to this proposition, 'Jesus is the Christ'; nor indeed to all the propositions contained in our creed, or in the Old and New Testament. It is not merely 'an assent to any, or all these credible things, as credible'. To say this were to say (which who could hear?) that the devils were born of God. For they have their faith. They trembling believe both that Jesus is the Christ and that all Scripture, having been given by inspiration of God, is true as God is true. It is not only 'an assent to divine truth, upon the testimony of God', or 'upon the evidence of miracles'. For they also heard the words of his mouth, and knew him to be a faithful and true witness. They could not but receive the testimony he gave, both of himself and of the Father

which sent him. They saw likewise the mighty works which he did, and thence believed that he 'came forth from God'. Yet notwithstanding this faith they are still 'reserved in chains of darkness unto the judgment of the great day'.

3. For all this is no more than a dead faith. The true, living, Christian faith, which whosoever hath is 'born of God', is not only an assent, an act of the understanding, but a disposition which God hath wrought in his heart; 'a sure trust and confidence in God that through the merits of Christ his sins are forgiven, and he reconciled to the favour of God'. This implies that a man first *renounce himself*; that, in order to be 'found in Christ', to be accepted through him, he totally reject all 'confidence in the flesh'; that, 'having nothing to pay', having no trust in his own works or righteousness of any kind, he come to God as a lost, miserable, self-destroyed, self-condemned, undone, helpless sinner, as one whose 'mouth' is utterly 'stopped', and who is altogether 'guilty before God'. Such a sense of sin (commonly called 'despair' by those who speak evil of the things they know not), together with a full conviction, such as no words can express, that of Christ only cometh our salvation, and an earnest desire of that salvation must precede a living faith: a trust in him who 'for us paid our ransom by his death, and for us fulfilled the law of his life'. This faith, then, whereby we are born of God, is 'not only a belief of all the articles of our faith, but also a true confidence of the mercy of God, through our Lord Jesus Christ'.

4. An immediate and constant fruit of this faith whereby we are born of God, a fruit which can in no wise be separated from it, no, not for an hour, is power over sin: power over outward sin of every kind; over every evil word and work; for wheresoever the blood of Christ is thus applied it 'purgeth the conscience from dead works'. And over inward sin; for it 'purifieth the heart' from every unholy desire and temper. This fruit of faith St. Paul has largely described in the sixth chapter of his Epistle to the Romans: 'How shall we (saith he) who' by faith 'are dead to sin, live any longer therein?' 'Our old man is crucified with Christ, that the body of sin might be destroyed, that henceforth we should not serve sin.' 'Likewise reckon ye yourselves to be dead unto sin, but alive unto God through Jesus Christ our Lord. . . . Let not sin therefore reign', even 'in your mortal body, but yield yourselves unto God, as those that are alive from the dead. For sin shall not have dominion over you. . . . God be thanked that ye were the servants of sin . . . , but being made free'—the plain meaning is, God be thanked that though ye were in the time past the servants of sin, yet now—'being free from sin, ye are become the servants of righteousness.'

5. The same invaluable privilege of the sons of God is as strongly asserted by St. John; particularly with regard to the former branch of it, namely, power over outward sin. After he had been crying out as one astonished at the depth of the riches of the goodness of God, 'Behold what manner of love the Father

hath bestowed upon us, that we should be called the sons of God! Beloved, now are we the sons of God; and it doth not yet appear what we shall be; but we know that when he shall appear we shall be like him; for we shall see him as he is'—he soon adds, 'Whosoever is born of God doth not commit sin; for his seed remaineth in him, and he cannot sin because he is born of God' (1 John 3:1–2, 9). But some men will say, 'True; "whosoever is born of God doth not commit sin" (1 John 3:9) *habitually*.' *Habitually*! Whence is that? I read it not. It is not written in the Book. God plainly saith, he 'doth not commit sin'. And thou addest, 'habitually'! Who art thou that *mendest* the oracles of God? That 'addest to the words of this Book'? Beware, I beseech thee, lest God 'add to thee all the plagues that are written therein'! Especially when the comment thou addest is such as quite swallows up the text: so that by this μεθοδεία πλάνης, this artful method of deceiving, the precious promise is utterly lost; by this κυβεία ἀνθρώπων, this tricking and shuffling of men, the Word of God is made of none effect. O beware thou that thus takest from the words of this Book, that taking away the whole meaning and spirit from them leavest only what may indeed be termed a dead letter, lest God take away thy part out of the book of life!

6. Suffer we the Apostle to interpret his own words by the whole tenor of his discourse. In the fifth verse of this chapter he had said, 'Ye know that he (Christ) was manifested to take away our sins; and in him is no sin.' What is the inference he draws from this? 'Whosoever abideth in him sinneth not; whosoever sinneth hath not seen him, neither known him.' To his enforcement of this important doctrine he premises an highly necessary caution: 'Little children, let no man deceive you' (for many will endeavour so to do; to persuade you that you may be unrighteous, that you may commit sin, and yet be children of God). 'He that doth righteousness is righteous, even as he is righteous. He that committeth sin is of the devil; for the devil sinneth from the beginning.' Then follows, 'Whosoever is born of God doth not commit sin; for his seed remaineth in him: and he cannot sin, because he is born of God. In this (adds the Apostle) the children of God are manifest, and the children of the devil' (1 John 3:7–10). By this plain mark (the committing or not committing sin) are they distinguished from each other. To the same effect are those words in his fifth chapter. 'We know that whosoever is born of God sinneth not; but he that is begotten of God keepeth himself, and that wicked one toucheth him not' (1 John 3:18).

7. Another fruit of this living faith is peace. For 'being justified by faith', having all our sins blotted out, 'we have peace with God, through our Lord Jesus Christ' (Rom. 5:1). This indeed our Lord himself, the night before his death, solemnly bequeathed to all his followers. 'Peace (saith he) I leave with you'; (you who 'believe in God', and 'believe also in me') 'my peace I give unto you. Not as the world giveth, give I unto you. Let not your heart be troubled,

neither let it be afraid' (John 14:27). And again, 'These things have I spoken unto you, that in me ye might have peace' (John 16:33). This is that 'peace of God which passeth all understanding'; that serenity of soul which it hath not entered into the heart of a natural man to conceive, and which it is not possible for even the spiritual man to utter. And it is a peace which all the powers of earth and hell are unable to take from him. Waves and storms beat upon it, but they shake it not; for it is founded upon a rock. It keepeth the hearts and minds of the children of God at all times and in all places. Whether they are in ease or in pain, in sickness or health, in abundance or want, they are happy in God. In every state they have learned to be content, yea, to give thanks unto God through Christ Jesus; being well assured that 'whatsoever is, is best'; because it is his will concerning them. So that in all the vicissitudes of life their 'heart standeth fast, believing in the Lord'.

II.1. A second scriptural mark of those who are born of God is hope. Thus St. Peter, speaking to all the children of God who were then 'scattered abroad', saith, 'Blessed be the God and Father of our Lord Jesus Christ, who according to his abundant mercy hath begotten us again unto a lively hope' (1 Pet. 1:3). Ἐλπίδα ζῶσαν, a *lively* or *living* hope, saith the Apostle: because there is also a *dead* hope (as well as a dead faith), a hope which is not from God but from the enemy of God and man—as evidently appears by its fruits. For as it is the offspring of pride, so it is the parent of every evil word and work. Whereas every man that hath in him this living hope is 'holy as he that calleth him is holy'. Every man that can truly say to his brethren in Christ, 'Beloved, now are we the sons of God; and we shall see him as he is'—'purifieth himself, even as he is pure'.

2. This hope (termed in the Epistle to the Hebrews πλεροφορία πίστεως, Heb. 10:22, and elsewhere πλεροφορία ἐλπίδος, Heb. 6:11—in our translation, the 'full assurance of faith', and the 'full assurance of hope'; expressions the best which our language could afford, although far weaker than those in the original), as described in Scripture, implies, first, the testimony of our own spirit or conscience that we walk 'in simplicity and godly sincerity'; but, secondly and chiefly, the testimony of the Spirit of God, 'bearing witness with', or to, 'our spirit, that we are the children of God; and if children, then heirs; heirs of God, and joint-heirs with Christ'.

3. Let us well observe what is here taught us by God himself touching this glorious privilege of his children. Who is it that is here said to 'bear witness'? Not our spirit only, but another; even the Spirit of God. He it is who 'beareth witness with our spirit'. What is it he beareth witness of? 'That we are the children of God; and if children, then heirs; heirs of God, and joint-heirs with Christ'—'if so be that we suffer with him' (if we deny ourselves, if we take up our cross daily, if we cheerfully endure persecution or reproach for his sake)

'that we may be also glorified together.' And in whom doth the Spirit of God bear this witness? In all who are the children of God. By this very argument does the Apostle prove in the preceding verses that they are so: 'As many', saith he, 'as are led by the Spirit of God, they are the sons of God. For ye have not received the spirit of bondage again to fear; but ye have received the Spirit of adoption, whereby we cry, Abba, Father!' It follows, 'The Spirit itself beareth witness with our spirit, that we are the children of God' (Rom. 8:14–16).

4. The variation of the phrase in the fifteenth verse is worthy our observation. '*Ye* have received the Spirit of adoption, whereby *we* cry, Abba, Father!' *Ye*—as many [as] are the sons of God—have, in virtue of your sonship, received that selfsame Spirit of adoption whereby *we* cry, Abba, Father. *We*, the apostles, prophets, teachers (for so the word may not improperly be understood); we, through whom you have believed, the 'ministers of Christ, and stewards of the mysteries of God'. As *we* and *you* have one Lord, so we have one Spirit; as we have one faith, so have we one hope also. We and you are sealed with one 'Spirit of promise', the earnest of *yours* and of *our* inheritance: the same Spirit bearing witness with yours and with our spirit, 'that we are the children of God'.

5. And thus is the Scripture fulfilled: 'Blessed are they that mourn, for they shall be comforted.' For 'tis easy to believe that though sorrow may precede this witness of God's Spirit with our spirit (indeed *must* in some degree while we groan under fear and a sense of the wrath of God abiding on us), yet as soon as any man feeleth it in himself his 'sorrow is turned into joy'. Whatsoever his pain may have been before, yet as soon as that 'hour is come, he remembereth the anguish no more, for joy' that he is born of God. It may be many of *you* have now sorrow, because you are 'aliens from the commonwealth of Israel', because you are conscious to yourselves that you have not this Spirit, that you are 'without hope and without God in the world'. But when the Comforter is come, then 'your heart shall rejoice'; yea, 'your joy shall be full', 'and that joy no man taketh from you' (John 16:22). 'We joy in God', will ye say, 'through our Lord Jesus Christ, by whom we have now received the atonement' (Rom. 5:11): 'by whom we have access into this grace'; this state of grace, of favour, of reconciliation with God, 'wherein we stand, and rejoice in hope of the glory of God.' Ye, saith St. Peter, whom God 'hath begotten again unto a lively hope', 'are kept by the power of God unto salvation. . . . Wherein ye greatly rejoice, though now for a season, if need be, ye are in heaviness through manifold temptations; that the trial of your faith . . . may be found unto praise, and honour, and glory, at the appearing of Jesus Christ, . . . in whom, though now ye see him not, ye rejoice with joy unspeakable, and full of glory' (1 Pet. 1:3–8). Unspeakable indeed! It is not for the tongue of man to describe this joy in the Holy Ghost. It is 'the hidden manna, which no man knoweth save he that receiveth it'. But this we know, it not only

remains, but overflows, in the depth of affliction. 'Are the consolations of God small' with his children, when all earthly comforts fail? Not so. But when sufferings most abound, the consolation of his Spirit doth much more abound: insomuch that the sons of God 'laugh at destruction when it cometh'; at want, pain, hell and the grave; as knowing him who 'hath the keys of death and hell', and will shortly 'cast them into the bottomless pit'; as hearing even now the 'great voice out of heaven' saying, 'Behold, the tabernacle of God is with men, and he will dwell with them, and they shall be his people, and God himself shall be with them, and be their God. And God shall wipe away all tears from their eyes, and there shall be no more death, neither sorrow, nor crying; neither shall there be any more pain; for the former things are passed away' (Rev. 21:3–4).

III.1. A third scriptural mark of those who are born of God, and the greatest of all, is love: even 'the love of God shed abroad in their hearts by the Holy Ghost which is given unto them' (Rom. 5:5). 'Because they are sons, God hath sent forth the Spirit of his Son into their hearts, crying, Abba Father!' (Gal. 4:6). By this Spirit, continually looking up to God as their reconciled and loving Father, they cry to him for their daily bread, for all things needful whether for their souls or bodies. They continually pour out their hearts before him, knowing 'they have the petitions which they ask of him' (1 John 5:15). Their delight is in him. He is the joy of their heart, 'their shield, and their exceeding great reward'. The desire of their soul is toward him; it is their 'meat and drink to do his will'; and they are 'satisfied as with marrow and fatness, while their mouth praiseth him with joyful lips' (Ps. 63:5).

2. And in this sense also 'everyone who loveth him that begat, loveth him that is begotten of him' (1 John 5:1). His spirit rejoiceth in God his Saviour. He 'loveth the Lord Jesus Christ in sincerity'. He is so 'joined unto the Lord' as to be 'one spirit'. His soul hangeth upon him, and chooseth him as altogether lovely, 'the chiefest among ten thousand'. He knoweth, he feeleth, what that means, 'My Beloved is mine, and I am his' (Cant. 2:16). 'Thou art fairer than the children of men; full of grace are thy lips, because God hath anointed thee for ever!' (Ps. 45:2).

3. The necessary fruit of this love of God is the love of our neighbour, of every soul which God hath made; not excepting our enemies, not excepting those who are now 'despitefully using and persecuting us'; a love whereby we love every man *as ourselves*—as we love our own souls. Nay, our Lord has expressed it still more strongly, teaching us to 'love one another even as he hath loved us'. Accordingly the commandment written in the hearts of all those that love God is no other than this, 'As I have loved you, so love ye one another.' Now 'herein perceive we the love of God, in that he laid down his life for us. We ought', then, as the Apostle justly infers, 'to lay down our lives

for our brethren' (1 John 3:16). If we feel ourselves ready to do this, then do we truly love our neighbour. Then 'we know that we have passed from death unto life, because we' thus 'love our brethren' (1 John 3:14). 'Hereby know we' that we are born of God, 'that we dwell in him, and he in us, because he hath given us of his loving Spirit' (1 John 4:13). 'For love is of God, and everyone that' thus 'loveth is born of God, and knoweth God' (1 John 4:7).

4. But some may possibly ask, 'Does not the Apostle say, "This is the love of God, that we keep his commandments"?' (1 John 5:3). Yea; and this is the love of our neighbour also, in the same sense as it is the love of God. But what would you infer from hence? That the keeping the outward commandments is all that is implied in loving God with all your heart, with all your mind, and soul, and strength, and in loving your neighbour as yourself? That the love of God is not an affection of the soul, but merely an *outward service*? And that the love of our neighbour is not a disposition of the heart, but barely a course of *outward works*? To mention so wild an interpretation of the Apostle's words is sufficiently to confute it. The plain indisputable meaning of that text is: 'this is the' sign or proof of the 'love of God', of our keeping the first and great commandment—to keep the rest of his commandments. For true love, if it be once shed abroad in our heart, will constrain us so to do; since whosoever loves God with all his heart cannot but serve him with all his strength.

5. A second fruit then of the love of God (so far as it can be distinguished from it) is universal obedience to him we love, and conformity to his will; obedience to all the commands of God, internal and external; obedience of the heart and of the life, in every temper and in all manner of conversation. And one of the tempers most obviously implied herein is the being 'zealous of good works'; the hungering and thirsting to do good, in every possible kind, unto all men; the rejoicing to 'spend and be spent for them', for every child of man, not looking for any recompense in this world, but only in the resurrection of the just.

IV.1. Thus have I plainly laid down those marks of the new birth which I find laid down in Scripture. Thus doth God himself answer that weighty question what it is to be born of God. Such, if the appeal be made to the oracles of God, is 'everyone that is born of the Spirit'. This it is, in the judgment of the Spirit of God, to be a son or a child of God. It is so to believe in God through Christ as 'not to commit sin', and to enjoy, at all times and in all places, that 'peace of God which passeth all understanding'. It is so to *hope* in God through the Son of his love as to have not only the 'testimony of a good conscience', but also 'the Spirit of God bearing witness with your spirits that ye are the children of God': whence cannot but spring the 'rejoicing evermore in him through whom ye have received the atonement'. It is so to *love* God, who hath thus loved you, as you never did love any creature: so that ye are constrained to love all men as yourselves; with a love not only ever burning in your hearts, but flaming out in all your actions and conversations, and making your whole life one 'labour of love', one continued obedience to those commands, 'Be ye merciful, as God is merciful'; 'Be ye holy, as I the Lord am holy'; 'Be ye perfect, as your Father which is in heaven is perfect.'

2. Who then are ye that are *thus* born of God? Ye 'know the things which are given to you of God'. Ye well know that ye are the children of God, and 'can assure your hearts before him'. And every one of you who has observed these words cannot but feel and know of a truth whether at this hour (answer to God and not to man!) you are thus a child of God or no! The question is not what you was made in baptism (do not evade!) but what you are now. Is the Spirit of adoption now in your heart? To your own heart let the appeal be made. I ask not whether you *was* born of water and the Spirit. But *are* you *now* the temple of the Holy Ghost which dwelleth in you? I allow you was 'circumcised with the circumcision of Christ' (as St. Paul emphatically terms baptism). But does the Spirit of Christ and of glory *now* rest upon you? Else 'your circumcision is become uncircumcision'.

3. Say not then in your heart, I *was once* baptized; therefore I *am now* a child of God. Alas, that consequence will by no means hold. How many are the baptized gluttons and drunkards, the baptized liars and common swearers, the baptized railers and evil-speakers, the baptized whoremongers, thieves, extortioners! What think you? Are these now the children of God? Verily I say unto you, whosoever you are, unto whom any of the preceding characters belong, 'Ye are of your father the devil, and the works of your father ye do.' Unto you I call in the name of him whom you crucify afresh, and in his words to your circumcised predecessors, 'Ye serpents, ye generation of vipers, how can you escape the damnation of hell?'

4. How indeed, except ye be born again! For ye are now dead in trespasses and sins. To say then that ye cannot be born again, that there is no new birth but in baptism, is to seal you all under damnation, to consign you to hell, without any help, without hope. And perhaps some may think this just and right. In their zeal for the Lord of Hosts they may say, 'Yea, cut off the sinners, the Amalekites! Let these Gibeonites be utterly destroyed! They deserve no less.' No; nor I, nor you—mine and your desert, as well as theirs, is hell. And it is mere mercy, free undeserved mercy, that *we* are not now in unquenchable fire. You will say, 'But we are washed, we were born again of water and of the Spirit.' So *were* they. This therefore hinders not at all, but that ye may *now* be even as they. Know ye not that 'what is highly esteemed of men is an abomination in the sight of God'? Come forth, ye 'saints of the world', ye that are honoured of men, and see who will cast the first stone at them, at these wretches not fit to live upon the earth, these common harlots, adulterers, murderers. Only learn ye first what that meaneth, 'He that hateth his brother

is a murderer' (1 John 3:15)—'He that looketh on a woman to lust after her hath committed adultery with her already in his heart' (Matt. 5:28)—'Ye adulterers and adulteresses, know ye not that the friendship of the world is enmity with God?' (Jas. 4:4).

5. 'Verily, verily, I say unto you, ye also must be born again.' 'Except' ye also 'be born again, ye cannot see the kingdom of God.' Lean no more on the staff of that broken reed, that ye *were* born again in baptism. Who denies that ye were then made 'children of God, and heirs of the kingdom of heaven'? But notwithstanding this, ye are now children of the devil; therefore ye must be born again. And let not Satan put it into your heart to cavil at a word, when the thing is clear. Ye have heard what are the marks of the children of God; all ye who have them not on your souls, baptized or unbaptized, must needs receive them, or without doubt ye will perish everlastingly. And if ye have been baptized, your only hope is this: that those who were made the children of God by baptism, but are now the children of the devil, may yet again receive 'power to become the sons of God'; that they may receive again what they have lost, even the 'Spirit of adoption, crying in their hearts, Abba, Father'!

6. Amen, Lord Jesus! May everyone who prepareth his heart yet again to seek thy face receive again that Spirit of adoption, and cry out, Abba, Father! Let him now again have power to believe in thy name as to become a child of God; as to know and feel he hath 'redemption in thy blood, even the forgiveness of sins', and that he 'cannot commit sin, because he is born of God'. Let him be now 'begotten again unto a living hope', so as to 'purify himself, as thou art pure'! And 'because he is a son', let the Spirit of love and of glory rest upon him, cleansing him 'from all filthiness of flesh and spirit', and teaching him to 'perfect holiness in the fear of God'!

THE GREAT PRIVILEGE OF THOSE THAT ARE BORN OF GOD

Sermon 19 – 1748

AN INTRODUCTORY COMMENT

Wesley must have realized that he had laid himself open to misinterpretation on the matter of 'sinless perfection' in his sermon on 'The Marks of the New Birth'. And so he proceeded to write 'The Great Privilege of those that are Born of God' for volume two of his collected *Sermons* (1748). With this sermon, he drew a more careful distinction between 'sin properly so called' and other shortfallings, i.e., between voluntary and involuntary sins, where 'voluntary' sounds suspiciously like 'habitual'. The two sermons are perhaps better read as a pair than apart.

He begins this sermon with a careful distinction between justification and the new birth: 'justification implies only a relative, the new birth a real, change.' Again he plays out the difference between a change in relationship (God doing something for us) and a change in condition (God doing something in us). Regeneration is thus understood as that act of grace concurrent with justification but not at all identical to it–a 'vast inward change' that opens up the lifelong quest for holiness. Then Wesley develops his idea of a spiritual sensorium, using the latency analogy of the senses at physical birth to point to the potential of the spiritual senses that are enlivened by their Creator Spirit at the new birth.

The main part of the sermon considers the sense in which the new-born Christian 'doth not commit sin'. The discussion hinges on Wesley's definition of sin as an outward action that is an actual, voluntary, transgression of the written law of God. In that sense, the Christian not only 'doth not' but 'cannot' commit sin. He goes on to show that, although some sin of omission and inward sin may precede a loss of faith, outward sin is always anticipated by a loss of faith. The idea of backsliding is central to Wesley's attack on the idea of 'once saved always saved'. Wesley ends the sermon with a description of how God continues to act upon the soul only as the soul continually re-acts upon God.

This sermon also seems to be a written version of one of Wesley's typical oral sermons from the early period of the Revival. His first recorded sermon from 1 John 3:9 comes on September 23, 1739; its last usage as a sermon text seems to have been in November 1756. In 1748, then, with these twin sermons, Wesley had laid out one of the undergirding premises of his vision of Christian existence.

The Great Privilege of those that are Born of God

Whosoever is born of God doth not commit sin.
John 3:9

1. It has been frequently supposed that the being born of God was all one with the being justified; that the new birth and justification were only different expressions denoting the same thing: it being certain on the one hand that whoever is justified is also born of God, and on the other that whoever is born of God is also justified; yea, that both these gifts of God are given to every believer in one and the same moment. In one point of time his sins are blotted out and he is born of God.

2. But though it be allowed that justification and the new birth are in point of time inseparable from each other, yet are they easily distinguished as being not the same, but things of a widely different nature. Justification implies only a relative, the new birth a real, change. God in justifying us does something *for* us: in begetting us again he does the work *in* us. The former changes our outward relation to God, so that of enemies we become children; by the latter our inmost souls are changed, so that of sinners we become saints. The one restores us to the favour, the other to the image of God. The one is the taking away the guilt, the other the taking away the power, of sin. So that although they are joined together in point of time, yet are they of wholly distinct natures.

3. The not discerning this, the not observing the wide difference there is between being justified and being born again, has occasioned exceeding great confusion of thought in many who have treated on this subject; particularly when they have attempted to explain this great privilege of the children of God, to show how 'whosoever is born of God doth not commit sin.'

4. In order to apprehend this clearly it may be necessary, first, to consider what is the proper meaning of that expression, 'whosoever is born of God'; and, secondly, to inquire in what sense he 'doth not commit sin'.

I.1. First, we are to consider what is the proper meaning of that expression, 'whosoever is born of God'. And in general, from all the passages of Holy Writ wherein this expression, the being 'born of God', occurs, we may learn that it implies not barely the being baptized, or any outward change whatever; but a vast inward change; a change wrought in the soul by the operation of the Holy Ghost, a change in the whole manner of our existence; for from the moment we are 'born of God' we live in quite another manner than we did before; we are, as it were, in another world.

2. The ground and reason of the expression is easy to be understood. When we undergo this great change we may with much propriety be said 'to be born again', because there is so near a resemblance between the circumstances of the natural and of the spiritual birth; so that to consider the circumstances of the natural birth is the most easy way to understand the spiritual.

3. The child which is not yet born subsists indeed by the air, as does everything which has life; but *feels* it not, nor anything else, unless in a very dull and imperfect manner. It *hears* little, if at all, the organs of hearing being as yet closed up. It *sees* nothing, having its eyes fast shut, and being surrounded with utter darkness. There are, it may be, some faint beginnings of life when the time of its birth draws nigh, and some motion consequent thereon, whereby it is distinguished from a mere mass of matter. But it has no *senses*; all these avenues of the soul are hitherto quite shut up. Of consequence it has scarce any intercourse with this visible world, nor any knowledge, conception, or idea of the things that occur therein.

4. The reason why he that is not yet born is wholly a stranger to the visible world is not because it is afar off—it is very nigh; it surrounds him on every side—but partly because he has not those senses (they are not yet opened in his soul) whereby alone it is possible to hold commerce with the material world; and partly because so thick a veil is cast between, through which he can discern nothing.

5. But no sooner is the child born into the world than he exists in a quite different manner. He now *feels* the air with which he is surrounded, and which pours into him from every side, as fast as he alternately breathes it back, to sustain the flame of life. And hence springs a continual increase of strength, of motion, and of sensation; all the bodily senses being now awakened and furnished with their proper objects.

His eyes are now opened to perceive the light, which silently flowing in upon them discovers not only itself but an infinite variety of things with which before he was wholly unacquainted. His ears are unclosed, and sounds rush in with endless diversity. Every sense is employed upon such objects as are peculiarly suitable to it. And by these inlets the soul, having an open intercourse with the visible world, acquires more and more knowledge of sensible things, of all the things which are under the sun.

6. So it is with him that is born of God. Before that great change is wrought, although he subsists by him in whom all that have life 'live and move and have their being', yet he is not *sensible* of God. He does not *feel*, he has no inward consciousness of his presence. He does not perceive that divine breath of life without which he cannot subsist a moment. Nor is he sensible of any of the things of God. They make no impression upon his soul. God is continually calling to him from on high, but he heareth not; his ears are shut; so that 'the

voice of the charmer' is lost to him, 'charm he never so wisely'. He seeth not the things of the Spirit of God, the eyes of his understanding being closed, and utter darkness covering his whole soul, surrounding him on every side. It is true he may have some faint dawnings of life, some small beginnings of spiritual motion; but as yet he has no spiritual senses capable of discerning spiritual objects. Consequently, he 'discerneth not the things of the Spirit of God. He cannot know them; because they are spiritually discerned.'

7. Hence he has scarce any knowledge of the invisible world, as he has scarce any intercourse with it. Not that it is afar off. No; he is in the midst of it: it encompasses him round about. The 'other world', as we usually term it, is not far from every one of us. It is above, and beneath, and on every side. Only the natural man discerneth it not; partly because he has no spiritual senses, whereby alone we can discern the things of God; partly because so thick a veil is interposed as he knows not how to penetrate.

8. But when he is born of God, born of the Spirit, how is the manner of his existence changed! His whole soul is now sensible of God, and he can say by sure experience, 'Thou art about my bed, and about my path'; I feel thee in 'all my ways'. 'Thou besettest me behind and before, and layest thy hand upon me.' The Spirit or breath of God is immediately inspired, breathed into the new-born soul; and the same breath which comes from, returns to God. As it is continually received by faith, so it is continually rendered back by love, by prayer, and praise, and thanksgiving–love and praise and prayer being the breath of every soul which is truly born of God. And by this new kind of spiritual respiration, spiritual life is not only sustained but increased day by day, together with spiritual strength and motion and sensation; all the senses of the soul being now awake, and capable of 'discerning' spiritual 'good and evil'.

9. 'The eyes of his understanding' are now open, and he 'seeth him that is invisible'. He sees what is 'the exceeding greatness of his power' and of his love toward them that believe. He sees that God is merciful to him a sinner; that he is reconciled through the Son of his love. He clearly perceives both the pardoning love of God and all his 'exceeding great and precious promises'. 'God, who commanded the light to shine out of the darkness, hath shined' and doth shine 'in his heart, to enlighten him with the knowledge of the glory of God in the face of Jesus Christ.' All the darkness is now passed away, and he abides in the light of God's countenance.

10. His ears are now opened, and the voice of God no longer calls in vain. He hears and obeys the heavenly calling: he 'knows the voice of his shepherd'. All his spiritual senses being now awakened, he has a clear intercourse with the invisible world. And hence he knows more and more of the things which before it 'could not enter into his heart to conceive'. He now knows what the peace of God is; what is joy in the Holy Ghost; what the love of God which

is shed abroad in the hearts of them that believe through Christ Jesus. Thus the veil being removed which before interrupted the light and voice, the knowledge and love of God, he who is born of the Spirit, 'dwelling in love, dwelleth in God and God in him'.

II.1. Having considered the meaning of that expression, 'whosoever is born of God', it remains in the second place to inquire in what sense he 'doth not commit sin'.

Now one who is so born of God as hath been above described, who continually receives into his soul the breath of life from God, the gracious influence of his Spirit, and continually renders it back; one who thus believes and loves, who by faith perceives the continual actings of God upon his spirit, and by a kind of spiritual re-action returns the grace he receives in unceasing love, and praise, and prayer; not only 'doth not commit sin' while he thus 'keepeth himself', but so long as this 'seed remaineth in him he cannot sin', because he is born of God.

2. By 'sin' I here understand outward sin, according to the plain, common acceptation of the word: an actual, voluntary 'transgression of the law'; of the revealed, written law of God; of any commandment of God acknowledged to be such at the time that it is transgressed. But 'whosoever is born of God', while he abideth in faith and love and in the spirit of prayer and thanksgiving, not only 'doth not', but 'cannot' thus 'commit sin'. So long as he thus believeth in God through Christ and loves him, and is pouring out his heart before him, he cannot voluntarily transgress any command of God, either by speaking or acting what he knows God hath forbidden—so long that 'seed' which 'remaineth in him' (that loving, praying, thankful faith) compels him to refrain from whatsoever he knows to be an abomination in the sight of God.

3. But here a difficulty will immediately occur, and one that to many has appeared insuperable, and induced them to deny the plain assertion of the Apostle, and give up the privilege of the children of God.

It is plain, in fact, that those whom we cannot deny to have been truly 'born of God' (the Spirit of God having given us in his Word this infallible testimony concerning them) nevertheless not only could but did commit sin, even gross, outward sin. They did transgress the plain, known laws of God, speaking or acting what they knew he had forbidden.

4. Thus David was unquestionably born of God or ever he was anointed king over Israel. He knew in whom he had believed; he was strong in faith, giving glory to God. 'The Lord', saith he, 'is my shepherd; therefore can I lack nothing. He shall feed me in green pastures, and lead me forth beside the waters of comfort. Yea, though I walk through the valley of the shadow of death, I will fear no evil; for thou art with me' (Ps. 23:1, 2, 4). He was filled with love, such as often constrained him to cry out, 'I will love thee, O Lord,

my God; the Lord is my stony rock, and my defence; the horn also of my salvation, and my refuge' (Ps. 18:1, 2). He was a man of prayer, pouring out his soul before God in all circumstances of life; and abundant in praises and thanksgiving. 'Thy praise', saith he, 'shall be ever in my mouth' (Ps. 34:1). 'Thou art my God, and I will thank thee; thou art my God, and I will praise thee' (Ps. 118:28). And yet such a child of God could and did commit sin; yea, the horrid sins of adultery and murder.

5. And even after the Holy Ghost was more largely given, after 'life and immortality were brought to light by the gospel', we want not instances of the same melancholy kind, which were also doubtless written for our instruction. Thus he who (probably from his selling all that he had, and bringing the price for the relief of his poor brethren) was 'by the apostles' themselves 'surnamed Barnabas', that is, 'the son of consolation' (Acts 4:36–37); who was so honoured at Antioch as to be selected with Saul out of all the disciples to carry their 'relief unto the brethren in Judea' (Acts 11:29): this Barnabas, who at his return from Judea was by the peculiar direction of the Holy Ghost solemnly 'separated' from the other 'prophets and teachers' 'for the work whereunto God had called him' (Acts 13:1–2), even to accompany the great Apostle among the Gentiles, and to be his fellow-labourer in every place; nevertheless was afterward so 'sharp' in his 'contention' with St. Paul (because he 'thought it not good to take with them' John in his 'visiting the brethren' a second time, 'who had departed from them from Pamphylia, and went not with them to the work') that he himself also departed from the work; that he 'took John, and sailed unto Cyprus' (Acts 15:35, 38, 39), forsaking him to whom he had been in so immediate a manner joined by the Holy Ghost.

6. An instance more astonishing than both these is given by St. Paul in his Epistle to the Galatians. 'When Peter', the aged, the zealous, the first of the apostles, one of the three most highly favoured by his Lord, 'was come to Antioch, I withstood him to the face, because he was to be blamed. For before that certain came from James he did eat with the Gentiles'—the heathens converted to the Christian faith—as having been peculiarly taught of God that he 'should not call any man common or unclean' (Acts 10:28). But 'when they were come, he separated himself, fearing them which were of the circumcision. And the other Jews dissembled likewise with him; insomuch that Barnabas also was carried away with their dissimulation. But when I saw that they walked not uprightly according to the truth of the gospel, I said unto Peter before them all, If thou, being a Jew, livest after the manner of the Gentiles', not regarding the ceremonial law of Moses, 'why compellest thou the Gentiles to live as do the Jews?' (Gal. 2:12–14). Here is also plain undeniable sin, committed by one who was undoubtedly 'born of God'. But how can this be reconciled with the assertion of St. John, if taken in the obvious literal meaning, that 'whosoever is born of God doth not commit sin'?

7. I answer, what has been long observed is this: so long as 'he that is born of God keepeth himself' (which he is able to do, by the grace of God) 'the wicked one toucheth him not.' But if he keepeth not himself, if he abide not in the faith, he may commit sin even as another man.

It is easy therefore to understand how any of these children of God might be moved from his own steadfastness, and yet the great truth of God, declared by the Apostle, remain steadfast and unshaken. He did not keep himself by that grace of God which was sufficient for him. He fell step by step, first into negative, inward sin—not 'stirring up the gift of God' which was in him, not 'watching unto prayer', not 'pressing on to the mark of the prize of his high calling'; then into positive, inward sin—inclining to wickedness with his heart, giving way to some evil desire or temper. Next he lost his faith, his sight of a pardoning God, and consequently his love of God. And being then weak and like another man he was capable of committing even outward sin.

8. To explain this by a particular instance. David was born of God, and saw God by faith. He loved God in sincerity. He could truly say, 'Whom have I in heaven but thee? And there is none upon earth' (neither person or thing) 'that I desire in comparison to thee!' But still there remained in his heart that corruption of nature which is the seed of all evil.

He was 'walking upon the roof of his house' (2 Sam. 11:2), probably praising the God whom his soul loved, when he looked and saw Bathsheba. He felt a temptation, a thought which tended to evil. The Spirit of God did not fail to convince him of this. He doubtless heard and knew the warning voice. But he yielded in some measure to the thought, and the temptation began to prevail over him. Hereby his spirit was sullied. He saw God still; but it was more dimly than before. He loved God still; but not in the same degree, not with the same strength and ardour of affection. Yet God checked him again, though his spirit was grieved; and his voice, though fainter and fainter, still whispered, 'Sin lieth at the door'; 'look unto me, and be thou saved.' But he would not hear. He looked again, not unto God, but unto the forbidden object, till nature was superior to grace, and kindled lust in his soul.

The eye of his mind was now closed again, and God vanished out of his sight. Faith, the divine, supernatural intercourse with God, and the love of God ceased together. He then rushed on as a horse into the battle, and knowingly committed the outward sin.

9. You see the unquestionable progress from grace to sin. Thus it goes on, from step to step. (1) The divine seed of loving, conquering faith remains in him that is 'born of God'. 'He keepeth himself', by the grace of God, and 'cannot commit' sin; (2) A temptation arises, whether from the world, the flesh, or the devil, it matters not; (3) The Spirit of God gives him warning that sin is near, and bids him more abundantly watch unto prayer; (4) He gives way in some degree to the temptation, which now begins to grow pleasing to him;

(5) The Holy Spirit is grieved; his faith is weakened, and his love of God grows cold; (6) The Spirit reproves him more sharply, and saith, 'This is the way; walk thou in it.' (7) He turns away from the painful voice of God and listens to the pleasing voice of the tempter; (8) Evil desire begins and spreads in his soul, till faith and love vanish away; (9) He is then capable of committing outward sin, the power of the Lord being departed from him.

10. To explain this by another instance. The Apostle Peter was full of faith and of the Holy Ghost; and hereby keeping himself he had a conscience void of offence toward God and toward man.

Walking thus in simplicity and godly sincerity, 'before that certain came from James he did eat with the Gentiles', knowing that what God had cleansed was not common or unclean.

But 'when they were come' a temptation arose in his heart to 'fear those of the circumcision' (the Jewish converts who were zealous for circumcision and the other rites of the Mosaic law) and regard the favour and praise of these men more than the praise of God.

He was warned by the Spirit that sin was near. Nevertheless, he yielded to it in some degree, even to sinful fear of man, and his faith and love were proportionably weakened.

God reproved him again for giving place to the devil. Yet he would not hearken to the voice of his Shepherd, but gave himself up to that slavish fear, and thereby quenched the Spirit.

Then God disappeared, and faith and love being extinct he committed the outward sin. 'Walking not uprightly, not according to the truth of the gospel', he 'separated himself' from his Christian brethren, and by his evil example, if not advice also, 'compelled' even 'the Gentiles to live after the manner of the Jews'; to entangle themselves again with that 'yoke of bondage' from which 'Christ had set them free'.

Thus it is unquestionably true that he who is born of God, keeping himself, doth not, cannot commit sin; and yet if he keepeth not himself he may commit all manner of sin with greediness.

III.1. From the preceding considerations we may learn, first, to give a clear and incontestable answer to a question which has frequently perplexed many who were sincere of heart. Does sin precede or follow the loss of faith? Does a child of God first commit sin, and thereby lose his faith? Or does he lose his faith first, before he can commit sin?

I answer: some sin, of omission at least, must necessarily precede the loss of faith—some inward sin. But the loss of faith must precede the committing outward sin.

The more any believer examines his own heart, the more will he be convinced of this: that 'faith working by love' excludes both inward and outward sin from a soul 'watching unto prayer'; that nevertheless we are even then liable to temptation, particularly to the sin that did easily beset us; that if the loving eye of the soul be steadily fixed on God the temptation soon vanishes away. But if not, if we are ἐξελκόμενοι (as the Apostle James speaks), 'drawn out' of God by our 'own desire', and δελεαζόμενοι, 'caught by the bait' of present or promised pleasure: then that 'desire conceived' in us 'brings forth sin'; and having by that inward sin destroyed our faith, it casts us headlong into the snare of the devil, so that we may commit any outward sin whatever.

2. From what has been said we may learn, secondly, what the life of God in the soul of a believer is, wherein it properly consists, and what is immediately and necessarily implied therein. It immediately and necessarily implies the continual inspiration of God's Holy Spirit: God's breathing into the soul, and the soul's breathing back what it first receives from God; a continual action of God upon the soul, and re-action of the soul upon God; an unceasing presence of God, the loving, pardoning God, manifested to the heart, and perceived by faith; and an unceasing return of love, praise, and prayer, offering up all the thoughts of our hearts, all the words of our tongues, all the works of our hands, all our body, soul, and spirit, to be an holy sacrifice, acceptable unto God in Christ Jesus.

3. And hence we may, thirdly, infer the absolute necessity of this re-action of the soul (whatsoever it be called) in order to the continuance of the divine life therein. For it plainly appears God does not continue to act upon the soul unless the soul re-acts upon God. He prevents us indeed with the blessings of his goodness. He first loves us, and manifests himself unto us. While we are yet afar off he calls us to himself, and shines upon our hearts. But if we do not then love him who first loved us; if we will not hearken to his voice; if we turn our eye away from him, and will not attend to the light which he pours upon us: his Spirit will not always strive; he will gradually withdraw, and leave us to the darkness of our own hearts. He will not continue to breathe into our soul unless our soul breathes toward him again; unless our love, and prayer, and thanksgiving return to him, a sacrifice wherewith he is well pleased.

4. Let us learn, lastly, to follow that direction of the great Apostle: 'Be not high-minded, but fear.' Let us fear sin more than death or hell. Let us have a jealous (though not painful) fear, lest we should lean to our own deceitful hearts. 'Let him that standeth take heed lest he fall.' Even he who now standeth fast in the grace of God, in the faith that 'overcometh the world', may nevertheless fall into inward sin, and thereby 'make shipwreck of his faith'. And how easily then will outward sin regain its dominion over him! Thou, therefore, O man of God, watch always, that thou mayest always hear the voice of God. Watch that thou mayest pray without ceasing, at all times and in all places pouring out thy heart before him. So shalt thou always believe, and always love, and never commit sin.

UPON OUR LORD'S SERMON ON THE MOUNT

DISCOURSE IV

Sermon 24 – 1748

AN INTRODUCTORY COMMENT

The unifying theme of Wesley's thirteen 'discourses' on the Sermon on the Mount (Matthew 5–7) is the Christian life understood as the fruit of justifying faith. These sermons are not, however, a thirteen-part essay, tightly organized and argued as a unit. Each is a discourse in its own right. Yet the series is designed so that each appears as a part of a whole and shares a common aim: 'every branch of gospel obedience is asserted and proved to be indispensably necessary to eternal salvation' (letter to John Downes, Nov. 17, 1759). Wesley conceived the design of Matthew 5–7 according to its three unfolding themes: (1) 'the sum of true religion'; (2) 'rules touching that right intention which we are to preserve in all our outward actions'; and (3) 'the main hindrances of this religion'.

After commenting on the Beatitudes in the first three sermons in the series, Discourse IV turns to Christianity as 'a social religion' in which inward holiness (our love of God) prompts outward holiness (love of neighbour). Here Wesley is fleshing out a long-time theme, that the Bible knows nothing of solitary religion. This theme he had stated vigorously against the mystics and Moravians in the introduction to *Hymns and Sacred Poems* (1739): 'The gospel of Christ knows of no religion but social; no holiness but social holiness.' In this instance, he also develops the contrary corollary: 'to turn it into a solitary religion is indeed to destroy it.' Developing the scriptural text further in the second section, Wesley also explains that if true religion abides in the heart, 'it is impossible to conceal it', in spite of all pretences to the contrary. The third section answers the various objections brought against 'being social, open, active Christians.' In some instances, Wesley seems to be answering objections to the specific expectations of the *General Rules*. In every instance, the ruling principle is that outward and inward religion are both necessary.

This sermon was first published in the second volume of his *Sermons on Several Occasions* (1748). Although never reprinted separately, it was published in all subsequent editions of his collected sermons.

Upon our Lord's Sermon on the Mount

Discourse IV

Ye are the salt of the earth. But if the salt hath lost its savour, wherewith shall it be salted? It is thenceforth good for nothing but to be cast out, and trodden under foot of men.

Ye are the light of the world. A city that is set on an hill cannot be hid.

Neither do men light a candle and put it under a bushel, but on a candlestick; and it giveth light to all that are in the house.

Let your light so shine before men that they may see your good works, and glorify your Father which is in heaven.

Matthew 5:13–16

1. The beauty of holiness, of that inward man of the heart which is renewed after the image of God, cannot but strike every eye which God hath opened, every enlightened understanding. The ornament of a meek, humble, loving spirit will at least excite the approbation of all those who are capable in any degree of discerning spiritual good and evil. From the hour men begin to emerge out of the darkness which covers the giddy, unthinking world, they cannot but perceive how desirable a thing it is to be thus transformed into the likeness of him that created us. This inward religion bears the shape of God so visibly impressed upon it that a soul must be wholly immersed in flesh and blood when he can doubt of its divine original. We may say of this, in a secondary sense, even as of the Son of God himself, that it is 'the brightness of his glory, the express image of his person': ἀπαύγασμα τῆς δόξης αὐτοῦ, 'the beaming forth of his' eternal 'glory'; and yet so tempered and softened that even the children of men may herein see God and live: χαρακτὴρ τῆς ὑποστάσεως αὐτοῦ, 'the character, the stamp, the living impression, of his person' who is the fountain of beauty and love, the original source of all excellency and perfection.

2. If religion therefore were carried no farther than this they could have no doubt concerning it—they should have no objection against pursuing it with the whole ardour of their souls. But why, say they, is it clogged with other things? What need of loading it with *doing* and *suffering*? These are what damps the vigour of the soul and sinks it down to earth again. Is it not enough to 'follow after charity'? To soar upon the wings of love? Will it not suffice to worship God, who is a Spirit, with the spirit of our minds, without encumber-

ing ourselves with outward things, or even thinking of them at all? Is it not better that the whole extent of our thought should be taken up with high and heavenly contemplation? And that instead of busying ourselves at all about externals, we should only commune with God in our hearts?

3. Many eminent men have spoken thus: have advised us 'to cease from all outward actions'; wholly to withdraw from the world; to leave the body behind us; to abstract ourselves from all sensible things—to have no concern at all about outward religion, but to 'work all virtues in the will', as the far more excellent way, more perfective of the soul, as well as more acceptable to God.

4. It needed not that any should tell our Lord of this masterpiece of the wisdom from beneath, this fairest of all the devices wherewith Satan hath ever perverted the right ways of the Lord! And Oh! what instruments hath he found from time to time to employ in this his service! To wield this grand engine of hell against some of the most important truths of God! Men that 'would deceive, if it were possible, the very elect', the men of faith and love. Yea, that have for a season deceived and led away no inconsiderable number of them who have fallen in all ages into the gilded snare, and hardly escaped with the skin of their teeth.

5. But has our Lord been wanting on his part? Has he not sufficiently guarded us against this pleasing delusion? Has he not armed us here with armour of proof against Satan 'transformed into an angel of light'? Yea, verily. He here defends, in the clearest and strongest manner, the active, patient religion he had just described. What can be fuller and plainer than the words he immediately subjoins to what he had said of doing and suffering? 'Ye are the salt of the earth. But if the salt have lost its savour, wherewith shall it be salted? It is thenceforth good for nothing but to be cast out and trodden under foot of men. Ye are the light of the world. A city that is set on an hill cannot be hid. Neither do men light a candle and put it under a bushel, but on a candlestick; and it giveth light to all that are in the house. Let your light so shine before men that they may see your good works, and glorify your Father which is in heaven.'

In order fully to explain and enforce these important words I shall endeavour to show, first, that Christianity is essentially a social religion, and that to turn it into a solitary one is to destroy it; secondly, that to conceal this religion is impossible, as well as utterly contrary to the design of its author. I shall, thirdly, answer some objections; and conclude the whole with a practical application.

I. 1. First, I shall endeavour to show that Christianity is essentially a social religion, and that to turn it into a solitary religion is indeed to destroy it.

By Christianity I mean that method of worshipping God which is here revealed to man by Jesus Christ. When I say this is essentially a social religion,

I mean not only that it cannot subsist so well, but that it cannot subsist at all without society, without living and conversing with other men. And in showing this I shall confine myself to those considerations which will arise from the very discourse before us. But if this be shown, then doubtless to turn this religion into a solitary one is to destroy it.

Not that we can in any wise condemn the intermixing solitude or retirement with society. This is not only allowable but expedient; nay, it is necessary, as daily experience shows, for everyone that either already is or desires to be a real Christian. It can hardly be that we should spend one entire day in a continued intercourse with men without suffering loss in our soul, and in some measure grieving the Holy Spirit of God. We have need daily to retire from the world, at least morning and evening, to converse with God, to commune more freely with our Father which is in secret. Nor indeed can a man of experience condemn even longer seasons of religious retirement, so they do not imply any neglect of the worldly employ wherein the providence of God has placed us.

2. Yet such retirement must not swallow up all our time; this would be to destroy, not advance, true religion. For that the religion described by our Lord in the foregoing words cannot subsist without society, without our living and conversing with other men, is manifest from hence, that several of the most essential branches thereof can have no place if we have no intercourse with the world.

3. There is no disposition, for instance, which is more essential to Christianity than meekness. Now although this, as it implies resignation to God, or patience in pain and sickness, may subsist in a desert, in a hermit's cell, in total solitude; yet as it implies (which it no less necessarily does) mildness, gentleness, and long-suffering, it cannot possibly have a being, it has no place under heaven, without an intercourse with other men. So that to attempt turning this into a solitary virtue is to destroy it from the face of the earth.

4. Another necessary branch of true Christianity is peacemaking, or doing of good. That this is equally essential with any of the other parts of the religion of Jesus Christ there can be no stronger argument to evince (and therefore it would be absurd to allege any other) than that it is here inserted in the original plan he has laid down of the fundamentals of his religion. Therefore to set aside this is the same daring insult on the authority of our great Master as to set aside mercifulness, purity of heart, or any other branch of his institution. But this is apparently set aside by all who call us to the wilderness, who recommend entire solitude either to the babes, or the young men, or the fathers in Christ. For will any man affirm that a solitary Christian (so called, though it is little less than a contradiction in terms) can be a merciful man—that is, one that takes every opportunity of doing all good to all men? What can be

more plain than that this fundamental branch of the religion of Jesus Christ cannot possibly subsist without society, without our living and conversing with other men?

5. But is it not expedient, however (one might naturally ask), to converse only with good men? Only with those whom we know to be meek and merciful, holy of heart and holy of life? Is it not expedient to refrain from any conversation or intercourse with men of the opposite character? Men who do not obey, perhaps do not believe, the gospel of our Lord Jesus Christ? The advice of St. Paul to the Christians at Corinth may seem to favour this: 'I wrote unto you in an epistle not to company with fornicators' (1 Cor. 5:9). And it is certainly not advisable so to company with them, or with any of the workers of iniquity, as to have any particular familiarity, or any strictness of friendship with them. To contract or continue an intimacy with any such is no way expedient for a Christian. It must necessarily expose him to abundance of dangers and snares, out of which he can have no reasonable hope of deliverance.

But the Apostle does not forbid us to have any intercourse at all, even with the men that know not God. For then, says he, 'ye must needs go out of the world,' which he could never advise them to do. But, he subjoins, 'If any man that is called a brother', that professes himself a Christian, 'be a fornicator, or covetous, or an idolater, or a railer, or a drunkard, or an extortioner', 'now I have written unto you not to keep company' with him; 'with such an one, no, not to eat' (1 Cor. 5:11). This must necessarily imply that we break off all familiarity, all intimacy of acquaintance with him. 'Yet count him not', saith the Apostle elsewhere, 'as an enemy, but admonish him as a brother' (2 Thess. 3:15): plainly showing that even in such a case as this we are not to renounce all fellowship with him; so that here is no advice to separate wholly, even from wicked men. Yea, these very words teach us quite the contrary.

6. Much more the words of our Lord, who is so far from directing us to break off all commerce with the world that without it, according to his account of Christianity, we cannot be Christians at all. It would be easy to show that some intercourse even with ungodly and unholy men is absolutely needful in order to the full exertion of every temper which he has described as the way of the kingdom; that it is indispensably necessary in order to the complete exercise of poverty of spirit, of mourning, and of every other disposition which has a place here in the genuine religion of Jesus Christ. Yea, it is necessary to the very being of several of them; of that meekness, for example, which instead of demanding 'an eye for an eye, or a tooth for a tooth', doth 'not resist evil', but causes us rather, when smitten 'on the right cheek, to turn the other also'; of that mercifulness whereby 'we love our enemies, bless them that curse us, do good to them that hate us, and pray for them which despitefully use us and persecute us'; and of that complication of love and all holy tempers which is

exercised in suffering for righteousness' sake. Now all these, it is clear, could have no being were we to have no commerce with any but real Christians.

7. Indeed, were we wholly to separate ourselves from sinners, how could we possibly answer that character which our Lord gives us in these very words: 'Ye' (Christians, ye that are lowly, serious and meek; ye that hunger after righteousness, that love God and man, that do good to all, and therefore suffer evil: Ye) 'are the salt of the earth.' It is your very nature to season whatever is round about you. It is the nature of the divine savour which is in you to spread to whatsoever you touch; to diffuse itself on every side, to all those among whom you are. This is the great reason why the providence of God has so mingled you together with other men, that whatever grace you have received of God may through you be communicated to others; that every holy temper, and word, and work of yours, may have an influence on them also. By this means a check will in some measure be given to the corruption which is in the world; and a small part, at least, saved from the general infection, and rendered holy and pure before God.

8. That we may the more diligently labour to season all we can with every holy and heavenly temper, our Lord proceeds to show the desperate state of those who do not impart the religion they have received; which indeed they cannot possibly fail to do, so long as it remains in their own hearts. 'If the salt have lost its savour, wherewith shall it be salted? It is thenceforth good for nothing but to be cast out, and trodden under foot of men.' If ye who were holy and heavenly-minded, and consequently zealous of good works, have no longer that savour in yourselves, and do therefore no longer season others; if you are grown flat, insipid, dead, both careless of your own soul and useless to the souls of other men, 'wherewith shall' ye 'be salted?' How shall ye be recovered? What help? What hope? Can tasteless salt be restored to its savour? No; 'it is thenceforth good for nothing but to be cast out', even as the mire in the streets, 'and to be trodden under foot of men,' to be overwhelmed with everlasting contempt. If ye had never known the Lord there might have been hope—if ye had never been 'found in him'. But what can you now say to that his solemn declaration, just parallel to what he hath here spoken? 'Every branch in me that beareth not fruit, he (the Father) taketh away. . . . He that abideth in me, and I in him, bringeth forth much fruit. . . . If a man abide not in me' (or, do not bring forth fruit) 'he is cast out as a branch, and withered; and men gather them' (not to plant them again, but) 'to cast them into the fire' (John 15:2, 5–6).

9. Toward those who have never tasted of the good word God is indeed pitiful and of tender mercy. But justice takes place with regard to those who have tasted that the Lord is gracious, and have afterwards 'turned back from the holy commandment then delivered to them'. 'For it is impossible for those who were once enlightened', in whose hearts God had once shined, to

enlighten them with the knowledge of the glory of God in the face of Jesus Christ; who 'have tasted of the heavenly gift' of redemption in his blood, the forgiveness of sins; 'and were made partakers of the Holy Ghost'—of lowliness, of meekness, and of the love of God and man shed abroad in their hearts by the Holy Ghost which was given unto them—'and have fallen away', καὶ παραπεσόντας (here is not a supposition, but a flat declaration of matter of fact), 'to renew them again unto repentance; seeing they crucify to themselves the Son of God afresh, and put him to an open shame' (Heb. 6:4, etc.).

But that none may misunderstand these awful words it should be carefully observed, (1) who they are that are here spoken of; namely they, and they only, who 'were once' thus 'enlightened'; they only 'who did taste of that heavenly gift, and were' thus 'made partakers of the Holy Ghost'. So that all who have not experienced these things are wholly unconcerned in this Scripture. (2) What that falling away is which is here spoken of. It is an absolute, total apostasy. A believer may fall, and not fall away. He may fall and rise again. And if he should fall, even into sin, yet this case, dreadful as it is, is not desperate. For 'we have an advocate with the Father, Jesus Christ the righteous; and he is the propitiation for our sins.' But let him above all things beware lest his 'heart be hardened by the deceitfulness of sin'; lest he should sink lower and lower till he wholly fall away, till he become as 'salt that hath lost its savour': 'For if we thus sin wilfully, after we have received the' experimental 'knowledge of the truth, there remaineth no more sacrifice for sins; but a certain, fearful looking for of fiery indignation, which shall devour the adversaries.'

II. 1. 'But although we may not wholly separate ourselves from mankind; although it be granted we ought to season them with the religion which God has wrought in our hearts; yet may not this be done insensibly? May we not convey this into others in a secret and almost imperceptible manner? So that scarce anyone shall be able to observe how or when it is done? Even as salt conveys its own savour into that which is seasoned thereby, without any noise, and without being liable to any outward observation. And if so, although we do not go out of the world, yet we may lie hid in it. We may thus far keep our religion to ourselves, and not offend those whom we cannot help.'

2. Of this plausible reasoning of flesh and blood our Lord was well aware also. And he has given a full answer to it in those words which come now to be considered: in explaining which I shall endeavour to show, as I proposed to do in the second place, that so long as true religion abides in our hearts it is impossible to conceal it, as well as absolutely contrary to the design of its great author.

And, first, it is impossible for any that have it to conceal the religion of Jesus Christ. This our Lord makes plain beyond all contradiction by a twofold comparison: 'Ye are the light of the world. A city set upon an hill cannot be hid.'

'Ye' Christians 'are the light of the world,' with regard both to your tempers and actions. Your holiness makes you as conspicuous as the sun in the midst of heaven. As ye cannot go out of the world, so neither can ye stay in it without appearing to all mankind. Ye may not flee from men, and while ye are among them it is impossible to hide your lowliness and meekness and those other dispositions whereby ye aspire to be perfect, as your Father which is in heaven is perfect. Love cannot be hid any more than light; and least of all when it shines forth in action, when ye exercise yourselves in the labour of love, in beneficence of every kind. As well may men think to hide a city as to hide a Christian: yea, as well may they conceal a city set upon a hill as a holy, zealous, active lover of God and man.

3. It is true, men who love darkness rather than light, because their deeds are evil, will take all possible pains to prove that the light which is in you is darkness. They will say evil, all manner of evil, falsely, of the good which is in you: they will lay to your charge that which is farthest from your thoughts, which is the very reverse of all you are and all you do. And your patient continuance in well-doing, your meek suffering all things for the Lord's sake, your calm, humble joy in the midst of persecution, your unwearied labour to overcome evil with good, will make you still more visible and conspicuous than ye were before.

4. So impossible it is to keep our religion from being seen, unless we cast it away; so vain is the thought of hiding the light, unless by putting it out. Sure it is that a secret, unobserved religion cannot be the religion of Jesus Christ. Whatever religion can be concealed is not Christianity. If a Christian could be hid, he could not be compared to a city set upon an hill; to the light of the world, the sun shining from heaven and seen by all the world below. Never therefore let it enter into the heart of him whom God hath renewed in the spirit of his mind to hide that light, to keep his religion to himself; especially considering it is not only impossible to conceal true Christianity, but likewise absolutely contrary to the design of the great Author of it.

5. This plainly appears from the following words: 'Neither do men light a candle, to put it under a bushel.' As if he had said, 'As men do not light a candle only to cover or conceal it, so neither does God enlighten any soul with his glorious knowledge and love to have it covered or concealed, either by prudence, falsely so called, or shame, or voluntary humility; to have it hid either in a desert, or in the world; either by avoiding men, or in conversing with them. "But they put it on a candlestick, and it giveth light to all that are in the house."' In like manner it is the design of God that every Christian should be in an open point of view; that he may give light to all around; that he may visibly express the religion of Jesus Christ.

6. Thus hath God in all ages spoken to the world, not only by precept but by example also. He hath 'not left himself without witness' in any nation where the sound of the gospel hath gone forth, without a few who testified his truth by their lives as well as their words. These have been 'as lights shining in a dark place'. And from time to time they have been the means of enlightening some, of preserving a remnant, a little seed, which was 'counted unto the Lord for a generation'. They have led a few poor sheep out of the darkness of the world, and guided their feet into the way of peace.

7. One might imagine that where both Scripture and the reason of things speak so clearly and expressly there could not be much advanced on the other side, at least not with any appearance of truth. But they who imagine thus know little of the depths of Satan. After all that Scripture and reason have said, so exceeding plausible are the pretences for solitary religion, for a Christian's going out of the world, or at least hiding himself in it, that we need all the wisdom of God to see through the snare, and all the power of God to escape it—so many and strong are the objections which have been brought against being social, open, active Christians.

III. 1. To answer these was the third thing which I proposed. And, first, it has been often objected that religion does not lie in outward things but in the heart, the inmost soul; that it is the union of the soul with God, the life of God in the soul of man; that outside religion is nothing worth; seeing God 'delighteth not in burnt offerings', in outward services, but a pure and holy heart is 'the sacrifice he will not despise'.

I answer, it is most true that the root of religion lies in the heart, in the inmost soul; that this is the union of the soul with God, the life of God in the soul of man. But if this root be really in the heart it cannot but put forth branches. And these are the several instances of outward obedience, which partake of the same nature with the root, and consequently are not only marks or signs, but substantial parts of religion.

It is also true that bare, outside religion, which has no root in the heart, is nothing worth; that God delighteth not in *such* outward services, no more than in Jewish burnt offerings, and that a pure and holy heart is a sacrifice with which he is always well pleased. But he is also well pleased with all that outward service which arises from the heart; with the sacrifice of our prayers (whether public or private), of our praises and thanksgivings; with the sacrifice of our goods, humbly devoted to him, and employed wholly to his glory; and with that of our bodies, which he peculiarly claims; which the Apostle 'beseeches us, by the mercies of God, to present unto him, a living sacrifice, holy, acceptable to God'.

2. A second objection, nearly related to this, is that love is all in all: that it is 'the fulfilling of the law', 'the end of the commandment', of every command-

ment of God; that all we do and all we suffer, if we have not charity or love, profiteth us nothing; and therefore the Apostle directs us to 'follow after charity', and terms this, the 'more excellent way'.

I answer, it is granted that the love of God and man arising from 'faith unfeigned' is all in all 'the fulfilling of the law', the end of every commandment of God. It is true that without this whatever we do, whatever we suffer, profits us nothing. But it does not follow that love is all [in all] in such a sense as to supersede either faith or good works. It is 'the fulfilling of the law', not by releasing us from but by constraining us to obey it. It is 'the end of the commandment' as every commandment leads to and centres in it. It is allowed that whatever we do or suffer, without love, profits us nothing. But withal whatever we do or suffer in love, though it were only the suffering reproach for Christ, or the giving a cup of cold water in his name, it shall in no wise lose its reward.

3. 'But does not the Apostle direct us to "follow after charity"? And does he not term it "a more excellent way"?' He does direct us to 'follow after charity'; but not after that alone. His words are, 'Follow after charity; and desire spiritual gifts' (1 Cor. 14:1). Yea, 'follow after charity,' and desire to spend and to be spent for your brethren. 'Follow after charity'; and as you have opportunity do good to all men.

In the same verse also wherein he terms this, the way of love, 'a more excellent way', he directs the Corinthians to desire other gifts besides it; yea, to desire them earnestly. 'Covet earnestly', saith he, 'the best gifts: and yet I show unto you a more excellent way' (1 Cor. 12:31). More excellent than what? Than the gifts of 'healing', of 'speaking with tongues', and of 'interpreting', mentioned in the preceding verse. But not more excellent than the way of obedience. Of this the Apostle is not speaking; neither is he speaking of outward religion at all. So that this text is quite wide of the present question.

But suppose the Apostle had been speaking of outward as well as inward religion, and comparing them together; suppose in the comparison he had given the preference ever so much to the latter; suppose he had preferred (as he justly might) a loving heart before all outward works whatever. Yet it would not follow that we were to reject either one or the other. No; God hath joined them together from the beginning of the world. And let not man put them asunder.

4. 'But "God is a Spirit, and they that worship him must worship him in spirit and in truth". And is not this enough? Nay, ought we not to employ the whole strength of our mind herein? Does not attending to outward things clog the soul, that it cannot soar aloft in holy contemplation? Does it not damp the vigour of our thought? Has it not a natural tendency to encumber and distract the mind? Whereas St. Paul would have us "to be without carefulness", and to "wait upon the Lord without distraction".'

I answer, 'God is a Spirit, and they that worship him must worship him in spirit and in truth.' Yea, and this is enough: we ought to employ the whole strength of our mind therein. But then I would ask, 'What is it to worship God, a Spirit, in spirit and in truth?' Why, it is to worship him with our spirit; to worship him in that manner which none but spirits are capable of. It is to believe in him as a wise, just, holy being, of purer eyes than to behold iniquity; and yet merciful, gracious, and long-suffering; forgiving iniquity and transgression and sin; casting all our sins behind his back, and accepting us in the beloved. It is to love him, to delight in him, to desire him, with all our heart and mind and soul and strength; to imitate him we love by purifying ourselves, even as he is pure; and to obey him whom we love, and in whom we believe, both in thought and word and work. Consequently one branch of the worshipping God in spirit and in truth is the keeping his outward commandments. To glorify him therefore with our bodies as well as with our spirits, to go through outward work with hearts lifted up to him, to make our daily employment a sacrifice to God, to buy and sell, to eat and drink to his glory: this is worshipping God in spirit and in truth as much as the praying to him in a wilderness.

5. But if so, then contemplation is only one way of worshipping God in spirit and in truth. Therefore to give ourselves up entirely to this would be to destroy many branches of spiritual worship, all equally acceptable to God, and equally profitable, not hurtful, to the soul. For it is a great mistake to suppose that an attention to those outward things whereto the providence of God hath called us is any clog to a Christian, or any hindrance at all to his always seeing him that is invisible. It does not at all damp the ardour of his thought; it does not encumber or distract his mind; it gives him no uneasy or hurtful care who does it all as unto the Lord: who hath learned whatsoever he doth, in word or deed, to do all in the name of the Lord Jesus; having only one eye of the soul which moves round on outward things, and one immovably fixed on God. Learn what this meaneth, ye poor recluses, that you may clearly discern your own littleness of faith. Yea, that you may no longer judge others by yourselves, go and learn what that meaneth:

> Thou, O Lord, in tender love
>   Dost all my burdens bear;
> Lift my heart to things above,
>   And fix it ever there.
> Calm on tumult's wheel I sit,
> Midst busy multitudes alone,
> Sweetly waiting at thy feet,
>   Till all thy will be done.

6. But the grand objection is still behind. 'We appeal', say they, 'to

experience. Our light did shine: we used outward things many years; and yet they profited nothing. We attended on all the ordinances; but we were no better for it–nor indeed anyone else. Nay, we were the worse. For we fancied ourselves Christians for so doing, when we knew not what Christianity meant.'

I allow the fact. I allow that you and ten thousand more have thus abused the ordinances of God, mistaking the means for the end, supposing that the doing these or some other outward works either was the religion of Jesus Christ or would be accepted in the place of it. But let the abuse be taken away and the use remain. Now use all outward things; but use them with a constant eye to the renewal of your soul in righteousness and true holiness.

7. But this is not all. They affirm: 'Experience likewise shows that the trying to do good is but lost labour. What does it avail to feed or clothe men's bodies if they are just dropping into everlasting fire? And what good can any man do to their souls? If these are changed, God doth it himself. Besides, all men are either good, at least desirous so to be, or obstinately evil. Now the former have no need of us. Let them ask help of God, and it shall be given them. And the latter will receive no help from us. Nay, and our Lord forbids to "cast our pearls before swine".'

I answer, (1) whether they will finally be lost or saved, you are expressly commanded to feed the hungry and clothe the naked. If you can and do not, whatever becomes of them, you shall go away into everlasting fire. (2) Though it is God only changes hearts, yet he generally doth it by man. It is our part to do all that in us lies as diligently as if we could change them ourselves, and then to leave the event to him. (3) God, in answer to their prayers, builds up his children by each other in every good gift, nourishing and strengthening the whole 'body by that which every joint supplieth'. So that 'the eye cannot say to the hand, I have no need of thee'; no, nor even 'the head to the feet, I have no need of you'. Lastly, how are you assured that the persons before you are dogs or swine? Judge them not until you have tried. 'How knowest thou, O man, but thou mayst gain thy brother,' but thou mayst, under God, save his soul from death? When he spurns thy love and blasphemes the good word, then it is time to give him up to God.

8. 'We have tried. We have laboured to reform sinners. And what did it avail? On many we could make no impression at all. And if some were changed for a while, yet their goodness was but as the morning dew, and they were soon as bad, nay worse than ever. So that we only hurt them–and ourselves too; for our minds were hurried and discomposed; perhaps filled with anger instead of love. Therefore we had better have kept our religion to ourselves.'

It is very possible this fact also may be true, that you have tried to do good and have not succeeded; yea, that those who seemed reformed relapsed into sin, and their last state was worse than the first. And what marvel? Is the servant above his master? But how often did he strive to save sinners! And they would not hear; or when they had followed him awhile they turned back as a dog to his vomit. But he did not therefore desist from striving to do good. No more should you, whatever your success be. It is your part to do as you are commanded: the event is in the hand of God. You are not accountable for this: leave it to him who orders all things well. 'In the morning sow thy seed, and in the evening withhold not thy hand; for thou knowest not whether shall prosper' (Eccles. 11:6).

'But the trial hurries and frets your own soul.' Perhaps it did so for this very reason, because you thought you was accountable for the event—which no man is, nor indeed can be. Or perhaps because you was off your guard; you was not watchful over your own spirit. But this is no reason for disobeying God. Try again; but try more warily than before. Do good (as you forgive) 'not seven times only; but until seventy times seven.' Only be wiser by experience: attempt it every time more cautiously than before. Be more humbled before God, more deeply convinced that of yourself you can do nothing. Be more jealous over your own spirit, more gentle and watchful unto prayer. Thus 'cast your bread upon the waters, and you shall find it again after many days.'

IV. 1. Notwithstanding all these plausible pretences for hiding it, 'Let your light so shine before men that they may see your good works, and glorify your Father which is in heaven.' This is the practical application which our Lord himself makes of the foregoing considerations.

'Let your light so shine'—your lowliness of heart, your gentleness and meekness of wisdom; your serious, weighty concern for the things of eternity, and sorrow for the sins and miseries of men; your earnest desire of universal holiness and full happiness in God; your tender goodwill to all mankind, and fervent love to your supreme benefactor. Endeavour not to conceal this light wherewith God hath enlightened your soul, but let it 'shine before men', before all with whom you are, in the whole tenor of your conversation. Let it shine still more eminently in your actions, in your doing all possible good to all men; and in your suffering for righteousness' sake, while you 'rejoice and are exceeding glad, knowing that great is your reward in heaven'.

2. 'Let your light so shine before men that they may see your good works': so far let a Christian be from ever designing or desiring to conceal his religion. On the contrary let it be your desire not to conceal it, not to put the 'light under a bushel'. Let it be your care to place it 'on a candlestick, that it may give light to all that are in the house'. Only take heed not to seek your own praise herein, not to desire any honour to yourselves. But let it be your sole aim that all who see your good works may 'glorify your Father which is in heaven'.

3. Be this your one ultimate end in all things. With this view be plain, open, undisguised. Let your love be without dissimulation. Why should you hide

fair, disinterested love? Let there be no guile found in your mouth: let your words be the genuine picture of your heart. Let there be no darkness or reservedness in your conversation, no disguise in your behaviour. Leave this to those who have other designs in view—designs which will not bear the light. Be ye artless and simple to all mankind, that all may see the grace of God which is in you. And although some will harden their hearts, yet others will take knowledge that ye have been with Jesus, and by returning themselves 'to the great Bishop of their souls', 'glorify your Father which is in heaven'.

4. With this one design, that men may 'glorify God in you', go on in his name and in the power of his might. Be not ashamed even to stand alone, so it be in the ways of God. Let the light which is in your heart shine in all good works, both works of piety and works of mercy. And in order to enlarge your ability of doing good, renounce all superfluities. Cut off all unnecessary expense, in food, in furniture, in apparel. Be a good steward of every gift of God, even of these his lowest gifts. Cut off all unnecessary expense of time, all needless or useless employments. And 'whatsoever thy hand findeth to do, do it with thy might.' In a word, be thou full of faith and love; do good; suffer evil. And herein be thou 'steadfast, unmovable'; yea, 'always abounding in the work of the Lord; forasmuch as thou knowest that thy labour is not in vain in the Lord.'

UPON OUR LORD'S SERMON ON THE MOUNT

DISCOURSE V

Sermon 25 – 1748

AN INTRODUCTORY TEXT

Wesley's interest in Matthew 5-7 was not with critical textual or historical problems. He felt that the Sermon on the Mount was the only Gospel passage where Christ designed 'to lay down at once the whole plan of his religion, to give us a full, prospect of Christianity'. We catch here then Wesley's sense of the wholeness of the message he is interpreting, his conviction of the honest integration of a profoundly ethical evangel with an ethic that is also vividly evangelical. This set of sermons, as much as any, highlight Wesley's distinctive concern for integration and balance–between the faith that justifies and the faith that works by love.

In Discourse V, Wesley is most concerned with the balance of law and gospel. The law points us to the gospel, and the gospel leads us to a 'more exact' fulfilling of the law. Wesley's manner of relating law and gospel hinges upon a view of grace that can prove the maxim he had long held: 'every command in Holy Writ is only a covered promise.' He is not hesitant to agree with Jesus' expectation that our righteousness should 'exceed the righteousness of the scribes and Pharisees', whom he then describes in some detail as being 'singularly good'. The specifics of this pattern coincide exactly with the three-fold structure of the *General Rules*: do no harm (avoid evil), do good, and attend the ordinances of God (use the means of grace). These external actions (the righteousness of the law) should then be both met and exceeded by the Christian, whose righteousness is manifest in the internal dispositions that comprise 'the religion of the heart', characterized by a list of virtues ranging from poverty of spirit to purity of heart.

This sermon was first published in the second volume of his *Sermons on Several Occasions* (1748), and like most of the other thirteen essays in this series, was reprinted only in collected rather than separate editions.

Upon our Lord's Sermon on the Mount
Discourse V

Think not that I am come to destroy the law or the prophets: I am not come to destroy, but to fulfil.

For verily I say unto you, Till heaven and earth pass, one jot or one tittle shall in no wise pass from the law, till all be fulfilled.

Whosoever therefore shall break one of these least commandments, and shall teach men so, he shall be called the least in the kingdom of heaven; but whosoever shall do and teach them, the same shall be called great in the kingdom of heaven.

For verily I say unto you, That except your righteousness shall exceed the righteousness of the scribes and Pharisees, ye shall in no case enter into the kingdom of heaven.

Matthew 5:17–20

1. Among the multitude of reproaches which fell upon him who was 'despised and rejected of men', it could not fail to be one that he was a teacher of novelties, an introducer of a *new religion*. This might be affirmed with the more colour because many of the expressions he had used were not common among the Jews: either they did not use them at all, or not in the same sense, not in so full and strong a meaning. Add to this that the worshipping God 'in spirit and in truth' must always appear a new religion to those who have hitherto known nothing but outside worship, nothing but the 'form of godliness'.

2. And 'tis not improbable some might hope it was so, that he was abolishing the old religion and bringing in another, one which they might flatter themselves would be an easier way to heaven. But our Lord refutes in these words both the vain hopes of the one and the groundless calumnies of the other.

I shall consider them in the same order as they lie, taking each verse for a distinct head of discourse.

I.1. And, first, 'think not that I am come to destroy the law or the prophets. I am not come to destroy, but to fulfil.'

The ritual or ceremonial law delivered by Moses to the children of Israel, containing all the injunctions and ordinances which related to the old sacrifices and service of the temple, our Lord indeed did come to destroy, to dissolve and utterly abolish. To this bear all the apostles witness: not only Barnabas and Paul, who vehemently withstood those who taught that Christians ought 'to keep the law of Moses' (Acts 15:5); not only St. Peter, who termed the insisting on this, on the observance of the ritual law, a[s] 'tempting God, and putting a yoke upon the neck of the disciples which neither our fathers (saith he) nor we were able to bear' (Acts 15:10); but 'all the apostles, elders, and brethren, being assembled with one accord', declared that to command them to keep this law was to 'subvert their souls'; and that 'it seemed good to the Holy Ghost and to them to lay no such burden upon them' (Acts 15:24, etc.). This 'handwriting of ordinances our Lord did blot out, take away, and nail to his cross.'

2. But the moral law, contained in the Ten Commandments, and enforced by the prophets, he did not take away. It was not the design of his coming to revoke any part of this. This is a law which never can be broken, which 'stands fast as the faithful witness in heaven'. The moral stands on an entirely different foundation from the ceremonial or ritual law, which was only designed for a temporary restraint upon a disobedient and stiff-necked people; whereas this was from the beginning of the world, being 'written not on tables of stone' but on the hearts of all the children of men when they came out of the hands of the Creator. And however the letters once wrote by the finger of God are now in a great measure defaced by sin, yet can they not wholly be blotted out while we have any consciousness of good and evil. Every part of this law must remain in force, upon all mankind, and in all ages; as not depending either on time or place, or any other circumstances liable to change, but on the nature of God and the nature of man, and their unchangeable relation to each other.

3. 'I am not come to destroy, but to fulfil.' Some have conceived our Lord to mean, I am come to fulfil this by my entire and perfect obedience to it. And it cannot be doubted but he did in this sense fulfil every part of it. But this does not appear to be what he intends here, being foreign to the scope of his present discourse. Without question his meaning in this place is (consistently with all that goes before and follows after): I am come to establish it in its fullness, in spite of all the glosses of men; I am come to place in a full and clear view whatsoever was dark or obscure therein; I am come to declare the true and full import of every part of it; to show the length and breadth, the entire extent of every commandment contained therein, and the height and depth, the inconceivable purity and spirituality of it in all its branches.

4. And this our Lord has abundantly performed in the preceding and subsequent parts of the discourse before us, in which he has not introduced a new religion into the world, but the same which was from the beginning: a religion the substance of which is, without question, 'as old as the creation'; being coeval with man, and having proceeded from God at the very time when

'man became a living soul'. (The substance, I say, for some circumstances of it now relate to man as a fallen creature); a religion witnessed to both by the law and by the prophets in all succeeding generations. Yet was it never so fully explained nor so thoroughly understood till the great Author of it himself condescended to give mankind this authentic comment on all the essential branches of it; at the same time declaring it should never be changed, but remain in force to the end of the world.

II.1. 'For verily I say unto you' (a solemn preface, which denotes both the importance and certainty of what is spoken), 'Till heaven and earth pass, one jot or one tittle shall in no wise pass from the law till all be fulfilled.'

'One jot'—it is literally, *not one iota,* not the most inconsiderable vowel; 'or one tittle', μία κεραία, one corner, or point of a consonant. It is a proverbial expression which signifies that no one commandment contained in the moral law, nor the least part of one, however inconsiderable it might seem, should ever be disannulled.

'Shall in no wise pass from the law'; οὐ μὴ παρέλθῃ ἀπὸ τοῦ νόμου. The double negative here used strengthens the sense so as to admit of no contradiction. And the word παρέλθῃ, it may be observed, is not barely *future,* declaring what *will* be; but has likewise the force of an *imperative,* ordering what *shall* be. It is a word of authority, expressing the sovereign will and power of him that spake, of him whose word is the law of heaven and earth, and stands fast for ever and ever.

'One jot or one tittle shall in no wise pass till heaven and earth pass'; or as it is expressed immediately after, ἕως ἂν πάντα γένηται, 'till all' (or rather, *all things*) 'be fulfilled', till the consummation of all things. Here is therefore no room for that poor evasion (with which some have delighted themselves greatly) that 'no part of the law was to pass away till *all the law* was fulfilled; but it has been fulfilled by Christ, and therefore now must pass, for the gospel to be established.' Not so; the word 'all' does not mean all the law, but all things in the universe; as neither has the term 'fulfilled' any reference to the law, but to all things in heaven and earth.

2. From all this we may learn that there is no contrariety at all between the law and the gospel; that there is no need for the law to pass away in order to the establishing of the gospel. Indeed neither of them supersedes the other, but they agree perfectly well together. Yea, the very same words, considered in different respects, are parts both of the law and of the gospel. If they are considered as commandments, they are parts of the law: if as promises, of the gospel. Thus, 'Thou shalt love the Lord thy God with all thy heart,' when considered as a commandment, is a branch of the law; when regarded as a promise, is an essential part of the gospel—the gospel being no other than the commands of the law proposed by way of promises. Accordingly poverty of

spirit, purity of heart, and whatever else is enjoined in the holy law of God, are no other, when viewed in a gospel light, than so many great and precious promises.

3. There is therefore the closest connection that can be conceived between the law and the gospel. On the one hand the law continually makes way for and points us to the gospel; on the other the gospel continually leads us to a more exact fulfilling of the law. The law, for instance, requires us to love God, to love our neighbour, to be meek, humble, or holy. We feel that we are not sufficient for these things, yea, that 'with man this is impossible.' But we see a promise of God to give us that love, and to make us humble, meek, and holy. We lay hold of this gospel, of these glad tidings: it is done unto us according to our faith, and 'the righteousness of the law is fulfilled in us' through faith which is in Christ Jesus.

We may yet farther observe that every command in Holy Writ is only a covered promise. For by that solemn declaration, 'This is the covenant I will make after those days, saith the Lord; I will put my laws in your minds, and write them in your hearts,' God hath engaged to give whatsoever he commands. Does he command us then to 'pray without ceasing'? To 'rejoice evermore'? To be 'holy as he is holy'? It is enough. He will work in us this very thing. It shall be unto us according to his word.

4. But if these things are so, we cannot be at a loss what to think of those who in all ages of the church have undertaken to change or supersede some commands of God, as they professed, by the peculiar direction of his Spirit. Christ has here given us an infallible rule whereby to judge of all such pretentions. Christianity, as it includes the whole moral law of God, both by way of injunction and of promise, if we will hear him, is designed of God to be the last of all his dispensations. There is no other to come after this. This is to endure till the consummation of all things. Of consequence all such new revelations are of Satan, and not of God; and all pretences to another more perfect dispensation fall to the ground of course. 'Heaven and earth shall pass away; but this word shall not pass away.'

III.1. 'Whosoever therefore shall break one of these least commandments, and shall teach men so, he shall be called the least in the kingdom of heaven; but whosoever shall do and teach them, the same shall be called great in the kingdom of heaven.'

Who, what are they that make 'the preaching of the law' a character of reproach? Do they not see on whom their reproach must fall? On whose head it must light at last? Whosoever on this ground despiseth us, despiseth him that sent us. For did ever any man preach the law like him? Even when he 'came not to condemn but to save the world'; when he came purposely to bring 'life and immortality to light through the gospel'. Can any 'preach the law' more expressly, more rigorously, than Christ does in these words? And who is he that shall amend them? Who is he that shall instruct the Son of God how to preach? Who will teach him a better way of delivering the message which he hath received of the Father?

2. 'Whosoever shall break one of these least commandments', or one of the least of these commandments. 'These commandments', we may observe, is a term used by our Lord as equivalent with 'the law', or the 'law and the prophets', which is the same thing, seeing the prophets added nothing to the law, but only declared, explained, or enforced it, as they were moved by the Holy Ghost.

'Whosoever shall break one of these least commandments', especially if it be done wilfully or presumptuously. *One*—for 'he that keepeth the whole law and' thus 'offends in one point, is guilty of all': the wrath of God abideth on him as surely as if he had broken every one. So that no allowance is made for one darling lust; no reserve for one idol; no excuse for refraining from all besides, and only giving way to one bosom sin. What God demands is an entire obedience; we are to have an eye to all his commandments; otherwise we lose all the labour we take in keeping some, and our poor souls for ever and ever.

'One of these least', or one of the least of these 'commandments'. Here is another excuse cut off, whereby many, who cannot deceive God, miserably deceive their own souls. 'This sin, saith the sinner, is it not a little one? Will not the Lord spare me in this thing? Surely he will not be extreme to mark this, since I do not offend in the greater matters of the law.' Vain hope! Speaking after the manner of men we may term these great, and those little commandments. But in reality they are not so. If we use propriety of speech there is no such thing as a little sin, every sin being a transgression of the holy and perfect law, and an affront of the great majesty of heaven.

3. 'And shall teach men so'—In some sense it may be said that whosoever openly breaks any commandment teaches others to do the same; for example speaks, and many times louder than precept. In this sense it is apparent every open drunkard is a teacher of drunkenness; every sabbath-breaker is constantly teaching his neighbour to profane the day of the Lord. But this is not all; an habitual breaker of the law is seldom content to stop here. He generally teaches other men to do so too, by word as well as example; especially when he hardens his neck, and hateth to be reproved. Such a sinner soon commences an advocate for sin: he defends what he is resolved not to forsake. He excuses the sin which he will not leave, and thus directly teaches every sin which he commits.

'He shall be called least in the kingdom of heaven'—that is, shall have no part therein. He is a stranger to the kingdom of heaven which is on earth; he hath no portion in that inheritance; no share of that righteousness and peace and joy in the Holy Ghost. Nor by consequence can he have any part in the glory which shall be revealed.

4. But if those who even thus break and teach others to break one of the least of these commandments shall be called least in the kingdom of heaven, shall have no part in the kingdom of Christ and of God; if even these 'shall be cast into outer darkness', where is 'wailing and gnashing of teeth', then where will they appear whom our Lord chiefly and primarily intends in these words? They who, bearing the character of teachers sent from God, do nevertheless themselves break his commandments, yea and openly teach others so to do, being corrupt both in life and doctrine?

5. These are of several sorts. Of the first sort are they who live in some wilful, habitual sin. Now if an ordinary sinner teaches by his example, how much more a sinful minister, even if he does not attempt to defend, excuse, or extenuate his sin! If he does he is a murderer indeed, yea, the murderer-general of his congregation! He peoples the regions of death. He is the choicest instrument of the prince of darkness. When he goes hence 'hell from beneath is moved to meet him at his coming.' Nor can he sink into the bottomless pit without dragging a multitude after him.

6. Next to these are the good-natured, good sort of men: who live an easy, harmless life, neither troubling themselves with outward sin, nor with inward holiness; men who are remarkable neither one way nor the other, neither for religion nor irreligion; who are very regular both in public and private, but don't pretend to be any stricter than their neighbours. A minister of this kind breaks not one, or a few only, of the least commandments of God, but all the great and weighty branches of his law which relate to the power of godliness, and all that require us to 'pass the time of our sojourning in fear'; to 'work out our salvation with fear and trembling'; to have our 'loins always girt and our lights burning'; to 'strive or "agonize" to enter in at the strait gate'. And he 'teaches men so', by the whole form of his life and the general tenor of his preaching, which uniformly tends to soothe those in their pleasing dream who imagine themselves Christians and are not; to persuade all who attend upon his ministry to sleep on and take their rest. No marvel, therefore, if both he and they that follow him wake together in everlasting burnings.

7. But above all these, in the highest rank of the enemies of the gospel of Christ are they who openly and explicitly 'judge the law' itself, and 'speak evil of the law'; who teach men to break (λῦσαι, to dissolve, to loose, to untie the obligation of) not one only—whether of the least or of the greatest—but all the commandments at a stroke; who teach, without any cover, in so many words: 'What did our Lord do with the law? He abolished it.' 'There is but one duty, which is that of believing.' 'All commands are unfit for our times.' 'From any demand of the law no man is obliged now to go one step, to give away one farthing, to eat or omit one morsel.' This is indeed carrying matters with a high hand. This is withstanding our Lord to the face, and telling him that he

understood not how to deliver the message on which he was sent. 'O Lord, lay not this sin to their charge!' 'Father, forgive them; for they know not what they do!'

8. The most surprising of all the circumstances that attend this strong delusion is that they who are given up to it really believe that they honour Christ by overthrowing his law, and that they are magnifying his office while they are destroying his doctrine! Yea, they honour him just as Judas did when he 'said, Hail, Master, and kissed him'. And he may as justly say to every one of them, 'Betrayest thou the Son of man with a kiss?' It is no other than betraying him with a kiss to talk of his blood and take away his crown; to set light by any part of his law under pretence of advancing his gospel. Nor indeed can anyone escape this charge who preaches faith in any such manner as either directly or indirectly tends to set aside any branch of obedience; who preaches Christ so as to disannul or weaken in any wise the least of the commandments of God.

9. It is impossible indeed to have too high an esteem for 'the faith of God's elect'. And we must all declare, 'By grace ye are saved through faith: . . . not of works, lest any man should boast.' We must cry aloud to every penitent sinner, 'Believe in the Lord Jesus Christ, and thou shalt be saved.' But at the same time we must take care to let all men know we esteem no faith but that 'which worketh by love'; and that we are not 'saved by faith' unless so far as we are delivered from the power as well as the guilt of sin. And when we say, 'Believe, and thou shalt be saved,' we do not mean, 'Believe, and thou shalt step from sin to heaven, without any holiness coming between, faith supplying the place of holiness'; but, believe and thou shalt be holy; believe in the Lord Jesus, and thou shalt have peace and power together. Thou shalt have power from him in whom thou believest to trample sin under thy feet; power to love the Lord thy God with all thy heart, and to serve him with all thy strength. Thou shalt have power 'by patient continuance in well-doing' to 'seek for glory and honour and immortality'. Thou shalt both 'do and teach' all the commandments of God, from the least even to the greatest. Thou shalt teach them by thy life as well as thy words, and so 'be called great in the kingdom of heaven'.

IV. 1. Whatever other way we teach to the kingdom of heaven, to glory, honour, and immortality, be it called 'the way of faith' or by any other name, it is in truth the way to destruction. It will not bring a man peace at the last. For thus saith the Lord, 'Verily I say unto you, except your righteousness shall exceed the righteousness of the scribes and Pharisees, ye shall in no case enter into the kingdom of heaven.'

The *scribes*, mentioned so often in the New Testament as some of the most constant and vehement opposers of our Lord, were not secretaries, or men employed in writing only, as that term might incline us to believe. Neither were they *lawyers*, in our common sense of the word (although the word νομικοί is so rendered in our translation). Their employment had no affinity at all to that of a lawyer among us. They were conversant with the laws of God, and not with the laws of man. These were their study: it was their proper and peculiar business to read and expound the law and the prophets, particularly in the synagogues. They were the ordinary, stated preachers among the Jews; so that if the sense of the original word was attended to we might render it, the divines. For these were the men who made divinity their profession; and they were generally (as their name literally imports) men of letters; men of the greatest account for learning that were then in the Jewish nation.

2. The Pharisees were a very ancient sect or body of men among the Jews: originally so called from the Hebrew word פרש, which signifies to 'separate' or 'divide'. Not that they made any formal separation from or division in the national church. They were only distinguished from others by greater strictness of life, by more exactness of conversation. For they were zealous of the law in the minutest points, paying tithes of mint, anise, and cummin. And hence they were had in honour of all the people and generally esteemed the holiest of men.

Many of the scribes were of the sect of the Pharisees. Thus St. Paul himself, who was educated for a scribe, first at the university of Tarsus, and after that in Jerusalem at the feet of Gamaliel (one of the most learned scribes or doctors of the law that were then in the nation), declares of himself before the council, 'I am a Pharisee, the son of a Pharisee' (Acts 23:6); and before King Agrippa, 'after the straitest sect of our religion I lived a Pharisee' (Acts 26:5). And the whole body of the scribes generally esteemed and acted in concert with the Pharisees. Hence we find our Saviour so frequently coupling them together, as coming in many respects under the same consideration. In this place they seem to be mentioned together as the most eminent professors of religion: the former of whom were accounted the wisest, the latter the holiest of men.

3. What 'the righteousness of the scribes and Pharisees' really was it is not difficult to determine. Our Lord has preserved an authentic account which one of them gave of himself. And he is clear and full in describing his own righteousness, and cannot be supposed to have omitted any part of it. He 'went up' indeed 'into the temple to pray', but was so intent upon his own virtues that he forgot the design upon which he came. For 'tis remarkable he does not properly pray at all. He only tells God how wise and good he was. 'God, I thank thee that I am not as other men are, extortioners, unjust, adulterers; or even as this publican. I fast twice in the week: I give tithes of all that I possess.' His righteousness therefore consisted of three parts: first, saith he, 'I am not as other men are.' I am not an 'extortioner', not 'unjust', not an 'adulterer'; not 'even as this publican'. Secondly, 'I fast twice in the week'; and thirdly,

'give tithes of all that I possess.'

'I am not as other men are.' This is not a small point. It is not every man that can say this. It is as if he had said, I do not suffer myself to be carried away by that great torrent, custom. I live not by custom but by reason; not by the examples of men but the word of God. 'I am not an extortioner, not unjust, not an adulterer'; however common these sins are, even among those who are called the people of God (extortion, in particular, a kind of legal injustice, not punishable by any human law, the making gain of another's ignorance or necessity, having filled every corner of the land); 'nor even as this publican', not guilty of any open or presumptuous sin, not an outward sinner, but a fair, honest man, of blameless life and conversation.

4. 'I fast twice in the week.' There is more implied in this than we may at first be sensible of. All the stricter Pharisees observed the weekly fasts, namely, every Monday and Thursday. On the former day they fasted in memory of Moses receiving on that day (as their tradition taught) the two tables of stone written by the finger of God; on the latter in memory of his casting them out of his hand when he saw the people dancing round the golden calf. On these days they took no sustenance at all till three in the afternoon, the hour at which they began to offer up the evening sacrifice in the temple. Till that hour it was their custom to remain in the temple—in some of the corners, apartments, or courts thereof—that they might be ready to assist at all the sacrifices and to join in all the public prayers. The time between they were accustomed to employ partly in private addresses to God, partly in searching the Scriptures, in reading the law and the prophets, and in meditating thereon. Thus much is implied in, 'I fast twice in the week', the second branch of the righteousness of a Pharisee.

5. 'I give tithes of all that I possess.' This the Pharisees did with the utmost exactness. They would not except the most inconsiderable thing, no, not mint, anise, or cummin. They would not keep back the least part of what they believed properly to belong to God, but gave a full tenth of their whole substance yearly, and of all their increase, whatsoever it was.

Yea, the stricter Pharisees (as has been often observed by those who are versed in the ancient Jewish writings), not content with giving one tenth of their substance to God in his priests and Levites, gave another tenth to God in the poor, and that continually. They gave the same proportion of all they had in alms as they were accustomed to give in tithes. And this likewise they adjusted with the utmost exactness, that they might not keep back any part, but might fully render unto God the things which were God's, as they accounted this to be. So that upon the whole they gave away from year to year an entire fifth of all that they possessed.

6. This was 'the righteousness of the scribes and Pharisees': a righteousness which in many respects went far beyond the conception which many have been

accustomed to entertain concerning it. But perhaps it will be said it was all false and feigned; for they were all a company of hypocrites. Some of them doubtless were; men who had really no religion at all, no fear of God, or desire to please him; who had no concern for the honour that cometh of God, but only for the praise of men. And these are they whom our Lord so severely condemns, so sharply reproves, on many occasions. But we must not suppose, because many Pharisees were hypocrites, therefore all were so. Nor indeed is hypocrisy by any means essential to the character of a Pharisee. This is not the distinguishing mark of their sect. It is rather this (according to our Lord's account)—they 'trusted in themselves that they were righteous, and despised others'. This is their genuine badge. But the Pharisee of this kind cannot be a hypocrite. He must be, in the common sense, sincere; otherwise he could not 'trust in himself that he is righteous'. The man who was here commending himself to God unquestionably thought himself righteous. Consequently, he was no hypocrite—he was not conscious to himself of any insincerity. He now spoke to God just what he thought, namely, that he was abundantly better than other men.

But the example of St. Paul, were there no other, is sufficient to put this out of all question. He could not only say, when he was a Christian, 'Herein do I exercise myself, to have always a conscience void of offence toward God and toward men' (Acts 24:16); but even concerning the time when he was a Pharisee, 'Men and brethren, I have lived in all good conscience before God until this day' (Acts 23:1). He was therefore sincere when he was a Pharisee, as well as when he was a Christian. He was no more an hypocrite when he persecuted the church than when he preached the faith which once he persecuted. Let this then be added to 'the righteousness of the scribes and Pharisees'—a sincere belief that they are righteous, and in all things 'doing God service'.

7. And yet, 'Except your righteousness', saith our Lord, 'shall exceed the righteousness of the scribes and Pharisees, ye shall in no case enter into the kingdom of heaven.' A solemn and weighty declaration! And which it behoves all who are called by the name of Christ seriously and deeply to consider. But before we inquire how our righteousness may exceed theirs, let us examine whether at present we come up to it.

First, a Pharisee was 'not as other men are'. In externals he was singularly good. Are we so? Do we dare to be singular at all? Do we not rather swim with the stream? Do we not many times dispense with religion and reason together because we would not 'look particular'? Are we not often more afraid of being out of the fashion than of being out of the way of salvation? Have we courage to stem the tide? To run counter to the world? 'To obey God rather than man'? Otherwise the Pharisee leaves us behind at the very first step. 'Tis well if we overtake him any more.

But to come closer. Can we use his first plea with God, which is in substance, 'I do no harm. I live in no outward sin. I do nothing for which my own heart condemns me.' Do you not? Are you sure of that? Do you live in no practice for which your own heart condemns you? If you are not an adulterer, if you are not unchaste either in word or deed, are you not unjust? The grand measure of justice, as well as of mercy, is, Do unto others as thou wouldst they should do unto thee. Do you walk by this rule? Do you never do unto any what you would not they should do unto you? Nay, are you not grossly unjust? Are you not an extortioner? Do you not make a gain of anyone's ignorance or necessity? Neither in buying nor selling? Suppose you are engaged in trade, do you demand, do you receive, no more than the real value of what you sell? Do you demand, do you receive, no more of the ignorant than of the knowing; of a little child than of an experienced trader? If you do, why does not your heart condemn you? You are a barefaced extortioner. Do you demand no more than the usual price of the goods of any who is in pressing want? Who must have, and that without delay, the things which you only can furnish him with? If you do, this also is flat extortion. Indeed you do not come up to the righteousness of a Pharisee.

8. A Pharisee, secondly (to express his sense in our common way), used all the means of grace. As he fasted *often* and *much*, 'twice in every week', so he attended all the sacrifices. He was constant in public and private prayer, and in reading and hearing the Scriptures. Do you go as far as this? Do you fast *much* and *often?* Twice in the week? I fear not! Once, at least: 'On all Fridays in the year.' (So our church clearly and peremptorily enjoins all her members to do, to observe all these as well as the vigils and the forty days of Lent as 'days of fasting, or abstinence'.) Do you fast twice in the year? I am afraid some among us cannot plead even this! Do you neglect no opportunity of attending and partaking of the Christian sacrifice? How many are they who call themselves Christians and yet are utterly regardless of it; yet do not eat of that bread or drink of that cup for months, perhaps years together? Do you every day either hear the Scriptures or read them and meditate thereon? Do you join in prayer with the great congregation? Daily, if you have opportunity? If not, whenever you can, particularly on that day which you 'remember to keep it holy'? Do you strive to *make* opportunities? Are you 'glad when they say unto you, we will go into the house of the Lord'? Are you zealous of, and diligent in, private prayer? Do you suffer no day to pass without it? Rather are not some of you so far from spending therein (with the Pharisee) several hours in one day that you think one hour full enough, if not too much? Do you spend an hour in a day, or in a week, in praying to your Father which is in secret? Yea, an hour in a month? Have you spent one hour together in private prayer ever since you was born? Ah, poor Christian! Shall not the Pharisee rise up in the judgment against thee and condemn thee? His righteousness is as far above

thine as the heaven is above the earth.

9. The Pharisee, thirdly, 'paid tithes' and gave alms 'of all that he possessed'. And in how ample a manner! So that he was (as we phrase it) 'a man that did much good'. Do we come up to him here? Which of us is so abundant as he was in good works? Which of us gives a fifth of all his substance to God? Both of the principal and of the increase? Who of us out of (suppose) an hundred pounds a year, gives twenty to God and the poor; out of fifty, ten: and so in a larger or a smaller proportion? When shall our righteousness, in using all the means of grace, in attending all the ordinances of God, in avoiding evil and doing good, equal at least the righteousness of the scribes and Pharisees?

10. Although if it only equalled theirs what would that profit? 'For verily I say unto you, except your righteousness shall exceed the righteousness of the scribes and Pharisees, ye shall in no case enter into the kingdom of heaven.' But how can it exceed theirs? Wherein does the righteousness of a Christian exceed that of a scribe or Pharisee?

Christian righteousness exceeds theirs, first, in the extent of it. Most of the Pharisees, though they were rigorously exact in many things, yet were emboldened by the traditions of the elders to dispense with others of equal importance. Thus they were extremely punctual in keeping the fourth commandment—they would not even 'rub an ear of corn' on the sabbath day—but not at all in keeping the third, making little account of light, or even false swearing. So that their righteousness was partial—whereas the righteousness of a real Christian is universal. He does not observe one, or some parts, of the law of God, and neglect the rest; but keeps all his commandments, loves them all, values them above gold or precious stones.

11. It may be indeed that some of the scribes and Pharisees endeavoured to keep all the commandments, and consequently were, as touching the righteousness of the law, that is, according to the letter of it, blameless. But still the righteousness of a Christian exceeds all this righteousness of a scribe or Pharisee by fulfilling the spirit as well as the letter of the law, by inward as well as outward obedience. In this, in the spirituality of it, it admits of no comparison. This is the point which our Lord has so largely proved in the whole tenor of this discourse. Their righteousness was external only; Christian righteousness is in the inner man. The Pharisee 'cleansed the outside of the cup and the platter'; the Christian is clean within. The Pharisee laboured to present God with a good life; the Christian with a holy heart. The one shook off the leaves, perhaps the fruits of sin; the other 'lays the axe to the root', as not being content with the outward form of godliness, how exact soever it be, unless the life, the spirit, the power of God unto salvation, be felt in the inmost soul.

Thus to do no harm, to do good, to attend the ordinances of God (the righteousness of a Pharisee) are all external; whereas, on the contrary, poverty of spirit, mourning, meekness, hunger and thirst after righteousness, the love of our neighbour, and purity of heart (the righteousness of a Christian) are all internal. And even peacemaking (or doing good) and suffering for righteousness' sake, stand entitled to the blessings annexed to them only as they imply these inward dispositions, as they spring from, exercise, and confirm them. So that whereas the righteousness of the scribes and Pharisees was external only, it may be said in some sense that the righteousness of a Christian is internal only—all his actions and sufferings being as nothing in themselves, being estimated before God only by the tempers from which they spring.

12. Whosoever therefore thou art who bearest the holy and venerable name of a Christian, see, first, that thy righteousness fall not short of the righteousness of the scribes and Pharisees. Be not thou 'as other men are'. Dare to stand alone, to be

Against example, singularly good!

If thou 'follow a multitude' at all it must be 'to do evil'. Let not custom or fashion be thy guide, but reason and religion. The practice of others is nothing to thee: 'Every man must give an account of himself to God.' Indeed if thou canst save the soul of another, do; but at least save one, thy own. Walk not in the path of death because it is broad, and many walk therein. Nay, by this very token thou mayst know it. Is the way wherein thou now walkest a broad, well-frequented, fashionable way? Then it infallibly leads to destruction. O be not thou 'damned for company'—'cease from evil'; fly from sin as from the face of a serpent. At least, do no harm. 'He that committeth sin is of the devil.' Be not thou found in that number. Touching outward sins, surely the grace of God is even now sufficient for thee. 'Herein' at least 'exercise thyself to have a conscience void of offence toward God and toward men.'

Secondly, let not thy righteousness fall short of theirs with regard to the ordinances of God. If thy labour or bodily strength will not allow of thy fasting 'twice in the week', however, deal faithfully with thy own soul, and fast as often as thy strength will permit. Omit no public, no private opportunity of pouring out thy soul in prayer. Neglect no occasion of eating that bread and drinking that cup which is the communion of the body and blood of Christ. Be diligent in searching the Scriptures: read as thou mayst, and meditate therein day and night. Rejoice to embrace every opportunity of hearing 'the word of reconciliation' declared by the 'ambassadors of Christ, the stewards of the mysteries of God'. In using all the means of grace, in a constant and careful attendance on every ordinance of God, live up to (at least, till thou canst go beyond) 'the righteousness of the scribes and Pharisees'.

Thirdly, fall not short of a Pharisee in doing good. Give alms of all thou dost possess. Is any hungry? Feed him. Is he athirst? Give him drink. Naked? Cover him with a garment. If thou hast this world's goods, do not limit thy beneficence to a scanty proportion. Be merciful to the uttermost of thy power. Why not, even as this Pharisee? 'Now make thyself friends', while the time is, 'of the mammon of unrighteousness, that when thou failest', when this earthly tabernacle is dissolved, 'they may receive thee into everlasting habitations.'

13. But rest not here. Let thy 'righteousness exceed the righteousness of the scribes and Pharisees'. Be not thou content to 'keep the whole law, and offend in one point'. 'Hold thou fast all his commandments, and all false ways do thou utterly abhor.' Do all the things whatsoever he hath commanded, and that with all thy might. Thou canst do all things through Christ strengthening thee, though without him thou canst do nothing.

Above all, let thy righteousness exceed theirs in the purity and spirituality of it. What is the exactest form of religion to thee? The most perfect outside righteousness? Go thou higher and deeper than all this. Let thy religion be the religion of the heart. Be thou poor in spirit; little and base and mean and vile in thy own eyes; amazed and humbled to the dust at the love of God which is in Christ Jesus thy Lord. Be serious: let the whole stream of thy thoughts, words, and works, be such as flows from the deepest conviction that thou standest on the edge of the great gulf, thou and all the children of men, just ready to drop in, either into everlasting glory, or everlasting burnings. Be meek: let thy soul be filled with mildness, gentleness, patience, long-suffering toward all men; at the same time that all which is in thee is athirst for God, the living God, longing to awake up after his likeness, and to be satisfied with it. Be thou a lover of God and of all mankind. In this spirit do and suffer all things. Thus 'exceed the righteousness of the scribes and Pharisees', and thou shalt be 'called great in the kingdom of heaven'.

UPON OUR LORD'S SERMON ON THE MOUNT

DISCOURSE VI

Sermon 26 – 1748

AN INTRODUCTORY COMMENT

Many commentators of the seventeenth and eighteenth centuries had devoted their talents to the interpretation of Matthew 5–7 as the principal summary of Christian ethics. Chief among these earlier authors who influenced Wesley's thought were Bishop Offspring Blackall, John Norris, James Blair (the American), John Cardinal Bona, and Henry Hammond. Echoes of all these are heard throughout Wesley's observations in this series of thirteen sermons, together with lesser borrowings from John Bengel, Matthew Poole, and Matthew Henry. Yet Wesley came up with a model of his own, both in form and substance. These sermons thus remind us of Wesley's ready appeal to tradition, even while he maintained his own originality and independence.

In Discourse VI, Wesley describes how actions that are otherwise indifferent in their nature may be made 'holy and good and acceptable to God' when performed with a pure and holy intention. His concern for 'purity of intention', the central theme in the holy living tradition, goes back to his Oxford days and his reading of Jeremy Taylor. In this sermonic context, however, holy tempers and affections are shown to be the necessary prerequisite for 'works of piety' and 'works of charity or mercy' that have any value before God. The sermon ends with a rather lengthy, phrase by phrase exposition of the Lord's Prayer that relies heavily upon traditional interpretations. It does provide the natural occasion, however, to stress the necessity of doing the will of God 'on earth as it is done in heaven'. His description of angelic obedience (the model for mankind) is threefold: the angels obey God willingly, continually, and perfectly, which is to say, entirely. Nothing less is prayed for on earth. In the previous decade, Wesley's sermon on this phrase of the Lord's Prayer had taken a slightly different turn, but both have a very high view of human potential–that mankind like the angels can 'do nothing but what is the will of God' and 'do the whole will of God in all things' (see Sermon 145 in the Bicentennial Edition).

This sermon was first published in the second volume of *Sermons on Several Occasions* (1748). The poetic paraphrase of the Lord's Prayer appended at the end was taken from *Hymns and Sacred Poems* (1742).

Upon our Lord's Sermon on the Mount

Discourse VI

Take heed that ye do not your alms before men, to be seen of them; otherwise ye have no reward of your Father which is in heaven.

Therefore when thou dost thine alms, do not sound a trumpet before thee, as the hypocrites do in the synagogues and in the streets, that they may have praise of men. Verily, I say unto you, they have their reward.

But when thou dost alms, let not thy left hand know what thy right hand doth: that thine alms may be in secret; and thy Father which seeth in secret, himself shall reward thee openly.

And when thou prayest, thou shalt not be as the hypocrites are; for they love to pray standing in the synagogues and in the corners of the streets, that they may be seen of men. Verily I say unto you, They have their reward.

But thou, when thou prayest, enter into thy closet, and when thou hast shut the door, pray to thy Father which is in secret; and thy Father which seeth in secret he shall reward thee openly.

But when ye pray, use not vain repetitions, as the heathen do; for they think that they shall be heard for their much speaking.

Be not ye therefore like unto them; for your Father knoweth what things ye have need of before you ask him.

After this manner therefore pray ye: Our Father, which art in heaven, hallowed be thy name. Thy kingdom come. Thy will be done on earth as it is in heaven. Give us this day our daily bread. And forgive us our trespasses, as we forgive them that trespass against us. And lead us not into temptation, but deliver us from evil. For thine is the kingdom and the power and the glory, for ever and ever. Amen.

For if ye forgive men their trespasses, your heavenly Father will also forgive you.

But if ye forgive not men their trespasses, neither will your Father forgive your trespasses.

Matthew 6:1–15

1. In the preceding chapter our Lord has described inward religion in its various branches. He has laid before us those dispositions of soul which constitute real Christianity: the inward tempers contained in that holiness 'without which no man shall see the Lord'—the affections which, when flowing

from their proper fountain, from a living faith in God through Christ Jesus, are intrinsically and essentially good, and acceptable to God. He proceeds to show in this chapter how all our actions likewise, even those that are indifferent in their own nature, may be made holy and good and acceptable to God, by a pure and holy intention. Whatever is done without this, he largely declares, is of no value before God. Whereas whatever outward works are thus consecrated to God, they are, in his sight, of great price.

2. The necessity of this purity of intention he shows, first, with regard to those which are usually accounted religious actions, and indeed are such when performed with a right intention. Some of these are commonly termed works of piety; the rest, works of charity or mercy. Of the latter sort he particularly names almsgiving; of the former, prayer and fasting. But the directions given for these are equally to be applied to every work, whether of charity or mercy.

I. 1. And, first, with regard to works of mercy. 'Take heed', saith he, 'that ye do not your alms before men, to be seen of them. Otherwise ye have no reward of your Father which is in heaven.' 'That ye do not your alms'—although this only is named, yet is every work of charity included, everything which we give, or speak, or do, whereby our neighbour may be profited, whereby another man may receive any advantage, either in his body or soul. The feeding the hungry, the clothing the naked, the entertaining or assisting the stranger, the visiting those that are sick or in prison, the comforting the afflicted, the instructing the ignorant, the reproving the wicked, the exhorting and encouraging the well-doer; and if there be any other work of mercy, it is equally included in this direction.

2. 'Take heed that ye do not your alms before men, to be seen of them.' The thing which is here forbidden is not barely the doing good in the sight of men. This circumstance alone, that others see what we do, makes the action neither worse nor better, but the doing it before men, 'to be seen of them'—with this view, from this intention only. I say, 'from this intention only', for this may in some cases be a part of our intention; we may design that some of our actions should be seen, and yet they may be acceptable to God. We may intend that our 'light' should 'shine before men', when our conscience bears us witness in the Holy Ghost that our ultimate end in designing they should 'see our good works' is 'that they may glorify our Father which is in heaven'. But take heed that ye do not the least thing with a view to your own glory. Take heed that a regard to the praise of men have no place at all in your works of mercy. If ye seek your own glory, if you have any design to gain the honour that cometh of men, whatever is done with this view is nothing worth; it is not done unto the Lord; he accepteth it not; 'ye have no reward' for this 'of our Father which is in heaven'.

3. 'Therefore when thou dost thine alms, do not sound a trumpet before

thee, as the hypocrites do in the synagogues and in the streets, that they may have praise of men.' The word 'synagogue' does not here mean a place of worship, but any place of public resort, such as the market-place or exchange. It was a common thing among the Jews who were men of large fortunes, particularly among the Pharisees, to cause a trumpet to be sounded before them in the most public parts of the city when they were about to give any considerable alms. The pretended reason for this was to call the poor together to receive it, but the real design that they might have praise of men. But be not thou like unto them. Do not thou cause a trumpet to be sounded before thee. Use no ostentation in doing good. Aim at the honour which cometh of God only. 'They' who seek the praise of men 'have their reward.' They shall have no praise of God.

4. 'But when thou dost alms, let not thy left hand know what thy right hand doth.' This is a proverbial expression, the meaning of which is, do it in as secret a manner as is possible: as secret as is consistent with the doing it at all (for it must not be left undone: omit no opportunity of doing good, whether secretly or openly) and with the doing it in the most effectual manner. For here is also an exception to be made. When you are fully persuaded in your own mind that by your not concealing the good which is done either you will yourself be enabled, or others excited, to do the more good, then you may not conceal it: then let your light appear, and 'shine to all that are in the house'. But unless where the glory of God and the good of mankind oblige you to the contrary, act in as private and unobserved a manner as the nature of the thing will admit: 'That thy alms may be in secret; and thy Father which seeth in secret, he shall reward thee openly.' Perhaps in the present world—many instances of this stand recorded in all ages—but infallibly in the world to come, before the general assembly of men and angels.

II. 1. From works of charity or mercy our Lord proceeds to those which are termed works of piety. 'And when thou prayest', saith he, 'thou shalt not be as the hypocrites are; for they love to pray standing in the synagogues, and in the corners of the streets, that they may be seen of men.' 'Thou shalt not be as the hypocrites are.' Hypocrisy then, or insincerity, is the first thing we are to guard against in prayer. Beware not to speak what thou dost not mean. Prayer is the lifting up of the heart to God: all words of prayer without this are mere hypocrisy. Whenever therefore thou attemptest to pray, see that it be thy one design to commune with God, to lift up thy heart to him, to pour out thy soul before him. Not 'as the hypocrites', who 'love', or are wont, 'to pray standing in the synagogues', the exchange or market-places, 'and in the corners of the streets', wherever the most people are, 'that they may be seen of men': this was the sole design, the motive and end, of the prayers which they there repeated. 'Verily I say unto you, They have their reward.' They are to expect none from your Father which is in heaven.

2. But it is not only the having an eye to the praise of men which cuts us off from any reward in heaven, which leaves us no room to expect the blessing of God upon our works, whether of piety or mercy; purity of intention is equally destroyed by a view to any temporal reward whatever. If we repeat our prayers, if we attend the public worship of God, if we relieve the poor, with a view to gain or interest, it is not a whit more acceptable to God than if it were done with a view to praise. Any temporal view, any motive whatever on this side eternity, any design but that of promoting the glory of God, and the happiness of men for God's sake, makes every action, however fair it may appear to men, an abomination unto the Lord.

3. 'But when thou prayest, enter into thy closet; and when thou hast shut the door, pray to thy Father which is in secret.' There is a time when thou art openly to glorify God, to pray and praise him in the great congregation. But when thou desirest more largely and more particularly to make thy requests known unto God, whether it be in the evening or in the morning or at noonday, 'enter into thy closet and shut the door.' Use all the privacy thou canst. (Only leave it not undone, whether thou hast any closet, any privacy, or no. Pray to God if it be possible when none seeth but he; but if otherwise, pray to God.) Thus 'pray to thy Father which is in secret'; pour out thy heart before him; 'and thy Father which seeth in secret, he shall reward thee openly.'

4. 'But when ye pray', even in secret, 'use not vain repetitions, as the heathen do.' Μὴ βατταλογήσητε. Do not use abundance of words without any meaning. Say not the same thing over and over again; think not the fruit of your prayers depends on the length of them, like the heathens; 'for they think they shall be heard for their much speaking.'

The thing here reproved is not simply the length, no more than the shortness of our prayers. But, first, length without meaning: the speaking much, and meaning little or nothing; the using (not all repetitions; for our Lord himself prayed thrice, repeating the same words; but) vain repetitions, as the heathens did, reciting the names of their gods over and over; as they do among Christians (vulgarly so called) and not among the Papists only, who say over and over the same string of prayers without ever feeling what they speak. Secondly, the thinking to be heard for our much speaking: the fancying God measures prayers by their length, and is best pleased with those which contain the most words, which sound the longest in his ears. These are such instances of superstition and folly as all who are named by the name of Christ should leave to the heathens, to them on whom the glorious light of the gospel hath never shined.

5. 'Be not ye therefore like unto them.' Ye who have tasted of the grace of God in Christ Jesus are thoroughly convinced 'your Father knoweth what things ye have need of before ye ask him.' So that the end of your praying is

not to inform God, as though he knew not your wants already; but rather to inform yourselves, to fix the sense of those wants more deeply in your hearts, and the sense of your continual dependence on him who only is able to supply all your wants. It is not so much to move God—who is always more ready to give than you to ask—as to move yourselves, that you may be willing and ready to receive the good things he has prepared for you.

III. 1. After having taught the true nature and ends of prayer our Lord subjoins an example of it: even that divine form of prayer which seems in this place to be proposed by way of pattern chiefly, as the model and standard of all our prayers—'After this manner therefore pray ye.' Whereas elsewhere he enjoins the use of these very words: 'He said unto them, When ye pray, say . . . ' (Luke 11:2).

2. We may observe in general concerning this divine prayer, first, that it contains all we can reasonably or innocently pray for. There is nothing which we have need to ask of God, nothing which we can ask without offending him, which is not included either directly or indirectly in this comprehensive form. Secondly, that it contains all we can reasonably or innocently desire; whatever is for the glory of God, whatever is needful or profitable, not only for ourselves, but for every creature in heaven and earth. And indeed our prayers are the proper test of our desires, nothing being fit to have a place in our desires which is not fit to have a place in our prayers; what we may not pray for, neither should we desire. Thirdly, that it contains all our duty to God and man; whatsoever things are pure and holy, whatsoever God requires of the children of men, whatsoever is acceptable in his sight, whatsoever it is whereby we may profit our neighbour, being expressed or implied therein.

3. It consists of three parts: the preface, the petitions, and the doxology or conclusion. The preface, 'Our Father which art in heaven', lays a general foundation for prayer; comprising what we must first know of God before we can pray in confidence of being heard. It likewise points out to us all those tempers with which we are to approach to God, which are most essentially requisite if we desire either our prayers or our lives should find acceptance with him.

4. 'Our *Father*.' If he is a Father, then he is good, then he is loving to his children. And here is the first and great reason for prayer. God is willing to bless; let us ask for a blessing. 'Our *Father*'—our Creator, the Author of our being; he who raised us from the dust of the earth, who breathed into us the breath of life, and we became living souls. But if he made us, let us ask, and he will not withhold any good thing from the work of his own hands. 'Our *Father*'—our Preserver, who day by day sustains the life he has given; of whose continuing love we now and every moment receive life and breath and all things. So much the more boldly let us come to him, and 'we shall find mercy

and grace to help in time of need.' Above all, the Father of our Lord Jesus Christ, and of all that believe in him; who justifies us 'freely by his grace, through the redemption that is in Jesus'; who hath 'blotted out all our sins', 'and healed all our infirmities'; who hath received us for 'his own children, by adoption and grace', 'and because we are sons, hath sent forth the Spirit of his Son into our hearts, crying Abba, Father'; 'who hath begotten us again of incorruptible seed', and 'created us anew in Christ Jesus'. Therefore we know that he heareth us always; therefore we 'pray' to him 'without ceasing'. We pray, because we love. And 'we love him, because he first loved us.'

5. '*Our* Father'—not *mine* only who now cry unto him; but *ours*, in the most extensive sense. The 'God and Father of the spirits of all flesh'; the Father of angels and men (so the very heathens acknowledged him to be, Πατὴρ ἀνδρῶν τε θεῶν τε), the Father of the universe, of all the families both in heaven and earth. Therefore with him there is no respect of persons. He loveth all that he hath made. He 'is loving unto every man, and his mercy is over all his works'. And 'the Lord's delight is in them that fear him, and put their trust in his mercy'; in them that trust in him through the Son of his love, knowing they are 'accepted in the Beloved'. But 'if God so loved us, we ought also to love one another.' Yea, all mankind; seeing 'God so loved the world, that he gave his only-begotten Son', even to die the death, that they 'might not perish, but have everlasting life'.

6. 'Which art in heaven'—high and lifted up; God over all, blessed for ever. Who, sitting on the circle of the heavens, beholdeth all things both in heaven and earth. Whose eye pervades the whole sphere of created being; yea, and of uncreated night; unto whom 'known are all his works', and all the works of every creature, not only 'from the beginning of the world' (a poor, low, weak translation) but ἀπ' αἰῶνος, from all eternity, from everlasting to everlasting. Who constrains the host of heaven, as well as the children of men, to cry out with wonder and amazement, O the depth!—'the depth of the riches both of the wisdom and of the knowledge of God!' 'Which art in heaven'—the Lord and ruler of all, superintending and disposing all things; who art the King of kings and Lord of lords, the blessed and only potentate; who art strong and girded about with power, doing whatsoever pleaseth thee! The Almighty, for whensoever thou willest, to do is present with thee. 'In heaven'—eminently there. Heaven is thy throne, the place where thine honour particularly dwelleth. But not there alone; for thou fillest heaven and earth, the whole expanse of space. Heaven and earth are full of thy glory. Glory be to thee, O Lord, most high!

Therefore should we 'serve the Lord with fear, and rejoice unto him with reverence'. Therefore should we think, speak, and act, as continually under the eye, in the immediate presence of the Lord, the King.

7. 'Hallowed be thy name.' This is the first of the six petitions whereof the

prayer itself is composed. The name of God is God himself–the nature of God so far as it can be discovered to man. It means, therefore, together with his existence, all his attributes or perfections–his eternity, particularly signified by his great and incommunicable name Jehovah, as the Apostle John translates it, τὸ 'Α καὶ τὸ 'Ω, ἀρχὴ καὶ τέλος, ὁ ὢν καὶ ὁ ἦν καὶ ὁ ἐρχόμενος, 'the Alpha and Omega, the Beginning and the End; he which is, and which was, and which is to come.' His 'fullness of being', denoted by his other great name, 'I am that I am'; his omnipresence;–his omnipotence;–who is indeed the only agent in the material world, all matter being essentially dull and inactive, and moving only as it is moved by the finger of God. And he is the spring of action in every creature, visible and invisible, which could neither act nor exist without the continued influx and agency of his almighty power;–his wisdom, clearly deduced from the things that are seen, from the goodly order of the universe;–his Trinity in Unity and Unity in Trinity, discovered to us in the very first line of his Written Word, ברא אלהים–literally 'the Gods created', a plural noun joined with a verb of the singular number; as well as in every part of his subsequent revelations, given by the mouth of all his holy prophets and apostles;–his essential purity and holiness;–and above all his love, which is the very brightness of his glory.

In praying that God, or his 'name', may 'be hallowed' or glorified, we pray that he may be known, such as he is, by all that are capable thereof, by all intelligent beings, and with affections suitable to that knowledge: that he may be duly honoured and feared and loved by all in heaven above and in the earth beneath; by all angels and men, whom for that end he has made capable of knowing and loving him to eternity.

8. 'Thy kingdom come.' This has a close connection with the preceding petition. In order that the name of God may be hallowed, we pray that his kingdom, the kingdom of Christ, may come. This kingdom then comes to a particular person when he 'repents and believes the gospel'; when he is taught of God not only to know himself but to know Jesus Christ and him crucified. As 'this is life eternal, to know the only true God, and Jesus Christ whom he hath sent', so it is the kingdom of God begun below, set up in the believer's heart. The Lord God omnipotent then reigneth, when he is known through Christ Jesus. He taketh unto himself his mighty power; that he may subdue all things unto himself. He goeth on in the soul conquering and to conquer, till he hath put all things under his feet, till 'every thought' is 'brought into captivity to the obedience of Christ'.

When therefore God shall 'give his Son the heathen for his inheritance, and the utmost parts of the earth for his possession'; when 'all kingdoms shall bow before him, and all nations shall do him service'; when 'the mountain of the Lord's house', the church of Christ, 'shall be established in the top of the mountains'; when 'the fullness of the Gentiles shall come in, and all Israel shall be saved'—then shall it be seen that 'the Lord is King, and hath put on glorious apparel', appearing to every soul of man as King of kings, and Lord of lords. And it is meet for all those who 'love his appearing' to pray that he would hasten the time; that this his kingdom, the kingdom of grace, may come quickly, and swallow up all the kingdoms of the earth; that all mankind receiving him for their king, truly believing in his name, may be filled with righteousness and peace and joy, with holiness and happiness, till they are removed hence into his heavenly kingdom, there to reign with him for ever and ever.

For this also we pray in those words, 'Thy kingdom come.' We pray for the coming of his everlasting kingdom, the kingdom of glory in heaven, which is the continuation and perfection of the kingdom of grace on earth. Consequently this, as well as the preceding petition, is offered up for the whole intelligent creation, who are all interested in this grand event, the final renovation of all things by God's putting an end to misery and sin, to infirmity and death, taking all things into his own hands, and setting up the kingdom which endureth throughout all ages.

Exactly answerable to this are those awful words in the prayer at the burial of the dead: 'Beseeching thee, that it may please thee, of thy gracious goodness, shortly to accomplish the number of thine elect, and to hasten thy kingdom; that we, with all those that are departed in the true faith of thy holy name, may have our perfect consummation and bliss, both in body and soul, in thy everlasting glory.'

9. 'Thy will be done on earth, as it is in heaven.' This is the necessary and immediate consequence wherever the kingdom of God is come; wherever God dwells in the soul by faith, and Christ reigns in the heart by love.

It is probable many, perhaps the generality of men, at the first view of these words are apt to imagine they are only an expression of, or petition for, resignation; for a readiness to suffer the will of God, whatsoever it be concerning us. And this is unquestionably a divine and excellent temper, a most precious gift of God. But this is not what we pray for in this petition, at least not in the chief and primary sense of it. We pray, not so much for a passive as for an active conformity to the will of God in saying, 'Thy will be done on earth as it is done in heaven.'

How is it done by the angels of God in heaven? Those who now circle his throne rejoicing? They do it willingly; they love his commandments, and gladly hearken to his words. It is their meat and drink to do his will; it is their highest glory and joy. They do it continually; there is no interruption in their willing service. They rest not day nor night, but employ every hour (speaking after the manner of men—otherwise our measures of duration, days and nights and hours, have no place in eternity) in fulfilling his commands, in executing his designs, in performing the counsel of his will. And they do it perfectly. No sin, no defect belongs to angelic minds. It is true, 'the stars are not pure in his sight,' even the morning stars that sing together before him. 'In his sight', that is, in comparison of him, the very angels are not pure. But this does not imply that they are not pure in themselves. Doubtless they are; they are without spot and blameless. They are altogether devoted to his will, and perfectly obedient in all things.

If we view this in another light, we may observe the angels of God in heaven do *all* the will of God. And they do nothing else, nothing but what they are absolutely assured is his will. Again, they do all the will of God *as* he willeth, in the manner which pleases him, and no other. Yea, and they do this only *because* it is his will; for this and no other reason.

10. When therefore we pray that the 'will of God' may 'be done on earth as it is in heaven', the meaning is that all the inhabitants of the earth, even the whole race of mankind, may do the will of their Father which is in heaven as *willingly* as the holy angels; that these may do it *continually*, even as they, without any interruption of their willing service. Yea, and that they may do it *perfectly*; that 'the God of peace, through the blood of the everlasting covenant, may make them perfect in every good work to do his will, and work in them all which is well-pleasing in his sight'.

In other words, we pray that we, and all mankind, may do the whole will of God in all things; and nothing else, not the least thing but what is the holy and acceptable will of God. We pray that we may do the whole will of God *as* he willeth, in the manner that pleases him; and lastly, that we may do it *because* it is his will; that this may be the sole reason and ground, the whole and only motive, of whatsoever we think, or whatsoever we speak, or do.

11. 'Give us this day our daily bread.' In the three former petitions we have been praying for all mankind. We come now more particularly to desire a supply for our own wants. Not that we are directed, even here, to confine our prayer altogether to ourselves; but this and each of the following petitions may be used for the whole church of Christ upon earth.

By 'bread' we may understand all things needful, whether for our souls or bodies: τὰ πρὸς ζωὴν καὶ εὐσέβειαν, 'the things pertaining to life and godliness'. We understand not barely the outward bread, what our Lord terms 'the meat which perisheth'; but much more the spiritual bread, the grace of God, the food 'which endureth unto everlasting life'. It was the judgment of many of the ancient Fathers that we are here *to understand* the sacramental bread also; daily received in the beginning by the whole church of Christ, and highly esteemed, till the love of many waxed cold, as the grand channel whereby the grace of his Spirit was conveyed to the souls of all the children of God.

'Our daily bread.' The word we render 'daily' has been differently explained by different commentators. But the most plain and natural sense of it seems to be this, which is retained in almost all translations, as well ancient as modern: what is sufficient for this day, and so for each day as it succeeds.

12. 'Give us'; for we claim nothing of right, but only of free mercy. We deserve not the air we breathe, the earth that bears, or the sun that shines upon us. All our desert, we own, is hell. But God loves us freely. Therefore we ask him to *give* what we can no more *procure* for ourselves than we can *merit* it at his hands.

Not that either the goodness or the power of God is a reason for us to stand idle. It is his will that we should use all diligence in all things, that we should employ our utmost endeavours, as much as if our success were the natural effect of our own wisdom and strength. And then, as though we had done nothing, we are to depend on him, the giver of every good and perfect gift.

'This day'; for we are to take no thought for the morrow. For this very end has our wise Creator divided life into these little portions of time, so clearly separated from each other; that we might look on every day as a fresh gift of God, another life which we may devote to his glory; and that every evening may be as the close of life, beyond which we are to see nothing but eternity.

13. 'And forgive us our trespasses, as we forgive them that trespass against us.' As nothing but sin can hinder the bounty of God from flowing forth upon every creature, so this petition naturally follows the former; that all hindrances being removed, we may the more clearly trust in the God of love for every manner of thing which is good.

'Our trespasses.' The word properly signifies 'our debts'. Thus our sins are frequently represented in Scripture; every sin laying us under a fresh debt to God, to whom we already owe, as it were, ten thousand talents. What then can we answer when he shall say, 'Pay me that thou owest'? We are utterly insolvent; we have nothing to pay; we have wasted all our substance. Therefore if he deal with us according to the rigour of his law, if he exact what he justly may, he must command us to be 'bound hand and foot', 'and delivered over to the tormentors'.

Indeed we are already bound hand and foot by the chains of our own sins. These, considered with regard to ourselves, are chains of iron and fetters of brass. They are wounds wherewith the world, the flesh, and the devil, have gashed and mangled us all over. They are diseases that drink up our blood and spirits, that bring us down to the chambers of the grave. But considered, as they are here, with regard to God, they are debts, immense and numberless. Well, therefore, seeing we have nothing to pay, may we cry unto him that he would 'frankly forgive' us all.

The word translated 'forgive' implies either to forgive a debt, or to unloose a chain. And if we attain the former, the latter follows of course: if our debts are forgiven, the chains fall off our hands. As soon as ever, through the free grace of God in Christ, we 'receive forgiveness of sins', we receive likewise 'a lot among those which are sanctified, by faith which is in him'. Sin has lost its power; it has no dominion over those who 'are under grace', that is, in favour with God. As 'there is now no condemnation for them that are in Christ Jesus', so they are freed from sin as well as from guilt. 'The righteousness of the law is fulfilled in them', and they 'walk not after the flesh, but after the Spirit'.

14. 'As we forgive them that trespass against us.' In these words our Lord clearly declares both on what condition and in what degree or manner we may look to be forgiven of God. All our trespasses and sins are forgiven us *if* we forgive, and *as* we forgive, others. First, God forgives us *if* we forgive others. This is a point of the utmost importance. And our blessed Lord is so jealous lest at any time we should let it slip out of our thoughts that he not only inserts it in the body of his prayer, but presently after repeats it twice over: 'If', saith he, 'ye forgive men their trespasses, your heavenly Father will also forgive you. But if ye forgive not men their trespasses, neither will your Father forgive your trespasses' (Matt. 6:14–15). Secondly, God forgives us *as* we forgive others. So that if any malice or bitterness, if any taint of unkindness or anger remains, if we do not clearly, fully, and from the heart, forgive all men their trespasses, we far cut short the forgiveness of our own. God cannot clearly and fully forgive us. He may show us some degree of mercy. But we will not suffer him to blot out all our sins, and forgive all our iniquities.

In the meantime, while we do not from our hearts forgive our neighbour his trespasses, what manner of prayer are we offering to God whenever we utter these words? We are indeed setting God at open defiance: we are daring him to do his worst. 'Forgive us our trespasses, as we forgive them that trespass against us!' That is, in plain terms, 'Do not thou forgive us at all; we desire no favour at thy hands. We pray that thou wilt keep our sins in remembrance, and that thy wrath may abide upon us.' But can you seriously offer such a prayer to God? And hath he not yet cast you quick into hell? O tempt him no longer! Now, even now, by his grace, forgive as you would be forgiven! Now have compassion on thy fellow-servant, as God hath had and will have pity on thee!

15. 'And lead us not into temptation, but deliver us from evil.' 'Lead us not into temptation.' The word translated 'temptation' means trial of any kind. And so the English word 'temptation' was formerly taken in an indifferent sense, although now it is usually understood of solicitation to sin. St. James uses the word in both these senses: first in its general, then its restrained acceptation. He takes it in the former sense when he saith, 'Blessed is the man that endureth temptation; for when he is tried', or approved of God, 'he shall receive the crown of life' (Jas. 1:12). He immediately adds, taking the word in the latter sense: 'Let no man say when he is tempted, I am tempted of God; for God cannot be tempted with evil, neither tempteth he any man. But every man is tempted, when he is drawn away of his own lust,' or desire, ἐξελκόμενος,

drawn out of God, in whom alone he is safe, 'and enticed', caught as a fish with a bait. Then it is, when he is thus 'drawn away and enticed', that he properly 'enters into temptation'. The temptation covers him as a cloud; it overspreads his whole soul. Then how hardly shall he escape out of the snare! Therefore we beseech God 'not to lead us into temptation', that is (seeing 'God tempteth no man') not to suffer us to be led into it. 'But deliver us from evil'; rather 'from the evil one'; ἀπὸ τοῦ πονηροῦ. Ὁ πονηρός is unquestionably 'the wicked one', emphatically so called, the prince and god of this world, who works with mighty power in the children of disobedience. But all those who are the children of God by faith are delivered out of his hands. He may fight against them; and so he will. But he cannot conquer, unless they betray their own souls. He may torment for a time, but he cannot destroy; for God is on their side, who will not fail in the end to 'avenge his own elect, that cry unto him day and night': 'Lord, when we are tempted, suffer us not to enter into temptation. Do thou make a way for us to escape, that the wicked one touch us not.'

16. The conclusion of this divine prayer, commonly called the doxology, is a solemn thanksgiving, a compendious acknowledgement of the attributes and works of God. 'For thine is the kingdom'—the sovereign right of all things that are or ever were created; yea, thy kingdom is an everlasting kingdom, and thy dominion endureth throughout all ages. 'The power'—the executive power whereby thou governest all things in thy everlasting kingdom, whereby thou dost whatsoever pleaseth thee, in all places of thy dominion. 'And the glory'—the praise due from every creature for thy power, and the mightiness of thy kingdom, and for all thy wondrous works which thou workest from everlasting, and shalt do, world without end, 'for ever and ever! Amen.' So be it!

I believe it will not be unacceptable to the serious reader, to subjoin

A
Paraphrase
on the
Lord's Prayer

I

Father of all, whose powerful voice
    Called forth this universal frame,
Whose mercies over all rejoice,
    Through endless ages still the same:

Thou by thy word upholdest all;
 Thy bounteous LOVE to all is showed,
Thou hear'st thy every creature call,
 And fillest every mouth with good.

II

In heaven thou reign'st, enthroned in light,
 Nature's expanse beneath thee spread;
Earth, air, and sea before thy sight,
 And hell's deep gloom are open laid.
Wisdom, and might, and love are thine,
 Prostrate before thy face we fall,
Confess thine attributes divine,
 And hail the sovereign Lord of all.

III

Thee, sovereign Lord, let all confess
 That moves in earth, or air, or sky,
Revere thy power, thy goodness bless,
 Tremble before thy piercing eye.
All ye who owe to him your birth
 In praise your every hour employ;
Jehovah reigns! Be glad, O earth,
 And shout, ye morning stars, for joy.

IV

Son of thy sire's eternal love,
 Take to thyself thy mighty power;
Let all earth's sons thy mercy prove,
 Let all thy bleeding grace adore.
The triumphs of thy love display;
 In every heart reign thou alone,
Till all thy foes confess thy sway,
 And glory ends what grace begun.

V

Spirit of grace, and health, and power,
 Fountain of light and love below,
Abroad thine healing influence shower,
 O'er all the nations let it flow.

Inflame our hearts with perfect love,
In us the work of faith fulfil;
So not heaven's hosts shall swifter move
Than we on earth to do thy will.

VI

Father, 'tis thine each day to yield
Thy children's wants a fresh supply;
Thou cloth'st the lilies of the field,
And hearest the young ravens cry.
On thee we cast our care; we live
Through thee, who know'st our every need;
O feed us with thy grace, and give
Our souls this day the living bread.

VII

Eternal, spotless Lamb of God,
Before the world's foundation slain,
Sprinkle us ever with thy blood,
O cleanse and keep us ever clean.
To every soul (all praise to thee!)
Our bowels of compassion move:
And all mankind by this may see
God is in us; for God is love.

VIII

Giver and Lord of life, whose power
And guardian care for all are free;
To thee in fierce temptation's hour
From sin and Satan let us flee.
Thine, Lord, we are, and ours thou art;
In us be all thy goodness showed;
Renew, enlarge, and fill our heart
With peace, and joy, and heaven, and God.

IX

Blessing and honour, praise and love,
Co-equal, co-eternal Three,
In earth below, in heaven above,
By all thy works be paid to Thee.

Thrice holy, thine the kingdom is,
    The power omnipotent is thine;
And when created nature dies,
    Thy never-ceasing glories shine.

UPON OUR LORD'S SERMON ON THE MOUNT

DISCOURSE VIII

Sermon 28 – 1748

AN INTRODUCTORY COMMENT

The scriptural texts in Matthew 5–7 had long fascinated Wesley. The second sermon he ever wrote was on Matthew 6:33, preached at Binsey (near Oxford), November 21, 1725. During his trip to Georgia in the mid-1730s, he exposited the Sermon on the Mount to the passengers aboard the *Simmonds*. In April 1739, it was the example of the Sermon on the Mount that encouraged Wesley to break out of his prejudices against field-preaching: 'I begun expounding our Lord's Sermon on the Mount (one pretty remarkable precedent of field preaching, though I suppose there were churches at that time also).' The records show that, between 1739 and 1746, Wesley preached more than one hundred sermons from separate texts in the Sermon on the Mount.

In Discourse VIII, Wesley has picked one of the most conspicuous passages in the Scripture whereby to present yet another denunciation of greed and surplus accumulation. But the outline of his discussion inverts the order of the verses so as to deal first with the necessity for the Christian to have 'a single eye' (fixed on God), an opportunity for Wesley to explain again the nature of holiness. Only then does he proceed to discuss what is and what is not forbidden by the phrase, 'Lay not up for yourselves treasures upon earth.' Although he suggests at one point that it would be better to throw surplus goods into the sea than to use them 'in folly and superfluity', Wesley goes on to emphasize his more characteristic view: 'disperse abroad, give to the poor: deal your bread to the hungry. Cover the naked with a garment, entertain the stranger, carry or send relief to them that are in prison. Heal the sick . . . defend the oppressed, plead the cause of the fatherless, and make the widow's heart sing for joy.'

A first draft of 'Discourse VIII' seems to have been written in 1736. This sermon was first published in the second volume of his *Sermons on Several Occasions* (1748) and included in all subsequent collections of his *Sermons* published during his lifetime.

Upon our Lord's Sermon on the Mount

Discourse VIII

Lay not up for yourselves treasures upon earth, where moth and rust doth corrupt, and where thieves break through and steal:

But lay up for yourselves treasures in heaven, where neither moth nor rust doth corrupt, and where thieves do not break through nor steal;

For where your treasure is, there will your heart be also.

The light of the body is the eye: if therefore thine eye be single, thy whole body shall be full of light.

But if thine eye be evil, thy whole body shall be full of darkness. If therefore the light that is in thee be darkness, how great is that darkness!

Matthew 6:19–23

1. From those which are commonly termed 'religious actions', and which are real branches of true religion where they spring from a pure and holy intention and are performed in a manner suitable thereto, our Lord proceeds to the actions of 'common life', and shows that the same purity of intention is as indispensably required in our ordinary business as in giving alms, or fasting, or prayer.

And without question the same purity of intention 'which makes our alms and devotions acceptable must also make our labour or employment a proper offering to God. If a man pursues his business that he may raise himself to a state of honour and riches in the world, he is no longer serving God in his employment, and has no more title to a reward from God than he who gives alms that he may be *seen*, or prays that he may be *heard* of men. For vain and earthly designs are no more allowable in our employments than in our alms and devotions. They are not only evil when they mix with our good works', with our religious actions, 'but they have the same evil nature when they enter into the common business of our employments. If it were allowable to pursue them in our worldly employments, it would be allowable to pursue them in our devotions. But as our alms and devotions are not an acceptable service but when they proceed from a pure intention, so our common employment cannot be reckoned a service to him but when it is performed with the same piety of heart.'

2. This our blessed Lord declares in the liveliest manner in those strong

and comprehensive words which he explains, enforces, and enlarges upon throughout this whole chapter. 'The light of the body is the eye. If therefore thine eye be single, thy whole body shall be full of light: but if thine eye be evil, thy whole body shall be full of darkness.' The eye is the intention: what the eye is to the body, the intention is to the soul. As the one guides all the motions of the body, so does the other those of the soul. This eye of the soul is then said to be 'single' when it looks at one thing only; when we have no other design but to 'know God, and Jesus Christ whom he hath sent'; to know him with suitable affections, loving him as he hath loved us; to please God in all things; to serve God (as we love him) with all our heart and mind and soul and strength; and to enjoy God in all and above all things, in time and in eternity.

3. 'If thine eye be' thus 'single', thus fixed on God, 'thy whole body shall be full of light.' 'Thy whole body'—all that is guided by the intention, as the body is by the eye. All thou art, all thou dost: thy desires, tempers, affections; thy thoughts and words and actions. The whole of these 'shall be full of light'; full of true, divine knowledge. This is the first thing we may here understand by light. 'In his light thou shalt see light.' 'He which' of old 'commanded light to shine out of darkness, shall shine in thy heart.' He shall enlighten the eyes of thy understanding with the knowledge of the glory of God. His Spirit shall reveal unto thee the deep things of God. The inspiration of the Holy One shall give thee understanding, and cause thee to know wisdom secretly. Yea, the anointing which thou receivest of him 'shall abide in thee and teach thee of all things'.

How does experience confirm this? Even after God hath opened the eyes of our understanding, if we seek or desire anything else than God, how soon is our foolish heart darkened! Then clouds again rest upon our souls. Doubts and fears again overwhelm us. We are tossed to and fro, and know not what to do, or which is the path wherein we should go. But when we desire and seek nothing but God, clouds and doubts vanish away. We 'who were sometime darkness are now light in the Lord'. The night now shineth as the day; and we find 'the path of the upright is light.' God showeth us the path wherein we should go, and 'maketh plain the way before our face'.

4. The second thing which we may here understand by 'light' is holiness. While thou seekest God in all things thou shalt find him in all, the fountain of all holiness, continually filling thee with his own likeness, with justice, mercy, and truth. While thou lookest unto Jesus and him alone thou shalt be filled with the mind that was in him. Thy soul shall be renewed day by day after the image of him that created it. If the eye of thy mind be not removed from him, if thou endurest 'as seeing him that is invisible', and seeking nothing else in heaven or earth, then as thou beholdest the glory of the Lord thou shalt be 'transformed into the same image, from glory to glory, by the Spirit of the Lord'.

And it is also matter of daily experience that 'by grace we are thus saved through faith.' It is by faith that the eye of the mind is opened to see the light of the glorious love of God. And as long as it is steadily fixed thereon, on God in Christ, reconciling the world unto himself, we are more and more filled with the love of God and man, with meekness, gentleness, long-suffering; with all the fruits of holiness, which are, through Christ Jesus, to the glory of God the Father.

5. This light which fills him who has a single eye implies, thirdly, happiness as well as holiness. Surely 'light is sweet, and a pleasant thing it is to see the sun.' But how much more to see the sun of righteousness continually shining upon the soul! And if there be any consolation in Christ, if any comfort of love, if any peace that passeth all understanding, if any rejoicing in hope of the glory of God, they all belong to him whose eye is single. Thus is his 'whole body full of light'. He walketh in the light as God is in the light, rejoicing evermore, praying without ceasing, and in everything giving thanks, *enjoying* whatever is the will of God concerning him in Christ Jesus.

6. 'But if thine eye be evil, thy whole body shall be full of darkness.' 'If thine eye be evil': we see there is no medium between a single and an evil eye. If the eye be not single, then it is evil. If the intention in whatever we do be not singly to God, if we seek anything else, then our 'mind and conscience are defiled'.

Our eye therefore is evil if in anything we do we aim at any other end than God; if we have any view but to know and to love God, to please and serve him in all things; if we have any other design than to enjoy God, to be happy in him both now and for ever.

7. If thine eye be not singly fixed on God, 'thy whole body shall be full of darkness.' The veil shall still remain on thy heart. Thy mind shall be more and more blinded by 'the God of this world, lest the light of the glorious gospel of Christ should shine upon thee'. Thou wilt be full of ignorance and error touching the things of God, not being able to receive or discern them. And even when thou hast some desire to serve God, thou wilt be full of uncertainty as to the manner of serving him; finding doubts and difficulties on every side, and not seeing any way to escape.

Yea, if thine eye be not single, if thou seek any of the things of earth, thou shalt be full of ungodliness and unrighteousness, thy desires, tempers, affections, being all out of course, being all dark, and vile, and vain. And thy conversation will be evil as well as thy heart, not 'seasoned with salt', or 'meet to minister grace unto the hearers', but idle, unprofitable, corrupt, grievous to the Holy Spirit of God.

8. Both 'destruction and unhappiness are in thy ways'; for 'the way of peace hast thou not known.' There is no peace, no settled, solid peace, for them that know not God. There is no true nor lasting content for any who do not seek him with their whole heart. While thou aimest at any of the things that perish,

'all that cometh is vanity.' Yea, not only vanity, but 'vexation of spirit', and that both in the pursuit and the enjoyment also. Thou walkest indeed in a vain shadow, and disquietest thyself in vain. Thou walkest in darkness that may be felt. 'Sleep on'; but thou canst not 'take thy rest.' The dreams of life can give pain, and that thou knowest; but ease they cannot give. There is no rest in this world or the world to come, but only in God, the centre of spirits.

'If the light which is in thee be darkness, how great is that darkness!' If the intention which ought to enlighten the whole soul, to fill it with knowledge, and love, and peace, and which in fact does so as long as it is single, as long as it aims at God alone—if this be darkness; if it aim at anything beside God, and consequently cover the soul with darkness instead of light, with ignorance and error, with sin and misery—O how great is that darkness! It is the very smoke which ascends out of the bottomless pit! It is the essential night which reigns in the lowest deep, in the land of the shadow of death.

9. Therefore 'lay not up for yourselves treasures upon earth, where moth and rust doth corrupt, and where thieves break through and steal.' If you do, it is plain your eye is evil; it is not singly fixed on God.

With regard to most of the commandments of God, whether relating to the heart or life, the heathens of Africa or America stand much on a level with those that are called Christians. The Christians observe them (a few only being excepted) very near as much as the heathens. For instance: the generality of the natives of England, commonly called Christians, are as sober and as temperate as the generality of the heathens near the Cape of Good Hope. And so the Dutch or French Christians are as humble and as chaste as the Choctaw or Cherokee Indians. It is not easy to say, when we compare the bulk of the nations in Europe with those in America, whether the superiority lies on the one side or the other. At least the American has not much the advantage. But we cannot affirm this with regard to the command now before us. Here the heathen has far the pre-eminence. He desires and seeks nothing more than plain food to eat and plain raiment to put on. And he seeks this only from day to day. He reserves, he lays up nothing; unless it be as much corn at one season of the year as he will need before that season returns. This command, therefore, the heathens, though they know it not, do constantly and punctually observe. They 'lay up for themselves no treasures upon earth'; no stores of purple or fine linen, of gold or silver, which either 'moth or rust may corrupt', or 'thieves break through and steal'. But how do the Christians observe what they profess to receive as a command of the most high God? Not at all; not in any degree; no more than if no such command had ever been given to man. Even the *good* Christians, as they are accounted by others as well as themselves, pay no manner of regard thereto. It might as well be still hid in its original Greek for any notice they take of it. In what Christian city do you find one man of five hundred who makes the least scruple of laying up just as much treasure as he can? Of increasing his goods just as far as he is able? There are indeed those who would not do this unjustly; there are many who will neither rob nor steal; and some who will not defraud their neighbour; nay, who will not gain either by his ignorance or necessity. But this is quite another point. Even these do not scruple the thing, but the manner of it. They do not scruple the 'laying up treasures upon earth', but the laying them up by dishonesty.

They do not start at disobeying Christ, but at a breach of heathen morality. So that even these honest men do no more obey this command than a highwayman or a housebreaker. Nay, they never designed to obey it. From their youth up it never entered into their thoughts. They were bred up by their Christian parents, masters, and friends, without any instruction at all concerning it; unless it were this, to break it as soon and as much as they could, and to continue breaking it to their life's end.

10. There is no one instance of spiritual infatuation in the world which is more amazing than this. Most of these very men read or hear the Bible read, many of them every Lord's day. They have read or heard these words an hundred times, and yet never suspect that they are themselves condemned thereby, any more than by those which forbid parents to offer up their sons or daughters unto Moloch.

O that God would speak to these miserable self-deceivers with his own voice, his mighty voice! That they may at last awake out of the snare of the devil, and the scales may fall from their eyes!

11. Do you ask what it is to 'lay up treasures on earth'? It will be needful to examine this thoroughly. And let us, first, observe what is not forbidden in this command, that we may then clearly discern what is.

We are not forbidden in this command, first, to 'provide things honest in the sight of all men,' to provide wherewith we may 'render unto all their due,' whatsoever they can justly demand of us. So far from it that we are taught of God to 'owe no man anything'. We ought therefore to use all diligence in our calling, in order to owe no man anything: this being no other than a plain law of common justice which our Lord came 'not to destroy but to fulfil'.

Neither, secondly, does he here forbid the providing for ourselves such things as are needful for the body; a sufficiency of plain, wholesome food to eat, and clean raiment to put on. Yea, it is our duty, so far as God puts it into our power, to provide these things also; to the end we may 'eat our own bread', and be 'burdensome to no man'.

Nor yet are we forbidden, thirdly, to provide for our children and for those of our own household. This also it is our duty to do, even upon principles of heathen morality. Every man ought to provide the plain necessaries of life both for his own wife and children, and to put them into a capacity of providing these for themselves when he is gone hence and is no more seen. I say, of providing *these*, the plain necessaries of life—not delicacies, not superfluities—

and that by their *diligent labour*; for it is no man's duty to furnish them any more than himself with the means either of luxury or idleness. But if any man provides not thus far for his own children (as well as for 'the widows of his own house', of whom primarily St. Paul is speaking in those well-known words to Timothy), 'he hath' practically 'denied the faith, and is worse than an infidel,' or heathen.

Lastly, we are not forbidden in these words to lay up from time to time what is needful for the carrying on our worldly business in such a measure and degree as is sufficient to answer the foregoing purposes: in such a measure as, first, to 'owe no man anything'; secondly, to procure for ourselves the necessaries of life; and, thirdly, to furnish those of our own house with them while we live, and with the means of procuring them when we are gone to God.

12. We may now clearly discern (unless we are unwilling to discern it) what that is which is forbidden here. It is the designedly procuring more of this world's goods than will answer the foregoing purposes; the labouring after a larger measure of worldly substance, a larger increase of gold and silver; the laying up any more than these ends require is what is here expressly and absolutely forbidden. If the words have any meaning at all, it must be this, for they are capable of no other. Consequently whoever he is that, owing no man anything, and having food and raiment for himself and his household, together with a sufficiency to carry on his worldly business so far as answers these reasonable purposes—whosoever, I say, being already in these circumstances, seeks a still larger portion on earth—he lives in an open habitual denial of the Lord that bought him. He hath practically 'denied the faith, and is worse than an' African or American 'infidel'.

13. Hear ye this, all ye that dwell in the world, and love the world wherein ye dwell. Ye may be 'highly esteemed of men'; but ye are an 'abomination in the sight of God'. How long shall your souls cleave to the dust? How long will ye load yourselves with thick clay? When will ye awake and see that the open, speculative heathens are nearer the kingdom of heaven than you? When will ye be persuaded to choose the better part; that which cannot be taken away from you? When will ye seek only to 'lay up treasures in heaven', renouncing, dreading, abhorring all other? If you aim at 'laying up treasures on earth' you are not *barely* losing your time and spending your strength for that which is not bread: for what is the fruit if you succeed? You have murdered your own soul. You have extinguished the last spark of spiritual life therein. Now indeed, in the midst of life you are in death. You are a living man, but a dead Christian. 'For where your treasure is, there will your heart be also.' Your heart is sunk into the dust; your soul cleaveth to the ground. Your affections are set, not on things above, but on things of the earth; on poor husks that may poison, but cannot satisfy an everlasting spirit made for God. Your love, your joy, your

desire are all placed on the things which perish in the using. You have thrown away the treasure in heaven: God and Christ are lost. You have gained riches, and hell-fire.

14. O 'how hardly shall they that have riches enter into the kingdom of God!' When our Lord's disciples were astonished at his speaking thus he was so far from retracting it that he repeated the same important truth in stronger terms than before. 'It is easier for a camel to go through the eye of a needle, than for a rich man to enter into the kingdom of God.' How hard is it for them whose very word is applauded not to be wise in their own eyes! How hard for them not to think themselves better than the poor, base, uneducated herd of men! How hard not to seek happiness in their riches, or in things dependent upon them; in gratifying the desire of the flesh, the desire of the eye, or the pride of life! O ye rich, how can ye escape the damnation of hell? Only, with God all things are possible.

15. And even if you do not succeed, what is the fruit of your *endeavouring* to lay up treasures on earth? 'They that will be rich' (οἱ βουλόμενοι πλουτεῖν, they that desire, that endeavour after it, whether they succeed or no) 'fall into a temptation and a snare', a gin, a trap of the devil, 'and into many foolish and hurtful lusts'—ἐπιθυμίας [πολλὰς] ἀνοήτους, desires with which reason hath nothing to do, such as properly belong, not to rational and immortal beings, but only to the brute beasts which have no understanding; 'which drown men in destruction and perdition', in present and eternal misery. Let us but open our eyes, and we may daily see the melancholy proofs of this: men who desiring, resolving to be rich, 'coveting after money, the root of all evil, have already pierced themselves through with many sorrows', and anticipated the hell to which they are going.

The cautiousness with which the Apostle here speaks is highly observable. He does not affirm this absolutely of *the rich*; for a man may possibly be rich without any fault of his, by an overruling providence, preventing his own choice. But he affirms it of οἱ βουλόμενοι πλουτεῖν, 'those who desire' or seek 'to be rich'. Riches, dangerous as they are, do not always 'drown men in destruction and perdition'. But the desire of riches does: those who calmly desire and deliberately seek to attain them, whether they do, in fact, gain the world or no, do infallibly lose their own souls. These are they that sell him who bought them with his blood, for a few pieces of gold or silver. These enter into a covenant with death and hell: and their covenant shall stand. For they are daily making themselves meet to partake of their inheritance with the devil and his angels.

16. O who shall warn this generation of vipers to flee from the wrath to come! Not those who lie at their gate, or cringe at their feet, desiring to be fed with the crumbs that fall from their tables. Not those who court their favour or fear their frown: none of those who mind earthly things. But if there be a

Christian upon earth, if there be a man who hath overcome the world, who desires nothing but God, and fears none but him that is able to destroy both body and soul in hell—thou, O man of God, speak and spare not; lift up thy voice like a trumpet. Cry aloud, and show these honourable sinners the desperate condition wherein they stand. It may be one in a thousand may have ears to hear, may arise and shake himself from the dust; may break loose from these chains that bind him to the earth, and at length lay up treasures in heaven.

17. And if it should be that one of these, by the mighty power of God, awoke and asked, What must I do to be saved? the answer, according to the oracles of God, is clear, full, and express. God doth not say to thee, 'Sell all that thou hast.' Indeed he who seeth the hearts of men saw it needful to enjoin this in one peculiar case, that of the *young, rich ruler*. But he never laid it down for a general rule to all rich men, in all succeeding generations. His general direction is, first, 'Be not highminded.' 'God seeth not as man seeth.' He esteems thee not for thy riches, for thy grandeur or equipage, for any qualification or accomplishment which is directly or indirectly owing to thy wealth, which can be bought or procured thereby. All these are with him as dung and dross: let them be so with thee also. Beware thou think not thyself to be one jot wiser or better for all these things. Weigh thyself in another balance: estimate thyself only by the measure of faith and love which God hath given thee. If thou hast more of the knowledge and love of God than he, thou art on this account, and no other, wiser and better, more valuable and honourable than him who is with the dogs of thy flock. But if thou hast not this treasure those art more foolish, more vile, more truly contemptible—I will not say, than the lowest servant under thy roof but—than the beggar laid at thy gate, full of sores.

18. Secondly, 'Trust not in uncertain riches.' Trust not in them for help; and trust not in them for happiness.

First, trust not in them for help. Thou art miserably mistaken if thou lookest for this in gold or silver. These are no more able to set thee *above the world* than to set thee above the devil. Know that both the world and the prince of this world laugh at all such preparations against them. These will little avail in the day of trouble—even if they remain in the trying hour. But it is not certain that they will; for how oft do they 'make themselves wings and fly away'? But if not, what support will they afford, even in the ordinary troubles of life? The desire of thy eyes, the wife of thy youth, thy son, thine only son, or the friend which was as thy own soul, is taken away at a stroke. Will thy riches reanimate the breathless clay, or call back its late inhabitant? Will they secure thee from sickness, diseases, pain? Do these visit the poor only? Nay; he that feeds thy flocks or tills thy ground has less sickness and pain than thou. He is more rarely visited by these unwelcome guests: and if they come there at all they are more easily driven away from the little cot than from 'the cloud-topped palaces'.

And during the time that thy body is chastened with pain, or consumes away with pining sickness, how do thy treasures help thee? Let the poor heathen answer:

Ut lippum pictae tabulae, fomenta podagrum,
*Auriculas citharae collecta sorde dolentes.**

19. But there is at hand a greater trouble than all these. *Thou* art to die. *Thou* art to sink into dust; to return to the ground from which thou wast taken, to mix with common clay. *Thy* body is to go to the earth as it was, while thy spirit returns to God that gave it. And the time draws on: the years slide away with a swift though silent pace. Perhaps your day is far spent: the noon of life is past, and the evening shadows begin to rest upon you. You feel in yourself sure approaching decay. The springs of life wear away apace. Now what help is there in your riches? Do they sweeten death? Do they endear that solemn hour? Quite the reverse. 'O death, how bitter art thou to a man that liveth at rest in his possessions!' How unacceptable to him is that awful sentence. 'This night shall thy soul be required of thee!' Or will they prevent the unwelcome stroke, or protract the dreadful hour? Can they deliver your soul that it should not see death? Can they restore the years that are past? Can they add to your appointed time a month, a day, an hour, a moment? Or will the good things you have chosen for your portion here follow you over the great gulf? Not so: naked came you into this world; naked must you return.

Linquenda tellus, et domus et placens
Uxor: nec harum quas seris arborum
Te, praeter invisam cupressum,
*Ulla brevem dominum sequetur.***

Surely, were not these truths too plain to be *observed*, because they are too plain to be *denied*, no man that is to die could possibly 'trust' for help 'in uncertain riches'.

20. And trust not in them for happiness. For here also they will be found 'deceitful upon the weights'. Indeed this every reasonable man may infer from what has been observed already. For if neither thousands of gold and silver, nor any of the advantages or pleasures purchased thereby, can prevent our being miserable, it evidently follows they cannot make us happy. What happiness can they afford to him who in the midst of all is constrained to cry out,

* ['Such pleasures as pictures can afford to weak eyes, or bounty-laden tables to a man with gout,' cf. Horace, *Epistles*, I. ii. 52–53.]

** ['You must take leave of lands, home, winsome wife; and no tree whose culture had pleased shall survive your brief reign except those mournful cypresses,' Horace, *Odes*, II. xiv. 21–24.]

> To my new courts sad thought does still repair,
> And round my gilded roofs hangs hovering care.

Indeed experience is here so full, strong, and undeniable, that it makes all other arguments needless. Appeal we therefore to fact. Are the rich and great the only happy men? And is each of them more or less happy in proportion to his measure of riches? Are they happy at all? I had wellnigh said, they are of all men most miserable! Rich man, for once, speak the truth from thy heart. Speak, both for thyself, and for thy brethren:

> Amidst our plenty something still . . .
> To me, to thee, to him is wanting!
> That cruel something unpossessed
> Corrodes and leavens all the rest.

Yea, and so it will, till thy wearisome days of vanity are shut up in the night of death.

Surely then, to trust in riches for happiness is the greatest folly of all that are under the sun! Are you not convinced of this? Is it possible you should still expect to find happiness in money or all it can procure? What! Can silver and gold, and eating and drinking, and horses and servants, and glittering apparel, and diversions and pleasures (as they are called) make thee happy? They can as soon make thee immortal.

21. These are all dead show. Regard them not. 'Trust' thou 'in the living God'; so shalt thou be safe under the shadow of the Almighty; his faithfulness and truth shall be thy shield and buckler. He is a very present help in time of trouble; such an help as can never fail. Then shalt thou say, if all thy other friends die, 'The Lord liveth, and blessed be my strong helper!' He shall remember thee when thou liest sick upon thy bed; when vain is the help of man; when all the things of earth can give no support, he will 'make all thy bed in thy sickness'. He will sweeten thy pain; the consolations of God shall cause thee to clap thy hands in the flames. And even when this house of earth is wellnigh shaken down, when it is just ready to drop into the dust, he will teach thee to say, 'O death, where is thy sting? O grave, where is thy victory? Thanks be unto God, who giveth me the victory, through my Lord Jesus Christ.'

O trust in him for happiness as well as for help. All the springs of happiness are in him. Trust in him 'who giveth us all things richly to enjoy', παρέχοντι [ἡμῖν] πλουσίως πάντα εἰς ἀπόλαυσιν; who of his own rich and free mercy holds them out to us as in his own hand, that receiving them as his gift, and as pledges of his love, we may 'enjoy all' that we possess. It is his love gives a relish to all we taste, puts life and sweetness into all, while every creature leads us up to the great Creator, and all earth is a scale to heaven. He transfuses the joys that are at his own right hand into all he bestows on his thankful children;

who, having fellowship with the Father and his Son Jesus Christ, enjoy him in all and above all.

22. Thirdly, seek not to *increase in goods.* 'Lay not up for thyself treasures upon earth.' This is a flat, positive command, full as clear as 'Thou shalt not commit adultery.' How then is it possible for a rich man to grow richer without denying the Lord that bought him? Yea, how can any man who has already the necessaries of life gain or aim at more, and be guiltless? 'Lay not up', saith our Lord, 'treasures upon earth.' If in spite of this you do and will lay up money or goods, what 'moth or rust' may 'corrupt, or thieves break through and steal'; if you will add house to house, or field to field, why do you call yourself a Christian? You do not obey Jesus Christ. You do not design it. Why do you name yourself by his name? 'Why call ye me, Lord, Lord', saith he himself, 'and do not the things which I say?'

23. If you ask, 'But what must we do with our goods, seeing we have more than we have occasion to use, if we must not lay them up? Must we throw them away?' I answer: if you threw them into the sea, if you were to cast them into the fire and consume them, they would be better bestowed than they are now. You cannot find so mischievous a manner of throwing them away as either the laying them up for your posterity or the laying them out upon yourselves in folly and superfluity. Of all possible methods of 'throwing them away' these two are the very worst—the most opposite to the gospel of Christ, and the most pernicious to your own soul.

How pernicious to your own soul the latter of these is has been excellently shown by a late writer:

> If we waste our money we are not only guilty of wasting a talent which God has given us, but we do ourselves this farther harm: we turn this useful talent into a powerful means of corrupting ourselves; because so far as it is spent wrong, so far it is spent in the support of some wrong temper, in gratifying some vain and unreasonable desires, which as Christians we are obliged to renounce.
>
> As wit and fine parts cannot be only trifled away, but will expose those that have them to greater follies, so money cannot be only trifled away, but if it is not used according to reason and religion, will make people live a more silly and extravagant life than they would have done without it. If therefore you don't spend your money in doing good to others, you must spend it to the hurt of yourself. You act like one that refuses the cordial to his sick friend which he cannot drink himself without inflaming his blood. For this is the case of superfluous money; if you give it to those who want it it is a cordial; if you spend it upon yourself in something that you do not want it only inflames and disorders your mind.
>
> In using riches where they have no real use, nor we any real want, we only use them to our great hurt, in creating unreasonable desires, in nourishing ill tempers, in indulging in foolish passions, and supporting a vain turn of mind. For high eating and drinking, fine clothes and fine houses, state and equipage,

gay pleasures and diversions, do all of them naturally hurt and disorder our heart. They are the food and nourishment of all the folly and weakness of our nature. They are all of them the support of something that ought not to be supported. They are contrary to that sobriety and piety of heart which relishes divine things. They are so many weights upon our mind, that makes us less able and less inclined to raise our thoughts and affections to things above.

So that money thus spent is not merely wasted or lost, but it is spent to bad purposes and miserable effects; to the corruption and disorder of our hearts; to the making us unable to follow the sublime doctrines of the gospel. It is but like keeping money from the poor to buy poison for ourselves.

24. Equally inexcusable are those who *lay up* what they do not need for any reasonable purposes:

> If a man had hands and eyes and feet that he could give to those that wanted them; if he should lock them up in a chest instead of giving them to his brethren that were blind and lame, should we not justly reckon him an inhuman wretch? If he should rather choose to amuse himself with hoarding them up than entitle himself to an eternal reward by giving them to those that wanted eyes and hands, might we not justly reckon him mad?
>
> Now money has very much the nature of eyes and feet. If therefore we lock it up in chests while the poor and distressed want it for their necessary uses we are not far from the cruelty of him that chooses rather to hoard up the hands and eyes than to give them to those that want them. If we choose to lay it up rather than to entitle ourselves to an eternal reward by disposing of our money well, we are guilty of his madness that rather chooses to lock up eyes and hands than to make himself for ever blessed by giving them to those that want them.

25. May not this be another reason why rich men shall so hardly enter into the kingdom of heaven? A vast majority of them are under a curse, under the peculiar curse of God; inasmuch as in the general tenor of their lives they are not only robbing God continually, embezzling and wasting their Lord's goods, and by that very means corrupting their own souls; but also robbing the poor, the hungry, the naked, wronging the widow and the fatherless, and making themselves accountable for all the want, affliction, and distress which they may but do not remove. Yea, doth not the blood of all those who perish for want of what they either lay up or lay out needlessly, cry against them from the earth? O what account will they give to him who is ready to judge both the quick and the dead!

26. The true way of employing what you do not want yourselves you may, fourthly, learn from those words of our Lord which are the counterpart of what went before: 'Lay up for yourselves treasures in heaven, where neither moth nor rust doth corrupt, and where thieves do not break through and steal.' Put out whatever thou canst spare upon better security than this world can afford. Lay up thy treasures in the bank of heaven; and God shall restore them in that

day. 'He that hath pity upon the poor lendeth unto the Lord,' and look, 'what he layeth out, it shall be paid him again.' Place that, saith he, unto my account. Howbeit, 'thou owest me thine own self also!'

Give to the poor with a single eye, with an upright heart, and write, 'So much given to God.' For 'Inasmuch as ye did it unto one of the least of these my brethren, ye have done it unto me.'

This is the part of a 'faithful and wise steward': not to sell either his houses or lands, or principal stock, be it more or less, unless some peculiar circumstance should require it; and not to desire or endeavour to increase it, any more than to squander it away in vanity; but to employ it wholly to those wise and reasonable purposes for which his Lord has lodged it in his hands. The wise steward, after having provided his own household with what is needful for life and godliness, 'makes' himself 'friends with' all that remains from time to time of the 'mammon of unrighteousness; that when he fails they may receive him into everlasting habitations'; that whensoever his earthly tabernacle is dissolved, they who were before carried into Abraham's bosom, after having eaten his bread, and worn the fleece of his flock, and praised God for the consolation, may welcome him into paradise, and to 'the house of God, eternal in the heavens'.

27. We 'charge you', therefore, 'who are rich in this world', as having authority from our great Lord and Master, ἀγαθοεργεῖν—'to be habitually doing good', to live in a course of good works. 'Be ye merciful as your Father which is in heaven is merciful,' who doth good and ceaseth not. 'Be ye merciful'—'How far?' *After your power,* with all the ability which God giveth. Make this your only measure of doing good, not any beggarly maxims or customs of the world. We charge you to 'be rich in good works'; as you have much, to *give plenteously.* Freely ye have received; freely give; so as to lay up no treasure but in heaven. Be ye 'ready to distribute' to everyone according to his necessity. Disperse abroad, give to the poor: deal your bread to the hungry. Cover the naked with a garment, entertain the stranger, carry or send relief to them that are in prison. Heal the sick; not by miracle, but through the blessing of God upon your seasonable support. Let the blessing of him that was ready to perish through pining want come upon thee. Defend the oppressed, plead the cause of the fatherless, and make the widow's heart sing for joy.

28. We exhort *you* in the name of the Lord Jesus Christ to be 'willing to communicate', κοινωνικοὺς εἶναι; to be of the same spirit (though not in the same outward state) with those believers of ancient times, who 'remained steadfast' ἐν τῇ κοινωνίᾳ, in that blessed and holy 'fellowship' wherein 'none said that anything was his own, but they had all things common.' Be a steward, a faithful and wise steward, of God and of the poor; differing from them in these two circumstances only, that your wants are first supplied out of the portion of your Lord's goods which remains in your hands, and that you have

the blessedness of giving. Thus 'lay up for yourselves a good foundation', not in the world which now is, but rather 'for the time to come, that ye may lay hold on eternal life.' The great foundation indeed of all the blessings of God, whether temporal or eternal, is the Lord Jesus Christ, his righteousness and blood, what he hath done, and what he hath suffered for us. And 'other foundation', in this sense, 'can no man lay'; no, not an apostle, no, not an angel from heaven. But through his merits, whatever we do in his name is a foundation for a good reward in the day when 'every man shall receive his own reward, according to his own labour.' Therefore 'labour' thou, 'not for the meat that perisheth, but for that which endureth unto everlasting life.' Therefore 'whatsoever thy hand' now 'findeth to do, do it with thy might'. Therefore let

> No fair occasion pass unheeded by;
> Snatching the golden moments as they fly,
> Thou by few fleeting years ensure eternity!

'By patient continuance in well-doing, seek' thou 'for glory and honour and immortality.' In a constant, zealous performance of all good works wait thou for that happy hour when 'the King shall say, I was an hungered, and ye gave me meat; I was thirsty, and ye gave me drink. I was a stranger, and ye took me in, naked, and ye clothed me. I was sick, and ye visited me; I was in prison, and ye came unto me.' 'Come, ye blessed of my Father, receive the kingdom prepared for you from the foundation of the world!'

THE ORIGINAL, NATURE, PROPERTIES, AND USE OF THE LAW

Sermon 34 – 1750

AN INTRODUCTORY COMMENT

The most patent danger in Wesley's delicate balancing of faith alone and holy living was its possible tilt toward moralism; something of this sort did occur in Methodism after Wesley's death, despite all his earnest efforts to safeguard against it. But the opposite extreme, antinomianism, was already being vigorously asserted during Wesley's day, as if antinomianism were a valid consequence of 'faith alone'. This controversy had emerged with the Revival itself, in Wesley's disagreements with the Moravians (1739–40). It had been carried forward by the reckless rhetoric of men like William Cudworth, although Wesley had found its substance in the more sophisticated teachings of James Hervey and others.

In the 1740s, Wesley had debated the issue of faith and good works with Count von Zinzendorf and William Cudworth. The urgency of this debate from Wesley's point of view is evident from the pamphlets that he published against Cudworth, as well as several questions and answers in the manuscript Minutes of the Conference in 1745. These publications, however, did not conclude the controversy, as can be seen from many *Journal* entries over the ensuing five years. It was therefore both urgent and appropriate for Wesley to follow his thirteen sermons on the Sermon on the Mount with some additional sermonic essays on the complex, dynamic interdependence of 'Law and Gospel' in his doctrine of salvation. That was the aim and occasion of the following three sermons.

This sermon has a plain and simple outline that follows its title. The 'original' of the Law is man's inborn moral sense—not 'natural' in the deist sense but rather as an aspect of the residual *imago Dei*. The 'nature' of the Law is Christological, as if Torah and Christ are in some sense to be equated. The 'properties' of the Law are threefold: it is holy, just, and good. Here Wesley follows the standard Puritan exegesis of Rom. 7:12 as to the Law's holiness and its instrumentality in the delineation of the just and the good. The 'uses' of the Law are likewise threefold: to convict, convert, and sustain the believer.

This essay is a 'tract for the times' and not the distillate of oral preaching; we have no record of Wesley's having ever preached on Rom. 7:12. This sermon was first published in volume three of *Sermons on Several Occasions* (1750).

The Original, Nature, Properties, and Use of the Law

Wherefore the law is holy, and the commandment holy, and just, and good.
Romans 7:12

1. Perhaps there are few subjects within the whole compass of religion so little understood as this. The reader of this Epistle is usually told, 'By "the law" St. Paul means the Jewish law'; and so, apprehending himself to have no concern therewith, passes on without farther thought about it. Indeed some are not satisfied with this account; but observing the Epistle is directed to the Romans, thence infer that the Apostle in the beginning of this chapter alludes to the old Roman law. But as they have no more concern with this than with the ceremonial law of Moses, so they spend not much thought on what they suppose is occasionally mentioned, barely to illustrate another thing.

2. But a careful observer of the Apostle's discourse will not be content with those slight explications of it. And the more he weighs the words, the more convinced he will be that St. Paul, by 'the law' mentioned in this chapter, does not mean either the ancient law of Rome or the ceremonial law of Moses. This will clearly appear to all who attentively consider the tenor of his discourse. He begins the chapter, 'Know ye not, brethren (for I speak to them that know the law)'—to them who have been instructed therein from their youth—'that the law hath dominion over a man as long as he liveth?' (Rom. 7:1). What? The law of Rome only, or the ceremonial law? No, surely; but the *moral* law. 'For', to give a plain instance, 'the woman that hath an husband is bound by the (moral) law to her husband as long as he liveth. But if her husband be dead, she is loosed from the law of her husband' (Rom. 7:2). 'So, then, if while her husband liveth she be married to another man, she shall be called an adulteress: but if her husband be dead she is free from that law, so that she is no adulteress, though she be married to another man' (Rom. 7:3). From this particular instance the Apostle proceeds to draw that general conclusion: 'Wherefore, my brethren', by a plain parity of reason, 'ye also are become dead to the law', the whole Mosaic institution, 'by the body of Christ' offered for you, and bringing you under a new dispensation: 'that ye should' without any blame 'be married to another, even to him who is raised from the dead', and hath thereby given proof of his authority to make the change, 'that ye should bring forth fruit unto God' (Rom. 7:4). And this we can do now, whereas

before we could not: 'For when we were in the flesh', under the power of the flesh, that is, of corrupt nature (which was necessarily the case till we knew the power of Christ's resurrection), 'the motions of sins which were by the law', which were shown and inflamed by the Mosaic law, not conquered, 'did work in our members', broke out various ways, 'to bring forth fruit unto death' (Rom. 7:5). 'But now we are delivered from the law', from that whole moral as well as ceremonial economy; 'that being dead whereby we were held'–that entire institution being now as it were dead, and having no more authority over us than the husband when dead hath over his wife–'that we should serve' him who died for us and rose again 'in newness of spirit', in a new spiritual dispensation, 'and not in the oldness of the letter' (Rom. 7:6)–with a bare outward service, according to the letter of the Mosaic institution.

3. The Apostle having gone thus far in proving that the Christian had set aside the Jewish dispensation, and that the moral law itself, though it could never pass away, yet stood on a different foundation from what it did before, now stops to propose and answer an objection. 'What shall we say then? Is the law sin?' So some might infer from a misapprehension of those words, 'the motions of sin which were by the law'. 'God forbid!' saith the Apostle, that we should say so. 'Nay', the law is an irreconcilable enemy to sin, searching it out wherever it is. 'I had not known sin but by the law. I had not known lust', evil desire, to be sin, 'except the law had said, Thou shalt not covet' (Rom. 7:7). After opening this farther in the four following verses, he subjoins this general conclusion with regard more especially to the moral law, from which the preceding instance was taken: 'Wherefore the law is holy, and the commandment holy, and just, and good.'

4. In order to explain and enforce these deep words, so little regarded because so little understood, I shall endeavour to show, first, the original of this law; secondly, the nature thereof; thirdly, the properties, that it is 'holy, and just, and good'; and fourthly, the uses of it.

I.1. I shall, first, endeavour to show the original of the moral law, often called 'the law' by way of eminence. Now this is not, as some may possibly have imagined, of so late an institution as the time of Moses. Noah declared it to men long before that time, and Enoch before him. But we may trace its original higher still, even beyond the foundation of the world to that period, unknown indeed to men, but doubtless enrolled in the annals of eternity, when 'the morning stars' first 'sang together', being newly called into existence. It pleased the great Creator to make these his first-born sons intelligent beings, that they might know him that created them. For this end he endued them with understanding, to discern truth from falsehood, good from evil; and as a necessary result of this, with liberty, a capacity of choosing the one and refusing the other. By this they were likewise enabled to offer him a free and willing service: a service rewardable in itself, as well as most acceptable to their gracious Master.

2. To employ all the faculties which he had given them, particularly their understanding and liberty, he gave them a law, a complete model of all truth, so far as was intelligible to a finite being, and of all good, so far as angelic minds were capable of embracing it. It was also the design of their beneficent Governor herein to make way for a continual increase of their happiness; seeing every instance of obedience to that law would both add to the perfection of their nature and entitle them to an higher reward, which the righteous Judge would give in its season.

3. In like manner, when God in his appointed time had created a new order of intelligent beings, when he had raised man from the dust of the earth, breathed into him the breath of life, and caused him to become a living soul, endued with power to choose good or evil, he gave to this free, intelligent creature the same law as to his first-born children—not wrote indeed upon tables of stone, or any corruptible substance, but engraven on his heart by the finger of God, wrote in the inmost spirit both of men and of angels—to the intent it might never be far off, never hard to be understood; but always at hand, and always shining with clear light, even as the sun in the midst of heaven.

4. Such was the original of the law of God. With regard to man, it was coeval with his nature. But with regard to the elder sons of God, it shone in its full splendour 'or ever the mountains were brought forth, or the earth and the round world were made'. But it was not long before man rebelled against God, and by breaking this glorious law wellnigh effaced it out of his heart; 'the eyes of his understanding' being *darkened* in the same measure as his soul was 'alienated from the life of God'. And yet God did not despise the work of his own hands; but being reconciled to man through the Son of his love, he in some measure re-inscribed the law on the heart of his dark, sinful creature. 'He' again 'showed thee, O man, what is good' (although not as in the beginning), 'even to do justly, and to love mercy, and to walk humbly with thy God.'

5. And this he showed not only to our first parents, but likewise to all their posterity, by 'that true light which enlightens every man that cometh into the world'. But notwithstanding this light, all flesh had in process of time 'corrupted their way before him'; till he chose out of mankind a peculiar people, to whom he gave a more perfect knowledge of his law. And the heads of this, because they were slow of understanding, he wrote on two tables of stone; which he commanded the fathers to teach their children through all succeeding generations.

6. And thus it is that the law of God is now made known to them that know not God. They hear, with the hearing of the ear, the things that were written

aforetime for our instruction. But this does not suffice. They cannot by this means comprehend the height and depth and length and breadth thereof. God alone can reveal this by his Spirit. And so he does to all that truly believe, in consequence of that gracious promise made to all the Israel of God: 'Behold, the days come, saith the Lord, that I will make a new covenant with the house of Israel. . . . And this shall be the covenant that I will make. . . . I will put my law in their inward parts, and write it in their hearts; and I will be their God, and they shall be my people' (Jer. 31:31, 33).

II.1. The nature of that law which was originally given to angels in heaven and man in paradise, and which God has so mercifully promised to write afresh in the hearts of all true believers, was the second thing I proposed to show. In order to which I would first observe that although 'the law' and 'the commandment' are sometimes differently taken (the commandment meaning but a part of the law) yet in the text they are used as equivalent terms, implying one and the same thing. But we cannot understand here, either by one or the other, the ceremonial law. 'Tis not the ceremonial law whereof the Apostle says, in the words above recited, 'I had not known sin but by the law': this is too plain to need a proof. Neither is it the ceremonial law which saith, in the words immediately subjoined, 'Thou shalt not covet.' Therefore the ceremonial law has no place in the present question.

2. Neither can we understand by the law mentioned in the text the Mosaic dispensation. 'Tis true the word is sometimes so understood: as when the Apostle says, speaking to the Galatians, 'The covenant which was confirmed before' (namely with Abraham the father of the faithful), 'the law', i.e. the Mosaic dispensation, 'which was four hundred and thirty years after, cannot disannul' (Gal. 3:17). But it cannot be so understood in the text; for the Apostle never bestows so high commendations as these upon that imperfect and shadowy dispensation. He nowhere affirms the Mosaic to be a *spiritual* law; or that it is 'holy, and just, and good'. Neither is it true that God 'will write that law in the hearts' of them whose 'iniquities he remembers no more'. It remains that 'the law', eminently so termed, is no other than the moral law.

3. Now this law is an incorruptible picture of the high and holy One that inhabiteth eternity. It is he whom in his essence no man hath seen or can see, made visible to men and angels. It is the face of God unveiled; God manifested to his creatures as they are able to bear it; manifested to give and not to destroy life; that they may see God and live. It is the heart of God disclosed to man. Yea, in some sense we may apply to this law what the Apostle says of his Son—it is 'the streaming forth' or outbeaming 'of his glory, the express image of his person'.

4. 'If virtue', said the ancient heathen, 'could assume such a shape as that we could behold her with our eyes, what wonderful love would she excite in

us!' If virtue could do this! It is done already. The law of God is all virtues in one, in such a shape as to be beheld with open face by all those whose eyes God hath enlightened. What is the law but divine virtue and wisdom assuming a visible form? What is it but the original ideas of truth and good, which were lodged in the uncreated mind from eternity, now drawn forth and clothed with such a vehicle as to appear even to human understanding?

5. If we survey the law of God in another point of view, it is supreme, unchangeable reason; it is unalterable rectitude; it is the everlasting fitness of all things that are or ever were created. I am sensible what a shortness, and even impropriety, there is in these and all other human expressions, when we endeavour by these faint pictures to shadow out the deep things of God. Nevertheless we have no better, indeed no other way, during this our infant state of existence. As 'we' now 'know' but 'in part', so we are constrained to 'prophesy', i.e. speak of the things of God, 'in part' also. 'We cannot order our speech by reason of darkness' while we are in this house of clay. While I am 'a child' I must 'speak as a child'. But I shall soon 'put away childish things'. For 'when that which is perfect is come, that which is in part shall be done away.'

6. But to return. The law of God (speaking after the manner of men) is a copy of the eternal mind, a transcript of the divine nature; yea, it is the fairest offspring of the everlasting Father, the brightest efflux of his essential wisdom, the visible beauty of the Most High. It is the delight and wonder of cherubim and seraphim and all the company of heaven, and the glory and joy of every wise believer, every well instructed child of God upon earth.

III.1. Such is the nature of the ever-blessed law of God. I am, in the third place, to show the properties of it. Not all, for that would exceed the wisdom of an angel; but those only which are mentioned in the text. These are three: It is 'holy, just, and good'. And first, 'the law is holy.'

2. In this expression the Apostle does not appear to speak of its effects, but rather of its nature. As St. James, speaking of the same thing under another name, says, 'The wisdom from above' (which is no other than this law, written in our heart) 'is first pure' (Jas. 3:17), ἁγνή—chaste, spotless, internally and essentially holy. And consequently, when it is transcribed into the life, as well as the soul, it is (as the same Apostle terms it), θρησκεία καθαρὰ καὶ ἀμίαντος, 'pure religion and undefiled' (Jas. 1:27); or, the pure, clean, unpolluted worship of God.

3. It is indeed in the highest degree pure, chaste, clean, holy. Otherwise it could not be the immediate offspring, and much less the express resemblance of God, who is essential holiness. It is pure from all sin, clean and unspotted from any touch of evil. It is a chaste virgin, incapable of any defilement, of any mixture with that which is unclean or unholy. It has no fellowship with sin of

any kind; for 'what communion hath light with darkness?' As sin is in its very nature enmity to God, so his law is enmity to sin.

4. Therefore it is that the Apostle rejects with such abhorrence that blasphemous supposition that the law of God is either sin itself or the cause of sin. 'God forbid' that we should suppose it is the cause of sin because it is the discoverer of it; because it detects the hidden things of darkness, and drags them out into open day. 'Tis true, by this means (as the Apostle observes, verse 13) 'sin appears to be sin.' All its disguises are torn away, and it appears in its native deformity. 'Tis true likewise that 'sin by the commandment becomes exceeding sinful.' Being now committed against light and knowledge, being stripped even of the poor plea of ignorance, it loses its excuse as well as disguise, and becomes far more odious both to God and man. Yea, and it is true that 'sin worketh death by that which is good,' which in itself is pure and holy. When it is dragged out to light it rages the more: when it is restrained it bursts out with greater violence. Thus the Apostle, speaking in the person of one who was convinced of sin but not yet delivered from it, 'sin taking occasion by the commandment', detecting and endeavouring to restrain it, disdained the restraint, and so much the more 'wrought in me all manner of concupiscence' (verse 8)—all manner of foolish and hurtful desire, which that commandment sought to restrain. Thus 'when the commandment came, sin revived' (verse 9). It fretted and raged the more. But this is no stain on the commandment. Though it is abused it cannot be defiled. This only proves that 'the heart' of man 'is desperately wicked.' But 'the law' of God 'is holy' still.

5. And it is, secondly, *just*. It renders to all their due. It prescribes exactly what is right, precisely what ought to be done, said, or thought, both with regard to the Author of our being, with regard to ourselves, and with regard to every creature which he has made. It is adapted in all respects to the nature of things, of the whole universe and every individual. It is suited to all the circumstances of each, and to all their mutual relations, whether such as have existed from the beginning, or such as commenced in any following period. It is exactly agreeable to the fitnesses of things, whether essential or accidental. It clashes with none of these in any degree, nor is ever unconnected with them. If the word be taken in that sense, there is nothing *arbitrary* in the law of God: although still the whole and every part thereof is totally dependent upon his will, so that 'Thy will be done' is the supreme universal law both in earth and heaven.

6. 'But is the will of God the cause of his law? Is his will the original of right and wrong? Is a thing therefore right because God wills it? Or does he will it because it is right?'

I fear this celebrated question is more curious than useful. And perhaps in the manner it is usually treated of it does not so well consist with the regard that is due from a creature to the Creator and Governor of all things. 'Tis hardly decent for man to call the supreme God to give an account to him! Nevertheless, with awe and reverence we may speak a little. The Lord pardon us if we speak amiss!

7. It seems, then, that the whole difficulty arises from considering God's will as distinct from God. Otherwise it vanishes away. For none can doubt but God is the cause of the law of God. But the will of God is God himself. It is God considered as willing thus or thus. Consequently, to say that the will of God, or that God himself, is the cause of the law, is one and the same thing.

8. Again: if the law, the immutable rule of right and wrong, depends on the nature and fitnesses of things, and on their essential relations to each other (I do not say their eternal relations; because the eternal relations of things existing in time is little less than a contradiction); if, I say, this depends on the nature and relations of things, then it must depend on God, or the will of God; because those things themselves, with all their, relations, are the work of his hands. By his will, 'for his pleasure' alone, they all 'are and were created'.

9. And yet it may be granted (which is probably all that a considerate person would contend for) that in every particular case God wills this or this (suppose that men should honour their parents) because it is right, agreeable to the fitness of things, to the relation wherein they stand.

10. The law then is right and just concerning all things. And it is *good* as well as *just*. This we may easily infer from the fountain whence it flowed. For what was this but the goodness of God? What but goodness alone inclined him to impart that divine copy of himself to the holy angels? To what else can we impute his bestowing upon man the same transcript of his own nature? And what but tender love constrained him afresh to manifest his will to fallen man? Either to Adam or any of his seed, who like him were 'come short of the glory of God'? Was it not mere love that moved him to publish his law, after the understandings of men were darkened? And to send his prophets to declare that law to the blind, thoughtless children of men? Doubtless his goodness it was which raised up Enoch and Noah to be preachers of righteousness; which caused Abraham, his friend, and Isaac and Jacob, to bear witness to his truth. It was his goodness alone which, when 'darkness' had 'covered the earth, and thick darkness the people', gave a written law to Moses, and through him to the nation whom he had chosen. It was his love which explained these living oracles by David and all the prophets that followed; until, when the fullness of time was come, he sent his only-begotten Son, 'not to destroy the law, but to fulfil', to confirm every jot and tittle thereof, till having wrote it in the hearts of all his children, and put all his enemies under his feet, 'he shall deliver up' his mediatorial 'kingdom to the Father', 'that God may be all in all'.

11. And this law which the goodness of God gave at first, and has preserved through all ages, is, like the fountain from whence it springs, full of goodness and benignity. It is mild and kind; it is (as the Psalmist expresses it) 'sweeter

than honey and the honeycomb'. It is winning and amiable. It includes 'whatsoever things are lovely or of good report. If there be any virtue, if there be any praise' before God and his holy angels, they are all comprised in this: wherein are hid all the treasures of the divine wisdom and knowledge and love.

12. And it is *good* in its effects, as well as in its nature. As the tree is, so are its fruits. The fruits of the law of God written in the heart are 'righteousness and peace and assurance for ever'. Or rather, the law itself is righteousness, filling the soul with a peace that passeth all understanding, and causing us to rejoice evermore in the testimony of a good conscience toward God. It is not so properly a pledge as an 'earnest of our inheritance', being a part of the purchased possession. It is God made manifest in our flesh, and bringing with him eternal life; assuring us by that pure and perfect love that we are 'sealed unto the day of redemption'; that he will 'spare us, as a man spareth his own son that serveth him, in the day when he maketh up his jewels', and that there remaineth for us 'a crown of glory which fadeth not away'.

IV.1. It remains only to show, in the fourth and last place, the uses of the law. And the first use of it, without question, is to convince the world of sin. This is indeed the peculiar work of the Holy Ghost, who can work it without any means at all, or by whatever means it pleaseth him, however insufficient in themselves, or even improper to produce such an effect accordingly, some there are whose hearts have been broken in pieces in a moment, either in sickness or in health, without any visible cause, or any outward means whatever. And others (one in an age) have been awakened to a sense of 'the wrath of God abiding on them' by hearing that 'God was in Christ, reconciling the world unto himself'. But it is the ordinary method of the Spirit of God to convict sinners by the law. It is this which, being set home on the conscience, generally breaketh the rocks in pieces. It is more especially this part of 'the word of God' which 'is' ζῶν καὶ ἐνεργής, 'quick and powerful', full of life and energy, 'and sharper than any two-edged sword'. This, in the hand of God and of those whom he hath sent, 'pierces' through all the folds of a deceitful heart, and 'divides asunder even the soul and spirit', yea, as it were, the very 'joints and marrow'. By this is the sinner discovered to himself. All his fig leaves are torn away, and he sees that he is 'wretched, and poor, and miserable, and blind, and naked'. The law flashes conviction on every side. He feels himself a mere sinner. He has nothing to pay. His 'mouth is stopped,' and he stands 'guilty before God'.

2. To slay the sinner is then the first use of the law; to destroy the life and strength wherein he trusts, and convince him that he is dead while he liveth; not only under sentence of death, but actually dead unto God, void of all spiritual life, 'dead in trespasses and sins'. The second use of it is to bring him unto life, unto Christ, that he may live. 'Tis true, in performing both these

offices it acts the part of a severe schoolmaster. It drives us by force, rather than draws us by love. And yet love is the spring of all. It is the spirit of love which, by this painful means, tears way our confidence in the flesh, which leaves us no broken reed whereon to trust, and so constrains the sinner, stripped of all, to cry out in the bitterness of his soul, or groan in the depth of his heart,

> I give up every plea beside
> 'Lord, I am damned–but thou hast died.'

3. The third use of the law is to keep us alive. It is the grand means whereby the blessed Spirit prepares the believer for larger communications of the life of God.

I am afraid this great and important truth is little understood, not only by the world, but even by many whom God hath taken out of the world, who are real children of God by faith. Many of these lay it down as an unquestioned truth that when we come to Christ we have done with the law; and that in *this* sense, 'Christ is the end of the law to everyone that believeth.' 'The end of the law'. So he is, 'for righteousness', for justification, 'to everyone that believeth'. Herein the law is at an end. It justifies none, but only brings them to Christ; who is also, in another respect, 'the end' or scope 'of the law'–the point at which it continually aims. But when it has brought us to him it has yet a farther office, namely, to keep us with him. For it is continually exciting all believers, the more they see of its height and depth and length and breadth, to exhort one another so much the more:

> Closer and closer let us cleave
> To his beloved embrace;
> Expect his fullness to receive,
> And grace to answer grace.

4. Allowing then that every believer has done with the law, as it means the Jewish ceremonial law, or the entire Mosaic dispensation (for these Christ 'hath taken out of the way'); yea, allowing we have done with the moral law as a means of procuring our justification (for we are 'justified freely by his grace, through the redemption that is in Jesus'); yet in another sense we have not done with this law. For it is still of unspeakable use, first, in convincing us of the sin that yet remains both in our hearts and lives, and thereby keeping us close to Christ, that his blood may cleanse us every moment; secondly, in deriving strength from our Head into his living members, whereby he empowers them to do what his law commands; and thirdly, in confirming our hope of whatsoever it commands and we have not yet attained, of receiving grace upon grace, till we are in actual possession of the fullness of his promises.

5. How clearly does this agree with the experience of every true believer! While he cries out: 'O what love have I unto thy law! All the day long is my

study in it,' he sees daily in that divine mirror more and more of his own sinfulness. He sees more and more clearly that he is still a sinner in all things; that neither his heart nor his ways are right before God; and that every moment sends him to Christ. This shows him the meaning of what is written: 'Thou shalt make a plate of pure gold, and grave upon it, Holiness to the Lord. And it shall be upon Aaron's forehead' (the type of our great High Priest) 'that Aaron may bear the iniquities of the holy things, which the children of Israel shall hallow in all their holy gifts' (so far are our prayers or holy things from atoning for the rest of our sins); 'and it shall be always upon his forehead, that they may be accepted before the Lord' (Exod. 28:36, 38).

6. To explain this by a single instance. The law says, 'Thou shalt not kill,' and hereby (as our Lord teaches) forbids not only outward acts but every unkind word or thought. Now the more I look into this perfect law, the more I feel how far I come short of it; and the more I feel this, the more I feel my need of his blood to atone for all my sin, and of his Spirit to purify my heart, and make me 'perfect and entire, lacking nothing'.

7. Therefore I cannot spare the law one moment, no more than I can spare Christ; seeing I now want it as much to keep me to Christ as ever I wanted it to bring me to him. Otherwise this 'evil heart of unbelief' would immediately 'depart from the living God'. Indeed each is continually sending me to the other–the law to Christ, and Christ to the law. On the one hand, the height and depth of the law constrain me to fly to the love of God in Christ; on the other, the love of God in Christ endears the law to me 'above gold or precious stones'; seeing I know every part of it is a gracious promise, which my Lord will fulfil in its season.

8. Who art thou then, O man, that 'judgest the law, and speakest evil of the law'? That rankest it with sin, Satan, and death, and sendest them all to hell together? The Apostle James esteemed 'judging' or 'speaking evil of the law' so enormous a piece of wickedness that he knew not how to aggravate the guilt of judging our brethren more than by showing it included this. So now, says he, 'thou art not a doer of the law but a judge!' A judge of that which God hath ordained to judge thee. So thou hast set up thyself in the judgment seat of Christ, and cast down the rule whereby he will judge the world! O take knowledge what advantage Satan hath gained over thee! And for the time to come never think or speak lightly of, much less dress up as a scarecrow, this blessed instrument of the grace of God. Yea, love and value it for the sake of him from whom it came, and of him to whom it leads. Let it be thy glory and joy, next to the cross of Christ. Declare its praise, and make it honourable before all men.

9. And if thou art thoroughly convinced that it is the offspring of God, that it is the copy of all his imitable perfections, and that it 'is holy, and just, and good', but especially to them that believe; then instead of casting it away as a

polluted thing, see that thou cleave to it more and more. Never let the law of mercy and truth, of love to God and man, of lowliness, meekness, and purity forsake thee. 'Bind it about thy neck: write it on the table of thy heart.' Keep close to the law if thou wilt keep close to Christ; hold it fast; let it not go. Let this continually lead thee to the atoning blood, continually confirm thy hope, till all 'the righteousness of the law is fulfilled in thee', and thou art 'filled with all the fullness of God'.

10. And if thy Lord hath already fulfilled his word, if he hath already 'written his law in thy heart', then 'stand fast in the liberty wherewith Christ hath made thee free.' Thou art not only made free from Jewish ceremonies, from the guilt of sin and the fear of hell (these are so far from being the whole, that they are the least and lowest part of Christian liberty), but what is infinitely more, from the power of sin, from serving the devil, from offending God. O stand fast in this liberty, in comparison of which all the rest is not even worthy to be named. Stand fast in loving God with all thy heart and serving him with all thy strength. This is perfect freedom; thus to keep his law and to walk in all commandments blameless. 'Be not entangled again with the yoke of bondage.' I do not mean of Jewish bondage; nor yet of bondage to the fear of hell: these, I trust, are far from thee. But beware of being entangled again with the yoke of sin, of any inward or outward transgression of the law. Abhor sin far more than death or hell; abhor sin itself far more than the punishment of it. Beware of the bondage of pride, of desire, of anger; of every evil temper or word or work. 'Look unto Jesus', and in order thereto 'look' more and more 'into the perfect law, the law of liberty', and 'continue therein'; so shalt thou daily 'grow in grace, and in the knowledge of our Lord Jesus Christ.'

THE LAW ESTABLISHED THROUGH FAITH

DISCOURSE I

Sermon 35 – 1750

AN INTRODUCTORY COMMENT

The twin discourses entitled 'The Law Established through Faith' amount to a single essay in two parts. In this first essay, Wesley turns on his critics and charges them with 'voiding the Law' by (1) 'not preaching it at all', (2) by preaching 'faith' so as to 'supersede the necessity of holiness', or (3) by making it void in fact by 'living as if faith was designed to excuse us from holiness'.

The danger in discounting the Law, of course, was the concomitant moral and spiritual laxity of antinomianism. Wesley had discovered this tendency to 'make void the whole law' especially in the Moravians and Calvinists, as others before him had seen a certain lawlessness in the Puritan Commonwealth of the previous century. Their way of 'preaching Christ', Wesley felt, often magnified the Gospel by lifting up Christ's promises and omitting his commands in such a way as to make void both the Law and the Gospel.

In this discourse, Wesley is careful to distinguish the ways in which a believer 'under grace' is and is not still under the Law. He grants that obedience to the ceremonial law, the whole of the Mosaic institution, or even the whole moral law are no longer conditions of our acceptance with God. But acceptance comes by God's grace to the believer who has 'such a faith as, working by love, produces all obedience and holiness'. Wesley's tightest logic appears in the second part where he challenges the 'main pillar of antinomianism' based on Rom. 4:5–the believer's faith 'is counted for righteousness'. He grants that it may count for 'preceding righteousness' but certainly not 'subsequent righteousness'. Wesley ends the sermon with a typical litany of questions for self-examination that test the reader's zeal for and diligence in Christian living.

This work is probably not the distillate of Wesley's oral preaching, since there are only two clear references to his use of Rom. 3:31, both in 1741. This sermon was first published in the third volume of Wesley's *Sermons on Several Occasions* (1750). It was reprinted separately (with the other two sermons on the Law) four times during Wesley's lifetime and was included in all the successive collections of his published sermons.

The Law Established through Faith

Discourse I

Do we then make void the law through faith?
God forbid! Yea, we establish the law.
Romans 3:31

1. St. Paul having in the beginning of this Epistle laid down his general proposition, namely, that 'the gospel of Christ is the power of God unto salvation to everyone that believeth'—the powerful means whereby God makes every believer a partaker of present and eternal salvation—goes on to show that there is no other way under heaven whereby men can be saved. He speaks particularly of salvation from the guilt of sin, which he commonly terms justification. And that all men stood in need of this, that none could plead their own innocence, he proves at large by various arguments addressed to the Jews as well as the heathens. Hence he infers (in the nineteenth verse of this chapter) 'that every mouth', whether of Jew or heathen, must 'be stopped' from excusing or justifying himself, 'and all the world become guilty before God. Therefore', saith he, by his own obedience, 'by the works of the law, shall no flesh be justified in his sight' (Rom.3:20). 'But now the righteousness of God without the law', without our previous obedience thereto, 'is manifested (Rom 3:21); even the righteousness of God which is by faith of Jesus Christ unto all and upon all that believe; for there is no difference' (Rom. 3:22) as to their need of justification, or the manner wherein they attain it. 'For all have sinned, and come short of the glory of God' (Rom. 3:23), the glorious image of God wherein they were created: and all (who attain) 'are justified freely by his grace, through the redemption that is in Jesus Christ (Rom. 3:24); whom God hath set forth to be a propitiation through faith in his blood (Rom. 3:25); . . . that he might be just, and yet the justifier of him which believeth in Jesus' (Rom. 3:26); that without any impeachment to his justice he might show him mercy for the sake of that propitiation. 'Therefore we conclude' (which was the grand position he had undertaken to establish) 'that a man is justified by faith, without the works of the law' (Rom. 3:28).

2. It was easy to foresee an objection which might be made, and which has in fact been made in all ages; namely, that to say 'we are justified without the works of the law' is to abolish the law. The Apostle, without entering into a formal dispute, simply denies the charge. 'Do we then', says he, 'make void the law through faith? God forbid! Yea, we establish the law.'

3. The strange imagination of some that St. Paul, when he says, 'A man is justified without the works of the law,' means only the *ceremonial* law, is abundantly confuted by these very words. For did St. Paul 'establish' the *ceremonial* law? It is evident he did not. He did 'make void' that law through faith, and openly avowed his doing so. It was the *moral* law only of which he might truly say, we do not make void but 'establish' this 'through faith'.

4. But all men are not herein of his mind. Many there are who will not agree to this. Many in all ages of the church, even among those who bore the name of Christians, have contended that 'the faith once delivered to the saints' was designed to make void the whole law. They would no more spare the moral than the ceremonial law, but were for 'hewing', as it were, 'both in pieces before the Lord': vehemently maintaining, 'If you establish any law, "Christ shall profit you nothing. Christ is become of no effect to you; ye are fallen from grace."'

5. But is the zeal of these men according to knowledge? Have they observed the connection between the law and faith? And that, considering the close connection between them, to destroy one is indeed to destroy both? That to abolish the moral law is, in truth, to abolish faith and the law together, as leaving no proper means either of bringing us to faith or of 'stirring up that gift of God' in our soul?

6. It therefore behoves all who desire either to come to Christ, or to 'walk in him whom they have received', to take heed how they 'make void the law through faith'; to secure us effectually against which let us inquire, first, which are the most usual ways of 'making void the law through faith'; and, secondly, how we may follow the Apostle, and by faith 'establish the law'.

I.1. Let us, first, inquire which are the most usual ways of 'making void the law through faith'. Now the way for a preacher to make it all void at a stroke is not to preach it at all. This is just the same thing as to blot it out of the oracles of God. More especially when it is done with design; when it is made a rule, 'not to preach the law'—and the very phrase, 'a preacher of the law', is used as a term of reproach, as though it meant little less than 'an enemy to the gospel'.

2. All this proceeds from the deepest ignorance of the nature, properties, and use of the law; and proves that those who act thus either know not Christ, are utter strangers to the living faith, or at least that they are but babes in Christ, and as such 'unskilled in the word of righteousness'.

3. Their grand plea is this, that preaching the gospel (that is, according to their judgment, the speaking of nothing but the sufferings and merits of Christ) answers all the ends of the law. But this we utterly deny. It does not answer the very first end of the law, namely, the convincing men of sin, the awakening those who are still asleep on the brink of hell. There may have been here and

there an exempt case. One in a thousand may have been awakened by the gospel. But this is no general rule. The ordinary method of God is to convict sinners by the law, and that only. The gospel is not the means which God hath ordained, or which our Lord himself used, for this end. We have no authority in Scripture for applying it thus, nor any ground to think it will prove effectual. Nor have we any more ground to expect this from the nature of the thing. 'They that be whole', as our Lord himself observes, 'need not a physician, but they that be sick.' It is absurd therefore to offer a physician to them that are whole, or that at least imagine themselves so to be. You are first to convince them that they are sick; otherwise they will not thank you for your labour. It is equally absurd to offer Christ to them whose heart is whole, having never yet been broken. It is, in the proper sense, 'casting pearls before swine'. Doubtless 'they will trample them under foot'; and it is no more than you have reason to expect if they also 'turn again and rend you'.

4. 'But although there is no command in Scripture to offer Christ to the careless sinner, yet are there not scriptural precedents for it?' I think not: I know not any. I believe you can't produce one, either from the four evangelists, or the Acts of the Apostles. Neither can you prove this to have been the practice of any of the apostles from any passage in all their writings.

5. 'Nay, does not the Apostle Paul say, in his former Epistle to the Corinthians, "We preach Christ crucified"? (1 Cor. 1:23) and in his latter, "We preach not ourselves, but Christ Jesus the Lord"?' (2 Cor. 4:5).

We consent to rest the cause on this issue: to tread in his steps, to follow his example. Only preach you just as St. Paul preached, and the dispute is at an end.

For although we are certain he *preached Christ* in as perfect a manner as the very chief of the apostles, yet who *preached the law* more than St. Paul? Therefore he did not think the gospel answered the same end.

6. The very first sermon of St. Paul's which is recorded concludes in these words: 'By him all that believe are justified from all things, from which ye could not be justified by the law of Moses. Beware therefore lest that come upon you which is spoken of in the Prophets: Behold, ye despisers, and wonder and perish; for I work a work in your days, a work which you will in no wise believe, though a man declare it unto you' (Acts 13:39–45). Now it is manifest, all this is 'preaching the law', in the sense wherein you understand the term; even although great part of, if not all, his hearers were either 'Jews or religious proselytes' (Acts 13:43), and therefore probably many of them, in some degree at least, convinced of sin already. He first reminds them that they could not be justified by the law of Moses, but only by faith in Christ; and then severely threatens them with the judgments of God, which is, in the strongest sense, 'preaching the law'.

7. In his next discourse, that to the heathens at Lystra (Acts 14:15, etc.), we

do not find so much as the name of Christ. The whole purport of it is that they should 'turn from those vain idols unto the living God'. Now confess the truth. Do not you think if you had been there you could have preached much better than he? I should not wonder if you thought too that his *preaching so ill* occasioned his being *so ill treated*; and that his being *stoned* was a just judgment upon him for not *preaching Christ!*

8. To the jailer indeed, when he 'sprang in and came trembling, and fell down before Paul and Silas, and said, Sirs, What must I do to be saved?', he immediately 'said, Believe in the Lord Jesus Christ' (Acts 16:29-31). And in the case of one so deeply convinced of sin, who would not have said the same? But to the men of Athens you find him speaking in a quite different manner, reproving their superstition, ignorance, and idolatry, and strongly moving them to repent, from the consideration of a future judgment, and of the resurrection from the dead (Acts 17:22-31). Likewise 'when Felix sent for Paul', on purpose that he might 'hear him concerning the faith in Christ'; instead of preaching Christ in *your* sense (which would probably have caused the governor either to mock or to contradict and blaspheme) 'he reasoned of righteousness, temperance, and judgment to come', till 'Felix' (hardened as he was) 'trembled' (Acts 24:24-25). Go thou and tread in his steps. *Preach* Christ to the careless sinner by 'reasoning of righteousness, temperance, and judgment to come'!

9. If you say, 'But he *preached Christ* in a different manner in his epistles,' I answer, [1] he did not there preach at all, not in that sense wherein we speak; for 'preaching' in our present question means speaking before a congregation. But waiving this I answer, (2) his epistles are directed, not to unbelievers, such as those we are now speaking of, but to 'the saints of God' in Rome, Corinth, Philippi, and other places. Now unquestionably he would speak more of Christ to these than to those who were without God in the world. And yet, (3) every one of these is full of the law, even the Epistles to the Romans and the Galatians, in both of which he does what you term preaching the law, and that to believers as well as unbelievers.

10. From hence 'tis plain you know not what it is to 'preach Christ', in the sense of the Apostle. For doubtless St. Paul judged himself to be preaching Christ both to Felix, and at Antioch, Lystra, and Athens: from whose example every thinking man must infer that not only the declaring the love of Christ to sinners, but also the declaring that he will come from heaven in flaming fire, is, in the Apostle's sense, 'preaching Christ'. Yea, in the full scriptural meaning of the word. To preach Christ is to preach what he hath revealed, either in the Old or New Testament; so that you are then as really preaching Christ when you are saying, 'The wicked shall be turned into hell, and all the people that forget God,' as when you are saying, 'Behold the Lamb of God, which taketh away the sin of the world!'

11. Consider this well: that to 'preach Christ' is to preach all things that Christ hath spoken: all his promises; all his threatenings and commands; all that is written in his Book. And then you will know how to preach Christ without making void the law.

12. 'But does not the greatest blessing attend those discourses wherein we peculiarly preach the merits and sufferings of Christ?' Probably, when we preach to a congregation of mourners or of believers, these will be attended with the greatest blessing; because such discourses are peculiarly suited to their state. At least these will usually convey the most comfort. But this is not always the greatest blessing. I may sometimes receive a far greater by a discourse that cuts me to the heart and humbles me to the dust. Neither should I receive that comfort if I were to preach or to hear no discourses but on the sufferings of Christ. These by constant repetition would lose their force, and grow more and more flat and dead, till at length they would become a dull round of words, without any spirit or life or virtue. So that thus to 'preach Christ' must, in process of time, make void the gospel as well as the law.

II.1. A second way of 'making void the law through faith' is the teaching that faith supersedes the necessity of holiness. This divides itself into a thousand smaller paths—and many there are that walk therein. Indeed there are few that wholly escape it; few who are convinced we 'are saved by faith' but are sooner or later, more or less, drawn aside into this by-way.

2. All those are drawn into this by-way who, if it be not their settled judgment that faith in Christ entirely sets aside the necessity of keeping his law, yet suppose either, (1) that holiness is less necessary now than it was before Christ came; or, (2) that a less degree of it is necessary; or, (3) that it is less necessary to believers than to others. Yea, and so are all those who, although their judgment be right in the general, yet think they may take more liberty in particular cases than they could have done before they believed. Indeed the using the term *liberty* in such a manner for 'liberty from obedience or holiness' shows at once that their judgment is perverted, and that they are guilty of what they imagined to be far from them; namely, of 'making void the law through faith', by supposing faith to supersede holiness.

3. The first plea of those who teach this expressly is that we are now under the covenant of grace, not works; and therefore we are no longer under the necessity of performing the works of the law.

And who ever was under the covenant of works? None but Adam before the fall. He was fully and properly under that covenant, which required perfect, universal obedience, as the one condition of acceptance, and left no place for pardon, upon the very least transgression. But no man else was ever under this, neither Jew nor Gentile, neither before Christ nor since. All his sons were and are under the covenant of grace. The manner of their acceptance is this:

the free grace of God, through the merits of Christ, gives pardon to them that believe, that believe with such a faith as, working by love, produces all obedience and holiness.

4. The case is not therefore, as you suppose, that men were *once* more obliged to obey God, or to work the works of his law, than they are *now*. This is a supposition you cannot make good. But we should have been obliged, if we had been under the covenant of works, to have done those works antecedent to our acceptance. Whereas now all good works, though as necessary as ever, are not antecedent to our acceptance, but consequent upon it. Therefore the nature of the covenant of grace gives you no ground, no encouragement at all, to set aside any instance or degree of obedience, any part or measure of holiness.

5. 'But are we not "justified by faith, without the works of the law"?' Undoubtedly we are, without the works either of the ceremonial or the moral law. And would to God all men were convinced of this! It would prevent innumerable evils: antinomianism in particular—for, generally speaking, they are the Pharisees who make the antinomians. Running into an extreme so palpably contrary to Scripture, they occasion others to run into the opposite one. These, seeking to be justified by works, affright those from allowing any place for them.

6. But the truth lies between both. We are, doubtless, 'justified by faith'. This is the corner-stone of the whole Christian building. 'We are justified without the works of the law' as any previous condition of justification. But they are an immediate fruit of that faith whereby we are justified. So that if good works do not follow our faith, even all inward and outward holiness, it is plain our faith is nothing worth; we are yet in our sins. Therefore that we are 'justified by faith', even by 'faith without works', is no ground for 'making void the law through faith'; or for imagining that faith is a dispensation from any kind or degree of holiness.

7. 'Nay, but does not St. Paul expressly say, "Unto him that worketh not, but believeth on him that justifieth the ungodly, his faith is counted for righteousness"? And does it not follow from hence that faith is to a believer in the room, in the place, of righteousness? But if faith is in the room of righteousness or holiness, what need is there of this too?'

This, it must be acknowledged, comes home to the point, and is indeed the main pillar of antinomianism. And yet it needs not a long or laboured answer. We allow, (1) that God 'justifies the ungodly', him that till that hour is totally ungodly, full of all evil, void of all good; (2) that he justifies 'the ungodly that worketh not', that till that moment worketh no good work—neither can he: for an evil tree cannot bring forth good fruit; (3) that he justifies him 'by faith alone', without any goodness or righteousness preceding; and (4) that 'faith is' then 'counted to him for righteousness', namely, for *preceding righteousness*; i.e. God, through the merits of Christ, accepts him that believes as if he had already fulfilled all righteousness. But what is all this to your point? The Apostle does not say either here or elsewhere that this faith is counted to him for *subsequent righteousness.* He does teach that there is no righteousness *before* faith; but where does he teach that there is none *after* it? He does assert holiness cannot *precede* justification; but not that it need not *follow* it. St. Paul therefore gives you no colour for 'making void the law' by teaching that faith supersedes the necessity of holiness.

III.1. There is yet another way of 'making void the law through faith', which is more common than either of the former. And that is, the doing it practically; the making it void in *fact,* though not in *principle;* the *living* as if faith was designed to excuse us from holiness.

How earnestly does the Apostle guard us against this, in those well-known words: 'What then? Shall we sin, because we are not under the law, but under grace? God forbid!' (Rom. 6:15). A caution which it is needful thoroughly to consider, because it is of the last importance.

2. The being 'under the law' may here mean, (1) the being obliged to observe the ceremonial laws; (2) the being obliged to conform to the whole Mosaic institution; (3) the being obliged to keep the whole moral law as the condition of our acceptance with God; and, (4) the being under the wrath and curse of God, under sentence of eternal death; under a sense of guilt and condemnation, full of horror and slavish fear.

3. Now although a believer is 'not without law to God, but under the law to Christ', yet from the moment he believes he is not 'under the law', in any of the preceding senses. On the contrary, he is 'under grace', under a more benign, gracious dispensation. As he is no longer under the ceremonial law, nor under the Mosaic institution; as he is not obliged to keep even the moral law as the condition of his acceptance, so he is delivered from the wrath and the curse of God, from all sense of guilt and condemnation, and from all that horror and fear of death and hell whereby he was 'all his life' before 'subject to bondage'. And he now performs (which while 'under the law' he could not do) a willing and universal obedience. He obeys, not from the motive of slavish fear, but on a nobler principle, namely, the grace of God ruling in his heart, and causing all his works to be wrought in love.

4. What then? Shall this evangelical principle of action be less powerful than the legal? Shall we be less obedient to God from filial love than we were from servile fear?

'Tis well if this is not a common case; if this practical antinomianism, this unobserved way of 'making void the law through faith', has not infected thousands of believers.

Has it not infected you? Examine yourself honestly and closely. Do you not do now what you durst not have done when you was 'under the law', or (as we commonly call it) 'under conviction'? For instance: you durst not then indulge yourself in food. You took just what was needful, and that of the cheapest kind. Do you not allow yourself more latitude now? Do you not indulge yourself a *little* more than you did? O beware lest you 'sin because you are not under the law, but under grace'!

5. When you was under conviction, you durst not indulge the lust of the eye in any degree. You would not do anything, great or small, merely to gratify your curiosity. You regarded only cleanliness and necessity, or at most very moderate convenience, either in furniture or apparel; superfluity and finery of whatever kind, as well as fashionable elegance, were both a terror and an abomination to you.

Are they so still? Is your conscience as tender now in these things as it was then? Do you still follow the same rule both in furniture and apparel, trampling all finery, all superfluity, everything useless, everything merely ornamental, however fashionable, under foot? Rather, have you not resumed what you had once laid aside, and what you could not then use without wounding your conscience? And have you not learned to say, 'Oh, I am not *so scrupulous* now.' I would to God you were! Then you would not sin thus 'because you are not under the law, but under grace'.

6. You was once scrupulous, too, of commending any to their face; and still more of suffering any to commend *you*. It was a stab to your heart; you could not bear it; you sought the honour that cometh of God only. You could not endure such conversation, nor any conversation which was not good to the use of edifying. All idle talk, all trifling discourse, you abhorred; you hated as well as feared it, being deeply sensible of the value of time, of every precious fleeting moment. In like manner you dreaded and abhorred idle expense; valuing your money only less than your time, and trembling lest you should be found an unfaithful steward even of the mammon of unrighteousness.

Do you now look upon praise as deadly poison, which you can neither give nor receive but at the peril of your soul? Do you still dread and abhor all conversation which does not tend to the use of edifying, and labour to improve every moment that it may not pass without leaving you better than it found you? Are not you less careful as to the expense both of money and time? Cannot you now lay out either as you could not have done once? Alas! How has that 'which should have been for your health proved to you an occasion of falling'! How have you 'sinned, because you was not under the law, but under grace'!

7. God forbid you should any longer continue thus to 'turn the grace of God into lasciviousness'! O remember how clear and strong a conviction you once had concerning all these things! And at the same time you was fully satisfied from whom that conviction came. The world told you you was in a delusion; but you knew it was the voice of God. In these things you was not *too scrupulous* then; but you are not now *scrupulous enough*. God kept you longer

in that painful school that you might learn those great lessons the more perfectly. And have you forgot them already? O recollect them, before it is too late. Have you suffered so many things in vain? I trust it is not yet in vain. Now use the conviction without the pain. Practise the lesson without the rod. Let not the mercy of God weigh less with you now than his fiery indignation did before. Is love a less powerful motive than fear? If not, let it be an invariable rule, 'I will do nothing now I am *under grace* which I durst not have done when *under the law*'.

8. I cannot conclude this head without exhorting you to examine yourself, likewise, touching sins of omission. Are you as clear of these, now you are 'under grace', as you was when 'under the law'? How diligent was you then in hearing the Word of God! Did you neglect any opportunity? Did you not attend thereon day and night? Would a small hindrance have kept you away? A little business? A visitant? A slight indisposition? A soft bed? A dark or cold morning? Did not you then fast often? Or use abstinence to the uttermost of your power? Was not you much in prayer (cold and heavy as you was) while you was hanging over the mouth of hell? Did you not speak and not spare, even for an unknown God? Did you not boldly plead his cause? Reprove sinners? And avow the truth before an adulterous generation? And are you now a believer in Christ? Have you the 'faith that overcometh the world'? What! and are less zealous for your Master now than you was when you knew him not? Less diligent in fasting, in prayer, in hearing his Word, in calling sinners to God? O repent! See and feel your grievous loss! Remember from whence you are fallen! Bewail your unfaithfulness! Now be zealous and do the first works; lest, if you continue to 'make void the law through faith', God cut you off, and 'appoint' you your 'portion with the unbelievers'!

THE LAW ESTABLISHED THROUGH FAITH
DISCOURSE II

Sermon 36 – 1750

What we have in this and the previous sermon is yet a further variation on the central theme of the series on the Sermon on the Mount: the distinctive character of evangelical ethics in which the *fides caritate formata* is always the consequent of the *sola fide*, never its alternative. For two decades, Wesley had challenged some of the more radical Protestant interpretations of what it meant for Christians to be under the 'new covenant' of grace as distinguished from the 'old covenant' of works. This set of sermons on the Law is a careful attempt by Wesley to delineate his view of the relationship between the two.

In this second discourse, Wesley argues that the Law is and ought to be 'established by faith': (1) by preaching 'our doctrine' in its whole extent, explaining and enforcing it in the same manner as our great Teacher did while upon earth—this goal is accomplished by 'preaching Christ' in all his offices, Priest, Prophet, and King; (2) by preaching 'faith alone' so as to promote holiness rather than to supersede or subordinate it—faith is still only the 'handmaid of love'; and (3) by manifesting holy living in Christian hearts and lives—'without this, what would all the rest avail?'

This sermon has one of Wesley's most interesting and original proposals: that faith is in order to love and, therefore, that 'love will exist after faith' (II.1-6). This idea seems to echo St. Ignatius of Antioch, 'The beginning [of the Christian life] is faith but the end is love' (*Epistle to the Ephesians*, 14:1). Here, as in the previous sermon, Wesley comes down rather hard on those who 'magnify faith beyond all proportion' and assume that being 'under grace' excuses a multitude of evils. Wesley turns the idea of grace around and shows that we are not thereby freed from the law but rather are thereby enabled to fulfill the law—empowered 'to fulfill all righteousness.' The sermon ends with a typical appeal to the reader to apply this message personally through careful self-examination.

This sermon was first published in volume three of Wesley's *Sermons on Several Occasions* (1750). It was reprinted separately (together with the other two sermons on the Law) four times during Wesley's lifetime and was also included in the subsequent collections of his published sermons.

The Law Established through Faith
Discourse II

Do we then make void the law through faith?
God forbid! Yea, we establish the law.
Romans 3:31

1. It has been shown in the preceding discourse which are the most usual ways of 'making void the law through faith'. Namely, first, the not preaching it at all, which effectually makes it all void at a stroke, and this under colour of 'preaching Christ' and magnifying the gospel—though it be, in truth, destroying both the one and the other. Secondly, the teaching (whether directly or indirectly) that faith supersedes the necessity of holiness, that this is less necessary now, or a less degree of it necessary, than before Christ came; that it is less necessary to us because we believe than otherwise it would have been; or that Christian liberty is a liberty from any kind or degree of holiness—so perverting those great truths that we are now under the *covenant of grace* and not of *works*; that 'a man is justified by faith, without the works of the law'; and that 'to him that worketh not, but believeth, his faith is counted for righteousness'. Or, thirdly, the doing this practically: the making void the law in practice though not in principle; the living or acting as if faith was designed to excuse us from holiness; the allowing ourselves in sin 'because we are not under the law, but under grace'. It remains to inquire how we may follow a better pattern, how we may be able to say with the Apostle, 'Do we then make void the law through faith? God forbid! Yea, we establish the law.'

2. We do not indeed establish the old ceremonial law: we know that is abolished for ever. Much less do we establish the whole Mosaic dispensation—this, we know, our Lord has 'nailed to his cross'. Nor yet do we so establish the moral law (which, it is to be feared, too many do) as if the fulfilling it, the keeping all the commandments, were the condition of our justification. If it were so, surely 'in his sight should no man living be justified'. But all this being allowed, we still, in the Apostle's sense, 'establish the law', the moral law.

I.1. We 'establish the law', first, by our doctrine: by endeavouring to preach it in its whole extent, to explain and enforce every part of it in the same manner as our great Teacher did while upon earth. We establish it by following St. Peter's advice, 'If any man speak, let him speak as the oracles of God'; as the holy men of old, moved by the Holy Ghost, spoke and wrote for our instruction; and as the apostles of our blessed Lord, by the direction of the same Spirit. We establish it whenever we speak in his name, by keeping back nothing from them that hear; by declaring to them without any limitation or reserve the whole counsel of God. And in order the more effectually to establish it we use herein great plainness of speech. 'We are not as many that corrupt the word of God', καπηλεύουσι (as artful men their bad wines); we do not cauponize, mix, adulterate, or soften it to make it suit the taste of the hearers. 'But as of sincerity, but as of God, in the sight of God speak we in Christ,' as having no other aim than by 'manifestation of the truth to commend ourselves to every man's conscience in the sight of God'.

2. We then, by our doctrine, establish the law when we thus openly declare it to all men, and that in the fullness wherein it is delivered by our blessed Lord and his apostles; when we publish it in the height and depth and length and breadth thereof. We then establish the law when we declare every part of it, every commandment contained therein, not only in its full, literal sense, but likewise in its spiritual meaning; not only with regard to the outward actions which it either forbids or enjoins, but also with respect to the inward principle, to the thoughts, desires, and intents of the heart.

3. And indeed this we do the more diligently, not only because it is of the deepest importance—inasmuch as all the fruit, every word and work, must be only evil continually if the tree be evil, if the dispositions and tempers of the heart be not right before God—but likewise because, as important as these things are, they are little considered or understood; so little that we may truly say of the law, too, when taken in its full spiritual meaning, it is 'a mystery which was hid from ages and generations since the world began'. It was utterly hid from the heathen world. They, with all their boasted wisdom, neither 'found out God' nor the law of God, not in the letter, much less in the spirit of it. 'Their foolish hearts were' more and more 'darkened'; while 'professing themselves wise, they became fools'. And it was almost equally hid, as to its spiritual meaning, from the bulk of the Jewish nation. Even these, who were so ready to declare concerning others, 'this people that know not the law is accursed', pronounced their own sentence therein, as being under the same curse, the same dreadful ignorance. Witness our Lord's continual reproof of the wisest among them for their gross misinterpretations of it. Witness the supposition, almost universally received among them, that they needed only to make clean the outside of the cup, that the paying tithe of mint, anise, and cummin, outward exactness, would atone for inward unholiness, for the total neglect both of justice and mercy, of faith and the love of God. Yea, so absolutely was the spiritual meaning of the law hidden from the wisest of them, that one of their most eminent rabbis comments thus on those words of the Psalmist, 'If I incline unto iniquity with my heart, the Lord will not hear me.'

'That is', saith he, 'if it be only in my heart, if I do not commit outward wickedness, the Lord will not regard it; he will not punish me unless I proceed to the outward act!'

4. But alas! the law of God, as to its inward spiritual meaning, is not hid from the Jews or heathens only, but even from what is called the Christian world; at least, from a vast majority of them. The spiritual sense of the commandments of God is still a mystery to these also. Nor is this observable only in those lands which are overspread with Romish darkness and ignorance. But this is too sure, that the far greater part, even of those who are called 'Reformed Christians', are utter strangers at this day to the law of Christ, in the purity and spirituality of it.

5. Hence it is that to this day 'the scribes and Pharisees'—the men who have the form but not the power of religion, and who are generally wise in their own eyes, and righteous in their own conceits—'hearing these things are offended', are deeply offended when we speak of the religion of the heart, and particularly when we show that without this, were we to 'give all our goods to feed the poor', it would profit us nothing. But offended they must be, for we cannot but speak the truth as it is in Jesus. It is our part, whether they will hear or whether they will forbear, to deliver our own soul. All that is written in the Book of God we are to declare, not as pleasing men, but the Lord. We are to declare not only all the promises but all the threatenings, too, which we find therein. At the same time that we proclaim all the blessings and privileges which God had prepared for his children, we are likewise to 'teach all the things whatsoever he hath commanded'. And we know that all these have their use; either for the awakening those that sleep, the instructing the ignorant, the comforting the feeble-minded, or the building up and perfecting of the saints. We know that 'all Scripture given by inspiration of God is profitable' either 'for doctrine' or 'for reproof', either 'for correction' or 'for instruction in righteousness'; and 'that the man of God', in the process of the work of God in his soul, has need of every part thereof, that he 'may' at length 'be perfect, thoroughly furnished unto all good works'.

6. It is our part thus to 'preach Christ' by preaching all things whatsoever he hath revealed. We may indeed, without blame, yea, and with a peculiar blessing from God, declare the love of our Lord Jesus Christ. We may speak in a more especial manner of 'the Lord our righteousness'. We may expatiate upon the grace of 'God in Christ, reconciling the world unto himself'. We may, at proper opportunities, dwell upon his praise, as bearing 'the iniquities of us all', as 'wounded for our transgressions' and 'bruised for our iniquities', that 'by his stripes we might be healed'. But still we should not 'preach Christ' according to his word if we were wholly to confine ourselves to this. We are not ourselves clear before God unless we proclaim him in all his offices. To preach Christ as a workman that needeth not to be ashamed is to preach him

not only as our great 'High Priest, taken from among men, and ordained for men, in things pertaining to God'; as such, 'reconciling us to God by his blood', and 'ever living to make intercession for us'; but likewise as the Prophet of the Lord, 'who of God is made unto us wisdom', who by his word and his Spirit 'is with us always', 'guiding us into all truth'; yea, and as remaining a King for ever; as giving laws to all whom he has bought with his blood; as restoring those to the image of God whom he had first reinstated in his favour; as reigning in all believing hearts until he has 'subdued all things to himself'; until he hath utterly cast out all sin, and 'brought in everlasting righteousness.'

II.1. 'We establish the law', secondly, when we so preach faith in Christ as not to supersede but produce holiness: to produce all manner of holiness, negative and positive, of the heart and of the life.

In order to this we continually declare (what should be frequently and deeply considered by all who would not 'make void the law through faith') that faith itself, even Christian faith, the faith of God's elect, the faith of the operation of God, still is only the handmaid of love. As glorious and honourable as it is, it is not the end of the commandment. God hath given this honour to love alone. Love is the end of all the commandments of God. Love is the end, the sole end, of every dispensation of God, from the beginning of the world to the consummation of all things. And it will endure when heaven and earth flee away; for 'love' alone 'never faileth'. Faith will totally fail; it will be swallowed up in sight, in the everlasting vision of God. But even then love,

> Its nature and its office still the same,
> Lasting its lamp and unconsumed its flame,
> In deathless triumph shall for ever live,
> And endless good diffuse, and endless praise receive.

2. Very excellent things are spoken of faith, and whosoever is a partaker thereof may well say with the Apostle, 'Thanks be to God for his unspeakable gift.' Yet still it loses all its excellence when brought into a comparison with love. What St. Paul observes concerning the superior glory of the gospel above that of the law may with great propriety be spoken of the superior glory of love above that of faith: 'Even that which was made glorious hath no glory in this respect, by reason of the glory that excelleth. For if that which is done away is glorious, much more doth that which remaineth exceed in glory.' Yea, all the glory of faith before it is done away arises hence, that it ministers to love. It is the great temporary means which God has ordained to promote that eternal end.

3. Let those who magnify faith beyond all proportion, so as to swallow up all things else, and who so totally misapprehend the nature of it as to imagine it stands in the place of love, consider farther that as love will exist after faith,

so it did exist long before it. The angels, who from the moment of their creation beheld the face of their Father that is in heaven, had no occasion for faith in its general notion, as it is the evidence of things not seen. Neither had they need of faith in its more particular acceptation, faith in the blood of Jesus; for he took not upon him the nature of angels, but only the seed of Abraham. There was therefore no place before the foundation of the world for faith either in the general or particular sense. But there was for love. Love existed from eternity, in God, the great ocean of love. Love had a place in all the children of God, from the moment of their creation. They received at once from their gracious Creator to exist, and to love.

4. Nor is it certain (as ingeniously and plausibly as many have descanted upon this) that faith, even in the general sense of the word, had any place in paradise. It is highly probable, from that short and uncircumstantial account which we have in Holy Writ, that Adam, before he rebelled against God, walked with him by sight and not by faith.

For then his reason's eye was strong and clear,
  And as an eagle can behold the sun,
Might have beheld his Maker's face as near
  As th' intellectual angels could have done.

He was then able to talk with him face to face, whose face we cannot now see and live; and consequently had no need of that faith whose office it is to supply the want of sight.

5. On the other hand, it is absolutely certain, faith, in its particular sense, had then no place. For in that sense it necessarily presupposes sin, and the wrath of God declared against the sinner; without which there is no need of an atonement for sin in order to the sinner's reconciliation with God. Consequently, as there was no need of an atonement before the fall, so there was no place for faith in that atonement; man being then pure from every stain of sin, holy as God is holy. But love even then filled his heart. It reigned in him without a rival. And it was only when love was lost by sin that faith was added, not for its own sake, nor with any design that it should exist any longer than until it had answered the end for which it was ordained—namely, to restore man to the love from which he was fallen. At the fall therefore was added this evidence of things unseen, which before was utterly needless; this confidence in redeeming love, which could not possibly have any place till the promise was made that the seed of the woman should bruise the serpent's head.

6. Faith then was originally designed of God to re-establish the law of love. Therefore, in speaking thus, we are not undervaluing it, or robbing it of its due praise, but on the contrary showing its real worth, exalting it in its just proportion, and giving it that very place which the wisdom of God assigned it from the beginning. It is the grand means of restoring that holy love wherein

man was originally created. It follows, that although faith is of no value in itself (as neither is any other means whatsoever) yet as it leads to that end—the establishing anew the law of love in our hearts—and as in the present state of things it is the only means under heaven for effecting it, it is on that account an unspeakable blessing to man, and of unspeakable value before God.

III.1. And this naturally brings us to observe, thirdly, the most important way of 'establishing the law'; namely, the establishing it in our own hearts and lives. Indeed, without this, what would all the rest avail? We might establish it by our doctrine; we might preach it in its whole extent; might explain and enforce every part of it. We might open it in its most spiritual meaning, and declare the mysteries of the kingdom; we might preach Christ in all his offices, and faith in Christ as opening all the treasures of his love. And yet, all this time, if the law we preached were not established in our hearts we should be of no more account before God than 'sounding brass or tinkling cymbals'. All our preaching would be so far from profiting ourselves that it would only increase our damnation.

2. This is therefore the main point to be considered: How may we establish the law in our own hearts so that it may have its full influence on our lives? And this can only be done by faith.

Faith alone it is which effectually answers this end, as we learn from daily experience. For so long as we walk by faith, not by sight, we go swiftly on in the way of holiness. While we steadily look, not at the things which are seen, but at those which are not seen, we are more and more crucified to the world and the world crucified to us. Let but the eye of the soul be constantly fixed, not on the things which are temporal, but on those which are eternal, and our affections are more and more loosened from earth and fixed on things above. So that faith in general is the most direct and effectual means of promoting all righteousness and true holiness; of establishing the holy and spiritual law in the hearts of them that believe.

3. And by faith, taken in its more particular meaning for a confidence in a pardoning God, we establish his law in our own hearts in a still more effectual manner. For there is no motive which so powerfully inclines us to love God as the sense of the love of God in Christ. Nothing enables us like a piercing conviction of this to give our hearts to him who was given for us. And from this principle of grateful love to God arises love to our brother also. Neither can we avoid loving our neighbour, if we truly believe the love wherewith God hath loved us. Now this love to man, grounded on faith and love to God, 'worketh no ill to our neighbour'. Consequently it is, as the Apostle observes, 'the fulfilling of the' whole negative 'law'. 'For this, Thou shalt not commit adultery, Thou shalt not kill, Thou shalt not steal, Thou shalt not bear false witness, Thou shalt not covet; and if there be any other commandment, it is

briefly comprehended in this saying, Thou shalt love thy neighbour as thyself.' Neither is love content with barely working no evil to our neighbour. It continually incites us to do good: as we have time and opportunity, to do good in every possible kind and in every possible degree to all men. It is therefore the fulfilling of the positive, likewise, as well as of the negative law of God.

4. Nor does faith fulfil either the negative or positive law as to the external part only; but it works inwardly by love to the purifying of the heart, the cleansing it from all vile affections. 'Everyone that hath this' faith 'in him purifieth himself, even as he is pure'—purifieth himself from every earthly, sensual desire, from all vile and inordinate affections; yea, from the whole of that carnal mind which is enmity against God. At the same time, if it have its perfect work, it fills him with all goodness, righteousness, and truth. It brings all heaven into his soul, and causes him to walk in the light, even as God is in the light.

5. Let us thus endeavour to establish the law in ourselves; not sinning 'because we are under grace', but rather using all the power we receive thereby 'to fulfil all righteousness'. Calling to mind what light we received from God while his Spirit was convincing us of sin, let us beware we do not put out that light. What we had then attained let us hold fast. Let nothing induce us to build again what we have destroyed; to resume anything, small or great, which we then clearly saw was not for the glory of God or the profit of our own soul; or to neglect anything, small or great, which we could not then neglect without a check from our own conscience. To increase and perfect the light which we had before, let us now add the light of faith. Confirm we the former gift of God by a deeper sense of whatever he had then shown us, by a greater tenderness of conscience, and a more exquisite sensibility of sin. Walking now with joy and not with fear, in a clear, steady sight of things eternal, we shall look on pleasure, wealth, praise—all the things of earth—as on bubbles upon the water; counting nothing important, nothing desirable, nothing worth a deliberate thought, but only what is 'within the veil', where 'Jesus sitteth at the right hand of God'.

6. Can *you* say, 'Thou art merciful to my unrighteousness; my sins thou rememberest no more'? Then for the time to come see that you fly from sin, as from the face of a serpent. For how exceeding sinful does it appear to you now! How heinous above all expression! On the other hand, in how amiable a light do you now see the holy and perfect will of God! Now, therefore, labour that it may be fulfilled, both in you, by you, and upon you. Now watch and pray that you may sin no more, that you may see and shun the least transgression of his law. You see the motes which you could not see before when the sun shines into a dark place. In like manner you see the sins which you could not see before, now the sun of righteousness shines in your heart. Now, then, do all diligence to walk in every respect according to the light you

have received. Now be zealous to receive more light daily, more of the knowledge and love of God, more of the Spirit of Christ, more of his life, and of the power of his resurrection. Now use all the knowledge and love and life and power you have already attained. So shall you continually go on from faith to faith. So shall you daily increase in holy love, till faith is swallowed up in sight, and the law of love established to all eternity.

A CAUTION AGAINST BIGOTRY

Sermon 38 – 1750

AN INTRODUCTORY COMMENT

Part of the price of peace in eighteenth-century Britain, after the bitter quarrels of Civil War and Restoration, was a general lessening of partisan zeal and bigotry. The main concern of all, in both church and civil state, was surcease from religious turmoil. It was, therefore, inevitable that the Methodist Revival should revive fears of new religious disruptions; and Wesley's claim to an extraordinary vocation, his blithe disregard for parish boundaries and for the conventions of ministerial courtesy, along with his employment of lay preachers in busy rotation across the three kingdoms, did nothing to allay such fears.

In much the same way that the Methodists had come by the label 'enthusiasts', they also had come to be regarded as 'bigots' in the current general sense of 'excessive or irrational zealots'. With the Revival in full flood and with Wesley as sole head of a tightly organized, highly partisan group of zealous preachers and people, there was an obvious occasion for a carefully considered statement about proper and improper zeal addressed to critics and to Methodists alike—'a caution against bigotry', defined as 'too strong an attachment to, or fondness for, our own party, opinion, church, and religion'.

In this sermon Wesley studiously avoids an apologetic stance. Rather, he redefines the problem by asking about the proper business of true apostles and answering it by reference to the gospel story of the casting out of devils (taken here as a metaphor for the whole conflict between Christ and the forces of evil and also for the ministry of salvation). Wesley argues that valid ministry should be measured by fruits rather than forms. Further, he implies that churchmen might indeed be actually grateful for the work of the Methodists and that, in their turn, the Methodists should renounce all bigotry discovered within themselves. In effect, he gives a positive, if also indirect, plea for a carefully considered religious pluralism both in theology and praxis.

There is no record of any other instance of Wesley's using Mark 9:38–39 as a sermon text—from which we may infer that it was written on purpose for the third volume of his collected sermons. But its underlying pragmatism can be seen as essential in Wesley's concepts of theological method and of Christian community-in-diversity. Thus, it was a useful rejoinder to those who took Methodist bigotry as a matter of course and yet also a timely antidote to Methodist 'zeal without knowledge'.

A Caution against Bigotry

And John answered him, saying, Master, we saw one casting out devils in thy name, and we forbade him, because he followeth not us. And Jesus said, Forbid him not.
Mark 9:38–39

1. In the preceding verses we read that after the twelve had been disputing 'which of them should be the greatest', Jesus 'took a little child, and set him in the midst of them, and taking him in his arms said unto them, Whosoever shall receive one of these little children in my name receiveth me; and whosoever receiveth me receiveth not me (only), but him that sent me.' Then 'John answered' (that is, said with reference to what our Lord had spoken just before), 'Master, we saw one casting out devils in thy name, and we forbade him, because he followeth not us.' As if he had said: 'Ought we to have received him? In receiving him, should we have received thee? Ought we not rather to have forbidden him? Did not we do well therein?' 'But Jesus said, Forbid him not.'

2. The same passage is recited by St. Luke, and almost in the same words. But it may be asked: 'What is this to us? Seeing no man now "casts out devils". Has not the power of doing this been withdrawn from the church for twelve or fourteen hundred years? How then are *we* concerned in the case here proposed, or in our Lord's decision of it?'

3. Perhaps more nearly than is commonly imagined, the case proposed being no uncommon case. That we may reap our full advantage from it I design to show, first, in what sense men may, and do now, 'cast out devils'; secondly, what we may understand by, 'He followeth not us.' I shall, thirdly, explain our Lord's direction, 'Forbid him not,' and conclude with an inference from the whole.

I.1. I am, in the first place, to show in what sense men may, and do now, 'cast out devils'.

In order to have the clearest view of this we should remember that (according to the scriptural account) as God dwells and works in the children of light, so the devil dwells and works in the children of darkness. As the Holy Spirit possesses the souls of good men, so the evil spirit possesses the souls of the wicked. Hence it is that the Apostle terms him 'the god of this world'—from the uncontrolled power he has over worldly men. Hence our blessed Lord styles him 'the prince of this world'—so absolute is his dominion over it. And hence St. John, 'We know that we are of God,' and all who are not of God, 'the whole world', ἐν τῷ πονηρῷ κεῖται—not, lieth in wickedness, but 'lieth in the wicked one'—lives and moves in him, as they who are not of the world do in God.

2. For the devil is not to be considered only as 'a roaring lion, going about seeking whom he may devour'; nor barely as a subtle enemy who cometh unawares upon poor souls and 'leads them captive at his will'; but as he who dwelleth in them and walketh in them; who 'ruleth the darkness' or wickedness 'of this world', of worldly men and all their dark designs and actions, by keeping possession of their hearts, setting up his throne there, and bringing every thought into obedience to himself. Thus the 'strong one armed keepeth his house'; and if this 'unclean spirit' sometime 'go out of a man', yet he often returns with 'seven spirits worse than himself; and they enter in and dwell there.' Nor can he be idle in his dwelling. He is continually 'working in' these 'children of disobedience'. He works in them with power, with mighty energy, transforming them into his own likeness, effacing all the remains of the image of God, and preparing them for every evil word and work.

3. It is therefore an unquestionable truth that the god and prince of this world still possesses all who know not God. Only the manner wherein he possesses them now differs from that wherein he did it of old time. Then he frequently tormented their bodies as well as souls, and that openly, without any disguise; now he torments their souls only (unless in some rare cases) and that as covertly as possible. The reason of this difference is plain. It was then his aim to drive mankind into superstition. Therefore he wrought as openly as he could. But 'tis his aim to drive *us* into infidelity. Therefore he works as privately as he can; for the more secret he is, the more he prevails.

4. Yet if we may credit historians there are countries even now where he works as openly as aforetime. 'But why in savage and barbarous countries only? Why not in Italy, France, or England?' For a very plain reason: he knows his men. And he knows what he hath to do with each. To Laplanders he appears barefaced; because he is to fix them in superstition and gross idolatry. But with you he is pursuing a different point. He is to make you idolize yourselves, to make you wiser in your own eyes than God himself, than all the oracles of God. Now in order to this he must not appear in his own shape. That would frustrate his design. No; he uses all his art to make you deny his being, till he has you safe in his own place.

5. He reigns, therefore, although in a different way, yet as absolute in one land as in the other. He has the gay Italian infidel in his teeth as sure as the wild Tartar. But he is fast asleep in the mouth of the lion, who is too wise to wake him out of sleep. So he only plays with him for the present, and when he pleases swallows him up.

The god of this world holds his English worshippers full as fast as those in Lapland. But it is not his business to affright them, lest they should fly to the God of heaven. The prince of darkness therefore does not appear while he rules over these his willing subjects. The conqueror holds his captives so much the safer because they imagine themselves at liberty. Thus the 'strong one armed keepeth his house, and his goods are in peace': neither the deist nor nominal Christian suspects he is there; so he and they are perfectly at peace with each other.

6. All this while he works with energy in them. He blinds the eyes of their understanding so that the light of the glorious gospel of Christ cannot shine upon them. He chains their souls down to earth and hell with the chains of their own vile affections. He binds them down to the earth by love of the world, love of money, of pleasure, of praise. And by pride, envy, anger, hate, revenge, he causes their souls to draw nigh unto hell; acting the more secure and uncontrolled because they know not that he acts at all.

7. But how easily may we know the cause from its effects! These are sometimes gross and palpable. So they were in the most refined of the heathen nations. Go no farther than the admired, the virtuous Romans. And you will find these, when at the height of their learning and glory, 'filled with all unrighteousness, fornication, wickedness, covetousness, maliciousness; full of envy, murder, debate, deceit, malignity; whisperers, backbiters, despiteful, proud, boasters, disobedient to parents, covenant-breakers, without natural affection, implacable, unmerciful'.

8. The strongest parts of this description are confirmed by one whom some may think a more unexceptionable witness. I mean their brother heathen, Dion Cassius, who observes that before Caesar's return from Gaul not only gluttony and lewdness of every kind were open and barefaced; not only falsehood, injustice, and unmercifulness abounded in public courts as well as private families; but the most outrageous robberies, rapine, and murders were so frequent in all parts of Rome that few men went out of doors without making their wills, as not knowing if they should return alive.

9. As gross and palpable are the works of the devil among many (if not all) the modern heathens. The *natural religion* of the Creeks, Cherokees, Chicasaws, and all other Indians bordering on our southern settlements (not of a few single men, but of entire nations) is to torture all their prisoners from morning to night, till at length they roast them to death; and upon the slightest undesigned provocation to come behind and shoot any of their own countrymen. Yea, it is a common thing among them for the son, if he thinks his father lives too long, to knock out his brains; and for a mother, if she is tired of her children, to fasten stones about their necks, and throw three or four of them into the river one after another.

10. It were to be wished that none but heathens had practised such gross,

palpable works of the devil. But we dare not say so. Even in cruelty and bloodshed, how little have the Christians come behind them! And not the Spaniards or Portuguese alone, butchering thousands in South America. Not the Dutch only in the East Indies, or the French in North America, following the Spaniards step by step. Our own countrymen, too, have wantoned in blood, and exterminated whole nations: plainly proving thereby what spirit it is that dwells and works in the children of disobedience.

11. These monsters might almost make us overlook the works of the devil that are wrought in our own country. But, alas! We cannot open our eyes even here without seeing them on every side. Is it a small proof of his power that common swearers, drunkards, whoremongers, adulterers, thieves, robbers, sodomites, murderers, are still found in every part of our land? How triumphant does the prince of this world reign in all these children of disobedience!

12. He less openly but no less effectually works in dissemblers, talebearers, liars, slanderers; in oppressors and extortioners; in the perjured, the seller of his friend, his honour, his conscience, his country. And yet these may talk of religion or conscience still! Of honour, virtue, and public spirit. But they can no more deceive Satan than they can God. He likewise knows those that are his: and a great multitude they are, out of every nation and people, of whom he has full possession at this day.

13. If you consider this you cannot but see in what sense men may now also 'cast out devils'; yea, and every minister of Christ does cast them out, if his Lord's work prosper in his hand.

By the power of God attending his Word he brings these sinners to repentance: an entire inward as well as outward change, from all evil to all good. And this is in a sound sense to 'cast out devils', out of the souls wherein they had hitherto dwelt. The strong one can no longer keep his house. A stronger than he is come upon him, and hath cast him out, and taken possession for himself, and made it an habitation of God through his Spirit. Here then the energy of Satan ends, and the Son of God 'destroys the works of the devil'. The understanding of the sinner is now enlightened, and his heart sweetly drawn to God. His desires are refined, his affections purified; and being filled with the Holy Ghost he grows in grace till he is not only holy in heart, but in all manner of conversation.

14. All this is indeed the work of God. It is God alone who can cast out Satan. But he is generally pleased to do this by man, as an instrument in his hand, who is then said to 'cast out devils in his name'—by his power and authority. And he sends whom he will send upon this great work; but usually such as man would never have thought of. For 'his ways are not as our ways, neither his thoughts as our thoughts.' Accordingly he chooses the weak to confound the mighty; the foolish to confound the wise: for this plain reason, that he may secure the glory to himself, that 'no flesh may glory in his sight'.

II.1. But shall we not *forbid* one who thus 'casteth out devils', if 'he followeth not us'? This it seems was both the judgment and practice of the Apostle, till he referred the case to his Master. 'We forbade him', saith he, 'because he followeth not us,' which he supposed to be a very sufficient reason. What we may understand by this expression, 'He followeth not us,' is the next point to be considered.

The lowest circumstance we can understand thereby is, 'He has no outward connection with us. We do not labour in conjunction with each other. He is not our fellow-helper in the gospel.' And indeed whensoever our Lord is pleased to send many labourers into his harvest, they cannot all act in subordination to, or connection with, each other. Nay, they cannot all have personal acquaintance with, nor be so much as known to, one another. Many there will necessarily be in different parts of the harvest, so far from having any mutual intercourse that they will be as absolute strangers to each other, as if they had lived in different ages. And concerning any of these whom we know not we may doubtless say, 'He followeth not us.'

2. A second meaning of this expression may be, 'He is *not of our party.*' It has long been matter of melancholy consideration to all who pray for the peace of Jerusalem that so many several parties are still subsisting among those who are all styled Christians. This has been particularly observable in our own countrymen, who have been continually dividing from each other upon points of no moment, and many times such as religion had no concern in. The most trifling circumstances have given rise to different parties, which have continued for many generations. And each of these would be ready to object to one who was on the other side, 'He followeth not us.'

3. That expression may mean, thirdly, 'He differs from us in our *religious opinions.*' There was a time when all Christians were of one mind, as well as of one heart. So great grace was upon them all when they were first filled with the Holy Ghost. But how short a space did this blessing continue! How soon was that unanimity lost, and difference of opinion sprang up again, even in the church of Christ! And that not in nominal but in real Christians; nay, in the very chief of them, the apostles themselves! Nor does it appear that the difference which then began was ever entirely removed. We do not find that even those pillars in the temple of God, so long as they remained upon earth, were ever brought to think alike, to be of one mind, particularly with regard to the ceremonial law. 'Tis therefore no way surprising that infinite varieties of opinion should now be found in the Christian church. A very probable consequence of this is that whenever we see any 'casting out devils' he will be one that in this sense 'followeth not us'—that is not of our opinion. 'Tis scarce to be imagined he will be of our mind in all points, even of religion. He may very probably think in a different manner from us even on several subjects of importance, such as the nature and use of the moral law, the eternal decrees

of God, the sufficiency and efficacy of his grace, and the perseverance of his children.

4. He may differ from us, fourthly, not only in opinion, but likewise in some points of practice. He may not approve of that manner of worshipping God which is practised in our congregation, and may judge that to be more profitable for his soul which took its rise from Calvin, or Martin Luther. He may have many objections to that liturgy which we approve of beyond all others, many doubts concerning that form of church government which we esteem both apostolical and scriptural. Perhaps he may go farther from us yet: he may, from a principle of conscience, refrain from several of those which we believe to be the ordinances of Christ. Or if we both agree that they are ordained of God, there may still remain a difference between us either as to the manner of administering those ordinances or the persons to whom they should be administered. Now the unavoidable consequence of any of these differences will be that he who thus differs from us must separate himself with regard to those points from our society. In this respect therefore 'he followeth not us'; he is 'not (as we phrase it) of our church'.

5. But in a far stronger sense 'he followeth not us' who is not only of a different church, but of such a church as we account to be in many respects antiscriptural and antichristian: a church which we believe to be utterly false and erroneous in her doctrines, as well as very dangerously wrong in her practice, guilty of gross superstition as well as idolatry; a church that has added many articles to the faith which was once delivered to the saints; that has dropped one whole commandment of God, and made void several of the rest by her traditions; and that pretending the highest veneration for, and strictest conformity to, the ancient church, has nevertheless brought in numberless innovations without any warrant either from antiquity or Scripture. Now most certainly 'he followeth not us' who stands at so great a distance from us.

6. And yet there may be a still wider difference than this. He who differs from us in judgment or practice may possibly stand at a greater distance from us in affection than in judgment. And this indeed is a very natural and a very common effect of the other. The differences which begin in points of opinion seldom terminate there. They generally spread into the affections, and then separate chief friends. Nor are any animosities so deep and irreconcilable as those that spring from disagreement in religion. For this cause the bitterest enemies of a man are those of his own household. For this the father rises against his own children, and the children against the father; and perhaps persecute each other even to the death, thinking all the time they are doing God service. It is therefore nothing more than we may expect if those who differ from us either in religious opinions or practice soon contract a sharpness, yea, bitterness toward us; if they are more and more prejudiced against us, till they conceive as ill an opinion of our persons as of our principles. An almost

necessary consequence of this will be, they will speak in the same manner as they think of us. They will set themselves in opposition to us, and, as far as they are able hinder our work, seeing it does not appear to them to be the work of God, but either of man or of the devil. He that thinks, speaks, and acts in such a manner as this, in the highest sense 'followeth not us'.

7. I do not indeed conceive that the person of whom the Apostle speaks in the text (although we have no particular account of him either in the context or in any other part of Holy Writ) went so far as this. We have no ground to suppose that there was any material difference between him and the apostles; much less that he had any prejudice either against them or their Master. It seems we may gather thus much from our Lord's own words which immediately follow the text, 'There is no man which shall do a miracle in my name that can lightly speak evil of me.' But I purposely put the case in the strongest light, adding all the circumstances which can well be conceived; that being forewarned of the temptation in its full strength we may in no case yield to it and fight against God.

III.1. Suppose then a man have no intercourse with us, suppose he be not of our party, suppose he separate from our Church, yea, and widely differ from us both in judgment, practice, and affection; yet if we see even this man 'casting out devils' Jesus saith, 'Forbid him not.' This important direction of our Lord, I am, in the third place, to explain.

2. If we see this man casting out devils—but 'tis well if in such a case we would believe even what we saw with our eyes, if we did not give the lie to our own senses. He must be little acquainted with human nature who does not immediately perceive how extremely unready we should be to believe that any man does cast out devils who 'followeth not us' in all or most of the senses above recited. I had almost said, in any of them; seeing we may easily learn even from what passes in our own breasts how unwilling men are to allow anything good in those who do not in all things agree with themselves.

3. 'But what is a sufficient, reasonable proof that a man does (in the sense above) cast out devils?' The answer is easy. Is there full proof, first, that a person before us was a gross, open sinner? Secondly, that he is not so now; that he has broke off his sins, and lives a Christian life? And thirdly, that his change was wrought by his hearing this man preach? If these three points be plain and undeniable, then you have sufficient, reasonable proof, such as you cannot resist without wilful sin, that this man casts out devils.

4. Then 'forbid him not.' Beware how you attempt to hinder him, either by your authority or arguments or persuasions. Do not in any wise strive to prevent his using all the power which God has given him. If you have *authority* with him, do not use that authority to stop the work of God. Do not furnish him with *reasons* why he ought not any more to speak in the name of Jesus.

Satan will not fail to supply him with these if you do not second him therein. *Persuade* him not to depart from the work. If he should give place to the devil and you, many souls might perish in their iniquity, but their blood would God require at *your* hands.

5. 'But what if he be only a *layman* who casts out devils? Ought I not to forbid him then?'

Is the fact allowed? Is there reasonable proof that this man has or does 'cast out devils'? If there is, forbid him not; no, not at the peril of your soul. Shall not God work by whom he will work? 'No man can do these works unless God is with him'—unless God hath sent him for this very thing. But if God hath sent him, will you call him back? Will you forbid him to go?

6. 'But I do not know that he is sent of God.' 'Now herein is a marvellous thing' (may any of the seals of his mission say, any whom he hath brought from Satan to God) 'that ye know not whence this man is, and behold he hath opened mine eyes! If this man were not of God, he could do nothing.' If you doubt the fact, send for the parents of the man; send for his brethren, friends, acquaintance. But if you cannot doubt this, if you must needs acknowledge that 'a notable miracle hath been wrought', then with what conscience, with what face can you charge him whom God hath sent 'not to speak any more in his name'?

7. I allow that it is *highly expedient,* whoever preaches in his name should have an outward as well as an inward call; but that it is *absolutely necessary* I deny.

'Nay, is not the Scripture express? "No man taketh this honour unto himself, but he that is called of God, as was Aaron"' (Heb. 5:4).

Numberless times has this text been quoted on the occasion, as containing the very strength of the cause. But surely never was so unhappy a quotation. For, first, Aaron was not called to preach at all. He was called to 'offer gifts and sacrifice for sin'. That was his peculiar employment. Secondly, these men do not offer sacrifice at all, but only preach, which Aaron did not. Therefore it is not possible to find one text in all the Bible which is more wide of the point than this.

8. 'But what was the practice of the apostolic age?' You may easily see in the Acts of the Apostles. In the eighth chapter we read: 'There was a great persecution against the church which was at Jerusalem; and they were all scattered abroad throughout the regions of Judea and Samaria, except the apostles' (Acts 8:1). 'Therefore they that were scattered abroad went everywhere preaching the word' (Acts 8:4). Now, were all these outwardly called to preach? No man in his senses can think so. Here then is an undeniable proof what was the practice of the apostolic age. Here you see not one but a multitude of 'lay preachers', men that were only sent of God.

9. Indeed so far is the practice of the apostolic age from inclining us to think

it was *unlawful* for a man to preach before he was ordained, that we have reason to think it was then accounted *necessary*. Certainly the practice and the direction of the Apostle Paul was to *prove* a man before he was ordained at all. 'Let these' (the deacons), says he, 'first be proved; then let them use the office of a deacon' (1 Tim. 3:10). Proved? How? By setting them to construe a sentence of Greek? And asking them a few commonplace questions? O amazing proof of a minister of Christ! Nay; but by making a clear, open trial (as is still done by most of the Protestant Churches in Europe) not only whether their lives be holy and unblameable, but whether they have such gifts as are absolutely and indispensably necessary in order to edify the church of Christ.

10. 'But what if a man has these? And has brought sinners to repentance? And yet the bishop will not ordain him?' Then the bishop does 'forbid him to cast out devils'. But I dare not forbid him. I have published my reasons to all the world. Yet 'tis still insisted I ought to do it. You who insist upon it, answer those reasons. I know not that any have done this yet, or even made a feint of doing it. Only some have spoken of them as very weak and trifling. And this was prudent enough. For 'tis far easier to despise—at least, seem to despise—an argument than to answer it. Yet till this is done I must say, when I have reasonable proof that any man does cast out devils, whatever others do I dare not forbid him, lest I be found even to fight against God.

11. And whosoever thou art that fearest God, 'forbid him not,' either directly or indirectly. There are many ways of doing this. You indirectly forbid him if you either wholly deny, or despise and make little account of the work which God has wrought by his hands. You indirectly forbid him when you discourage him in his work by drawing him into disputes concerning it, by raising objections against it, or frighting him with consequences which very possibly will never be. You forbid him when you show any unkindness toward him either in language or behaviour; and much more when you speak of him to others either in an unkind or a contemptuous manner, when you endeavour to represent him to any either in an odious or a despicable light. You are forbidding him all the time you are speaking evil of him or making no account of his labours. O forbid him not in any of these ways; nor by forbidding others to hear him, by discouraging sinners from hearing that word which is able to save their souls.

12. Yea, if you would observe our Lord's direction in its full meaning and extent, then remember his word, 'He that is not for us is against us, and he that gathereth not with me, scattereth.' He that gathereth not men into the kingdom of God assuredly scatters them from it. For there can be no neuter in this war: everyone is either on God's side or on Satan's. Are you on God's side? Then you will not only not forbid any man that 'casts out devils', but you will labour to the uttermost of your power to forward him in the work. You will readily acknowledge the work of God, and confess the greatness of

it. You will remove all difficulties and objections, as far as may be, out of his way. You will strengthen his hands by speaking honourably of him before all men, and avowing the things which you have seen and heard. You will encourage others to attend upon his word, to hear him whom God hath sent. And you will omit no actual proof of tender love which God gives you an opportunity of showing him.

IV.1. If we willingly fail in any of these points, if we either directly or indirectly forbid him 'because he followeth not us', then we are 'bigots'. This is the inference I draw from what has been said. But the term 'bigotry', I fear, as frequently as it is used, is almost as little understood as 'enthusiasm'. It is too strong an attachment to, or fondness for, our own party, opinion, Church, and religion. Therefore he is a bigot who is so fond of any of these, so strongly attached to them, as to forbid any who casts out devils, because he differs from himself in any or all these particulars.

2. Do *you* beware of this. Take care, first, that you do not convict yourself of bigotry by your unreadiness to believe that any man does cast out devils who differs from you. And if you are clear thus far, if you acknowledge the fact, then examine yourself, secondly: 'Am I not convicted of bigotry in this, in forbidding him directly or indirectly? Do I not directly forbid him on this ground, because he is not of my *party*? Because he does not fall in with my *opinions*? Or because he does not worship God according to that scheme of religion which I have received from my fathers?'

3. Examine yourself: 'Do I not indirectly, at least, forbid him on any of these grounds? Am I not sorry that God should thus own and bless a man that holds such erroneous opinions? Do I not discourage him because he is not of my Church? By disputing with him concerning it, by raising objections, and by perplexing his mind with distant consequences? Do I show no anger, contempt, or unkindness of any sort, either in my words or actions? Do I not mention behind his back his (real or supposed) faults? His defects or infirmities? Do not I hinder sinners from hearing his word?' If you do any of these things you are a bigot to this day.

4. 'Search me, O Lord, and prove me. Try out my reins and my heart.' 'Look well if there be any way of *bigotry* in me, and lead me in the way everlasting.' In order to examine ourselves thoroughly let the case be proposed in the strongest manner. What if I were to see a Papist, an Arian, a Socinian casting out devils? If I did, I could not forbid even him without convicting myself of bigotry. Yea, if it could be supposed that I should see a Jew, a deist, or a Turk doing the same, were I to forbid him either directly or indirectly I should be no better than a bigot still.

5. O stand clear of this. But be not content with not forbidding any that casts out devils. 'Tis well to go thus far; but do not stop here. If you will avoid

all bigotry, go on. In every instance of this kind, whatever the instrument be, acknowledge the finger of God. And not only acknowledge but rejoice in his work, and praise his name with thanksgiving. Encourage whomsoever God is pleased to employ, to give himself wholly up thereto. Speak well of him wheresoever you are; defend his character and his mission. Enlarge as far as you can his sphere of action. Show him all kindness in word and deed. And cease not to cry to God in his behalf, that he may save both himself and them that hear him.

6. I need add but one caution. Think not the bigotry of another is any excuse for your own. 'Tis not impossible that one who casts out devils himself may yet forbid you so to do. You may observe this is the very case mentioned in the text. The apostles forbade another to do what they did themselves. But beware of retorting. It is not your part to return evil for evil. Another's not observing the direction of our Lord is no reason why you should neglect it. Nay, but let him have all the bigotry to himself. If he forbids *you*, do not you forbid *him*. Rather labour and watch and pray the more, to confirm your love toward him. If he speaks all manner of evil of *you*, speak all manner of good (that is true) of *him*. Imitate herein that glorious saying of a great man (O that he had always breathed the same spirit!) 'Let Luther call me an hundred devils; I will still reverence him as a messenger of God.'

CATHOLIC SPIRIT

Sermon 39 – 1750

AN INTRODUCTORY COMMENT

There was a nondogmatic strain in Anglicanism that had discouraged the formulation of creeds, confessions, and systematic treatises. Wesley was certainly opinionated and partisan himself, with a stubborn loyalty to what he understood to be the essential core of Christian truth. But he also agreed with the Cambridge Platonists before him that most of the cruel controversies in religion that had spilled so much blood and ink were quarrels about 'opinions', i.e., subsidiary doctrines affecting the fullness and variety of religious language, not its primary object. He also agreed with William of St. Thierry that love is the surest way to truth and the highest goal of thought. He had a clear enough view for himself of the Christian essentials but never ever tried to formulate them in an unrevisable statement. He had ventured his most elaborate summary of them in an open *Letter to a Roman Catholic* (1749); his least elaborate ('love of God and love of neighbour') is repeated endlessly throughout the sermons. In every case, his concern is to narrow the field of irreducible disagreement between professing, practising Christians and to transfer their concerns from argument about faith in Christ to faith itself and to its consequences.

'Catholic Spirit' is the most formal articulation of this nondogmatic method in theology. In it we find yet another statement of 'essentials', and it goes with his method that Wesley believes he could presuppose a consensus here. Then we come to Wesley's effort to redeem controversy in general by the spirit of Christian love and forbearance. Given clarity as to the essentials and liberty as to opinions, he is glad for Methodists 'to think and let think'.

There are only three other recorded instances of his preaching from this text, all between 1740 and 1749. This sermon was republished separately in 1755 and 1770, with an appended hymn by Charles Wesley on 'Catholic Love' that includes the stanza:

> Weary of all this wordy strife,
> These notions, forms, and modes, and names,
> To Thee, the Way, the Truth, the Life
> Whose love my simple heart inflames,
> Divinely taught, at last I fly,
> With thee and thine to live and die.

In some ears such language and the attitude behind it would inevitably sound soft-headed. Its deeper concern, however, may represent Wesley's most important contribution to the cause of Christian unity and to the requisite spirit in which that cause may best be served.

Catholic Spirit

And when he was departed thence, he lighted on Jehonadab the son of Rechab coming to meet him. And he saluted him and said, Is thine heart right, as my heart is with thy heart? And Jehonadab answered, It is. If it be, give me thine hand.
2 Kings 10:15

1. It is allowed even by those who do not pay this great debt that love is due to all mankind, the royal law, 'Thou shalt love thy neighbour as thyself,' carrying its own evidence to all that hear it. And that, not according to the miserable construction put upon it by the zealots of old times, 'Thou shalt love thy neighbour', thy relation, acquaintance, friend, 'and hate thine enemy.' Not so. 'I say unto you', said our Lord, 'Love your enemies, bless them that curse you, do good to them that hate you, and pray for them that despitefully use you and persecute you; that ye may be the children'—may appear so to all mankind—'of your Father which is in heaven, who maketh his sun to rise on the evil and on the good, and sendeth rain on the just and on the unjust.'

2. But it is sure, there is a peculiar love which we owe to those that love God. So David: 'All my delight is upon the saints that are in the earth, and upon such as excel in virtue.' And so a greater than he: 'A new commandment I give unto you, that ye love one another: as I have loved you, that ye also love one another. By this shall all men know that ye are my disciples, if ye have love one to another' (John 13:34–35). This is that love on which the Apostle John so frequently and strongly insists. 'This', said he, 'is the message that ye heard from the beginning, that we should love one another' (1 John 3:11). 'Hereby perceive we the love of God, because he laid down his life for us. And we ought', if love should call us thereto, 'to lay down our lives for the brethren' (1 John 3:16). And again, 'Beloved, let us love one another; for love is of God. He that loveth not, knoweth not God; for God is love' (1 John 4:7–8). 'Not that we loved God, but that he loved us, and sent his Son to be the propitiation for our sins. Beloved, if God so loved us, we ought also to love one another' (1 John 4:10–11).

3. All men approve of this. But do all men practise it? Daily experience shows the contrary. Where are even the Christians who 'love one another, as he hath given us commandment'? How many hindrances lie in the way! The two grand, general hindrances are, first, that they can't all think alike; and in consequence of this, secondly, they can't all walk alike; but in several smaller

points their practice must differ in proportion to the difference of their sentiments.

4. But although a difference in opinions or modes of worship may prevent an entire external union, yet need it prevent our union in affection? Though we can't think alike, may we not love alike? May we not be of one heart, though we are not of one opinion? Without all doubt we may. Herein all the children of God may unite, notwithstanding these smaller differences. These remaining as they are, they may forward one another in love and in good works.

5. Surely in this respect the example of Jehu himself, as mixed a character as he was of, is well worthy both the attention and imitation of every serious Christian. 'And when he was departed thence, he lighted on Jehonadab the son of Rechab coming to meet him. And he saluted him and said, Is thine heart right, as my heart is with thy heart? And Jehonadab answered, It is. If it be, give me thine hand.'

The text naturally divides itself into two parts. First a question proposed by Jehu to Jehonadab, 'Is thine heart right, as my heart is with thy heart?' Secondly, an offer made on Jehonadab's answering, 'It is.'—'If it be, give me thine hand.'

I.1. And, first, let us consider the question proposed by Jehu to Jehonadab, 'Is thine heart right, as my heart is with thy heart?'

The very first thing we may observe in these words is that here is no inquiry concerning Jehonadab's opinions. And yet 'tis certain he held some which were very uncommon, indeed quite peculiar to himself; and some which had a close influence upon practice, on which likewise he laid so great a stress as to entail them upon his children's children, to their latest posterity. This is evident from the account given by Jeremiah, many years after his death. 'I took Jaazaniah and his brethren, and all his sons, and the whole house of the Rechabites; . . . and set before them pots full of wine, and cups, and said unto them, Drink ye wine. But they said, We will drink no wine; for Jonadab (or Jehonadab) the son of Rechab our father' (it would be less ambiguous if the words were placed thus: Jehonadab 'our father the son of Rechab', out of love and reverence to whom he probably desired his descendants might be called by his name) 'commanded us, saying, Ye shall drink no wine, neither ye nor your sons for ever. Neither shall ye build house, nor sow seed, nor plant vineyard, nor have any; but all your days ye shall dwell in tents. . . . And we have obeyed, and done according to all that Jonadab our father commanded us' (Jer. 35:3–10).

2. And yet Jehu (although it seems to have been his manner, both in things secular and religious, to 'drive furiously') does not concern himself at all with any of these things, but lets Jehonadab abound in his own sense. And neither of them appears to have given the other the least disturbance touching the opinions which he maintained.

3. 'Tis very possible that many good men now also may entertain peculiar opinions; and some of them may be as singular herein as even Jehonadab was. And 'tis certain, so long as 'we know' but 'in part', that all men will not see all things alike. It is an unavoidable consequence of the present weakness and shortness of human understanding that several men will be of several minds, in religion as well as in common life. So it has been from the beginning of the world, and so it will be 'till the restitution of all things'.

4. Nay farther: although every man necessarily believes that every particular opinion which he holds is true (for to believe any opinion is not true is the same thing as not to hold it) yet can no man be assured that all his own opinions taken together are true. Nay, every thinking man is assured they are not, seeing *humanum est errare et nescire*–to be ignorant of many things, and to mistake in some, is the necessary condition of humanity. This therefore, he is sensible, is his own case. He knows in the general that he himself is mistaken; although in what particulars he mistakes he does not, perhaps cannot, know.

5. I say, perhaps he cannot know. For who can tell how far invincible ignorance may extend? Or (what comes to the same thing) invincible prejudice; which is often so fixed in tender minds that it is afterwards impossible to tear up what has taken so deep a root. And who can say, unless he knew every circumstance attending it, how far any mistake is culpable? Seeing all guilt must suppose some concurrence of the will–of which he only can judge who searcheth the heart.

6. Every wise man therefore will allow others the same liberty of thinking which he desires they should allow him; and will no more insist on their embracing his opinions than he would have them to insist on his embracing theirs. He bears with those who differ from him, and only asks him with whom he desires to unite in love that single question. 'Is thine heart right, as my heart is with thy heart?'

7. We may, secondly, observe that here is no inquiry made concerning Jehonadab's mode of worship, although 'tis highly probable there was in this respect also a very wide difference between them. For we may well believe Jehonadab, as well as all his posterity, worshipped God at Jerusalem, whereas Jehu did not; he had more regard to state policy than religion. And therefore although he slew the worshippers of Baal, and 'destroyed Baal out of Israel', yet 'from the' convenient 'sin of Jeroboam', the worship of 'the golden calves, he departed not' (2 Kgs. 10:28–29).

8. But even among men of an upright heart, men who desire 'to have a conscience void of offence', it must needs be that as long as there are various opinions there will be various ways of worshipping God; seeing a variety of opinion necessarily implies a variety of practice. And as in all ages men have differed in nothing more than in their opinions concerning the Supreme Being, so in nothing have they more differed from each other than in the

manner of worshipping him. Had this been only in the heathen world it would not have been at all surprising, for we know these 'by their wisdom knew not God'; nor therefore could they know how to worship him. But is it not strange that even in the Christian world, although they all agree in the general, 'God is a Spirit, and they that worship him must worship him in spirit and in truth,' yet the particular modes of worshipping God are almost as various as among the heathens?

9. And how shall we choose among so much variety? No man can choose for or prescribe to another. But everyone must follow the dictates of his own conscience in simplicity and godly sincerity. He must be fully persuaded in his own mind, and then act according to the best light he has. Nor has any creature power to constrain another to walk by his own rule. God has given no right to any of the children of men thus to lord it over the conscience of his brethren. But every man must judge for himself, as every man must give an account of himself to God.

10. Although therefore every follower of Christ is obliged by the very nature of the Christian institution to be a member of some particular congregation or other, some church, as it is usually termed (which implies a particular manner of worshipping God; for 'two cannot walk together unless they be agreed'); yet none can be obliged by any power on earth but that of his own conscience to prefer this or that congregation to another, this or that particular manner of worship. I know it is commonly supposed that the place of our birth fixes the church to which we ought to belong; that one, for instance, who is born in England ought to be a member of that which is styled 'the Church of England', and consequently to worship God in the particular manner which is prescribed by that church. I was once a zealous maintainer of this, but I find many reasons to abate of this zeal. I fear it is attended with such difficulties as no reasonable man can get over. Not the least of which is that if this rule had took place, there could have been no Reformation from popery, seeing it entirely destroys the right of private judgment on which that whole Reformation stands.

11. I dare not therefore presume to impose my mode of worship on any other. I believe it is truly primitive and apostolical. But my belief is no rule for another. I ask not therefore of him with whom I would unite in love, 'Are you of my Church? Of my congregation? Do you receive the same form of church government and allow the same church officers with me? Do you join in the same form of prayer wherein I worship God?' I inquire not, 'Do you receive the Supper of the Lord in the same posture and manner that I do?' Nor whether, in the administration of baptism, you agree with me in admitting sureties for the baptized, in the manner of administering it, or the age of those to whom it should be administered. Nay, I ask not of you (as clear as I am in my own mind) whether you allow baptism and the Lord's Supper at all. Let

all these things stand by: we will talk of them, if need be, at a more convenient season. My only question at present is this, 'Is thine heart right, as my heart is with thy heart?'

12. But what is properly implied in the question? I do not mean what did Jehu imply therein, but what should a follower of Christ understand thereby when he proposes it to any of his brethren?

The first thing implied is this: Is thy heart right with God? Dost thou believe his being, and his perfections? His eternity, immensity, wisdom, power; his justice, mercy, and truth? Dost thou believe that he now 'upholdeth all things by the word of his power'? And that he governs even the most minute, even the most noxious, to his own glory, and the good of them that love him? Hast thou a divine evidence, a supernatural conviction, of the things of God? Dost thou 'walk by faith, not by sight'? 'Looking not at temporal things, but things eternal'?

13. Dost thou believe in the Lord Jesus Christ, 'God over all, blessed for ever'? Is he 'revealed in' thy soul? Dost thou 'know Jesus Christ and him crucified'? Does he 'dwell in thee, and thou in him'? Is he 'formed in thy heart by faith'? Having absolutely disclaimed all thy own works, thy own righteousness, hast thou 'submitted thyself unto the righteousness of God', 'which is by faith in Christ Jesus'? Art thou 'found in him, not having thy own righteousness, but the righteousness which is by faith'? And art thou, through him, 'fighting the good fight of faith, and laying hold of eternal life'?

14. Is thy faith ἐνεργουμένη δι' ἀγάπης—filled with the energy of love? Dost thou love God? I do not say 'above all things', for it is both an unscriptural and an ambiguous expression, but 'with all thy heart, and with all thy mind, and with all thy soul, and with all thy strength'? Dost thou seek all thy happiness in him alone? And dost thou find what thou seekest? Does thy soul continually 'magnify the Lord, and thy spirit rejoice in God thy Saviour'? Having learned 'in everything to give thanks', dost thou find it is 'a joyful and a pleasant thing to be thankful'? Is God the centre of thy soul? The sum of all thy desires? Art thou accordingly 'laying up' thy 'treasure in heaven', and 'counting all things else dung and dross'? Hath the love of God cast the love of the world out of thy soul? Then thou art 'crucified to the world'. 'Thou art dead' to all below, 'and thy life is hid with Christ in God.'

15. Art thou employed in doing 'not thy own will, but the will of him that sent thee'? Of him that sent thee down to sojourn here a while, to spend a few days in a strange land, till having finished the work he hath given thee to do thou return to thy Father's house? Is it thy meat and drink 'to do the will of thy Father which is in heaven'? Is 'thine eye single' in all things? Always fixed on him? Always 'looking unto Jesus'? Dost thou point at him in whatsoever thou dost? In all thy labour, thy business, thy conversation? Aiming only at the glory of God in all? 'Whatsoever' thou dost, either 'in word or deed, doing

it all in the name of the Lord Jesus, giving thanks unto God, even the Father, through him'?

16. Does the love of God constrain thee to 'serve' him 'with fear'? To 'rejoice unto him with reverence'? Art thou more afraid of displeasing God than either of death or hell? Is nothing so terrible to thee as the thought of 'offending the eyes of his glory'? Upon this ground dost thou 'hate all evil ways', every transgression of his holy and perfect law? And herein 'exercise' thyself 'to have a conscience void of offence toward God and toward man'?

17. Is thy heart right toward thy neighbour? Dost thou 'love as thyself' all mankind without exception? 'If you love those only that love you, what thank have you?' Do you 'love your enemies'? Is your soul full of goodwill, of tender affection toward them? Do you love even the enemies of God? The unthankful and unholy? Do your bowels yearn over them? Could you 'wish yourself (temporally) accursed' for their sake? And do you show this by 'blessing them that curse you, and praying for those that despitefully use you and persecute you'?

18. Do you show your love by your works? While you have time, as you have opportunity, do you in fact 'do good to all men'—neighbours or strangers, friends or enemies, good or bad? Do you do them all the good you can? Endeavouring to supply all their wants, assisting them both in body and soul to the uttermost of your power? If thou art thus minded, may every Christian say—yea, if thou art but sincerely desirous of it, and following on till thou attain—then 'thy heart is right, as my heart is with thy heart.'

II.1. 'If it be, give me thine hand.' I do not mean, 'Be of my opinion.' You need not. I do not expect nor desire it. Neither do I mean, 'I will be of your opinion.' I cannot. It does not depend on my choice. I can no more think than I can see or hear as I will. Keep you your opinion, I mine; and that as steadily as ever. You need not even endeavour to come over to me, or bring me over to you. I do not desire you to dispute those points, or to hear or speak one word concerning them. Let all opinions alone on one side and the other. Only 'give me thine hand.'

2. I do not mean, 'Embrace my modes of worship,' or, 'I will embrace yours.' This also is a thing which does not depend either on your choice or mine. We must both act as each is fully persuaded in his own mind. Hold you fast that which you believe is most acceptable to God, and I will do the same. I believe the episcopal form of church government to be scriptural and apostolical. If you think the presbyterian or independent is better, think so still, and act accordingly. I believe infants ought to be baptized, and that this may be done either by dipping or sprinkling. If you are otherwise persuaded, be so still, and follow your own persuasion. It appears to me that forms of prayer are of excellent use, particularly in the great congregation. If you judge

extemporary prayer to be of more use, act suitably to your own judgment. My sentiment is that I ought not to forbid water wherein persons may be baptized, and that I ought to eat bread and drink wine as a memorial of my dying Master. However, if you are not convinced of this, act according to the light you have. I have no desire to dispute with you one moment upon any of the preceding heads. Let all these smaller points stand aside. Let them never come into sight. 'If thine heart is as my heart', if thou lovest God and all mankind, I ask no more: 'Give me thine hand.'

3. I mean, first, love me. And that not only as thou lovest all mankind; not only as thou lovest thine enemies or the enemies of God, those that hate thee, that 'despitefully use thee and persecute thee'; not only as a stranger, as one of whom thou knowest neither good nor evil. I am not satisfied with this. No; 'If thine heart be right, as mine with thy heart', then love me with a very tender affection, as a friend that is closer than a brother; as a brother in Christ, a fellow-citizen of the new Jerusalem, a fellow-soldier engaged in the same warfare, under the same Captain of our salvation. Love me as a companion in the kingdom and patience of Jesus, and a joint-heir of his glory.

4. Love me (but in an higher degree than thou dost the bulk of mankind) with the love that is 'long-suffering and kind'; that is patient if I am ignorant or out of the way, bearing and not increasing my burden; and is tender, soft, and compassionate still; that 'envieth not' if at any time it please God to prosper me in his work even more than thee. Love me with the love that 'is not provoked' either at my follies or infirmities, or even at my acting (if it should sometimes so appear to thee) not according to the will of God. Love me so as to 'think no evil' of me, to put away all jealousy and evil surmising. Love me with the love that 'covereth all things', that never reveals either my faults or infirmities; that 'believeth all things', is always willing to think the best, to put the fairest construction on all my words and actions; that 'hopeth all things', either that the thing related was never done, or not done with such circumstances as are related, or, at least, that it was done with a good intention, or in sudden stress of temptation. And hope to the end that whatever is amiss will, by the grace of God, be corrected, and whatever is wanting supplied, through the riches of his mercy in Christ Jesus.

5. I mean, secondly, commend me to God in all thy prayers; wrestle with him in my behalf, that he would speedily correct what he sees amiss and supply what is wanting in me. In thy nearest access to the throne of grace beg of him who is then very present with thee that my heart may be more as thy heart, more right both toward God and toward man; that I may have a fuller conviction of things not seen, and a stronger view of the love of God in Christ Jesus; may more steadily walk by faith, not by sight, and more earnestly grasp eternal life. Pray that the love of God and of all mankind may be more largely poured into my heart; that I may be more fervent and active in doing the will

of my Father which is in heaven, more zealous of good works, and more careful to abstain from all appearance of evil.

6. I mean, thirdly, provoke me to love and to good works. Second thy prayer as thou hast opportunity by speaking to me in love whatsoever thou believest to be for my soul's health. Quicken me in the work which God has given me to do, and instruct me how to do it more perfectly. Yea, 'smite me friendly and reprove me' whereinsoever I appear to thee to be doing rather my own will than the will of him that sent me. O speak and spare not, whatever thou believest may conduce either to the amending my faults, the strengthening my weakness, the building me up in love, or the making me more fit in any kind for the Master's use.

7. I mean, lastly, love me not in word only, but in deed and in truth. So far as in conscience thou canst (retaining still thy own opinions and thy own manner of worshipping God), join with me in the work of God, and let us go on hand in hand. And thus far, it is certain, thou mayst go. Speak honourably, wherever thou art, of the work of God, by whomsoever he works, and kindly of his messengers. And if it be in thy power, not only sympathize with them when they are in any difficulty or distress, but give them a cheerful and effectual assistance, that they may glorify God on thy behalf.

8. Two things should be observed with regard to what has been spoken under this last head. The one, that whatsoever love, whatsoever offices of love, whatsoever spiritual or temporal assistance, I claim from him whose heart is right, as my heart is with his, the same I am ready, by the grace of God, according to my measure, to give him. The other, that I have not made this claim in behalf of myself only, but of all whose heart is right toward God and man, that we may all love one another as Christ hath loved us.

III.1. One inference we may make from what has been said. We may learn from hence what is a 'catholic spirit'.

There is scarce any expression which has been more grossly misunderstood and more dangerously misapplied than this. But it will be easy for any who calmly consider the preceding observations to correct any such misapprehensions of it, and to prevent any such misapplication.

For from hence we may learn, first, that a catholic spirit is not *speculative latitudinarianism*. It is not an indifference to all opinions. This is the spawn of hell, not the offspring of heaven. This unsettledness of thought, this being 'driven to and fro, and tossed about with every wind of doctrine', is a great curse, not a blessing; an irreconcilable enemy, not a friend, to true catholicism. A man of a truly catholic spirit has not now his religion to seek. He is fixed as the sun in his judgment concerning the main branches of Christian doctrine. 'Tis true he is always ready to hear and weigh whatsoever can be offered against his principles. But as this does not show any wavering in his own mind, so neither does it occasion any. He does not halt between two opinions, nor vainly endeavour to blend them into one. Observe this, you who know not what spirit ye are of, who call yourselves men of a catholic spirit only because you are of a muddy understanding; because your mind is all in a mist; because you have no settled, consistent principles, but are for jumbling all opinions together. Be convinced that you have quite missed your way: you know not where you are. You think you are got into the very spirit of Christ, when in truth you are nearer the spirit of antichrist. Go first and learn the first elements of the gospel of Christ, and then shall you learn to be of a truly catholic spirit.

2. From what has been said we may learn, secondly, that a catholic spirit is not any kind of *practical latitudinarianism.* It is not indifference as to public worship or as to the outward manner of performing it. This likewise would not be a blessing but a curse. Far from being an help thereto it would, so long as it remained, be an unspeakable hindrance to the worshipping of God in spirit and in truth. But the man of a truly catholic spirit, having weighed all things in the balance of the sanctuary, has no doubt, no scruple at all concerning that particular mode of worship wherein he joins. He is clearly convinced that *this* manner of worshipping God is both scriptural and rational. He knows none in the world which is more scriptural, none which is more rational. Therefore without rambling hither and thither he cleaves close thereto, and praises God for the opportunity of so doing.

3. Hence we may, thirdly, learn that a catholic spirit is not indifference to all congregations. This is another sort of latitudinarianism, no less absurd and unscriptural than the former. But it is far from a man of a truly catholic spirit. He is fixed in his congregation as well as his principles. He is united to one, not only in spirit, but by all the outward ties of Christian fellowship. There he partakes of all the ordinances of God. There he receives the Supper of the Lord. There he pours out his soul in public prayer, and joins in public praise and thanksgiving. There he rejoices to hear the word of reconciliation, the gospel of the grace of God. With these his nearest, his best beloved brethren, on solemn occasions he seeks God by fasting. These particularly he watches over in love, as they do over his soul, admonishing, exhorting, comforting, reproving, and every way building up each other in the faith. These he regards as his own household, and therefore according to the ability God has given him naturally cares for them, and provides that they may have all the things that are needful for life and godliness.

4. But while he is steadily fixed in his religious principles, in what he believes to be the truth as it is in Jesus; while he firmly adheres to that worship of God which he judges to be most acceptable in his sight; and while he is united by the tenderest and closest ties to one particular congregation; his heart is enlarged toward all mankind, those he knows and those he does not; he

embraces with strong and cordial affection neighbours and strangers, friends and enemies. This is catholic or universal love. And he that has this is of a catholic spirit. For love alone gives the title to this character—catholic love is a catholic spirit.

5. If then we take this word in the strictest sense, a man of a catholic spirit is one who in the manner above mentioned 'gives his hand' to all whose 'hearts are right with his heart'. One who knows how to value and praise God for all the advantages he enjoys: with regard to the knowledge of the things of God, the true, scriptural manner of worshipping him; and above all his union with a congregation fearing God and working righteousness. One who, retaining these blessings with the strictest care, keeping them as the apple of his eye, at the same time loves as friends, as brethren in the Lord, as members of Christ and children of God, as joint partakers now of the present kingdom of God, and fellow-heirs of his eternal Kingdom, all of whatever opinion or worship or congregation who believe in the Lord Jesus Christ; who love God and man; who, rejoicing to please and fearing to offend God, are careful to abstain from evil and zealous of good works. He is the man of a truly catholic spirit who bears all these continually upon his heart, who having an unspeakable tenderness for their persons, and longing for their welfare, does not cease to commend them to God in prayer, as well as to plead their cause before men; who speaks comfortably to them, and labours by all his words to strengthen their hands in God. He assists them to the uttermost of his power in all things, spiritual and temporal. He is ready 'to spend and be spent for them'; yea, 'to lay down his life for' their sake.

6. Thou, O man of God, think on these things. If thou art already in this way, go on. If thou hast heretofore mistook the path, bless God who hath brought thee back. And now run the race which is set before thee, in the royal way of universal love. Take heed lest thou be either wavering in thy judgment or straitened in thy bowels. But keep an even pace, rooted in the faith once delivered to the saints and grounded in love, in true, catholic love, till thou art swallowed up in love for ever and ever.

THE GREAT ASSIZE

Sermon 15 – 1758

AN INTRODUCTORY COMMENT

Wesley wrote this sermon at the home of his friend and benefactor Ebenezer Blackwell in Lewisham, to which he had retired in late February 1758. This work was the only Wesley sermon to a civil court that was ever published and also the only one in what may fairly be labelled an ornate style. The sermon was preached in St. Paul's, Bedford, on Friday, March 10. It was published, by request, in the summer of 1758 and then inserted into the 1771 edition of his *Sermons*. Twenty years later, Wesley avowed that even then he could not 'write a better sermon on the Great Assize than I did [in 1758]' (*Journal*, Sept. 1, 1778).

In this sermon, Wesley has accommodated his carefully cultivated 'plain style' to a new and special occasion; very little of the revival preacher appears here. There are no quotations from hymns, but lines from Virgil, Ovid, and Edward Young instead. There is scant recourse to any evangelical emphasis, no reference to Methodism, and only a passing hat-tipping to 'faith alone'. The rhetoric of the introduction and conclusion is frankly exalted, and an earthly commonplace becomes the analogue for the cosmic climax of human destiny and the occasion for Wesley's most explicit exposition of his eschatology.

This, of course, is the central concern of the sermon: Wesley's vivid sense of the Christian life as lived under God's constant judgment and oriented toward his Final Judgment. The analogy between earthly assizes and 'the Great Assize' was at least as old in English preaching as *The Pricke of Conscience*, formerly attributed to Richard Rolle of Hampole (c.1300–49). Here, the dominant metaphors are all forensic, and Wesley's depiction of the end-time is as stark and decisive as he could make it. The reader must judge as to the consonance of Wesley's views of 'The Last Day' with New Testament and traditional Christian eschatologies as they have evolved. But it would be well to recognize the influence of Joseph Mede and J. A. Bengel, his main sources for eschatology besides the Scriptures. *The Great Assize* may better be appraised as an implicit statement about 'the way of salvation' rather than a speculation reaching out beyond faith's basic surety that God's final purposes for his human creation are already validly revealed in Jesus Christ.

The Great Assize

We shall all stand before the judgment seat of Christ.
Romans 14:10

1. How many circumstances concur to raise the awfulness of the present solemnity! The general concourse of people of every age, sex, rank, and condition of life, willingly or unwillingly gathered together, not only from the neighbouring, but from distant parts: *criminals*, speedily to be brought forth, and having no way to escape; *officers*, waiting in their various posts to execute the orders which shall be given; and the *representative* of our gracious Sovereign, whom we so highly reverence and honour. The *occasion* likewise of this assembly adds not a little to the solemnity of it: to hear and determine causes of every kind, some of which are of the most important nature; on which depends no less than life or death—death, that uncovers the face of eternity! It was doubtless in order to increase the serious sense of these things, and not in the minds of the vulgar only, that the wisdom of our forefathers did not disdain to appoint even several minute circumstances of this solemnity. For these also, by means of the eye or ear, may more deeply affect the heart. And when viewed in this light, trumpets, staves, apparel, are no longer trifling or insignificant, but subservient in their kind and degree to the most valuable ends of society.

2. But as awful as this solemnity is, one far more awful is at hand. For yet a little while and 'we shall all stand before the judgment seat of Christ. For, As I live, saith the Lord, every knee shall bow to me, and every tongue shall confess to God.' And in that day 'every one of us shall give account of himself to God.'

3. Had all men a deep sense of this, how effectually would it secure the interests of society! For what more forcible motive can be conceived to the practice of genuine morality? To a steady pursuit of solid virtue, an uniform walking in justice, mercy, and truth? What could strengthen our hands in all that is good, and deter us from all evil, like a strong conviction of this—'The judge standeth at the door,' and we are shortly to *stand before* him?

4. It may not therefore be improper, or unsuitable to the design of the present assembly, to consider,

I. The chief circumstances which will precede our standing before the judgment seat of Christt.

II. The judgment itself, and
III. A few of the circumstances which will follow it.

I. Let us, in the first place, consider the chief circumstances which will precede our standing before the judgment seat of Christ.

And first, 1. 'God will show signs in the earth beneath' (Acts 2:19): particularly, he will 'arise to shake terribly the earth'. 'The earth shall reel to and fro like a drunkard, and shall be removed like a cottage.' 'There shall be earthquakes' κατὰ τόπους (not in divers only, but) 'in all places' (Luke 21:11)—not in one only, or a few, but in every part of the habitable world—even 'such as were not since men were upon the earth, so mighty earthquakes and so great'. In one of these 'every island shall flee away, and the mountains will not be found' (Rev. 16:20). Meantime all the waters of the terraqueous globe will feel the violence of those concussions: 'the sea and waves roaring' (Luke 21:25), with such an agitation as had never been known before since the hour that 'the fountains of the great deep were broken up,' to destroy the earth which then 'stood out of the water and in the water'. The air will be all storm and tempest, full of dark 'vapours and pillars of smoke' (Joel 2:30); resounding with thunder from pole to pole, and torn with ten thousand lightnings. But the commotion will not stop in the region of the air: 'The powers of heaven also shall be shaken.' 'There shall be signs in the sun and in the moon and in the stars' (Luke 21:25, 26)—those fixed as well as those that move round them. 'The sun shall be turned into darkness and the moon into blood, before the great and terrible day of the Lord come' (Joel 2:31). 'The stars shall withdraw their shining' (Joel 3:15), yea and 'fall from heaven', being thrown out of their orbits. And then shall be heard the universal 'shout' from all the companies of heaven, followed by 'the voice of the archangel' proclaiming the approach of the Son of God and man, 'and the trumpet of God' (1 Thess. 4:16) sounding an alarm to all 'that sleep in the dust of the earth'. In consequence of this all the graves shall open, and the bodies of men arise. 'The sea also shall give up the dead which are therein' (Rev. 20:13), and everyone shall rise with his own body—his own in substance, although so changed in its properties as we cannot now conceive. For 'this corruptible will then put on incorruption, and this mortal put on immortality' (1 Cor. 15:53). Yea, 'death and Hades', the invisible world, shall 'deliver up the dead that are in them' (Rev. 20:13); so that all who ever lived and died since God created man shall be raised incorruptible and immortal.

2. At the same time 'the Son of man shall send forth his angels' over all the earth, 'and they shall gather his elect from the four winds, from one end of heaven to the other' (Matt. 24:31). And the Lord himself shall 'come with clouds, in his own glory and the glory of his Father, with ten thousand of his saints, even myriads of angels', and 'shall sit upon the throne of his glory. And

before him shall be gathered all nations, and he shall separate them one from another, and shall set the sheep' (the good) 'on his right hand, and the goats' (the wicked) 'upon the left' (Matt. 25:31–33). Concerning this general assembly it is that the beloved disciple speaks thus: 'I saw the dead' (all that had been dead) 'small and great, stand before God. And the books were opened (a figurative expression, plainly referring to the manner of proceeding among men), and the dead were judged out of those things which were written in the books according to their works' (Rev. 20:12).

II. These are the chief circumstances which are recorded in the oracles of God as preceding the general judgment. We are, secondly, to consider the judgment itself, so far as it hath pleased God to reveal it.

1. The person by whom God 'will judge the world' is his only-begotten Son, whose 'goings forth are from everlasting', 'who is God over all, blessed for ever'. Unto him, 'being the out-beaming of his Father's glory, the express image of his person' (Heb. 1:3), the Father 'hath committed all judgment, because he is the Son of man' (John 5:22, 27); because, though he was 'in the form of God, and thought it not robbery to be equal with God, yet he emptied himself, taking upon him the form of a servant, being made in the likeness of men' (Phil. 2:6–7). Yea, because 'being found in fashion as a man, he humbled himself' yet farther, 'becoming obedient unto death, even the death of the cross. Wherefore God hath highly exalted him,' even in his human nature, and 'ordained him' as man to try the children of men, to be the 'judge both of the quick and dead'; both of those who shall be found alive at his coming, and of those who were before 'gathered to their fathers'.

2. The time termed by the prophet 'the great and the terrible day' is usually in Scripture styled 'the day of the Lord'. The space from the creation of man upon the earth to the end of all things is *the day of the sons of men*. The time that is now passing over us is properly *our day*. When this is ended, the day of the Lord will begin. But who can say how long it will continue? 'With the Lord one day is as a thousand years, and a thousand years as one day' (2 Pet. 3:8). And from this very expression some of the ancient Fathers drew that inference, that what is commonly called 'the day of judgment' would be indeed a thousand years. And it seems they did not go beyond the truth; nay, probably they did not come up to it. For if we consider the number of persons who are to be judged, and of actions which are to be inquired into, it does not appear that a thousand years will suffice for the transactions of that day. So that it may not improbably comprise several thousand years. But God shall reveal this also in its season.

3. With regard to the place where mankind will be judged we have no explicit account in Scripture. An eminent writer (but not he alone; many have been of the same opinion) supposes it will be on earth, where the works were

done according to which they shall be judged, and that God will in order thereto employ the angels of his strength,

> To smooth and lengthen out the boundless space,
> And spread an area for all human race.

But perhaps it is more agreeable to our Lord's own account of his 'coming in the clouds' to suppose it will be above the earth, if not 'twice a planetary height'. And this supposition is not a little favoured by what St. Paul writes to the Thessalonians. 'The dead in Christ shall rise first. Then we who remain alive shall be caught up together with them, in the clouds, to meet the Lord in the air' (1 Thess. 4:16–17). So that it seems most probable the 'great white throne' will be high exalted above the earth.

4. The persons to be judged who can count, any more than the drops of rain or the sands of the sea? I beheld, saith St. John, 'a great multitude which no man can number, clothed with white robes, and palms in their hands'. How immense then must be the total multitude of all nations, and kindreds, and people, and tongues! Of all that have sprung from the loins of Adam since the world began, till time shall be no more! If we admit the common supposition, which seems noways absurd, that the earth bears at any one time no less than four hundred millions of living souls—men, women, and children—what a congregation must all those generations make who have succeeded each other for seven thousand years!

> Great Xerxes' world in arms, proud Cannae's host, . . .
> They all are here, and here they all are lost:
> Their numbers swell to be discerned in vain;
> Lost as a drop in the unbounded main.

Every man, every woman, every infant of days that ever breathed the vital air will then hear the voice of the Son of God, and start into life, and appear before him. And this seems to be the natural import of that expression, 'the dead, small and great': all universally, all without exception, all of every age, sex, or degree; all that ever lived and died, or underwent such a change as will be equivalent with death. For long before that day the phantom of human greatness disappears and sinks into nothing. Even in the moment of death that vanishes away. Who is rich or great in the grave?

5. And every man shall there 'give an account of his own works', yea, a full and true account of all that he ever did while in the body, whether it was good or evil. O what a scene will then be disclosed in the sight of angels and men! While not the fabled Rhadamanthus, but the Lord God Almighty, who knoweth all things in heaven and earth,

Castigatque, auditque dolos; subigitque fateri
Quae quis apud superos, furto laetatus inani,
*Distulit in seram commissa piacula mortem.**

Nor will all the actions alone of every child of man be then brought to open view, but all their words, seeing 'every idle word which men shall speak, they shall give account thereof in the day of judgment.' So that, 'By thy words' (as well as works) 'thou shalt be justified; or by thy words thou shalt be condemned' (Matt. 12:36–37). Will not God then bring to light every circumstance also that accompanied every word or action, and if not altered the nature, yet lessened or increased the goodness or badness of them? And how easy is this to him who is 'about our bed and about our path, and spieth out all our ways'! We know 'the darkness is no darkness to him, but the night shineth as the day.'

6. Yea, he 'will bring to light' not 'the hidden works of darkness' only, but the very 'thoughts and intents of the heart'. And what marvel? For he 'searcheth the reins', and 'understandeth all our thoughts'. 'All things are naked and open to the eyes of him with whom we have to do.' 'Hell and destruction are before him' without a covering; 'how much more the hearts of the children of men!'

7. And in that day shall be discovered every inward working of every human soul: every appetite, passion, inclination, affection, with the various combinations of them, with every temper and disposition that constitute the whole complex character of each individual. So shall it be clearly and infallibly seen who was righteous, and who unrighteous; and in what degree every action or person or character was either good or evil.

8. 'Then the king will say to them upon his right hand, Come, ye blessed of my Father. For I was hungry and ye gave me meat; thirsty and ye gave me drink; I was a stranger and ye took me in; naked and ye clothed me.' In like manner, all the good they did upon earth will be recited before men and angels: whatsoever they had done either 'in word or deed, in the name', or for the sake 'of the Lord Jesus'. All their good desires, intentions, thoughts, all their holy dispositions, will also be then remembered; and it will appear that though they were unknown or forgotten among men, yet God 'noted' them 'in his book'. All their sufferings likewise for the name of Jesus and for the testimony of a good conscience will be displayed, unto their *praise* from the righteous judge, their *honour* before saints and angels, and the increase of that 'far more exceeding and eternal weight of glory'.

9. But will their evil deeds too—since if we take in his whole life 'there is

* ['O'er these drear realms stern Rhadamanthus reigns, / Detects each artful villain and constrains / To own the crimes, long veiled from human sight: / In vain! Now all stand forth in hated light.' Thus Wesley's own translation of the full quatrain from Virgil, *Aeneid*, vi. 567–69.]

not a man on earth that liveth and sinneth not'—will these be remembered in that day, and mentioned in the great congregation? Many believe they will not, and ask, 'Would not this imply that their sufferings were not at an end, even when life ended? Seeing they would still have sorrow, and shame, and confusion of face to endure?' They ask farther, 'How can this be reconciled with God's declaration by the Prophet, "If the wicked will turn from all his sins that he hath committed, and keep all my statutes, and do that which is lawful and right; . . . all his transgressions that he hath committed, they shall not be once mentioned unto him"? (Ezek. 18:21–22). How is it consistent with the promise which God has made to all who accept of the gospel covenant, "I will forgive their iniquities, and remember their sin no more"? (Jer. 31:34). Or as the Apostle expresses it, "I will be merciful to their unrighteousness, and their sins and iniquities will I remember no more"?' (Heb. 8:12).

10. It may be answered, it is apparently and absolutely necessary, for the full display of the glory of God, for the clear and perfect manifestation of his wisdom, justice, power, and mercy toward the heirs of salvation, that all the circumstances of their life should be placed in open view, together with all their tempers, and all the desires, thoughts, and intents of their hearts. Otherwise how would it appear out of what a depth of sin and misery the grace of God had delivered them? And, indeed, if the whole lives of all the children of men were not manifestly discovered, the whole amazing contexture of divine providence could not be manifested; nor should we yet be able in a thousand instances to 'justify the ways of God to man'. Unless our Lord's words were fulfilled in their utmost sense, without any restriction or limitation, 'there is nothing covered that shall not be revealed, or hid that shall not be known' (Matt. 10:26), abundance of God's dispensations under the sun would still appear without their reasons. And then only when God hath brought to light all the hidden things of darkness, whosoever were the actors therein, will it be seen that wise and good were all his ways; that he 'saw through the thick cloud', and governed all things by the wise 'counsel of his own will'; that nothing was left to chance or the caprice of men, but God disposed all 'strongly and sweetly', and wrought all into one connected chain of justice, mercy, and truth.

11. And in the discovery of the divine perfections the righteous will rejoice with joy unspeakable; far from feeling any painful sorrow or shame for any of those past transgressions which were long since blotted out as a cloud, washed away by the blood of the Lamb. It will be abundantly sufficient for them that 'all the transgressions which they had committed shall not be once mentioned unto them' to their disadvantage; that 'their sins and transgressions and iniquities shall be remembered no more' to their condemnation. This is the plain meaning of the promise; and this all the children of God shall find true, to their everlasting comfort.

12. After the righteous are judged, the king will turn to them upon his left

hand, and they shall also be judged, every man 'according to his works'. But not only their outward works will be brought into the account, but all the evil words which they have ever spoken; yea, all the evil desires, affections, tempers, which have or have had a place in their souls, and all the evil thoughts or designs which were ever cherished in their hearts. The joyful sentence of acquittal will then be pronounced upon those on the right hand, the dreadful sentence of condemnation upon those on the left—both of which must remain fixed and unmovable as the throne of God.

III.1. We may, in the third place, consider a few of the circumstances which will follow the general judgment. And the first is the execution of the sentence pronounced on the evil and on the good. 'These shall go away into eternal punishment, and the righteous into life eternal.' It should be observed, it is the very same word which is used both in the former and the latter clause: it follows that either the punishment lasts for ever, or the reward too will come to an end. No, never, unless God could come to an end, or his mercy and truth could fail. 'Then shall the righteous shine forth as the sun in the kingdom of their Father,' and shall 'drink of those rivers of pleasure which are at God's right hand for evermore'. But here all description falls short; all human language fails! Only one who is caught up into the third heaven can have a just conception of it. But even such an one cannot express what he hath seen—these things 'it is not possible for man to utter.'

'The wicked', meantime, 'shall be turned into hell,' even 'all the people that forget God'. They will be 'punished with everlasting destruction from the presence of the Lord, and from the glory of his power'. They will be 'cast into the lake of fire burning with brimstone', originally 'prepared for the devil and his angels'; where they will 'gnaw their tongues' for anguish and pain; they will 'curse God, and look upward': there the dogs of hell—pride, malice, revenge, rage, horror, despair—continually devour them. There 'they have no rest day or night, but the smoke of their torment ascendeth for ever and ever.' 'For their worm dieth not, and the fire is not quenched.'

2. Then the heavens will be shrivelled up 'as a parchment scroll', and 'pass away with a great noise'; they will 'flee from the face of him that sitteth on the throne, and there will be found no place for them' (Rev. 20:11). The very manner of their passing away is disclosed to us by the Apostle Peter: 'In the day of God, the heavens, being on fire, shall be dissolved' (2 Pet. 3:12). The whole beautiful fabric will be overthrown by that raging element, the connection of all its parts destroyed, and every atom torn asunder from the others. By the same 'the earth also and the works that are therein shall be burnt up' (2 Pet. 3:10). The enormous works of nature, 'the everlasting hills', mountains that have defied the rage of time, and stood unmoved so many thousand years, will sink down in fiery ruin. How much less will the works of art, though of

the most durable kind, the utmost efforts of human industry—tombs, pillars, triumphal arches, castles, pyramids—be able to withstand the flaming conqueror. All, all will die, perish, vanish away, like a dream when one awaketh!

3. It has indeed been imagined by some great and good men that as it requires that same almighty power to annihilate things as to create, to speak into nothing or out of nothing; so no part of, no atom in the universe will be totally or finally destroyed. Rather, they suppose that as the last operation of fire which we have yet been able to observe is to reduce into glass what by a smaller force it had reduced to ashes; so in the day God hath ordained the whole earth, if not the material heavens also, will undergo this change, after which the fire can have no farther power over them. And they believe this is intimated by that expression in the Revelation made to St. John: 'Before the throne there was a sea of glass like unto crystal' (Rev. 4:6). We cannot now either affirm or deny this; but we shall know hereafter.

4. If it be inquired by the scoffers, the minute philosophers: 'How can these things be? Whence should come such an immense quantity of fire as would consume the heavens and the whole terraqueous globe?' we would beg leave, first, to remind them that this difficulty is not peculiar to the Christian system. The same opinion almost universally obtained among the *unbigoted* heathens. So one of those celebrated 'free-thinkers' speaks according to the generally received sentiment:

> *Esse quoque in fatis reminiscitur, affore tempus,*
> *Quo mare, quo tellus, correptaque regia coeli*
> *Ardeat, et mundi moles operosa laboret.**

But, secondly, it is easy to answer, even from our slight and superficial acquaintance with natural things, that there are abundant magazines of fire ready prepared, and treasured up against the day of the Lord. How soon may a comet, commissioned by him, travel down from the most distant parts of the universe? And were it to fix upon the earth in its return from the sun, when it is some thousand times hotter than a red-hot cannon-ball, who does not see what must be the immediate consequence? But, not to ascend so high as the ethereal heavens, might not the same lightnings which give 'shine to the world', if commanded by the Lord of nature give ruin and utter destruction? Or, to go no farther than the globe itself, who knows what huge reservoirs of liquid fire are from age to age contained in the bowels of the earth? Aetna, Hecla, Vesuvius, and all the other volcanoes that belch out flames and coals of fire, what are they but so many proofs and mouths of those fiery furnaces? And at the same time so many evidences that God hath in readiness wherewith

* ['He remembered also that 'twas in the fates that a time would come when sea and land, the unkindled palace of the sky, and the beleaguered structure of the universe, should be destroyed by fire,' Ovid, *Metamorphoses*, i.256–58.]

to fulfil his word. Yea, were we to observe no more than the surface of the earth, and the things that surround us on every side, it is most certain (as a thousand experiments prove beyond all possibility of denial) that we ourselves, our whole bodies, are full of fire, as well as everything round about us. Is it not easy to make this ethereal fire visible even to the naked eye? And to produce thereby the very same effects on combustible matter which are produced by culinary fire? Needs there then any more than for God to unloose that secret chain whereby this irresistible agent is now bound down, and lies quiescent in every particle of matter? And how soon would it tear the universal frame in pieces, and involve all in one common ruin?

5. There is one circumstance more which will follow the judgment that deserves our serious consideration. 'We look', says the Apostle, 'according to his promise, for new heavens and a new earth, wherein dwelleth righteousness' (2 Pet. 3:13). The promise stands in the prophecy of Isaiah: 'Behold, I create new heavens and a new earth. And the former shall not be remembered' (Isa. 65:17); so great shall the glory of the latter be. These St. John did behold in the visions of God. 'I saw', saith he, 'a new heaven and a new earth; for the first heaven and the first earth were passed away' (Rev. 21:1). And only 'righteousness dwelt therein.' Accordingly he adds, 'And I heard a great voice from' the third 'heaven, saying, Behold, the tabernacle of God is with men, and he will dwell with them, and they shall be his people, and God himself shall be with them, and be their God' (Rev. 21:3). Of necessity, therefore, they will all be happy: 'God shall wipe away all tears from their eyes, and there shall be no more death, neither sorrow, nor crying; neither shall there be any more pain' (Rev. 21:4). 'There shall be no more curse; but they shall see his face' (Rev. 22:3,4), shall have the nearest access to, and thence the highest resemblance of him. This is the strongest expression in the language of Scripture to denote the most perfect happiness. 'And his name shall be on their foreheads.' They shall be openly acknowledged as God's own property; and his glorious nature shall most visibly shine forth in them. 'And there shall be no night there; and they need no candle, neither light of the sun; for the Lord God giveth them light, and they shall reign for ever and ever.'

IV. It remains only to apply the preceding considerations to all who are here before God. And are we not directly led so to do by the present solemnity, which so naturally points us to that day when the Lord 'will judge the world in righteousness'? This, therefore, by reminding us of that more awful season, may furnish many lessons of instruction. A few of these I may be permitted just to touch on. May God write them on all our hearts!

1. And, first, 'how beautiful are the feet' of those who are sent by the wise and gracious providence of God to execute justice on earth, to defend the injured, and punish the wrongdoer! Are they not 'the ministers of God to us

for good', the grand supporters of the public tranquillity, the patrons of innocence and virtue, the great security of all our temporal blessings? And does not every one of these represent not only an earthly prince, but the Judge of the earth; him whose 'name is written upon his thigh, King of Kings, and Lord of Lords'! O that all these sons 'of the right hand of the Most High' may be holy as he is holy! Wise with the 'wisdom that sitteth by his throne', like him who is the eternal wisdom of the Father! No respecters of persons, as he is none; but 'rendering to every man according to his works': like him inflexibly, inexorably just, though pitiful and of tender mercy! So shall they be terrible indeed to them that do evil, as 'not bearing the sword in vain'. So shall the laws of our land have their full use and due honour, and the throne of our King be still 'established in righteousness'.

2. Ye truly honourable men, whom God and the King have commissioned in a lower degree to administer justice, may not ye be compared to those ministering spirits who will attend the Judge coming in the clouds? May you, like them, burn with love to God and man! May you love righteousness and hate iniquity! May ye all minister in your several spheres (such honour hath God given you also!) to them that shall be heirs of salvation, and to the glory of your great Sovereign! May ye remain the establishers of peace, the blessing and ornaments of your country, the protectors of a guilty land, the guardian angels of all that are round about you!

3. You whose office it is to execute what is given you in charge by him before whom you stand, how nearly are you concerned to resemble those that stand before the face of the Son of man! Those 'servants of his that do his pleasure', 'and hearken to the voice of his words'. Does it not highly import *you* to be as uncorrupt as *them*? To approve yourselves the servants of God? To do justly and love mercy; to do to all as ye would they should do to you? So shall that great Judge, under whose eye you continually stand, say to you also, 'Well done, good and faithful servants: enter ye into the joy of your Lord!'

4. Suffer me to add a few words to all of you who are this day present before the Lord. Should not you bear it in your minds all the day long that a more awful day is coming? A large assembly this! But what is it to that which every eye will then behold—the general assembly of all the children of men that ever lived on the face of the whole earth! A few will stand at the judgment seat this day, to be judged touching what shall be laid to their charge. And they are now reserved in prison, perhaps in chains, till they are brought forth to be tried and sentenced. But we shall all, I that speak and you that hear, 'stand at the judgment seat of Christ'. And we are now reserved on this earth, which is not our home, in this prison of flesh and blood, perhaps many of us in chains of darkness too, till we are ordered to be brought forth. Here a man is questioned concerning one or two facts which he is supposed to have committed. There we are to give an account of all our works, from the cradle to the grave: of all

our words; of all our desires and tempers, all the thoughts and intents of our hearts; of all the use we have made of our various talents, whether of mind, body, or fortune, till God said, 'Give an account of thy stewardship; for thou mayest be no longer steward.' In this court it is possible some who are guilty may escape for want of evidence. But there is no want of evidence in that court. All men with whom you had the most secret intercourse, who were privy to all your designs and actions, are ready before your face. So are all the spirits of darkness, who inspired evil designs, and assisted in the execution of them. So are all the angels of God—those 'eyes of the Lord that run to and fro over all the earth'—who watched over your soul, and laboured for your good so far as you would permit. So is your own conscience, a thousand witnesses in one, now no more capable of being either blinded or silenced, but constrained to know and to speak the naked truth touching all your thoughts and words and actions. And is conscience as a thousand witnesses? Yea, but God is as a thousand consciences! O who can stand before the face of 'the great God, even our Saviour, Jesus Christ'!

See, see! He cometh! He maketh the clouds his chariots. He rideth upon the wings of the wind! A devouring fire goeth before him, and after him a flame burneth! See, he sitteth upon his throne, clothed with light as with a garment, arrayed with majesty and honour! Behold his eyes are as a flame of fire, his voice as the sound of many waters!

How will ye escape? Will ye call to the mountains to fall on you, the rocks to cover you? Alas, the mountains themselves, the rocks, the earth, the heavens, are just ready to flee away! Can ye prevent the sentence? Wherewith? With all the substance of thy house, with thousands of gold and silver? Blind wretch! Thou camest naked from thy mother's womb, and [shalt move] naked into eternity. Hear the Lord, the Judge! 'Come ye blessed of my Father! Inherit the kingdom prepared for you from the foundation of the world.' Joyful sound! How widely different from that voice which echoes through the expanse of heaven, 'Depart, ye cursed, into everlasting fire, prepared for the devil and his angels!' And who is he that can prevent or retard the full execution of either sentence? Vain hope! Lo, 'hell is moved from beneath' to receive those who are ripe for destruction! And the 'everlasting doors lift up their heads' that the heirs of glory may come in!

5. 'What manner of persons (then) ought we to be, in all holy conversation and godliness?' We know it cannot be long before the Lord will descend 'with the voice of the archangel, and the trumpet of God'; when every one of us shall appear before him and 'give account of his own works'. 'Wherefore, beloved, seeing ye look for these things', seeing ye know he will come and will not tarry, 'be diligent that ye may be found of him in peace, without spot, and blameless.' Why should ye not? Why should one of you be found on the left hand at his appearing? He 'willeth not that any should perish, but that all should come to

repentance'; by repentance to faith in a bleeding Lord; by faith to spotless love, to the full image of God renewed in the heart, and producing all holiness of conversation. Can you doubt of this when you remember the Judge of all is likewise 'the Saviour of all'? Hath he not bought you with his own blood, that ye might 'not perish, but have everlasting life'? O make proof of his mercy rather than his justice! Of his love rather than the thunder of his power! 'He is not far from every one of us'; and he is now come, 'not to condemn, but to save the world'. He standeth in the midst! Sinner, doth he not now, even now, knock at the door of thy heart? O that thou mayst know, at least '*in this thy day*', the things that belong unto thy peace! O that ye may now give yourselves to him who 'gave himself for you', in humble faith, in holy, active, patient love! So shall ye rejoice with exceeding joy *in his day*, when he cometh in the clouds of heaven.

ORIGINAL SIN

Sermon 44 – 1759

AN INTRODUCTORY COMMENT

One of the prime targets in orthodox Christianity for the deists and other apostles of enlightenment was the doctrine of original sin, with its corollary, total depravity. It was a cherished conviction of theirs that humans could recover their innate moral virtue, their power to will and to do the good. The early Wesley was never more than lightly touched by these attacks. His view of mankind's primal ruin is delineated in his very early sermon on Gen. 1:27 (1729), a view that is presupposed elsewhere in his comments on anthropology. But when a new optimism about man's innate virtue, with a corresponding denial of the notions of 'the Fall' and 'original sin', began to be urged by professed Christians, Wesley was quick to sense a radical challenge and to react appropriately. To him, Article IX, 'Of Original or Birth Sin', had always seemed beyond exception.

The issue had come into focus for Wesley in 1740, when Dr. John Taylor, an eminent Dissenting minister and Hebrew scholar, published an influential treatise, *The Scripture Doctrine of Original Sin*. It had been quickly answered by two other Dissenting ministers, Samuel Hebden and David Jennings. Wesley joined the fray in 1757 with the longest treatise that he ever wrote, *The Doctrine of Original Sin: According to Scripture, Reason, and Experience*. Its first part is most nearly Wesley's own answer to Taylor; in the others he borrows heavily from Jennings, Hebden, Isaac Watts, Thomas Boston, and others. Meanwhile, between 1751 and 1758, he preached on Genesis 6:5 ten times. Even so, he realized that oral preaching would not suffice in the circumstances and that his full length volume was more than most people would read. Accordingly, in 1759, he reformulated Part I of *The Doctrine of Original Sin* in sermon form and published it separately. In 1760 he placed it at the head of his fourth volume of *Sermons*.

In the logic of his soteriology, this sermon was a major doctrinal statement in which he sought to compound the Latin tradition of total depravity with the Eastern Orthodox view of sin as disease and of salvation as *therapeia*. Thus, it still stands as a sufficient answer to all simple-minded references to Wesley as a Pelagian.

Original Sin

And God saw that the wickedness of man was great in the earth, and that every imagination of the thoughts of his heart was only evil continually.
Genesis 6:5

1. How widely different is this from the fair pictures of human nature which men have drawn in all ages! The writings of many of the ancients abound with gay descriptions of the dignity of man; whom some of them paint as having all virtue and happiness in his composition, or at least entirely in his power, without being beholden to any other being; yea, as self-sufficient, able to live on his own stock, and little inferior to God himself.

2. Nor have heathens alone, men who were guided in their researches by little more than the dim light of reason, but many likewise of them that bear the name of Christ, and to whom are entrusted the oracles of God, spoke as magnificently concerning the nature of man, as if it were all innocence and perfection. Accounts of this kind have particularly abounded in the present century; and perhaps in no part of the world more than in our own country. Here not a few persons of strong understanding, as well as extensive learning, have employed their utmost abilities to show what they termed 'the fair side of human nature'. And it must be acknowledged that if their accounts of him be just, man is still but 'a little lower than the angels', or (as the words may be more literally rendered), 'a little less than God'.

3. Is it any wonder that these accounts are very readily received by the generality of men? For who is not easily persuaded to think favourably of himself? Accordingly writers of this kind are almost universally read, admired, applauded. And innumerable are the converts they have made, not only in the gay but the learned world. So that it is now quite unfashionable to talk otherwise, to say anything to the disparagement of human nature; which is generally allowed, notwithstanding a few infirmities, to be very innocent and wise and virtuous.

4. But in the meantime, what must we do with our Bibles? For they will never agree with this. These accounts, however pleasing to flesh and blood, are utterly irreconcilable with the scriptural. The Scripture avers that 'by one man's disobedience all men were constituted sinners'; that 'in Adam all died', spiritually died, lost the life and the image of God; that fallen, sinful Adam then 'begat a son in his own likeness'; nor was it possible he should beget him

in any other, for 'who can bring a clean thing out of an unclean?' That consequently *we*, as well as other men, 'were by nature' 'dead in trespasses and sins', 'without hope, without God in the world', and therefore 'children of wrath'; that every man may say, 'I was shapen in wickedness, and in sin did my mother conceive me'; that 'there is no difference, in that all have sinned, and come short of the glory of God,' of that glorious image of God wherein man was originally created. And hence, when 'the Lord looked down from heaven upon the children of men, he saw they were all gone out of the way, they were altogether become abominable, there was none righteous, no not one', none that truly 'sought after God'. Just agreeable, this, to what is declared by the Holy Ghost in the words above recited: 'God saw', when he looked down from heaven before, 'that the wickedness of man was great in the earth'; so great that 'every imagination of the thoughts of his heart was only evil continually'.

This is God's account of man: from which I shall take occasion, first, to show what men were before the flood; secondly, to inquire whether they are not the same now; and, thirdly, to add some inferences.

I.1. I am, first, by opening the words of the text, to show what men were before the flood. And we may fully depend on the account here given. For God saw it, and he cannot be deceived. He 'saw that the wickedness of man was great'. Not of this or that man; not of a few men only; not barely of the greater part, but of *man in general*, of men universally. The word includes the whole human race, every partaker of human nature. And it is not easy for us to compute their numbers, to tell how many thousands and millions they were. The earth then retained much of its primeval beauty and original fruitfulness. The face of the globe was not rent and torn as it is now; and spring and summer went hand in hand. 'Tis therefore probable it afforded sustenance for far more inhabitants than it is now capable of sustaining. And these must be immensely multiplied while men begat sons and daughters for seven or eight hundred years together. Yet among all this inconceivable number *only* Noah 'found favour with God'. He alone (perhaps including part of his household) was an exception from the universal wickedness, which by the just judgment of God in a short time after brought on universal destruction. All the rest were partakers in the same guilt, as they were in the same punishment.

2. 'God saw all the imaginations of the thoughts of his heart'—of his soul, his inward man, the spirit within him, the principle of all his inward and outward motions. He 'saw all the imaginations'. It is not possible to find a word of a more extensive signification. It includes whatever is formed, made, fabricated within; all that is or passes in the soul: every inclination, affection, passion, appetite; every temper, design, thought. It must of consequence include every word and action, as naturally flowing from the fountains, and

being either good or evil according to the fountain from which they severally flow.

3. Now God 'saw that all' this, the whole thereof, 'was evil', contrary to moral rectitude; contrary to the nature of God, which necessarily includes all good; contrary to the divine will, the eternal standard of good and evil; contrary to the pure, holy image of God, wherein man was originally created, and wherein he stood when God, surveying the works of his hands, saw them all to be 'very good'; contrary to justice, mercy, and truth, and to the essential relations which each man bore to his Creator and his fellow creatures.

4. But was there not good mingled with the evil? Was there not light intermixed with the darkness? No, none at all: 'God saw that the whole imagination of the heart' of man 'was *only* evil.' It cannot indeed be denied but many of them, perhaps all, had good motions put into their hearts. For the spirit of God did then also 'strive with man', if haply he might repent; more especially during that gracious reprieve, the hundred and twenty years while the ark was preparing. But still 'in his flesh dwelt no good thing': all his nature was purely evil. It was wholly consistent with itself, and unmixed with anything of any opposite nature.

5. However, it may still be matter of inquiry, 'Was there no intermission of this evil? Were there no lucid intervals, wherein something good might be found in the heart of man?' We are not here to consider what the grace of God might occasionally work in his soul. And abstracting from this, we have no reason to believe there was any intermission of that evil. For God, who 'saw the whole imagination of the thoughts of his heart to be *only* evil', saw likewise that it was always the same, that it 'was only evil *continually*'—every year, every day, every hour, every moment. He never deviated into good.

II. Such is the authentic account of the whole race of mankind, which he who knoweth what is in man, who searcheth the heart and trieth the reins, hath left upon record for our instruction. Such were all men before God brought the flood upon the earth. We are, secondly, to inquire whether they are the same now.

1. And this is certain, the Scripture gives us no reason to think any otherwise of them. On the contrary, all the above-cited passages of Scripture refer to those who lived after the flood. It was above a thousand years after that God declared by David concerning the children of men, 'They are all gone out of the way' of truth and holiness; 'there is none righteous, no, not one.' And to this bear all the prophets witness in their several generations. So Isaiah concerning God's peculiar people (and certainly the heathens were in *no better* condition): 'The whole head is sick, and the whole heart faint. From the sole of the foot even unto the head there is no soundness, but wounds and bruises and putrifying sores.' The same account is given by all the apostles, yea, by the

whole tenor of the oracles of God. From all these we learn concerning man in his natural state, unassisted by the grace of God, that 'all the imaginations of the thoughts of his heart' are still 'evil, only evil', and that 'continually'.

2. And this account of the present state of man is confirmed by daily experience. It is true the natural man discerns it not. And this is not to be wondered at. So long as a man born blind continues so, he is scarce sensible of his want. Much less, could we suppose a place where all were born without sight, would they be sensible of the want of it. In like manner, so long as men remain in their natural blindness of understanding they are not sensible of their spiritual wants, and of this in particular. But as soon as God opens the eyes of their understanding they see the state they were in before; they are then deeply convinced that 'every man living', themselves especially, are by nature 'altogether vanity'; that is, folly and ignorance, sin and wickedness.

3. We see, when God opens our eyes, that we were before ἄθεοι ἐν τῷ κόσμῳ—'without God', or rather, 'atheists in the world'. We had by nature no knowledge of God, no acquaintance with him. It is true, as soon as we came to the use of reason we learned 'the invisible things of God, even his eternal power and godhead', from 'the things that are made'. From the things that are seen we inferred the existence of an eternal, powerful being that is not seen. But still, although we acknowledged his being, we had no acquaintance with him. As we know there is an emperor of China, whom yet we do not know, so we knew there was a King of all the earth; but yet we knew him not. Indeed we could not, by any of our natural faculties. By none of these could we attain the knowledge of God. We could no more perceive him by our natural understanding than we could see him with our eyes. For 'no one knoweth the Father but the Son, and he to whom the Son willeth to reveal him. And no one knoweth the Son but the Father, and he to whom the Father revealeth him.'

4. We read of an ancient king who, being desirous to know what was the *natural language* of men, in order to bring the matter to a certain issue made the following experiment: he ordered two infants, as soon as they were born, to be conveyed to a place prepared for them, where they were brought up without any instruction at all, and without ever hearing an human voice. And what was the event? Why, that when they were at length brought out of their confinement, they spake no language at all, they uttered inarticulate sounds, like those of other animals. Were two infants in like manner to be brought up from the womb without being instructed in any religion, there is little room to doubt but (unless the grace of God interposed) the event would be just the same. They would have no religion at all: they would know no more of God than the beasts of the field, than the 'wild ass's colt'. Such is *natural religion*, abstracted from traditional, and from the influences of God's spirit!

5. And having no knowledge, we can have no love of God: we cannot love

him we know not. Most men *talk* indeed of loving God, and perhaps imagine that they do. At least few will acknowledge they do not love him. But the fact is too plain to be denied. No man loves God by nature, no more than he does a stone, or the earth he treads upon. What we love, we delight in: but no man has naturally any delight in God. In our natural state we cannot conceive how anyone should delight in him. We take no pleasure in him at all; he is utterly tasteless to us. To love God! It is far above, out of our sight. We cannot naturally attain unto it.

6. We have by nature not only no love, but no fear of God. It is allowed, indeed, that most men have, sooner or later, a kind of senseless, irrational fear, properly called 'superstition'; though the blundering Epicureans gave it the name of 'religion'. Yet even this is not natural, but acquired; chiefly by conversation or from example. By nature 'God is not in all our thoughts.' We leave him to manage his own affairs, to sit quietly, as we imagine, in heaven, and leave us on earth to manage ours. So that we have no more of the fear of God before our eyes than of the love of God in our hearts.

7. Thus are all men 'atheists in the world'. But atheism itself does not screen us from *idolatry*. In his natural state every man born into the world is a rank idolater. Perhaps indeed we may not be such in the vulgar sense of the word. We do not, like the idolatrous heathens, worship molten or graven images. We do not bow down to the stock of a tree, to the work of our own hands. We do not pray to the angels or saints in heaven, any more than to the saints that are upon earth. But what then? We 'have set up our idols in our heart'; and to these we bow down, and worship them. We worship ourselves when we pay that honour to ourselves which is due to God only. Therefore all pride is idolatry; it is ascribing to ourselves what is due to God alone. And although pride was not made for man, yet where is the man that is born without it? But hereby we rob God of his unalienable right, and idolatrously usurp his glory.

8. But pride is not the only sort of idolatry which we are all by nature guilty of. Satan has stamped his own image on our heart in *self-will* also. 'I will', said he, before he was cast out of heaven, 'I will sit upon the sides of the north.' I will do my own will and pleasure, independently on that of my Creator. The same does every man born into the world say, and that in a thousand instances. Nay, and avow it, too, without ever blushing upon the account, without either fear or shame. Ask the man, 'Why did you do this?' He answers, 'Because I had a mind to it.' What is this but, 'Because it was my will'; that is, in effect, because the devil and I are agreed; because Satan and I govern our actions by one and the same principle. The will of God meantime is not in his thoughts, is not considered in the least degree; although it be the supreme rule of every intelligent creature, whether in heaven or earth, resulting from the essential, unalterable relation which all creatures bear to their Creator.

9. So far we bear the image of the devil, and tread in his steps. But at the

next step we leave Satan behind, we run into an idolatry whereof he is not guilty: I mean *love of the world*, which is now as natural to every man as to love his own will. What is more natural to us than to seek happiness in the creature instead of the Creator? To seek that satisfaction in the works of his hands which can be found in God only? What more natural than the desire of the flesh? That is, of the pleasure of sense in every kind? Men indeed talk magnificently of despising these low pleasures, particularly men of learning and education. They affect to sit loose to the gratification of those appetites wherein they stand on a level with the beasts that perish. But it is mere affectation; for every man is conscious to himself that in this respect he is by nature a very beast. Sensual appetites, even those of the lowest kind, have, more or less, the dominion over him. They lead him captive, they drag him to and fro, in spite of his boasted reason. The man, with all his good breeding and other accomplishments, has no pre-eminence over the goat. Nay, it is much to be doubted whether the beast has not the pre-eminence over him! Certainly he has, if we may hearken to one of their modern oracles, who very decently tells us:

> Once in a season, beasts too taste of love:
> Only the beast of reason is its slave
> And in that folly drudges all the year.

A considerable difference indeed, it must be allowed, there is between man and man, arising (beside that wrought by preventing grace) from difference of constitution and of education. But notwithstanding this, who that is not utterly ignorant of himself can here cast the first stone at another? Who can abide the test of our blessed Lord's comment on the seventh commandment: 'He that looketh upon a woman to lust after her hath committed adultery with her already in his heart'? So that one knows not which to wonder at most, the ignorance or the insolence of those men who speak with such disdain of them that are overcome by desires which every man has felt in his own breast! The desire of every pleasure of sense, innocent or not, being natural to every child of man.

10. And so is 'the desire of the eye', the desire of the pleasures of the imagination. These arise either from great, or beautiful, or uncommon objects—if the two former do not coincide with the latter; for perhaps it would appear upon a diligent inquiry that neither *grand* nor *beautiful* objects please any longer than they are *new*; that when the novelty of them is over, the greatest part, at least, of the pleasure they give is over; and in the same proportion as they become familiar they become flat and insipid. But let us experience this ever so often, the same desire will remain still. The inbred thirst continues fixed in the soul. Nay, the more it is indulged, the more it increases, and incites us to follow after another and yet another object; although we leave every one

with an abortive hope and a deluded expectation. Yea,

> The hoary fool, who many days
> Has struggled with continued sorrow,
> Renews his hope, and fondly lays
> The desperate bet upon tomorrow!
>
> Tomorrow comes! 'Tis noon! 'Tis night!
> This day like all the former flies:
> Yet on he goes, to seek delight
> Tomorrow, till tonight he dies!

11. A third symptom of this fatal disease, the love of the world, which is so deeply rooted in our nature, is 'the pride of life', the desire of praise, of 'the honor that cometh of men'. This the greatest admirers of human nature allow to be strictly natural—as natural as the sight or hearing, or any other of the external senses. And are they ashamed of it, even men of letters, men of refined and improved understanding? So far from it that they glory therein; they applaud themselves for their love of applause! Yea, eminent Christians, so called, make no difficulty of adopting the saying of the old, vain heathen, *Animi dissoluti est et nequam negligere quid de se homines sentiant*: 'Not to regard what men think of us is the mark of a wicked and abandoned mind.' So that to go calm and unmoved 'through honour and dishonour, through evil report and good report', is with them a sign of one that is indeed 'not fit to live; away with such a fellow from the earth.' But would one imagine that these men had ever heard of Jesus Christ or his apostles? Or that they knew who it was that said, 'How can ye believe, who receive honour one of another, and seek not that honour which cometh of God only?' But if this be really so; if it be impossible to believe, and consequently to please God, so long as we 'receive (or *seek*) honour one of another, and seek not the honour which cometh of God only'; then in what a condition are all mankind! The Christians as well as the heathens! Since they all seek 'honour one of another'! Since it is as natural for them so to do, themselves being the judges, as it is to see the light which strikes upon their eye, or to hear the sound which enters their ear; yea, since they account it the sign of a virtuous mind to seek the praise of men, and of a vicious one to be content with 'the honour which cometh of God only'!

III.1. I proceed to draw a few inferences from what has been said. And, first, from hence we may learn one grand, fundamental difference between Christianity, considered as a system of doctrines, and the most refined heathenism. Many of the ancient heathens have largely described the vices of particular men. They have spoken much against their covetousness or cruelty, their luxury or prodigality. Some have dared to say that 'no man is born without vices of one kind or another.' But still, as none of them were apprised of the fall of man, so none of them knew his total corruption. They knew not that all men were empty of all good, and filled with all manner of evil. They were wholly ignorant of the entire depravation of the whole human nature, of every man born into the world, in every faculty of his soul, not so much by those particular vices which reign in particular persons as by the general flood of atheism and idolatry, of pride, self-will, and love of the world. This, therefore, is the first, grand, distinguishing point between heathenism and Christianity. The one acknowledges that many men are infected with many vices, and even born with a proneness to them; but supposes withal that in some the natural good much overbalances the evil. The other declares that all men are 'conceived in sin', and 'shapen in wickedness'; that hence there is in every man a 'carnal mind which is enmity against God, which is not, cannot be, subject to his law', and which so infects the whole soul that 'there dwelleth in him, in his flesh', in his natural state, 'no good thing'; but 'all the imagination of the thoughts of his heart is evil', '*only* evil', and that 'continually.'

2. Hence we may, secondly, learn that all who deny this—call it 'original sin' or by any other title—are but heathens still in the fundamental point which differences heathenism from Christianity. They may indeed allow that men have many vices; that some are born with us; and that consequently we are not born altogether so wise or so virtuous as we should be; there being few that will roundly affirm we are born with as much propensity to good as to evil, and that every man is by nature as virtuous and wise as Adam was at his creation. But here is the shibboleth: Is man by nature filled with all manner of evil? Is he void of all good? Is he wholly fallen? Is his soul totally corrupted? Or, to come back to the text, is 'every imagination of the thoughts of his heart evil continually'? Allow this, and you are so far a Christian. Deny it, and you are but an heathen still.

3. We may learn from hence, in the third place, what is the proper nature of religion, of the religion of Jesus Christ. It is θεραπεία ψυχῆς, God's method of healing a soul which is *thus diseased.* Hereby the great Physician of souls applies medicine to heal *this sickness*; to restore human nature, totally corrupted in all its faculties. God heals all our atheism by the knowledge of himself, and of Jesus Christ whom he hath sent; by giving us faith, a divine evidence and conviction of God and of the things of God—in particular of this important truth: Christ loved *me*, and gave himself for *me.* By repentance and lowliness of heart the deadly disease of pride is healed; that of self-will by resignation, a meek and thankful submission to the will of God. And for the love of the world in all its branches the love of God is the sovereign remedy. Now this is properly religion, 'faith thus working by love', working the genuine, meek humility, entire deadness to the world, with a loving, thankful acquiescence in and conformity to the whole will and Word of God.

4. Indeed if man were not thus fallen there would be no need of all this.

There would be no occasion for this work in the heart, this 'renewal in the spirit of our mind'. The 'superfluity of godliness' would then be a more proper expression than the 'superfluity of naughtiness'. For an outside religion without any godliness at all would suffice to all rational intents and purposes. It does accordingly suffice, in the judgment of those who deny this corruption of our nature. They make very little more of religion than the famous Mr. Hobbes did of reason. According to him, reason is only 'a well-ordered train of words': according to them, religion is only a well-ordered train of words and actions. And they speak consistently with themselves; for if the inside be not 'full of wickedness', if this be clean already, what remains but to 'cleanse the outside of the cup'? Outward reformation, if their supposition be just, is indeed the one thing needful.

5. But ye have not so learned the oracles of God. Ye know that he who seeth what is in man gives a far different account both of nature and grace, of our fall and our recovery. Ye know that the great end of religion is to renew our hearts in the image of God, to repair that total loss of righteousness and true holiness which we sustained by the sin of our first parent. Ye know that all religion which does not answer this end, all that stops short of this, the renewal of our soul in the image of God, after the likeness of him that created it, is no other than a poor farce and a mere mockery of God, to the destruction of our own soul. O beware of all those teachers of lies who would palm this upon you for Christianity! Regard them not, though they should come unto you with 'all the deceivableness of unrighteousness', with all smoothness of language, all decency, yea, beauty and elegance of expression, all professions of earnest goodwill to you, and reverence for the Holy Scriptures. Keep to the plain, old 'faith, once delivered to the saints', and delivered by the Spirit of God to your hearts. Know your disease! Know your cure! Ye were born in sin; therefore 'ye must be born again', 'born of God'. By nature ye are wholly corrupted; by grace ye shall be wholly renewed. 'In Adam ye all died'; in the second Adam, 'in Christ, ye all are made alive.' You 'that were dead in sins hath he quickened'. He hath already given you a principle of life, even 'faith in him who loved *you*, and gave himself for *you*'! Now 'go on' 'from faith to faith', until your whole sickness be healed, and all that 'mind be in you which was also in Christ Jesus'!

THE NEW BIRTH

Sermon 45 – 1760

AN INTRODUCTORY TEXT

In conventional Anglican soteriology the basic remedy for original sin had always lain in the church and the sacrament of baptism, as it had in the ancient church. The young Wesley had grown up with this tradition and had reproduced it in his publication of 'A Treatise on Baptism' (1758), without any acknowledgement that it was an abridgement of his father's *Short Discourse of Baptism* (1700). Even the mature Wesley had remarked, in 'The Marks of the New Birth' (1748), 'that these privileges [of being "born again"] by the free mercy of God, are ordinarily annexed to baptism'. But as tensions in the Revival mounted, between the claims of nominal Christians to baptismal regeneration and the claims of the evangelicals to 'conversion', the whole problem of regeneration in relation both to justification and sanctification became more and more urgent. And now that Wesley had restated his doctrine of original sin, there was an obvious logic in producing an updated version of his doctrine of 'new birth', with special reference, in the new situation, to some of his revisions of the conventional notions of baptismal regeneration.

Wesley answers three basic questions: why must we be born again? how must we be born again? and to what ends is it necessary that we be born again? He then proceeds to draw a few inferences from the above, especially distinguishing the new birth from baptism (admitting that regeneration does not always accompany baptism) and from sanctification. In the end, the necessity of the text's appeal ('Ye must be born again') is played off against the inadequate but commonplace view of religion as doing good, avoiding evil, and attending the ordinances of God (cf. the *General Rules*).

This written sermon, then, is a distillate of more than sixty oral sermons on John 3:7, reaching back to 1740 and continuing with increasing frequency in the 1750s. We may see here a rough measure of the importance of the point about 'conversion' as perceived by Wesley and his people. 'The New Birth' is Wesley's conscious effort to provide them with a formal statement of the issue, even though, as an essay, it is clearly incomplete in both its form and argument. In addition to its first appearance in the fourth volume of Wesley's *Sermons on Several Occasions* (1760) and subsequently in the *Works* (1771), this sermon was printed separately at least five times during Wesley's lifetime.

The New Birth

Ye must be born again.
John 3:7

1. If any doctrines within the whole compass of Christianity may be properly termed fundamental they are doubtless these two—the doctrine of justification, and that of the new birth: the former relating to that great work which God does *for us*, in forgiving our sins; the latter to the great work which God does *in us*, in renewing our fallen nature. In order of time neither of these is before the other. In the moment we are justified by the grace of God through the redemption that is in Jesus we are also 'born of the Spirit'; but in order of thinking, as it is termed, justification precedes the new birth. We first conceive his wrath to be turned away, and then his Spirit to work in our hearts.

2. How great importance, then, must it be of to every child of man thoroughly to understand these fundamental doctrines! From a full conviction of this, many excellent men have wrote very largely concerning justification, explaining every point relating thereto, and opening the Scriptures which treat upon it. Many likewise have wrote on the new birth—and some of them largely enough—but yet not so clearly as might have been desired, nor so deeply and accurately; having either given a dark, abstruse account of it, or a slight and superficial one. Therefore a full and at the same time a clear account of the new birth seems to be wanting still. Such as may enable us to give a satisfactory answer to these three questions: First, why must we be born again? What is the foundation of this doctrine of the new birth? Secondly, how must we be born again? What is the nature of the new birth? And thirdly, wherefore must we be born again? To what end is it necessary? These questions, by the assistance of God, I shall briefly and plainly answer, and then subjoin a few inferences which will naturally follow.

I.1. And, first, why must we be born again? What is the foundation of this doctrine? The foundation of it lies near as deep as the creation of the world, in the scriptural account whereof we read, 'And God', the three-one God, 'said, Let us make man in our image, after our likeness. So God created man in his own image, in the image of God created he him' (Gen. 1:26-27). Not barely in his *natural image*, a picture of his own immortality, a spiritual being endued with understanding, freedom of will, and various affections; nor merely in his *political image*, the governor of this lower world, having 'dominion over the fishes of the sea, and over the fowl of the air, and over the cattle, and over all the earth'; but chiefly in his *moral image*, which, according to the Apostle, is 'righteousness and true holiness' (Eph. 4:24). In this image of God was man made. 'God is love': accordingly man at his creation was full of love, which was the sole principle of all his tempers, thoughts, words, and actions. God is full of justice, mercy, and truth: so was man as he came from the hands of his Creator. God is spotless purity: and so man was in the beginning pure from every sinful blot. Otherwise God could not have pronounced *him* as well as all the other works of his hands, 'very good' (Gen. 1:31). This he could not have been had he not been pure from sin, and filled with righteousness and true holiness. For there is no medium. If we suppose an intelligent creature not to love God, not to be righteous and holy, we necessarily suppose him not to be good at all; much less to be 'very good'.

2. But although man was made in the image of God, yet he was not made immutable. This would have been inconsistent with that state of trial in which God was pleased to place him. He was therefore created able to stand, and yet liable to fall. And this God himself apprised him of, and gave him a solemn warning against it. Nevertheless 'man did not abide in honour.' He fell from his high estate. He 'ate of the tree whereof the Lord had commanded him, Thou shalt not eat thereof.' By this wilful act of disobedience to his Creator, this flat rebellion against his sovereign, he openly declared that he would no longer have God to rule over him; that he would be governed by his own will, and not the will of him that created him, and that he would not seek his happiness in God, but in the world, in the works of his hands. Now God had told him before, 'In the day that thou eatest' of that fruit 'thou shalt surely die.' And the word of the Lord cannot be broken. Accordingly in that day he did die: he died to God, the most dreadful of all deaths. He lost the life of God: he was separated from him in union with whom his spiritual life consisted. The body dies when it is separated from the soul, the soul when it is separated from God. But this separation from God Adam sustained in the day, the hour, he ate of the forbidden fruit. And of this he gave immediate proof; presently showing by his behaviour that the love of God was extinguished in his soul, which was now 'alienated from the life of God'. Instead of this he was now under the power of servile fear, so that he fled from the presence of the Lord. Yea, so little did he retain even of the knowledge of him who filleth heaven and earth that he endeavoured to 'hide himself from the Lord God, among the trees of the garden' (Gen. 3:8). So had he lost both the knowledge and the love of God, without which the image of God would not subsist. Of this therefore he was deprived at the same time, and became unholy as well as unhappy. In the room of this he had sunk into pride and self-will, the very image of the devil, and into sensual appetites and desires, the image of the beasts that perish.

3. If it be said, 'Nay, but that threatening, "In the day that thou eatest thereof thou shalt surely die," refers to temporal death, and that alone, to the death of the body only'; the answer is plain: to affirm this is flatly and palpably to make God a liar—to aver that the God of truth positively affirmed a thing contrary to truth. For it is evident Adam did not *die* in this sense 'in the day that he ate thereof'. He lived, in the sense opposite to this death, above nine hundred years after; so that this cannot possibly be understood of the death of the body without impeaching the veracity of God. It must therefore be understood of spiritual death, the loss of the life and image of God.

4. And 'in Adam all died,' all humankind, all the children of men who were then in Adam's loins. The natural consequence of this is that everyone descended from him comes into the world spiritually dead, dead to God, wholly 'dead in sin'; entirely void of the life of God, void of the image of God, of all that 'righteousness and holiness' wherein Adam was created. Instead of this every man born into the world now bears the image of the devil, in pride and self-will; the image of the beast, in sensual appetites and desires. This then is the foundation of the new birth—the entire corruption of our nature. Hence it is that being 'born in sin' we 'must be born again'. Hence everyone that is born of a woman must be born of the Spirit of God.

II.1. But how must a man be born again? What is the nature of the new birth? This is the second question. And a question it is of the highest moment that can be conceived. We ought not, therefore, in so weighty a concern, to be content with a slight inquiry, but to examine it with all possible care, and to ponder it in our hearts, till we fully understand this important point, and clearly see how we are to be born again.

2. Not that we are to expect any minute, philosophical account of the *manner how* this is done. Our Lord sufficiently guards us against any such expectation by the words immediately following the text: wherein he reminds Nicodemus of as indisputable a fact as any in the whole compass of nature—which, notwithstanding, the wisest man under the sun is not able fully to explain. 'The wind bloweth where it listeth', not by thy power or wisdom, 'and thou hearest the sound thereof.' Thou art absolutely assured, beyond all doubt, that it doth blow. 'But thou canst not tell whence it cometh, neither whither it goeth.' The precise manner how it begins and ends, rises and falls, no man can tell. 'So is everyone that is born of the Spirit.' Thou mayst be as absolutely assured of the fact as of the blowing of the wind; but the precise manner how it is done, how the Holy Spirit works this in the soul, neither thou nor the wisest of the children of men is able to explain.

3. However, it suffices for every rational and Christian purpose that without descending into curious, critical inquiries, we can give a plain scriptural account of the nature of the new birth. This will satisfy every reasonable man who

desires only the salvation of his soul. The expression, 'being born again', was not first used by our Lord in his conversation with Nicodemus. It was well known before that time, and was in common use among the Jews when our Saviour appeared among them. When an adult heathen was convinced that the Jewish religion was of God, and desired to join therein, it was the custom to baptize him first, before he was admitted to circumcision. And when he was baptized he was said to be 'born again': by which they meant that he who was before a child of the devil was now adopted into the family of God, and accounted one of his children. This expression therefore which Nicodemus, being 'a teacher in Israel', ought to have understood well, our Lord uses in conversing with him; only in a stronger sense than he was accustomed to. And this might be the reason of his asking, 'How can these things be?' They cannot be literally. 'A man' cannot 'enter a second time into his mother's womb and be born'. But they may, spiritually. A man may be 'born from above', 'born of God', 'born of the Spirit'—in a manner which bears a very near analogy to the natural birth.

4. Before a child is born into the world he has eyes, but sees not; he has ears, but does not hear. He has a very imperfect use of any other sense. He has no knowledge of any of the things of the world, nor any natural understanding. To that manner of existence which he then has we do not even give the name of life. It is then only when a man is born that we say, he begins to live. For as soon as he is born he begins to see the light and the various objects with which he is encompassed. His ears are then opened, and he hears the sounds which successively strike upon them. At the same time all the other organs of sense begin to be exercised upon their proper objects. He likewise breathes and lives in a manner wholly different from what he did before. How exactly does the parallel hold in all these instances! While a man is in a mere natural state, before he is born of God, he has, in a spiritual sense, eyes and sees not; a thick impenetrable veil lies upon them. He has ears, but hears not; he is utterly deaf to what he is most of all concerned to hear. His other spiritual senses are all locked up; he is in the same condition as if he had them not. Hence he has no knowledge of God, no intercourse with him; he is not at all acquainted with him. He has no true knowledge of the things of God, either of spiritual or eternal things. Therefore, though he is a living man, he is a dead Christian. But as soon as he is born of God there is a total change in all these particulars. The 'eyes of his understanding are opened' (such is the language of the great Apostle). And he who of old 'commanded light to shine out of darkness shining on his heart', he sees 'the light of the glory of God', his glorious love, 'in the face of Jesus Christ'. His ears being opened, he is now capable of hearing the inward voice of God, saying, 'Be of good cheer, thy sins are forgiven thee': 'Go and sin no more.' This is the purport of what God speaks to his heart; although perhaps not in these very words. He is now ready

to hear whatsoever 'he that teacheth man knowledge' is pleased from time to time to reveal to him. He 'feels in his heart' (to use the language of our Church) 'the mighty working of the Spirit of God'. Not in a gross, carnal sense, as the men of the world stupidly and wilfully misunderstand the expression, though they have been told again and again, we mean thereby neither more nor less than this: he feels, is inwardly sensible of, the graces which the Spirit of God works in his heart. He feels, he is conscious of, a 'peace which passeth all understanding'. He many times feels such a joy in God as is 'unspeakable and full of glory'. He feels 'the love of God shed abroad in his heart by the Holy Ghost which is given unto him'. And all his spiritual senses are then 'exercised to discern' spiritual 'good and evil'. By the use of these he is daily increasing in the knowledge of God, of Jesus Christ whom he hath sent, and of all the things pertaining to his inward kingdom. And now he may properly be said *to live:* God having quickened him by his Spirit, he is alive to God through Jesus Christ. He lives a life which the world knoweth not of, a 'life' which 'is hid with Christ in God'. God is continually breathing, as it were, upon his soul, and his soul is breathing unto God. Grace is descending into his heart, and prayer and praise ascending to heaven. And by this intercourse between God and man, this fellowship with the Father and the Son, as by a kind of spiritual respiration, the life of God in the soul is sustained: and the child of God grows up, till he comes to 'the full measure of the stature of Christ'.

5. From hence it manifestly appears what is the nature of the new birth. It is that great change which God works in the soul when he brings it into life: when he raises it from the death of sin to the life of righteousness. It is the change wrought in the whole soul by the almighty Spirit of God when it is 'created anew in Christ Jesus', when it is 'renewed after the image of God', 'in righteousness and true holiness', when the love of the world is changed into the love of God, pride into humility, passion into meekness; hatred, envy, malice, into a sincere, tender, disinterested love for all mankind. In a word, it is that change whereby the 'earthly, sensual, devilish' mind is turned into 'the mind which was in Christ'. This is the nature of the new birth. 'So is everyone that is born of the Spirit.'

III.1. It is not difficult for any who has considered these things to see the necessity of the new birth, and to answer the third question: Wherefore, to what ends, is it necessary that we should be born again? It is very easily discerned that this is necessary, first, in order to holiness. For what is holiness, according to the oracles of God? Not a bare external religion, a round of outward duties, how many soever they be, and how exactly soever performed. No; gospel holiness is no less than the image of God stamped upon the heart. It is no other than the whole mind which was in Christ Jesus. It consists of all heavenly affections and tempers mingled together in one. It implies such a continual, thankful love to him who hath not withheld from us his Son, his only Son, as makes it natural, and in a manner necessary to us, to love every child of man; as fills us with 'bowels of mercies, kindness, gentleness, long-suffering'. It is such a love of God as teaches us to be blameless in all manner of conversation; as enables us to present our souls and bodies, all we are and all we have, all our thoughts, words, and actions, a continual sacrifice to God, acceptable through Christ Jesus. Now this holiness can have no existence till we are renewed in the image of our mind. It cannot commence in the soul till that change be wrought, till by the power of the highest overshadowing us we are brought 'from darkness to light, from the power of Satan unto God'; that is, till we are born again; which therefore is absolutely necessary in order to holiness.

2. But 'without holiness no man shall see the Lord,' shall see the face of God in glory. Of consequence the new birth is absolutely necessary in order to eternal salvation. Men may indeed flatter themselves (so desperately wicked and so deceitful is the heart of man!) that they may live in their sins till they come to the last gasp, and yet afterward live with God. And thousands do really believe that they have found a 'broad way which leadeth' not 'to destruction'. What danger, say they, can a woman be in, that is so *harmless* and so *virtuous?* What fear is there that so *honest* a man, one of so strict *morality*, should miss of heaven? Especially if over and above all this they constantly attend on church and sacrament. One of these will ask with all assurance, 'What, shall not I do as well as my neighbours?' Yes, as well as your unholy neighbours; as well as your neighbours that die in their sins. For you will all drop into the pit together, into the nethermost hell. You will all lie together in the lake of fire, 'the lake of fire burning with brimstone'. Then at length you will see (but God grant you may see it before!) the necessity of holiness in order to glory—and consequently of the new birth, since none can be holy except he be born again.

3. For the same reason, except he be born again none can be happy even in this world. For it is not possible in the nature of things that a man should be happy who is not holy. Even the poor ungodly poet could tell us,

Nemo malus felix—

no wicked man is happy. The reason is plain: all unholy tempers are uneasy tempers. Not only malice, hatred, envy, jealousy, revenge, create a present hell in the breast, but even the softer passions, if not kept within due bounds, give a thousand times more pain than pleasure. Even 'hope', when 'deferred' (and how often must this be the case!) 'maketh the heart sick.' And every desire which is not according to the will of God is liable to 'pierce us through with many sorrows'. And all those general sources of sin, pride, self-will, and idolatry, are, in the same proportion as they prevail, general sources of misery. Therefore as long as these reign in any soul happiness has no place there. But they must reign till the bent of our nature is changed, that is, till we are born again. Consequently the new birth is absolutely necessary in order to happiness in this world, as well as in the world to come.

IV. I proposed in the last place to subjoin a few inferences which naturally follow from the preceding observations.

1. And, first, it follows that baptism is not the new birth: they are not one and the same thing. Many indeed seem to imagine they are just the same; at least, they speak as if they thought so. But I do not know that this opinion is publicly avowed by any denomination of Christians whatever. Certainly it is not by any within these kingdoms, whether of the Established Church, or dissenting from it. The judgment of the latter is clearly declared in their *Larger Catechism*: 'Q. What are the parts of a sacrament? A. The parts of a sacrament are two: the one, an outward and sensible sign; the other, an inward and spiritual grace thereby signified. Q. What is baptism? A. Baptism is a sacrament wherein Christ hath ordained the washing with water to be a sign and seal of regeneration by his Spirit' (*Qq*. 163, 165). Here it is manifest [that] baptism, the sign, is spoken of as distinct from regeneration, the thing signified.

In the Church Catechism likewise the judgment of our Church is declared with the utmost clearness. 'What meanest thou by this word, "sacrament"? I mean an outward and visible sign of an inward and spiritual grace. What is the outward part or form in baptism? Water, wherein the person is baptized, "In the name of the Father, Son, and Holy Ghost". What is the inward part or thing signified? A death unto sin, and a new birth unto righteousness.' Nothing therefore is plainer than that, according to the Church of England, baptism is not the new birth.

But indeed the reason of the thing is so clear and evident as not to need any other authority. For what can be more plain than that the one is an external, the other an internal work? That the one is a visible, the other an invisible thing, and therefore wholly different from each other: the one being an act of man, purifying the body, the other a change wrought by God in the soul. So that the former is just as distinguishable from the latter as the soul from the body, or water from the Holy Ghost.

2. From the preceding reflections we may, secondly, observe that as the new birth is not the same thing with baptism, so it does not always accompany baptism; they do not constantly go together. A man may possibly be 'born of water', and yet not be 'born of the Spirit'. There may sometimes be the outward sign where there is not the inward grace. I do not now speak with regard to infants: it is certain, our Church supposes that all who are baptized in their infancy are at the same time born again. And it is allowed that the whole office for the baptism of infants proceeds upon this supposition. Nor is it an objection of any weight against this that we cannot comprehend how this work can be

wrought in infants: for neither can we comprehend *how* it is wrought in a person of riper years. But whatever be the case with infants, it is sure all of riper years who are baptized are not at the same time born again. 'The tree is known by its fruits.' And hereby it appears too plain to be denied that divers of those who were children of the devil before they were baptized continue the same after baptism: 'For the works of' their 'father they do'; they continue servants of sin, without any pretence either to inward or outward holiness.

3. A third inference which we may draw from what has been observed is that the new birth is not the same with sanctification. This is indeed taken for granted by many; particularly by an eminent writer in his late treatise on 'the nature and grounds of Christian regeneration'. To waive several other weighty objections which might be made to that tract, this is a palpable one: it all along speaks of regeneration as a progressive work carried on in the soul by slow degrees from the time of our first turning to God. This is undeniably true of sanctification; but of regeneration, the new birth, it is not true. This is a part of sanctification, not the whole; it is the gate of it, the entrance into it. When we are born again, then our sanctification, our inward and outward holiness, begins. And thenceforward we are gradually to 'grow up in him who is our head'. This expression of the Apostle admirably illustrates the difference between one and the other, and farther points out the exact analogy there is between natural and spiritual things. A child is born of a woman in a moment, or at least in a very short time. Afterward he gradually and slowly grows till he attains the stature of a man. In like manner a child is born of God in a short time, if not in a moment. But it is by slow degrees that he afterward grows up to the measure of the full stature of Christ. The same relation therefore which there is between our natural birth and our growth there is also between our new birth and our sanctification.

4. One point more we may learn from the preceding observations. But it is a point of so great importance as may excuse the considering it the more carefully, and prosecuting it at some length. What must one who loves the souls of men, and is grieved that any of them should perish, say to one whom he sees living in sabbath-breaking, drunkenness, or any other wilful sin? What can he say, if the foregoing observations are true, but 'you must be born again.' 'No', says a zealous man, 'that cannot be. How can you talk so uncharitably to the man? Has he not been baptized already? He cannot be born again now.' Can he not be born again? Do you affirm this? Then he cannot be saved. Though he be as old as Nicodemus was, yet, 'except he be born again, he cannot see the kingdom of God.' Therefore in saying, 'he cannot be born again,' you in effect deliver him over to damnation. And where lies the uncharitableness now? On my side, or on yours? I say, 'He may be born again, and so become an heir of salvation.' You say, 'He cannot be born again.' And if so, he must inevitably perish. So you utterly block up his way to salvation,

and send him to hell out of mere charity!

But perhaps the sinner himself, to whom in real charity we say, 'You must be born again,' has been taught to say, 'I defy your new doctrine; I need not be born again. I was born again when I was baptized. What! Would you have me deny my baptism?' I answer, first, there is nothing under heaven which can excuse a lie. Otherwise I should say to an open sinner, 'If you have been baptized, do not own it.' For how highly does this aggravate your guilt! How will it increase your damnation! Was you devoted to God at eight days old, and have you been all these years devoting yourself to the devil? Was you, even before you had the use of reason, consecrated to God the Father, the Son, and the Holy Ghost? And have you, ever since you had the use of it, been flying in the face of God, and consecrating yourself to Satan? Does the abomination of desolation, the love of the world, pride, anger, lust, foolish desire, and a whole train of vile affections, stand where it ought not? Have you set up all these accursed things in that soul which was once a 'temple of the Holy Ghost'? Set apart for 'an habitation of God through the Spirit'? Yea, solemnly given up to him? And do you glory in this, that you once belonged to God? O, be ashamed! Blush! Hide yourself in the earth! Never boast more of what ought to fill you with confusion, to make you ashamed before God and man! I answer, secondly, you have already denied your baptism; and that in the most effectual manner. You have denied it a thousand and a thousand times; and you do so still day by day. For in your baptism you renounced the devil and all his works. Whenever therefore you give place to him again, whenever you do any of the works of the devil, then you deny your baptism. Therefore you deny it by every wilful sin; by every act of uncleanness, drunkenness, or revenge; by every obscene or profane word; by every oath that comes out of your mouth. Every time you profane the day of the Lord you thereby deny your baptism; yea, every time you do anything to another which you would not he should do to you. I answer, thirdly, be you baptized or unbaptized, you must be born again. Otherwise it is not possible you should be inwardly holy: and without inward as well as outward holiness you cannot be happy even in this world; much less in the world to come. Do you say, 'Nay, but I do no harm to any man; I am honest and just in all my dealings; I do not curse, or take the Lord's name in vain; I do not profane the Lord's day; I am no drunkard, I do not slander my neighbour, nor live in any wilful sin'? If this be so, it were much to be wished that all men went as far as you do. But you must go farther yet, or you cannot be saved. Still you must be born again. Do you add, 'I do go farther yet; for I not only do no harm, but do all the good I can.' I doubt that fact; I fear you have had a thousand opportunities of doing good which you have suffered to pass by unimproved, and for which therefore you are accountable to God. But if you had improved them all, if you really had done all the good you possibly could to all men, yet this does not at all alter the case. Still you must be born again. Without this nothing will do any good to your poor, sinful, polluted soul. 'Nay, but I constantly attend all the ordinances of God: I keep to my church and sacrament.' It is well you do. But all this will not keep you from hell, except you be born again. Go to church twice a day, go to the Lord's table every week, say ever so many prayers in private; hear ever so many sermons, good sermons, excellent sermons, the best that ever were preached; read ever so many good books–still you must be born again. None of these things will stand in the place of the new birth. No, nor anything under heaven. Let this, therefore, if you have not already experienced this inward work of God, be your continual prayer, 'Lord, add this to all thy blessings: let me be "born again". Deny whatever thou pleasest, but deny not this: let me be "born from above". Take away whatsoever seemeth thee good, reputation, fortune, friends, health. Only give me this: to be "born of the Spirit"! To be received among the children of God. Let me be born, "not of corruptible seed, but incorruptible, by the Word of God, which liveth and abideth for ever". And then let me daily "grow in grace, and in the knowledge of our Lord and Saviour Jesus Christ"!'

THE USE OF MONEY

Sermon 50 – 1760

AN INTRODUCTORY COMMENT

This sermon, the last in volume four of his *Sermons* (1760), is the clearest of Wesley's summaries of his economic views, greatly oversimplified but with a prophet's confidence. He had already preached on Luke 16:9 at least twenty-seven times between 1741 and 1758 (sometimes under the title of 'The Mammon of Unrighteousness'), which indicates that this topic was a constant concern and a perplexing problem.

The new capitalism of Wesley's world had resulted in a steady accumulation of venture capital and, correspondingly, a shocking contrast between the splendid lifestyle of the newly rich and the grinding misery of the perennial poor. The impoverished masses were Wesley's self-chosen constituency: 'Christ's poor'. At the same time, Wesley was deeply committed to a work ethic that saw sloth as sin and that condemned self-indulgence as a faithless stewardship of God's bounties in creation. He did not see money as anything evil in itself. Thrift, industry, honesty, sobriety, generosity were all Christian virtues; their warrants rested in the twin love of God and neighbour, and thus they were included in the agenda of holy living.

In this sense, Wesley shared a broad tradition of economic discipline and philanthropy long understood as essential in the Christian ethic. Its first premise was the flat rejection of the notion 'that men may use their possessions as they list'; this view, so ran both medieval and Reformation ethics, was tantamount to atheism. The basic ideas of gaining, saving, and sharing the wealth ran back at least to William Perkins. This sermon also echoes sentiments found in Richard Lucas, John Tillotson, Giovanni Bona, Jeremy Collier, and John Chappelow. Wesley's formula, however, has a different final focus than one can find in any of its sources: an insistence on 'giving all you can'. This radical exhortation brought even the ordinary conventions of generosity and philanthropy into question. It is as if Wesley regarded surplus accumulation as sinful in itself or at the very least as an irresistible temptation to sin.

The break here with the economic wisdom of the day is drastic and deliberate; he challenged his own people and others to a more stringent form of self-denial than most of them were prepared for. His inability to persuade the Methodists on this point did not deter Wesley, as we can see from his later sermons, 'The Danger of Riches', 'On Riches', and 'The Danger of Increasing Riches'. On no other single point, save only faith alone and holy living, is Wesley more insistent, consistent, and out of step with the bourgeois spirit of his age.

The Use of Money

I say unto you, Make unto yourselves friends
of the mammon of unrighteousness, that when ye fail,
they may receive you into the everlasting habitations.
Luke 16:9

1. Our Lord, having finished the beautiful parable of the Prodigal Son, which he had particularly addressed to those who murmured at his receiving publicans and sinners, adds another relation of a different kind, addressed rather to the children of God. 'He said unto his disciples'—not so much to the scribes and Pharisees to whom he had been speaking before—'There was a certain rich man, who had a steward, and he was accused to him of wasting his goods. And calling him he said, Give an account of thy stewardship, for thou canst be no longer steward' (Luke 16:1-2). After reciting the method which the bad steward used to provide against the day of necessity, our Saviour adds, 'His lord commended the unjust steward'—namely in this respect, that he used timely precaution—and subjoins this weighty reflection, 'The children of this world are wiser in their generation than the children of light' (Luke 16:8). Those who seek no other portion than 'this world are wiser' (not absolutely; for they are one and all the veriest fools, the most egregious madmen under heaven, but) 'in their generation', in their own way; they are more consistent with themselves, they are truer to their acknowledged principles, they more steadily pursue their end, 'than the children of light', than they who see 'the light of the glory of God in the face of Jesus Christ'. Then follow the words above recited: 'And I'—the only-begotten Son of God, the Creator, Lord and Possessor of heaven and earth, and all that is therein; the Judge of all, to whom ye are to 'give an account of your stewardship' when ye 'can be no longer stewards'—'I say unto you' (learn in this respect even of the unjust steward), 'make yourselves friends', by wise, timely precaution, 'of the mammon of unrighteousness.' 'Mammon' means riches or money. It is termed 'the mammon of unrighteousness' because of the unrighteous manner wherein it is frequently procured, and wherein even that which was honestly procured is generally employed. 'Make yourselves friends' of this by doing all possible good, particularly to the children of God; 'that when ye fail', when ye return to dust, when ye have no more place under the sun, those of them who are gone before 'may receive you', may welcome you 'into the everlasting habitations'.

2. An excellent branch of Christian wisdom is here inculcated by our Lord on all his followers, namely, the right use of money—a subject largely spoken of, after their manner, by men of the world, but not sufficiently considered by those whom God hath chosen out of the world. These generally do not consider as the importance of the subject requires the use of this excellent talent. Neither do they understand how to employ it to the greatest advantage; the introduction of which into the world is one admirable instance of the wise and gracious providence of God. It has indeed been the manner of poets, orators, and philosophers, in almost all ages and nations, to rail at this as the grand corrupter of the world, the bane of virtue, the pest of human society. Hence nothing so commonly heard as:

Ferrum, ferroque nocentius aurum—

'And gold, more mischievous than keenest steel.' Hence the lamentable complaint,

*Effodiuntur opes, irritamenta malorum.**

Nay, one celebrated writer gravely exhorts his countrymen, in order to banish all vice at once, to 'throw all their money into the sea':

. . . in mare proximum
*Summi materiem mali!***

But is not all this mere empty rant? Is there any solid reason therein? By no means. For let the world be as corrupt as it will, is gold or silver to blame? 'The love of money', we know, 'is the root of all evil'; but not the thing itself. The fault does not lie in the money, but in them that use it. It may be used ill; and what may not? But it may likewise be used well; it is full as applicable to the best as to the worst uses. It is of unspeakable service to all civilized nations in all the common affairs of life. It is a most compendious instrument of transacting all manner of business, and (if we use it according to Christian wisdom) of doing all manner of good. It is true, were man in a state of innocence, or were all men 'filled with the Holy Ghost', so that, like the infant church at Jerusalem, 'no man counted anything he had his own', but 'distribution was made to everyone as he had need,' the use of it would be superseded; as we cannot conceive there is anything of the kind among the inhabitants of heaven. But in the present state of mankind it is an excellent gift of God, answering the noblest ends. In the hands of his children it is food for the hungry, drink for the thirsty, raiment for the naked. It gives to the traveller and the stranger where to lay his head. By it we may supply the place of an husband to the widow, and of a father to the fatherless; we may be a

* ['Wealth is dug up, incentive to all ill,' Ovid, *Metamorphoses*, I.i.141.]
** ['Into the *nearest* sea . . .,' Horace, *Odes*, III.xxiv.47, 49.]

defence for the oppressed, a means of health to the sick, of ease to them that are in pain. It may be as eyes to the blind, as feet to the lame; yea, a lifter up from the gates of death.

3. It is therefore of the highest concern that all who fear God know how to employ this valuable talent; that they be instructed how it may answer these glorious ends, and in the highest degree. And perhaps all the instructions which are necessary for this may be reduced to three plain rules, by the exact observance whereof we may approve ourselves faithful stewards of 'the mammon of unrighteousness'.

I.1. The first of these is (he that heareth let him understand!) *Gain all you can*. Here we may speak like the children of the world. We meet them on their own ground. And it is our bounden duty to do this. We ought to gain all we can gain without buying gold too dear, without paying more for it than it is worth. But this it is certain we ought not to do: we ought not to gain money at the expense of life; nor (which is in effect the same thing) at the expense of our health. Therefore no gain whatsoever should induce us to enter into, or to continue in, any employ which is of such a kind, or is attended with so hard or so long labour, as to impair our constitution. Neither should we begin or continue in any business which necessarily deprives us of proper seasons for food and sleep in such a proportion as our nature requires. Indeed there is a great difference here. Some employments are absolutely and totally unhealthy—as those which imply the dealing much with arsenic or other equally hurtful minerals, or the breathing an air tainted with steams of melting lead, which must at length destroy the firmest constitution. Others may not be absolutely unhealthy, but only to persons of a weak constitution. Such are those which require many hours to be spent in writing, especially if a person write sitting, and lean upon his stomach, or remain long in an uneasy posture. But whatever it is which reason or experience shows to be destructive of health or strength, that we may not submit to; seeing 'the life is more' valuable 'than meat, and the body than raiment.' And if we are already engaged in such an employ, we should exchange it as soon as possible for some which, if it lessen our gain, will however not lessen our health.

2. We are, secondly, to gain all we can without hurting our mind any more than our body. For neither may we hurt this. We must preserve, at all events, the spirit of an healthful mind. Therefore we may not engage or continue in any sinful trade, any that is contrary to the law of God, or of our country. Such are all that necessarily imply our robbing or defrauding the king of his lawful customs. For it is at least as sinful to defraud the King of his right as to rob our fellow subjects. And the king has full as much right to his customs as we have to our houses and apparel. Other businesses there are, which however innocent *in themselves*, cannot be followed with innocence *now* (at least, not

in England): such, for instance, as will not afford a competent maintenance without cheating or lying, or conformity to some custom which is not consistent with a good conscience. These likewise are sacredly to be avoided, whatever gain they may be attended with provided we follow the custom of the trade; for to gain money we must not lose our souls. There are yet others which many pursue with perfect innocence without hurting either their body or mind. And yet perhaps *you* cannot: either they may entangle you in that company which would destroy your soul—and by repeated experiments it may appear that you cannot separate the one from the other—or there may be an idiosyncrasy, a peculiarity in your constitution of soul (as there is in the bodily constitution of many) by reason whereof that employment is deadly to *you* which another may safely follow. So I am convinced, from many experiments, I could not study to any degree of perfection either mathematics, arithmetic, or algebra, without being a deist, if not an atheist. And yet others may study them all their lives without sustaining any inconvenience. None therefore can here determine for another, but every man must judge for himself, and abstain from whatever he in particular finds to be hurtful to his soul.

3. We are, thirdly, to gain all we can without hurting our neighbour. But this we may not, cannot do, if we love our neighbour as ourselves. We cannot, if we love everyone as ourselves, hurt anyone *in his substance*. We cannot devour the increase of his lands, and perhaps the lands and houses themselves, by gaming, by overgrown bills (whether on account of physic, or law, or anything else), or by requiring or taking such interest as even the laws of our country forbid. Hereby all *pawnbroking* is excluded, seeing whatever good we might do thereby all unprejudiced men see with grief to be abundantly overbalanced by the evil. And if it were otherwise, yet we are not allowed to 'do evil that good may come'. We cannot, consistent with brotherly love, sell our goods below the market price. We cannot study to ruin our neighbour's trade in order to advance our own. Much less can we entice away or receive any of his servants or workmen whom he has need of. None can gain by swallowing up his neighbour's substance, without gaining the damnation of hell.

4. Neither may we gain by hurting our neighbour *in his body*. Therefore we may not sell anything which tends to impair health. Such is, eminently, all that liquid fire commonly called 'drams' or 'spirituous liquor'. It is true, these may have a place in medicine; they may be of use in some bodily disorders (although there would rarely be occasion for them were it not for the unskillfulness of the practitioner). Therefore such as prepare and sell them *only for this end* may keep their conscience clear. But who are they? Who prepare and sell them *only for this end?* Do you know ten such distillers in England? Then excuse these. But all who sell them in the common way, to any that will buy, are poisoners-general. They murder his Majesty's subjects by wholesale, neither does their eye pity or spare. They drive them to hell like sheep. And

what is their gain? Is it not the blood of these men? Who then would envy their large estates and sumptuous palaces? A curse is in the midst of them: the curse of God cleaves to the stones, the timber, the furniture of them. The curse of God is in their gardens, their walks, their groves; a fire that burns to the nethermost hell. Blood, blood is there–the foundation, the floor, the walls, the roof are stained with blood! And canst thou hope, O thou man of blood, though thou art 'clothed in scarlet and fine linen, and farest sumptuously every day', canst thou hope to deliver down thy 'fields of blood' to the third generation? Not so; for there is a God in heaven. Therefore thy name shall soon be rooted out. Like as those whom thou hast destroyed, body and soul, 'thy memorial shall perish with thee.'

5. And are not they partakers of the same guilt, though in a lower degree, whether surgeons, apothecaries, or physicians, who play with the lives or health of men to enlarge their own gain? Who purposely lengthen the pain or disease which they are able to remove speedily? Who protract the cure of their patient's body in order to plunder his substance? Can any man be clear before God who does not shorten every disorder *as much as he can*, and remove all sickness and pain *as soon as he can*. He cannot. For nothing can be more clear than that he does not 'love his neighbour as himself'; than that he does not 'do unto others as he would they should do unto himself'.

6. This is dear-bought gain. And so is whatever is procured by hurting our neighbour *in his soul*: by ministering, suppose either directly or indirectly, to his unchastity or intemperance, which certainly none can do who has any fear of God, or any real desire of pleasing him. It nearly concerns all those to consider this who have anything to do with taverns, victualling-houses, operahouses, playhouses, or any other places of public, fashionable diversion. If these profit the souls of men, you are clear; your employment is good, and your gain innocent. But if they are either sinful in themselves, or natural inlets to sin of various kinds, then it is to be feared you have a sad account to make. O beware lest God say in that day, 'These have perished in their iniquity, but their blood do I require at thy hands!'

7. These cautions and restrictions being observed, it is the bounden duty of all who are engaged in worldly business to observe that first and great rule of Christian wisdom with respect to money, 'Gain all you can.' Gain all you can by honest industry: use all possible diligence in your calling. Lose no time. If you understand yourself and your relation to God and man, you know you have none to spare. If you understand your particular calling as you ought, you will have no time that hangs upon your hands. Every business will afford some employment sufficient for every day and every hour. That wherein *you* are placed, if you follow it in earnest, will leave you no leisure for silly, unprofitable diversions. You have always something better to do, something that will profit you, more or less. And 'whatsoever thy hand findeth to do, do it with thy

might.' Do it *as soon* as possible. No delay! No putting off from day to day, or from hour to hour. Never leave anything till tomorrow which you can do today. And do it *as well* as possible. Do not sleep or yawn over it. Put your whole strength to the work. Spare no pains. Let nothing be done by halves, or in a slight and careless manner. Let nothing in your business be left undone if it can be done by labour or patience.

8. Gain *all* you can, by common sense, by using in your business all the understanding which God has given you. It is amazing to observe how few do this; how men run on in the same dull track with their forefathers. But whatever they do who know not God, this is no rule for *you*. It is a shame for a Christian not to improve upon *them* in whatever he takes in hand. *You* should be continually learning from the experience of others or from your own experience, reading, and reflection, to do everything you have to do better today than you did yesterday. And see that you practise whatever you learn, that you may make the best of all that is in your hands.

II.1. Having gained all you can, by honest wisdom and unwearied diligence, the second rule of Christian prudence is, *Save all you can.* Do not throw the precious talent into the sea: leave that folly to heathen philosophers. Do not throw it away in idle expenses, which is just the same as throwing it into the sea. Expend no part of it merely to gratify the desire of the flesh, the desire of the eye, or the pride of life.

2. Do not waste any part of so precious a talent merely in gratifying the desires of the flesh; in procuring the pleasures of sense of whatever kind; particularly, in enlarging the pleasure of tasting. I do not mean, avoid gluttony and drunkenness only: an honest heathen would condemn these. But there is a regular, reputable kind of sensuality, an elegant epicurism, which does not immediately disorder the stomach, nor (sensibly, at least) impair the understanding. And yet (to mention no other effects of it now) it cannot be maintained without considerable expense. Cut off all this expense. Despise delicacy and variety, and be content with what plain nature requires.

3. Do not waste any part of so precious a talent merely in gratifying the desire of the eye by superfluous or expensive apparel, or by needless ornaments. Waste no part of it in curiously adorning your houses in superfluous or expensive furniture; in costly pictures, painting, gilding, books; in elegant (rather than useful) gardens. Let your neighbours, who know nothing better, do this: 'Let the dead bury their dead.' But 'What is that to thee?' says our Lord: 'Follow thou me.' Are you willing? Then you are able so to do.

4. Lay out nothing to gratify the pride of life, to gain the admiration or praise of men. This motive of expense is frequently interwoven with one or both of the former. Men are expensive in diet, or apparel, or furniture, not barely to please their appetite, or to gratify their eye, their imagination, but their vanity

too. 'So long as thou dost well unto thyself, men will speak good of thee.' So long as thou art 'clothed in purple and fine linen, and farest sumptuously every day', no doubt many will applaud thy elegance of taste, thy generosity and hospitality. But do not buy their applause so dear. Rather be content with the honour that cometh from God.

5. Who would expend anything in gratifying these desires if he considered that to gratify them is to increase them? Nothing can be more certain than this: daily experience shows, the more they are indulged, they increase the more. Whenever therefore you expend anything to please your taste or other senses, you pay so much for sensuality. When you lay out money to please your eye, you give so much for an increase of curiosity, for a stronger attachment to these pleasures, which perish in the using. While you are purchasing anything which men use to applaud, you are purchasing more vanity. Had you not then enough of vanity, sensuality, curiosity before? Was there need of any addition? And would you pay for it, too? What manner of wisdom is this? Would not the literally throwing your money into the sea be a less mischievous folly?

6. And why should you throw away money upon your children, any more than upon yourself, in delicate food, in gay or costly apparel, in superfluities of any kind? Why should you purchase for them more pride or lust, more vanity, or foolish and hurtful desires? They do not want any more; they have enough already; nature has made ample provision for them. Why should you be at farther expense to increase their temptations and snares, and to 'pierce them through with more sorrows'?

7. Do not *leave* it to them, to throw away. If you have good reason to believe that they would waste what is now in your possession in gratifying and thereby increasing the desire of the flesh, the desire of the eye, or the pride of life (at the peril of theirs and your own soul), do not set these traps in their way. Do not offer your sons or your daughters unto Belial any more than unto Moloch. Have pity upon them, and remove out of their way what you may easily foresee would increase their sins, and consequently plunge them deeper into everlasting perdition. How amazing then is the infatuation of those parents who think they can never leave their children enough? What! cannot you leave them enough of arrows, firebrands, and death? Not enough of foolish and hurtful desires? Not enough of pride, lust, ambition, vanity? Not enough of everlasting burnings! Poor wretch! Thou fearest where no fear is. Surely both thou and they, when ye are lifting up your eyes in hell, will have enough both of the 'worm that never dieth', and of 'the fire that never shall be quenched'.

8. 'What then would you do if you was in my case? If you had a considerable fortune to leave?' Whether I *would* do it or no, I know what I *ought* to do: this will admit of no reasonable question. If I had one child, elder or younger, who knew the value of money, one who I believed would put it to the true use, I should think it my absolute, indispensable duty to leave that child the bulk of

my fortune; and to the rest just so much as would enable them to live in the manner they had been accustomed to do. 'But what if all your children were equally ignorant of the true use of money?' I ought then (hard saying! Who can hear it?) to give each what would keep him above want, and to bestow all the rest in such a manner as I judged would be most for the glory of God.

III.1. But let not any man imagine that he has done anything barely by going thus far, by *gaining and saving all he can*, if he were to stop here. All this is nothing if a man go not forward, if he does not point all this at a farther end. Nor indeed can a man properly be said to *save* anything if he only *lays it up*. You may as well throw your money into the sea as bury it in the earth. And you may as well bury it in the earth as in your chest, or in the Bank of England. Not to use, is effectually to throw it away. If therefore you would indeed 'make yourselves friends of the mammon of unrighteousness', add the third rule to the two preceding. Having first gained all you can, and secondly saved all you can, then give all you can.

2. In order to see the ground and reason of this, consider: when the possessor of heaven and earth brought you into being and placed you in this world, he placed you here not as a proprietor, but a steward. As such he entrusted you for a season with goods of various kinds. But the sole property of these still rests in him, nor can ever be alienated from him. As you yourself are not your own, but his, such is likewise all that you enjoy. Such is your soul, and your body—not your own, but God's. And so is your substance in particular. And he has told you in the most clear and express terms how you are to employ it for him, in such a manner that it may be all an holy sacrifice, acceptable through Christ Jesus. And this light, easy service he has promised to reward with an eternal weight of glory.

3. The directions which God has given us touching the use of our worldly substance may be comprised in the following particulars. If you desire to be a faithful and a wise steward, out of that portion of your Lord's goods which he has for the present lodged in your hands, but with the right of resuming whenever it pleases him, first, provide things needful for yourself—food to eat, raiment to put on, whatever nature moderately requires for preserving the body in health and strength. Secondly, provide these for your wife, your children, your servants, or any others who pertain to your household. If when this is done there be an overplus left, then 'do good to them that are of the household of faith.' If there be an overplus still, 'as you have opportunity, do good unto all men.' In so doing, you *give all you can*; nay, in a sound sense, all you have. For all that is laid out in this manner is really given to God. You 'render unto God the things that are God's', not only by what you give to the poor, but also by that which you expend in providing things needful for yourself and your household.

4. If then a doubt should at any time arise in your mind concerning what you are going to expend, either on yourself or any part of your family, you have an easy way to remove it. Calmly and seriously inquire: (1) In expending this, am I acting according to my character? Am I acting herein, not as a proprietor, but as a steward of my Lord's goods? (2) Am I doing this in obedience to his Word? In what Scripture does he require me so to do? (3) Can I offer up this action, this expense, as a sacrifice to God through Jesus Christ? (4) Have I reason to believe that for this very work I shall have a reward at the resurrection of the just? You will seldom need anything more to remove any doubt which arises on this head; but by this fourfold consideration you will receive clear light as to the way wherein you should go.

5. If any doubt still remain, you may farther examine yourself by prayer according to those heads of inquiry. Try whether you can say to the Searcher of hearts, your conscience not condemning you: 'Lord, thou seest I am going to expend this sum on that food, apparel, furniture. And thou knowest I act herein with a single eye as a steward of thy goods, expending this portion of them thus in pursuance of the design thou hadst in entrusting me with them. Thou knowest I do this in obedience to thy Word, as thou commandest, and because thou commandest it. Let this, I beseech thee, be an holy sacrifice, acceptable through Jesus Christ! And give me a witness in myself that for this labour of love I shall have a recompense when thou rewardest every man according to his works.' Now if your conscience bear you witness in the Holy Ghost that this prayer is well-pleasing to God, then have you no reason to doubt but that expense is right and good, and such as will never make you ashamed.

6. You see then what it is to 'make [unto] yourselves friends of the mammon of unrighteousness', and by what means you may procure 'that when ye fail they may receive you into the everlasting habitations'. You see the nature and extent of truly Christian prudence so far as it relates to the use of that great talent-money. *Gain all you can,* without hurting either yourself or your neighbour, in soul or body, by applying hereto with unintermitted diligence, and with all the understanding which God has given you. *Save all you can,* by cutting off every expense which serves only to indulge foolish desire, to gratify either the desire of the flesh, the desire of the eye, or the pride of life. Waste nothing, living or dying, on sin or folly, whether for yourself or your children. And then, *Give all you can,* or in other words give all you have to God. Do not stint yourself, like a Jew rather than a Christian, to this or that proportion. 'Render unto God', not a tenth, not a third, not half, but 'all that is God's', be it more or less, by employing all on yourself, your household, the household of faith, and all mankind, in such a manner that you may give a good account of your stewardship when ye can be no longer stewards; in such a manner as the oracles of God direct, both by general and particular precepts; in such a

manner that whatever ye do may be 'a sacrifice of a sweet-smelling savour to God', and that every act may be rewarded in that day when the Lord cometh with all his saints.

7. Brethren, can we be either wise or faithful stewards unless we thus manage our Lord's goods? We cannot, as not only the oracles of God, but our own conscience beareth witness. Then why should we delay? Why should we confer any longer with flesh and blood, or men of the world? Our kingdom, our wisdom 'is not of this world'. Heathen custom is nothing to us. We follow no men any farther than they are followers of Christ. Hear ye him. Yea, today, while it is called today, hear and obey his voice. At this hour and from this hour, do his will; fulfil his word in this and in all things. I entreat you, in the name of the Lord Jesus, act up to the dignity of your calling. No more sloth! Whatsoever your hand findeth to do, do it with your might. No more waste! Cut off every expense which fashion, caprice, or flesh and blood demand. No more covetousness! But employ whatever God has entrusted you with in doing good, all possible good, in every possible kind and degree, to the household of faith, to all men. This is no small part of 'the wisdom of the just'. Give all ye have, as well as all ye are, a spiritual sacrifice to him who withheld not from you his Son, his only Son; so 'laying up in store for yourselves a good foundation against the time to come, that ye may attain eternal life'.

ON SIN IN BELIEVERS

Sermon 13 – 1763

AN INTRODUCTORY COMMENT

Wesley's reiteration of the idea of the Christian's grace-bestowed power not to commit sin, found in several of his early sermons, was bound to generate controversy and confusion among both critics and some disciples. The Lutherans had taught that the justified believer, burdened by the ineradicable 'remains of sin', was at the same time justified and a sinner, but also that with repentance, sins were covered by the imputed righteousness of Christ and thus inculpable. With similar premises with respect to the 'remains' (the Christian is 'a sinner saved by grace'), the Calvinists stressed rigorous examination of consciences, repentance, the final perseverance of the elect, and the perfect and immutable freedom 'in the state of glory only'. On the other side, the Moravians and some of Wesley's own disciples had taken the claim that 'those born of God do not commit sin' to its antinomian extreme of sinless (even guiltless) perfection, as if the power not to sin meant the extirpation of all 'remains of sin'. Moreover, they had appealed to Wesley's basic soteriology as the logical ground for their interpretation.

Wesley, caught in the controversy generated by these two polarities, came up with what he regarded as a valid third alternative. Its root notion was a distinction between 'sin properly so called' (i.e., the deliberate violation of a known law of God) and all 'involuntary transgressions' (culpable only if unrepented and knowingly repeated). This distinction already had a history in Catholic moral theory ('mortal' versus 'venial') and a special development among Anglican moralists as well.

Thus, there was an unstable tension between the claims that a Christian may be delivered from sin's bondage and that 'sin *remains* but no longer *reigns*'. Wesley insisted on holding to both traditions (*sola fide* and *holy living*) without forfeiting the essence of either. He was concerned to face the dreadful realities of sin while never yielding to any defeatist notion that God's grace is intrinsically impotent to save souls 'to the utmost' in this life.

In 1763, in an effort to counter the distortions and bring the controversy more nearly back to balance, Wesley wrote and published this sermon 'in order to remove a mistake which some were labouring to propagate: that there is no sin in any that are justified'. This sermon is designed for the encouragement of 'the weaker brethren' whose Christian assurance had been all too easily shaken by their awareness of sin's residues in their hearts, even in their uncertain pilgrimage of grace toward 'perfect love'.

On Sin in Believers

If any man be in Christ, he is a new creature.
2 Corinthians 5:17

I.1. Is there then sin in him that is in Christ? Does sin *remain* in one that 'believes in him'? Is there any sin in them that are 'born of God', or are they wholly delivered from it? Let no one imagine this to be a question of mere curiosity, or that it is of little importance whether it be determined one way or the other. Rather it is a point of the utmost moment to every serious Christian, the resolving of which very nearly concerns both his present and eternal happiness.

2. And yet I do not know that ever it was controverted in the primitive Church. Indeed there was no room for disputing concerning it, as all Christians were agreed. And so far as I have observed, the whole body of ancient Christians who have left us anything in writing declare with one voice that even believers in Christ, till they are 'strong in the Lord, and in the power of his might', have need to 'wrestle with flesh and blood', with an evil nature, as well as 'with principalities and powers'.

3. And herein our own Church (as indeed in most points) exactly copies after the primitive; declaring (in her Ninth Article), 'Original sin is the corruption of the nature of every man, whereby man is in his own nature inclined to evil, so that the flesh lusteth contrary to the Spirit. And this infection of nature doth remain, yea, in them that are regenerated; whereby the lust of the flesh, called in Greek φρόνημα σαρκός, is not subject to the law of God. And although there is no condemnation for them that believe, yet this lust hath of itself the nature of sin.'

4. The same testimony is given by all other churches; not only by the Greek and Romish Church, but by every Reformed Church in Europe, of whatever denomination. Indeed some of these seem to carry the thing too far; so describing the corruption of heart in a believer as scarce to allow that he has dominion over it, but rather is in bondage thereto. And by this means they leave hardly any distinction between a believer and an unbeliever.

5. To avoid this extreme many well-meaning men, particularly those under the direction of the late Count Zinzendorf, ran into another, affirming that 'all true believers are not only saved from the *dominion* of sin but from the *being* of inward as well as outward sin, so that it no longer *remains* in them.' And from them, about twenty years ago, many of our countrymen imbibed the same

opinion, that even the corruption of nature *is no more* in those who believe in Christ.

6. It is true that when the Germans were pressed upon this head they soon allowed (many of them at least) that sin did still remain *in the flesh,* but not *in the heart* of a believer. And after a time, when the absurdity of this was shown, they fairly gave up the point; allowing that sin did still *remain,* though not *reign,* in him that is born of God.

7. But the English who had received it from them (some directly, some at second or third hand) were not so easily prevailed upon to part with a favourite opinion. And even when the generality of them were convinced it was utterly indefensible, a few could not be persuaded to give it up, but maintain it to this day.

II.1. For the sake of these who really fear God and desire to know 'the truth as it is in Jesus', it may not be amiss to consider the point with calmness and impartiality. In doing this I use indifferently the words 'regenerate', 'justified', or 'believers'; since, though they have not precisely the same meaning (the first implying an inward, *actual* change; the second a *relative* one; and the third the means whereby both the one and the other are wrought) yet they come to one and the same thing, as everyone that 'believes' is both 'justified' and 'born of God'.

2. By 'sin' I here understand inward sin: any sinful temper, passion, or affection; such as pride, self-will, love of the world, in any kind or degree; such as lust, anger, peevishness; any disposition contrary to the mind which was in Christ.

3. The question is not concerning *outward sin,* whether a child of God *commits sin* or no. We all agree and earnestly maintain, 'He that committeth sin is of the devil.' We agree, 'Whosoever is born of God doth not commit sin.' Neither do we now inquire whether inward sin will *always* remain in the children of God; whether sin will continue in the soul *as long as* it continues in the body. Nor yet do we inquire whether a justified person may *relapse* either into inward or outward sin. But simply this: is a justified or regenerate man freed from *all sin* as soon as he is justified? Is there then no sin in his heart? Nor ever after, unless he fall from grace?

4. We allow that the state of a justified person is inexpressibly great and glorious. He is 'born again, not of blood, nor of the flesh, nor of the will of man, but of God'. He is a child of God, a member of Christ, an heir of the kingdom of heaven. 'The peace of God which passeth all understanding keepeth his heart and mind in Christ Jesus.' His very 'body is a temple of the Holy Ghost', and 'an habitation of God through the Spirit'. He is 'created anew in Christ Jesus'; he is *washed;* he is *sanctified.* His 'heart is purified by faith'; he is cleansed from 'the corruption that is in the world'. 'The love of

God is shed abroad in his heart by the Holy Ghost which is given unto him.' And so long as he 'walketh in love' (which he may always do) he 'worships God in spirit and in truth'. He 'keepeth the commandments of God, and doth those things that are pleasing in his sight': so 'exercising himself as to have a conscience void of offence toward God and toward man'. And he has power both over outward and inward sin, even from the moment he is justified.

III.1. 'But was he not then "freed from all sin", so that there is no sin in his heart?' I cannot say this: I cannot believe it, because St. Paul says the contrary. He is speaking to believers, and describing the state of believers in general, when he says, 'The flesh lusteth against the spirit, and the spirit against the flesh: these are contrary the one to the other' (Gal. 5:17). Nothing can be more express. The Apostle here directly affirms that 'the flesh', evil nature, opposes 'the spirit', even in believers; that even in the regenerate there are two principles 'contrary the one to the other'.

2. Again: when he writes to the believers at Corinth, to those who were 'sanctified in Christ Jesus' (1 Cor. 1:2), says: 'I, brethren, could not speak unto you as unto spiritual, but as unto carnal, as unto babes in Christ. . . . Ye are yet carnal: for whereas there is among you envying and strife, are ye not carnal?' (1 Cor. 3:1, 3.) Now here the Apostle speaks unto those who were unquestionably believers, whom in the same breath he styles his 'brethren in Christ', as being still in a measure *carnal*. He affirms there was 'envying' (an evil temper) occasioning 'strife' among them, and yet does not give the least intimation that they had lost their faith. Nay, he manifestly declares they had not; for then they would not have been 'babes in Christ'. And (what is most remarkable of all) he speaks of being 'carnal' and 'babes in Christ' as one and the same thing; plainly showing that every believer is (in a degree) 'carnal' while he is only a 'babe in Christ'.

3. Indeed this grand point, that there are two contrary principles in believers—nature and grace, the flesh and the spirit—runs through all the epistles of St. Paul, yea, through all the Holy Scriptures. Almost all the directions and exhortations therein are founded on this supposition, pointing at wrong tempers or practices in those who are, notwithstanding, acknowledged by the inspired writers to be believers. And they are continually exhorted to fight with and conquer these, by the power of the faith which was in them.

4. And who can doubt but there was faith in the angel of the church of Ephesus when our Lord said to him: 'I know thy works, and thy labour, and thy patience. . . . Thou hast patience, and for my name's sake hast laboured and hast not fainted.' But was there meantime no sin in his heart? Yea, or Christ would not have added, 'Nevertheless I have somewhat against thee, because thou hast left thy first love' (Rev. 2:2–4). This was real sin which God saw in his heart, of which accordingly he is exhorted to *repent*. And yet we

have no authority to say that even then he had no faith.

5. Nay, the angel of the church at Pergamos also is exhorted to 'repent', which implies sin, though our Lord expressly says, 'Thou hast not denied my faith' (Rev. 2:13, 16). And to the angel of the church in Sardis he says, 'Strengthen the things which remain that are ready to die' (Rev. 3:2). The good which remained was 'ready to die', but was not actually dead. So there was still a spark of faith even in him; which he is accordingly commanded to 'hold fast' (Rev. 3:3).

6. Once more: when the Apostle exhorts believers to 'cleanse' themselves 'from all filthiness of flesh and spirit' (2 Cor. 7:1), he plainly teaches that those believers were not yet cleansed therefrom. Will you answer, 'He that "abstains from all appearance of evil" does *ipso facto* cleanse himself from all filthiness'? Not in any wise. For instance, a man reviles me; I feel resentment, which is 'filthiness of spirit'; yet I say not a word. Here I 'abstain from all appearance of evil', but this does not cleanse me from that filthiness of spirit, as I experience to my sorrow.

7. And as this position, 'there is no sin in a believer, no carnal mind, no bent to backsliding,' is thus contrary to the Word of God, so it is to the *experience* of his children. These continually feel an heart bent to backsliding, a natural tendency to evil, a proneness to depart from God, and cleave to the things of earth. They are daily sensible of sin remaining in their heart, pride, self-will, unbelief, and of sin cleaving to all they speak and do, even their best actions and holiest duties. Yet at the same time they 'know that they are of God'; they cannot doubt of it for a moment. They feel 'his Spirit clearly witnessing with their spirit that they are the children of God'. They 'rejoice in God through Christ Jesus, by whom they have now received the atonement'. So that they are equally assured that sin is in them and that 'Christ is in them, the hope of glory.'

8. 'But can Christ be in the same heart where sin is?' Undoubtedly he can; otherwise it never could be saved therefrom. Where the sickness is, there is the physician,

> Carrying on his work within,
> Striving till he cast out sin.

Christ indeed cannot *reign* where sin *reigns*; neither will he *dwell* where any sin is *allowed*. But he *is* and *dwells* in the heart of every believer who is fighting against all sin; although it be 'not' yet 'purified according to the purification of the sanctuary'.

9. It has been observed before, that the opposite doctrine, 'that there is no sin in believers', is quite *new* in the church of Christ; that it was never heard of for seventeen hundred years, never till it was discovered by Count Zinzendorf. I do not remember to have seen the least intimation of it either in

any ancient or modern writer, unless perhaps in some of the wild, ranting antinomians. And these likewise say and unsay, acknowledging there is sin 'in their flesh', although no sin 'in their heart'. But whatever doctrine is *new* must be *wrong*; for the *old* religion is the only *true* one; and no doctrine can be right unless it is the very same 'which was from the beginning'.

10. One argument more against this new, unscriptural doctrine may be drawn from the dreadful consequences of it. One says, 'I felt anger today.' Must I reply, 'Then you have no faith'? Another says, 'I know what you advise is good; but my will is quite averse to it.' Must I tell him, 'Then you are an unbeliever, under the wrath and the curse of God'? What will be the natural consequence of this? Why, if he believe what I say, his soul will not only be grieved and wounded but perhaps utterly destroyed; inasmuch as he will 'cast away that confidence which hath great recompense of reward'. And having cast away his shield, how shall he 'quench the fiery darts of the wicked one'? How shall he overcome the world? Seeing 'this is the victory that overcometh the world, even our faith.' He stands disarmed in the midst of his enemies, open to all their assaults. What wonder then if he be utterly overthrown, if they take him captive at their will; yea, if he fall from one wickedness to another, and never see good any more? I cannot therefore by any means receive this assertion 'that there is no sin in a believer from the moment he is justified'. First, because it is contrary to the whole tenor of Scripture; secondly, because it is contrary to the experience of the children of God; thirdly, because it is absolutely new, never heard of in the world till yesterday; and lastly, because it is naturally attended with the most fatal consequences, not only grieving those whom God hath not grieved, but perhaps dragging them into everlasting perdition.

IV.1. However, let us give a fair hearing to the chief arguments of those who endeavour to support it. And it is, first, from Scripture they attempt to prove that there is no sin in a believer. They argue thus: 'The Scripture says every believer is "born of God", is "clean", is "holy", is "sanctified"; is "pure in heart", has a new heart, is a temple of the Holy Ghost. Now, as "that which is born of the flesh is flesh", is altogether evil, so "that which is born of the Spirit is spirit", is altogether good. Again: a man cannot be clean, sanctified, holy, and at the same time unclean, unsanctified, unholy. He cannot be pure and impure, or have a new and an old heart together. Neither can his soul be unholy while it is a temple of the Holy Ghost.'

I have put this objection as strong as possible, that its full weight may appear. Let us now examine it, part by part. And (1) '"That which is born of the Spirit is spirit," is altogether good.' I allow the text, but not the comment; for the text affirms this, and no more, that every man who is 'born of the Spirit' is a *spiritual man*. He is so. But so he may be, and yet not be *altogether* spiritual.

The Christians at *Corinth* were *spiritual* men; else they had been no Christians at all. And yet they were not *altogether* spiritual: they were still (in part) *carnal.* 'But they were fallen from grace.' St. Paul says, 'No: they were even then "babes in Christ".' (2) 'But a man cannot be clean, sanctified, holy, and at the same time unclean, unsanctified, unholy.' Indeed he may. So the Corinthians were. 'Ye are washed,' says the Apostle, 'ye are sanctified'; namely cleansed from 'fornication, idolatry, drunkenness', and all other outward sin (1 Cor 6:9, 10, 11). And yet at the same time, in another sense of the word, they were *unsanctified:* they were not *washed,* not inwardly *cleansed* from envy, evil surmising, partiality. 'But sure they had not a new heart and an old heart together.' It is most sure they had; for at that very time their hearts were *truly,* yet not *entirely,* renewed. Their carnal mind was nailed to the cross; yet it was not wholly destroyed. 'But could they be *unholy* while they were "temples of the Holy Ghost"?' (1 Cor. 6:19.) Yes, that they were 'temples of the Holy Ghost' is certain. And it is equally certain they were, in some degree, *carnal,* that is, *unholy.*

2. 'However, there is one Scripture more which will put the matter out of question: "If any man be (a believer) in Christ, he is a new creature. Old things are passed away; behold all things are become new" (2 Cor. 5:17). Now certainly a man cannot be a *new creature* and an *old creature* at once.' Yes, he may: he may be *partly renewed,* which was the very case with those at Corinth. They were doubtless 'renewed in the spirit of their mind', or they could not have been so much as 'babes in Christ'. Yet they had not the whole mind which was in Christ, for they *envied* one another. 'But it is said expressly, "Old things are passed away: all things are become new."' But we must not so interpret the Apostle's words as to make him contradict himself. And if we will make him consistent with himself the plain meaning of the words is this: his *old judgment* (concerning justification, holiness, happiness, indeed concerning the things of God in general) is now 'passed away'; so are his *old desires, designs, affections, tempers,* and *conversation.* All these are undeniably 'become new', greatly changed from what they were. And yet, though they are *new,* they are not *wholly* new. Still he feels, to his sorrow and shame, remains of the 'old man', too manifest taints of his former tempers and affections, a law in his members which frequently *fights* against that law of his mind, though it cannot 'gain any advantage' over him as long as he 'watches unto prayer'.

3. This whole argument, 'If he is clean, he is clean,' 'if he is holy, he is holy' (and twenty more expressions of the same kind may easily be heaped together) is really no better than playing upon words: it is the fallacy of arguing from a *particular* to a *general,* of inferring a general conclusion from particular premises. Propose the sentence entire, and it runs thus: 'If he is holy *at all,* he is holy *altogether.*' That does not follow: every babe in Christ is holy, and yet not altogether so. He is saved from sin; yet not entirely: it *remains,* though it

does not *reign*. If you think it does not *remain* (in *babes* at least, whatever be the case with *young men*, or *fathers*) you certainly have not considered the height and depth and length and breadth of the law of God (even the law of love laid down by St. Paul in the thirteenth of Corinthians); and that 'every ἀνομία', disconformity to, or deviation from this law, 'is sin.' Now, is there no disconformity to this in the heart or life of a believer? What may be in an adult Christian is another question. But what a stranger must he be to human nature who can possibly imagine that this is the case with every babe in Christ!

4.* 'But believers "walk after the Spirit" (Rom. 8:1), and the Spirit of God *dwells* in them. Consequently they are delivered from the guilt, the power, *or, in one word*, the being of sin.'

These are coupled together as if they were the same thing. But they are not the same thing. The *guilt* is one thing, the *power* another, and the *being* yet another. That believers are delivered from the *guilt* and *power* of sin we allow; that they are delivered from the *being* of it we deny. Nor does it in any wise follow from these texts. A man may have the Spirit of God *dwelling in* him, and may 'walk after the Spirit', though he still feels 'the flesh lusting against the Spirit'.

5. 'But the "church is the body of Christ" (Col. 1:24). This implies that its members are washed from all filthiness; otherwise it will follow that Christ and Belial are incorporated with each other.'

Nay, it will not follow from hence—'Those who are the mystical body of Christ still feel the flesh lusting against the Spirit'—that Christ has any fellowship with the devil, or with that sin which he enables them to resist and overcome.

6. 'But are not Christians "come to the heavenly Jerusalem", where "nothing defiled can enter"?' Yes; 'and to an innumerable company of angels', 'and to the spirits of just men made perfect' (Heb. 12:22–23): that is,

> Earth and heaven all agree,
> All his one great family.

And they are likewise holy and *undefiled* while they 'walk after the Spirit'; although sensible there is another principle in them, and that 'these are contrary to each other'.

7. 'But Christians are "reconciled to God". Now this could not be if any of the "carnal mind" remained; for this "is enmity against God". Consequently no reconciliation can be effected but by its total destruction.'

We 'are reconciled to God through the blood of the cross'. And in that moment, the φρόνημα σαρκός, the corruption of nature which is 'enmity with

* What follows for some pages is an answer to a paper published in the *Christian Magazine* [1762], pp. 577–82. I am surprised Mr. [William] Dodd should give such a paper a place in his magazine which is directly contrary to our Ninth Article.

God', is put under our feet. The flesh has 'no more dominion over us'. But it still *exists;* and it is still in its nature enmity with God, lusting against his Spirit.

8. 'But "they that are Christ's have crucified the flesh, with its affections and lusts"' (Gal. 5:24). They have so; yet it remains in them still, and often struggles to break from the cross. 'Nay, but they have "put off the old man with his deeds"' (Col. 3:9). They have; and in the sense above-described, 'old things are passed away; all things are become new.' An hundred texts may be cited to the same effect. And they will all admit of the same answer. 'But, to say all in one word, "Christ gave himself for the church, that . . . it might be holy and without blemish"' (Eph. 5:25, 27). And so it will be in the end: but it never was yet, from the beginning to this day.

9. 'But let *experience* speak: all who are justified do at that time find an absolute freedom from all sin.' That I doubt; but if they do, do they find it ever after? Else you gain nothing. 'If they do not, it is their own fault.' That remains to be proved.

10. 'But, in the very nature of things, can a man have pride in him, and not be proud? Anger, and yet not be angry?'

A man may have *pride* in him, may think of himself in *some particulars* above what he ought to think (and so be *proud* in that particular) and yet not be a proud man in his *general* character. He may have *anger* in him, yea, and a strong propensity to furious anger, without *giving way* to it. 'But can anger and pride be in that heart where *only* meekness and humility are felt?' No; but *some* pride and anger may be in that heart where there is *much* humility and meekness.

'It avails not to say these tempers *are* there, but they do not *reign*; for sin cannot in any kind or degree *exist* where it does not *reign*; for *guilt* and *power* are essential properties of sin. Therefore where one of them is, all must be.'

Strange indeed! 'Sin cannot in any kind or degree *exist* where it does not *reign*'? Absolutely contrary this to all experience, all Scripture, all common sense. Resentment of an affront is sin. It is ἀνομία, disconformity to the law of love. This has existed in me a thousand times. Yet it did not, and does not, *reign*. But '*guilt* and *power* are essential properties of sin; therefore where one is, all must be.' No; in the instance before us, if the resentment I feel is not yielded to, even for a moment, there is no *guilt* at all, no condemnation from God upon that account. And in this case it has no *power*: though it 'lusteth against the Spirit' it cannot prevail. Here, therefore, as in ten thousand instances, there is *sin* without either *guilt* or *power*.

11. 'But the supposing sin in a believer is pregnant with everything frightful and discouraging. It implies the contending with a power that has the possession of our strength, maintains his usurpation of our hearts, and there prosecutes the war in defiance of our Redeemer.' Not so. The supposing sin

is *in* us does not imply that it has the possession of our strength; no more than a man crucified has the possession of those that crucify him. As little does it imply that sin 'maintains its usurpation of our hearts'. The usurper is dethroned. He *remains* indeed where he once reigned; but remains *in chains.* So that he does in some sense 'prosecute the war', yet he grows weaker and weaker, while the believer goes on from strength to strength, conquering and to conquer.

12. 'I am not satisfied yet. He that has sin in him is a slave to sin. Therefore you suppose a man to be justified while he is a slave to sin. Now if you allow men may be justified while they have pride, anger, or unbelief in them—nay if you aver these are (at least for a time) in all that are justified—what wonder that we have so many proud, angry, unbelieving believers!'

I do not suppose any man who is justified is a slave to sin. Yet I do suppose sin remains (at least for a time) in all that are justified. 'But if sin remains in a believer he is a sinful man: if pride, for instance, then he is proud; if self-will, then he is self-willed; if unbelief, then he is an unbeliever—consequently, no believer at all. How then does he differ from unbelievers, from unregenerate men?'

This is still mere playing upon words. It means no more than, 'If there is sin, pride, self-will in him, then—there is sin, pride, self-will.' And this nobody can deny. In *that sense,* then, he is proud or self-willed. But he is not proud or self-willed in the same sense that unbelievers are, that is, *governed* by pride or self-will. Herein he differs from unregenerate men. They *obey* sin; he does not. Flesh is in them both. But they 'walk after the flesh'; he 'walks after the Spirit'.

'But how can *unbelief* be in a *believer*?' That word has two meanings. It means either *no faith,* or *little faith;* either the *absence* of faith, or the *weakness* of it. In the former sense, unbelief is not in a believer; in the latter, it is in all babes. Their faith is commonly mixed with doubt or fear, that is (in the latter sense) with unbelief. 'Why are ye fearful,' says our Lord, 'O ye of little faith?' Again, 'O thou of little faith, wherefore didst thou doubt?' You see, here was *unbelief* in *believers:* little faith and much unbelief.

13. 'But this doctrine—that sin remains in a believer, that a man may be in the favour of God while he has sin in his heart—certainly tends to encourage men in sin.' Understand the proposition right, and no such consequence follows. A man may be in God's favour though he *feel* sin; but not if he *yields* to it. *Having sin* does not forfeit the favour of God; *giving way to sin* does. Though the flesh in *you* 'lust against the Spirit', you may still be a child of God. But if you 'walk after the flesh', you are a child of the devil. Now, this doctrine does not encourage to *obey* sin, but to *resist* it with all our might.

V.1. The sum of all is this: there are in every person, even after he is justified, two contrary principles, nature and grace, termed by St. Paul the 'flesh' and the 'spirit'. Hence although even babes in Christ are *sanctified*, yet it is only *in part*. In a degree, according to the measure of their faith, they are *spiritual*; yet in a degree they are *carnal*. Accordingly, believers are continually exhorted to watch against the flesh, as well as the world and the devil. And to this agrees the constant experience of the children of God. While they feel this witness in themselves they feel a will not wholly resigned to the will of God. They know they are in him, and yet find an heart ready to depart from him, a proneness to evil in many instances, and a backwardness to that which is good. The contrary doctrine is wholly *new*; never heard of in the church of Christ from the time of his coming into the world till the time of Count Zinzendorf. And it is attended with the most fatal consequences. It cuts off all watching against our evil nature, against the Delilah which we are told is gone, though she is still lying in our bosom. It tears away the shield of weak believers, deprives them of their faith, and so leaves them exposed to all the assaults of the world, the flesh, and the devil.

2. Let us therefore hold fast the sound doctrine 'once delivered to the saints', and delivered down by them with the written word to all succeeding generations: that although we are renewed, cleansed, purified, sanctified, the moment we truly believe in Christ, yet we are not then renewed, cleansed, purified altogether; but the flesh, the evil nature, still remains (though subdued) and wars against the Spirit. So much the more let us use all diligence in 'fighting the good fight of faith'. So much the more earnestly let us 'watch and pray' against the enemy within. The more carefully let us 'take to' ourselves and 'put on the whole armour of God'; that although 'we wrestle' both with 'flesh and blood, and with principalities and powers, and wicked spirits in high places, we may be able to withstand in the evil day, and having done all, to stand'.

THE SCRIPTURE WAY OF SALVATION

Sermon 43 – 1765

AN INTRODUCTORY COMMENT

During the 1750s, Wesley had become embroiled in an unpleasant controversy with Scottish dissenters, Robert Sandeman and his disciples, on the relative merits of 'a faith of *adherence*' (Sandeman's notion of faith as an act of will) and 'a faith of *assurance*' (Wesley's 'heart religion'). Sandeman's advocacy of salvation by assent had seemed dangerous to Wesley; already it had encouraged Thomas Maxfield and George Bell in their rush into antinomianism. Between 1757 and 1763, Wesley wrote several treatises in vehement reaction to this threatening position.

The controversy, of course, had a history. Nathaniel Culverwell had explored it a century before and concluded that 'assurance consists only in the mind, and so there you have the difference between the faith of adherence and the faith of assurance. . . . A man may be a true child of God and certainly saved, though he have not assurance.' Wesley could never have agreed, especially after 1738. When he published an extract from Culverwell in the *Christian Library* (1752), he omitted these sentiments from the work. He would also have known of William Allen's threefold distinction in *The Glass of Justification* (1658): 'Faith, as it justifies, hath three acts: credence, adherence, confidence'; this view is very close to his own idea. And he also knew the famous summary of the question in Arthur Bedford's *The Doctrine of Assurance* (1738): 'The "faith of adherence" is a saving faith, wrought in the heart of a sinner by the Spirit and Word of God. . . . And thus he hopes, though he hath no certainty. The "faith of assurance" is that whereby a man absolutely knows all this to be true in his own particular case.'

Given, however, the still unsettled state of mind among the Methodists in 1765, Wesley decided to sum up the matter yet once more: to correlate the faith that saves with the faith that sanctifies. In this sermon, then, he gathered up the best residues of earlier sermons–*Salvation by Faith*, 'Justification by Faith', and 'The Circumcision of the Heart'. Here he could reemphasize the point that in the Christian life, all is of grace–'preventing', 'justifying', 'accompanying', and 'sanctifying'. The result is the most successful summary of the Wesleyan vision of the 'way of salvation' in the entire sermon corpus.

This essay had the most extensive history of oral preaching behind it: over forty instances of Wesley's using Eph. 2:8 before 1765, including his first written sermon on it, *Salvation by Faith*. The text continued to be a favourite: over fifty recorded instances in the quarter century following 1765.

The Scripture Way of Salvation

Ye are saved through faith.
Ephesians 2:8

1. Nothing can be more intricate, complex, and hard to be understood, than religion as it has been often described. And this is not only true concerning the religion of the heathens, even many of the wisest of them, but concerning the religion of those also who were in some sense Christians; yea, and men of great name in the Christian world, men 'who seemed to be pillars' thereof. Yet how easy to be understood, how plain and simple a thing, is the genuine religion of Jesus Christ! Provided only that we take it in its native form, just as it is described in the oracles of God. It is exactly suited by the wise Creator and Governor of the world to the weak understanding and narrow capacity of man in his present state. How observable is this both with regard to the end it proposes and the means to attain that end! The end is, in one word, salvation: the means to attain it, faith.

2. It is easily discerned that these two little words—I mean faith and salvation—include the substance of all the Bible, the marrow, as it were, of the whole Scripture. So much the more should we take all possible care to avoid all mistake concerning them, and to form a true and accurate judgment concerning both the one and the other.

Let us then seriously inquire,

I. What is salvation?
II. What is that faith whereby we are saved? and
III. How we are saved by it.

I.1. And first let us inquire, What is *salvation*? The salvation which is here spoken of is not what is frequently understood by that word, the going to heaven, eternal happiness. It is not the soul's going to paradise, termed by our Lord 'Abraham's bosom'. It is not a blessing which lies on the other side death, or (as we usually speak) in the other world. The very words of the text itself put this beyond all question. 'Ye *are* saved.' It is not something at a distance: it is a present thing, a blessing which, through the free mercy of God, ye are now in possession of. Nay, the words may be rendered, and that with equal propriety, 'Ye *have been* saved.' So that the salvation which is here spoken of might be extended to the entire work of God, from the first dawning of grace in the soul till it is consummated in glory.

2. If we take this in its utmost extent it will include all that is wrought in the soul by what is frequently termed 'natural conscience', but more properly, 'preventing grace'; all the 'drawings' of 'the Father', the desires after God, which, if we yield to them, increase more and more; all that 'light' wherewith the Son of God 'enlighteneth everyone that cometh into the world', *showing* every man 'to do justly, to love mercy, and to walk humbly with his God'; all the *convictions* which his Spirit from time to time works in every child of man. Although it is true the generality of men stifle them as soon as possible, and after a while forget, or at least deny, that ever they had them at all.

3. But we are at present concerned only with that salvation which the Apostle is directly speaking of. And this consists of two general parts, justification and sanctification.

Justification is another word for pardon. It is the forgiveness of all our sins, and (what is necessarily implied therein) our acceptance with God. The price whereby this hath been procured for us (commonly termed the 'meritorious cause' of our justification) is the blood and righteousness of Christ, or (to express it a little more clearly) all that Christ hath done and suffered for us till 'he poured out his soul for the transgressors.' The immediate effects of justification are, the peace of God, a 'peace that passeth all understanding', and a 'rejoicing in *hope* of the glory of God', 'with *joy* unspeakable and full of glory'.

4. And at the same time that we are justified, yea, in that very moment, *sanctification begins*. In that instant we are 'born again', 'born from above', 'born of the Spirit'. There is a *real* as well as a *relative* change. We are inwardly renewed by the power of God. We feel the 'love of God shed abroad in our heart by the Holy Ghost which is given unto us', producing love to all mankind, and more especially to the children of God; expelling the love of the world, the love of pleasure, of ease, of honour, of money; together with pride, anger, self-will, and every other evil temper—in a word, changing the 'earthly, sensual, devilish' mind into 'the mind which was in Christ Jesus'.

5. How naturally do those who experience such a change imagine that all sin is gone! That it is utterly rooted out of their heart, and has no more any place therein! How easily do they draw that inference, 'I *feel* no sin; therefore I *have* none.' It does not *stir*; therefore it does not *exist*: it has no *motion*; therefore it has no *being*.

6. But it is seldom long before they are undeceived, finding sin was only suspended, not destroyed. Temptations return and sin revives, showing it was but stunned before, not dead. They now feel two principles in themselves, plainly contrary to each other: 'the flesh lusting against the spirit', nature opposing the grace of God. They cannot deny that although they still feel power to believe in Christ and to love God, and although his 'Spirit' still 'witnesses with' their 'spirits that' they 'are the children of God'; yet they feel in

themselves, sometimes pride or self-will, sometimes anger or unbelief. They find one or more of these frequently *stirring* in their heart, though not *conquering*; yea, perhaps 'thrusting sore at them, that they' may 'fall; but the Lord is' their 'help'.

7. How exactly did Macarius, fourteen hundred years ago, describe the present experience of the children of God! 'The unskilful (or unexperienced), when grace operates, presently imagine they have no more sin. Whereas they that have discretion cannot deny that even we who have the grace of God may be molested again. . . . For we have often had instances of some among the brethren who have experienced such grace as to affirm that they had no sin in them. And yet after all, when they thought themselves entirely freed from it, the corruption that lurked within was stirred up anew, and they were well-nigh burnt up.'

8. From the time of our being 'born again' the gradual work of sanctification takes place. We are enabled 'by the Spirit' to 'mortify the deeds of the body', of our evil nature. And as we are more and more dead to sin, we are more and more alive to God. We go on from grace to grace, while we are careful to 'abstain from all appearance of evil', and are 'zealous of good works', 'as we have opportunity, doing good to all men'; while we walk in all his ordinances blameless, therein worshipping him in spirit and in truth; while we take up our cross and deny ourselves every pleasure that does not lead us to God.

9. It is thus that we wait for entire sanctification, for a full salvation from all our sins, from pride, self-will, anger, unbelief, or, as the Apostle expresses it, 'Go on to perfection.' But what is perfection? The word has various senses: here it means perfect love. It is love excluding sin; love filling the heart, taking up the whole capacity of the soul. It is love 'rejoicing evermore, praying without ceasing, in everything giving thanks'.

II. But what is that 'faith through which we are saved'? This is the second point to be considered.

1. Faith in general is defined by the Apostle, ἔλεγχος πραγμάτων οὐ βλεπομένων—'an evidence', a divine 'evidence and conviction' (the word means both), 'of things not seen'—not visible, not perceivable either by sight or by any other of the external senses. It implies both a supernatural *evidence* of God and of the things of God, a kind of spiritual *light* exhibited to the soul, and a supernatural *sight* or perception thereof. Accordingly the Scripture speaks sometimes of God's giving light, sometimes a power of discerning it. So St. Paul: 'God, who commanded light to shine out of darkness, hath shined in our hearts, to give us the light of the knowledge of the glory of God in the face of Jesus Christ.' And elsewhere the same Apostle speaks 'of the eyes of' our 'understanding being opened'. By this twofold operation of the Holy Spirit—having the eyes of our soul both *opened* and *enlightened*—we see the things which

the natural 'eye hath not seen, neither the ear heard'. We have a prospect of the invisible things of God. We see the *spiritual world*, which is all round about us, and yet no more discerned by our natural faculties than if it had no being; and we see the *eternal world*, piercing through the veil which hangs between time and eternity. Clouds and darkness then rest upon it no more, but we already see the glory which shall be revealed.

2. Taking the word in a more particular sense, faith is a divine evidence and conviction, not only that 'God was in Christ, reconciling the world unto himself', but also that Christ 'loved *me*, and gave himself for *me*'. It is by this faith (whether we term it the *essence*, or rather a *property* thereof) that we 'receive Christ'; that we receive him in all his offices, as our Prophet, Priest, and King. It is by this that he 'is made of God unto us wisdom, and righteousness, and sanctification, and redemption'.

3. 'But is this the "faith of assurance" or "faith of adherence"?' The Scripture mentions no such distinction. The Apostle says: 'There is one faith, and one hope of our calling,' one Christian, saving faith, as 'there is one Lord' in whom we believe, and 'one God and Father of us all.' And it is certain this faith necessarily implies an *assurance* (which is here only another word for *evidence*, it being hard to tell the difference between them) that 'Christ loved *me*, and gave himself for *me*.' For 'he that believeth' with the true, living faith, 'hath the witness in himself.' 'The Spirit witnesseth with his spirit that he is a child of God.' 'Because he is a son, God hath sent forth the Spirit of his Son into his heart, crying, Abba, Father'; giving him an assurance that he is so, and a childlike confidence in him. But let it be observed that, in the very nature of the thing, the assurance goes before the confidence. For a man cannot have a childlike confidence in God till he knows he is a child of God. Therefore confidence, trust, reliance, adherence, or whatever else it be called, is not the first, as some have supposed, but the second branch or act of faith.

4. It is by this faith we 'are saved', justified and sanctified, taking that word in its highest sense. But how are we justified and sanctified by faith? This is our third head of inquiry. And this being the main point in question, and a point of no ordinary importance, it will not be improper to give it a more distinct and particular consideration.

III.1. And first, how are we justified by faith? In what sense is this to be understood? I answer, faith is the condition, and the only condition, of justification. It is the condition: none is justified but he that believes; without faith no man is justified. And it is the only condition: this alone is sufficient for justification. Everyone that believes is justified, whatever else he has or has not. In other words: no man is justified till he believes; every man when he believes is justified.

2. 'But does not God command us to *repent* also? Yea, and to "bring forth

fruits meet for repentance"? To "cease", for instance, "from doing evil", and "learn to do well"? And is not both the one and the other of the utmost necessity? Insomuch that if we willingly neglect either we cannot reasonably expect to be justified at all? But if this be so, how can it be said that faith is the only condition of justification?'

God does undoubtedly command us both to repent and to bring forth fruits meet for repentance; which if we willingly neglect we cannot reasonably expect to be justified at all. Therefore both repentance and fruits meet for repentance are in some sense necessary to justification. But they are not necessary in the *same sense* with faith, nor in the *same degree.* Not in the *same degree*; for those fruits are only necessary *conditionally*, if there be time and opportunity for them. Otherwise a man may be justified without them, as was the 'thief' upon the cross (if we may call him so; for a late writer has discovered that he was no thief, but a very honest and respectable person!). But he cannot be justified without faith: this is impossible. Likewise let a man have ever so much repentance, or ever so many of the fruits meet for repentance, yet all this does not at all avail: he is not justified till he believes. But the moment he believes, with or without those fruits, yea, with more or less repentance, he is justified. Not in the *same sense*: for repentance and its fruits are only *remotely* necessary, necessary in order to faith; whereas faith is *immediately* and *directly* necessary to justification. It remains that faith is the only condition which is *immediately* and *proximately* necessary to justification.

3. 'But do you believe we are sanctified by faith? We know you believe that we are justified by faith; but do not you believe, and accordingly teach, that we are sanctified by our works?'

So it has been roundly and vehemently affirmed for these five and twenty years. But I have constantly declared just the contrary, and that in all manner of ways. I have continually testified in private and in public that we are sanctified, as well as justified, by faith. And indeed the one of these great truths does exceedingly illustrate the other. Exactly as we are justified by faith, so are we sanctified by faith. Faith is the condition, and the only condition of sanctification, exactly as it is of justification. It is the condition: none is sanctified but he that believes; without faith no man is sanctified. And it is the only condition: this alone is sufficient for sanctification. Everyone that believes is sanctified, whatever else he has or has not. In other words: no man is sanctified till he believes; every man when he believes is sanctified.

4. 'But is there not a repentance consequent upon, as well as a repentance previous to, justification? And is it not incumbent on all that are justified to be "zealous of good works"? Yea, are not these so necessary that if a man willingly neglect them he cannot reasonably expect that he shall ever be sanctified in the full sense, that is, "perfected in love"? Nay, can he "grow" at all "in grace, in the" loving "knowledge of our Lord Jesus Christ"? Yea, can

he retain the grace which God has already given him? Can he continue in the faith which he has received, or in the favour of God? Do not you yourself allow all this, and continually assert it? But if this be so, how can it be said that faith is the only condition of sanctification?'

5. I do allow all this, and continually maintain it as the truth of God. I allow there is a repentance consequent upon, as well as a repentance previous to, justification. It is incumbent on all that are justified to be zealous of good works. And these are so necessary that if a man willingly neglect them, he cannot reasonably expect that he shall ever be sanctified. He cannot 'grow in grace', in the image of God, the mind which was in Christ Jesus; nay, he cannot retain the grace he has received, he cannot continue in faith, or in the favour of God.

What is the inference we must draw herefrom? Why, that both repentance, rightly understood, and the practice of all good works, works of piety, as well as works of mercy (now properly so called, since they spring from faith) are in some sense necessary to sanctification.

6. I say 'repentance rightly understood'; for this must not be confounded with the former repentance. The repentance consequent upon justification is widely different from that which is antecedent to it. This implies no guilt, no sense of condemnation, no consciousness of the wrath of God. It does not suppose any doubt of the favour of God, or any 'fear that hath torment'. It is properly a conviction wrought by the Holy Ghost of the 'sin' which still 'remains' in our heart, of the φρόνημα σαρκός, 'the carnal mind', which 'does still remain', as our Church speaks, 'even in them that are regenerate'—although it does no longer *reign*, it has not now dominion over them. It is a conviction of our proneness to evil, of an heart 'bent to backsliding', of the still continuing tendency of the 'flesh' to 'lust against the Spirit'. Sometimes, unless we continually watch and pray, it lusteth to pride, sometimes to anger, sometimes to love of the world, love of ease, love of honour, or love of pleasure more than of God. It is a conviction of the tendency of our heart to self-will, to atheism, or idolatry; and above all to unbelief, whereby in a thousand ways, and under a thousand pretences, we are ever 'departing' more or less 'from the living God'.

7. With this conviction of the sin *remaining* in our hearts there is joined a clear conviction of the sin remaining in our lives, still *cleaving* to all our words and actions. In the best of these we now discern a mixture of evil, either in the spirit, the matter, or the manner of them; something that could not endure the righteous judgment of God, were he 'extreme to mark what is done amiss'. Where we least suspected it we find a taint of pride of self-will, of unbelief or idolatry; so that we are now more ashamed of our best duties than formerly of our worst sins. And hence we cannot but feel that these are so far from having anything meritorious in them, yea, so far from being able to stand in sight of the divine justice, that for those also we should be guilty before God were it

not for the blood of the covenant.

8. Experience shows that together with this conviction of sin *remaining* in our hearts and *cleaving* to all our words and actions, as well as the guilt which on account thereof we should incur were we not continually sprinkled with the atoning blood, one thing more is implied in this repentance, namely, a conviction of our helplessness, of our utter inability to think one good thought, or to form one good desire; and much more to speak one word aright, or to perform one good action but through his free, almighty grace, first preventing us, and then accompanying us every moment.

9. 'But what good works are those, the practice of which you affirm to be necessary to sanctification?' First, all works of piety, such as public prayer, family prayer, and praying in our closet; receiving the Supper of the Lord; searching the Scriptures by hearing, reading, meditating; and using such a measure of fasting or abstinence as our bodily health allows.

10. Secondly, all works of mercy, whether they relate to the bodies or souls of men; such as feeding the hungry, clothing the naked, entertaining the stranger, visiting those that are in prison, or sick, or variously afflicted; such as the endeavouring to instruct the ignorant, to awaken the stupid sinner, to quicken the lukewarm, to confirm the wavering, to comfort the feebleminded, to succour the tempted, or contribute in any manner to the saving of souls from death. This is the repentance, and these the fruits meet for repentance, which are necessary to full sanctification. This is the way wherein God hath appointed his children to wait for complete salvation.

11. Hence may appear the extreme mischievousness of that seemingly innocent opinion that 'there is no sin in a believer; that all sin is destroyed, root and branch, the moment a man is justified.' By totally preventing that repentance it quite blocks up the way to sanctification. There is no place for repentance in him who believes there is no sin either in his life or heart. Consequently there is no place for his being 'perfected in love', to which that repentance is indispensably necessary.

12. Hence it may likewise appear that there is no possible danger in *thus* expecting full salvation. For suppose we were mistaken, suppose no such blessing ever was or can be attained, yet we lose nothing. Nay, that very expectation quickens us in using all the talents which God has given us; yea, in improving them all, so that when our Lord cometh he will 'receive his own with increase'.

13. But to return. Though it be allowed that both this repentance and its fruits are necessary to full salvation, yet they are not necessary either in the *same sense* with faith or in the *same degree*. Not in the same degree; for these fruits are only necessary *conditionally*, if there be time and opportunity for them. Otherwise a man may be sanctified without them. But he cannot be sanctified without faith. Likewise let a man have ever so much of this repentance, or ever

so many good works, yet all this does not at all avail: he is not sanctified till he believes. But the moment he believes, with or without those fruits, yea, with more or less of this repentance, he is sanctified. Not in the *same sense*; for this repentance and these fruits are only *remotely* necessary, necessary in order to the continuance of his faith, as well as the increase of it; whereas faith is *immediately* and *directly* necessary to sanctification. It remains that faith is the only condition which is *immediately* and *proximately* necessary to sanctification.

14. 'But what is that faith whereby we are sanctified, saved from sin and perfected in love?' It is a divine evidence and conviction, first, that God hath promised it in the Holy Scripture. Till we are thoroughly satisfied of this there is no moving one step farther. And one would imagine there needed not one word more to satisfy a reasonable man of this than the ancient promise, 'Then will I circumcise thy heart, and the heart of thy seed, to love the Lord your God with all your heart, and with all your soul.' How clearly does this express the being perfected in love! How strongly imply the being saved from all sin! For as long as love takes up the whole heart, what room is there for sin therein?

15. It is a divine evidence and conviction, secondly, that what God hath promised he is *able* to perform. Admitting therefore that 'with men it is impossible' to bring a clean thing out of an unclean, to purify the heart from all sin, and to fill it with all holiness, yet this creates no difficulty in the case, seeing 'with God all things are possible.' And surely no one ever imagined it was possible to any power less than that of the Almighty! But if God speaks, it shall be done. God saith, 'Let there be light: and there is light.'

16. It is, thirdly, a divine evidence and conviction that he is able and willing to do it *now*. And why not? Is not a moment to him the same as a thousand years? He cannot want more time to accomplish whatever is his will. And he cannot want or stay for any more *worthiness* or *fitness* in the persons he is pleased to honour. We may therefore boldly say, at any point of time, 'Now is the day of salvation.' '*Today* if ye will hear his voice, harden not your hearts.' 'Behold! all things are now ready! Come unto the marriage!'

17. To this confidence, that God is both able and willing to sanctify us *now*, there needs to be added one thing more, a divine evidence and conviction that *he doth it*. In that hour it is done. God says to the inmost soul, 'According to thy faith be it unto thee!' Then the soul is pure from every spot of sin; 'it is clean from all unrighteousness.' The believer then experiences the deep meaning of those solemn words, 'If we walk in the light, as he is in the light, we have fellowship one with another, and the blood of Jesus Christ his Son cleanseth us from all sin.'

18. 'But does God work this great work in the soul *gradually* or *instantaneously*?' Perhaps it may be gradually wrought in some. I mean in this sense–they do not advert to the particular moment wherein sin ceases to be. But it is infinitely desirable, were it the will of God, that it should be done instantane-

ously; that the Lord should destroy sin 'by the breath of his mouth' in a moment, in the twinkling of an eye. And so he generally does, a plain fact of which there is evidence enough to satisfy any unprejudiced person. *Thou* therefore look for it every moment. Look for it in the way above described; in all those 'good works' whereunto thou art 'created anew in Christ Jesus'. There is then no danger. You can be no worse, if you are no better for that expectation. For were you to be disappointed of your hope, still you lose nothing. But you shall not be disappointed of your hope: it will come, and will not tarry. Look for it then every day, every hour, every moment. Why not this hour, this moment? Certainly you may look for it *now*, if you believe it is by faith. And by this token may you surely know whether you seek it by faith or by works. If by works, you want something to be done *first, before* you are sanctified. You think, 'I must first *be* or *do* thus or thus.' Then you are seeking it by works unto this day. If you seek it by faith, you may expect it *as you are*: and if as you are, then expect it *now*. It is of importance to observe that there is an inseparable connection between these three points—expect it *by faith*, expect it *as you are*, and expect it *now!* To deny one of them is to deny them all: to allow one is to allow them all. Do *you* believe we are sanctified by faith? Be true then to your principle, and look for this blessing just as you are, neither better, nor worse; as a poor sinner that has still nothing to pay, nothing to plead but 'Christ died.' And if you look for it as you are, then expect it *now*. Stay for nothing. Why should you? Christ is ready. And he is all you want. He is waiting for you. He is at the door! Let your inmost soul cry out,

Come in, come in, thou heavenly Guest!
   Nor hence again remove:
But sup with me, and let the feast
   Be everlasting love.

THE LORD OUR RIGHTEOUSNESS

Sermon 20 – 1765

AN INTRODUCTORY COMMENT

An extended comment on faith's positive fruits, this sermon was inspired by the worsening conflict between Wesley and the Calvinists after mid-century, which gave rise to the need for a clearer statement of Wesley's position on 'imputation' and 'impartation' in justification by faith. The conflict stretched back to the breach between the Wesleys and George Whitefield in 1739. Continued criticism of Wesley was climaxed in 1755 by a three-volume 'dialogue' by a former 'Oxford Methodist', James Hervey, since turned Calvinist. In his *Theron and Aspasio*, Hervey had laid out the differences between Arminians (Theron) and English Calvinists (Aspasio) who argue plausibly for 'the imputed righteousness of Christ' as the prime reality in justification. 'Theron' comes off rather badly in the 'dialogue'. Wesley's private criticism wounded the gentle-spirited Hervey, who replied in a series of long letters to Wesley that he wisely left unposted and unpublished at his death in 1758. However, they fell into the hands of William Cudworth, who promptly put them in print. *The Lord Our Righteousness* was Wesley's response. It was preached on Sunday, November 24, 1765, in the chapel in West Street, near Seven Dials, and published at least four times shortly thereafter. It was also included in Wesley's *Works* (1771) and his eight-volume collection of *Sermons* (1787–88).

At issue was whether Christ's atoning death is to be understood as the 'formal' or the 'meritorious' cause of a sinner's justification. This issue had divided British theologians since the days of John Davenant and George Downame. The doctrine of 'formal cause' implied some sort of correlated view of predestination and irresistible grace. The idea of 'meritorious cause' allowed for prevenience, free will, and 'universal redemption'. To the Calvinists, however, the latter was merely a subtler form of works-righteousness. Hervey suggested that Wesley's principles halted 'between Protestantism and Popery' and that his views were closely associated with the papists' on several points.

Wesley begins the sermon with a forceful assertion of the premises of 'faith alone'. But his conclusions develop quite differently from anything in the Lutheran and Calvinist traditions based on those same premises. This sermon signals the end of Wesley's efforts to avoid an open rift with the Calvinists; it marks the beginning of 'the later Wesley'. Moreover, it is a sample of Wesley's efforts to agree and disagree in matters of 'theological *opinions*' while still holding fast to the Christian unity made possible by shared beliefs in the essentials of Christian doctrine.

The Lord Our Righteousness

This is his name whereby he shall be called,
The Lord our righteousness.
Jeremiah 23:6

1. How dreadful and how innumerable are the contests which have arisen about religion! And not only among the children of this world, among those who knew not what true religion was; but even among the children of God, those who had experienced 'the kingdom of God within them', who had tasted of 'righteousness, and peace, and joy in the Holy Ghost'. How many of these in all ages, instead of joining together against the common enemy, have turned their weapons against each other, and so not only wasted their precious time but hurt one another's spirits, weakened each other's hands, and so hindered the great work of their common Master! How many of the weak have hereby been offended! How many of the 'lame turned out of the way'! How many sinners confirmed in their disregard of all religion, and their contempt of those that profess it! And how many of 'the excellent ones upon earth' have been constrained to 'weep in secret places'!

2. What would not every lover of God and his neighbour do, what would he not suffer, to remedy this sore evil? To remove contention from the children of God? To restore or preserve peace among them? What but a good conscience would he think too dear to part with in order to promote this valuable end? And suppose we cannot 'make these wars to cease in all the world', suppose we cannot reconcile all the children of God to each other; however, let each do what he can, let him contribute if it be but two mites toward it. Happy are they who are able in any degree to promote 'peace and goodwill among men'! Especially among good men; among those that are all listed under the banner of 'the Prince of Peace'; and are therefore peculiarly engaged, 'as much as lies in them, to live peaceably with all men'.

3. It would be a considerable step toward this glorious end if we could bring good men to understand one another. Abundance of disputes arise purely from the want of this, from mere misapprehension. Frequently neither of the contending parties understands what his opponent means; whence it follows that each violently attacks the other while there is no real difference between them. And yet it is not always an easy matter to convince them of this. Particularly when their passions are moved: it is then attended with the utmost difficulty. However, it is not impossible; especially when we attempt it, not

trusting in ourselves, but having all our dependence upon him with whom all things are possible. How soon is he able to disperse the cloud, to shine upon their hearts, and to enable them both to understand each other and 'the truth as it is in Jesus'!

4. One very considerable article of this truth is contained in the words above recited, 'This is his name whereby he shall be called, The Lord our righteousness': a truth this which enters deep into the nature of Christianity, and in a manner supports the whole frame of it. Of this undoubtedly may be affirmed what Luther affirms of a truth closely connected with it: it is *articulus stantis vel cadentis ecclesiae*—the Christian church stands or falls with it. It is certainly the pillar and ground of that faith of which alone cometh salvation—of that *catholic* or universal faith which is found in all the children of God, and which 'unless a man keep whole and undefiled, without doubt he shall perish everlastingly'.

5. Might not one therefore reasonably expect, that however they differed in others, all those who name the name of Christ should agree in this point? But how far is this from being the case! There is scarce any wherein they are so little agreed, wherein those who all profess to follow Christ seem so widely and irreconcilably to differ. I say 'seem', because I am thoroughly convinced that many of them only seem to differ. The disagreement is more in words than in sentiments: they are much nearer in judgment than in language. And a wide difference in language there certainly is, not only between Protestants and Papists, but between Protestant and Protestant; yea, even between those who all believe justification by faith, who agree as well in this as every other fundamental doctrine of the gospel.

6. But if the difference be more in *opinion* than real *experience*, and more in *expression* than in *opinion*, how can it be that even the children of God should so vehemently contend with each other on the point? Several reasons may be assigned for this: the chief is their not understanding one another, joined with too keen an attachment to their *opinions* and particular modes of *expression*.

In order to remove this, at least in some measure, in order to our understanding one another on this head, I shall by the help of God endeavour to show,

I. What is the righteousness of Christ;
II. When, and in what sense, it is imputed to us;

And conclude with a short and plain application.

And, I. What is the righteousness of Christ? It is twofold, either his divine or his human righteousness.

1. His divine righteousness belongs to his divine nature, as he is ὁ ὤν, 'He that existeth, over all, God, blessed for ever': the supreme, the eternal, 'equal with the Father as touching his godhead, though inferior to the Father as

touching his manhood'. Now this is his eternal, essential, immutable holiness; his infinite justice, mercy, and truth: in all which 'he and the Father are one.'

But I do not apprehend that the divine righteousness of Christ is immediately concerned in the present question. I believe few, if any, do now contend for the *imputation* of *this* righteousness to us. Whoever believes the doctrine of imputation understands it chiefly, if not solely, of his human righteousness.

2. The *human righteousness* of Christ belongs to him in his human nature, as he is 'the mediator between God and man, the man Christ Jesus'. This is either *internal* or *external*. His internal righteousness is the image of God stamped on every power and faculty of his soul. It is a copy of his divine righteousness, as far as it can be imparted to a human spirit. It is a transcript of the divine purity, the divine justice, mercy, and truth. It includes love, reverence, resignation to his Father; humility, meekness, gentleness; love to lost mankind, and every other holy and heavenly temper: and all these in the highest degree, without any defect, or mixture of unholiness.

3. It was the least part of his *external righteousness* that he did nothing amiss; that he knew no outward sin of any kind, 'neither was guile found in his mouth'; that he never spoke one improper word, nor did one improper action. Thus far it is only a *negative* righteousness, though such an one as never did nor ever can belong to anyone that is born of a woman, save himself alone. But even his outward righteousness was *positive* too. 'He did all things well.' In every word of his tongue, in every work of his hands, he did precisely the 'will of him that sent him'. In the whole course of his life he did the will of God on earth as the angels do it in heaven. All he acted and spoke was exactly right in every circumstance. The whole and every part of his obedience was complete. 'He fulfilled all righteousness.'

4. But his obedience implied more than all this. It implied not only doing, but suffering: suffering the whole will of God from the time he came into the world till 'he bore our sins in his own body upon the tree'; yea, till having made a full atonement for them 'he bowed his head and gave up the ghost.' This is usually termed the *passive* righteousness of Christ, the former, his *active* righteousness. But as the active and passive righteousness of Christ were never in fact separated from each other, so we never need separate them at all, either in speaking or even in thinking. And it is with regard to both these conjointly that Jesus is called, 'the Lord our righteousness'.

II. But when is it that any of us may truly say, 'the Lord our righteousness'? In other words, when is it that the righteousness of Christ is *imputed* to us, and in what sense is it imputed?

1. Look through all the world, and all the men therein are either believers or unbelievers. The first thing then which admits of no dispute among

reasonable men is this: to all believers the righteousness of Christ is imputed; to unbelievers it is not.

'But when is it imputed?' When they believe. In that very hour the righteousness of Christ is theirs. It is imputed to every one that believes, as soon as he believes: faith and the righteousness of Christ are inseparable. For if he believes according to Scripture, he believes in the righteousness of Christ. There is no true faith, that is, justifying faith, which hath not the righteousness of Christ for its object.

2. It is true believers may not all speak alike; they may not all use the same language. It is not to be expected that they should; we cannot reasonably require it of them. A thousand circumstances may cause them to vary from each other in the manner of expressing themselves. But a difference of expression does not necessarily imply a difference of sentiment. Different persons may use different expressions, and yet mean the same thing. Nothing is more common than this, although we seldom make sufficient allowance for it. Nay, it is not easy for the same persons, when they speak of the same thing at a considerable distance of time, to use exactly the same expressions, even though they retain the same sentiments. How then can we be rigorous in requiring others to use just the same expressions with us?

3. We may go a step farther yet. Men may differ from us in their opinions as well as their expressions, and nevertheless be partakers with us of the same precious faith. 'Tis possible they may not have a *distinct apprehension* of the very blessing which they enjoy. Their *ideas* may not be so *clear*, and yet their experience may be as sound as ours. There is a wide difference between the natural faculties of men, their understandings in particular. And that difference is exceedingly increased by the manner of their education. Indeed, this alone may occasion an inconceivable difference in their opinions of various kinds. And why not upon this head as well as on any other? But still, though their opinions as well as expressions may be confused and inaccurate, their hearts may cleave to God through the Son of his love, and be truly interested in his righteousness.

4. Let us then make all that allowance to others which, were we in their place, we would desire for ourselves. Who is ignorant (to touch again on that circumstance only) of the amazing power of education? And who that knows it can expect, suppose, a member of the Church of Rome either to think or speak clearly on this subject? And yet if we had heard even dying Bellarmine cry out, when he was asked, 'Unto which of the saints wilt thou turn?'—'*Fidere meritis Christi tutissimum*: It is safest to trust in the merits of Christ'—would we have affirmed that notwithstanding his wrong opinions he had no share in his righteousness?

5. 'But in what sense is this righteousness imputed to believers?' In this: all believers are forgiven and accepted, not for the sake of anything in them, or

of anything that ever was, that is, or ever can be done by them, but wholly and solely for the sake of what Christ hath done and suffered for them. I say again, not for the sake of anything in them or done by them, of their own righteousness or works. 'Not for works of righteousness which we have done, but of his own mercy he saved us.' 'By grace ye are saved through faith. . . . Not of works, lest any man should boast'; but wholly and solely for the sake of what Christ hath done and suffered for us. We are 'justified freely by his grace, through the redemption that is in Jesus Christ'. And this is not only the means of our *obtaining* the favour of God, but of our continuing therein. It is thus we come to God at first: it is by the same we come unto him ever after. We walk in one and the same 'new and living way' till our spirit returns to God.

6. And this is the doctrine which I have constantly believed and taught for near eight and twenty years. This I published to all the world in the year 1738, and ten or twelve times since, in those words, and many others to the same effect, extracted from the *Homilies* of our Church:

> These things must necessarily go together in our justification: upon God's part his great mercy and grace, upon Christ's part the satisfaction of God's justice, and on our part faith in the merits of Christ. So that the grace of God doth not shut out the righteousness of God in our justification, but only shutteth out the righteousness of man, as to *deserving* our justification.
>
> That we are justified by faith alone is spoken to take away clearly all merit of our works, and wholly to ascribe the *merit* and *deserving* of our justification to Christ only. Our justification comes freely of the mere mercy of God. For whereas all the world was not able to pay any part toward our ransom, it pleased him, without any of our deserving, to prepare for us Christ's body and blood, whereby our ransom might be paid, and his justice satisfied. Christ therefore is now the righteousness of all them that truly believe in him.

7. The hymns published a year or two after this, and since republished several times (a clear testimony that my judgment was still the same) speak full to the same purpose. To cite all the passages to this effect would be to transcribe a great part of the volumes. Take one for all, which was reprinted seven years ago, five years ago, two years ago, and some months since:

> Jesu, thy blood and righteousness
> My beauty are, my glorious dress:
> Midst flaming worlds in these arrayed
> With joy shall I lift up my head.

The whole expresses the same sentiment from the beginning to the end.

8. In the sermon on justification published nineteen, and again seven or eight years ago, I express the same thing in these words:

> In consideration of this, that the Son of God hath 'tasted death for every man',

> God hath now 'reconciled the world unto himself, not imputing to them their former trespasses'. So that for the sake of his well-beloved Son, of what he hath done and suffered for us, God now vouchsafes on one only condition (which himself also enables us to perform) both to remit the punishment due to our sins, to reinstate us in his favour, and to restore our dead souls to spiritual life, as the earnest of life eternal ([*Sermons on Several Occasions* (1746), I], p. 87).

9. This is more largely and particularly expressed in the *Treatise on Justification* which I published last year:

> If we take the phrase of 'imputing Christ's righteousness' for the bestowing (as it were) the righteousness of Christ, including his obedience, as well passive as active, in the return of it—that is, in the privileges, blessings, and benefits purchased by it—so a believer may be said to be justified by *the righteousness of Christ imputed*. The meaning is, God justifies the believer for the sake of Christ's righteousness, and not for any righteousness of his own. So Calvin: 'Christ by his obedience procured and merited for us grace or favour with God the Father' (*Institutes*, II.xvii.[3]). Again, 'Christ by his obedience procured or purchased righteousness for us.' And yet again: 'All such expressions as these—that we are justified by the grace of God, that Christ is our righteousness, that righteousness was procured for us by the death and resurrection of Christ—import the same thing': namely, that the righteousness of Christ, both his active and passive righteousness, is the meritorious cause of our justification, and has procured for us at God's hand that upon our believing we should be accounted righteous by him (p. 5).

10. But perhaps some will object, 'Nay, but you affirm that "faith is imputed to us for righteousness."' St. Paul affirms this over and over; therefore I affirm it too. Faith is imputed for righteousness to every believer; namely, faith in the righteousness of Christ. But this is exactly the same thing which has been said before. For by that expression I mean neither more nor less than that we are justified by faith, not by works; or that every believer is forgiven and accepted merely for the sake of what Christ has done and suffered.

11. 'But is not a believer invested or clothed with the righteousness of Christ?' Undoubtedly he is. And accordingly the words above-recited are the language of every believing heart:

> Jesu, thy blood and righteousness
> My beauty are, my glorious dress.

That is, for the sake of thy active and passive righteousness I am forgiven and accepted of God.

'But must not we put off the filthy rags of our own righteousness before we can put on the spotless righteousness of Christ?' Certainly we must; that is, in plain terms, we must 'repent' before we can 'believe the gospel'. We must be cut off from dependence upon ourselves before we can truly depend upon

Christ. We must cast away all confidence in our own righteousness, or we cannot have a true confidence in his. Till we are delivered from trusting in anything that we do, we cannot thoroughly trust in what he has done and suffered. First 'we receive the sentence of death in ourselves'; then we trust in him that lived and died for us.

12. 'But do not you believe *inherent* righteousness?' Yes, in its proper place; not as the *ground* of our acceptance with God, but as the *fruit* of it; not in the place of *imputed* righteousness, but as consequent upon it. That is, I believe God *implants* righteousness in every one to whom he has *imputed* it. I believe 'Jesus Christ is made of God unto us sanctification' as well as righteousness; or that God sanctifies, as well as justifies, all them that believe in him. They to whom the righteousness of Christ is imputed are made righteous by the spirit of Christ, are renewed in the image of God 'after the likeness wherein they were created, in righteousness and true holiness'.

13. 'But do not you put faith in the room of Christ, or of his righteousness?' By no means. I take particular care to put each of these in its proper place. The righteousness of Christ is the whole and sole *foundation* of all our hope. It is by faith that the Holy Ghost enables us to build upon this foundation. God gives this faith. In that moment we are accepted of God; and yet not for the sake of that faith, but of what Christ has done and suffered for us. You see, each of these has its proper place, and neither clashes with the other: we believe, we love; we endeavour to walk in all the commandments of the Lord blameless. Yet,

> While thus we bestow
> Our moments below,
> Ourselves we forsake
> And refuge in Jesus's righteousness take.
>
> His passion alone,
> The foundation we own:
> And pardon we claim,
> And eternal redemption in Jesus's name.

14. I therefore no more deny the righteousness of Christ than I deny the godhead of Christ. And a man may full as justly charge me with denying the one as the other. Neither do I deny *imputed righteousness:* this is another unkind and unjust accusation. I always did, and do still continually affirm, that the righteousness of Christ is imputed to every believer. But who do deny it? Why, all *infidels,* whether baptized or unbaptized; all who affirm the glorious gospel of our Lord Jesus Christ to be a *cunningly* devised fable; all Socinians and Arians; all who deny the supreme godhead of the Lord that bought them. They of consequence deny his divine righteousness, as they suppose him to be a mere creature. And they deny his human righteousness as imputed to any man,

seeing they believe everyone is accepted *for his own righteousness.*

15. The human righteousness of Christ, at least the imputation of it as the whole and sole meritorious cause of the justification of a sinner before God, is likewise denied by the members of the Church of Rome—by all of them who are true to the principles of their own church. But undoubtedly there are many among them whose experience goes beyond their principles; who, though they are far from expressing themselves justly, yet feel what they know not how to express. Yea, although their conceptions of this great truth be as crude as their expressions, yet 'with their heart they believe'; they rest on Christ alone, both 'unto' present and eternal 'salvation'.

16. With these we may rank those even in the Reformed Churches who are usually termed *mystics.* One of the chief of these in the present century (at least in England) was Mr. Law. It is well known that he absolutely and zealously denied the imputation of the righteousness of Christ; as zealously as Robert Barclay, who scruples not to say, 'Imputed righteousness, imputed nonsense!' The body of the people known by the name of Quakers espouse the same sentiment. Nay, the generality of those who profess themselves members of the Church of England are either totally ignorant of the matter and know nothing about *imputed righteousness,* or deny this and justification by faith together as destructive of good works. To these we may add a considerable number of the people vulgarly styled Anabaptists, together with thousands of Presbyterians and Independents lately enlightened by the writings of Dr. Taylor. On the last I am not called to pass any sentence: I leave them to him that made them. But will anyone dare to affirm that all mystics (such as was Mr. Law in particular), all Quakers, all Presbyterians or Independents, and all members of the Church of England, who are not clear in their opinions or expressions, are void of all Christian experience? That consequently they are all in a state of damnation, 'without hope, without God in the world'? However confused their ideas may be, however improper their language, may there not be many of them whose heart is right toward God and who effectually know 'the Lord our righteousness'?

17. But, blessed be God, we are not among those who are so dark in their conceptions and expressions. We no more deny the *phrase* than the *thing;* but we are unwilling to obtrude it on other men. Let them use either this or such other expressions as they judge to be more exactly scriptural, provided their *heart* rests only on what Christ hath done and suffered for pardon, grace, and glory. I cannot express this better than in Mr. Hervey's words, worthy to be wrote in letters of gold: 'We are not solicitous as to any *particular set of phrases.* Only let men be humbled as repenting criminals at Christ's feet, let them rely as devoted pensioners on his merits, and they are undoubtedly in the way to a blessed immortality.'

18. Is there any need, is there any possibility of saying more? Let us only

abide by this declaration, and all the contention about this or that 'particular phrase' is torn up by the roots. Keep to this: 'All who are humbled as repenting criminals at Christ's feet and rely as devoted pensioners on his merits are in the way to a blessed immortality.' And what room for dispute? Who denies this? Do we not all meet on this ground? What then shall we wrangle about? A man of peace here proposes terms of accommodation to all the contending parties. We desire no better. We accept of the terms. We subscribe to them with heart and hand. Whoever refuses so to do, set a mark upon that man! He is an enemy of peace, and a troubler of Israel, a disturber of the church of God.

19. In the meantime what we are afraid of is this: lest any should use the phrase, 'the righteousness of Christ', or, 'the righteousness of Christ is "imputed to me",' as a cover for his unrighteousness. We have known this done a thousand times. A man has been reproved, suppose, for drunkenness. 'Oh, said he, I pretend to no righteousness of *my own*: Christ is *my righteousness*.' Another has been told that 'the extortioner, the unjust, shall not inherit the kingdom of God.' He replies with all assurance, 'I am unjust in myself, but I have a spotless righteousness in Christ.' And thus though a man be as far from the practice as from the tempers of a Christian, though he neither has the mind which was in Christ nor in any respect walks as he walked, yet he has armour of proof against all conviction in what he calls the 'righteousness of Christ'.

20. It is the seeing so many deplorable instances of this kind which makes us sparing in the use of these expressions. And I cannot but call upon all of you who use them frequently, and beseech you in the name of God our Saviour, whose you are and whom you serve, earnestly to guard all that hear you against this accursed abuse of it. O warn them (it may be they will hear *your* voice) against 'continuing in sin that grace may abound'! Warn them against making 'Christ the minister of sin'! Against making void that solemn decree of God, 'without holiness no man shall see the Lord,' by a vain imagination of being *holy in Christ*. O warn them that if they remain unrighteous, the righteousness of Christ will profit them nothing! Cry aloud (is there not a cause?) that for this very end the righteousness of Christ is imputed to us, that 'the righteousness of the law may be fulfilled in us,' and that we may 'live soberly, religiously, and godly in this present world.'

It remains only to make a short and plain application. And first I would address myself to you who violently oppose these expressions, and are ready to condemn all that use them as antinomians. But is not this bending the bow too much the other way? Why should you condemn all who do not speak just as you do? Why should you quarrel with *them* for using the phrases they like, any more than they with *you* for taking the same liberty? Or if they do quarrel with you upon that account, do not imitate the bigotry which you blame. At least allow *them* the liberty which they ought to allow *you*. And why should you be angry at an *expression?* 'Oh, it has been abused.' And what expression has not? However, the abuse may be removed, and at the same time the use remain. Above all be sure to retain the important sense which is couched under that expression. All the blessings I enjoy, all I hope for in time and in eternity, are given wholly and solely for the sake of what Christ has done and suffered for me.

I would, secondly, add a few words to you who are fond of these expressions. And permit me to ask, Do not I allow enough? What can any reasonable man desire more? I allow the whole *sense* which you contend for: that we have every blessing 'through the righteousness of God our Saviour'. I allow *you* to use whatever expressions you choose, and that a thousand times over; only guarding them against that dreadful abuse which you are as deeply concerned to prevent as I am. I myself frequently use the expression in question, 'imputed righteousness'; and often put this and the like expressions into the mouth of a whole congregation. But allow me liberty of conscience herein: allow me the right of private judgment. Allow me to use it just as often as I judge it preferable to any other expression. And be not angry with me if I cannot judge it proper to use any one expression every two minutes. *You* may if you please; but do not condemn me because I do not. Do not for this represent me as a Papist, or 'an enemy to the righteousness of Christ'. Bear with *me*, as I do with *you*; else how shall we 'fulfil the law of Christ'? Do not make tragical outcries, as though I was 'subverting the very foundations of Christianity'. Whoever does this does me much wrong: the Lord lay it not to his charge! I lay, and have done for many years, the very same foundation with you. And indeed 'other foundation can no man lay than that which is laid, even Jesus Christ.' I build inward and outward holiness thereon, as you do, even by faith. Do not therefore suffer any distaste, or unkindness, no, nor any shyness or coldness in your heart. If there were *a difference of opinion*, where is our religion if we cannot *think and let think?* What hinders but you may forgive *me* as easily as I may forgive *you*? How much more when there is only *a difference of expression*? Nay, hardly so much as that—all the dispute being only whether a particular mode of expression shall be used *more or less frequently!* Surely we must earnestly desire to contend with one another before we can make this a bone of contention! O let us not any more for such very trifles as these give our common enemies room to blaspheme! Rather let us at length cut off occasion from them that seek occasion! Let us at length (O why was it not done before?) join hearts and hands in the service of our great Master. As we have 'one Lord, one faith, one hope of our calling', let us all strengthen each other's hands in God, and with one heart and one mouth declare to all mankind, 'the Lord our righteousness'.

THE WITNESS OF THE SPIRIT
DISCOURSE II

Sermon 11 – 1767

AN INTRODUCTORY COMMENT

The following essay was written more than twenty years after the first discourse of the same title. A postscript to this sermon indicates that Wesley finished the work while in Ireland, at 'Newry, April 4, 1767'; he published it the same year. That the two sermons belong together was recognized by Wesley in the collection of his *Works* (1771), where they appear as Sermons 10 and 11. Although there is no record that either sermon was ever preached in the form published, this second publication shows that the ground and character of Christian assurance was still a central concern of his theology.

But why two discourses of this sort, on the same text, with most of the same arguments? Any answer must be circumstantial; it will illustrate Wesley's understanding of the sermon genre as a way of repeating himself with fresh and refined nuances. Discourse I is the basic statement; it seeks a middle course between 'enthusiasm' and 'rationalism' by recourse to the idea of the inner witness of the Holy Spirit. But what Wesley had intended as a moderating formulation had drawn a storm of criticism that repeated the charge of 'enthusiasm' and ignored Wesley's stress on objectivity. Moreover, as the Revival was moving on into its second generation, there were cases of real enthusiasm that lent credence to these other criticisms (e.g., by William Cudworth and James Relly).

By the mid-1760s, the time was ripe for a restatement of the doctrine of the 'twofold testimony', the idea that the Spirit's testimony is conveyed conjointly, through Scripture by divine illumination and also by the Spirit's gracious sanctifying presence. Wesley was also prepared to rehearse and refute the main objections that had been raised against this position over the controversy's course. The inference he draws from the whole discussion attempts to safeguard his notion from subjectivity by insisting that the gifts of the Spirit, including the gift of assurance, are always to be judged by reference to the fruit of the Spirit (Gal. 5:22–23). Discourse II is, therefore, more than a mere sequel; it is a significant revision of Discourse I. Thus, the two essays are designed to be read together with one eye on the arguments themselves and the other on their theological context in the ongoing Revival.

The Witness of the Spirit
Discourse II

The Spirit itself beareth witness with our spirit,
that we are the children of God.
Romans 8:16

I.1. None who believes the Scriptures to be the Word of God can doubt the *importance* of such a truth as this: a truth revealed therein not once only, not obscurely, not incidentally, but frequently, and that in express terms; but solemnly and of set purpose, as denoting one of the peculiar privileges of the children of God.

2. And it is the more necessary to explain and defend this truth, because there is a danger on the right hand and on the left. If we deny it, there is a danger lest our religion degenerate into mere formality; lest, 'having a form of godliness', we neglect if not 'deny, the power of it'. If we allow it, but do not understand what we allow, we are liable to run into all the wildness of enthusiasm. It is therefore needful in the highest degree to guard those who fear God from both these dangers by a scriptural and rational illustration and confirmation of this momentous truth.

3. It may seem something of this kind is the more needful because so little has been wrote on the subject with any clearness, unless some discourses on the wrong side of the question, which explain it quite away. And it cannot be doubted but these were occasioned, at least in great measure, by the crude, unscriptural, irrational explications of others, who 'knew not what they spake, nor whereof they affirmed'.

4. It more clearly concerns the Methodists, so called, clearly to understand, explain, and defend this doctrine, because it is one grand part of the testimony which God has given them to bear to all mankind. It is by his peculiar blessing upon them in searching the Scriptures, confirmed by the experience of his children, that this great evangelical truth has been recovered, which had been for many years well-nigh lost and forgotten.

II.1. But what is 'the witness of the Spirit'? The original word, μαρτυρία, may be rendered either (as it is in several places) 'the witness', or less ambiguously 'the testimony' or 'the record': so it is rendered in our translation, 'This is the record' (the testimony, the sum of what God testifies in all the inspired writings), 'that God hath given unto us eternal life, and this life is in his Son' (1 John 5:11). The testimony now under consideration is given by the Spirit of God to and with our spirit. He is the person testifying. What he testifies to us is 'that we are the children of God'. The immediate result of this testimony is 'the fruit of the Spirit'; namely, 'love, joy, peace; longsuffering, gentleness, goodness'. And without these the testimony itself cannot continue. For it is inevitably destroyed, not only by the commission of any outward sin, or the omission of known duty, but by giving way to any inward sin—in a word, by whatever grieves the Holy Spirit of God.

2. I observed many years ago:

> It is hard to find words in the language of men to explain the deep things of God. Indeed there are none that will adequately express what the Spirit of God works in his children. But perhaps one might say (desiring any who are taught of God to correct, soften, or strengthen the expression), by 'the testimony of the Spirit' I mean an inward impression of the soul, whereby the Spirit of God immediately and directly witnesses to my spirit that I am a child of God, that 'Jesus Christ hath loved me, and given himself for me'; that all my sins are blotted out, and I, even I, am reconciled to God (*Sermons*, Vol. 1 ['The Witness of the Spirit', I]).

3. After twenty years' farther consideration I see no cause to retract any part of this. Neither do I conceive how any of these expressions may be altered so as to make them more intelligible. I can only add, that if any of the children of God will point out any other expressions which are more clear, and more agreeable to the Word of God, I will readily lay these aside.

4. Meantime let it be observed, I do not mean hereby that the Spirit of God testifies this by any outward voice; no, nor always by an inward voice, although he may do this sometimes. Neither do I suppose that he always applies to the heart (though he often may) one or more texts of Scripture. But he so works upon the soul by his immediate influence, and by a strong though inexplicable operation, that the stormy wind and troubled waves subside, and there is a sweet calm; the heart resting as in the arms of Jesus, and the sinner being clearly satisfied that God is reconciled, that all his 'iniquities are forgiven, and his sins covered'.

5. Now what is the matter of dispute concerning this? Not whether there be a witness or testimony of the Spirit? Not whether the Spirit does testify with our spirit that we are the children of God? None can deny this without flatly contradicting the Scripture, and charging a lie upon the God of truth. Therefore that there is a testimony of the Spirit is acknowledged by all parties.

6. Neither is it questioned whether there is an *indirect* witness or testimony that we are the children of God. This is nearly, if not exactly, the same with 'the testimony of a good conscience toward God', and is the result of reason or reflection on what we feel in our own souls. Strictly speaking, it is a conclusion drawn partly from the Word of God, and partly from our own

experience. The Word of God says everyone who has the fruit of the Spirit is a child of God. Experience, or inward consciousness, tells me that I have the fruit of the Spirit. And hence I rationally conclude: therefore I am a child of God. This is likewise allowed on all hands, and so is no matter of controversy.

7. Nor do we assert that there can be any real testimony of the Spirit without the fruit of the Spirit. We assert, on the contrary, that the fruit of the Spirit immediately springs from this testimony. Not always, indeed, in the same degree, even when the testimony is first given, and much less afterwards. Neither joy nor peace are always at one stay; no, nor love; as neither is the testimony itself always equally strong and clear.

8. But the point in question is whether there be any *direct testimony* of the Spirit at all; whether there be any other testimony of the Spirit than that which arises from a consciousness of the fruit.

III.1. I believe there is, because that is the plain, natural meaning of the text, 'The Spirit itself beareth witness with our spirit, that we are the children of God.' It is manifest, here are two witnesses mentioned, who together testify the same thing—the Spirit of God, and our own spirit. The late Bishop of London, in his sermon on this text, seems astonished that anyone can doubt of this, which appears upon the very face of the words. Now 'the testimony of our own spirit', says the bishop, is one which is 'the consciousness of our own sincerity'; or, to express the same thing a little more clearly, the consciousness of the fruit of the Spirit. When our spirit is conscious of this—of love, joy, peace, long-suffering, gentleness, goodness—it easily infers from these premises that we are the children of God.

2. It is true, that great man supposes the other witness to be 'the consciousness of our own good works'. This, he affirms, is 'the testimony of God's Spirit'. But this is included in the testimony of our own spirit; yea, and in sincerity, even according to the common sense of the word. So the Apostle: 'Our rejoicing is this, the testimony of our conscience, that in simplicity and godly sincerity we have had our conversation in the world': where, it is plain, sincerity refers to our words and actions at least as much as to our inward dispositions. So that this is not another witness, but the very same that he mentioned before, the consciousness of our good works being only one branch of the consciousness of our sincerity. Consequently here is only one witness still. If therefore the text speaks of two witnesses, one of these is not the consciousness of good works, neither of our sincerity, all this being manifestly contained in 'the testimony of our own spirit'.

3. What then is the other witness? This might easily be learned, if the text itself were not sufficiently clear, from the verse immediately preceding: 'Ye have received, not the spirit of bondage, but the Spirit of adoption, whereby we cry, Abba, Father.' It follows, 'The Spirit itself beareth witness with our spirit, that

we are the children of God.'

4. This is farther explained by the parallel text, 'Because ye are sons, God hath sent forth the Spirit of his Son into your hearts, crying Abba, Father' (Gal. 4:6). Is not this something *immediate* and *direct*, not the result of reflection or argumentation? Does not this Spirit cry 'Abba, Father', in our hearts the moment it is given—antecedently to any reflection upon our sincerity; yea, to any reasoning whatsoever? And is not this the plain, natural sense of the words, which strikes anyone as soon as he hears them? All these texts, then, in their most obvious meaning, describe a direct testimony of the Spirit.

5. That 'the testimony of the Spirit of God' must, in the very nature of things, be antecedent to 'the testimony of our own spirit', may appear from this single consideration: we must be holy in heart and life before we can be conscious that we are so. But we must love God before we can be holy at all, this being the root of all holiness. Now we cannot love God till we know he loves us: 'We love him, because he first loved us.' And we cannot know his love to us till his Spirit witnesses it to our spirit. Till then we cannot believe it; we cannot say, 'The life which I now live, I live by faith in the Son of God, who loved me, and gave himself for me.'

> Then, only then we feel
> Our interest in his blood,
> And cry, with joy unspeakable,
> Thou art my Lord, my God.

Since therefore the testimony of his Spirit must precede the love of God and all holiness, of consequence it must precede our consciousness thereof.

6. And here properly comes in, to confirm this scriptural doctrine, the experience of the children of God—the experience not of two or three, not of a few, but of a great multitude which no man can number. It has been confirmed, both in this and in all ages, by 'a cloud of' living and dying 'witnesses'. It is confirmed by *your* experience and *mine*. The Spirit itself bore witness to my spirit that I was a child of God, gave me an *evidence* hereof, and I immediately cried, 'Abba, Father!' And this I did (and so did you) before I reflected on, or was conscious of, any fruit of the Spirit. It was from this testimony received that love, joy, peace, and the whole fruit of the Spirit flowed. First I heard,

> 'Thy sins are forgiven! Accepted thou art!'
> I listened, and heaven sprung up in my heart.

7. But this is confirmed, not only by the experience of the children of God—thousands of whom can declare that they never did know themselves to be in the favour of God till it was directly witnessed to them by his Spirit—but by all those who are convinced of sin, who feel the wrath of God abiding on

them. These cannot be satisfied with anything less than a direct testimony from his Spirit that he is 'merciful to their unrighteousness, and remembers their sins and iniquities no more'. Tell any of these, 'You are to know you are a child by reflecting on what he has wrought in you, on your love, joy, and peace'; and will he not immediately reply, 'By all this I know I am a child of the devil. I have no more love to God than the devil has; my carnal mind is enmity against God. I have no joy in the Holy Ghost; my soul is sorrowful even unto death. I have no peace; my heart is a troubled sea; I am all storm and tempest.' And which way can these souls possibly be comforted but by a divine testimony (not that they are good, or sincere, or conformable to the Scripture in heart and life, but) that God 'justifieth the ungodly'—him that, till the moment he is justified, is all ungodly, void of all true holiness? 'Him that worketh not', that worketh nothing that is truly good till he is conscious that he is accepted, 'not for any works of righteousness which he hath done', but by the mere free mercy of God? Wholly and solely for what the Son of God hath done and suffered for him? And can it be otherwise if 'a man is justified by faith, without the works of the law'? If so, what inward or outward goodness can he be conscious of antecedent to his justification? Nay, is not the 'having nothing to pay', that is, the being conscious that 'there dwelleth in us no good thing,' neither inward nor outward goodness, essentially, indispensably necessary before we can be 'justified freely through the redemption that is in Jesus Christ'? Was ever any man justified since his coming into the world, or can any man ever be justified till he is brought to that point,

> I give up every plea, beside
> 'Lord, I am damned—but thou hast died!'

8. Everyone therefore who denies the existence of such a testimony does, in effect, deny justification by faith. It follows that either he never experienced this, either he never was justified, or that he has forgotten (as St. Peter speaks) τοῦ καθαρισμοῦ τῶν πάλαι αὐτοῦ ἁμαρτιῶν, 'the purification from his former sins', the experience he then had himself, the manner wherein God wrought in his own soul, when his former sins were blotted out.

9. And the experience even of the children of the world here confirms that of the children of God. Many of these have a desire to please God: some of them take much pains to please him. But do they not, one and all, count it the highest absurdity for any to talk of *knowing* his sins are forgiven? Which of *them* even pretends to any such thing? And yet many of them are conscious of their own sincerity. Many of them undoubtedly have, in a degree, the testimony of their own spirit, a consciousness of their own uprightness. But this brings them no consciousness that they are forgiven, no knowledge that they are the children of God. Yea, the more sincere they are, the more uneasy they generally are for want of knowing it: plainly showing that this cannot be

known in a satisfactory manner by the bare testimony of our own spirit, without God's directly testifying that we are his children.

IV. But abundance of objections have been made to this, the chief of which it may be well to consider.

1. It is objected, first, 'Experience is not sufficient to prove a doctrine which is not founded on Scripture.' This is undoubtedly true, and it is an important truth. But it does not affect the present question, for it has been shown that this doctrine is founded on Scripture. Therefore experience is properly alleged to confirm it.

2. 'But madmen, French prophets, and enthusiasts of every kind have imagined they experienced this witness.' They have so, and perhaps not a few of them did, although they did not retain it long. But if they did not, this is no proof at all that others have not experienced it: as a madman's *imagining* himself a king does not prove that there are no *real* kings.

'Nay, many who pleaded strongly for this have utterly decried the Bible.' Perhaps so, but this was no necessary consequence: thousands plead for it who have the highest esteem for the Bible.

'Yea, but many have fatally deceived themselves hereby, and got above all conviction.'

And yet a scriptural doctrine is no worse, though men abuse it to their own destruction.

3. 'But I lay it down as an undoubted truth, the fruit of the Spirit is the witness of the Spirit.' Not undoubted; thousands doubt of, yea flatly deny it: but to let that pass, 'If this witness be sufficient there is no need of any other. But it is sufficient, unless in one of these cases: (1) The *total absence* of the fruit of the Spirit.' And this is the case when the direct witness is first given. '(2) The *not perceiving it*. But to contend for it in this case is to contend for being in the favour of God and not knowing it.' True, not knowing it at that time any otherwise than by the testimony which is given for that end. And this we do contend for: we contend that the direct witness may shine clear, even while the indirect one is under a cloud.

4. It is objected, secondly: 'the design of the witness contended for is to prove that the profession we make is genuine. But it does not prove this.' I answer, the proving this is not the design of it. It is antecedent to our making any profession at all, but that of being lost, undone, guilty, helpless sinners. It is designed to assure those to whom it is given that they are the children of God; that they are 'justified freely by his grace, through the redemption that is in Jesus Christ'. And this does not suppose that their preceding thoughts, words, and actions are conformable to the rule of the Scripture. It supposes quite the reverse, namely, that they are sinners all over, sinners both in heart and life. Were it otherwise God would 'justify the godly', and their own works

would be 'counted to them for righteousness'. And I cannot but fear that a supposition of our being justified by works is at the root of all these objections. For whoever cordially believes that God *imputes* to all that are justified 'righteousness without works', will find no difficulty in allowing the witness of his Spirit preceding the fruit of it.

5. It is objected, thirdly: 'One evangelist says, "Your heavenly Father will give the Holy Spirit to them that ask him." The other evangelist calls the same thing "good gifts", abundantly demonstrating that the Spirit's way of bearing witness is by giving good gifts.' Nay, here is nothing at all about 'bearing witness', either in one text or the other. Therefore till this demonstration is more abundantly demonstrated, I let it stand as it is.

6. It is objected, fourthly: 'The Scripture says, "The tree is known by its fruit"; "Prove all things"; "Try the spirits"; "Examine yourselves."' Most true: therefore let every man who believes he 'hath the witness in himself *try* whether it be of God. If the fruit follow, it is; otherwise, it is not. For certainly 'the tree is known by its fruit.' Hereby we *prove* if it be of God. 'But the direct witness is never referred to in the Book of God.' Not as standing alone, not as a single witness, but as connected with the other; as giving a *joint testimony*, testifying *with our spirit* that we are children of God. And who is able to prove that it is not *thus* referred to in this very Scripture: 'Examine yourselves whether ye be in the faith; prove your own selves. Know ye not your own selves that Jesus Christ is in you?' It is by no means clear that they did not know this by a *direct* as well as a *remote* witness. How is it proved that they did not know it, first, by inward consciousness, and then by love, joy, and peace?

7. 'But the testimony arising from the internal and external change is constantly referred to in the Bible.' It is so. And we constantly refer thereto to confirm the testimony of the Spirit.

'Nay, all the marks *you* have given whereby to distinguish the operations of God's Spirit from delusion refer to the change wrought in us and upon us.' This likewise is undoubtedly true.

8. It is objected, fifthly, that 'the direct witness of the Spirit does not secure us from the greatest delusions. And is that a witness fit to be trusted whose testimony cannot be depended on, that is forced to fly to something else to prove what it asserts?' I answer: to secure us from all delusion, God gives us two witnesses that we are his children. And this they testify conjointly. Therefore 'what God hath joined together, let not man put asunder.' And while they are joined we cannot be deluded: their testimony can be depended on. They are fit to be trusted in the highest degree, and need nothing else to prove what they assert.

'Nay, the direct witness only asserts, but does not prove anything.' By two witnesses shall every word be established. And when the Spirit 'witnesses with our spirit', as God designs it to do, then it fully proves that we are children of God.

9. It is objected, sixthly: 'You own the change wrought is a sufficient testimony, unless in the case of severe trials, such as that of our Saviour upon the cross. But none of us can be tried in that manner.' But you or I may be tried in such a manner, and so may any other child of God, that it will be impossible for us to keep our filial confidence in God without the direct witness of his Spirit.

10. It is objected, lastly, 'The greatest contenders for it are some of the proudest and most uncharitable of men.' Perhaps some of the *hottest* contenders for it are both proud and uncharitable. But many of the *firmest* contenders for it are eminently meek and lowly in heart, and, indeed, in all other respects also,

True followers of their lamb-like Lord.

The preceding objections are the most considerable that I have heard, and I believe contain the strength of the cause. Yet I apprehend whoever calmly and impartially considers those objections and the answers together, will easily see that they do not destroy, no, nor weaken the evidence of that great truth, that the Spirit of God does *directly* as well as *indirectly* testify that we are children of God.

V.1. The sum of all is this: the testimony of the Spirit is an inward impression on the souls of believers, whereby the Spirit of God directly testifies to their spirit that they are children of God. And it is not questioned whether there is a testimony of the Spirit, but whether there is any *direct testimony*, whether there is any other than that which arises from a consciousness of the fruit of the Spirit. We believe there is: because this is the plain, natural meaning of the text, illustrated both by the preceding words and by the parallel passage in the Epistle to the Galatians; because, in the nature of the thing, the testimony must precede the fruit which springs from it, and because this plain meaning of the Word of God is confirmed by the experience of innumerable children of God; yea, and by the experience of all who are convinced of sin, who can never rest till they have a direct witness; and even of the children of the world who, not having the witness in themselves, one and all declare none can *know* his sins forgiven.

2. And whereas it is objected that experience is not sufficient to prove a doctrine unsupported by Scripture; that madmen and enthusiasts of every kind have imagined such a witness; that the design of that witness is to prove our profession genuine, which design it does not answer; that the Scripture says, 'The tree is known by its fruit,' 'Examine yourselves: . . . prove your own selves,' and meantime the direct witness is never referred to in all the Book of God; that it does not secure us from the greatest delusions; and, lastly, that the change wrought in us is a sufficient testimony, unless in such trials as

Christ alone suffered—we answer, (1) Experience is sufficient to *confirm* a doctrine which is grounded on Scripture. (2) Though many fancy they experience what they do not, this is no prejudice to real experience. (3) The design of that witness is to assure us we are children of God; and this design it does answer. (4) The true witness of the Spirit is known by its fruit—love, peace, joy—not indeed preceding, but following it. (5) It cannot be proved that the direct as well as the indirect witness is not referred to in that very text, 'Know ye not your own selves . . . that Jesus Christ is in you?' (6) The Spirit of God, 'witnessing with our spirit', does secure us from all delusion. And, lastly, we are all liable to trials wherein the testimony of our own spirit is not sufficient, wherein nothing less than the direct testimony of God's Spirit can assure us we are his children.

3. Two inferences may be drawn from the whole. The first: let none ever presume to rest in any supposed testimony of the Spirit which is separate from the fruit of it. If the Spirit of God does really testify that we are children of God, the immediate consequence will be the fruit of the Spirit, even 'love, joy, peace, long-suffering, gentleness, goodness, fidelity, meekness, temperance'. And however this fruit may be clouded for a while during the time of strong temptation, so that it does not appear to the tempted person while 'Satan is sifting him as wheat,' yet the substantial part of it remains, even under the thickest cloud. It is true, joy in the Holy Ghost may be withdrawn during the hour of trial. Yea, the soul may be 'exceeding sorrowful' while 'the hour and power of darkness' continues. But even this is generally restored with increase, and he rejoices 'with joy unspeakable and full of glory'.

4. The second inference is: let none rest in any supposed fruit of the Spirit without the witness. There may be foretastes of joy, of peace, of love—and those not delusive, but really from God—long before we have the witness in ourselves, before the Spirit of God witnesses with our spirits that we have 'redemption in the blood of Jesus, even the forgiveness of sins'. Yea, there may be a degree of long-suffering, of gentleness, of fidelity, meekness, temperance (not a shadow thereof, but a real degree, by the preventing grace of God) before we are 'accepted in the Beloved', and consequently before we have a testimony of our acceptance. But it is by no means advisable to rest here; it is at the peril of our souls if we do. If we are wise we shall be continually crying to God, until his Spirit cry in our heart, 'Abba, Father!' This is the privilege of all the children of God, and without this we can never be assured that we are his children. Without this we cannot retain a steady peace, nor avoid perplexing doubts and fears. But when we have once received this 'Spirit of adoption', that 'peace which passes all understanding', and which expels all painful doubt and fear, will 'keep our hearts and minds in Christ Jesus'. And when this has brought forth its genuine fruit, all inward and outward holiness, it is undoubtedly the will of him that calleth us to give us always what he has once given. So that

there is no need that we should ever more be deprived of either the testimony of God's Spirit or the testimony of our own, the consciousness of our walking in all righteousness and true holiness.

THE REPENTANCE OF BELIEVERS

Sermon 14 – 1767

AN INTRODUCTORY COMMENT

This sermon is a sequel to *On Sin in Believers* and builds upon its basic assumption that believers who are justified are not thereby wholly sanctified; they are therefore still sinners in need of continued repentance. At justification, the believer is delivered from the dominion of outward sin, but although the power of inward sin is broken, it is by no means destroyed. Having drawn out that point in the earlier sermon, Wesley here explains more fully the nature and consequences of repentance and belief after justification.

Repentance, at times considered to be an inward change, is here considered as 'one kind of self-knowledge—the knowing ourselves sinners, yea, guilty, helpless sinners, even though we know we are children of God' (see also 'The Way to the Kingdom'). Wesley rings the changes on the types of sin that still tend to remain in the heart of the believer, sins that a person can by no means expel through self-effort, even 'by all the grace which is given at justification'. With no such instantaneous deliverance in evidence, the believer must be content with a gradual work of God. Belief then takes on a new sense also, for through faith the repentant believer is now saved from the sin that still remains in the heart: 'By faith we receive not only mercy, but "grace to help in every time of need",' thereby 'purifying the heart and cleansing the hands'. Wesley is wont to press home three lessons: that our hearts are not wholly cleansed from sin at justification, that a conviction of our demerit after justification is necessary to a full acceptance of the atonement, and that a deep conviction of our utter helplessness teaches us 'truly to live upon Christ by faith'.

A postscript indicates that Wesley finished writing this sermon in 'Londonderry, April 24, 1767'. It was first published as a pamphlet that same year and went through two more editions before Wesley incorporated it in his collected *Works* in 1771. Like some of the other sermons included in that edition of the *Works*, this sermon was inexplicably omitted from the subsequent eight-volume collection of *Sermons* (1787–88).

The Repentance of Believers

Repent and believe the gospel.
Mark 1:15

1. It is generally supposed that repentance and faith are only the gate of religion; that they are necessary only at the beginning of our Christian course, when we are setting out in the way of the kingdom. And this may seem to be confirmed by the great Apostle, where exhorting the Hebrew Christians to 'go on to perfection' he teaches them to 'leave' these first 'principles of the doctrine of Christ: not laying again the foundation of repentance from dead works and faith toward God'; which must at least mean that they should comparatively leave these, that at first took up all their thoughts, in order to 'press forward toward the prize of the high calling of God in Christ Jesus'.

2. And this is undoubtedly true, that there is a repentance and a faith which are more especially necessary at the beginning: a repentance which is a conviction of our utter sinfulness and guiltiness and helplessness, and which precedes our receiving that kingdom of God which our Lord observes 'is within us'; and a faith whereby we receive that kingdom, even 'righteousness, and peace, and joy in the Holy Ghost'.

3. But notwithstanding this, there is also a repentance and a faith (taking the words in another sense, a sense not quite the same, nor yet entirely different) which are requisite after we have 'believed the gospel'; yea, and in every subsequent stage of our Christian course, or we cannot 'run the race which is set before us'. And this repentance and faith are full as necessary, in order to our continuance and growth in grace, as the former faith and repentance were in order to our entering into the kingdom of God.

But in what sense are we to repent and believe, after we are justified? This is an important question, and worthy of being considered with the utmost attention.

I. And first, in what sense are we to repent?

1. Repentance frequently means an inward change, a change of mind from sin to holiness. But we now speak of it in a quite different sense, as it is one kind of self-knowledge—the knowing ourselves sinners, yea, guilty, helpless sinners, even though we know we are children of God.

2. Indeed when we first know this, when we first find redemption in the blood of Jesus, when the love of God is first shed abroad in our hearts and

his kingdom set up therein, it is natural to suppose that we are no longer sinners, that all our sins are not only covered but destroyed. As we do not then feel any evil in our hearts, we readily imagine none is there. Nay, some well-meaning men have imagined this, not only at that time, but ever after; having persuaded themselves that when they were justified they were entirely sanctified. Yea, they have laid it down as a general rule, in spite of Scripture, reason, and experience. These sincerely believe and earnestly maintain that all sin is destroyed when we are justified, and that there is no sin in the heart of a believer, but that it is altogether clean from that moment. But though we readily acknowledge, 'he that believeth is born of God,' and 'he that is born of God doth not commit sin,' yet we cannot allow that he does not *feel* it within: it does not *reign*, but it does *remain*. And a conviction of the sin which *remains* in our heart is one great branch of the repentance we are now speaking of.

3. For it is seldom long before he who imagined all sin was gone feels there is still *pride* in his heart. He is convinced, both that in many respects he has thought of himself more highly than he ought to think, and that he has taken to himself the praise of something he had received, and gloried in it as though he had not received it. And yet he knows he is in the favour of God. He cannot and ought not to 'cast away his confidence'. 'The Spirit still witnesses with his spirit, that he is a child of God.'

4. Nor is it long before he feels *self-will* in his heart, even a will contrary to the will of God. A will every man must inevitably have, as long as he has an understanding. This is an essential part of human nature, indeed of the nature of every intelligent being. Our blessed Lord himself had a will as a man; otherwise he had not been a man. But his human will was invariably subject to the will of his Father. At all times, and on all occasions, even in the deepest affliction, he could say, 'Not as I will, but as thou wilt.' But this is not the case at all times, even with a true believer in Christ. He frequently finds his will more or less exalting itself against the will of God. He wills something, because it is pleasing to nature, which is not pleasing to God. And he wills (is averse from) something because it is painful to nature, which is the will of God concerning him. Indeed (suppose he continues in the faith) he fights against it with all his might. But this very thing implies that it really exists, and that he is conscious of it.

5. Now self-will, as well as pride, is a species of idolatry; and both are directly contrary to the love of God. The same observation may be made concerning *the love of the world*. But this likewise even true believers are liable to feel in themselves; and every one of them does feel it, more or less, sooner or later, in one branch or another. It is true, when he first passes from death unto life he desires nothing more but God. He can truly say, 'All my desire is unto thee,' 'and unto the remembrance of thy name.' 'Whom have I in heaven but thee? And there is none upon earth that I desire besides thee?' But it is not so

always. In process of time he will feel again (though perhaps only for a few moments) either 'the desire of the flesh, or the desire of the eye, or the pride of life'. Nay, if he does not continually watch and pray he may find *lust* reviving, yea, and thrusting sore at him that he may fall, till he has scarce any strength left in him. He may feel the assaults of *inordinate affection*, yea, a strong propensity to 'love the creature more than the Creator'—whether it be a child, a parent, an husband or wife, or 'the friend that is as his own soul'. He may feel in a thousand various ways a desire of earthly things or pleasures. In the same proportion he will forget God, not seeking his happiness in him, and consequently being a 'lover of pleasure more than a lover of God'.

6. If he does not keep himself every moment he will again feel 'the desire of the eye', the desire of gratifying his imagination with something great, or beautiful, or uncommon. In how many ways does this desire assault the soul! Perhaps with regard to the poorest trifles, such as dress, or furniture—things never designed to satisfy the appetite of an immortal spirit. Yet how natural it is for us, even after we 'have tasted of the powers of the world to come', to sink again into these foolish, low desires of things that perish in the using! How hard is it, even for those who know in whom they have believed, to conquer but one branch of the desire of the eye, curiosity; constantly to trample it under their feet, to desire nothing merely because it is new!

7. And how hard is it even for the children of God wholly to conquer 'the pride of life'! St. John seems to mean by this nearly the same with what the world terms 'the sense of honour'. This is no other than a desire of and delight in 'the honour that cometh of men'—a desire and love of praise, and (which is always joined with it) a proportionable *fear of dispraise.* Nearly allied to this is *evil shame,* the being ashamed of that wherein we ought to glory. And this is seldom divided from 'the fear of man', which brings a thousand snares upon the soul. Now where is he, even among those that seem strong in faith, who does not find in himself a degree of all these evil tempers? So that even these are but in part 'crucified to the world'; for the evil root remains in their heart.

8. And do we not feel other tempers, which are as contrary to the love of our neighbour as these are to the love of God? The love of our neighbour 'thinketh no evil'. Do not we find anything of the kind? Do we never find any *jealousies,* any evil surmisings, any groundless or unreasonable suspicions? He that is clear in these respects, let him cast the first stone at his neighbour. Who does not sometimes feel other tempers or inward motions which he knows are contrary to brotherly love? If nothing of malice, hatred, or bitterness, is there no touch of envy? Particularly toward those who enjoy some (real or supposed) good which we desire but cannot attain? Do we never find any degree of *resentment* when we are injured or affronted? Especially by those whom we peculiarly loved, and whom we had most laboured to help or oblige. Does injustice or ingratitude never excite in us any desire of *revenge*; any desire of

returning evil for evil, instead of 'overcoming evil with good'? This also shows how much is still in our heart which is contrary to the love of our neighbour.

9. *Covetousness* in every kind and degree is certainly as contrary to this as to the love of God. Whether φιλαργυρία, 'the love of money' which is too frequently 'the root of all evils', or πλεονεξία, literally, a desire of having more, or increasing in substance. And how few even of the real children of God are entirely free from both! Indeed one great man, Martin Luther, used to say he 'never had any covetousness in him (not only in his converted state, but) ever since he was born'. But if so, I would not scruple to say he was the only man born of a woman (except him that was God as well as man) who had not, who was born without it. Nay, I believe, never was anyone born of God, that lived any considerable time after, who did not feel more or less of it many times, especially in the latter sense. We may therefore set it down as an undoubted truth that *covetousness*, together with pride, and self-will, and anger, *remain* in the hearts even of them that are justified.

10. It is their experiencing this which has inclined so many serious persons to understand the latter part of the seventh chapter to the Romans, not of them that 'are under the law'—that are convinced of sin, which is undoubtedly the meaning of the Apostle—but of them that 'are under grace', that are 'justified freely, through the redemption that is in Jesus Christ'. And it is most certain they are thus far right; there does still *remain*, even in them that are justified, a 'mind' which is in some measure 'carnal' (so the Apostle tells even the believers at Corinth, 'Ye are carnal'); an heart 'bent to backsliding', still ever ready to 'depart from the living God'; a propensity to pride, self-will, anger, revenge, love of the world, yea, and all evil: a root of bitterness which, if the restraint were taken off for a moment, would instantly spring up; yea, such a depth of corruption as without clear light from God we cannot possibly conceive. And a conviction of all this sin *remaining* in their hearts is the repentance which belongs to them that are justified.

11. But we should likewise be convinced that as sin remains in our hearts, so it *cleaves* to our words and actions. Indeed it is to be feared that many of our words are more than mixed with sin, that they are sinful altogether. For such undoubtedly is all *uncharitable conversation*, all which does not spring from brotherly love, all which does not agree with that golden rule, 'What ye would that others should do to you, even so do unto them.' Of this kind is all backbiting, all talebearing, all whispering, all evil-speaking; that is, repeating the faults of absent persons—for none would have others repeat his faults when he is absent. Now how few are there, even among believers, who are in no degree guilty of this? Who steadily observe the good old rule, 'Of the dead and the absent—nothing but good.' And suppose they do, do they likewise abstain from *unprofitable conversation*? Yet all this is unquestionably sinful, and 'grieves the Holy Spirit of God'. Yea, and for 'every idle word that men shall speak

they shall give an account in the day of judgment'.

12. But let it be supposed that they continually 'watch and pray', and so do 'not enter into this temptation'; that they constantly set a watch before their mouth, and keep the door of their lips: suppose they exercise themselves herein, that *all* their 'conversation may be in grace seasoned with salt', and meet 'to minister grace to the hearers'; yet do they not daily slide into useless discourse, notwithstanding all their caution? And even when they endeavour to speak for God, are their words pure, free from unholy mixtures? Do they find nothing wrong in their very *intention?* Do they speak merely to please God, and not partly to please themselves? Is it wholly to do the will of God, and not their own will also? Or, if they begin with a single eye, do they go on 'looking unto Jesus', and talking with him all the time they are with their neighbour? When they are reproving sin do they feel no anger or unkind temper to the sinner? When they are instructing the ignorant do they not find any pride, any self-preference? When they are comforting the afflicted, or provoking one another to love and to good works, do they never perceive any inward self-commendation—'Now you have spoken well'? Or any vanity, a desire that others should think so, and esteem them on the account? In some or all of these respects how much sin *cleaves* to the best conversation even of believers! The conviction of which is another branch of the repentance which belongs to them that are justified.

13. And how much sin, if their conscience is thoroughly awake, may they find *cleaving to their actions* also? Nay, are there not many of these which, though they are such as the world would not condemn, yet cannot be commended, no, nor excused, if we judge by the Word of God? Are there not many of their actions which they themselves know are not 'to the glory of God'? Many wherein they did not even aim at this, which were not undertaken with an eye to God? And of those that were, are there not many wherein their eye is not singly fixed on God? Wherein they are doing their own will at least as much as his, and seeking to please themselves as much if not more than to please God? And while they are endeavouring to do good to their neighbour, do they not feel wrong tempers of various kinds? Hence their good actions, so called, are far from being strictly such, being polluted with such a mixture of evil! Such are their works of *mercy!* And is there not the same mixture in their works of *piety?* While they are hearing the word which is able to save their souls, do they not frequently find such thoughts as make them afraid lest it should turn to their condemnation rather than their salvation? Is it not often the same case while they are endeavouring to offer up their prayers to God, whether in public, or private? Nay, while they are engaged in the most solemn service. Even while they are at the table of the Lord, what manner of thoughts arise in them? Are not their hearts sometimes wandering to the ends of the earth, sometimes filled with such imaginations as make them fear lest all their

sacrifice should be an abomination to the Lord? So that they are more ashamed of their best duties than they were once of their worst sins.

14. Again: how many *sins of omission* are they chargeable with? We know the words of the Apostle, 'To him that knoweth to do good, and doth it not, to him it is sin.' But do they not know a thousand instances wherein they might have done good, to enemies, to strangers, to their brethren, either with regard to their bodies or their souls, and they did it not? How many omissions have they been guilty of in their duty toward God? How many opportunities of communicating, of hearing his word, of public or private prayer have they neglected? So great reason had even that holy man Archbishop Ussher, after all his labours for God, to cry out, almost with his dying breath, 'Lord, forgive me my sins of omission.'

15. But besides these outward omissions, may they not find in themselves *inward defects* without number? Defects of every kind: they have not the love, the fear, the confidence they ought to have toward God. They have not the love which is due to their neighbour, to every child of man; no, nor even that which is due to their brethren, to every child of God, whether those that are at a distance from them, or those with whom they are immediately connected. They have no holy temper in the degree they ought; they are defective in everything: in a deep consciousness of which they are ready to cry out with Mr. de Renty, 'I am a ground all overrun with thorns'; or with Job, 'I am vile'; 'I abhor myself, and repent as in dust and ashes.'

16. A conviction of their *guiltiness* is another branch of that repentance which belongs to the children of God. But this is cautiously to be understood, and in a peculiar sense. For it is certain, 'there is no condemnation for them that are in Christ Jesus', that believe in him, and in the power of that faith 'walk not after the flesh, but after the Spirit'. Yet can they no more bear the *strict justice* of God now than before they believed. This pronounces them to be still *worthy of death* on all the preceding accounts. And it would absolutely condemn them thereto, were it not for the atoning blood. Therefore, they are thoroughly convinced that they still *deserve* punishment, although it is hereby turned aside from them. But here there are extremes on one hand and on the other, and few steer clear of them. Most men strike on one or the other, either thinking themselves condemned when they are not, or thinking they *deserve* to be acquitted. Nay, the truth lies between: they still *deserve*, strictly speaking, only the damnation of hell. But what they deserve does not come upon them because they 'have an advocate with the Father'. His life and death and intercession still interpose between them and condemnation.

17. A conviction of their *utter helplessness* is yet another branch of this repentance. I mean hereby two things: (1) That they are no more able now *of themselves* to think one good thought, to form one good desire, to speak one good word, or do one good work, than before they were justified; that they

have still no kind or degree of strength *of their own*, no power either to do good or resist evil; no ability to conquer or even withstand the world, the devil, or their own evil nature. They 'can', it is certain, 'do all these things'; but it is not by *their own strength*. They have power to overcome all these enemies; 'for sin hath no dominion over' them. But it is not from nature, either in whole or in part; 'it is the *mere* gift of God.' Nor is it given all at once, as if they had a stock laid up for many years, but from moment to moment.

18. By this helplessness I mean, secondly, an absolute inability to deliver ourselves from that guiltiness or desert of punishment whereof we are still conscious; yea, and an inability to remove by all the grace we have (to say nothing of our natural powers) either the pride, self-will, love of the world, anger, and general proneness to *depart from God* which we experimentally know to *remain* in the heart, even of them that are regenerate; or the evil which, in spite of all our endeavours, *cleaves* to all our words and actions. Add to this an utter inability wholly to avoid *uncharitable* and, much more, *unprofitable conversation*. Add an inability to avoid *sins of omission*, or to supply the numberless *defects* we are convinced of, especially the want of love and other right tempers both to God and man.

19. If any man is not satisfied of this, if any believes that whoever is justified is able to remove these sins out of his heart and life, let him make the experiment. Let him try whether, by the grace he has already received, he can expel pride, self-will, or inbred sin in general. Let him try whether he can cleanse his words and actions from all mixture of evil; whether he can avoid all uncharitable and unprofitable conversation, with all sins of omission; and lastly, whether he can supply the numberless defects which he still finds in himself. Let him not be discouraged by one or two experiments, but repeat the trial again and again. And the longer he tries the more deeply will he be convinced of his utter helplessness in all these respects.

20. Indeed this is so evident a truth that well-nigh all the children of God scattered abroad, however they differ in other points, yet generally agree in this, that although we may 'by the Spirit mortify the deeds of the body', resist and conquer both outward and inward sin, although we may *weaken* our enemies day by day, yet we cannot *drive them out*. By all the grace which is given at justification we cannot extirpate them. Though we watch and pray ever so much, we cannot wholly cleanse either our hearts or hands. Most sure we cannot, till it shall please our Lord to speak to our hearts again, to 'speak the second time, "Be clean."' And then only 'the leprosy is cleansed.' Then only the evil root, the carnal mind, is destroyed, and inbred sin subsists no more. But if there be no such second change, if there be no instantaneous deliverance after justification, if there be none but a gradual work of God (that there is a gradual work none denies) then we must be content, as well as we can, to remain full of sin till death. And if so, we must remain *guilty* till death,

continually *deserving* punishment. For it is impossible the guilt or desert of punishment should be removed from us as long as all this sin remains in our heart, and cleaves to our words and actions. Nay, in rigorous justice, all we think, and speak, and act, continually increases it.

II.1. In this sense we are to *repent* after we are justified. And till we do so we can go no farther. For till we are sensible of our disease it admits of no cure. But supposing we do thus repent, then are we called to 'believe the gospel'.

2. And this also is to be understood in a peculiar sense, different from that wherein we believed in order to justification. Believe the 'glad tidings of great salvation' which God hath prepared for all people. Believe that he who is 'the brightness of his Father's glory, the express image of his person', 'is able to save unto the uttermost all that come unto God through him'. He is able to save you from all the sin that still remains in your heart. He is able to save you from all the sin that cleaves to all your words and actions. He is able to save you from sins of omission, and to supply whatever is wanting in you. It is true, 'This is impossible with man; but with [the] God-man all things are possible.' For what can be too hard for him who hath 'all power in heaven and in earth'? Indeed his bare power to do this is not a sufficient foundation for our faith that he *will* do it, that he will thus exert his power, unless he hath promised it. But this he has done: he has promised it over and over, in the strongest terms. He has given us these 'exceeding great and precious promises', both in the Old and the New Testament. So we read in the law, in the most ancient part of the oracles of God, 'The Lord thy God will circumcise thy heart, and the heart of thy seed, to love the Lord thy God with all thy heart and all thy soul' (Deut. 30:6). So in the Psalms: 'He shall redeem Israel (the Israel of God) from all his sins.' So in the Prophet: 'Then will I sprinkle clean water upon you, and ye shall be clean; from all your filthiness, and from all your idols, will I cleanse you. . . . And I will put my Spirit within you, and ye shall keep my judgments and do them. I will also save you from all your uncleannesses' (Ezek. 36:25, 27, 29). So likewise in the New Testament: 'Blessed be the Lord God of Israel; for he hath visited and redeemed his people, and hath raised up an horn of salvation for us. . . . To perform the oath which he swore to our father Abraham, that he would grant unto us that we, being delivered out of the hands of our enemies, should serve him without fear, in holiness and righteousness before him, all the days of our life' (Luke 1:68-69, 72-75).

3. You have therefore good reason to believe he is not only able but *willing* to do this—to 'cleanse you from all your filthiness of flesh and spirit', to 'save you from all your uncleannesses'. This is the thing which you now long for: this is the faith which you now particularly need, namely, that the great physician, the lover of my soul, is willing to 'make me clean'. But is he willing to do this tomorrow or today? Let him answer for himself: 'Today, if ye will

hear my voice, harden not your hearts.' If you put it off till tomorrow, you 'harden your hearts'; you refuse to 'hear his voice'. Believe therefore that he is willing to save you *today*. He is willing to save you *now*. 'Behold, now is the accepted time.' He now saith, 'Be thou clean!' Only believe; and you also will immediately find, 'All things are possible to him that believeth.'

4. Continue to believe in him 'that loved thee, and gave himself for thee', that 'bore all thy sins in his own body on the tree'; and he saveth thee from all condemnation, by his blood continually applied. Thus it is that we continue in a justified state. And when we go 'from faith to faith', when we have a faith to be cleansed from indwelling sin, to be saved from all our uncleannesses, we are likewise saved from all that *guilt*, that *desert* of punishment, which we felt before. So that then we may say, not only,

> Every moment, Lord, I *want*
> The merit of thy death:

but likewise, in the full assurance of faith,

> Every moment, Lord, I *have*
> The merit of thy death.

For by that faith in his life, death, and intercession for us, renewed from moment to moment, we are every whit clean, and there is not only now no condemnation for us, but no such desert of punishment as was before, the Lord cleansing both our hearts and lives.

5. By the same faith we feel the power of Christ every moment resting upon us, whereby alone we are what we are, whereby we are enabled to continue in spiritual life, and without which, notwithstanding all our present holiness, we should be devils the next moment. But as long as we retain our faith in him we 'draw water out of the wells of salvation'. Leaning on our Beloved, even Christ in us the hope of glory, who dwelleth in our hearts by faith, who likewise is ever interceding for us at the right hand of God, we receive help from him to think and speak and act what is acceptable in his sight. Thus does he 'prevent them that believe in all their doings, and further them with his continual help', so that all their designs, conversations, and actions are 'begun, continued, and ended in him'. Thus doth he 'cleanse the thoughts of their hearts, by the inspiration of his Holy Spirit, that they may perfectly love him, and worthily magnify his holy name'.

6. Thus it is that in the children of God repentance and faith exactly answer each other. By repentance we feel the sin remaining in our hearts, and cleaving to our words and actions. By faith we receive the power of God in Christ, purifying our hearts and cleansing our hands. By repentance we are still sensible that we deserve punishment for all our tempers and words and actions. By faith we are conscious that our advocate with the Father is continually

pleading for us, and thereby continually turning aside all condemnation and punishment from us. By repentance we have an abiding conviction that there is no help in us. By faith we receive not only mercy, but 'grace to help in *every* time of need'. Repentance disclaims the very possibility of any other help. Faith accepts all the help we stand in need of from him that hath all power in heaven and earth. Repentance says, 'Without him I can do nothing': faith says, 'I can do all things through Christ strengthening me.' Through him I cannot only overcome, but expel all the enemies of my soul. Through him I can 'love the Lord my God with all my heart, mind, soul, and strength'; yea, and walk in holiness and righteousness before him all the days of my life.

III.1. From what has been said we may easily learn the mischievousness of that opinion that we are *wholly* sanctified when we are justified; that our hearts are then cleansed from all sin. It is true we are then delivered (as was observed before) from the dominion of outward sin: and at the same time the power of inward sin is so broken that we need no longer follow or be led by it. But it is by no means true that inward sin is then totally destroyed, that the root of pride, self-will, anger, love of the world, is then taken out of the heart, or that the carnal mind and the heart bent to backsliding are entirely extirpated. And to suppose the contrary is not, as some may think, an innocent, harmless mistake. No: it does immense harm; it entirely blocks up the way to any farther change. For it is manifest, 'They that are whole do not need a physician, but they that are sick.' If therefore we think we are quite made whole already, there is no room to seek any farther healing. On this supposition it is absurd to expect a farther deliverance from sin, whether gradual or instantaneous.

2. On the contrary, a deep conviction that we are not yet whole, that our hearts are not fully purified, that there is yet in us 'a carnal mind' which is still in its nature 'enmity against God'; that a whole body of sin remains in our heart, weakened indeed, but not destroyed, shows beyond all possibility of doubt the absolute necessity of a farther change. We allow that at the very moment of justification we are 'born again': in that instant we experience that inward change from 'darkness into marvellous light'; from the image of the brute and the devil into the image of God, from the earthly, sensual, devilish mind, to the mind which was in Christ Jesus. But are we then *entirely* changed? Are we *wholly* transformed into the image of him that created us? Far from it: we still retain a depth of sin; and it is the consciousness of this which constrains us to groan for a full deliverance to him that is mighty to save. Hence it is that those believers who are not convinced of the deep corruption of their hearts, or but slightly and as it were notionally convinced, have little concern about *entire sanctification*. They may possibly hold the opinion that such a thing is to be, either at death, or some time (they know not when) before it. But they have no great uneasiness for the want of it, and no great hunger or thirst after

it. They cannot, until they know themselves better, until they repent in the sense above described, until God unveils the inbred monster's face, and shows them the real state of their souls. Then only, when they feel the burden, will they groan for deliverance from it. Then and not till then will they cry out, in the agony of their soul,

> Break off the yoke of inbred sin,
> And fully set my spirit free!
> I cannot rest till pure within,
> Till I am wholly lost in thee!

3. We may learn from hence, secondly, that a deep conviction of our *demerit* after we are accepted (which in one sense may be termed *guilt*) is absolutely necessary in order to our seeing the true value of the atoning blood; in order to our feeling that we need this as much after we are justified as ever we did before. Without this conviction we cannot but account the blood of the covenant *as a common thing*, something of which we have not now any great need, seeing all our past sins are blotted out. Yea, but if both our hearts and lives are thus unclean, there is a kind of guilt which we are contracting every moment, and which of consequence would every moment expose us to fresh condemnation, but that

> He ever lives above,
> For us to intercede,
> His all-atoning love,
> His precious blood to plead.

It is this repentance, and the faith intimately connected with it, which are expressed in those strong lines:

> I sin in every breath I draw,
> Nor do thy will, nor keep thy law
> On earth as angels do above:
> But still the Fountain open stands,
> Washes my feet, my heart, my hands,
> Till I am perfected in love.

4. We may observe, thirdly, a deep conviction of our utter *helplessness*—of our total inability to retain anything we have received, much more to deliver ourselves from the world of iniquity remaining both in our hearts and lives—teaches us truly to live upon Christ by faith, not only as our Priest, but as our King. Hereby we are brought to 'magnify him', indeed, to 'give him all the glory of his grace', to 'make him a whole Christ, an entire Saviour', and truly to 'set the crown upon his head'. These excellent words, as they have frequently been used, have little or no meaning. But they are fulfilled in a

strong and a deep sense when we thus, as it were, go out of ourselves, in order to be swallowed up in him; when we sink into nothing that he may be all in all. Then, his almighty grace having abolished 'every high thing which exalted itself against' him, every temper, and thought, and word, and work is 'brought to the obedience of Christ'.

THE GOOD STEWARD

Sermon 51 – 1768

AN INTRODUCTORY COMMENT

In its substance and theme this sermon follows as a sequel to 'The Use of Money', but its form is different and so also is its style. It is one of the very few of Wesley's sermons to the nobility, the fruit of a brief period of closer cooperation between Wesley and the Countess of Huntingdon and her circle of high-born friends at the end of the 1760s, an alliance shortly to be disrupted by the Calvinist controversies of the 1770s. 'The Use of Money' is clearly to 'plain people'. *The Good Steward* is an 'inaugural sermon' marking Wesley's somewhat unlikely appointment as Chaplain to the Countess Dowager of Buchan.

The Dowager seems to have been persuaded by Lady Huntingdon to appoint Mr. Wesley. This benefice was promptly acknowledged in a mildly stilted letter from Wesley to Lady Huntingdon on January 4, 1768. Five months later, Wesley finished writing this sermon, which he dated with a postscript, 'Edinburgh, May 14, 1768'. The following day, he preached there to a 'sufficiently crowded house, even with the rich and honourable', and one may suppose that his topic for that occasion was *The Good Steward*. He had already spoken on this same theme in 'Sermon on the Mount, VIII'. He and the well-read in his audience would have recognized the echoes here from William Law's classic description of 'the stewardship of life itself' in his *Serious Call*. The special obligations of Christian stewardship amongst 'the rich and honourable' had already been analysed in quite genteel fashion by John Chappelow, *The Right Way to be Rich*. What Wesley adds is a vivid description of 'The Last Judgment', echoing his earlier sermon, *The Great Assize*.

Wesley's style is noticeably more formal than in the generality of his sermons, his learning slightly more in evidence. Even more notable, however, are his brief excursions into speculation (e.g., the controverted question about 'the sleep of death'). The basic message is, of course, familiar from Wesley's earliest interest in holy living: all of life is from God, and our use of all its gifts and bounties are to be received gratefully and administered faithfully as 'good stewards'. This sermon was first published in Newcastle in 1768 and then inserted into Wesley's *Works* (1771).

The Good Steward

Give an account of thy stewardship;
for thou canst be no longer steward.
Luke 16:2

1. The relation which man bears to God, the creature to his Creator, is exhibited to us in the oracles of God under various representations. Considered as a sinner, a fallen creature, he is there represented as a *debtor* to his Creator. He is also frequently represented as a *servant*, which indeed is essential to him as a creature, insomuch that this appellation is given to the Son of God when in his state of humiliation: he 'took upon him the form of a servant, being made in the likeness of men'.

2. But no character more exactly agrees with the present state of man than that of a *steward*. Our blessed Lord frequently represents him as such; and there is a peculiar propriety in the representation. It is only in one particular respect, namely, as he is a sinner, that he is styled a 'debtor'; and when he is styled a 'servant' the appellation is general and indeterminate. But a'steward' is a servant of a particular kind; such a one as man is in all respects. This appellation is exactly expressive of his situation in the present world, specifying what kind of servant he is to God, and what kind of service his divine master expects from him.

It may be of use, then, to consider this point thoroughly, and to make our full improvement of it. In order to this let us, first, inquire in what respects we are now God's 'stewards'. Let us, secondly, observe that when he requires our souls of us we 'can be no longer stewards'. It will then only remain, as we may in the third place observe, to 'give an account of our stewardship'.

I.1. And, first, we are to inquire in what respects we are now God's stewards. We are now indebted to him for all we have; but although a debtor is obliged to return what he has received, yet until the time of payment comes he is at liberty to use it as he pleases. It is not so with a steward: he is not at liberty to use what is lodged in his hands as *he* pleases, but as his master pleases. He has no right to dispose of anything which is in his hands but according to the will of his lord. For he is not the proprietor of any of these things, but barely entrusted with them by another: and entrusted on this express condition, that he shall dispose of all as his master orders. Now this is exactly the case of every man with relation to God. We are not at liberty to use what he has lodged in our hands as *we* please, but as he pleases, who alone is the Possessor of heaven and earth, and the Lord of every creature. We have no right to dispose of anything we have but according to his will, seeing we are not proprietors of any of these things. They are all, as our Lord speaks, ἀλλότρια, 'belonging to another person'; nor is anything properly 'our own' in the land of our pilgrimage. We shall not receive τὰ ἴδια, 'our own things', till we come to our own country. Eternal things only are our own: with all these temporal things we are barely entrusted by another—the Disposer and Lord of all. And he entrusts us with them on this express condition, that we use them only as our Master's goods, and according to the particular directions which he has given us in his Word.

2. On this condition he hath entrusted us with souls, our bodies, our goods, and whatever other talents we have received: but in order to impress this weighty truth on our hearts it will be needful to come to particulars.

And first, God has entrusted us with our *soul*, an immortal spirit made in the image of God, together with all the powers and faculties thereof—understanding, imagination, memory; will, and a train of affections either included in it or closely dependent upon it; love and hatred, joy and sorrow, respecting present good and evil; desire and aversion, hope and fear, respecting that which is to come. All these St. Paul seems to include in two words when he says, 'The peace of God shall keep your *hearts* and *minds*.' Perhaps, indeed the latter word, νοήματα, might rather be rendered 'thoughts', provided we take that word in its most extensive sense, for every perception of the mind, whether active or passive.

3. Now of all these it is certain we are only stewards. God has entrusted us with these powers and faculties, not that we may employ them according to our own will, but according to the express orders which he has given us; although it is true that in doing his will we most effectually secure our own happiness, seeing it is herein only that we can be happy either in time or in eternity. Thus we are to use our understanding, our imagination, our memory, wholly to the glory of him that gave them. Thus our will is to be wholly given up to him, and all our affections to be regulated as he directs. We are to love and hate, to rejoice and grieve, to desire and shun, to hope and fear, according to the rule which he prescribes whose we are, and whom we are to serve in all things. Even our thoughts are not our own in this sense: they are not at our own disposal, but for every deliberate motion of our mind we are accountable to our great Master.

4. God has, secondly, entrusted us with our *bodies* (those exquisitely wrought machines, so 'fearfully and wonderfully made'), with all the powers and members thereof. He has entrusted us with the organs of *sense*, of sight, hearing, and the rest: but none of these are given us as our own, to be employed according to our own will. None of these are *lent* us in such a sense as to leave

us at liberty to use them as we please for a season. No; we have received them on these very terms, that as long as they abide with us we should employ them all in that very manner, and no other, which he appoints.

5. It is on the same terms that he has imparted to us that most excellent talent of *speech*. 'Thou has given me a tongue', says the ancient writer, 'that I may praise thee therewith.' For this purpose was it given to all the children of men, to be employed in glorifying God. Nothing therefore is more ungrateful, or more absurd, than to think or say, 'our tongues are our own.' That cannot be, unless we have created ourselves, and so are independent on the Most High. Nay, but 'it is he that hath made us, and not we ourselves.' The manifest consequence is that he is still *Lord over us*, in this as in all other respects. It follows that there is not a word of our tongue for which we are not accountable to him.

6. To him we are equally accountable for the use of our *hands* and *feet*, and all the *members* of our body. These are so many talents which are committed to our trust, until the time appointed by the Father. Until then we have the use of all these; but as stewards, not as proprietors: to the end we should 'render them, not as instruments of unrighteousness unto sin, but as instruments of righteousness unto God'.

7. God has entrusted us, thirdly, with a portion of *worldly goods*, with food to eat, raiment to put on, and a place where to lay our head, with not only the necessaries but the conveniences of life. Above all, he has committed to our charge that precious talent which contains all the rest, *money*. Indeed, it is unspeakably precious if we are 'wise and faithful stewards' of it; if we employ every part of it for such purposes as our blessed Lord has commanded us to do.

8. God has entrusted us, fourthly, with several talents which do not properly come under any of these heads: such is bodily *strength*; such are *health*, a pleasing *person*, an agreeable *address*; such are *learning* and *knowledge* in their various degrees, with all the other advantages of *education*. Such is the *influence* which we have over others, whether by their *love* and *esteem* of us, or by *power*—power to do them good or hurt, to help or hinder them in the circumstances of life. Add to these that invaluable talent of *time*, with which God entrusts us from moment to moment. Add, lastly, that on which all the rest depend, and without which they would all be curses, not blessings: namely, the *grace* of God, the power of his Holy Spirit, which alone worketh in us all that is acceptable in his sight.

II.1. In so many respects are the children of men stewards of the Lord, 'the possessor of heaven and earth'. So large a portion of his goods of various kinds hath he committed to their charge. But it is not for ever, nor indeed for any considerable time. We have this trust reposed in us only during the short, uncertain space that we sojourn here below; only so long as we remain on earth, as this fleeting breath is in our nostrils. The hour is swiftly approaching, it is just at hand, when we 'can be no longer stewards'. The moment the body 'returns to the dust as it was, and the spirit to God that gave it', we bear that character no more; the time of our stewardship is at an end. Part of those goods wherewith we were before entrusted are now come to an end; at least they are so with regard to *us*; nor are we longer entrusted with them—and that part which remains can no longer be employed or improved as it was before.

2. Part of what we were entrusted with before is at an end, at least with regard to us. What have we to do after this life with food, and raiment, and houses, and earthly possessions? The food of the dead is the dust of the earth: they are clothed only with worms and rottenness. They dwell in 'the house prepared for all flesh': their lands know them no more. All their worldly goods are delivered into other hands, and they have 'no more portion under the sun'.

3. The case is the same with regard to the *body*. The moment the spirit returns to God we are no longer stewards of this machine, which is then sown in corruption and dishonour. All the parts and members of which it was composed lie mouldering in the clay. The hands have no longer power to move; the feet have forgot their office; the flesh, the sinews, the bones are all hasting to be dissolved into common dust.

4. Here end also the talents of a mixed nature: our *strength*, our *health*, our *beauty*; our *eloquence* and *address*; our faculty of pleasing, of persuading or convincing others. Here end likewise all the *honours* we once enjoyed, all the *power* which was lodged in our hands, all the *influence* which we once had over others, either by the love or the esteem which they bore us. 'Our love, our hatred, our desire is perished': none regard how we were once affected toward them. They look upon the dead as neither able to help nor hurt them; so that 'a living dog is better than a dead lion.'

5. Perhaps a doubt may remain concerning some of the other talents wherewith we are now entrusted, whether they will cease to exist when the body returns to dust, or only cease to be improvable. Indeed there is no doubt but the kind of *speech* which we now use, by means of these bodily organs, will then be entirely at an end, when those organs are destroyed. It is certain the tongue will no more occasion any vibrations in the air; neither will the ear convey these tremulous motions to the common sensory. Even the *sonus exilis*, the low, shrill voice which the poet supposes to belong to a separate spirit, we cannot allow to have a real being; it is a mere flight of imagination. Indeed it cannot be questioned but separate spirits have some way to communicate their sentiments to each other; but what inhabitant of flesh and blood can explain that way? What we term 'speech' they cannot have. So that we can no longer be stewards of this talent when we are numbered with the dead.

6. It may likewise admit of a doubt whether our *senses* will exist when the

organs of sense are destroyed. Is it not probable that those of the lower kind will cease—the feeling, the smell, the taste—as they have a more immediate reference to the body, and are chiefly, if not wholly, intended for the preservation of it? But will not some kind of *sight* remain, although the eye be closed in death? And will there not be something in the soul equivalent to the present sense of *hearing?* Nay, is it not probable that these will not only exist in the separate state, but exist in a far greater degree, in a more eminent manner than now. When the soul, disentangled from its clay, is no longer

A dying sparkle in a cloudy place;

when it no longer

Looks through the windows of the eye and ear,

but rather is all eye, all ear, all sense, in a manner we cannot yet conceive. And have we not a clear proof of the possibility of this, of seeing without the use of the eye, and hearing without the use of the ear? Yea, and an earnest of it continually? For does not the soul see, in the clearest manner, when the eye is of no use, namely in dreams? Does she not then enjoy the faculty of hearing without any help from the ear? But however this be, certain it is that neither will our *senses,* any more than our *speech,* be entrusted to us in the manner they are now, when the body lies in the silent grave.

7. How far the *knowledge* or *learning* which we have gained by *education* will then remain, we cannot tell. Solomon indeed says, 'There is no work, nor device, nor knowledge, nor wisdom, in the grave whither thou goest.' But it is evident, these words cannot be understood in an absolute sense; for it is so far from being true that there is *no knowledge* after we have quitted the body that the doubt lies on the other side, whether there be any such thing as real knowledge till then? Whether it be not a plain, sober truth, not a mere poetical fiction, that

. . . all these shadows which for things we take,
Are but the empty dreams which in death's sleep we make—

only excepting those things which God himself has been pleased to reveal to man? I will speak for one. After having sought for truth with some diligence for half a century I am at this day hardly sure of anything but what I learn from the Bible. Nay, I positively affirm I know nothing else so certainly that I would dare to stake my salvation upon it.

So much, however, we may learn from Solomon's words, that 'there is no' *such* 'knowledge or wisdom in the grave' as will be of any use to an unhappy spirit; there is 'no device' there whereby he can now improve those talents with which he was once entrusted. For *time* is no more: the time of our trial for everlasting happiness or misery is past. *Our day,* the day of man, is over; 'the day of salvation' is ended. Nothing now remains but the day of the Lord, ushering in wide, unchangeable eternity.

8. But still our souls, being incorruptible and immortal, of a nature 'little lower than the angels' (even if we are to understand that phrase of our original nature, which may well admit of a doubt), when our bodies are mouldered into earth, will remain with all their faculties. Our *memory*, our *understanding*, will be so far from being destroyed, yea, or impaired by the dissolution of the body, that on the contrary we have reason to believe they will be inconceivably strengthened. Have we not the clearest reason to believe that they will then be wholly freed from those defects which now naturally result from the union of the soul with the corruptible body? It is highly probable that from the time these are disunited our memory will let nothing slip; yea, that it will faithfully exhibit everything to our view which was ever committed to it. It is true that the invisible world is in Scripture termed 'the land of forgetfulness'; or, as it is still more strongly expressed in the old translation, 'the land where all things are forgotten'. They are forgotten; but by whom? Not by the inhabitants of that land, but by the inhabitants of the earth. It is with regard to them that the unseen world is 'the land of forgetfulness'. All things therein are too frequently forgotten by these; but not by disembodied spirits. From the time they have put off the earthly tabernacle we can hardly think they forget anything.

9. In like manner the *understanding* will doubtless be freed from the defects that are now inseparable from it. For many ages it has been an unquestioned maxim, *humanum est errare et nescire*—'ignorance and mistake are inseparable from human nature.' But the whole of this assertion is only true with regard to living men, and holds no longer than while 'the corruptible body presses down the soul'. Ignorance indeed belongs to every finite understanding (seeing there is none beside God that knoweth all things), but not mistake. When the body is laid aside, this also is laid aside for ever.

10. What then can we say to an ingenious man who has lately made a discovery that disembodied spirits have not only no senses (not even sight or hearing), but no memory or understanding, no thought or perception, not so much as a consciousness of their own existence! That they are in a dead sleep from death to the resurrection! *Consanguineus lethi sopor* indeed! Such a sleep we may well call 'a near kinsman of death', if it be not the same thing. What can we say but that ingenious men have strange dreams; and these they sometimes mistake for realities.

11. But to return. As the soul will retain its understanding and memory, notwithstanding the dissolution of the body, so undoubtedly the *will*, including all the *affections*, will remain in its full vigour. If our love or anger, our hope or desire, perish, it is only with regard to those whom we leave behind. To them it matters not whether they were the objects of our love or hate, of our desire or aversion. But in separate spirits themselves we have no reason to

believe that any of these are extinguished. It is more probable that they work with far greater force than while the soul was clogged with flesh and blood.

12. But although all these, although both our knowledge and senses, our memory and understanding, together with our will, our love, hate, and all our affections, remain after the body is dropped off, yet in this respect they are as though they were not; we are no longer stewards of them. The things continue, but our stewardship does not; we no more act in that capacity. Even the *grace* which was formerly entrusted with us, in order to enable us to be faithful and wise stewards, is now no longer entrusted for that purpose. The days of our stewardship are ended.

III.1. It now remains that, being 'no longer stewards', we 'give an account of our stewardship'. Some have imagined, this is to be done immediately after death, as soon as we enter into the world of spirits. Nay, the Church of Rome does absolutely assert this; yea, makes it an article of faith. And thus much we may allow: the moment a soul drops the body, and stands naked before God, it cannot but know what its portion will be to all eternity. It will have full in its view either everlasting joy or everlasting torment, as it is no longer possible to be deceived in the judgment which we pass upon ourselves. But the Scripture gives us no reason to believe that God will than sit in judgment upon us. There is no passage in all the oracles of God which affirms any such thing. That which has been frequently alleged for this purpose seems rather to prove the contrary; namely, 'It is appointed for men once to die, and after this, the judgment' (Heb. 9:27). For in all reason, the word 'once' is here to be applied to judgment as well as death. So that the fair inference to be drawn from this very text is, not that there are two judgments, a particular and a general, but that we are to be judged, as well as to die, once only; not once immediately after death, and again after the general resurrection, but then only 'when the Son of Man shall come in his glory, and all his holy angels with him'. The imagination therefore of one judgment at death, and another at the end of the world, can have no place with those who make the written Word of God the whole and sole standard of their faith.

2. The time then when we are to give this account is when the 'great white throne comes down from heaven, and he that sitteth thereon, from whose face the heavens and the earth flee away, and there is found no place for them'. It is then 'the dead, small, and great,' will 'stand before God; and the books' will be 'opened'—the book of Scripture, to them who were entrusted therewith, the book of conscience to all mankind. The 'book of remembrance' likewise (to use another scriptural expression), which had been writing from the foundation of the world, will then be laid open to the view of all the children of men. Before all these, even the whole human race, before the devil and his angels, before an innumerable company of holy angels, and before God the Judge of

all; thou wilt appear without any shelter or covering, without any possibility of disguise, to give a particular account of the manner wherein thou hast employed all thy Lord's goods.

3. The Judge of all will then inquire: 'How didst thou employ thy *soul?* I entrusted thee with an immortal spirit, endowed with various powers and faculties, with understanding, imagination, memory, will, affections. I gave thee withal full and express directions how all these were to be employed. Didst thou employ thy *understanding,* as far as it was capable, according to those directions, namely, in the knowledge of thyself and me? My nature, my attributes? My works, whether of creation, of providence, or of grace? In acquainting thyself with my Word? In using every means to increase thy knowledge thereof? In meditating thereon day and night? Didst thou employ thy *memory* according to my will? In treasuring up whatever knowledge thou hadst acquired which might conduce to my glory, to thy own salvation, or the advantage of others? Didst thou store up therein, not things of no value, but whatever instruction thou hadst learned from my Word; and whatever experience thou hadst gained of my wisdom, truth, power, and mercy? Was thy *imagination* employed, not in painting vain images, much less such as nourished foolish and hurtful desires, but in representing to thee whatever would profit thy soul, and awaken thy pursuit of wisdom and holiness? Didst thou follow my directions with regard to thy *will?* Was it wholly given up to me? Was it swallowed up in mine, so as never to oppose, but always run parallel with it? Were thy *affections* placed and regulated in such a manner as I appointed in my Word? Didst thou give me thy heart? Didst thou not love the world, neither the things of the world? Was I the object of thy love? Was all thy desire unto me, and unto the remembrance of my name? Was I the joy of thy heart, the delight of thy soul, the chief among ten thousand? Didst thou sorrow for nothing but what grieved my spirit? Didst thou fear and hate nothing but sin? Did the whole stream of thy affections flow back to the ocean from whence they came? Were thy *thoughts* employed according to my will? Not in ranging to the ends of the earth, not on folly, or sin; but on "whatsoever things were pure, whatsoever things were holy", on whatsoever was conducive to my "glory", and to "peace and goodwill among men"?'

4. Thy Lord will then inquire, 'How didst thou employ the *body* wherewith I entrusted thee? I gave thee a *tongue* to praise me therewith. Didst thou use it to the end for which it was given? Didst thou employ it, not in evil-speaking or idle-speaking, not in uncharitable or unprofitable conversation; but in such as was good, as was necessary or useful, either to thyself or others? Such as always tended, directly or indirectly, to "minister grace to the hearers"? I gave thee, together with thy other senses, those grand avenues of knowledge, *sight,* and *hearing.* Were these employed to those excellent purposes for which they were bestowed upon thee? In bringing thee in more and more instruction in

righteousness and true holiness? I gave thee hands and feet and various *members* wherewith to perform the works which were prepared for thee. Were they employed, not in doing "the will of the flesh", of thy evil nature, or "the will of the mind", the things to which thy reason or fancy led thee, but "the will of him that sent" thee into the world, merely to work out thy own salvation? Didst thou present all thy members, not to sin, as instruments of unrighteousness, but to me alone, through the Son of my love, "as instruments of righteousness"?'

5. The Lord of all will next inquire, 'How didst thou employ the *worldly goods* which I lodged in thy hands? Didst thou use thy food, not so as to seek or place thy happiness therein, but so as to preserve thy body in health, in strength and vigour, a fit instrument for the soul? Didst thou use apparel, not to nourish pride or vanity, much less to tempt others to sin, but conveniently and decently to defend thyself from the injuries of the weather? Didst thou prepare and use thy house and all other conveniences with a single eye to my glory? In every point seeking not thy own honour, but mine; studying to please, not thyself, but me? Once more: in what manner didst thou employ that comprehensive talent, *money*? Not in gratifying the desire of the flesh, the desire of the eye, or the pride of life? Not squandering it away in vain expenses, the same as throwing it into the sea? Not hoarding it up to leave behind thee, the same as burying it in the earth? But first supplying thy own reasonable wants, together with those of thy family; then restoring the remainder to me, through the poor, whom I had appointed to receive it; looking upon thyself as only one of that number of poor whose wants were to be supplied out of that part of my substance which I had placed in thy hands for this purpose; leaving thee the right of being supplied first, and the blessedness of giving rather than receiving? Wast thou accordingly a general benefactor to mankind? Feeding the hungry, clothing the naked, comforting the sick, assisting the stranger, relieving the afflicted according to their various necessities? Wast thou eyes to the blind, and feet to the lame? A father to the fatherless, and an husband to the widow? And didst thou labour to improve all outward works of mercy, as means of saving souls from death?'

6. Thy Lord will farther inquire: 'Hast thou been a wise and faithful steward with regard to the talents of a mixed nature which I lent thee? Didst thou employ thy health and strength, not in folly or sin, not in pleasures which perished in the using, "not in making provision for the flesh, to fulfil the desires thereof", but in a vigorous pursuit of that better part which none could take away from thee? Didst thou employ whatever was pleasing in thy person or address, whatever advantages thou hadst by education, whatever share of learning, whatever knowledge of things or men was committed thee, for the promoting of virtue in the world, for the enlargement of my kingdom? Didst thou employ whatever share of power thou hadst, whatever influence over

others, by the love or esteem of thee which they had conceived, for the increase of their wisdom and holiness? Didst thou employ that inestimable talent of time with wariness and circumspection, as duly weighing the value of every moment, and knowing that all were numbered in eternity? Above all, wast thou a good steward of my grace, preventing, accompanying, and following thee? Didst thou duly observe and carefully improve all the influences of my Spirit? Every good desire? Every measure of light? All his sharp or gentle reproofs? How didst thou profit by "the spirit of bondage and fear" which was previous to "the Spirit of adoption"? And when thou wast made a partaker of this Spirit, "crying in thy heart, Abba, Father", didst thou stand fast in the glorious liberty wherewith I made thee free? Didst thou from thenceforth present thy soul and body, all thy thoughts, thy words, and actions, in one flame of love, as an holy sacrifice, glorifying me with thy body and thy spirit? Then "well done, good and faithful servant! Enter thou into the joy of thy Lord!"' And what will remain either to the faithful or unfaithful steward? Nothing but the execution of that sentence which has been passed by the righteous Judge; fixing thee in a state which admits of no change, through everlasting ages. It remains only that thou be rewarded to all eternity according to thy works.

IV.1. From these plain considerations we may learn, first, how important is this short, uncertain day of life! How precious, above all utterance, above all conception, in every portion of it!

> The least of these a serious care demands;
> For though they are little, they are golden sands!

How deeply does it concern every child of man to let none of these run to waste; but to improve them all to the noblest purposes as long as the breath of God is in his nostrils!

2. We learn from hence, secondly, that there is no employment of our time, no action or conversation, that is purely *indifferent*. All is good or bad, because all our time, as everything we have, is *not our own*. All these are, as our Lord speaks, τὰ ἀλλότρια, the property of another—of God, our Creator. Now these either are or are not employed according to his will. If they are so employed, all is good; if they are not, all is evil. Again: it is his will that we should continually grow in grace and in the living knowledge of our Lord Jesus Christ. Consequently every thought, word, and work whereby this knowledge is increased, whereby we grow in grace, is good; and every one whereby this knowledge is not increased is truly and properly evil.

3. We learn from hence, thirdly, that there are no works of supererogation, that we can never do more than our duty; seeing all we have is not our own, but God's, all we can do is due to him. We have not received this or that, or

many things only, but everything from him: therefore everything is his due. He that gives us all must needs have a right to all. So that if we pay him anything less than all we cannot be 'faithful stewards'. And considering 'every man shall receive his own reward, according to his own labour,' we cannot be 'wise stewards' unless we labour to the uttermost of our power; not leaving anything undone which we possibly can do, but putting forth all our strength.

4. Brethren, 'Who is an understanding man and endued with knowledge among you? Let him show the wisdom from above by walking suitably to his character. If he so account of himself as a steward of the manifold gifts of God, let him see that all his thoughts, and words, and works be agreeable to the post God has assigned him. It is no small thing to lay out for God all which you have received from God. It required all your wisdom, all your resolution, all your patience and constancy; for more than ever you had by nature, but not more than you may have by grace. For his grace is sufficient for you, and 'all things', you know, 'are possible to him that believeth.' By faith, then, 'put on the Lord Jesus Christ'; 'put on the whole armour of God,' and you shall be enabled to glorify him in all your words and works, yea, to bring every thought into captivity to the obedience of Christ.

SPIRITUAL WORSHIP

Sermon 77 – 1780

AN INTRODUCTORY COMMENT

The theme of this sermon is the very fundament of all Wesley's theology: the valid worship of the one true God incarnate in the Son. In the sequence of Wesley's collected sermons, this sermon is followed by one on the folly of 'spiritual idolatry', which is to say, any other focus of human devotion than God in Christ. Together, they add up to a single essay in a Christocentric doctrine of spirituality.

'Spiritual Worship' was published without title in the *Arminian Magazine* (1781); a postscript dates it as 'London, Dec. 22, 1780'. This period, of course, would have been in the still tense aftermath of the tragic Gordon Riots of the previous June. Wesley had been absent from London at the time of the riots, but his sympathies with Gordon and the Protestant Association are hard to reconcile with his repeated disavowals of any intention to persecute Catholics, since there is no denying that the riots themselves were savagely anti-Catholic.

The sermon itself, however, is a sermonic essay in theology proper: the reality of God in trinitarian terms, 'the essence of true religion' understood as 'our happy knowledge of God', with knowledge being defined less as acquaintance than as communion. Although the sermon is formed around the questions, 'How is he the true God?' and 'How is he eternal life?' the concluding inferences all focus on Wesley's characteristic theme of 'happiness'.

There is in this essay a special stress on divine prevenience and many an echo from his earlier Oxford sermon, 'The Circumcision of the Heart'. In addition, Wesley's discussion of God as Creator, Preserver, Author, Redeemer, Governor, and End of all things leads to a treatment of the 'threefold circle of divine providence', an idea derived from Thomas Crane and developed more fully by Wesley in his sermon 'On Divine Providence'.

The present title was supplied for the sermon's republication in volume six of the eight-volume collected *Sermons* (1788). There is no record of any other editions during Wesley's lifetime.

Spiritual Worship

This is the true God, and eternal life.
1 John 5:20

1. In this epistle St. John speaks, not to any particular church, but to all the Christians of that age; although more especially to them among whom he then resided. And in them he speaks to the whole Christian church in all succeeding ages.

2. In this letter, or rather tract (for he was present with those to whom it was more immediately directed, probably being not able to preach to them any longer, because of his extreme old age) he does not treat directly of faith, which St. Paul had done; neither of inward and outward holiness, concerning which both St. Paul, St. James, and St. Peter had spoken; but of the foundation of all, the happy and holy communion which the faithful have with God the Father, Son, and Holy Ghost.

3. In the preface he describes the authority by which he wrote and spoke, and expressly points out the design of his present writing (1 John 1:1–4). To the preface exactly answers the conclusion of the Epistle, more largely explaining the same design, and recapitulating the marks of our communion with God, by 'we know', thrice repeated (1 John 5:18–20).

4. The tract itself treats,

First, severally, of communion with the Father, chapter one, verses 5–10; of communion with the Son, chapters two and three; of communion with the Spirit, chapter four.

Secondly, conjointly, of the testimony of the Father, Son, and Holy Ghost, on which faith in Christ, the being born of God, love to God and his children, the keeping his commandments, and victory over the world, are founded, chapter five, verses 1–12.

5. The recapitulation begins, chapter five, verse 18: 'We know that he who is born of God', who sees and loves God, 'sinneth not,' so long as this loving faith abideth in him. 'We know that we are of God', children of God, by the witness and the fruit of the Spirit; 'and the whole world', all who have not the Spirit, 'lieth in the wicked one.' They are, and live, and dwell in him, as the children of God do in the Holy One. 'We know that the Son of God is come; and hath given us a' spiritual 'understanding, that we may know the true one', the faithful and true witness. 'And we are in the true one', as branches in the vine. 'This is the true God, and eternal life.'

In considering these important words we may inquire,
First, how is he the true God?
Secondly, how is he eternal life?
I shall then, in the third place, add a few inferences.

I.[1.] And first we may inquire, how is he the true God? He is 'God over all, blessed for ever'. 'He was with God', with God the Father, 'from the beginning', from eternity, 'and was God.' 'He and the Father are one'; and consequently he 'thought it not robbery to be equal with God'. Accordingly the inspired writers give him all the titles of the most high God. They call him over and over by the incommunicable name, Jehovah, never given to any creature. They ascribe to him all the attributes and all the works of God. So that we need not scruple to pronounce him God of God, Light of Light, very God of very God: in glory equal with the Father, in majesty coeternal.

2. He is 'the true God', the only Cause, the sole Creator of all things. 'By him', saith the Apostle Paul, 'were created all things that are in heaven, and that are on earth'—yea, earth and heaven themselves; but the inhabitants are named, because more noble than the house—'visible and invisible'. The several species of which are subjoined: 'Whether they be thrones, or dominions, or principalities, or powers.' So St. John, 'All things were made by him, and without him was not anything made that was made.' And accordingly St. Paul applies to him those strong words of the Psalmist, 'Thou, Lord, in the beginning hast laid the foundation of the earth, and the heavens are the work of thy hands.'

3. And as 'the true God' he is also the *Supporter* of all the things that he hath made. He 'beareth', upholdeth, sustaineth, 'all' created 'things by the word of his power', by the same powerful word which brought them out of nothing. As this was absolutely necessary for the beginning of their existence, it is equally so for the continuance of it: were his almighty influence withdrawn they could not subsist a moment longer. Hold up a stone in the air; the moment you withdraw your hand it naturally falls to the ground. In like manner, were he to withdraw his hand for a moment the creation would fall into nothing.

4. As 'the true God' he is likewise the *Preserver* of all things. He not only keeps them in being, but preserves them in that degree of well-being which is suitable to their several natures. He preserves them in their several relations, connections, and dependences, so as to compose one system of beings, to form one entire universe, according to the counsel of his will. How strongly and beautifully is this expressed! Τὰ πάντα ἐν αὐτῷ, συνέστηκεν—'By him all things consist'; or, more literally, 'By and in him are all things compacted into one system.' He is not only the support but also the cement of the whole universe.

5. I would particularly remark (what perhaps has not been sufficiently

observed) that he is the true '*Author* of all' the *motion* that is in the universe. To spirits, indeed, he has given a small degree of self-moving power, but not to matter. All matter, of whatever kind it be, is absolutely and totally inert. It does not, cannot in any case move itself; and whenever any part of it seems to move it is in reality moved by something else. See that log which, vulgarly speaking, *moves* on the sea! It is in reality *moved* by the water. The water is moved by the wind, that is, a current of air. And the air itself owes all its motion to the ethereal fire, a particle of which is attached to every particle of it. Deprive it of that fire and it moves no longer: it is fixed; it is as inert as sand. Remove fluidity (owing to the ethereal fire intermixed with it) from water, and it has no more motion than the log. Impact fire into iron by hammering it when red hot, and it has no more motion than fixed air, or frozen water. But when it is unfixed, when it is in its most active state, what gives motion to fire? The very heathen will tell you. It is,

Magnam mens agitans molem, et vasto se corpore miscens.[*]

6. To pursue this a little farther: we say the moon moves round the earth, the earth and the other planets move round the sun, the sun moves round its own axis. But these are only vulgar expressions. For if we speak the truth of [them], neither the sun, moon, nor stars *move*. None of these move themselves. They are all *moved* every moment by the almighty hand that made them.

'Yes', says Sir Isaac, 'the sun, moon, and all the heavenly bodies do move, do gravitate toward each other.' Gravitate! What is that? 'Why, they all *attract* each other, in proportion to the quantity of matter they contain.' 'Nonsense all over', says Mr. Hutchinson, 'Jargon! self-contradiction! Can anything *act, where it is not?* No, they are continually *impelled* toward each other.' Impelled, by what? 'By the subtle matter, the ether, or electric fire.' But remember! Be it ever so subtle, it is matter still. Consequently it is as inert in itself as either sand or marble. It cannot therefore move itself; but probably it is the first material mover, the main spring whereby the Creator and Preserver of all things is pleased to move the universe.

7. 'The true God' is also the *Redeemer* of all the children of men. It pleased the Father to 'lay upon him the iniquities of us all', that by the one oblation of himself once offered, when he tasted death for every man, he might make a full and sufficient sacrifice, oblation, and satisfaction for the sins of the whole world.

8. Again: the true God is the *Governor* of all things; 'his kingdom ruleth over all.' 'The government' rests 'upon his shoulder', throughout all ages. He is the Lord and Disposer of the whole creation, and every part of it. And in how astonishing a manner does he govern the world! How far are his ways

* [Cf. Virgil, *Aeneid*, vi.726–27: 'The all-informing soul that fills, pervades, and actuates the whole.']

above human thought! How little do we know of his methods of government! Only this we know, *Ita praesides singulis sicut universis, et universis sicut singulis!*—thou presidest over each creature as if it were the universe, and over the universe as over each individual creature. Dwell a little upon this sentiment. What a glorious mystery does it contain! It is paraphrased in the words recited above.

> Father, how wide thy glories shine!
> Lord of the universe—and mine:
> Thy goodness watches o'er the whole,
> As all the world were but one soul:
> Yet keeps my ev'ry sacred hair,
> As I remained thy single care!

9. And yet there is a difference, as was said before, in his providential government over the children of men. A pious writer observes, there is a threefold circle of divine providence. The *outermost circle* includes all the sons of men—heathens, Mahometans, Jews, and Christians. He causeth his sun to rise upon all. He giveth them rain and fruitful seasons. He pours ten thousand benefits upon them, and fills their hearts with food and gladness. With an *interior circle* he encompasses the whole visible Christian church, all that name the name of Christ. He has an additional regard to these, and a nearer attention to their welfare. But the *innermost circle* of his providence encloses only the invisible church of Christ—all real Christians, wherever dispersed in all corners of the earth; all that worship God (whatever denomination they are of) in spirit and in truth. He keeps these as the apple of an eye: he hides them under the shadow of his wings. And it is to these in particular that our Lord says, 'Even the hairs of your head are all numbered.'

10. Lastly, being the true God he is the *End* of all things, according to that solemn declaration of the Apostle: 'Of him, and through him, and to him, are all things' (Rom. 11:36)—*of him* as the Creator; *through him* as the Sustainer and Preserver; and *to him* as the ultimate End of all.

II. In all these senses Jesus Christ is 'the true God'. But how is he 'eternal life'?

1. The thing directly intended in this expression is not that he *will be* eternal life—although this is a great and important truth, and never to be forgotten. 'He is the author of eternal salvation to all them that obey him.' He is the purchaser of that 'crown of life' which will be given to all that are 'faithful unto death'. And he will be the soul of all their joys to all the saints in glory.

The flame of angelical love
Is kindled at Jesus's face;
And all the enjoyment above
Consists in the rapturous gaze!

2. The thing directly intended is not that he is the resurrection; although this also is true, according to his own declaration, 'I am the resurrection and the life': agreeable to which are St. Paul's words, 'As in Adam all died, even so in Christ shall all be made alive.' So that we may well say, 'Blessed be the God and Father of our Lord Jesus Christ, who hath begotten us again unto a lively hope by the resurrection of Christ from the dead, to an inheritance incorruptible and undefiled, and that fadeth not away.'

3. But waiving what he *will be* hereafter, we are here called to consider what he *is now*. He is now the life of everything that lives in any kind or degree. He is the source of the lowest species of life, that of *vegetables*; as being the source of all the motion on which vegetation depends. He is the fountain of the life of *animals*, the power by which the heart beats, and the circulating juices flow. He is the fountain of all the life which man possesses in common with other animals. And if we distinguish the *rational* from the animal life, he is the source of this also.

4. But how infinitely short does all this fall of the life which is here directly intended! And of which the Apostle speaks so explicitly in the preceding verses: 'This is the testimony, that God *hath* given us eternal life; and this life is in his Son. He that hath the Son *hath* life' (the eternal life here spoken of), 'and he that hath not the Son of God, hath not this life' (1 John 5:11, 12). As if he had said, 'This is' the sum of 'the testimony which God hath' testified 'of his Son, that God *hath* given us', not only a title to but the real beginning of 'eternal life. And this life is' purchased by, and treasured up 'in his Son', who has all the springs and the fullness of it in himself, to communicate to his body, the church.

5. This eternal life then commences when it pleases the Father to reveal his Son in our hearts; when we first know Christ, being enabled to 'call him Lord by the Holy Ghost'; when we can testify, our conscience bearing us witness in the Holy Ghost, 'the life which I now live, I live by faith in the Son of God, who loved me, and gave himself for me.' And then it is that happiness begins—happiness real, solid, substantial. Then it is that heaven is opened in the soul, that the proper, heavenly state commences, while the love of God, as loving us, is shed abroad in the heart, instantly producing love to all mankind: general, pure benevolence, together with its genuine fruits, lowliness, meekness, patience, contentedness in every state; an entire, clear, full acquiescence in the whole will of God, enabling us to 'rejoice evermore, and in everything to give thanks'.

6. As our knowledge and our love of him increase by the same degrees, and

in the same proportion, the kingdom of an inward heaven must necessarily increase also; while we 'grow up in all things into him who is our head'. And when we are ἐν αὐτῷ πεπληρωμένοι, 'complete in him', as our translators render it—but more properly when we are 'filled with him'; when 'Christ in us, the hope of glory', is our God and our all; when he has taken the full possession of our heart; when he reigns therein, without a rival, the Lord of every motion there; when we dwell in Christ, and Christ in us, we are one with Christ, and Christ with us; then we are completely happy; then we live all 'the life that is hid with Christ in God'. Then, and not till then, we properly experience what that word meaneth, 'God is love; and whosoever dwelleth in love, dwelleth in God, and God in him.'

III. I have now only to add a few inferences from the preceding observations.

1. And we may learn from hence, first, that as there is but one God in heaven above and in the earth beneath, so there is only one happiness for created spirits, either in heaven or earth. This one God made our heart for himself; and it cannot rest till it resteth in him. It is true that while we are in the vigour of youth and health; while our blood dances in our veins; while the world smiles upon us and we have all the conveniences, yea, and superfluities of life—we frequently have pleasing dreams and enjoy a kind of happiness. But it cannot continue; it flies away like a shadow: and even while it lasts it is not solid or substantial; it does not satisfy the soul. We still pant after something else, something which we have not. Give a man everything that this world can give, still, as Horace observed near two thousand years ago,

*Curtae nescio quid semper abest rei.**

Still

Amidst our plenty something still
To me, to thee, to him is wanting!

That *something* is neither more nor less than the knowledge and love of God—without which no spirit can be happy either in heaven or earth.

2. Permit me to cite my own experience in confirmation of this. I distinctly remember that even in my childhood, even when I was at school, I have often said: 'They say the life of a schoolboy is the happiest in the world, but I am sure I am not happy. For I always want something which I have not; therefore I am not content, and so cannot be happy.' When I had lived a few years longer, being in the vigour of youth, a stranger to pain and sickness, and particularly to lowness of spirits (which I do not remember to have felt one quarter of an hour since I was born), having plenty of all things, in the midst

* ['. . . Something is always lacking to make one's fortune incomplete,' Horace, *Odes*, III. xxiv.64.]

of sensible and amiable friends who loved me, and I loved them; and being in the way of life which of all others suited my inclinations; still I was not happy! I wondered why I was not, and could not imagine what the reason was. The reason certainly was: I did not know God, the source of present as well as eternal happiness. What is a clear proof that I was not then happy is that, upon the coolest reflection, I knew not one week which I would have thought it worthwhile to have lived over again; taking it with every inward and outward sensation, without any variation at all.

3. But a pious man affirms, 'When I was young I was happy, though I was utterly without God in the world.' I do not believe you; though I doubt not but you believe yourself. But you are deceived, as I have been over and over. Such is the condition of human life!

> Flowerets and myrtles fragrant seem to rise;
> All is at distance fair; but near at hand,
> The gay deceit mocks the desiring eyes
> With thorns, and desert heath, and barren sand.

Look forward on any distant prospect! how beautiful does it appear: Come up to it; and the beauty vanishes away, and it is rough and disagreeable. Just so is life! But when the scene is past it resumes its former appearance; and we seriously believe that we were then very happy, though in reality we were far otherwise. For as none is now, so none ever was happy without the loving knowledge of the true God.

4. We may learn hence, secondly, that this happy knowledge of the true God is only another name for *religion*; I mean *Christian religion*, which indeed is the only one that deserves the name. Religion, as to the nature or essence of it, does not lie in this or that set of notions, vulgarly called 'faith'; nor in a round of duties, however carefully 'reformed' from error and superstition. It does not consist in any number of outward actions. No; it properly and directly consists in the knowledge and love of God, as manifested in the Son of his love, through the eternal Spirit. And this naturally leads to every heavenly temper, and to every good word and work.

5. We learn hence, thirdly, that none but a Christian is happy; none but a real, inward Christian. A glutton, a drunkard, a gamester may be 'merry'; but he cannot be happy. The beau, the belle, may eat and drink, and rise up to play; but still they feel they are not happy. Men or women may adorn their own dear persons with all the colours of the rainbow. They may dance and sing, and hurry to and fro, and flutter hither and thither. They may roll up and down in their splendid carriages and talk insipidly to each other. They may hasten from one diversion to another; but happiness is not there. They are still 'walking in a vain shadow, and disquieting themselves in vain'. One of their own poets has truly pronounced concerning the whole life of these

sons of pleasure:

> 'Tis a dull farce, and empty show:
> Powder, and pocketglass, and beau.

I cannot but observe of that fine writer that he came near the mark, and yet fell short of it. In his *Solomon* (one of the noblest poems in the English tongue) he clearly shows where happiness *is not*; that it is not to be found in natural knowledge, in power, or in the pleasures of sense or imagination. But he does not show where it is to be found. He could not, for he did not know it himself. Yet he came near it when he said,

> Restore, great Father, thy instructed son;
> And in my act may thy great will be done!

6. We learn hence, fourthly, that every Christian is happy, and that he who is not happy is not a Christian. If (as was observed above) religion is happiness, everyone that has it must be happy. This appears from the very nature of the thing; for if religion and happiness are in fact the same, it is impossible that any man can possess the former without possessing the latter also. He cannot have religion without having happiness, seeing they are utterly inseparable.

And it is equally certain, on the other hand, that he who is not happy is not a Christian; seeing if he was a real Christian he could not but be happy. But I allow an exception here in favour of those who are under violent temptation; yea, and of those who are under deep nervous disorders, which are indeed a species of insanity. The clouds and darkness which then overwhelm the soul suspend its happiness; especially if Satan is permitted to second those disorders by pouring in his fiery darts. But excepting these cases the observation will hold, and it should be well attended to: whoever is not happy, yea, happy in God, is not a Christian.

7. Are not *you* a living proof of this? Do not you still wander to and fro, seeking rest, but finding none? Pursuing happiness, but never overtaking it? And who can blame you for pursuing it? It is the very end of your being. The great Creator made nothing to be miserable, but every creature to be happy in its kind. And upon a general review of the works of his hands he pronounced them all 'very good'; which they would not have been had not every intelligent creature—yea, everyone capable of pleasure and pain—been happy in answering the end of its creation. If *you* are now unhappy, it is because you are in an unnatural state: and shall you not sigh for deliverance from it? 'The whole creation', being now 'subject to vanity', 'groaneth and travaileth in pain together.' I blame you only, or pity you, rather, for taking a wrong way to a right end: for seeking happiness where it never was and never can be found. You seek happiness in your fellow-creatures instead of your Creator. But these can no more make you happy than they can make you immortal. If you have

ears to hear, every creature cries aloud, 'Happiness is not in *me*.' All these are, in truth, 'broken cisterns, that can hold no water'. O turn unto your rest! Turn to him in whom are hid all the treasures of happiness! Turn unto him 'who giveth liberally unto all men', and he will give you 'to drink of the water of life freely'.

8. You cannot find your long sought happiness in all the *pleasures of the world.* Are they not 'deceitful upon the weights'? Are they not 'lighter than vanity itself'? How long will ye 'feed upon that which is not bread', which may *amuse*, but cannot satisfy? You cannot find it in the *religion of the world,* either in opinions or a mere round of outward duties. Vain labour! Is not 'God a spirit'? And therefore to be 'worshipped in spirit and in truth'? In this alone can you find the happiness you seek–in the union of your spirit with the Father of spirits; in the knowledge and love of him who is the fountain of happiness, sufficient for all the souls he has made.

9. But where is he to be found? Shall we 'go up into heaven' or 'down into hell' to seek him? Shall we 'take the wings of the morning' and search for him 'in the uttermost parts of the sea'? Nay,

Quod petis, hic est!

What a strange word to fall from the pen of a heathen–'What you seek is here!' He is 'about your bed'! He is 'about your path'. He 'besets you behind and before'. He 'lays his hand upon you'. Lo! God is here! Not afar off! Now, believe and feel him near! May he now reveal himself in your heart! Know him! Love him! And you are happy.

10. Are you already happy in him? Then see that you 'hold fast' 'whereunto you have attained'! 'Watch and pray,' that you may never be 'moved from your steadfastness'. 'Look unto yourselves, that ye lose not what you have gained, but that ye receive a full reward.' In so doing, expect a continual growth in grace, in the loving knowledge of our Lord Jesus Christ. Expect that the power of the Highest shall suddenly overshadow you, that all sin may be destroyed, and nothing may remain in your heart but holiness unto the Lord. And this moment, and every moment, 'present yourselves a living sacrifice, holy, acceptable to God,' and 'glorify him with your body, and with your spirit, which are God's.'

THE END OF CHRIST'S COMING

Sermon 62 – 1781

AN INTRODUCTORY COMMENT

This sermon is yet another explanatory comment on 'the problem of evil'. Wesley describes in some detail his understanding of human freedom, reason, and will as the backdrop for a discussion of the origin of sin, 'the works of the devil', countering the suggestion that evil was part of the natural creation (as Soame Jenyns had claimed). He then considers how 'the Son of God was manifested' as a saving remedy and the manner in which those works of the devil (sin and its fruits) could be destroyed. In the end, this sermon is another reiteration of what Wesley calls 'real religion': the restoration of humanity not only to the favour but also to the image of God, through a "'faith that worketh by love" all inward and outward holiness'.

Wesley describes this theme as the heart of real religion, still overlooked by most of the Christian world even though it 'runs through the Bible from the beginning to the end, in one connected chain'. This concept of an inherent consistency in the Bible provides the basis for one of his primary guidelines for the interpretation of the Scriptures: 'the agreement of every part of it with every other is properly the analogy of *faith*'. He also takes another swipe at those who 'dream that orthodoxy, right opinion (vulgarly called "faith"), is religion'.

Wesley finished writing this sermon on January 20, 1781 (as noted by a postscript at the end) and published it without a title in the July and August issues of the *Arminian Magazine* of that same year. In the following year, he published in the *Magazine* three or four more sermons that dealt with issues related to the creation and Fall. He then gathered these sermons together and included them in volume five of his collected *Sermons* (1788).

Judging from the record of Wesley's use of 1 John 3:8 in his oral preaching, it was a staple theme; twenty-seven instances are reported, spread rather evenly over the years from 1742 to 1789. This frequency confirms the impression of Wesley's serious preoccupation, both early and late, with the problem of evil, especially moral evil.

The End of Christ's Coming

For this purpose was the Son of God manifested,
that he might destroy the works of the devil.
1 John 3:8

1. Many eminent writers, heathen as well as Christian, both in earlier and later ages, have employed their utmost labour and art in painting the beauty of virtue. And the same pains they have taken to describe, in the liveliest colours, the deformity of vice; both of vice in general, and of those particular vices which were most prevalent in their respective ages and countries. With equal care they have placed in a strong light the happiness that attends virtue and the misery which usually accompanies vice, and always follows it. And it may be acknowledged that treatises of this kind are not wholly without their use. Probably hereby some on the one hand have been stirred up to desire and follow after virtue, and some on the other hand checked in their career of vice; perhaps reclaimed from it, at least for a season. But the change effected in men by these means is seldom either deep or universal. Much less is it durable: in a little space it vanishes away as the morning cloud. Such motives are far too feeble to overcome the numberless temptations that surround us. All that can be said of the beauty and advantage of virtue and the deformity and ill effects of vice cannot resist, and much less overcome and heal, one irregular appetite or passion.

> All these fences, and their whole array,
> One cunning bosom-sin sweeps quite away.

2. There is therefore an absolute necessity, if ever we would conquer vice, or steadily persevere in the practice of virtue, to have arms of a better kind than these; otherwise we may *see* what is right, but we cannot attain it. Many of the men of reflection among the very heathens were deeply sensible of this. The language of their heart was that of Medea:

> *Video meliora proboque,*
> *Deteriora sequor.**

How exactly agreeing with the words of the Apostle (personating a man convinced of sin, but not yet conquering it): 'The good that I would I do not;

* [Ovid, *Metamorphoses*, vii.21: 'I see the better and approve of it, but I follow the worse.']

but the evil I would not, that I do.' The impotence of the human mind even the Roman philosopher could discover: 'There is in every man', says he, 'this weakness (he might have said, this sore disease) *gloriae sitis*—a thirst for glory. Nature points out the disease; but nature shows us no remedy.'

3. Nor is it strange that though they sought for a remedy, yet they found none. For they sought it where it never was and never will be found, namely, in themselves—in reason, in philosophy. Broken reeds! Bubbles! Smoke! They did not seek it in God, in whom alone it is possible to find it. In God! No; they totally disclaim this, and that in the strongest terms. For although Cicero, one of their oracles, once stumbled upon that strange truth, *Nemo unquam vir magnus sine afflatu divino fuit* ('there never was any great man who was not divinely inspired'), yet in the very same tract he contradicts himself, and totally overthrows his own assertion by asking, *Quis pro virtute aut sapientia gratias dedit Deis unquam?*—whoever returned thanks to God for his virtue or wisdom? The Roman poet is (if possible) more express still; who, after mentioning several outward blessings, honestly adds:

> *Haec satis est orare Jovem, quae donat et aufert:*
> *Det vitam, det opes: aequum, mi animum ipse parabo.*
> We ask of God, what he can give or take—
> Life, wealth: but virtuous I myself will make.

4. The best of them either sought virtue partly from God and partly from themselves; or sought it from those gods who were indeed but devils, and so not likely to make their votaries better than themselves. So dim was the light of the wisest of men till 'life and immortality were brought to light by the gospel'; till 'the Son of God was manifested, to destroy the works of the devil.'

But what are 'the works of the devil' here mentioned? How was 'the Son of God manifested' to destroy them? And how, in what manner, and by what steps, does he actually destroy them? These three very important points we may consider in their order.

I.[1.] And, first, what these works of the devil are we learn from the words preceding and following the text: 'We know that he was manifested to take away our sins' (1 John 3:5). 'Whosoever abideth in him, sinneth not: whosoever sinneth, seeth him not, neither knoweth him' (1 John 3:6). 'He that committeth sin is of the devil; for the devil sinneth from the beginning. For this purpose was the Son of God manifested, that he might destroy the works of the devil' (1 John 3:8). 'Whosoever is born of God doth not commit sin' (1 John 3:9). From the whole of this it appears that 'the works of the devil' here spoken of are sin and the fruits of sin.

2. But since the wisdom of God has now dissipated the clouds which so long covered the earth, and put an end to the childish conjectures of men

concerning these things, it may be of use to take a more distinct view of these 'works of the devil', so far as the oracles of God instruct us. It is true, the design of the Holy Spirit was to assist our faith, not gratify our curiosity. And therefore the account he has given in the first chapters of Genesis is exceeding short. Nevertheless, it is so clear that we may learn therefrom whatsoever it concerns us to know.

3. To take the matter from the beginning: 'The Lord God' (literally Jehovah, the Gods'; that is, One and Three) 'created man in his own image'—in his own *natural* image (as to his better part) that is, a spirit, as God is a spirit: endued with *understanding,* which, if not the essence, seems to be the most essential property of a spirit. And probably the human spirit, like the angelical, then discerned truth by intuition. Hence he named every creature as soon as he saw it according to its inmost nature. Yet his knowledge was limited, as he was a creature; ignorance therefore was inseparable from him. But error was not: it does not appear that he was mistaken in anything. But he was capable of mistaking, of being deceived, although not necessitated to it.

4. He was endued also with a *will* with various affections (which are only the will exerting itself various ways) that he might love, desire, and delight in that which is good; otherwise his understanding had been to no purpose. He was likewise endued with *liberty,* a power of choosing what was good, and refusing what was not so. Without this both the will and the understanding would have been utterly useless. Indeed without liberty man had been so far from being a *free agent* that he could have been no *agent* at all. For every *unfree being* is purely passive, not active in any degree. Have you a sword in your hand? Does a man stronger than you seize your hand, and force you to wound a third person? In this you are no agent, any more than the sword: the hand is as passive as the steel. So in every possible case. He that is not free is not an *agent,* but a *patient.*

5. It seems therefore that every spirit in the universe, as such, is endued with *understanding,* and in consequence with a will and with a measure of *liberty;* and that these three are inseparably united in every intelligent nature. And observe: 'liberty necessitated', or overruled, is really no liberty at all. It is a contradiction in terms. It is the same as 'unfree freedom', that is, downright nonsense.

6. It may be farther observed (and it is an important observation) that where there is no liberty there can be no moral good or evil, no virtue or vice. The fire warms us, yet it is not capable of virtue; it burns us, yet this is no vice. There is no virtue but where an intelligent being knows, loves, and chooses what is good; nor is there any vice but where such a being knows, loves, and chooses what is evil.

7. And God created man, not only in his *natural,* but likewise in his own *moral* image. He created him not only *in knowledge,* but also in righteousness

and true holiness. As his understanding was without blemish, perfect in its kind, so were all his affections. They were all set right, and duly exercised on their proper objects. And as a free agent he steadily chose whatever was good, according to the direction of his understanding. In so doing he was unspeakably happy, dwelling in God and God in him, having an uninterrupted fellowship with the Father and the Son through the eternal Spirit; and the continual testimony of his conscience that all his ways were good and acceptable to God.

8. Yet his liberty (as was observed before) necessarily included a power of choosing or refusing either good or evil. Indeed it has been doubted whether man could then choose evil, knowing it to be such. But it cannot be doubted he might mistake evil for good. He was not infallible; therefore not impeccable. And this unravels the whole difficulty of the grand question, *unde malum?* 'How came evil into the world?' It came from 'Lucifer, son of the morning': it was 'the work of the devil'. 'For the devil', saith the Apostle, 'sinneth from the beginning'; that is, was the first sinner in the universe; the author of sin; the first being who by the abuse of his liberty introduced evil into the creation.

> He, of the first,
> If not the first archangel,

was self-tempted to think too highly of himself. He freely yielded to the temptation, and gave way first to pride, then to self-will. He said, 'I will sit upon the sides of the north; I will be like the Most High.' He did not fall alone, but soon drew after him a third part of the stars of heaven; in consequence of which they lost their glory and happiness, and were driven from their former habitation.

9. 'Having great wrath', and perhaps envy at the happiness of the creatures whom God had newly created, it is not strange that he should desire and endeavour to deprive them of it. In order to this he concealed himself in the serpent, who was 'the most subtle', or intelligent, of all the brute creatures, and on that account the least liable to raise suspicion. Indeed some have (not improbably) supposed that the serpent was then endued with reason and speech. Had not Eve known he was so, would she have admitted any parley with him? Would she not have been frighted rather than 'deceived', as the Apostle observes she was? To deceive her Satan mingled truth with falsehood: 'Hath God said, ye may not eat of every tree of the garden?' And soon after persuaded her to disbelieve God, to suppose his threatening should not be fulfilled. She then lay open to the whole temptation: to 'the desire of the flesh', for the tree was 'good for food'; to 'the desire of the eyes', for it was 'pleasant to the eyes'; and to 'the pride of life', for it was 'to be desired to make one wise', and consequently honoured. So unbelief begot pride. She thought herself wiser than God, capable of finding a better way to happiness than God

had taught her. It begot self-will: she was determined to do her own will, not the will of him that made her. It begot foolish desires, and completed all by outward sin: 'she took of the fruit and did eat.'

10. She then 'gave to her husband, and he did eat'. And 'in that day' yea, that moment, he 'died'. The life of God was extinguished in his soul. The glory departed from him. He lost the whole moral image of God, righteousness and true holiness. He was unholy; he was unhappy; he was full of sin, full of guilt and tormenting fears. Being broke off from God, and looking upon him as an angry judge, 'he was afraid.' But how was his understanding darkened, to think he could 'hide himself from the presence of the Lord among the trees of the garden'! Thus was his soul utterly dead to God! And in that day his body likewise began to die; became obnoxious to weakness, sickness, pain—all preparatory to the death of the body, which naturally led to eternal death.

II. Such are 'the works of the devil', sin and its fruits, considered in their order and connection. We are in the second place to consider how 'the Son of God was manifested' in order to 'destroy' them.

1. He was manifested as the only-begotten Son of God, in glory equal with the Father, to the inhabitants of heaven, before and at the foundation of the world. These 'morning-stars sang together', all these 'sons of God shouted for joy', when they heard him pronounce, 'Let there be light; and there was light'; when he 'spread the north over the empty space', and 'stretched out the heavens like a curtain'. Indeed it was the universal belief of the ancient church that God the Father none hath seen, nor can see; that from all eternity he hath dwelt in light unapproachable; and it is only in and by the Son of his love that he hath at any time revealed himself to his creatures.

2. How the Son of God was manifested to our first parents in paradise it is not easy to determine. It is generally, and not improbably, supposed that he appeared to them in the form of a man, and conversed with them face to face. Not that I can at all believe the ingenious dream of Dr. Watts concerning 'the glorious humanity of Christ', which he supposes to have existed before the world began, and to have been endued with I know not what astonishing powers. Nay, I look upon this to be an exceeding dangerous, yea, mischievous hypothesis, as it quite excludes the force of very many Scriptures which have been hitherto thought to prove the Godhead of the Son. And I am afraid it was the grand means of turning that great man aside from the faith once delivered to the saints; that is, if he was turned aside, if that beautiful soliloquy be genuine which is printed among his posthumous works, wherein he so earnestly beseeches the Son of God not to be displeased 'because he cannot believe him to be coequal and coeternal with the Father'.

3. May we not reasonably believe it was by similar appearances that he was manifested in succeeding ages to Enoch, while he 'walked with God'; to Noah,

before and after the deluge; to Abraham, Isaac, and Jacob on various occasions; and, to mention no more, to Moses. This seems to be the natural meaning of the word: 'My servant Moses is faithful in all my house. With him will I speak mouth to mouth, even apparently, and not in dark speeches; and the similitude of Jehovah shall he behold'—namely, the Son of God.

4. But all these were only types of his grand manifestation. It was in the fullness of time (in just the middle age of the world, as a great man largely proves) that God 'brought his first-begotten into the world, made of a woman', by the power of the Highest overshadowing her. He was afterwards manifested to the shepherds; to devout Simeon; to Anna, the prophetess; and to 'all that waited for redemption in Jerusalem'.

5. When he was of due age for executing his priestly office he was manifested to Israel, 'preaching the gospel of the kingdom of God in every town and in every city'. And for a time he was glorified by all, who acknowledged that he 'spake as never man spake'; that he 'spake as one having authority', with all the wisdom of God, and the power of God. He was manifested by numberless 'signs and wonders, and mighty works which he did'; as well as by his whole life, being the only one born of a woman 'who knew no sin'; who from his birth to his death 'did all things well', doing continually 'not his own will, but the will of him that sent him'.

6. After all, 'Behold the Lamb of God, taking away the sin of the world!' This was a more glorious manifestation of himself than any he had made before. How wonderfully was he manifested to angels and men when he 'was wounded for *our* transgressions', when he 'bore all our sins in his own body on the tree'; when, having by that one oblation of himself once offered, made a full, perfect, and sufficient sacrifice, oblation, and satisfaction for the sins of the whole world, he cried out, 'It is finished; and bowed his head, and gave up the ghost.' We need but just mention those farther manifestations—his resurrection from the dead, his ascension into heaven, into the glory which he had before the world began; and his pouring out the Holy Ghost on the day of Pentecost; both of which are beautifully described in those well-known words of the Psalmist: 'He hath ascended up on high; he hath led captivity captive; he hath received gifts for men; yea, even for his enemies, that the Lord God might dwell among, or in them.'

7. 'That the Lord God might dwell in them.' This refers to a yet farther manifestation of the Son of God, even his inward manifestation of himself. When he spoke of this to his apostles, but a little before his death, one of them immediately asked, 'Lord, how is it that thou wilt manifest thyself to us, and not unto the world?' By enabling us to believe in his name. For he is then inwardly manifested to us when we are enabled to say with confidence, 'My Lord, and my God!' Then each of us can boldly say, 'The life which I now live, I live by faith in the Son of God, who loved *me* and gave himself for *me*.'

And it is by thus manifesting himself in our hearts that he effectually 'destroys the works of the devil'.

III.1. How he does this, in what manner, and by what steps he does actually destroy them, we are now to consider. And, first, as Satan began his work in Eve by tainting her with unbelief, so the Son of God begins his work in man by enabling us to believe in him. He both opens and enlightens the eyes of our understanding. Out of darkness he commands light to shine, and takes away the veil which the god of this world had spread over our hearts. And we then see, not by a chain of *reasoning*, but by a kind of *intuition*, by a direct view, that 'God was in Christ, reconciling the world to himself, not imputing to them their former trespasses,' not imputing them to *me*. In that day 'we know that we are of God,' children of God by faith, 'having redemption through the blood' of Christ, 'even the forgiveness of sins'. 'Being justified by faith, we have peace with God, through our Lord Jesus Christ': that peace which enables us in every state therewith to be content; which delivers us from all perplexing doubts, from all tormenting fears, and in particular from that 'fear of death whereby we were all our lifetime subject to bondage'.

2. At the same time the Son of God strikes at the root of that grand work of the devil, pride; causing the sinner to humble himself before the Lord, to abhor himself as it were in dust and ashes. He strikes at the root of self-will, enabling the humbled sinner to say in all things, 'Not as I will, but as thou wilt.' He destroys the love of the world, delivering them that believe in him from 'every foolish and hurtful desire'; from 'the desire of the flesh, the desire of the eyes, and the pride of life'. He saves them from seeking or expecting to find happiness in any creature. As Satan turned the heart of man from the Creator to the creature; so the Son of God turns his heart back again from the creature to the Creator. Thus it is, by manifesting himself, he destroys the works of the devil, restoring the guilty outcast from God to his favour, to pardon and peace; the sinner in whom dwelleth no good thing, to love and holiness; the burdened, miserable sinner, to joy unspeakable, to real, substantial happiness.

3. But it may be observed that the Son of God does not destroy the whole work of the devil in man, as long as he remains in this life. He does not yet destroy bodily weakness, sickness, pain, and a thousand infirmities incident to flesh and blood. He does not destroy all that weakness of understanding which is the natural consequence of the soul's dwelling in a corruptible body; so that still

Humanum est errare et nescire:

both ignorance and error belong to humanity. He entrusts us with only an exceeding small share of knowledge in our present state, lest our knowledge should interfere with our humility, and we should again affect to be as gods.

It is to remove from us all temptation to pride, and all thought of independency (which is the very thing that men in general so earnestly covet, under the name of 'liberty') that he leaves us encompassed with all these infirmities—particularly weakness of understanding—till the sentence takes place, 'Dust thou art, and unto dust thou shalt return!'

4. Then error, pain, and all bodily infirmities cease: all these are destroyed by death. And death itself, 'the last enemy' of man, shall be destroyed at the resurrection. The moment that we hear the voice of the archangel and the trump of God, 'then shall be fulfilled the saying that is written, Death is swallowed up in victory. This corruptible body shall put on incorruption; this mortal body shall put on immortality'; and the Son of God, manifested in the clouds of heaven, shall destroy this last work of the devil.

5. Here then we see in the clearest, strongest light, what is real religion: a restoration of man, by him that bruises the serpent's head, to all that the old serpent deprived him of; a restoration not only to the favour, but likewise to the image of God; implying not barely deliverance from sin but the being filled with the fullness of God. It is plain, if we attend to the preceding considerations, that nothing short of this is Christian religion. Everything else, whether negative or external, is utterly wide of the mark. But what a paradox is this! How little is it understood in the Christian world! Yea, or this enlightened age, wherein it is taken for granted, the world is wiser than ever it was from the beginning of the world. Among all our discoveries, who has discovered this? How few either among the learned or unlearned? And yet, if we believe the Bible, who can deny it? Who can doubt of it? It runs through the Bible from the beginning to the end, in one connected chain. And the agreement of every part of it with every other is properly the *analogy* of *faith*. Beware of taking anything else, or anything less than this for religion. Not anything else: do not imagine an *outward form*, a round of duties, both in public and private, is religion. Do not suppose that honesty, justice, and whatever is called 'morality' (though excellent in its place) is religion. And least of all dream that orthodoxy, right opinion (vulgarly called 'faith'), is religion. Of all religious dreams this is the vainest, which takes hay and stubble for gold tried in the fire!

6. O do not take anything less than this for the religion of Jesus Christ! Do not take part of it for the whole. What God hath joined together, put not asunder. Take no less for his religion than the 'faith that worketh by love' all inward and outward holiness. Be not content with any religion which does not imply the destruction of all the works of the devil, that is, of all sin. We know weakness of understanding, and a thousand infirmities, will remain while this corruptible body remains. But sin need not remain: this is that work of the devil, eminently so called, which the Son of God was manifested to destroy in this present life. He is able, he is willing, to destroy it now in all

that believe in him. Only be not straitened in your own bowels! Do not distrust his power or his love! Put his promise to the proof! He hath spoken: and is he not ready likewise to perform? Only 'come boldly to the throne of grace,' trusting in his mere mercy: and you shall find, 'He saveth to the uttermost all those that come to God through him!'

THE DANGER OF RICHES

Sermon 87 – 1781

AN INTRODUCTORY COMMENT

Wesley's followers accepted most of his demands for disciplined Christian living (good works as the fruit and proof of faith). Moreover, given his stress on a self-denying moral rigorism, together with the general economic expansion in the Hanoverian era, it was natural enough that more than a few Methodists moved upward on the economic scale from erstwhile poverty toward modest affluence. In such a setting Wesley's first two rules about 'the use of money' ('gaining' and 'saving') made eminently good sense. It was the third rule against surplus accumulation ('giving') that made for trouble.

Many, if not most, of the newly rich Methodists were stubbornly unconvinced that their affluence was a fatal inlet to sin. Therefore they simply ignored Wesley's insistence that they part with all but their 'necessaries and conveniences'. Moreover, their views had lately been fortified by the immense influence of Adam Smith's *Wealth of Nations* (1776). This turn of events was, for Wesley, both perplexing and frustrating. Something of this mood is suggested by the fact that the first newly-written sermon that Wesley published in the *Arminian Magazine* is this one. He had written it in the late autumn of 1780 and published it in the January and February issues of 1781, without a title. In 1788, he added the present title to the work and included it in volume seven of his collected *Sermons*.

That same year, he wrote and published yet another sermon, 'On Riches'. Then, in the very last year of his life, he wrote out yet another anguished warning on 'The Danger of Increasing Riches'. This trio of 'late sermons', in addition to his 'Sermon on the Mount, VIII', 'The Use of Money', and *The Good Steward*, along with other frequent blasts against riches in other writings, suggest an intriguing generalization: surplus accumulation leads Wesley's inventory of sins in praxis. It was, in his eyes, an offence before God and man, an urgent and dire peril to any Christian's profession and hope of salvation. This view is in clear contrast to the notion, proffered by the Puritans (but approved by others), that honestly earned wealth is a sign and measure of divine favour. What is interesting is that Wesley's economic radicalism on this point has been ignored, not only by most Methodists, but by the economic historians as well.

The Danger of Riches

They that will be rich fall into temptation and a snare,
and into many foolish and hurtful desires, which
drown men in destruction and perdition.
1 Timothy 6:9

1. How innumerable are the ill consequences which have followed from men's not knowing or not considering this great truth! And how few are there even in the Christian world that either know or duly consider it! Yea, how small is the number of those, even among real Christians, who understand and lay it to heart! Most of these too pass it very lightly over, scarce remembering there is such a text in the Bible. And many put such a construction upon it as makes it of no manner of effect. '"They that will be rich"', say they, 'that is, will be rich at all events, who will be rich right or wrong, that are resolved to carry their point, to compass this end, whatever means they use to attain it—"they fall into temptation," and into all the evils enumerated by the Apostle.' But truly if this were all the meaning of the text it might as well have been out of the Bible.

2. This is so far from being the whole meaning of the text that it is no part of its meaning. The Apostle does not here speak of gaining riches unjustly, but of quite another thing: his words are to be taken in their plain, obvious sense, without any restriction or qualification whatsoever. St. Paul does not say, 'They that will be rich *by evil means*', by theft, robbery, oppression, or extortion; they that will be rich by fraud, or dishonest art; but simply, 'they that will be rich'; these, allowing, supposing the means they use to be ever so innocent, 'fall into temptation, and a snare, and into many foolish and hurtful desires, which drown men in destruction and perdition.'

3. But who believes that? Who receives it as the truth of God? Who is deeply convinced of it? Who preaches this? Great is the company of preachers at this day, regular and irregular. But who of them all openly and explicitly preaches this strange doctrine? It is the keen observation of a great man, 'The pulpit is a fearful preacher's stronghold.' But who, even in his stronghold, has the courage to declare so unfashionable a truth? I do not remember that in threescore years I have heard one sermon preached upon this subject. And what author within the same term has declared it from the press? At least in the English tongue? I do not know one. I have neither seen nor heard of any such author. I have seen two or three who just touch upon it, but none that

treats of it professedly. I have myself frequently touched upon it in preaching, and twice in what I have published to the world: once in explaining our Lord's Sermon on the Mount, and once in the discourse on the 'mammon of unrighteousness'. But I have never yet either published or preached any sermon expressly upon the subject. It is high time I should, that I should at length speak as strongly and explicitly as I can, in order to leave a full and clear testimony behind me whenever it pleases God to call me hence.

4. O that God would give me to speak *right* and *forcible* words! And you to receive them in honest and humble hearts! Let it not be said: 'They sit before thee as my people, and they hear thy words; but they will not do them. Thou art unto them as one that hath a pleasant voice, and can play well on an instrument; for they hear thy words, but they do them not!' O that ye may 'not be forgetful hearers, but doers of the word, that ye may be blessed in your deed'! In this hope I shall endeavour:

First, to explain the Apostle's words. And,

Secondly, to apply them.

But Oh! 'Who is sufficient for these things?' Who is able to stem the general torrent? To combat all the prejudices, not only of the vulgar, but of the learned and the religious world? Yet nothing is too hard for God! Still his grace is sufficient for us. In his name, then, and by his strength I will endeavour,

I. To explain the words of the Apostle.

1. And, first, let us consider what it is to 'be rich'. What does the Apostle mean by this expression?

The preceding verse fixes the meaning of this: 'Having food and raiment' (literally 'coverings', for the word includes *lodging* as well as *clothes*) 'let us be therewith content. But they that will be rich . . . '—that is, who will have more than these, more than 'food and coverings'. It plainly follows, whatever is more than these is, in the sense of the Apostle, *riches*—whatever is above the plain necessaries or (at most) conveniences of life. Whoever has sufficient food to eat and raiment to put on, with a place where to lay his head, and something over, is *rich*.

2. Let us consider, secondly, what is implied in that expression, 'they that will be rich'. And does not this imply, first, 'they that desire to be rich', to have more than 'food and coverings'; they that seriously and deliberately desire more than food to eat and raiment to put on, and a place where to lay their head; more than the plain necessaries and conveniences of life? All, at least, who allow themselves in this desire, who see no harm in it, 'desire to be rich'.

3. And so do, secondly, all those that calmly, deliberately, and of set purpose *endeavour* after more than 'food and coverings'; that aim at and endeavour after, not only so much worldly substance as will procure them the necessaries and conveniences of life, but more than this, whether to lay it up, or lay it out

in superfluities. All these undeniably prove their 'desire to be rich' by their endeavours after it.

4. Must we not, thirdly, rank among those 'that desire to be rich' all that in fact 'lay up treasures on earth'—a thing as expressly and clearly forbidden by our Lord as either adultery or murder. It is allowed, (1) that we are to provide necessaries and conveniences for those of our own household; (2) that men in business are to lay up as much as is necessary for the carrying on of that business; (3) that we are to leave our children what will supply them with necessaries and conveniences after we have left the world; and (4) that we are to provide things honest in the sight of all men, so as to 'owe no man anything'. But to lay up any more, when this is done, is what our Lord has flatly forbidden. When it is calmly and deliberately done, it is a clear proof of our desiring to be rich. And thus to lay up money is no more consistent with good conscience than to throw it into the sea.

5. We must rank among them, fourthly, all who *possess* more of this world's goods than they use according to the will of the Donor—I should rather say of the Proprietor, for he only *lends* them to us; or, to speak more strictly, *entrusts* them to us as stewards, reserving the property of them to himself. And indeed he cannot possibly do otherwise, seeing they are the work of his hands; he is and must be the Possessor of heaven and earth. This is his inalienable right, a right he cannot divest himself of. And together with that portion of his goods which he hath lodged in our hands he has delivered to us a writing, specifying the purposes for which he has entrusted us with them. If therefore we keep more of them in our hands than is necessary for the preceding purposes, we certainly fall under the charge of 'desiring to be rich'. Over and above that we are guilty of burying our Lord's talent in the earth, and on that account are liable to be pronounced 'wicked', because 'unprofitable servants'.

6. Under this imputation of 'desiring to be rich' fall, fifthly, all 'lovers of money'. The word properly means those that *delight in money*, those that take pleasure in it, those that seek their happiness therein, that brood over their gold and silver, bills or bonds. Such was the man described by the fine Roman painter, who broke out into that natural soliloquy,

> *. . . Populus me sibilat, at mihi plaudo*
> *Ipse domi quoties nummos contemplor in arca.**

If there are any vices which are not natural to man, I should imagine this is one; as money of itself does not seem to gratify any natural desire or appetite of the human mind; and as, during an observation of sixty years, I do not remember one instance of a man given up to the love of money till he had neglected to employ this precious talent according to the will of his master.

* ['The people hiss, but at home I congratulate myself even as I gaze on the moneys in my treasure chest,' Horace, *Satires*, I.i.66–67.]

After this, sin was punished by sin, and this evil spirit was permitted to enter into him.

7. But beside this gross sort of covetousness, 'the love of money', there is a more refined species of covetousness, termed by the great Apostle, πλεονεξία, which literally means 'a desire of having more'—more than we have already. And those also come under the denomination of 'they that will be rich'. It is true that this desire, under proper restrictions, is innocent; nay, commendable. But when it exceeds the bounds (and how difficult is it not to exceed them!) then it comes under the present censure.

8. But who is able to receive these hard sayings? Who can believe that they are the great truths of God? Not many wise, not many noble, not many famed for learning; none indeed who are not taught of God. And who are they whom God teaches? Let our Lord answer: 'If any man be willing to do his will, he shall know of the doctrine whether it be of God.' Those who are otherwise minded will be so far from receiving it that they will not be able to understand it. Two as sensible men as most in England sat down together, some time since, to read over and consider that plain discourse on, 'Lay not up for yourselves treasures upon earth.' After much deep consideration one of them broke out: 'Positively, I cannot understand it. Pray, do *you* understand it, Mr. L.?' Mr. L. honestly replied: 'Indeed, not I. I cannot conceive what Mr. W[esley] means. I can make nothing at all of it.' So utterly blind is our natural understanding touching the truth of God!

9. Having explained the former part of the text, 'they that will be rich', and pointed out in the clearest manner I could the persons spoken of, I will now endeavour, God being my helper, to explain what is spoken of them: 'They fall into temptation, and a snare, and into many foolish and hurtful desires, which drown men in destruction and perdition.'

'They fall into temptation.' This seems to mean much more than simply, 'they are tempted.' They 'enter into the temptation': they fall plump down into it. The waves of it compass them about, and cover them all over. Of those who thus enter into temptation very few escape out of it. And the few that do are sorely scorched by it, though not utterly consumed. If they escape at all it is with the skin of their teeth, and with deep wounds that are not easily healed.

10. They fall, secondly, 'into a snare', the snare of the devil, which he hath purposely set in their way. I believe the Greek word properly means a gin, a steel trap, which shows no appearance of danger. But as soon as any creature touches the spring it suddenly closes, and either crushes its bones in pieces or consigns it to inevitable ruin.

11. They fall, thirdly, 'into many foolish and hurtful desires': ανοήτους, silly, senseless, fantastic; as contrary to reason, to sound understanding, as they are to religion; 'hurtful', both to body and soul, tending to weaken, yea, destroy every gracious and heavenly temper; destructive of that faith which is

of the operation of God; of that hope which is full of immortality; of love to God and to our neighbour, and of every good word and work.

12. But what desires are these? This is a most important question, and deserves the deepest consideration.

In general they may all be summed up in one—the desiring happiness out of God. This includes, directly or remotely, every foolish and hurtful desire. St. Paul expresses it by 'loving the creature more than the Creator'; and by being 'lovers of pleasure more than lovers of God'. In particular they are (to use the exact and beautiful enumeration of St. John) 'the desire of the flesh, the desire of the eyes, and the pride of life': all of which 'the desire of riches' naturally tends both to beget and to increase.

13. 'The desire of the flesh' is generally understood in far too narrow a meaning. It does not, as is commonly supposed, refer to one of the senses only, but takes in all the pleasures of sense, the gratification of any of the outward senses. It has reference to the *taste* in particular. How many thousands do we find at this day in whom the ruling principle is the desire to enlarge the pleasure of *tasting*? Perhaps they do not gratify this desire in a gross manner, so as to incur the imputation of intemperance; much less so as to violate health or impair their understanding by gluttony or drunkenness. But they live in a genteel, regular sensuality; in an elegant epicurism, which does not hurt the body, but only destroys the soul, keeping it at a distance from all true religion.

14. Experience shows that the imagination is gratified chiefly by means of the eye. Therefore 'the desire of the eyes', in its natural sense, is the desiring and seeking happiness in gratifying the imagination. Now the imagination is gratified either by grandeur, by beauty, or by novelty—chiefly by the last, for neither grand nor beautiful objects please any longer than they are new.

15. Seeking happiness in *learning*, of whatever kind, falls under 'the desire of the eyes'; whether it be in history, languages, poetry, or any branch of natural or experimental philosophy; yea, we must include the several kinds of learning, such as geometry, algebra, and metaphysics. For if our supreme delight be in any of these, we are herein gratifying 'the desire of the eyes'.

16. 'The pride of life' (whatever else that very uncommon expression ἡ ἀλαζονεία τοῦ βίου may mean) seems to imply chiefly the *desire of honour*, of the esteem, admiration, and applause of men; as nothing more directly tends both to beget and cherish pride than the honour that cometh of men. And as *riches* attract much admiration, and occasion much applause, they proportionably minister food for pride, and so may also be referred to this head.

17. *Desire of ease* is another of these foolish and hurtful desires; desire of avoiding every cross, every degree of trouble, danger, difficulty; a desire of slumbering out of life, and going to heaven (as the vulgar say) upon a feather-bed. Everyone may observe how riches first beget and then confirm and increase this desire, making men more and more soft and delicate, more

unwilling, and indeed more unable, to 'take up' their 'cross daily', to 'endure hardship as good soldiers of Jesus Christ', 'and to take the kingdom of heaven by violence'.

18. Riches, either desired or possessed, naturally lead to some or other of these foolish and hurtful desires; and by affording the means of gratifying them all, naturally tend to increase them. And there is a near connection between unholy desires and every other unholy passion and temper. We easily pass from these to pride, anger, bitterness, envy, malice, revengefulness; to an headstrong, unadvisable, unreprovable spirit–indeed to every temper that is earthly, sensual, or devilish. All these the desire or possession of riches naturally tends to create, strengthen, and increase.

19. And by so doing, in the same proportion as they prevail, they 'pierce men through with many sorrows'; sorrows from remorse, from a guilty conscience; sorrows flowing from all the evil tempers which they inspire or increase; sorrows inseparable from those desires themselves, as every unholy desire is an uneasy desire; and sorrows from the contrariety of those desires to each other, whence it is impossible to gratify them all. And in the end 'they drown' the body in pain, disease, 'destruction', and the soul in everlasting 'perdition'.

II. 1. I am, in the second place, to apply what has been said. And this is the principal point. For what avails the clearest knowledge, even of the most excellent things, even of the things of God, if it go no farther than speculation, if it be not reduced to practice? He that hath ears to hear, let him hear! And what he hears, let him instantly put in practice. O that God would give me the thing which I long for–that before I go hence and am no more seen, I may see a people wholly devoted to God, crucified to the world, and the world crucified to them! A people truly given up to God, in body, soul, and substance! How cheerfully should I then say, 'Now lettest thou thy servant depart in peace!'

2. I ask, then, in the name of God, who of *you* 'desire to be rich'? Which of *you* (ask your own hearts in the sight of God) seriously and deliberately desire (and perhaps applaud yourselves for so doing, as no small instance of your *prudence*) to have more than food to eat, and raiment to put on, and a house to cover you? Who of you desires to have more than the plain necessaries and conveniences of life? Stop! Consider! What are you doing? Evil is before you! Will you rush upon the point of a sword? By the grace of God, turn and live!

3. By the same authority I ask, who of you are *endeavouring* to be rich? To procure for yourselves more than the plain necessaries and conveniences of life? Lay, each of you, your hand to your heart, and seriously inquire, Am I of that number? Am I labouring, not only for what I want, but for more than I want? May the Spirit of God say to everyone whom it concerns, 'Thou art the man!'

4. I ask, thirdly, who of you are in fact 'laying up for yourselves treasures upon earth'? Increasing in goods? Adding, as fast as you can, house to house, and field to field? 'As long as thou' thus 'dost well unto thyself, men will speak good of thee.' They will call thee a 'wise', a 'prudent' man! A man that 'minds the main chance'. Such is, and always has been, the wisdom of the world. 'But God saith unto' thee, 'Thou fool!' Art thou not 'treasuring up to thyself wrath against the day of wrath', and 'revelation of the righteous judgment of God'?

5. Perhaps you will ask, 'But do not you yourself advise, To gain all we can, and to save all we can? And is it possible to do this without both "desiring" and "endeavouring to be rich"? Nay, suppose our endeavours are successful, without actually "laying up treasures upon earth"?'

I answer, it is possible. You may gain all you can without hurting either your soul or body; you may save all you can, by carefully avoiding every needless expense, and yet never 'lay up treasures on earth', nor either desire or endeavour so to do.

6. Permit me to speak as freely of myself as I would of another man. I 'gain all I can' (namely, by writing) without hurting either my soul or body. I 'save all I can', not willingly wasting anything, not a sheet of paper, not a cup of water. I do not lay out anything, not a shilling, unless as a sacrifice to God. Yet by 'giving all I can' I am effectually secured from 'laying up treasures upon earth'. Yea, and I am secured from either desiring or endeavouring it as long as I 'give all I can'. And that I do this I call all that know me, both friends and foes, to testify.

7. But some may say, 'Whether you endeavour it or no, you are undeniably *rich*. You have more than the necessaries of life.' I have. But the Apostle does not fix the charge barely on *possessing* any quantity of goods, but on possessing more than we employ according to the will of the Donor.

Two and forty years ago, having a desire to furnish poor people with cheaper, shorter, and plainer books than any I had seen, I wrote many small tracts, generally a penny apiece; and afterwards several larger. Some of these had such a sale as I never thought of; and by this means I unawares became rich. But I never desired or endeavoured after it. And now that it is come upon me unawares I lay up no treasures upon earth: I lay up nothing at all. My desire and endeavour in this respect is to 'wind my bottom round the year'. I cannot help leaving my books behind me whenever God calls me hence. But in every other respect my own hands will be my executors.

8. Herein, my brethren, let you that are rich be even as I am. Do you that possess more than food and raiment ask: 'What shall we do? Shall we throw into the sea what God hath given us?' God forbid that you should! It is an excellent talent: it may be employed much to the glory of God. Your way lies plain before your face; if you have courage, walk in it. Having 'gained' (in a right sense) 'all you can', and 'saved all you can'; in spite of nature, and custom,

and worldly prudence, 'give all you can'. I do not say, 'Be a good Jew,' giving a tenth of all you possess. I do not say, 'Be a good Pharisee,' giving a fifth of all your substance. I dare not advise you to give half of what you have; no, nor three-quarters—but all! Lift up your hearts and you will see clearly in what sense this is to be done.

> If you desire to be a 'faithful and a wise steward', out of that portion of your Lord's goods which he has for the present lodged in your hands, but with the right of resumption whenever it pleaseth him, (1) provide things needful for yourself—food to eat, raiment to put on, whatever nature moderately requires for preserving you both in health and strength; (2) provide these for your wife, your children, your servants, or any others who pertain to your household. If when this is done there is an overplus left, then do good to 'them that are of the household of faith'. If there be an overplus still, 'as you have opportunity, do good unto all men'. In so doing, you *give all you can*; nay, in a sound sense, all you have. For all that is laid out in this manner is really given to God. You render unto God the things that are God's, not only by what you give to the poor, but also by that which you expend in providing things needful for yourself and your household.*

9. O ye Methodists, hear the word of the Lord! I have a message from God to all men; but to *you* above all. For above forty years I have been a servant to you and to your fathers. And I have not been as a reed shaken with the wind: I have not varied in my testimony. I have testified to you the very same thing from the first day even until now. But 'who hath believed our report?' I fear, not many rich. I fear there is need to apply to some of *you* those terrible words of the Apostle: 'Go to, now, ye rich men! Weep and howl for the miseries which shall come upon you. Your gold and silver is cankered, and the rust of them shall witness against you, and shall eat your flesh, as it were fire.' Certainly it will, unless ye both save all you can and give all you can. But who of you hath considered this since you first heard the will of the Lord concerning it? Who is now determined to consider and practise it? By the grace of God begin today!

10. O ye 'lovers of money', hear the word of the Lord! Suppose ye that money, though multiplied as the sand of the sea, can give happiness? Then you are 'given up to a strong delusion, to believe a lie'; a palpable lie, confuted daily by a thousand experiments. Open your eyes! Look all around you! Are the richest men the happiest? Have those the largest share of content who have the largest possessions? Is not the very reverse true? Is it not a common observation that the richest of men are in general the most discontented, the most miserable? Had not the far greater part of them more content when they had less money? Look into your breasts. If you are increased in goods, are you proportionably increased in happiness? You have more substance; but have

* *Works* [1771], Vol. 4, p. 56 [cf. Sermon 50, 'The Use of Money,' III. 3].

you more content? You know the contrary. You know that in seeking happiness from riches you are only striving to drink out of empty cups. And let them be painted and gilded ever so finely, they are empty still.

11. O ye that 'desire' or endeavour 'to be rich', hear ye the word of the Lord! Why should ye be stricken any more? Will not even experience teach you wisdom? Will ye leap into a pit with your eyes open? Why should you any more 'fall into temptation'? It cannot be but temptation will beset you as long as you are in the body. But though it should beset you on every side, why will you *enter into* it? There is no necessity for this; it is your own voluntary act and deed. Why should you any more plunge yourselves 'into a snare', into the trap Satan has laid for you, that is ready to break your bones in pieces, to crush your soul to death? After fair warning, why should you sink any more into 'foolish and hurtful desires'? Desires as foolish, as inconsistent with reason as they are with religion itself! Desires that have done you more hurt already than all the treasures upon earth can countervail.

12. Have they not hurt you already, have they not wounded you in the tenderest part, by slackening, if not utterly destroying your 'hunger and thirst after righteousness'? Have you now the same longing that you had once for the whole image of God? Have you the same vehement desire as you formerly had of 'going on unto perfection'? Have they not hurt you by weakening your *faith?* Have you now faith's 'abiding impression, realizing things to come'? Do you endure in all temptations from pleasure or pain, 'seeing him that is invisible'? Have you every day, and every hour, an uninterrupted sense of his presence? Have they not hurt you with regard to your *hope?* Have you now a hope full of immortality? Are you still big with earnest expectation of all the great and precious promises? Do you now 'taste the powers of the world to come'? Do you 'sit in heavenly places with Christ Jesus'?

13. Have they not so hurt you as to stab your religion to the heart? Have they not cooled (if not quenched) your *love of God?* This is easily determined. Have you the same delight in God which you once had? Can you now say,

> I nothing want beneath, above:
> Happy, happy in thy love!

I fear not. And if your love of God is in any wise decayed, so is also your love of your neighbour. You are then hurt in the very life and spirit of your religion! If you lose love, you lose all.

14. Are not you hurt with regard to your *humility?* If you are increased in goods, it cannot well be otherwise. Many will think you a better, because you are a richer man; and how can you help thinking so yourself? Especially considering the commendations which some will give you in simplicity, and many with a design to serve themselves of you.

If you are hurt in your humility it will appear by this token: you are not so teachable as you were, not so advisable; you are not so easy to be convinced, not so easy to be persuaded. You have a much better opinion of your own judgment, and are more attached to your own will. Formerly one might guide you with a thread; now one cannot turn you with a cart-rope. You were glad to be admonished or reproved; but that time is past. And you now account a man your enemy because he tells you the truth. O let each of you calmly consider this, and see if it be not your own picture!

15. Are you not equally hurt with regard to your *meekness?* You had once learned an excellent lesson of him that was meek as well as lowly in heart. When you were reviled, you reviled not again. You did not return railing for railing, but contrariwise, blessing. Your love was 'not provoked', but enabled you on all occasions to overcome evil with good. Is this your case now? I am afraid not. I fear you cannot 'bear all things'. Alas, it may rather be said you can bear nothing—no injury, nor even affront! How quickly are you ruffled! How readily does that occur: 'What! to use *me* so! What insolence is this! How did he dare to do it! I am not now what I was once. Let him know I am now able to defend myself.' You mean, to revenge yourself. And it is much if you are not willing as well as able; if you do not take your fellow servant by the throat.

16. And are you not hurt in your *patience* too? Does your love now 'endure all things'? Do you still 'in patience possess your soul', as when you first believed? O what a change is here! You have again learned to be frequently out of humour. You are often fretful; you feel, nay, and give way to peevishness. You find abundance of things go so cross that you cannot tell how to bear them!

Many years ago I was sitting with a gentleman in London who feared God greatly, and generally gave away, year by year, nine-tenths of his yearly income. A servant came in and threw some coals on the fire. A puff of smoke came out. The baronet threw himself back in his chair and cried out, 'Oh! Mr. Wesley, these are the crosses I meet with daily!' Would he not have been less impatient if he had had fifty, instead of five thousand pounds a year?

17. But to return. Are not you who have been successful in your endeavours to increase in substance, insensibly sunk into softness of mind, if not of body too? You no longer rejoice to 'endure hardship, as good soldiers of Jesus Christ'. You no longer 'rush into the kingdom of heaven, and take it as by storm'. You do not cheerfully and gladly 'deny yourselves', and 'take up your cross daily'. You cannot deny yourself the poor pleasure of a little sleep, or of a soft bed, in order to hear the word that is able to save your souls! Indeed, you 'cannot go out so early in the morning; besides it is dark; nay, cold; perhaps rainy too. Cold, darkness, rain—all these together. I can never think of it.' You did not say so when you were a poor man. You then regarded none of these things. It is the change of circumstances which has occasioned this melancholy

change in your body and mind; you are but the shadow of what you were. What have riches done for you?

'But it cannot be expected I should do as I have done; for I am now grown old.' Am not I grown old as well as you? Am not I in my seventy-eighth year? Yet by the grace of God I do not slack my pace yet. Neither would *you*, if you were a poor man still.

18. You are so deeply hurt that you have well-nigh lost your zeal for works of mercy, as well as of piety. You once pushed on, through cold or rain, or whatever cross lay in your way, to see the poor, the sick, the distressed. You went about doing good, and found out those who were not able to find you. You cheerfully crept down into their cellars, and climbed up into their garrets, to

> Supply all their wants,
> And spend and be spent in assisting his saints.

You found out every scene of human misery, and assisted according to your power:

> Each form of woe your generous pity moved;
> Your Saviour's face you saw, and seeing, loved.

Do you now tread in the same steps? What hinders? Do you fear spoiling your silken coat? Or is there another lion in the way? Are you afraid of catching vermin? And are you not afraid lest the roaring lion should catch *you*? Are you not afraid of him that hath said, 'Inasmuch as ye have not done it unto the least of these, ye have not done it unto me'? What will follow? 'Depart, ye cursed, into everlasting fire prepared for the devil and his angels.'

19. In time past how mindful were you of that word: 'Thou shalt not hate thy brother in thy heart. Thou shalt in any wise reprove thy brother, and not suffer sin upon him.' You *did* reprove, directly or indirectly, all those that sinned in your sight. And happy consequences quickly followed. How good was a word spoken in season! It was often as an arrow from the hand of a giant. Many a heart was pierced. Many of the stout-hearted, who scorned to hear a sermon,

> Fell down before his cross subdued,
> And felt his arrows dipped in blood.

But which of you now has that compassion for the ignorant, and for them that are out of the way? They may wander on for *you*, and plunge into the lake of fire without let or hindrance. Gold hath steeled your hearts. You have something else to do.

> Unhelped, unpitied let the wretches fall.

20. Thus have I given you, O ye gainers, lovers, possessors of riches, one more (it may be the last) warning. O that it may not be in vain! May God write it upon all your hearts! Though 'it is easier for a camel to go through the eye of a needle, than for a rich man to enter into the kingdom of heaven,' yet the things impossible with men are possible with God. Lord, speak! And even the rich men that hear these words shall enter thy kingdom! Shall 'take the kingdom of heaven by violence'; shall 'sell all for the pearl of great price': Shall be 'crucified to the world', 'and count all things dung, that they may win Christ'!

ON ZEAL

Sermon 92 – 1781

AN INTRODUCTORY COMMENT

This sermon is a comment on love in a single, crucial aspect. Wesley focuses on the much misunderstood impulse labelled 'religious zeal' and then proceeds to show that true 'zeal' is actually an expression of love or else it is both false and destructive. This framework allows him then to distinguish between the zeal that fuels the fires of controversy and persecution, and the special quality of holy love that is, as he says, 'the queen of all graces'. That this idea was a favourite in his mid-career is suggested by the fact that Wesley used Gal. 4:18 as a preaching text eighteen times between 1758 and 1779.

Wesley sets the stage by running through a list of the most atrocious episodes of misguided religious zeal from the Marian persecutions to the Irish Rising of 1641 to the wars of religion, accounting in Europe alone for some forty million deaths since 1520. Wesley then describes the nature or essence of true Christian zeal as 'the flame of love'. Therefore, his description of the properties of zeal unfolds a familiar list: humility, meekness, and patience. Wesley then shows how true Christian zeal relates to all the parts of religion, seen in terms of comparative concentric circles of categories that become more important as one approaches the center. He begins with zeal for the church universal, then zeal for the means of grace, for works of piety and works of mercy, for holy tempers, and finally (at the center) the choicest zeal is reserved for love itself. Never once is zeal associated with ideas or actions that could be misunderstood as 'enthusiasm' of any sort.

The written sermon first appeared in the *Arminian Magazine* (1781), without a title but with a postscript: 'Haverford West, May 6, 1781'. This notation agrees with his account in the *Journal* (April 29–May 7) of his visit for that year to Haverfordwest, seventeen miles from St. David's, Wales. Wesley remarked on one occasion during his visit that the listeners at Haverfordwest were 'the liveliest congregation I have seen in Wales'. The sermon was included in volume seven of Wesley's collected *Sermons* (1788), but was not thereafter reprinted in Wesley's lifetime.

On Zeal

It is good to be always zealously affected in a good thing.
Galatians 4:18

1. There are few subjects in the whole compass of religion that are of greater importance than this. For without zeal it is impossible either to make any considerable progress in religion ourselves, or to do any considerable service to our neighbour, whether in temporal or spiritual things. And yet nothing has done more disservice to religion, or more mischief to mankind, than a sort of zeal which has for several ages prevailed, both in pagan, Mahometan, and Christian nations. Insomuch that it may truly be said: pride, covetousness, ambition, revenge, have in all parts of the world slain their thousands, but zeal its ten thousands. Terrible instances of this have occurred in ancient times, in the most civilized heathen nations. To this chiefly were owing the inhuman persecutions of the primitive Christians; and in later ages the no less inhuman persecutions of the Protestants by the Church of Rome. It was zeal that kindled fires in our nation during the reign of bloody Queen Mary. It was zeal that soon after made so many provinces of France a field of blood. It was zeal that murdered so many thousand unresisting Protestants in the never to be forgotten massacre of Paris. It was zeal that occasioned the still more horrid massacre in Ireland; the like whereof, both with regard to the number of the murdered, and the shocking circumstances wherewith many of those murders were perpetrated, I verily believe never occurred before, since the world began. As to the other parts of Europe, an eminent German writer has taken immense pains to search both the records in various places, and the most authentic histories, in order to gain some competent knowledge of the blood which has been shed since the Reformation; and computes that, partly by private persecution, partly by religious wars in the course of forty years, reckoning from the year 1520, above forty millions of persons have been destroyed.

2. But is it not possible to distinguish right zeal from wrong? Undoubtedly it is possible. But it is difficult—such is the deceitfulness of the human heart! So skilfully do the passions justify themselves. And there are exceeding few treatises on the subject; at least in the English language. To this day I have seen or heard of only one sermon; and that was wrote above a hundred years ago by Dr. Sprat, then Bishop of Rochester, so that it is now exceeding scarce.

3. I would gladly cast in my mite, by God's assistance, toward the clearing up this important question, in order to enable well-meaning men who are

desirous of pleasing God to distinguish true Christian zeal from its various counterfeits. And this is more necessary at this time than it has been for many years. Sixty years ago there seemed to be scarce any such thing as religious zeal left in the nation. People in general were wonderfully cool and undisturbed about 'that trifle, religion'. But since then, it is easy to observe, there has been a very considerable alteration. Many thousands almost in every part of the nation have felt a real desire to save their souls. And I am persuaded there is at this day more religious zeal in England than there has been for a century past.

4. But has this zeal been of the right or the wrong kind? Probably both the one and the other. Let us see if we cannot separate these, that we may avoid the latter and cleave to the former. In order to this, I would first inquire what is the nature of true Christian zeal; secondly, what are the properties of it; and thirdly, draw some practical inferences.

I. And first, what is the nature of zeal in general, and of true Christian zeal in particular?

1. The original word, in its primary signification, means *heat*, such as the heat of boiling water. When it is figuratively applied to the mind it means any warm emotion or affection. Sometimes it is taken for *envy*. So we render it, Acts 5:17, where we read, 'The high priest and all that were with him were filled with envy'—ἐπλήσθησαν ζήλου (although it might as well be rendered were filled with zeal.) Sometimes it is taken for anger and indignation; sometimes for vehement desire. And when any of our passions are strongly moved on a religious account, whether for anything good, or against anything which we conceive to be evil, this we term, 'religious zeal'.

2. But it is not all that is called religious zeal which is worthy of that name. It is not properly religious or Christian zeal if it be not joined with charity. A fine writer (Bishop Sprat) carries the matter farther still. 'It has been affirmed', says that great man, 'no zeal is right which is not charitable. But this is not saying enough. I affirm that true zeal is not only charitable, but is mostly so. Charity or love is not only one ingredient, but the chief ingredient, in its composition.' May we not go farther still? May we not say that true zeal is not mostly charitable, but wholly so? That is, if we take charity in St. Paul's sense, for love—the love of God and our neighbour. For it is a certain truth (although little understood in the world) that Christian zeal is all love. It is nothing else. The love of God and man fills up its whole nature.

3. Yet it is not every degree of that love to which this appellation is given. There may be some love, a small degree of it, where there is no zeal. But it is properly love in a higher degree. It is 'fervent love'. True Christian zeal is no other than *the flame of love*. This is the nature, the inmost essence of it.

II.1. From hence it follows that the properties of love are the properties of zeal also. Now one of the chief properties of love is *humility*—'love is not puffed up.' Accordingly this is a property of true zeal: humility is inseparable from it. As is the degree of zeal, such is the degree of humility: they must rise and fall together. The same love which fills a man with zeal for God makes him little, and poor, and vile in his own eyes.

2. Another of the properties of love is *meekness:* consequently it is one of the properties of zeal. It teaches us to be meek as well as lowly; to be equally superior to anger and pride. Like as the wax melteth at the fire, so before this sacred flame all turbulent passions melt away, and leave the soul unruffled and serene.

3. Yet another property of love, and consequently of zeal, is unwearied *patience*; for 'love endureth all things'. It arms the soul with entire resignation to all the disposals of divine providence, and teaches us to say in every occurrence, 'It is the Lord; let him do what seemeth him good.' It enables us, in whatever state we are, therewith to be content; to repine at nothing; to murmur at nothing; but 'in everything to give thanks'.

4. There is a fourth property of Christian zeal, which deserves to be more particularly considered. This we learn from the very words of the Apostle: 'It is good to be zealously affected' (not to have transient touches of zeal, but a steady, rooted disposition) 'in a good thing'—in that which is good; for the proper object of zeal is good in general, that is, everything that is good, really such, in the sight of God.

5. But what is good in the sight of God? What is that religion wherewith God is always well pleased? How do the parts of this rise one above another? And what is the comparative value of them?

This is a point exceeding little considered, and therefore little understood. Positive divinity many have some knowledge of. But few know anything of comparative divinity. I never saw but one tract wrote upon this head; a sketch of which it may be of use to subjoin.

In a Christian believer *love* sits upon the throne, which is erected in the inmost soul; namely, love of God and man, which fills the whole heart, and reigns without a rival. In a circle near the throne are all *holy tempers:* long-suffering, gentleness, meekness, goodness, fidelity, temperance—and if any other is comprised in 'the mind which was in Christ Jesus'. In an exterior circle are all the *works of mercy,* whether to the souls or bodies of men. By these we exercise all holy tempers; by these we continually improve them, so that all these are real *means of grace,* although this is not commonly adverted to. Next to these are those that are usually termed *works of piety:* reading and hearing the Word, public, family, private prayer, receiving the Lord's Supper, fasting or abstinence. Lastly, that his followers may the more effectually provoke one another to love, holy tempers, and good works, our blessed Lord has united them together in one—*the church*, dispersed all over the earth; a little emblem of which, of the church universal, we have in every particular Christian congregation.

6. This is that religion which our Lord has established upon earth, ever since the descent of the Holy Ghost on the day of Pentecost. This is the entire, connected system of Christianity: and thus the several parts of it rise one above another, from that lowest point, 'the assembling ourselves together', to the highest, love enthroned in the heart. And hence it is easy to learn the comparative value of every branch of religion. Hence also we learn a fifth property of true zeal—that as it is always exercised ἐν καλῷ, 'in that which is good', so it is always *proportioned* to that good, to the degree of goodness that is in its object.

7. For example: every Christian ought undoubtedly to be zealous for *the church*, bearing a strong affection to it, and earnestly desiring its prosperity and increase. He ought to be thus zealous, as for the church universal, praying for it continually, so especially for that particular church or Christian society whereof he himself is a member. For this he ought to wrestle with God in prayer; meantime using every means in his power to enlarge its borders, and to strengthen his brethren, that they may adorn the doctrine of God our Saviour.

8. But he should be more zealous for the *ordinances of Christ* than for the church itself: for prayer in public and private, for the Lord's Supper, for reading, hearing, and meditating on his Word; and for the much neglected duty of fasting. These he should earnestly recommend, first, by his example, and then by advice, by argument, persuasion, and exhortation, as often as occasion offers.

9. Thus should he show his zeal for works of piety; but much more for *works of mercy*; seeing 'God will have mercy and not sacrifice'—that is, rather than sacrifice. Whenever, therefore, one interferes with the other, works of mercy are to be preferred. Even reading, hearing, prayer, are to be omitted, or to be postponed, 'at charity's almighty call'—when we are called to relieve the distress of our neighbour, whether in body or soul.

10. But as zealous as we are for all good works, we should be still more zealous for *holy tempers*; for planting and promoting both in our souls, and in all we have any intercourse with, lowliness of mind, meekness, gentleness, long-suffering, contentedness, resignation unto the will of God, deadness to the world and the things of the world, as the only means of being truly alive to God. For these proofs and fruits of living faith we cannot be too zealous. We should 'talk of them as we sit in our house, and when we walk by the way, and when we lie down, and when we rise up'. We should make them continual matter of prayer, as being far more excellent than any outward works whatever; seeing those will fail when the body drops off, but these will accompany us

into eternity.

11. But our choicest zeal should be reserved for *love* itself, the end of the commandment, the fulfilling of the law. The church, the ordinances, outward works of every kind, yea, all other holy tempers, are inferior to this, and rise in value only as they approach nearer and nearer to it. Here then is the great object of Christian zeal. Let every true believer in Christ apply with all fervency of spirit to the God and Father of our Lord Jesus Christ, that his heart may be more and more enlarged in love to God and to all mankind. This one thing let him do: let him 'press on to this prize of our high calling of God in Christ Jesus'.

III. It remains only to draw some practical inferences from the preceding observations.

1. And, first, if zeal, true Christian zeal, be nothing but the flame of love, then *hatred*, in every kind and degree, then every sort of *bitterness* toward them that oppose us, is so far from deserving the name of zeal that it is directly opposite to it. If zeal be only fervent love, then it stands at the utmost distance from *prejudice*, jealousy, evil surmising; seeing 'love thinketh no evil'. Then *bigotry* of every sort, and above all the spirit of *persecution*, are totally inconsistent with it. Let not, therefore, any of these unholy tempers screen themselves under that sacred name. As all these are the works of the devil, let them appear in their own shape, and no longer under that specious disguise deceive the unwary children of God.

2. Secondly; if lowliness be a property of zeal, then pride is inconsistent with it. It is true some degree of pride may remain after the love of God is shed abroad in the heart; as this is one of the last evils that is rooted out when God creates all things new. But it cannot reign, nor retain any considerable power, where fervent love is found. Yea, were we to give way to it but a little, it would damp that holy fervour; and if we did not immediately fly back to Christ, would utterly quench the Spirit.

3. Thirdly; if meekness be an inseparable property of zeal, what shall we say of those who call their anger by that name? Why, that they mistake the truth totally; that they in the fullest sense put darkness for light, and light for darkness. We cannot be too watchful against this delusion, because it spreads over the whole Christian world. Almost in all places zeal and anger pass for equivalent terms; and exceeding few persons are convinced that there is any difference between them. How commonly do we hear it said, 'See how zealous the man is!' Nay, he cannot be zealous: that is impossible; for he is in a passion. And passion is as inconsistent with zeal as light with darkness, or heaven with hell.

It were well that this point were thoroughly understood. Let us consider it a little farther. We frequently observe one that bears the character of a religious man vehemently angry at his neighbour. Perhaps he calls his brother 'Raca', or 'Thou fool': he brings a railing accusation against him. You mildly admonish him of his warmth. He answers, 'It is my zeal!' No, it is your sin; and unless you repent of it, will sink you lower than the grave. There is much such zeal as this in the bottomless pit. Thence all zeal of this kind comes. And thither it will go, and you with it, unless you are saved from it before you go hence.

4. Fourthly; if patience, contentedness, and resignation, are the properties of zeal, then murmuring, fretfulness, discontent, impatience, are wholly inconsistent with it. And yet how ignorant are mankind of this! How often do we see men fretting at the ungodly, or telling you they are 'out of patience' with such or such things, and terming all this their zeal! O spare no pains to undeceive them! If it be possible, show them what zeal is; and convince them that all murmuring, or fretting at sin, is a species of sin, and has no resemblance of, or connection with, the true zeal of the gospel.

5. Fifthly; if the object of zeal be 'that which is good', then fervour for any *evil thing* is not Christian zeal. I instance in *idolatry*—worshipping of angels, saints, images, the cross. Although therefore a man were so earnestly attached to any kind of idolatrous worship that he would even 'give his body to be burned' rather than refrain from it, call this bigotry or superstition if you please, but call it not zeal. That is quite another thing.

From the same premises it follows that fervour for *indifferent things* is not Christian zeal. But how exceedingly common is this mistake too! Indeed one would think that men of understanding could not be capable of such weakness. But alas! the history of all ages proves the contrary. Who were men of stronger understandings than Bishop Ridley and Bishop Hooper? And how warmly did these and other great men of that age dispute about the *sacerdotal vestments?* How eager was the contention for almost a hundred years for and against wearing a *surplice!* O shame to man! I would as soon have disputed about a straw or a barley-corn! And this, indeed, shall be called zeal! And why was it not rather called wisdom or holiness?

6. It follows also from the same premises that fervour for *opinions* is not Christian zeal. But how few are sensible of this! And how innumerable are the mischiefs which even this species of false zeal has occasioned in the Christian world! How many thousand lives have been cast away by those who were zealous for the Romish opinions! How many of the excellent ones of the earth have been cut off by zealots for the senseless opinion of transubstantiation! But does not every unprejudiced person see that this zeal is 'earthly, sensual, devilish'? And that it stands at the utmost contrariety to the zeal which is here recommended by the Apostle?

What an excess of charity is it then which our great poet expresses in his poem on the last day! Where he talks of meeting in heaven,

> Those who by mutual wounds expired,
> By *zeal* for their distinct persuasions fired?

Zeal indeed! What manner of zeal was this which led them to cut one another's throats? Those who were *fired* with this spirit, and died therein, will undoubtedly have their portion, not in heaven—only love is there—but in 'the fire that never shall be quenched'.

7. Lastly, if true zeal be always proportioned to the degree of goodness which is in its object, then should it rise higher and higher according to the scale mentioned above; according to the comparative value of the several parts of religion. For instance, all that truly fear God should be zealous for the *church*: both for the catholic or universal church, and for that part of it whereof they are members. This is not the appointment of men, but of God. He saw 'it was not good for men to be alone', even in this sense, but that the whole body of his children should be 'knit together, and strengthened, by that which every joint supplieth'. At the same time they should be more zealous for the *ordinances* of God: for public and private prayer, for hearing and reading the Word of God, and for fasting, and the Lord's Supper. But they should be more zealous for 'works of mercy' than even for works of piety. Yet ought they to be more zealous still for *holy tempers*—lowliness, meekness, resignation; but most zealous of all for that which is the sum and the perfection of religion—the *love* of God and man.

8. It remains only to make a close and honest application of these things to our own souls. We all know the general truth that 'it is good to be always zealously affected in a good thing.' Let us now, every one of us, apply it to his own soul in particular.

9. Those indeed who are still dead in trespasses and sins have neither part nor lot in this matter; nor those that live in any open sin, such as drunkenness, sabbath-breaking, or profane swearing. These have nothing to do with zeal; they have no business at all even to take the word in their mouth. It is utter folly and impertinence for any to talk of zeal for God while he is doing the works of the devil. But if you have renounced the devil and all his works, and have settled it in your heart, I will 'worship the Lord my God, and him only will I serve', then beware of being neither cold nor hot; then be zealous for God! You may begin at the lowest step. Be zealous for *the church*; more especially for that particular branch thereof wherein your lot is cast. Study the welfare of this, and carefully observe all the rules of it, for conscience' sake. But in the meantime take heed that you do not neglect any of the *ordinances* of God; for the sake of which, in a great measure, the church itself was constituted; so that it would be highly absurd to talk of zeal for the church if you were not more zealous for them. But are you more zealous for 'works of mercy' than even for works of piety? Do *you* follow the example of your Lord,

and prefer mercy even before sacrifice? Do you use all diligence in feeding the hungry, clothing the naked, visiting them that are sick and in prison? And above all, do you use every means in your power to save souls from death? If, as you have time, 'you do good unto all men', though 'especially to them that are of the household of faith', your zeal for the church is pleasing to God; but if not, if you are not 'careful to maintain good works', what have you to do with the church? If you have not 'compassion on your fellow-servants', neither will your Lord have pity on *you*. 'Bring no more vain oblations.' All your service is 'an abomination to the Lord'.

10. Are you better instructed than to put asunder what God has joined? Than to separate works of piety from works of mercy? Are you uniformly zealous of both? So far you walk acceptably to God: that is, if you continually bear in mind that God 'searcheth the heart and reins'; that 'He is a Spirit, and they that worship him, must worship him in spirit and in truth'; that consequently no outward works are acceptable to him unless they spring from *holy tempers,* without which no man can have a place in the kingdom of Christ and of God.

11. But of all holy tempers, and above all others, see that you be most zealous for *love!* Count all things loss in comparison of this, the love of God and all mankind. It is most sure that if you give all your goods to feed the poor, yea, and your body to be burned, and have not humble, gentle, patient love, it profiteth you nothing. O let this be deep engraven upon your heart: all is nothing without love.

12. Take then the whole of religion together, just as God has revealed it in his Word, and be uniformly zealous for every part of it, according to its degree of excellence, grounding all your zeal on the one foundation, 'Jesus Christ and him crucified'; holding fast this one principle, 'The life I now live, I live by faith in the Son of God who loved *me,* and gave himself for *me*'; proportion your zeal to the value of its object. Be calmly zealous therefore, first, for the *church*—'the whole state of Christ's church militant here on earth', and in particular for that branch thereof with which you are more immediately connected. Be more zealous for all those *ordinances* which our blessed Lord hath appointed to continue therein to the end of the world. Be more zealous for those *works of mercy,* those 'sacrifices wherewith God is well pleased', those marks whereby the Shepherd of Israel will know his sheep at the last day. Be more zealous still for *holy tempers,* for 'long-suffering, gentleness, goodness, meekness, lowliness, and resignation'; but be most zealous of all for *love,* the queen of all graces, the highest perfection in earth or heaven, the very image of the invisible God, as in men below, so in angels above. For 'God is love; and he that dwelleth in love, dwelleth in God and God in him.'

GOD'S LOVE TO FALLEN MAN

Sermon 59 – 1782

AN INTRODUCTORY COMMENT

The theme of this sermon, though not its text, is a constant in Wesley's soteriology: that without creating man to sin, God's omnipotent grace has wrought an even more wonderful glory for creation than if man had continued in his original innocence and obedience ('if Adam had not fallen, Christ had not died'). And not only are the potentialities of holiness and happiness thereby enhanced in a positive way through faith and love, but even the seemingly negative consequences of the Fall can be viewed as opportunities for exercising the 'passive graces' that promote holiness: in oneself, suffering leads to resignation, natural evil leads to patience, sickness leads to fortitude; in others, these present opportunities for doing works of mercy. So in the end, Wesley is able to answer Soame Jenyns's claim that evil necessarily entered the world by 'the nature of matter, which God was not able to alter' (*Free Inquiry into the Nature and Origin of Evil*, 1757): evil came into the world through mankind's free disobedience, which God 'permitted', thereby allowing for 'an infinitely greater happiness than they could possibly have attained if Adam had not fallen.' Wesley confidently proclaims this conclusion with almost no hint at the complex debate on the controversial issue that ran back into patristic theology.

There is only one reference to his oral preaching from 'Romans 5:14, etc.' (January 23, 1741), with no certain indication of his topic. He had extracted a sizeable fraction of Samuel Hoard's *God's Love to Mankind* (1633) and printed it in five instalments in the first year of the *Arminian Magazine* (1778). Wesley finished writing this sermon, according to a postscript, in 'Birmingham, July 9, 1782'; it appeared in the *Arminian Magazine* for September and October 1782. In its first form this sermon had no title. In volume seven of his collected *Sermons* (1788), Wesley entitled it 'God's Love to Fallen Man: A Sermon on Romans 5:15.' It was twice reprinted in separate pamphlets in 1791.

That its message lay close to Wesley's heart is confirmed by Elizabeth Ritchie's memoir of his last days: 'The next pleasing, awful scene was the great exertion he made in order to make Mr. Broadbent understand that he fervently desired a sermon he had written on the Love of God should be scattered abroad and given away to everybody.' We also have James Rogers's note to this event: 'He said, "Where is my sermon on The Love of God? Take it and spread it abroad; give it to everyone."' Ten thousand were printed and given away.

God's Love to Fallen Man

Not as the transgression, so is the free gift.
Romans 5:15

1. How exceeding common, and how bitter, is the outcry against our first parent for the mischief which he not only brought upon himself, but entailed upon his latest posterity! It was by his wilful rebellion against God that 'sin entered into the world'. 'By one man's disobedience', as the Apostle observes, 'the many', οἱ πολλοί, as many as were then in the loins of their forefather, 'were made', or constituted, 'sinners': not only deprived of the favour of God, but also of his image; of all virtue, righteousness, and true holiness; and sunk partly into the image of the devil, in pride, malice, and all other diabolical tempers; partly into the image of the brute, being fallen under the dominion of brutal passions and grovelling appetites. Hence also death entered into the world, with all his forerunners and attendants, pain, sickness, and a whole train of uneasy as well as unholy passions and tempers.

2. 'For all this we may thank Adam,' has echoed down from generation to generation. The selfsame charge has been repeated in every age, and in every nation where the oracles of God are known, in which alone this grand and important event has been discovered to the children of men. Has not *your* heart, and probably your lips too, joined in the general charge? How few are there of those who believe the scriptural relation of the fall of man that have not entertained the same thought concerning our first parent! Severely condemning him that through wilful disobedience to the sole command of his Creator

Brought death into the world, and all our woe.

3. Nay, it were well if the charge rested here: but it is certain it does not. It cannot be denied that it frequently glances from Adam to his Creator. Have not thousands, even of those that are called Christians, taken the liberty to call his mercy, if not his justice also, into question on this very account? Some indeed have done this a little more modestly, in an oblique and indirect manner. But others have thrown aside the mask and asked, 'Did not God foresee that Adam would abuse his liberty? And did he not know the baneful consequences which this must naturally have on all his posterity? And why then did he permit that disobedience? Was it not easy for the Almighty to have prevented it?' He certainly did foresee the whole. This cannot be denied. For

'known unto God are all his works from the beginning of the world.' (Rather, from all eternity, as the words ἀπ' αἰῶνος properly signify.) And it was undoubtedly in his power to prevent it: for he hath all power both in heaven and earth. But it was known to him at the same time that it was best, upon the whole, not to prevent it. He knew that 'not as the transgression, so the free gift'; that the evil resulting from the former was not as the good resulting from the latter, not worthy to be compared with it. He saw that to permit the fall of the first man was far best for mankind in general; that abundantly more good than evil would accrue to the posterity of Adam by his fall; that if 'sin abounded' thereby over all the earth, yet 'grace would much more abound'; yea, and that to every individual of the human race, unless it was his own choice.

4. It is exceeding strange that hardly anything has been written, or at least published, on this subject; nay, that it has been so little weighed or understood by the generality of Christians; especially considering that it is not a matter of mere curiosity, but a truth of the deepest importance; it being impossible on any other principle

> To assert a gracious providence,
> And justify the ways of God with men;

and considering withal how plain this important truth is to all sensible and candid inquirers. May the Lover of men open the eyes of our understanding to perceive clearly that by the fall of Adam mankind in general have gained a capacity,

First, of being more holy and happy on earth; and

Secondly, of being more happy in heaven, than otherwise they could have been.

[I.] 1. And, first, mankind in general have gained by the fall of Adam a capacity of attaining more holiness and happiness on earth than it would have been possible for them to attain if Adam had not fallen. For if Adam had not fallen Christ had not died. Nothing can be more clear than this; nothing more undeniable. The more thoroughly we consider the point, the more deeply shall we be convinced of it. Unless all the partakers of human nature had received that deadly wound in Adam it would not have been needful for the Son of God to take our nature upon him. Do you not see that this was the very ground of his coming into the world? 'By one man sin entered into the world, and death by sin. And thus death passed upon all', through him 'in whom all men sinned' (Rom. 5:12). Was it not to remedy this very thing that 'the Word was made flesh'? That 'as in Adam all died, so in Christ all might be made alive'? Unless then *many* had been made sinners by the disobedience of one, by the obedience of one many would not have been 'made righteous' (Rom 5:18-19). So there would have been no room for that amazing display of the Son of

God's love to mankind. There would have been no occasion for his 'being obedient unto death, even the death of the cross'. It could not then have been said, to the astonishment of all the hosts of heaven, 'God so loved the world,' yea, the ungodly world which had no thought or desire of returning to him, 'that he gave his Son' out of his bosom, his only-begotten Son, 'to the end that whosoever believeth on him should not perish, but have everlasting life.' Neither could we then have said, 'God was in Christ reconciling the world unto himself'; or that he 'made him to be sin' (that is, a sin-offering) 'for us who knew no sin, that we might be made the righteousness of God through him'. There would have been no such occasion is for such 'an advocate with the Father' as 'Jesus Christ the righteous'; neither for his appearing 'at the right hand of God to make intercession for us'.

2. What is the necessary consequence of this? It is this—there could then have been no such thing as faith in God, 'thus loving the world', giving his only Son for us men and for our salvation. There could have been no such thing as faith in the Son of God, 'as loving us and giving himself for us'. There could have been no faith in the Spirit of God, as renewing the image of God in our hearts, as raising us from the death of sin unto the life of righteousness. Indeed the whole privilege of justification by faith could have had no existence; there could have been no redemption in the blood of Christ; neither could Christ have been 'made of God unto us either wisdom, righteousness, sanctification, or redemption'.

3. And the same grand blank which was in our faith must likewise have been in our love. We might have loved the Author of our being, the Father of angels and men, as our Creator and Preserver; we might have said, 'O Lord, our Governor, how excellent is thy name in all the earth.' But we could not have loved him under the nearest and dearest relation, as 'delivering up his Son for us all'. We might have loved the Son of God as being 'the brightness of his Father's glory, the express image of his person' (although this ground seems to belong rather to the inhabitants of heaven than of earth). But we could not have loved him as 'bearing our sins in his own body on the tree', and 'by that one oblation of himself once offered making a full oblation, sacrifice, and satisfaction for the sins of the whole world'. We could not have been 'made conformable to his death', nor have 'known the power of his resurrection'. We could not have loved the Holy Ghost as revealing to us the Father and the Son, as opening the eyes of our understanding, bringing us out of darkness into his marvellous light, renewing the image of God in our soul, and sealing us unto the day of redemption. So that in truth what is now 'in the sight of God, even the Father', not of fallible men, 'pure religion and undefiled', would then have had no being; inasmuch as it wholly depends on those grand principles 'By grace ye are saved through faith'; and 'Jesus Christ is of God made unto us wisdom and righteousness, and sanctification and

redemption.'

4. We see then what unspeakable advantage we derive from the fall of our first parent, with regard to faith—faith both in God the Father, who spared not his own Son,' his only Son, but 'wounded him for our transgressions, and bruised him for our iniquities'; and in God the Son, who poured out his soul for us transgressors, and washed us in his own blood.' We see what advantage we derive therefrom with regard to the love of God, both of God the Father and God the Son. The chief ground of this love, as long as we remain in the body, is plainly declared by the Apostle: 'We love him, because he first loved us.' But the greatest instance of his love had never been given if Adam had not fallen.

5. And as our faith both in God the Father and the Son receives an unspeakable increase, if not its very being, from this grand event, as does also our love both of the Father and the Son; so does the love of our neighbour also, our benevolence to all mankind, which cannot but increase in the same proportion with our faith and love of God. For who does not apprehend the force of that inference drawn by the loving Apostle, 'Beloved, if God so loved us, we ought also to love one another.' 'If God *so* loved us'—observe, the stress of the argument lies on this very point—'so loved us' as to deliver up his only Son to die a cursed death for our salvation! 'Beloved, what manner of love is this', wherewith God hath loved us! So as to give his *only Son!* In glory equal with the Father; in majesty coeternal! What manner of love is this wherewith the only-begotten Son of God hath loved us! So as to 'empty himself', as far as possible, of his eternal Godhead! As to divest himself of that glory which he had with the Father before the world began! As to 'take upon him the form of a servant, being found in fashion as a man'! And then to humble himself still farther, 'being obedient unto death, yea, the death of the cross'! If God *so* loved us, how ought we to love one another! But this motive to brotherly love had been totally wanting if Adam had not fallen. Consequently we could not then have loved one another in so high a degree as we may now. Nor could there have been that height and depth in the command of our blessed Lord, 'As I have loved you, so love one another.'

6. Such gainers may we be by Adam's fall with regard both to the love of God and of our neighbour. But there is another grand point which, though little adverted to, deserves our deepest consideration. By that one act of our first parent not only 'sin entered into the world', but pain also, and was alike entailed on his whole posterity. And herein appeared not only the justice but the unspeakable goodness of God! For how much good does he continually bring out of this evil! How much holiness and happiness out of pain!

7. How innumerable are the benefits which God conveys to the children of men through the channel of sufferings! So that it might well be said, 'What are termed afflictions in the language of men are in the language of God styled

blessings.' Indeed had there been no suffering in the world a considerable part of religion, yea, and in some respects the most excellent part, could have had no place therein; since the very existence of it depends on our suffering; so that had there been no pain it could have had no being. Upon this foundation, even our suffering, it is evident all our passive graces are built—yea, the noblest of all Christian graces, love 'enduring all things'. Here is the ground for resignation to God, enabling us to say from the heart, in every trying hour, 'It is the Lord: let him do what seemeth him good.' 'Shall we receive good at the hand of the Lord, and shall we not receive evil?' And what a glorious spectacle is this! Did it not constrain even a heathen to cry out, *Ecce spectaculum Deo dignum!*: 'See a sight worthy of God—a good man struggling with adversity and superior to it.' Here is the ground for confidence in God, both with regard to what we feel, and with regard to what we should fear, were it not that our soul is calmly stayed on him. What room could there be for trust in God if there was no such thing as pain or danger? Who might not say then, 'The cup which my Father hath given me, shall I not drink it?' It is by sufferings that our faith is tried, and therefore made more acceptable to God. It is in the day of trouble that we have occasion to say, 'Though he slay me, yet will I trust in him.' And this is well-pleasing to God, that we should own him in the face of danger, in defiance of sorrow, sickness, pain, or death.

8. Again: had there been neither natural nor moral evil in the world, what must have become of patience, meekness, gentleness, long-suffering? It is manifest they could have had no being, seeing all these have evil for their object. If therefore evil had never entered into the world, neither could these have had any place in it. For who could have 'returned good for evil' had there been no evil-doer in the universe? How had it been possible on that supposition to 'overcome evil with good'? Will you say, 'But all these graces might have been divinely infused into the hearts of men.' Undoubtedly they might: but if they had, there would have been no use or exercise for them. Whereas in the present state of things we can never long want occasion to exercise them. And the more they are exercised, the more all our graces are strengthened and increased. And in the same proportion as our resignation, our confidence in God, our patience and fortitude, our meekness, gentleness, and long-suffering, together with our faith and love of God and man increase, must our happiness increase, even in the present world.

9. Yet again: as God's permission of Adam's fall gave all his posterity a thousand opportunities of *suffering*, and thereby of exercising all those passive graces which increase both their holiness and happiness; so it gives them opportunities of *doing good* in numberless instances, of exercising themselves in various good works which otherwise could have had no being. And what exertions of benevolence, of compassion, of godlike mercy, had then been totally prevented! Who could then have said to the Lover of men,

Thy mind throughout my life be shown,
  While listening to the wretch's cry,
The widow's or the orphan's groan,
  On mercy's wings I swiftly fly,
The poor and needy to relieve;
  Myself, my all, for them to give?

It is the just observation of a benevolent man,

All worldly joys go less,
Than that one joy of doing kindnesses.

Surely 'in keeping' this commandment, if no other, 'there is great reward'. 'As we have time, let us do good unto all men'; good of every kind, and in every degree. Accordingly the more good we do (other circumstances being equal) the happier we shall be. The more we deal our bread to the hungry, and cover the naked with garments, the more we relieve the stranger, and visit them that are sick or in prison; the more kind offices we do to those that groan under the various evils of human life; the more comfort we receive even in the present world; the greater recompense we have in our own bosom.

10. To sum up what has been said under his head. As the more holy we are upon earth the more happy we must be (seeing there is an inseparable connection between holiness and happiness); as the more good we do to others the more of present reward redounds into our own bosom; even as our sufferings for God lead us to 'rejoice' in him 'with joy unspeakable and full of glory'. Therefore the fall of Adam, first, by giving us an opportunity of being far more holy; secondly, by giving us the occasions of doing innumerable good works which otherwise could not have been done; and thirdly, by putting it into our power to suffer for God, whereby 'the spirit of glory and of God rests upon us'; may be of such advantage to the children of men, even in the present life, as they will not thoroughly comprehend till they attain life everlasting.

[II.] 11. It is then we shall be enabled fully to comprehend, not only the advantages which accrue at the present time to the sons of men by the fall of their first parent, but the infinitely greater advantages which they may reap from it in eternity. In order to form some conception of this we may remember the observation of the Apostle: 'As one star differeth from another star in glory, so also is the resurrection of the dead.' The most glorious stars will undoubtedly be those who are the most holy; who bear most of that image of God wherein they were created. The next in glory to these will be those who have been most abundant in good works; and next to them those that have suffered most according to the will of God. But what advantages in every one of these respects will the children of God receive in heaven by God's permitting the introduction of pain upon earth, in consequence of sin! By occasion of this they attained many holy tempers which otherwise could have had no being: resignation to God, confidence in him in times of trouble and danger, patience, meekness, gentleness, long-suffering, and the whole train of passive virtues. And on account of this superior holiness they will then enjoy superior happiness. Again: everyone will then 'receive his own reward according to his own labour'. Every individual will be 'rewarded according to his works'. But the fall gave rise to innumerable good works which could otherwise never have existed, such as ministering to the necessities of saints, yea, relieving the distressed in every kind. And hereby innumerable stars will be added to their eternal crown. Yet again. There will be an abundant reward in heaven for suffering as well as for doing the will of God: 'These light afflictions, which are but for a moment, work out for us a far more exceeding and eternal weight of glory.' Therefore that event which occasioned the entrance of suffering into the world has thereby occasioned to all the children of God an increase of glory to all eternity. For although the sufferings themselves will be at an end; although

> The pain of life shall then be o'er,
> The anguish and distracting care;
> There sighing grief shall weep no more;
> And sin shall never enter there;

yet the joys occasioned thereby shall never end, but flow at God's right hand for evermore.

12. There is one advantage more that we reap from Adam's fall which is not unworthy our attention. Unless in Adam all had died, being in the loins of their first parent, every descendant of Adam, every child of man, must have personally answered for himself to God. It seems to be a necessary consequence of this that if he had once fallen, once violated any command of God, there would have been no possibility of his rising again; there was no help, but he must have perished without remedy. For that covenant knew not to show mercy: the word was, 'The soul that sinneth, it shall die.' Now who would not rather be on the footing he is now? Under a covenant of mercy? Who would wish to hazard a whole eternity upon one stake? Is it not infinitely more desirable to be in a state wherein, though encompassed with infirmities, yet we do not run such a desperate risk, but if we fall we may rise again? Wherein we may say,

> My trespass is grown up to heaven!
> But far above the skies,
> In Christ abundantly forgiven,
> I see thy mercies rise!

13. In Christ! Let me entreat every serious person once more to fix his attention here. All that has been said, all that can be said on these subjects,

centres in this point. The fall of Adam produced the death of Christ! Hear, O heavens, and give ear, O earth! Yea,

> Let earth and heaven agree,
>   Angels and men be joined,
> To celebrate with me
>   The Saviour of mankind;
> T' adore the all-atoning Lamb,
> And bless the sound of Jesu's name!

If God had prevented the fall of man, 'the Word' had never been 'made flesh'; nor had we ever 'seen his glory, the glory as of the only-begotten of the Father'. Those mysteries never had been displayed 'which the very angels desire to look into'. Methinks this consideration swallows up all the rest, and should never be out of our thoughts. Unless 'by one man judgment had come upon all men to condemnation' neither angels nor men could ever have known 'the unsearchable riches of Christ'.

14. See then, upon the whole, how little reason we have to repine at the fall of our first parent, since herefrom we may derive such unspeakable advantages both in time and eternity. See how small pretence there is for questioning the mercy of God in permitting that event to take place! Since therein mercy, by infinite degrees, rejoices over judgment! Where then is the man that presumes to blame God for not preventing Adam's sin? Should we not rather bless him from the ground of the heart for therein laying the grand scheme of man's redemption, and making way for that glorious manifestation of his wisdom, holiness, justice, and mercy? If indeed God had decreed before the foundation of the world that millions of men should dwell in everlasting burnings because Adam sinned hundreds or thousands of years before they had a being, I know not who could thank him for this, unless the devil and his angels; seeing on this supposition all those millions of unhappy spirits would be plunged into hell by Adam's sin, without any possible advantage from it. But, blessed be God, this is not the case. Such a decree never existed. On the contrary, every one born of a woman may be an unspeakable gainer thereby; and none ever was or can be a loser but by his own choice.

15. We see here a full answer to that plausible account 'of the origin of evil' published to the world some years since, and supposed to be unanswerable— 'that it necessarily resulted from the nature of matter, which God was not able to alter'. It is very kind in this sweet-tongued orator to make an excuse for God! But there is really no occasion for it: God hath answered for himself. He made man in his own image, a spirit endued with understanding and liberty. Man abusing that liberty produced evil, brought sin and pain into the world. This God permitted in order to a fuller manifestation of his wisdom, justice, and mercy, by bestowing on all who would receive it an infinitely greater happiness

than they could possibly have attained if Adam had not fallen.

16. 'O the depth of the riches both of the wisdom and knowledge of God!' Although a thousand particulars of 'his judgments, and of his ways, are unsearchable' to us, and 'past' our 'finding out', yet may we discern the general scheme running through time into eternity. 'According to the counsel of his own will', the plan he had laid before the foundation of the world, he created the parent of all mankind in his own image. And he permitted 'all men' to be 'made sinners by the disobedience of' this one man, that 'by the obedience of one' all who receive 'the free gift' may be infinitely holier and happier to all eternity!

ON WORKING OUT OUR OWN SALVATION

Sermon 85 – 1785

AN INTRODUCTORY COMMENT

This sermon is the late Wesley's most complete and careful exposition of the mystery of divine-human interaction, his subtlest probing of the paradox of prevenient grace and human agency. In the first two parts of this sermon, Wesley inverts the order of the clauses in the scriptural text and examines each in turn. Part of his description of the steps of 'working out' this salvation entails a quotation from Isa. 1:16–17 that echoes the first two General Rules: 'Cease to do evil; learn to do well.'

In the third part Wesley then deals with the connection between the two clauses of the text. Wesley is attempting to answer a question that was no doubt put to him often during the Revival, by friends and critics alike: 'If it is God that worketh in us both to will and to do, what need is there of our working?' His answer is simple: 'First, God works; therefore you *can* work. Secondly, God works; therefore you *must* work.' Wesley highlights the pervasiveness of God's grace 'preventing, accompanying, and following' the believer. If there were ever a question as to Wesley's alleged Pelagianism, this sermon alone should suffice to dispose of it decisively.

Wesley had preached from this text four times in the 1730s at the Castle prison in Oxford, using a two-part sermon that he had abridged from William Tilly's works. At that point, Wesley was most interested in showing that the preventing (prevenient) and assisting grace of God were both fully consistent with human liberty. His only other recorded use of Phil. 2:12–13 as a preaching text was at Norwich in 1781.

The written version of this sermon bears almost no resemblance to the Tilly work, other than its natural tie to the scriptural text. It appeared in the *Arminian Magazine* (1785), with no title. It was later included in volume seven of his collected *Sermons* (1788), but never reprinted separately in Wesley's lifetime. And yet, in any dozen of his sermons most crucial for an accurate assay of Wesley's theology, this one would certainly deserve inclusion.

On Working Out Our Own Salvation

Work out your own salvation with fear and trembling; for it is God that worketh in you, both to will and to do of his good pleasure.
Philippians 2:12–13

1. Some great truths, as the being and attributes of God, and the difference between moral good and evil, were known in some measure to the heathen world; the traces of them are to be found in all nations; so that in some sense it may be said to every child of man: 'He hath showed thee, O man, what is good; even to do justly, to love mercy, and to walk humbly with thy God.' With this truth he has in some measure 'enlightened everyone that cometh into the world'. And hereby they that 'have not the law', that have no written law, 'are a law unto themselves'. They show 'the work of the law', the substance of it, though not the letter, 'written in their hearts', by the same hand which wrote the commandments on the tables of stone; 'their conscience also bearing them witness', whether they act suitably thereto or not.

2. But there are two grand heads of doctrine, which contain many truths of the most important nature, of which the most enlightened heathens in the ancient world were totally ignorant; as are also the most intelligent heathens that are now on the face of the earth: I mean those which relate to the eternal Son of God, and the Spirit of God—to the Son, giving himself to be 'a propitiation for the sins of the world', and to the Spirit of God, renewing men in that image of God wherein they were created. For after all the pains which ingenious and learned men have taken (that great man the Chevalier Ramsay in particular), to find some resemblance of these truths in the immense rubbish of heathen authors, the resemblance is so exceeding faint as not to be discerned but by a very lively imagination. Beside that even this resemblance, faint as it was, is only to be found in the discourses of a very few, and those were the most improved and deeply thinking men in their several generations; while the innumerable multitudes that surrounded them were little better for the knowledge of the philosophers, but remained as totally ignorant, even of these capital truths, as were the beasts that perish.

3. Certain it is that these truths were never known to the vulgar, the bulk of mankind, to the generality of men in any nation, till they were brought to light by the gospel. Notwithstanding a spark of knowledge glimmering here and there, the whole earth was covered with darkness till the Sun of Righteousness arose and scattered the shades of night. Since this Day-spring from on

high has appeared, a great light hath shined unto those who till then sat in darkness and in the shadow of death. And thousands of them in every age have known, 'that God so loved the world' as to 'give his only Son, to the end that whosoever believeth on him should not perish, but have everlasting life.' And being entrusted with the oracles of God, they have known that 'God hath also given us his Holy Spirit,' who 'worketh in us both to will and to do of his good pleasure'.

4. How remarkable are those words of the Apostle which precede these! 'Let this mind be in you, which was also in Christ Jesus: who, being in the form of God', the incommunicable nature of God from eternity, 'counted it no act of robbery' (that is the precise meaning of the word), no invasion of any other's prerogative, but his own unquestionable right, 'to be equal with God.' The word implies both the *fullness* and the supreme *height* of the Godhead. To which are opposed the two words, he 'emptied', and he 'humbled himself'. He 'emptied himself' of that divine fullness, veiled his fullness from the eyes of men and angels, 'taking'—and by that very act emptying himself—'the form of a servant, being made in the likeness of man', a real man like other men. 'And being found in fashion as a man', a common man, without any peculiar beauty or excellency, 'he humbled himself' to a still greater degree, 'becoming obedient' to God, though equal with him, 'even unto death, yea the death of the cross'—the greatest instance both of humiliation and obedience.

Having proposed the example of Christ, the Apostle exhorts them to secure the salvation which Christ hath purchased for them: 'Wherefore work out your own salvation with fear and trembling; for it is God that worketh in you both to will and to do of his good pleasure.'

In these comprehensive words we may observe,

First, that grand truth, which ought never to be out of our remembrance, 'It is God that worketh in us, both to will and to do of his own good pleasure';

Secondly, the improvement we ought to make of it: 'Work out your own salvation with fear and trembling';

Thirdly, the connection between them: 'It is God that worketh in you'; therefore 'work out your own salvation.'

I.1. First, we are to observe that great and important truth which ought never to be out of our remembrance, 'It is God that worketh in us both to will and to do of his good pleasure.' The meaning of these words may be made more plain by a small transposition of them: 'It is God that of his good pleasure worketh in you both to will and to do.' This position of the words, connecting the phrase of 'his good pleasure' with the word 'worketh', removes all imagination of merit from man, and gives God the whole glory of his own work. Otherwise we might have had some room for boasting, as if it were our own desert, some goodness in us, or some good thing done by us, which first moved God to work. But this expression cuts off all such vain conceits, and clearly shows his motive to work lay wholly in himself—in his own mere grace, in his unmerited mercy.

2. It is by this alone he is impelled to work in man both to will and to do. The expression is capable of two interpretations, both of which are unquestionably true. First, 'to will' may include the whole of inward, 'to do' the whole of outward religion. And if it be thus understood, it implies that it is God that worketh both inward and outward holiness. Secondly, 'to will' may imply every good desire, 'to do' whatever results therefrom. And then the sentence means, God breathes into us every good desire, and brings every good desire to good effect.

3. The original words τὸ θέλειν and τὸ ἐνεργεῖν, seem to favour the latter construction; τὸ θέλειν, which we render 'to will', plainly including every good desire, whether relating to our tempers, words, or actions, to inward or outward holiness. And τὸ ἐνεργεῖν, which we render 'to do', manifestly implies all that power from on high; all that energy which works in us every right disposition, and then furnishes us for every good word and work.

4. Nothing can so directly tend to hide pride from man as a deep, lasting conviction of this. For if we are thoroughly sensible that we have nothing which we have not received, how can we glory as if we had not received it? If we know and feel that the very first motion of good is from above, as well as the power which conducts it to the end—if it is God that not only infuses every good desire, but that accompanies and follows it, else it vanishes away—then it evidently follows that 'he who glorieth must glory in the Lord.'

II.1. Proceed, we now to the second point: if God 'worketh in you', then 'work out your own salvation.' The original word rendered, 'work out', implies the doing a thing thoroughly. 'Your own'—for you yourselves must do this, or it will be left undone for ever. 'Your *own salvation*'—salvation begins with what is usually termed (and very properly) 'preventing grace'; including the first wish to please God, the first dawn of light concerning his will, and the first slight, transient conviction of having sinned against him. All these imply some tendency toward life, some degree of salvation, the beginning of a deliverance from a blind, unfeeling heart, quite insensible of God and the things of God. Salvation is carried on by 'convincing grace', usually in Scripture termed 'repentance', which brings a larger measure of self-knowledge, and a farther deliverance from the heart of stone. Afterwards we experience the proper Christian salvation, whereby 'through grace' we 'are saved by faith', consisting of those two grand branches, justification and sanctification. By justification we are saved from the guilt of sin, and restored to the favour of God: by sanctification we are saved from the power and root of sin, and restored to the image of God. All experience, as well as Scripture, shows this salvation to be both instantaneous and gradual. It begins the moment we are justified, in the holy, humble, gentle, patient love of God and man. It gradually increases from that moment, as a 'grain of mustard seed, which at first is the least of all seeds, but' gradually 'puts forth large branches', and becomes a great tree; till in another instant the heart is cleansed from all sin, and filled with pure love to God and man. But even that love increases more and more, till we 'grow up in all things into him that is our head', 'till we attain the measure of the stature of the fullness of Christ'.

2. But how are we to 'work out' this salvation? The Apostle answers, 'With fear and trembling'. There is another passage of St. Paul wherein the same expression occurs, which may give light to this: 'Servants, obey your masters according to the flesh,' according to the present state of things, although sensible that in a little time the servant will be free from his master, 'with fear and trembling'. This is a proverbial expression, which cannot be understood literally. For what master could bear, much less require, his servant to stand trembling and quaking before him? And the following words utterly exclude this meaning: 'in singleness of heart', with a single eye to the will and providence of God, 'not with eye-service, as men-pleasers, but as servants of Christ, doing the will of God from the heart'; doing whatever they do as the will of God, and therefore with their might (Eph. 6:5–6). It is easy to see that these strong expressions of the Apostle clearly imply two things: first, that everything be done with the utmost earnestness of spirit, and with all care and caution—perhaps more directly referring to the former word, μετὰ φόβου, 'with fear'; secondly, that it be done with the utmost diligence, speed, punctuality, and exactness—not improbably referring to the latter word, μετὰ τρόμου, 'with trembling'.

3. How easily may we transfer this to the business of life, the working out our own salvation! With the same temper and in the same manner that Christian servants serve their masters that are upon earth, let other Christians labour to serve their Master that is in heaven: that is, first, with the utmost earnestness of spirit, with all possible care and caution; and, secondly, with the utmost diligence, speed, punctuality, and exactness.

4. But what are the steps which the Scripture directs us to take, in the working out of our own salvation? The prophet Isaiah gives us a general answer touching the first steps which we are to take: 'Cease to do evil; learn to do well.' If ever you desire that God should work in you that faith whereof cometh both present and eternal salvation, by the grace already given, fly from all sin as from the face of a serpent; carefully avoid every evil word and work; yea, abstain from all appearance of evil. And 'learn to do well'; be zealous of good works, of works of piety, as well as works of mercy. Use family prayer, and cry to God in secret. Fast in secret, and 'your Father which seeth in secret, he will reward you openly.' 'Search the Scriptures'; hear them in public, read them in

private, and meditate therein. At every opportunity be a partaker of the Lord's Supper. 'Do this in remembrance of him,' and he will meet you at his own table. Let your conversation be with the children of God, and see that it 'be in grace, seasoned with salt'. As ye have time, do good unto all men, to their souls and to their bodies. And herein 'be ye steadfast, unmovable, always abounding in the work of the Lord.' It then only remains that ye deny yourselves and take up your cross daily. Deny yourselves every pleasure which does not prepare you for taking pleasure in God, and willingly embrace every means of drawing near to God, though it be a cross, though it be grievous to flesh and blood. Thus when you have redemption in the blood of Christ, you will 'go on to perfection'; till, 'walking in the light, as he is in the light', you are enabled to testify that 'he is faithful and just', not only 'to forgive your sins', but 'to cleanse you from all unrighteousness.'

III. 1. 'But', say some, 'what connection is there between the former and the latter clause of this sentence? Is there not rather a flat opposition between the one and the other? If it is God that worketh in us both to will and to do, what need is there of our working? Does not his working thus supersede the necessity of our working at all? Nay, does it not render our working impracticable, as well as unnecessary? For if we allow that God does all, what is there left for us to do?'

2. Such is the reasoning of flesh and blood. And at first hearing it is exceeding plausible. But it is not solid, as will evidently appear if we consider the matter more deeply. We shall then see there is no opposition between these—'God works; therefore do ye work'—but on the contrary the closest connection, and that in two respects. For, first, God works; therefore you *can* work. Secondly, God works; therefore you *must* work.

3. First, God worketh in you; therefore you can work—otherwise it would be impossible. If he did not work it would be impossible for you to work out your own salvation. 'With man this is impossible', saith our Lord, 'for a rich man to enter into the kingdom of heaven.' Yea, it is impossible for any man; for any that is born of a woman, unless God work in him. Seeing all men are by nature not only sick, but 'dead in trespasses, and sins', it is not possible for them to do anything well till God raises them from the dead. It was impossible for Lazarus to 'come forth' till the Lord had given him life. And it is equally impossible for us to 'come' out of our sins, yea, or to make the least motion toward it, till he who hath all power in heaven and earth calls our dead souls into life.

4. Yet this is no excuse for those who continue in sin, and lay the blame upon their Maker by saying: 'It is God only that must quicken us; for we cannot quicken our own souls.' For allowing that all the souls of men are dead in sin by *nature,* this excuses none, seeing there is no man that is in a state of mere

nature; there is no man, unless he has quenched the Spirit, that is wholly void of the grace of God. No man living is entirely destitute of what is vulgarly called 'natural conscience'. But this is not natural; it is more properly termed 'preventing grace'. Every man has a greater or less measure of this, which waiteth not for the call of man. Everyone has sooner or later good desires, although the generality of men stifle them before they can strike deep root or produce any considerable fruit. Everyone has some measure of that light, some faint glimmering ray, which sooner or later, more or less, enlightens every man that cometh into the world. And everyone, unless he be one of the small number whose conscience is seared as with a hot iron, feels more or less uneasy when he acts contrary to the light of his own conscience. So that no man sins because he has not grace, but because he does not use the grace which he hath.

5. Therefore inasmuch as God works in you, you are now able to work out your own salvation. Since he worketh in you of his own good pleasure, without any merit of yours, both to will and to do, it is possible for you to fulfil all righteousness. It is possible for you to 'love God, because he hath first loved us', and to 'walk in love', after the pattern of our great Master. We know indeed that word of his to be absolutely true, 'Without me ye can do nothing.' But on the other hand we know, every believer can say, 'I can do all things through Christ that strengtheneth me.'

6. Meantime let us remember that God has joined these together in the experience of every believer. And therefore we must take care not to imagine they are ever to be put asunder. We must beware of that mock humility which teacheth us to say, in excuse for our wilful disobedience, 'Oh, I can do nothing,' and stops there, without once naming the grace of God. Pray think twice. Consider what you say. I hope you wrong yourself. For if it be really true that you can do nothing, then you have no faith. And if you have not faith you are in a wretched condition. Surely it is not so. You can do something, through Christ strengthening you. Stir up the spark of grace which is now in you, and he will give you more grace.

7. Secondly, God worketh in you; therefore you *must* work: you must be 'workers together with him' (they are the very words of the Apostle); otherwise he will cease working. The general rule on which his gracious dispensations invariably proceed is this: 'Unto him that hath shall be given; but from him that hath not', that does not improve the grace already given, 'shall be taken away what he assuredly hath' (so the words ought to be rendered). Even St. Augustine, who is generally supposed to favour the contrary doctrine, makes that just remark, *Qui fecit nos sine nobis, non salvabit nos sine nobis*: 'he that made us without ourselves, will not save us without ourselves.' He will not save us unless we 'save ourselves from this untoward generation'; unless we ourselves 'fight the good fight of faith, and lay hold on eternal life'; unless we 'agonize to enter in at the strait gate,' 'deny ourselves, and take up our cross

daily', and labour, by every possible means, to 'make our own calling and election sure'.

8. 'Labour' then, brethren, 'not for the meat that perisheth, but for that which endureth to everlasting life.' Say with our blessed Lord, though in a somewhat different sense, 'My Father worketh hitherto, and I work.' In consideration that he still worketh in you, be never 'weary of well-doing'. Go on, in virtue of the grace of God preventing, accompanying, and following you, in 'the work of faith, in the patience of hope, and in the labour of love'. 'Be ye steadfast and immovable; always abounding in the work of the Lord.' And 'the God of peace, who brought again from the dead the great Shepherd of the sheep'—Jesus—'make you perfect in every good work to do his will, working in you what is well-pleasing in his sight, through Jesus Christ, to whom be glory for ever and ever!'

THE NEW CREATION

Sermon 64 – 1785

AN INTRODUCTORY COMMENT

The aged Wesley returned again and again to his vision of cosmic redemption: the restoration of all creation including the entire human family, as the final, full benefit of God's unbounded love. This sermon was written in 1785 for inclusion in the November and December issues of the *Arminian Magazine* for that year, without a title and no further indication of place or date. The only prior reference to a sermon on Rev. 21:5 comes just two years earlier (January 1, 1783); the only other recorded instance comes five years later (August 4, 1790). Wesley placed this sermon in volume five of his collected *Sermons* (1788), with its present title and in the series of essays in Wesleyan eschatology that had begun with 'God's Love to Fallen Man'.

Wesley begins by taking the implied future tense seriously, showing that he is talking about 'the universal restoration which is to succeed the universal destruction'. Surprisingly, the bulk of the sermon describes how the qualities (though not the nature) of air, fire, water, and earth (the four Greek elements) will be new. The climax, of course, is the description of the changes anticipated throughout all animated nature. The picture is not only one of the 'peaceable kingdom' in the animal realm (Isa. 11:6), but also of humanity enjoying an 'unmixed state of holiness and happiness far superior to that which Adam enjoyed in paradise': without death, or pain, or sickness, or sorrow–'for there will be nor more sin' (see also 'God's Love to Fallen Man').

This sermon is remarkable for its unusual level of speculation (more than Wesley was wont to allow himself) and for its numerous allusions to the speculations of others, including an almost casual passing reference to a then quite lively controversy about 'the plurality of [inhabited] worlds'. Wesley's endorsement of the then novel idea of progress reflects his unfaltering optimism, in his case an optimism of grace rather than of nature.

The New Creation

Behold, I make all things new.
Revelation 21:5

1. What a strange scene is here opened to our view! How remote from all our natural apprehensions! Not a glimpse of what is here revealed was ever seen in the heathen world. Not only the modern, barbarous, uncivilized heathens have not the least conception of it; but it was equally unknown to the refined, polished heathens of ancient Greece and Rome. And it is almost as little thought of or understood by the generality of Christians: I mean, not barely those that are nominally such, that have the form of godliness without the power; but even those that in a measure fear God and study to work righteousness.

2. It must be allowed that after all the researches we can make, still our knowledge of the great truth which is delivered to us in these words is exceedingly short and imperfect. As this is a point of mere revelation, beyond the reach of all our natural faculties, we cannot penetrate far into it, nor form any adequate conception of it. But it may be an encouragement to those who have in any degree tasted of the powers of the world to come to go as far as we can go, interpreting Scripture by Scripture, according to the analogy of faith.

3. The Apostle, caught up in the visions of God, tells us in the first verse of the chapter, 'I saw a new heaven and a new earth'; and adds, 'He that sat upon the throne said (I believe the only words which he is said to utter throughout the whole book), Behold, I make all things new' (Rev. 21:5).

4. Very many commentators entertain a strange opinion that this relates only to the present state of things, and gravely tell us that the words are to be referred to the flourishing state of the church, which commenced after the heathen persecutions. Nay, some of them have discovered that all which the Apostle speaks concerning the 'new heaven and the new earth' was fulfilled when Constantine the Great poured in riches and honours upon the Christians. What a miserable way is this of making void the whole counsel of God with regard to all that grand chain of events, in reference to his church, yea, and to all mankind, from the time that John was in Patmos unto the end of the world! Nay, the line of this prophecy reaches farther still. It does not end with the present world, but shows us the things that will come to pass when this world is no more.

5. Thus saith the Creator and Governor of the universe, 'Behold, I make

all things new': all which are included in that expression of the Apostle, 'a new heaven and a new earth'. 'A new heaven': the original word in Genesis (chapter one) is in the plural number. And indeed this is the constant language of Scripture—not *heaven*, but *heavens*. Accordingly the ancient Jewish writers are accustomed to reckon three heavens. In conformity to which the apostle Paul speaks of his being 'caught up into the third heaven'. It is this, the third heaven, which is usually supposed to be the more immediate residence of God—so far as any residence can be ascribed to his omnipresent Spirit, who pervades and fills the whole universe. It is here (if we speak after the manner of men) that the Lord sitteth upon his throne, surrounded by angels and archangels, and by all his flaming ministers.

6. We cannot think that this heaven will undergo any change, any more than its great inhabitant. Surely this palace of the Most High was the same from eternity, and will be world without end. Only the inferior heavens are liable to change; the highest of which we usually call the starry heaven. This, St. Peter informs us, is 'reserved unto fire, against the day of judgment and destruction of ungodly men'. In that day, 'being on fire', it shall first shrivel as a parchment scroll; then it shall 'be dissolved', and 'shall pass away with a great noise'; lastly it shall 'flee from the face of him that sitteth on the throne', 'and there shall be found no place for it.'

7. At the same time 'the stars shall fall from heaven,' the secret chain being broken which had retained them in their several orbits from the foundation of the world. In the meanwhile the lower or sublunary 'heaven', with 'the elements' (or principles that compose it), 'shall melt with fervent heat,' while 'the earth with the works that are therein shall be burnt up.' This is the introduction to a far nobler state of things, such as it has not yet entered into the heart of men to conceive—the universal restoration which is to succeed the universal destruction. For 'we look for', says the Apostle, 'new heavens and a new earth, wherein dwelleth righteousness' (2 Pet. 3:7, etc.).

8. One considerable difference there will undoubtedly be in the starry heaven when it is created anew; there will be no blazing stars, no comets there. Whether those horrid, eccentric orbs are half-formed planets, in a chaotic state (I speak on the supposition of a plurality of worlds) or such as have undergone their general conflagration, they will certainly have no place in the new heaven, where all will be exact order and harmony. There may be many other differences between the heaven that now is and that which will be after the renovation. But they are above our apprehension: we must leave eternity to explain them.

9. We may more easily conceive the changes which will be wrought in the lower heaven, in the region of the air. It will be no more torn by hurricanes, or agitated by furious storms or destructive tempests. Pernicious or terrifying meteors will have no more place therein. We shall have no more occasion to say,

There like a trumpet, loud and strong,
  Thy thunder shakes our coast;
While the red lightnings wave along,
  The banners of thy host!

No; all will be then light, fair, serene—a lively picture of the eternal day.

10. All the elements (taking that word in the common sense for the principles of which all natural beings are compounded) will be new indeed; entirely changed as to their qualities, although not as to their nature. *Fire* is at present the general destroyer of all things under the sun; dissolving all things that come within the sphere of its action, and reducing them to their primitive atoms. But no sooner will it have performed its last great office of destroying the heavens and the earth (whether you mean thereby one system only, or the whole fabric of the universe—the difference between one and millions of worlds being nothing before the great Creator); when, I say, it has done this, the destruction wrought by fire will come to a perpetual end. It will destroy no more; it will consume no more; it will forget its power to burn, which it possesses only during the present state of things, and be as harmless in the new heavens and earth as it is now in the bodies of men and other animals, and the substance of trees and flowers; in all which (as late experiments show) large quantities of ethereal fire are lodged—if it be not rather an essential component part of every material being under the sun. But it will probably retain its vivifying power, though divested of its power to destroy.

11. It has been already observed that the calm, placid *air* will be no more disturbed by storms and tempests. There will be no more meteors with their horrid glare, affrighting the poor children of men. May we not add (though at first it may sound like a paradox) that there will be no more rain. It is observable that there was none in paradise; a circumstance which Moses particularly mentions: 'The Lord God had not caused it to rain upon the earth. But there went up a mist from the earth,' which then covered up the abyss of waters, 'and watered the whole face of the ground' (Gen. 2:5-6) with moisture sufficient for all the purposes of vegetation. We have all reason to believe that the case will be the same when paradise is restored. Consequently there will be no more clouds or fogs; but one bright, refulgent day. Much less will there be any poisonous damps or pestilential blasts. There will be no sirocco in Italy; no parching or suffocating winds in Arabia; no keen north-east winds in our own country,

Shattering the graceful locks of yon fair trees;

but only pleasing, healthful breezes,

Fanning the earth with odoriferous wings.

12. But what change will the element of *water* undergo when all things are made new? It will be in every part of the world clear and limpid, pure from all unpleasing or unhealthful mixtures; rising here and there in crystal fountains to refresh and adorn the earth 'with liquid lapse of murmuring stream'. For undoubtedly, as there were in paradise, there will be various rivers gently gliding along, for the use and pleasure of both man and beast. But the inspired writer has expressly declared, 'there will be no more sea' (Rev. 21:1). We have reason to believe that at the beginning of the world, when God said, 'Let the waters under the heaven be gathered together unto one place, and let the dry land appear' (Gen. 1:9), the dry land spread over the face of the water, and covered it on every side. And so it seems to have done till, in order to the general deluge which he had determined to bring upon the earth at once, 'the windows of heaven were opened, and the fountains of the great deep broken up.' But the sea will then retire within its primitive bounds, and appear on the surface of the earth no more. Neither indeed will there be any more need of the sea. For either as the ancient poet supposes,

Omnis feret omnia tellus–

every part of the earth will naturally produce whatever its inhabitants want—or all mankind will procure what the whole earth affords by a much easier and readier conveyance. For all the inhabitants of the earth, our Lord informs us, will then be ἰσάγγελοι, 'equal to angels'; on a level with them in swiftness as well as strength; so that they can quick as thought transport themselves or whatever they want from one side of the globe to the other.

13. But it seems a greater change will be wrought in the *earth* than even in the air and water. Not that I can believe that wonderful discovery of Jacob Boehme, which many so eagerly contend for, that the earth itself with all its furniture and inhabitants will then be transparent as glass. There does not seem to be the least foundation for this, either in Scripture or reason. Surely not in Scripture: I know not one text in the Old or New Testament which affirms any such thing. Certainly it cannot be inferred from that text in the Revelation, chapter the fourth, verse the sixth: 'And before the throne there was a sea of glass, like unto crystal.' And yet, if I mistake not, this is the chief, if not the only Scripture which has been urged in favour of this opinion! Neither can I conceive that it has any foundation in reason. It has indeed been warmly alleged that all things would be far more beautiful if they were quite transparent. But I cannot apprehend this; yea, I apprehend quite the contrary. Suppose every part of a human body were made transparent as crystal, would it appear more beautiful than it does now? Nay, rather it would shock us above measure. The surface of the body, and in particular 'the human face divine', is undoubtedly one of the most beautiful objects that can be found under heaven. But could you look through the rosy cheek, the smooth, fair forehead,

or the rising bosom, and distinctly see all that lies within, you would turn away from it with loathing and horror.

14. Let us next take a view of those changes which we may reasonably suppose will then take place in the *earth*. It will no more be bound up with intense cold, nor parched up with extreme heat; but will have such a temperature as will be most conducive to its fruitfulness. If in order to punish its inhabitants God did of old

Bid his angels turn askance
This oblique globe,

thereby occasioning violent cold on one part, and violent heat on the other; he will undoubtedly then order them to restore it to its original position; so that there will be a final end, on the one hand of the burning heat which makes some parts of it scarce habitable; and on the other of

The rage of Arctos, and eternal frost.

15. And it will then contain no jarring or destructive principles within its own bosom. It will no more have any of those violent convulsions in its own bowels. It will no more be shaken or torn asunder by the impetuous force of *earthquakes*; and will therefore need neither Vesuvius nor Etna, nor any *burning mountains* to prevent them. There will be no more horrid rocks or frightful precipices; no wild deserts or barren sands; no impassable morasses or unfaithful bogs to swallow up the unwary traveller. There will doubtless be inequalities on the surface of the earth, which are not blemishes, but beauties. For though I will not affirm that

earth hath this variety from heaven
Of pleasure situate in hill and dale;

yet I cannot think gently rising hills will be any defect, but an ornament of the new-made earth. And doubtless we shall then likewise have occasion to say:

Lo there his wondrous skill arrays
The fields in cheerful green!
A thousand herbs his hand displays,
A thousand flowers between!

16. And what will the general produce of the earth be? Not thorns, briars, or thistles. Not any useless or fetid weed; not any poisonous, hurtful, or unpleasant plant; but every one that can be conducive in any wise either to our use or pleasure. How far beyond all that the most lively imagination is now able to conceive! We shall no more regret the loss of the terrestrial paradise, or sigh at that well-devised description of our great poet;

Then shall this mount
Of paradise by might of waves be moved
Out of his place, pushed by the horned flood,
With all its verdure spoiled, and trees adrift,
Down the great river to the opening gulf,
And there take root, an island salt and bare!

For all the earth shall then be a more beautiful paradise than Adam ever saw.

17. Such will be the state of the new earth with regard to the meaner, the inanimate parts of it. But great as this change will be, it is little, it is nothing, in comparison of that which will then take place throughout all animated nature. In the living part of the creation were seen the most deplorable effects of Adam's apostasy. The whole animated creation, whatever has life, from leviathan to the smallest mite, was thereby 'made subject' to such 'vanity' as the inanimate creatures could not be. They were subject to that fell monster, death, the conqueror of all that breathe. They were made subject to its forerunner, pain, in its ten thousand forms; although 'God made not death, neither hath he pleasure in the death of any living.' How many millions of creatures in the sea, in the air, and on every part of the earth, can now no otherwise preserve their own lives than by taking away the lives of others; by tearing in pieces and devouring their poor, innocent, unresisting fellow-creatures! Miserable lot of such innumerable multitudes, who, insignificant as they seem, are the offspring of one common Father, the creatures of the same God of love! It is probable not only two-thirds of the animal creation, but ninety-nine parts out of a hundred, are under a necessity of destroying others in order to preserve their own life! But it shall not always be so. He that sitteth upon the throne will soon change the face of all things, and give a demonstrative proof to all his creatures that 'his mercy is over all his works.' The horrid state of things which at present obtains will soon be at an end. On the new earth no creature will kill or hurt or give pain to any other. The scorpion will have no poisonous sting, the adder no venomous teeth. The lion will have no claws to tear the lamb; no teeth to grind his flesh and bones. Nay, no creature, no beast, bird, or fish, will have any inclination to hurt any other. For cruelty will be far away, and savageness and fierceness be forgotten. So that violence shall be heard no more, neither wasting or destruction seen on the face of the earth. 'The wolf shall dwell with the lamb' (the words may be literally as well as figuratively understood) 'and the leopard shall lie down with the kid.' 'They shall not hurt or destroy,' from the rising up of the sun to the going down of the same.

18. But the most glorious of all will be the change which then will take place on the poor, sinful, miserable children of men. These had fallen in many respects, as from a greater height, so into a lower depth than any other part of the creation. But they shall 'hear a great voice out of heaven, saying, Behold,

the tabernacle of God is with men, and he will dwell with them, and they shall be his people, and God himself shall be their God.' Hence will arise an unmixed state of holiness and happiness far superior to that which Adam enjoyed in paradise. In how beautiful and affecting a manner is this described by the Apostle! 'God shall wipe away all tears from their eyes; and there shall be no more death, neither sorrow nor crying, neither shall there be any more pain: for the former things are done away' (Rev. 21:3–4). As there will be no more death, and no more pain or sickness preparatory thereto; as there will be no more grieving for or parting with friends; so there will be no more sorrow or crying. Nay, but there will be a greater deliverance than all this; for there will be no more sin. And to crown all, there will be a deep, an intimate, an uninterrupted union with God; a constant communion with the Father and his Son Jesus Christ, through the Spirit; a continual enjoyment of the Three-One God, and of all the creatures in him!

THE DUTY OF CONSTANT COMMUNION

Sermon 101 – 1787

AN INTRODUCTORY COMMENT

This sermon represents Wesley's fullest and most explicit statement of his eucharistic doctrine and praxis as well as his untroubled reliance upon a classic expression of the 'catholic tradition' in current Anglican doctrine at that time.

In 1732, Wesley wrote an extract of *The Great Duty of Frequenting the Christian Sacrifice* (1707) by Robert Nelson, the most celebrated Anglican liturgist of the day. Wesley designed to use the treatise primarily with his own students and friends at Oxford. In his extract, Wesley actually rewrote a good deal of Nelson's text, incorporated a few portions from other authors such as William Beveridge, and added some original material of his own. The shift of emphasis from Nelson's 'frequenting the Christian sacrifice' to Wesley's 'constant communion' seems to have been suggested by a tract of Arthur Bury's, the controversial rector of Exeter College, Oxford, entitled *The Constant Communicant* (1681), which was also read by the Oxford Methodists.

Fifty-five years later, Wesley proceeded to abridge the earlier extract and to revise it still further. He then presented the result as an 'original sermon' in the *Arminian Magazine* (1787), with the postscript, 'Oxon., Feb. 19, 1732'. It has no title but has a heading 'To the Reader', claiming the text as Wesley's own. This assertion, however, raises a nice question, since there is too much of Nelson here for it to be acknowledged as truly 'original' and too much of Wesley for it to be labelled as wholly 'borrowed'. When Wesley decided to include the *Magazine* revision of his earlier revision of Nelson in volume eight of his collected *Sermons*, he gave it its present title and repeated the earlier heading, 'To the Reader':

> The following discourse was written above five and fifty years ago, for the use of my pupils at Oxford. I have added very little, but retrenched much; as I then used more words than I do now. But I thank God I have not yet seen cause to alter my sentiments in any point which is therein delivered.

The Duty of Constant Communion

Do this in remembrance of me.
Luke 22:19

It is no wonder that men who have no fear of God should never think of doing this. But it is strange that it should be neglected by any that do fear God, and desire to save their souls. And yet nothing is more common. One reason why any neglect it is, they are so much afraid of 'eating and drinking unworthily' that they never think how much greater the danger is when they do not eat or drink it at all. That I may do what I can to bring these well-meaning men to a more just way of thinking, I shall,

First, show that it is the duty of every Christian to receive the Lord's Supper as often as he can; and secondly, answer some objections.

I. I am to show that it is the duty of every Christian to receive the Lord's Supper as often as he can.

1. The first reason why it is the duty of every Christian so to do is because it is a plain command of Christ. That this is his command appears from the words of the text, 'Do this in remembrance of me': by which, as the Apostles were obliged to bless, break, and give the bread to all that joined with them in those holy things, so were all Christians obliged to receive those signs of Christ's body and blood. Here therefore the bread and wine are commanded to be received, in remembrance of his death, to the end of the world. Observe, too, that this command was given by our Lord when he was just laying down his life for our sakes. They are therefore, as it were, his dying words to all his followers.

2. A second reason why every Christian should do this as often as he can is because the benefits of doing it are so great to all that do it in obedience to him; namely, the forgiveness of our past sins and the present strengthening and refreshing of our souls. In this world we are never free from temptations. Whatever way of life we are in, whatever our condition be, whether we are sick or well, in trouble or at ease, the enemies of our souls are watching to lead us into sin. And too often they prevail over us. Now when we are convinced of having sinned against God, what surer way have we of procuring pardon from him than the 'showing forth the Lord's death', and beseeching him, for the sake of his Son's sufferings, to blot out all our sins?

3. The grace of God given herein confirms to us the pardon of our sins by

enabling us to leave them. As our bodies are strengthened by bread and wine, so are our souls by these tokens of the body and blood of Christ. This is the food of our souls: this gives strength to perform our duty, and leads us on to perfection. If therefore we have any regard for the plain command of Christ, if we desire the pardon of our sins, if we wish for strength to believe, to love and obey God, then we should neglect no opportunity of receiving the Lord's Supper. Then we must never turn our backs on the feast which our Lord has prepared for us. We must neglect no occasion which the good providence of God affords us for this purpose. This is the true rule—so often are we to receive as God gives us opportunity. Whoever therefore does not receive, but goes from the holy table when all things are prepared, either does not understand his duty or does not care for the dying command of his Saviour, the forgiveness of his sins, the strengthening of his soul, and the refreshing it with the hope of glory.

4. Let everyone therefore who has either any desire to please God, or any love of his own soul, obey God and consult the good of his own soul by communicating every time he can; like the first Christians, with whom the Christian sacrifice was a constant part of the Lord's day's service. And for several centuries they received it almost every day. Four times a week always, and every saint's day beside. Accordingly those that joined in the prayers of the faithful never failed to partake of the blessed sacrament. What opinion they had of any who turned his back upon it we may learn from that ancient canon, 'If any believer join in the prayers of the faithful, and go away without receiving the Lord's Supper, let him be excommunicated, as bringing confusion into the church of God.'

5. In order to understand the nature of the Lord's Supper, it would be useful carefully to read over those passages in the Gospel and in the first Epistle to the Corinthians which speak of the institution of it. Hence we learn that the design of this sacrament is the continual remembrance of the death of Christ, by eating bread and drinking wine, which are the outward signs of the inward grace, the body and blood of Christ.

6. It is highly expedient for those who purpose to receive this, whenever their time will permit, to prepare themselves for this solemn ordinance by self-examination and prayer. But this is not absolutely necessary. And when we have not time for it, we should see that we have the habitual preparation which is absolutely necessary, and can never be dispensed with on any account or any occasion whatever. This is, first, a full *purpose* of heart to keep all the commandments of God. And secondly, a sincere *desire* to receive all his promises.

II. I am, in the second place, to answer the common objections against constantly receiving the Lord's Supper.

1. I say 'constantly' receiving. For as to the phrase of 'frequent communion', it is absurd to the last degree. If it means anything less than constant it means more than can be proved to be the duty of any man. For if we are not obliged to communicate 'constantly', by what argument can it be proved that we are obliged to communicate 'frequently'? Yea, more than once a year, or once in seven years? Or once before we die? Every argument brought for this either proves that we ought to do it *constantly*, or proves nothing at all. Therefore that indeterminate, unmeaning way of speaking ought to be laid aside by all men of understanding.

2. In order to prove that it is our duty to communicate constantly we may observe that the Holy Communion is to be considered either (1) as a command of God or (2) as a mercy to man.

First, as a command of God. God, our Mediator and Governor, from whom we have received our life and all things, on whose will it depends whether we shall be perfectly happy or perfectly miserable from this moment to eternity, declares to us that all who obey his commands shall be eternally happy; all who do not shall be eternally miserable. Now one of these commands is, 'Do this in remembrance of me.' I ask then, 'Why do you not do this, when you can do it if you will? When you have an opportunity before you, why do not you obey the command of God?'

3. Perhaps you will say, 'God does not command me to do this *as often as I can*'; that is, the words 'as often as you can' are not added in this particular place. What then? Are we not to obey every command of God as often as we can? Are not all the promises of God made to those, and those only, who 'give all diligence'; that is, to those who do all they can to obey his commandments? Our power is the one rule of our duty. Whatever we can do, that we ought. With respect either to this or any other command, he that when he may obey it if he will does not, will have no place in the kingdom of heaven.

4. And this great truth, that we are obliged to keep every command as far as we can, is clearly proved from the absurdity of the contrary opinion; for were we to allow that we are not obliged to obey every commandment of God as often as we can, we have no argument left to prove that any man is bound to obey any command at any time. For instance, should I ask a man why he does not obey one of the plainest commands of God–why, for instance, he does not help his parents–he might answer, 'I will not do it now, but I will at another time.' When that time comes, put him in mind of God's command again and he will say, 'I will obey it some time or other.' Nor is it possible ever to prove that he ought to do it now, unless by proving that he ought to do it as often as he can: and therefore he ought to do it now, because he can if he will.

5. Consider the Lord's Supper, secondly, as a mercy from God to man. As God, whose mercy is over all his works, and particularly over the children of

men, knew there was but one way for man to be happy like himself, namely, by being like him in holiness; as he knew we could do nothing toward this of ourselves, he has given us certain means of obtaining his help. One of these is the Lord's Supper, which of his infinite mercy he hath given for this very end: that through this means we may be assisted to attain those blessings which he hath prepared for us; that we may obtain holiness on earth and everlasting glory in heaven.

I ask, then, why do you not accept of his mercy as often as ever you can? God now offers you his blessing: why do you refuse it? You have an opportunity of receiving his mercy: why do you not receive it? You are weak: why do not you seize upon every opportunity of increasing your strength? In a word: considering this as a command of God, he that does not communicate as often as he can has no piety; considering it as a mercy, he that does not communicate as often as he can has no wisdom.

6. These two considerations will yield a full answer to all the common objections which have been made against constant communion; indeed to all that ever were or can be made. In truth nothing can be objected against it but upon supposition that at this particular time, either the communion would be no mercy, or I am not commanded to receive it. Nay, should we grant it would be no mercy, that is not enough; for still the other reason would hold: whether it does you any good or none, you are to obey the command of God.

7. However, let us see the particular excuses which men commonly make for not obeying it. The most common is, 'I am *unworthy*; and "he that eateth and drinketh unworthily, eateth and drinketh damnation to himself." Therefore I dare not communicate, lest I should eat and drink my own damnation.'

The case is this. God offers you one of the greatest mercies on this side heaven, and commands you to accept it. Why do not you accept this mercy in obedience to his command? You say, 'I am unworthy to receive it.' And what then? You are unworthy to receive any mercy from God. But is that a reason for refusing all mercy? God offers you a pardon for all your sins. You are unworthy of it, 'tis sure, and he knows it: but since he is pleased to offer it nevertheless, will not you accept of it? He offers to deliver your soul from death. You are unworthy to live. But will you therefore refuse life? He offers to endue your soul with new strength. Because you are unworthy of it, will you deny to take it? What can God himself do for us farther, if we refuse his mercy, even because we are unworthy of it?

8. But suppose this were no mercy to us (to suppose which is indeed giving God the lie; saying, that is not good for man which he purposely ordered for his good), still I ask, Why do not you obey God's command? He says, 'Do this.' Why do you not? You answer, 'I am unworthy to do it.' What! Unworthy to obey God? Unworthy to do what God bids you do? Unworthy to obey God's command? What do you mean by this? That those who are unworthy to obey

God ought not to obey him? Who told you so? If he were even 'an angel from heaven, let him be accursed'. If you think God himself has told you so by St. Paul, let us hear his words. They are these: 'He that eateth and drinketh unworthily, eateth and drinketh damnation to himself.'

Why, this is quite another thing. Here is not a word said of 'being unworthy' to eat and drink. Indeed he does speak of eating and drinking 'unworthily'; but that is quite a different thing—so he has told us himself. In this very chapter we are told that by eating and drinking unworthily is meant taking the holy sacrament in such a rude and disorderly way that one was 'hungry and another drunken'. But what is that to *you?* Is there any danger of *your* doing so? Of your eating and drinking *thus* 'unworthily'? However unworthy you are to communicate, there is no fear of your communicating thus. Therefore, whatever the punishment is of doing it thus unworthily, it does not concern *you*. You have no more reason from this text to disobey God than if there was no such text in the Bible. If you speak of 'eating and drinking unworthily' in the sense St. Paul uses the words you may as well say, 'I dare not communicate "for fear the church should fall" as for fear I should "eat and drink unworthily".'

9. If then you fear bringing *damnation* on yourself by this, you fear where no fear is. Fear it not for eating and drinking unworthily; for that, in St. Paul's sense, ye cannot do. But I will tell you for what you shall fear damnation: for not eating and drinking at all; for not obeying your Maker and Redeemer; for disobeying his plain command; for thus setting at nought both his mercy and authority. Fear ye this; for hear what his Apostle saith: 'Whosoever shall keep the whole law, and yet offend in one point, is guilty of all' (Jas. 2:10).

10. We see then how weak the objection is, 'I dare not receive (the Lord's Supper), because I am unworthy.' Nor is it any stronger, though the reason why you think yourself unworthy is that you have lately fallen into sin. It is true our Church forbids those 'who have done any grievous crime' to receive without repentance. But all that follows from this is that we should repent before we come; not that we should neglect to come at all.

To say, therefore, that 'a man may turn his back upon the altar because he has lately fallen into sin; that he may impose this penance upon himself', is talking without any warrant from Scripture. For where does the Bible teach to atone for breaking one commandment of God by breaking another? What advice is this—'Commit a new act of disobedience, and God will more easily forgive the past'!

11. Others there are who to excuse their disobedience plead that they are unworthy in another sense, that they 'cannot live up to it; they cannot pretend to lead so holy a life as constantly communicating would oblige them to do.' Put this into plain words. I ask: Why do not you accept the mercy which God commands you to accept? You answer, 'Because I cannot live up to the profession I must make when I receive it.' Then it is plain you ought never to

receive it at all. For it is no more lawful to promise once what you know you cannot perform than to promise it a thousand times. You know, too, that it is one and the same promise whether you make it every year or every day. You promise to do just as much whether you promise ever so often or ever so seldom.

If therefore you cannot live up to the profession they make who communicate once a week, neither can you come up to the profession you make who communicate once a year. But cannot you, indeed? Then it had been good for you that you had never been born. For all that you profess at the Lord's table you must both profess and keep, or you cannot be saved. For you profess nothing there but this, that you will diligently keep his commandments. And cannot you keep up to this profession? Then you cannot enter into life.

12. Think then what you say, before you say you cannot live up to what is required of constant communicants. This is no more than is required of any communicants, yea, of everyone that has a soul to be saved. So that to say you cannot live up to this is neither better nor worse than renouncing Christianity. It is in effect renouncing your baptism, wherein you solemnly promised to keep all his commandments. You now fly from that profession. You wilfully break one of his commandments, and to excuse yourself say you cannot keep his commandments! Then you cannot expect to receive the promises, which are made only to those that keep them.

13. What has been said on this pretence against constant communion is applicable to those who say the same thing in other words: 'We dare not do it, because it requires so perfect an obedience afterwards as we cannot promise to perform.' Nay, it requires neither more nor less perfect obedience than you promised in your baptism. You then undertook to keep the commandments of God by his help, and you promise no more when you communicate.

But observe upon the whole, this is not so properly an objection against constantly communicating as against communicating at all. For if we are not to receive the Lord's Supper till we are worthy of it, it is certain we ought never to receive it.

14. A second objection which is often made against constant communion is the having so much business as will not allow time for such a preparation as is necessary thereto. I answer: all the preparation that is absolutely necessary is contained in those words, 'Repent you truly of your sins past; have faith in Christ our Saviour' (and observe, that word is not here taken in its highest sense!); 'amend your lives, and be in charity with all men; so shall ye be meet partakers of these holy mysteries.' All who are thus prepared may draw near without fear, and receive the sacrament to their comfort. Now what business can hinder you from being thus prepared? From repenting of your past sins? From believing that Christ died to save sinners? From amending your lives, and being in charity with all men? No business can hinder you from this,

unless it be such as hinders you from being in a state of salvation. If you resolve and design to follow Christ you are fit to approach the Lord's table. If you do not design this, you are only fit for the table and company of devils.

15. No business therefore can hinder any man from having that preparation which alone is necessary, unless it be such as unprepares him for heaven, as puts him out of a state of salvation. Indeed every prudent man will, when he has time, examine himself before he receives the Lord's Supper: whether he repents him truly of his former sins; whether he believes the promises of God; whether he fully designs to walk in his ways, and be in charity with all men. In this, and in private prayer, he will doubtless spend all the time he conveniently can. But what is this to *you* who have not time? What excuse is this for not obeying God? He commands you to come, and prepare yourself by prayer if you have time; if you have not, however, come. Make not reverence to God's command a pretence for breaking it. Do not rebel against him for fear of offending him. Whatever you do or leave undone besides, be sure to do what God bids you do. Examining yourself, and using private prayer, especially before the Lord's Supper, is good. But behold! 'To obey is better than' self-examination, 'and to hearken' than the prayer of an angel.

16. A third objection against constant communion is that it abates our reverence for the sacrament. Suppose it did? What then! Will you thence conclude that you are not to receive it constantly? This does not follow. God commands you, 'Do this.' You may do it now, but will not; and to excuse yourself say, 'If I do it so often, it will abate the reverence with which I do it now.' Suppose it did. Has God ever told you that when the obeying his command abates your reverence to it then you may disobey it? If he has, you are guiltless; if not, what you say is just nothing to the purpose. The law is clear. Either show that the lawgiver makes this exception, or you are guilty before him.

17. Reverence for the sacrament may be of two sorts: either such as is owing purely to the newness of the thing, such as men naturally have for anything they are not used to; or such as is owing to our faith, or to the love or fear of God. Now the former of these is not properly a religious reverence, but purely natural. And this sort of reverence for the Lord's Supper the constantly receiving of it must lessen. But it will not lessen the true religious reverence, but rather confirm and increase it.

18. A fourth objection is, 'I have communicated constantly so long, but I have not found the benefit I expected.' This has been the case with many well-meaning persons, and therefore deserves to be particularly considered. And consider this first: whatever God commands us to do we are to do because he commands, whether we feel any benefit thereby or no. Now God commands, 'Do this in remembrance of me.' This therefore we are to do, because he commands, whether we find present benefit thereby or not. But undoubt-

edly we shall find benefit sooner or later, though perhaps insensibly. We shall be insensibly strengthened, made more fit for the service of God, and more constant in it. At least we are kept from falling back, and preserved from many sins and temptations. And surely this should be enough to make us receive this food as often as we can; though we do not presently feel the happy effects of it, as some have done, and we ourselves may when God sees best.

19. But suppose a man has often been at the sacrament, and yet received no benefit. Was it not his own fault? Either he was not rightly prepared, willing to obey all the commands, and to receive all the promises of God; or he did not receive it aright, trusting in God. Only see that you are duly prepared for it, and the oftener you come to the Lord's table the greater benefit you will find there.

20. A fifth objection which some have made against constant communion is that 'the Church enjoins it only three times a year.' The words of the Church are: 'Note, that every parishioner shall communicate at the least three times in the year.' To this I answer, first: What if the Church had not enjoined it at all? Is it not enough that God enjoins it? We obey the Church only for God's sake. And shall we not obey God himself? If then you receive three times a year because the Church commands it, receive every time you can because God commands it. Else your doing the one will be so far from excusing you for not doing the other that your own practice will prove your folly and sin, and leave you without excuse.

But, secondly, we cannot conclude from these words that the Church excuses him who receives only thrice a year. The plain sense of them is that he who does not receive thrice at least shall be cast out of the Church. But they do by no means excuse him who communicates no oftener. This never was the judgment of our Church. On the contrary, she takes all possible care that the sacrament be duly administered, wherever the Common Prayer is read, every Sunday and holiday in the year.

The Church gives a particular direction with regard to those that are in Holy Orders. 'In all cathedral and collegiate churches and colleges, where there are many priests and deacons, they shall all receive the communion with the priest, every Sunday at the least.'

21. It has been shown, first, that if we consider the Lord's Supper as a command of Christ, no man can have any pretence to Christian piety who does not receive it (not once a month, but) as often as he can; secondly, that if we consider the institution of it as a mercy to ourselves, no man who does not receive it as often as he can has any pretence to Christian prudence; thirdly, that none of the objections usually made can be any excuse for that man who does not at every opportunity obey his command and accept this mercy.

22. It has been particularly shown, first, that unworthiness is no excuse, because, though in one sense we are all unworthy, yet none of us need be

afraid of being unworthy in St. Paul's sense, of 'eating and drinking unworthily'; secondly, that the not having time enough for preparation can be no excuse, since the only preparation which is absolutely necessary is that which no business can hinder; nor indeed anything on earth, unless so far as it hinders our being in a state of salvation; thirdly, that its abating our reverence is no excuse, since he who gave the command, 'Do this', nowhere adds, 'unless it abates your reverence'; fourthly, that our not profiting by it is no excuse, since it is our own fault in neglecting that necessary preparation which is in our own power; lastly, that the judgment of our own Church is quite in favour of constant communion. If those who have hitherto neglected it on any of these pretences will lay these things to heart, they will, by the grace of God, come to a better mind, and never more forsake their own mercies.

THE MORE EXCELLENT WAY

Sermon 89 – 1787

AN INTRODUCTORY COMMENT

This sermon is a practical essay in Christian ethics that also illustrates how far the later Wesley had moved away from his earlier exclusivist standards of true faith and salvation. It should be read alongside *The Almost Christian*; the startling contrast between the two reflects a half-century's experience as leader of a revival movement and also a significant change in his mind and heart. Here, more explicitly than anywhere else in his writings, we see Wesley's acceptance of an older notion (seen in Clement of Alexandria) of 'two orders of Christians', each with its legitimate hope of salvation. At the same time as he admits that those on the lower road (simply avoiding evil, doing good, and attending the ordinances of God) are not headed for hell, he makes the somewhat remarkable claim that those on the higher road (seeking to attain the mind of Christ and walk as he walked) will have a higher place in heaven.

His particular concern in this essay, however, is to encourage 'the lower order of Christians' (i.e., 'the generality of Christians') to a more earnest striving for the shared goal of both orders: 'the more excellent way', a pure love of God and an humble 'love of all men for God's sake'. This position is the presupposition of his pastoral counsel on such mundane problems as the Christian's regulation of sleep, his daily round of prayer, his diligence in 'business', grace before and cheerfulness at meals, allowable 'diversions' and, as always, the proper 'use of money'. None of Wesley's lifelong aspirations to holiness is compromised here, nor is there any betrayal of his soteriological premise of justification by 'faith alone'. But there is a different spirit; there is an implied admission that he has changed his mind on this and other important points in his understanding of the Christian 'way of salvation'.

The sermon itself provides no definite clues as to date and provenance. It first appeared in the *Arminian Magazine* (1787) without a title and then reappeared the year following in the seventh volume of Wesley's collected *Sermons* with its present title. It was not reprinted in Wesley's lifetime.

The More Excellent Way

Covet earnestly the best gifts;
and yet I show unto you a more excellent way.
1 Corinthians 12:31

1. In the preceding verses St. Paul has been speaking of the extraordinary gifts of the Holy Ghost, such as healing the sick, prophesying (in the proper sense of the word; that is, foretelling things to come), speaking with strange tongues, such as the speaker had never learned, and the miraculous interpretation of tongues. And these gifts the Apostle allows to be desirable; yea, he exhorts the Corinthians, at least the teachers among them (to whom chiefly, if not solely, they were wont to be given in the first ages of the church) to 'covet' them 'earnestly', that thereby they might be qualified to be more useful either to Christians or heathens. 'And yet', says he, 'I show unto you a more excellent way'—far more desirable than all these put together, inasmuch as it will infallibly lead you to happiness both in this world and in the world to come; whereas you might have all those gifts, yea, in the highest degree, and yet be miserable both in time and eternity.

2. It does not appear that these extraordinary gifts of the Holy Ghost were common in the church for more than two or three centuries. We seldom hear of them after that fatal period when the Emperor Constantine called himself a Christian, and from a vain imagination of promoting the Christian cause thereby heaped riches, and power, and honour, upon the Christians in general; but in particular upon the Christian clergy. From this time they almost totally ceased; very few instances of the kind were found. The cause of this was not (as has been vulgarly supposed) 'because there was no more occasion for them' because all the world was become Christian. This is a miserable mistake: not a twentieth part of it was then nominally Christian. The real cause was: 'the love of many'—almost of all Christians, so called—was 'waxed cold.' The Christians had no more of the Spirit of Christ than the other heathens. The Son of man, when he came to examine his church, could hardly 'find faith upon earth'. This was the real cause why the extraordinary gifts of the Holy Ghost were no longer to be found in the Christian church—because the Christians were turned heathens again, and had only a dead form left.

3. However, I would not at present speak of these, of the extraordinary gifts of the Holy Ghost, but of the ordinary; and these likewise we may 'covet earnestly', in order to be more useful in our generation. With this view we

may covet 'the gift of *convincing* speech', in order to 'sound the unbelieving heart'; and the gift of *persuasion* to move the affections, as well as enlighten the understanding. We may covet *knowledge,* both of the word and of the works of God, whether of providence or grace. We may desire a measure of that faith which on particular occasions, wherein the glory of God or the happiness of men is nearly concerned, goes far beyond the power of natural causes. We may desire an easy elocution, a pleasing address, with resignation to the will of our Lord; yea, whatever would enable us, as we have opportunity, to be useful wherever we are. These gifts we may innocently desire: but there is a more excellent way.

4. The way of love, of loving all men for God's sake, of humble, gentle, patient love, is that which the Apostle so admirably describes in the ensuing chapter. And without this, he assures us, all eloquence, all knowledge, all faith, all works, and all sufferings, are of no more value in the sight of God than sounding brass or a rumbling cymbal; and are not of the least avail toward our eternal salvation. Without this all we know, all we believe, all we do, all we suffer, will profit us nothing in the great day of accounts.

5. But at present I would take a different view of the text, and point out a more excellent way in another sense. It is the observation of an ancient writer that there have been from the beginning two orders of Christians. The one lived an innocent life, conforming in all things not sinful to the customs and fashions of the world, doing many good works, abstaining from gross evils, and attending the ordinances of God. They endeavoured in general to have a conscience void of offence in their outward behaviour, but did not aim at any particular strictness, being in most things like their neighbours. The other sort of Christians not only abstained from all appearance of evil, were zealous of good works in every kind, and attended all the ordinances of God; but likewise used all diligence to attain the whole mind that was in Christ, and laboured to walk in every point as their beloved Master. In order to this they walked in a constant course of universal self-denial, trampling on every pleasure which they were not divinely conscious prepared them for taking pleasure in God. They took up their cross daily. They strove, they agonized without intermission, to enter in at the strait gate. This one thing they did; they spared no pains to arrive at the summit of Christian holiness: 'leaving the first principles of the doctrine of Christ, to go on to perfection'; 'to know all that love of God which passeth knowledge, and to be filled with all the fullness of God'.

6. From long experience and observation I am inclined to think that whoever finds redemption in the blood of Jesus, whoever is justified, has then the choice of walking in the higher or the lower path. I believe the Holy Spirit at that time sets before him the more excellent way, and incites him to walk therein, to choose the narrowest path in the narrow way, to aspire after the heights and depths of holiness, after the entire image of God. But if he does

not accept this offer, he insensibly declines into the lower order of Christians. He still goes on in what may be called a good way, serving God in his degree, and finds mercy in the close of life, through the blood of the covenant.

7. I would be far from quenching the smoking flax, from discouraging those that serve God in a low degree. But I would not wish them to stop here: I would encourage them to come up higher, without thundering hell and damnation in their ears, without condemning the way wherein they were, telling them it is the way that leads to destruction. I will endeavour to point out to them what is in every respect a more excellent way.

8. Let it be well remembered, I do not affirm that all who do not walk in this way are in the high road to hell. But thus much I must affirm: they will not have so high a place in heaven as they would have had if they had chosen the better part. And will this be a small loss? The having so many fewer stars in your crown of glory? Will it be a little thing to have a lower place than you might have had in the kingdom of your Father? Certainly there will be no sorrow in heaven: there all tears will be wiped from our eyes. But if it were possible grief could enter there, we should grieve at that irreparable loss! Irreparable then, but not now! Now, by the grace of God, we may choose the 'more excellent way'. Let us now compare this in a few particulars with the way wherein most Christians walk.

I. To begin at the beginning of the day. It is the manner of the generality of Christians, if they are not obliged to work for their living, *to rise*, particularly in winter, at eight or nine in the morning, after having lain in bed eight or nine, if not more hours. I do not say now (as I should have been very apt to do fifty years ago) that all who indulge themselves in this manner are in the way to hell. But neither can I say they are in the way to heaven, denying themselves, and taking up their cross daily. Sure I am, there is a more excellent way to promote health both of body and mind. From an observation of more than sixty years I have learned that men in health require, at an average, from six to seven hours' sleep, and healthy women a little more, from seven to eight, in four and twenty hours. I know this quantity of sleep to be most advantageous to the body as well as the soul. It is preferable to any medicine which I have known, both for preventing and removing nervous disorders. It is therefore undoubtedly the most excellent way, in defiance of fashion and custom, to take just so much sleep as experience proves our nature to require; seeing this is indisputably most conducive both to bodily and spiritual health. And why should not you walk in this way? Because it is difficult? Nay, with men it is impossible. But all things are possible with God; and by his grace all things will be possible to *you*. Only continue instant in prayer, and you will find this not only possible, but easy; yea, and it will be far easier to rise early constantly than to do it sometimes. But then you must begin at the right end: if you rise early, you must sleep early. Impose it upon yourself, unless when something extraordinary occurs, to go to bed at a fixed hour. Then the difficulty of it will soon be over; but the advantage of it will remain for ever.

II. The generality of Christians, as soon as they rise, are accustomed to use some kind of *prayer*; and probably to use the same form still which they learned when they were eight or ten years old. Now I do not condemn those who proceed thus (though many do) as mocking God, though they have used the same form, without any variation, for twenty or thirty years together. But surely there is a more excellent way of ordering our private devotions. What if you were to follow the advice given by that great and good man, Mr. Law, on this subject? Consider both your outward and inward state, and vary your prayers accordingly. For instance: suppose your outward state is prosperous; suppose you are in a state of health, ease, and plenty, having your lot cast among kind relations, good neighbours, and agreeable friends, that love you and you them; then your outward state manifestly calls for praise and thanksgiving to God. On the other hand, if you are in a state of adversity; if God has laid trouble upon your loins; if you are in poverty, in want, in outward distress; if you are in any imminent danger; if you are in pain and sickness: then you are clearly called to pour out your soul before God in such prayer as is suited to your circumstances. In like manner you may suit your devotions to your inward state, the present state of your mind. Is your soul in heaviness either from a sense of sin or through manifold temptations? Then let your prayer consist of such confessions, petitions, and supplications, as are agreeable to your distressed situation of mind. On the contrary, is your soul in peace? Are you rejoicing in God? Are his consolations not small with you? Then say with the Psalmist: 'Thou art my God, and I will thank thee; thou art my God, and I will praise thee.' You may likewise, when you have time, add to your other devotions a little reading and meditation, and perhaps a psalm of praise, the natural effusion of a thankful heart. You must certainly see that this is a more excellent way than the poor dry form which you used before.

III.1. The generality of Christians, after using some prayer, usually apply themselves to the *business* of their calling. Every man that has any pretence to be a Christian will not fail to do this; seeing it is impossible that an idle man can be a good man, sloth being inconsistent with religion. But with what view? For what end do you undertake and follow your worldly business? 'To provide things necessary for myself and my family.' It is a good answer as far as it goes; but it does not go far enough. For a Turk or a heathen goes so far, does his work for the very same ends. But a Christian may go abundantly farther: his end in all his labour is to please God; to do, not his own will, but the will of him that sent him into the world—for this very purpose, to do the will of God on earth as angels do in heaven. He works for eternity. He 'labours not for the meat that perisheth'—this is the smallest part of his motive—'but for that which endureth to everlasting life'. And is not this 'a more excellent way'?

2. Again: in what *manner* do you transact your worldly business? I trust, with *diligence*, whatever your hand findeth to do, doing it with your might; in justice, rendering to all their due, in every circumstance of life; yea, and in mercy, doing unto every man what you would he should do unto you. This is well; but a Christian is called to go still farther—to add piety to justice; to intermix prayer, especially the prayer of the heart, with all the labour of his hands. Without this all his diligence and justice only show him to be an honest heathen—and many there are who profess the Christian religion that go no farther than honest heathenism.

3. Yet again: in what *spirit* do you go through your business? In the spirit of the world, or the Spirit of Christ? I am afraid thousands of those who are called good Christians do not understand the question. If you act in the Spirit of Christ you carry the end you at first proposed through all your work from first to last. You do everything in the spirit of sacrifice, giving up your will to the will of God, and continually aiming, not at ease, pleasure, or riches; not at anything this short enduring world can give; but merely at the glory of God. Now can anyone deny that this is the most excellent way of pursuing worldly business?

IV.1. But these tenements of clay which we bear about us require constant reparation, or they will sink into the earth from which they were taken, even sooner than nature requires. Daily food is necessary to prevent this, to repair the constant decays of nature. It was common in the heathen world when they were about to use this, to take meat or even drink, *libare pateram Jovi*, to pour out a little to the honour of their god—although the gods of the heathens were but devils, as the Apostle justly observes. 'It seems', says a late writer, 'there was once some such custom as this in our own country. For we still frequently see a gentleman before he sits down to dinner in his own house, holding his hat before his face, and perhaps seeming to say something; though he generally does it in such a manner that no one can tell what he says.' Now what if instead of this, every head of a family, before he sat down to eat and drink, either morning, noon, or night (for the reason of the thing is the same at every hour of the day), was seriously to ask a blessing from God on what he was about to take; yea, and afterward seriously to return thanks to the Giver of all his blessings. Would not this be a more excellent way than to use that dull farce which is worse than nothing, being in reality no other than mockery both of God and man?

2. As to the *quantity* of their food, good sort of men do not usually eat to excess. At least not so far as to make themselves sick with meat, or to intoxicate themselves with drink. And as to the manner of taking it, it is usually innocent,

mixed with a little mirth, which is said to help digestion. So far, so good. And provided they take only that measure of plain, cheap, wholesome food, which most promotes health both of body and mind, there will be no cause of blame. Neither can I require you to take that advice of Mr. Herbert, though he was a good man:

> Take thy meat; think it dust; then eat a bit,
> And say with all, 'Earth to earth I commit.'

This is too melancholy: it does not suit with that cheerfulness which is highly proper at a Christian meal. Permit me to illustrate this subject with a little story. The King of France one day, pursuing the chase, outrode all his company, who after seeking him some time found him sitting in a cottage eating bread and cheese. Seeing them, he cried out: 'Where have I lived all my time? I never before tasted so good food in my life!' 'Sire', said one of them, 'you never had so *good sauce* before; for you were never hungry.' Now it is true, hunger is a good sauce: but there is one that is better still; that is, thankfulness. Sure that is the most agreeable food which is seasoned with this. And why should not yours at every meal? You need not then fix your eye on death, but receive every morsel as a pledge of life eternal. The Author of your being gives you in this food, not only a reprieve from death, but an earnest that in a little time 'death shall be swallowed up in victory.'

3. The time of taking our food is usually a time of *conversation* also, as it is natural to refresh our minds while we refresh our bodies. Let us consider a little in what manner the generality of Christians usually converse together. What are the ordinary subjects of their conversation? If it is harmless (as one would hope it is), if there be nothing in it profane, nothing immodest, nothing untrue, or unkind; if there be no talebearing, backbiting, or evil-speaking, they have reason to praise God for his restraining grace. But there is more than this implied in 'ordering our conversation aright'. In order to this it is needful, first, that 'your communication', that is, discourse or conversation, 'be good', that it be materially good, on good subjects; not fluttering about anything that occurs. For what have you to do with courts and kings? It is not your business to

> Fight o'er the wars, reform the state,

unless when some remarkable event calls for the acknowledgement of the justice or mercy of God. We *must* indeed sometimes talk of worldly things; otherwise we may as well go out of the world. But it should only be so far as is needful; then we should return to a better subject. Secondly, let your conversation be 'to the use of edifying'; calculated to edify either the speaker or the hearers or both; to build them up, as each has particular need, either in faith, or love, or holiness. Thirdly, see that it not only gives entertainment, but, in one kind or other, 'ministers grace to the hearers'. Now is not this a more excellent way of *conversing* than the harmless way above mentioned?

V.1. We have seen what is the more excellent way of ordering our conversation, as well as our business. But we cannot be always intent upon business; both our bodies and minds require some relaxation. We need intervals of diversion from business. It will be necessary to be very explicit upon this head, as it is a point which has been much misunderstood.

2. Diversions are of various kinds. Some are almost peculiar to men, as the sports of the field—hunting, shooting, fishing—wherein not many women (I should say, ladies) are concerned. Others are indifferently used by persons of both sexes; some of which are of a more public nature, as races, masquerades, plays, assemblies, balls. Others are chiefly used in private houses, as cards, dancing, and music; to which we may add the reading of plays, novels, romances, newspapers, and fashionable poetry.

3. Some diversions indeed which were formerly in great request are now fallen into disrepute. The nobility and gentry (in England at least) seem totally to disregard the once fashionable diversion of *hawking*; and the vulgar themselves are no longer diverted by men hacking and hewing each other in pieces at *broadsword*. The noble game of *quarterstaff* likewise is now exercised by very few. Yea, *cudgelling* has lost its honour, even in Wales itself. *Bear-baiting* also is now very seldom seen, and *bull-baiting* not very often. And it seems *cock-fighting* would totally cease in England, were it not for two or three right honourable patrons.

4. It is not needful to say anything more of these foul 'remains of Gothic barbarity' than that they are a reproach, not only to all religion, but even to human nature. One would not pass so severe a censure on the sports of the field. Let those who have nothing better to do, still run foxes and hares out of breath. Neither need much be said about horse-races, till some man of sense will undertake to defend them. It seems a great deal more may be said in defence of seeing a serious *tragedy*. I could not do it with a clear conscience; at least not in an English theatre, the sink of all profaneness and debauchery; but possibly others can. I cannot say quite so much for *balls* or *assemblies*, which are more reputable than *masquerades*, but must be allowed by all impartial persons to have exactly the same tendency. So undoubtedly have all public dancings. And the same tendency they must have, unless the same caution obtained among modern Christians which was observed among the ancient heathens. With them men and women never danced together, but always in separate rooms. This was always observed in ancient Greece, and for several ages at Rome, where a woman dancing in company with men would have at once been set down for a prostitute. Of playing at *cards* I say the same as of seeing plays. I could not do it with a clear conscience. But I am not obliged to pass sentences on those that are otherwise minded. I leave them to their

own Master: to him let them stand or fall.

5. But supposing these, as well as the reading of plays, novels, newspapers, and the like, to be quite 'innocent diversions', yet are there not 'more excellent ways' of diverting themselves for those that love or fear God? Would men of fortune divert themselves in the open air? They may do it by cultivating and improving their lands, by planting their grounds, by laying out, carrying on, and perfecting their gardens and orchards. At other times they may visit and converse with the most serious and sensible of their neighbours; or they may visit the sick, the poor, the widows, and fatherless in their affliction. Do they desire to divert themselves in the house? They may read useful history, pious and elegant poetry, or several branches of natural philosophy. If you have time, you may divert yourself by music, and perhaps by philosophical experiments. But above all, when you have once learned the use of prayer, you will find that as

> that which yields or fills
> All space, the ambient air, wide interfused
> Embraces round this florid earth;

so will this, till through every space of life it be interfused with all your employments, and wherever you are, whatever you do, embrace you on every side. Then you will be able to say boldly:

> With me no melancholy void,
> No moment lingers unemployed,
> Or unimproved below;
> My weariness of life is gone,
> Who live to serve my God alone,
> And only Jesus know.

VI. One point only remains to be considered; that is, the use of money. What is the way wherein the generality of Christians employ this? And is there not a more excellent way?

1. The generality of Christians usually set apart something yearly, perhaps a tenth or even one-eighth part of their income, whether it arise from yearly revenue, or from trade, for charitable uses. A few I have known who said like Zaccheus, 'Lord, the half of my goods I give to the poor.' O that it would please God to multiply these friends of mankind, these general benefactors! But,

2. Besides those who have a stated rule, there are thousands who give large sums to the poor; especially when any striking instance of distress is represented to them in lively colours.

3. I praise God for all of you who act in this manner. May you never be weary of well-doing! May God restore what you give sevenfold into your own bosom! But yet I show unto you a more excellent way.

4. You may consider yourself as one in whose hands the Proprietor of heaven and earth and all things therein has lodged a part of his goods, to be disposed of according to his direction. And his direction is, that you should look upon yourself as one of a certain number of indigent persons who are to be provided for out of that portion of his goods wherewith you are entrusted. You have two advantages over the rest: the one, that 'it is more blessed to give than to receive'; the other, that you are to serve yourself first, and others afterwards. This is the light wherein you are to see yourself and them. But to be more particular: first, if you have no family, after you have provided for yourself, give away all that remains; so that

> Each Christmas you accounts may clear,
> And wind your bottom round the year.

This was the practice of all the young men at Oxford who were called 'Methodists'. For example: one of them had thirty pounds a year. He lived on twenty-eight and gave away forty shillings. The next year receiving sixty pounds, he still lived on twenty-eight, and gave away two and thirty. The third year he received ninety pounds, and gave away sixty-two. The fourth year he received a hundred and twenty pounds. Still he lived as before on twenty-eight, and gave to the poor ninety-two. Was not this a more excellent way? Secondly, if you have a family, seriously consider before God how much each member of it wants in order to have what is needful for life and godliness. And in general do not allow them less, nor much more, than you allow yourself. Thirdly, this being done, fix your purpose to 'gain no more'. I charge you in the name of God, do not increase your substance! As it comes daily or yearly, so let it go; otherwise you 'lay up treasures upon earth'. And this our Lord as flatly forbids as murder and adultery. By doing it, therefore, you would 'treasure up to yourselves wrath against the day of wrath and revelation of the righteous judgment of God'.

5. But suppose it were not forbidden, how can you on principles of reason spend your money in a way which God may *possibly forgive*, instead of spending it in a manner which he will *certainly reward?* You will have no reward in heaven for what you *lay up*; you will for what you *lay out*. Every pound you put into the earthly bank is sunk: it brings no interest above. But every pound you give to the poor is put into the bank of heaven. And it will bring glorious interest; yea, and such as will be accumulating to all eternity.

6. Who then is a wise man, and endued with knowledge among you? Let him resolve this day, this hour, this moment, the Lord assisting him, to choose in all the preceding particulars the 'more excellent way'; and let him steadily keep it, both with regard to sleep, prayer, work, food, conversation, and diversions; and particularly with regard to the employment of that important 'talent', *money*. Let *your* heart answer to the call of God: 'From this moment,

God being my helper, I will lay up no more treasure upon earth; this one thing I will do, I will lay up treasure in heaven; I will render unto God the things that are God's; I will give him all my goods and all my heart.'

ON THE OMNIPRESENCE OF GOD

Sermon 118 – 1788

AN INTRODUCTORY COMMENT

This sermon is yet another contemplative essay, reflecting Wesley's vivid sense of the sacred: his vision of the Christian life as an immersion in the encompassing, suffusing personal presence of God. His complaint, at the outset, about the paucity of a proper treatment of this great theme, is scarcely more than a familiar literary device to justify himself as some sort of theological pioneer. His comment probably means that he judged the classical treatments of ubiquity (Augustine, Thomas Aquinas, Calvin, Taylor, Bérulle, Scougal) not to be sufficiently 'plain' or quite suited 'for general use'. There is a mild irony, though, in the fact that this work is not one of Wesley's plainer discourses; it is both more speculative and more heavily ornamented with quotations and learned allusions than usual. It is, however, 'pure Wesley', a moving description of the spiritual ambience in which he had lived and into which he had invited others to enter.

After attempting to explain the omnipresence of God, Wesley goes on to ask, 'What inference should we draw from hence?' Although said in a number of ways, the implication is always the same—'spare no pains to preserve always a deep, a continual, a lively, and a joyful sense of his gracious presence.' This sense of a pervasive consciousness of God's presence is evident in Wesley's diaries at Oxford in the late 1720s; for sixty years, then, it had established the spiritual environment for his own personal pilgrimage.

That this sermon is placed and dated (in a postscript) 'Portsmouth, Aug. 12, 1788,' is almost accidental; not much of it was written there. He had come to Portsmouth on the 11th after an all-night ride in the mail-coach from London and had then plunged into a busy round of sermons and class-meetings. The sermon is not 'occasional'; it is, rather, the distillate of long reflection, written down in the odd moments of a relentless schedule. It appeared first in the *Arminian Magazine* (1789) without a title. The present title was coined by Joseph Benson in his edition of the *Works* (1809-13) and was used by Thomas Jackson in his edition of the *Sermons* (1825) and thereafter.

On the Omnipresence of God

Do not I fill heaven and earth? saith the Lord.
Jeremiah 23:24

1. How strongly and beautifully do these words express the omnipresence of God! And can there be in the whole compass of nature a more sublime subject? Can there be any more worthy the consideration of every rational creature? Is there any more necessary to be considered, and to be understood, so far as our poor faculties will admit? How many excellent purposes may it answer! What deep instruction may it convey to all the children of men! And more directly to the children of God.

2. How is it then that so little has been wrote on so sublime and useful a subject? It is true that some of our most eminent writers have occasionally touched upon it, and have several strong and beautiful reflections which were naturally suggested by it. But which of them has published a regular treatise, or so much as a sermon, upon the head? Perhaps many were conscious of their inability to do justice to so vast a subject. It is possible there may some such lie hid in the voluminous writings of the last century. But if they are hid even in their own country, if they are already buried in oblivion, it is the same, for any use they are of, as if they had never been wrote.

3. What seems to be wanting still, for general use, is a plain discourse on the omnipresence or ubiquity of God, first in some manner explaining and proving that glorious truth, God is in this, and every place, and then applying it to the conscience of all thinking men in a few practical inferences.

I.1. Accordingly I will endeavour, by the assistance of his Spirit, first a little to explain the omnipresence of God: to show how we are to understand this glorious truth, God is in this, and every place. The Psalmist, you may remember, speaks strongly and beautifully upon it in the hundred and thirty-ninth Psalm; observing in the most exact order, first, God is in this place, and then, God is in every place. He observes, first, 'Thou art about my bed, and about my path, and spiest out all my ways' (Ps. 139:2). 'Thou hast fashioned me behind and before, and laid thine hand upon me' (Ps. 139:4). Although the manner thereof he could not explain—*how* it was he could not tell. 'Such knowledge', says he, 'is too wonderful for me: I cannot attain unto it' (Ps. 139:5). He next observes, in the most lively and affecting manner, that God is in every place. 'Whither shall I go then from thy Spirit, or whither shall

I go from thy presence? If I climb up into heaven, thou art there; if I go down to hell, thou art there also' (Ps 139:6–7). If I could ascend, speaking after the manner of men, to the highest part of the universe, or could I descend to the lowest point, thou art alike present both in one and the other. 'If I should take the wings of the morning, and remain in the uttermost parts of the sea; even there thy hand would lead me,' thy power and thy presence would be before me, 'and thy right hand would hold me,' seeing thou art equally in the length and breadth, and in the height and depth of the universe. Indeed thy presence and knowledge not only reach the utmost bounds of creation, but

> Thine omnipresent sight,
> Even to the pathless realms extends
> Of uncreated night.

In a word, there is no point of space, whether within or without the bounds of creation, where God is not.

2. Indeed this subject is far too vast to be comprehended by the narrow limits of human understanding. We can only say, 'The great God, the eternal, the almighty Spirit, is as unbounded in his presence as in his duration and power.' In condescension, indeed, to our weak understanding, he is said to 'dwell in heaven'; but strictly speaking the heaven of heavens cannot contain him, but he is in every part of his dominion. The universal God dwelleth in universal space; so that we may say,

> Hail, Father! whose creating call,
> Unnumbered worlds attend!
> Jehovah, comprehending all,
> Whom none can comprehend!

3. If we may dare attempt the illustrating this a little farther, what is the space occupied by a grain of sand, compared to that space which is occupied by the starry heavens? It is as a cipher; it is nothing; it vanishes away in the comparison. What is it then to the whole expanse of space, to which the whole creation is infinitely less than a grain of sand? And yet this space, to [which] the whole creation bears no proportion at all, is infinitely less in comparison of the great God than a grain of sand, yea, a millionth part of it, bears to that whole space.

II.1. This seems to be the plain meaning of those solemn words which God speaks of himself, 'Do not I fill heaven and earth?' And these sufficiently prove his omnipresence; which may be farther proved from this consideration: God acts everywhere, and therefore is everywhere; for it is an utter impossibility that any being, created or uncreated, should work where it is not. God acts in heaven, in earth, and under the earth, throughout the whole compass of his creation; by sustaining all things, without which everything would in an instant sink into its primitive nothing; by governing all, every moment superintending everything that he has made; strongly and sweetly influencing all, and yet without destroying the liberty of his rational creatures. The very heathens acknowledged that the great God governs the large and conspicuous parts of the universe; that he regulates the motions of the heavenly bodies, of the sun, moon, and stars; that he is

Vastem
Mens agitans molem, et toto se corpore miscens:

The all-informing soul,
That fills, pervades, and actuates the whole.

But they had no conception of his having a regard to the least things as well as the greatest; of his presiding over all that he has made, and governing atoms as well as worlds. This we could not have known unless it had pleased God to reveal it unto us himself. Had he not himself told us so, we should not have dared to think that 'not a sparrow falleth to the ground' without the 'will of our Father which is in heaven'; and much less affirm that 'even the very hairs of our head are all numbered'!

2. This comfortable truth, that God 'filleth heaven and earth', we learn also from the Psalm above recited. 'If I climb up into heaven, thou art there; if I go down to hell, thou art there also. If I take the wings of the morning, and remain in the uttermost parts of the sea; even there thy hand shall lead me.' The plain meaning is, if *I* remove to any distance whatever, thou art there; thou still besettest me, and layest thine hand upon me. Let me flee to any conceivable or inconceivable distance, above, beneath, or on any side, it makes no difference; thou art still equally there—in thee I still 'live and move and have my being'.

3. And where no creature is, still God is there. The presence or absence of any or all creatures makes no difference with regard to him. He is equally in all, or without all. Many have been the disputes among philosophers whether there be any such thing as empty space in the universe. And it is now generally supposed that all space is full. Perhaps it cannot be proved that all space is filled with matter. But the heathen himself will bear us witness, *Iovis omnis plena*, 'All things are full of God.' Yea, and whatever space exists beyond the bounds of creation (for creation must have bounds, seeing nothing is boundless, nothing can be but the great Creator), even that space cannot exclude him who fills the heaven and the earth.

4. Just equivalent to this is the expression of the Apostle (not as some have strangely supposed, concerning the church, but concerning the head of it), 'The fullness of him that filleth all in all' (Eph. 1:23)—τὰ πάντα ἐν πᾶσιν,

literally translated 'all things in all things', the strongest expression of universality which can possibly be conceived. It necessarily includes the last and the greatest of all things that exist. So that if any expression could be stronger, it would be stronger than even that, the 'filling heaven and earth'.

5. Indeed this very expression, 'Do not I fill heaven and earth?' (the question being equal to the strongest affirmation), implies the clearest assertion of God's being present everywhere, and filling all space. For it is well known the Hebrew phrase 'heaven and earth' includes the whole universe, the whole extent of space, created or uncreated, and all that is therein.

6. Nay, and we cannot believe the omnipotence of God unless we believe his omnipresence. For seeing (as was observed before) nothing can act where it is not, if there were any space where God was not present he would not be able to do anything there. Therefore to deny the omnipresence of God implies likewise the denial of his omnipotence. To set bounds to the one is undoubtedly to set bounds to the other also.

7. Indeed, wherever we suppose him not to be, there we suppose all his attributes to be in vain. He cannot exercise there either his justice or mercy, either his power or wisdom. In that extramundane space (so to speak) where we suppose God not to be present, we must of course suppose him to have no duration; but as it is supposed to be beyond the bounds of the creation, so it is beyond the bounds of the Creator's power. Such is the blasphemous absurdity which is implied in this supposition.

8. But to all that is or can be said of the omnipresence of God the world has one grand objection! They cannot see him. And this is really at the root of all their other objections. This our blessed Lord observed long ago: 'Whom the world cannot receive, because they see him not.' But is it not easy to reply, 'Can you see the wind? You cannot. But do you therefore deny its existence or its presence?' You say, 'No; for I can perceive it by my other senses.' But by which of your senses do you perceive your soul? Surely you do not deny either the existence or the presence of this! And yet it is not the object of your sight, or of any of your other senses. Suffice it then to consider that God is a spirit, as is your soul also. Consequently, 'him no man hath seen or can see' with eyes of flesh and blood.

III.1. But allowing that God is here, as in every place, that he is 'about our bed, and about our path', that he 'besets us behind and before, and lays his hand upon us', what inference should we draw from hence? What use should we make of this awful consideration? Is it not meet and right to humble ourselves before the eyes of his majesty? Should we not labour continually to acknowledge his presence 'with reverence and godly fear'? Not indeed with the fear of devils, that believe and tremble, but with the fear of angels, with something similar to that which is felt by the inhabitants of heaven, when

Dark with excessive bright his skirts appear,
Yet dazzles heaven, that brightest seraphim
Approach not, but with both wings veil their eyes.

2. Secondly, if you believe that God is about your bed and about your path, and spieth out all your ways, then take care not to do the least thing, not to speak the least word, not to indulge the least thought, which you have reason to think would offend him. Suppose that a messenger of God, an angel, be now standing at your right hand, and fixing his eyes upon you, would you not take care to abstain from every word or action that you knew would offend him? Yea, suppose one of your mortal fellow-servants, suppose only a holy man stood by you, would not you be extremely cautious how you conducted yourself, both in word and action? How much more cautious ought you to be when you know that not a holy man, not an angel of God, but God himself, the Holy One 'that inhabiteth eternity', is inspecting your heart, your tongue, your hand every moment! And that he himself will surely bring you into judgment for all you think, and speak, and act under the sun!

3. In particular. If there is not a word in your tongue, not a syllable you speak, but he 'knoweth it altogether', how exact should you be in 'setting a watch before your mouth, and in keeping the door of your lips'! How wary does it behove you to be in all your conversation, being forewarned by your Judge that 'By your words you shall be justified, or by your words you shall be condemned'! How cautious lest 'any corrupt communication', any uncharitable, yea, or unprofitable discourse, should 'proceed out of your mouth', instead of 'that which is good to the use of edifying', and meet to 'minister grace to the hearers'!

4. Yea, if God sees our hearts as well as our hands, and in all places, if he understandeth our thoughts long before they are clothed with words; how earnestly should we urge that petition, 'Search me, O Lord, and prove me; try out my reins and my heart.' 'Look well if there be any way of wickedness in me, and lead me in the way everlasting!' Yea, how needful is it to work together with him in 'keeping our hearts with all diligence', till he hath 'cast down imaginations, evil reasonings, and everything that exalteth itself against the knowledge of God, and brought into captivity every thought to the obedience of Christ'.

5. On the other hand, if you are already listed under the great captain of your salvation, seeing ye are continually under the eye of your captain, how zealous and active should you be to 'fight the good fight of faith, and lay hold on eternal life', 'to endure hardship as good soldiers of Jesus Christ', to use all diligence, to 'war a good warfare', and to do whatever is acceptable in his sight! How studious should you be to approve all your ways to his all-seeing eyes, that he may say to your hearts, what he will proclaim aloud in the great assembly of men and angels, 'Well done, good and faithful servants.'

6. In order to attain these glorious ends, spare no pains to preserve always a deep, a continual, a lively, and a joyful sense of his gracious presence. Never forget his comprehensive word to the great father of the faithful, 'I am the Almighty' (rather, the *All-sufficient*) 'God; walk before me, and be thou perfect!' Cheerfully expect that he before whom you stand will ever guide you with his eye, will support you by his guardian hand, will keep you from all evil. And 'when you have suffered a while' [he] will 'make you perfect', will 'stablish, strengthen, and settle you'; and then preserve you 'unblameable, unto the coming of our Lord Jesus Christ'.

THE UNITY OF THE DIVINE BEING

Sermon 120 – 1789

AN INTRODUCTORY COMMENT

This and the following two sermons were finished in Ireland during Wesley's last and longest visit there, from late March through mid-July 1789. This one is placed and dated (in a postscript), 'Dublin, April 9, 1789', where Wesley had been since March 29. None of the over-burdening busyness mentioned in his *Journal* for the period is reflected in this brief essay on the unity and attributes of 'the one God' and the corresponding essence of true religion ('right tempers towards God and man').

The theology here is standard orthodoxy of the day, and the tight linkage between right belief and authentic living is typically Wesleyan. It is no surprise to the reader that Wesley can so easily move from affirming 'there is one God' to claiming 'there is one religion and one happiness'. What is new, comparatively speaking, is Wesley's explicit identification of the threat to true religion coming from the wave of Enlightenment humanism in men like Rousseau, Voltaire, and David Hume ('the great triumvirate'), and even such lesser lights as William Wollaston and Jean-Jacques Burlamaqui. Although Wesley does not always do justice to their various positions in this brief treatment, he is very forceful in his assertion that their influence is no better than outright 'atheism', and his reaction is to assert that only true religion will motivate and sustain authentic morality. And true religion is not simply love of neighbour, as these writers would generally have one believe; it must be grounded in love of God. Thus, the themes here are commonplace in the Wesleyan theology, and yet he still can manage a certain freshness in his variations on them, even at age eighty-five.

The sermon appeared first without a title in the *Arminian Magazine* (1790). The title given it by Joseph Benson in the *Works* (1809–13) and followed by Thomas Jackson in the *Sermons* (1825) could readily be improved upon. Wesley rarely used such a phrase as 'the divine being', and the sermon's burden has less to do with God's unity than with its consequences for 'one religion and one happiness for all men'.

The Unity of the Divine Being

There is one God.
Mark 12:32

1. And as there is one God, so there is one religion and one happiness for all men. God never intended there should be any more; and it is not possible there should. Indeed, in another sense, as the Apostle observes, 'there are gods many, and lords many.' All the heathen nations had their gods, and many—whole shoals of them. And generally, the more polished they were, the more gods they heaped up to themselves. But *to us*, to all that are favoured with the Christian revelation, 'there is but one God,' who declares of himself, 'Is there any God beside me? There is none; I know not any.'

2. But who can search out this God to perfection? None of the creatures that he has made. Only some of his attributes he hath been pleased to reveal to us in his Word. Hence we learn that God is an eternal being: 'His goings forth are from everlasting,' and will continue to everlasting. As he ever was, so he ever will be; as there was no beginning of his existence, so there will be no end. This is universally allowed to be contained in his very name, 'Jehovah'; which the Apostle John accordingly renders, 'He that was, and that is, and that is to come'. Perhaps it would be as proper to say, 'He *is* from everlasting to everlasting.'

3. Nearly allied to the eternity of God is his omnipresence. As he exists through infinite duration, so he cannot but exist through infinite space; according to his own question, equivalent to the strongest assertion, 'Do not I fill heaven and earth, saith the Lord?' (heaven and earth, in the Hebrew idiom, implying the whole universe). Which therefore, according to his own declaration, is filled with his presence.

4. This one, eternal, omnipresent Being is likewise all-perfect. He has from eternity to eternity all the perfections, and infinitely more than it ever did or ever can enter into the heart of man to conceive; yea, infinitely more than the angels in heaven can conceive. These perfections we usually term the attributes of God.

5. And he is omnipotent as well as omnipresent: there can be no more bounds to his power than to his presence. He 'hath a mighty arm; strong is his hand, and high is his right hand.' He doth whatsoever pleaseth him, in the heaven, the earth, the sea, and in all deep places. With men, we know, many things are impossible; 'but not with God: with him all things are

possible.' Whensoever he willeth, to do is present with him.

6. The omniscience of God is a clear and necessary consequence of his omnipresence. If he is present in every part of the universe, he cannot but know whatever is, or is done there. According to the word of St. James: 'Known unto God are all his works', and the works of every creature, 'from the beginning of the world'; or rather, as the phrase literally implies, 'from eternity'. His eyes are not only 'over all the earth, beholding the evil and the good'; but likewise over the whole creation; yea, and the paths of uncreated night. Is there any difference between his knowledge and his wisdom? If there be, is not his knowledge the more general term (at least according to our weak conceptions), and his wisdom a particular branch of it? Namely, the knowing the end of everything that exists, and the means of applying it to that end.

7. Holiness is another of the attributes of the almighty, all-wise God. He is infinitely distant from every touch of evil. He 'is light, and in him is no darkness at all'. He is a God of unblemished justice and truth: but above all is his mercy. This we may easily learn from that beautiful passage in the thirty-fourth and -fifth chapters of Exodus: 'And Moses said, I beseech thee, show me thy glory. And the Lord descended in the cloud, and proclaimed the name of the Lord, the Lord, the Lord God, merciful and gracious, long-suffering, and abundant in goodness and truth; keeping mercy for thousands, and forgiving iniquity, and transgression, and sin.'

8. This God is a spirit; not having such a body, such parts, or passions, as men have. It was the opinion both of the ancient Jews and the ancient Christians that he alone is a pure spirit, totally separate from all matter; whereas they supposed all other spirits, even the highest angels, even cherubim and seraphim, to dwell in material vehicles, though of an exceeding light and subtle substance. At that point of duration which the infinite wisdom of God saw to be most proper, for reasons which lie hid in the abyss of his own understanding, not to be fathomed by any finite mind, God 'called into being all that is', created the heavens and the earth, together with all that they contain. 'All things were created by him, and without him was not anything made that was made.' He created man in particular, after his own image, to be 'a picture of his own eternity'. When he had raised man from the dust of the earth, he breathed into him an immortal spirit. Hence he is peculiarly called 'the Father of our spirits'; yea, 'the Father of the spirits of all flesh'.

9. He 'made all things', as the wise man observes, 'for himself'; for 'his glory they were created'. Not 'as if he needed anything', seeing 'he giveth to all life, and breath, and all things.' He made all things to be happy. He made man to be happy in himself. He is the proper centre of spirits, for whom every created spirit was made. So true is that well-known saying of the ancient fathers: *Fecisti nos ad te; et irrequietum est cor nostrum, donec requiescat in te*—Thou hast made us for thyself; and our heart cannot rest till it resteth in thee.

10. This observation gives us a clear answer to that question in the Assembly's Catechism, 'For what end did God create man?' The answer is, 'To glorify and enjoy him for ever.' This is undoubtedly true; but is it quite clear, especially to men of ordinary capacities? Do the generality of common people understand that expression, 'to glorify God'? No, no more than they understand Greek. And it is altogether above the capacity of children, to whom we can scarce ever speak plain enough. Now is not this the very principle that should be inculcated upon every human creature—'You are made to be happy in God'—as soon as ever reason dawns? Should not every parent, as soon as a child begins to talk or to run alone, say something of this kind: 'See! what is that which shines so over your head? That we call the sun. See how bright it is! Feel how it warms you! It makes the grass to spring and everything to grow. But God made the sun. The sun could not shine, nor warm, nor do any good, without him.' In this plain and familiar way a wise parent might many times in a day say something of God; particularly insisting, 'He made *you*; and he made you to be happy in him; and nothing else can make you happy.' We cannot press this too soon. If you say, 'Nay, but they cannot understand you when they are so young'; I answer, No, nor when they are fifty years old, unless God opens their understanding. And can he not do this at any age?

11. Indeed this should be pressed on every human creature, young and old, the more earnestly and diligently because so exceeding few, even of those that are called Christians, seem to know anything about it. Many indeed think of being happy with God in heaven; but the being happy in God on earth never entered into their thoughts. The less so because from the time they came into the world they are surrounded with idols. Such in turns are all 'the things that are seen' (whereas God is not seen), which all promise a happiness independent of God. Indeed it is true that

Upright both in heart and will
  We by our God were made.
But we turned from good to ill,
  And o'er the creatures strayed,
Multiplied our wand'ring thought,
Which first was fixed on God alone;
In ten thousand objects sought
  The bliss we lost in one.

12. These idols, these rivals of God, are innumerable: but they may be nearly reduced to three parts. First, objects of sense, such as gratify one or more of our outward senses. These excite the first kind of 'love of the world', which St. John terms 'the desire of the flesh'. Secondly, objects of the imagination, things that gratify our fancy, by grandeur, beauty, or novelty. All these make

us fair promises of happiness, and thereby prevent our seeking it in God. This the Apostle terms 'the desire of the eyes'; whereby chiefly the imagination is gratified. They are, thirdly, what St. John calls 'the pride of life'. He seems to mean honour, wealth, and whatever directly tends to engender pride.

13. But suppose we were guarded against all these, are there not other idols which we have need to be apprehensive of; and idols therefore the more dangerous, because we suspect no danger from them? For is there any danger to be feared from our friends and relations? From the mutual endearments of husbands and wives, or of parents and children? Ought we not to bear a very tender affection to them? Ought we not to love them only less than God? Yea, and is there not a tender affection due to those whom God has made profitable to our souls? Are we not commanded to 'esteem them very highly in love for their work's sake'? All this is unquestionably true. And this very thing makes the difficulty. Who is sufficient for this, to go far enough herein, and no farther? To love them enough, and not too much? Who can love a wife, a child, a friend well enough without loving the creature more than the Creator? Who is able to follow the caution which St. Paul gives to the Christians at Thessalonica, 1 Thess. 4:5?

14. I wish that weighty passage (so strangely disguised in our translation) were duly considered. 'Let every one of you know how to possess his vessel', his wife, 'in sanctification and honour'—so as neither to dishonour God or himself, nor to obstruct but farther holiness. St. Paul goes on, μὴ ἐν πάθει ἐπιθυμίας, which we render, 'not in the lust of concupiscence'—(What is this? It gives the English reader no conception at all. Πάθος means any *violent* or *impetuous affection*; ἐπιθυμία is desire. By the two words the Apostle undoubtedly means vehement and impetuous affections.)—as the 'Gentiles who know not God'; and so may naturally seek happiness in a creature.

15. If, by the grace of God, we have avoided or forsaken all these idols, there is still one more dangerous than all the rest, and that is, religion. It will easily be conceived I mean false religion; that is, any religion which does not imply *the giving the heart to God*. Such is, first, a religion of opinions, or what is commonly called orthodoxy. Into this snare fall thousands of those who profess to hold 'salvation by faith'; indeed all of those who by faith mean only a system of Arminian or Calvinian opinions. Such is, secondly, a religion of forms of barely outward worship, how constantly soever performed; yea, though we attended the church service every day, and the Lord's Supper every Sunday. Such is, thirdly, a religion of works, of seeking the favour of God by doing good to men. Such is, lastly, a religion of atheism; that is, every religion whereof God is not laid for the foundation. In a word, a religion wherein 'God in Christ, reconciling the world unto himself', is not the Alpha and Omega, the beginning and the end, the first and the last point.

16. True religion is right tempers towards God and man. It is, in two words,

gratitude and benevolence: gratitude to our Creator and supreme Benefactor, and benevolence to our fellow-creatures. In other words, it is the loving God with all our heart, and our neighbour as ourselves.

17. It is in consequence of our knowing God loves us that we love him, and love our neighbour as ourselves. Gratitude toward our Creator cannot but produce benevolence to our fellow-creatures. The love of Christ constrains us, not only to be harmless, to do no ill to our neighbour, but to be useful, to be 'zealous of good works', 'as we have time to do good unto all men', and be patterns to all of true genuine morality, of justice, mercy, and truth. This is religion, and this is happiness, the happiness for which we were made. This begins when we begin to know God, by the teaching of his own Spirit. As soon as the Father of spirits reveals his Son in our hearts, and the Son reveals his Father, the love of God is shed abroad in our hearts; then, and not till then, we are happy. We are happy, first, in the consciousness of his favour, which indeed is better than the life itself; next, in the constant communion with the Father, and with his Son, Jesus Christ; then in all the heavenly tempers which he hath wrought in us by his Spirit; again, in the testimony of his Spirit that all our works please him; and, lastly, in the testimony of our own spirit that 'in simplicity and godly sincerity we have had our conversation in the world.' Standing fast in this liberty from sin and sorrow, wherewith Christ hath made them free, real Christians 'rejoice evermore, pray without ceasing, and in everything give thanks'. And their happiness still increases as they 'grow up into the measure of the stature of the fullness of Christ'.

18. But how little is this religion experienced or even thought of in the Christian world! On the contrary, what reason have we to take up the lamentation of a dying saint (Mr. Haliburton, of St. Andrews in Scotland): 'O sirs, I am afraid a kind of *rational* religion is more and more prevailing amongst us, a religion that has nothing of Christ belonging to it; nay, that has not only nothing of Christ, but nothing of God in it!' And indeed how generally does this prevail, not only among professed infidels, but also among those who call themselves Christians, who profess to believe the Bible to be the Word of God. Thus our own countryman, Mr. Wollaston, in that elaborate work *The Religion of Nature Delineated*, presents us with a complete system of religion without anything of God about it, without being beholden in any degree to either the Jewish or Christian revelation. Thus Monsieur Burlamaqui (of Geneva), in his curious treatise on the law of nature, does not make any more use of the Bible than if he had never seen it. And thus the late Professor Hutcheson of Glasgow (a stronger writer than either of the other[s]) is so far from grounding virtue on either the fear or the love of God that he quite shuts God out of the question; not scrupling to declare in express terms that 'a regard to God is *inconsistent with* virtue; insomuch that if in doing a beneficent action you expect God to reward it, the virtue of the action is lost; it is then not a virtuous, but

a selfish action'!

19. Perhaps indeed there are not many who carry the matter to so great a length. But how great is the number of those who, allowing religion to consist of two branches, our duty to God and our duty to our neighbour, entirely forget the first part, and put the second part for the whole, for the entire duty of man. Thus almost all men of letters, both in England, France, Germany, yea, and all the civilized countries of Europe, extol 'humanity' to the skies, as the very essence of religion. To this the great triumvirate, Rousseau, Voltaire, and David Hume, have contributed all their labours, sparing no pains to establish a religion which should stand on its own foundation, independent on any revelation whatever, yea, not supposing even the being of a God. So leaving him, if he has any being, to himself, they have found out both a religion and a happiness which have no relation at all to God, nor any dependence upon him.

20. It is no wonder that this religion should grow fashionable, and spread far and wide in the world. But call it 'humanity', 'virtue', 'morality', or what you please, it is neither better nor worse than atheism. Men hereby wilfully and designedly put asunder what God has joined, the duties of the first and the second table. It is separating the love of our neighbour from the love of God. It is a plausible way of thrusting God out of the world he has made. They can do the business without him, and so either drop him entirely, not considering him at all; or suppose that since

> . . . he gave things their beginning,
> And set this whirligig a-spinning,

he has not concerned himself with these trifles, but let everything take its own course.

21. On the contrary, we have the fullest evidence that the eternal, omnipresent, almighty, all-wise Spirit, as he created all things, so he continually superintends whatever he has created. He governs all, not only to the bounds of creation, but through the utmost extent of space; and not only through the short time that is measured by the earth and sun, but from everlasting to everlasting. We know that as all nature, so all religion and all happiness depend on him; and we know that whoever teach to seek happiness without him are monsters and the pests of society.

22. But after all the vain attempts of learned or unlearned men it will be found, as there is but one God, so there is but one happiness, and one religion. And both of these centre in God. Both by Scripture and by experience we know that an unholy, and therefore an unhappy man, seeking rest but finding none, is sooner or later convinced that sin is the ground of his misery, and cries out of the deep to him that is able to save, 'God be merciful to me a sinner.' It is not long before he finds 'redemption in the blood of Jesus, even

the forgiveness of sins'. Then 'the Father reveals his Son' in his heart, and he 'calls Jesus Lord by the Holy Ghost'. And then the love of God is 'shed abroad in his heart, by the Holy Spirit which is given unto him'. From this principle springs real, disinterested benevolence to all mankind, making him humble, meek, gentle to all men, easy to be entreated, to be convinced of what is right, and persuaded to what is good, inviolably patient, with a thankful acquiescence in every step of his adorable providence. This is religion, even the whole mind which was also in Christ Jesus. And has any man the insolence or the stupidity to deny that this is happiness? Yea, that it

> Yields more of happiness below
> Than victors in a triumph know?

23. There can be no doubt but from this love to God and man a suitable conversation will follow. His 'communication', that is, discourse, will 'be always in grace, seasoned with salt', and meet to 'minister grace to the hearers'. He will always 'open his mouth with wisdom', and there will be 'in his tongue the law of kindness'. Hence his affectionate words will 'distil as the dew, and as the rain upon the tender herb'. And men will know 'it is not' he only 'that speaks, but the Spirit of the Father that speaketh in him'. His actions will spring from the same source with his words, even from the abundance of a loving heart. And while all these aim at the glory of God, and tend to this one point, whatever he does he may truly say:

> End of my every action thou,
> In all things thee I see!
> Accept my hallowed labour now!
> I do it as to thee!

24. He to whom this character belongs, and he alone, is a Christian. To him the one, eternal, omnipresent, all-perfect Spirit, is the Alpha and Omega, the first and the last. Not his Creator only, but his Sustainer, his Preserver, his Governor; yea, his Father, his Saviour, Sanctifier, and Comforter. This God is his God and his all, in time and in eternity. It is the benevolence springing from this root which is pure and undefiled religion. But if it be built on any other foundation, as it is of no avail in the sight of God, so it brings no real, solid, permanent happiness to man, but leaves him still a poor, dry, indigent, and dissatisfied creature.

25. Let all therefore that desire to please God condescend to be taught of God, and take care to walk in that path which God himself hath appointed. Beware of taking half of this religion for the whole, but take both parts of it together. And see that you begin where God himself begins: 'Thou shalt have no other God before me.' Is not this the first, our Lord himself being the judge, as well as the great commandment? First therefore see that ye love God; next

your neighbour, every child of man. From this fountain let every temper, every affection, every passion flow. So shall that 'mind be in you which was also in Christ Jesus'. Let all your thoughts, words, and actions spring from this. So shall you 'inherit the kingdom prepared for you from the beginning of the world'.

PROPHETS AND PRIESTS

Sermon 121 – 1789

AN INTRODUCTORY COMMENT

There were two points on which Wesley was never able to convince most of his people. One was the inherent sinfulness of 'riches'; the other was that they should remain content as a religious society (with their own lay preachers) within the Church of England (with her priests and sacraments). The issue of 'separation' had been raised by dissident Methodists as early as 1755 and simply would not disappear. It was, in fact, given fresh momentum by the constitution of 'the Conference' and the 'ordinations' of 1784.

The Irish Methodists were even more impatient than the English with Wesley's stubborn resistance to separation, and more eager to become visibly separate from the Church of England. Wesley's *Journal* entries for his trip to Ireland in the spring of 1789 reflect the urgency of this question and reiterate his longstanding decision not to 'ordain' lay preachers to administer the sacraments anywhere within the jurisdiction of the Church of England. The pressures were apparently strong enough to persuade him to write down his views on 'the degrees of the ministry' (Richard Hooker's phrase). He finished this project at 'Cork, May 9, 1789', according to his postscript. It was then published without a title in the *Arminian Magazine* (1790) as a sequel to his manifesto against separation in a previous issue. Although it was more an essay than a sermon, it quickly came to be called 'the Korah sermon' and was not well received. The drift among the Methodists toward 'separation' was by then irreversible, and this sermon seems to have changed no minds.

Its twin theses (no separation and no Methodist priesthood) reflect an unwavering Wesleyan standpoint based on a distinction between 'prophetic' and 'priestly' ministries that he had held since before his acceptance of 'lay assistants' in 1741. This distinction between 'prophets' free to preach and teach and 'priests' commissioned for sacramental administration went back at least to Hooker. Henry Moore, however, spoke for the Methodist majority in his bold rebuke to Wesley about such a sermon, claiming that its distinctions were not scriptural.

Since the sermon's first publication, Methodists have largely ignored it. George Story deliberately excluded it from the ninth volume of Wesley's collected *Sermons*, as did Joseph Benson from his edition of the *Works*. Thomas Jackson decided to include it in his edition of the *Sermons* (1825) and the 1829–31 edition of the *Works*, but with Moore's disparaging comments quoted in full as an introductory note. Jackson also gave it the title, 'The Ministerial Office', probably not a title that Wesley himself would have used.

Prophets and Priests

No man taketh this honour unto himself
but he that is called of God, as was Aaron.
Hebrews 5:4

1. There are exceeding few texts of Holy Scripture which have been more frequently urged than this against laymen, that are neither priests nor deacons, and yet take upon them to preach. Many have asked, 'How dare any take this honour to himself, unless he be called of God, as was Aaron?' And a pious and sensible clergyman some years ago published a sermon on these words, wherein he endeavours to show that it is not enough to be inwardly called of God to preach, as many imagine themselves to be, unless they are outwardly called by men sent of God for that purpose, as Aaron 'was called of God' by Moses.

2. But there is one grievous flaw in this argument, as often as it has been urged. 'Called of God, as was Aaron'! But Aaron did not preach at all: he was not called to it either by God or man. Aaron was called to minister in holy things; to offer up prayers and sacrifices; to execute the office of a priest. But he was never called to be a preacher.

3. In ancient times the office of a priest and that of a preacher were known to be entirely distinct. And so everyone will be convinced that impartially traces the matter from the beginning. From Adam to Noah it is allowed by all that the first-born in every family was of course the priest in that family, by virtue of his primogeniture. But this gave him no right to be a preacher or (in the scriptural language) a prophet. This office not infrequently belonged to the youngest branch of the family. For in this respect God always asserted his *right* to send by whom he *would* send.

4. From the time of Noah to that of Moses the same observation may be made. The eldest of the family was the priest, but any other might be the prophet. This, the office of priest, we find Esau inherited by virtue of his birthright, till he profanely sold it to Jacob 'for a mess of pottage'. And this it was which he could never recover, 'though he sought it carefully with tears'.

5. Indeed in the time of Moses a very considerable change was made with regard to the priesthood. God then appointed that instead of the first-born in every house a whole tribe should be dedicated to him; and that all that afterwards ministered unto him as priests should be of that tribe. Thus Aaron was of the tribe of Levi. And so likewise was Moses. But he was not a priest,

though he was the greatest prophet that ever lived before God brought his first-begotten into the world. Meantime not many of the Levites were prophets. And if any were, it was a mere accidental thing. They were not such as being of that tribe. Many, if not most of the prophets (as we are informed by the ancient Jewish writers), were of the tribe of Simeon. And some were of the tribe of Benjamin or Judah, and probably of other tribes also.

6. But we have reason to believe there were, in every age, two sorts of prophets. The extraordinary, such as Nathan, Isaiah, Jeremiah, and many others, on whom the Holy Ghost came in an extraordinary manner; such was Amos in particular, who saith of himself: 'I was no prophet, neither a prophet's son. But I was an herdman, and the Lord said unto me, Go, prophesy unto my people Israel' (Amos 7:14–15). The ordinary were those who were educated in 'the schools of the prophets', one of which was at Ramah, over which Samuel presided (1 Sam. 19:18). These were trained up to instruct the people, and were the ordinary preachers in their synagogues. In the New Testament they are usually termed scribes, or νομικοί, expounders of the law. But few, if any of them, were priests. These were all along a different order.

7. Many learned men have shown at large that our Lord himself, and all his apostles, built the Christian church as nearly as possible on the plan of the Jewish. So, the great High Priest of our profession sent apostles and evangelists to proclaim glad tidings to all the world, and then pastors, preachers, and teachers to build up in the faith the congregations that should be found. But I do not find that ever the office of an evangelist was the same with that of a pastor, frequently called a bishop. He presided over the flock, and administered the sacraments: the former assisted him, and preached the Word, either in one or more congregations. I cannot prove from any part of the New Testament, or from any author of the three first centuries, that the office of an evangelist gave any man a right to act as a pastor or bishop. I believe these offices were considered as quite distinct from each other till the time of Constantine.

8. Indeed in that evil hour when Constantine the Great called himself 'a Christian', and poured in honour and wealth upon the Christians, the case was widely altered. It soon grew common for one man to take the whole charge of a congregation, in order to engross the whole pay. Hence the same person acted as priest and prophet, as pastor and evangelist. And this gradually spread more and more throughout the whole Christian church. Yet even at this day, although the same person usually discharges both those offices, yet the office of an evangelist or teacher does not imply that of a pastor, to whom peculiarly belongs the administration of the sacraments—neither among the Presbyterians, nor in the Church of England, nor even among the Roman Catholics. All Presbyterian Churches, it is well known (that of Scotland in particular) license men to preach before they are ordained, throughout that whole

kingdom. And it is never understood that this appointment to preach gives them any right to administer the sacraments. Likewise in our own Church persons may be authorized to preach—yea, may be Doctors of Divinity (as was Dr. Alwood at Oxford when I resided there)—who are not ordained at all, and consequently have no right to administer the Lord's Supper. Yea, even in the Church of Rome itself, if a lay brother believes he is called to go a mission, as it is termed, he is sent out, though neither priest nor deacon, to execute that office, and not the other.

9. 'But may it not be thought that the case now before us is different from all these?' Undoubtedly in many respects it is. Such a phenomenon has now appeared as has not appeared in the Christian world before, at least not for many ages. Two young men 'sowed the word of God', not only in the churches, but likewise literally 'by the highway side', and indeed in every place where they saw an open door, where sinners had ears to hear. They were members of the Church of England, and had no design of separating from it. And they advised all that were of it to continue therein, although they joined the Methodist society; for this did not imply leaving their former congregation, but only leaving their sins. The churchmen might go to church still; the Presbyterian, Anabaptist, Quaker, might still retain their own opinions, and attend their own congregations. The having a real desire to flee from the wrath to come was the only condition required of them. Whosoever therefore 'feared God and worked righteousness' was qualified for this society.

10. Not long after a young man (Thomas Maxfield) offered himself to serve them as a son in the gospel. And then another, Thomas Richards, and a little after a third, Thomas Westell. Let it be well observed on what terms we received these, viz., as prophets, not as priests. We received them wholly and solely to preach; not to administer sacraments. And those who imagine these offices to be inseparably joined are totally ignorant of the constitution of the whole Jewish as well as Christian church. Neither the Romish, nor the English, nor the Presbyterian Churches, ever accounted them so. Otherwise we should never have accepted the service either of Mr. Maxfield, Richards, or Westell.

11. In 1744, all the Methodist preachers had their first Conference. But none of them dreamed that the being called to preach gave them any right to administer sacraments. And when that question was proposed, 'In what light are we to consider ourselves?' it was answered, 'As *extraordinary messengers*, raised up to provoke the *ordinary* ones to jealousy.' In order hereto one of our first rules was—given to each preacher—'You are to do *that part* of the work which we appoint.' But *what work* was this? Did we ever appoint you to administer sacraments, to exercise the priestly office? Such a design never entered into our mind; it was the farthest from our thoughts. And if any preacher had taken such a step we should have looked upon it as a palpable breach of this rule, and consequently as a recantation of our connexion.

12. For supposing (what I utterly deny) that the receiving you as a preacher at the same time gave an authority to administer the sacraments, yet it gave you no other authority than to do it, or anything else, *where I appoint.* But where did I appoint you to do this? Nowhere at all. Therefore by this very rule you are excluded from doing it. And in doing it you renounce the first principle of Methodism, which was wholly and solely to preach the gospel.

13. It was several years after our society was formed before any attempt of this kind was made. The first was, I apprehend, at Norwich. One of our preachers there yielded to the importunity of a few of the people, and baptized their children. But as soon as it was known, he was informed it must not be, unless he designed to leave our connexion. He promised to do it no more—and I suppose he kept his promise.

14. Now as long as the Methodists keep to this plan they cannot separate from the Church. And this is our peculiar glory. It is new upon the earth. Revolve all the histories of the church, from the earliest ages, and you will find, whenever there was a great work of God in any particular city or nation, the subjects of that work soon said to their neighbours, 'Stand by yourselves, for we are holier than you!' As soon as ever they separated themselves, either they retired into deserts, or they built religious houses; or at least formed parties, into which none was admitted but such as subscribed both to their judgment and practice. But with the Methodists it is quite otherwise. They are not a sect or party. They do not separate from the religious community to which they at first belonged. They are still members of the Church; such they desire to live and to die. And I believe one reason why God is pleased to continue my life so long is to confirm them in their present purpose not to separate from the Church.

15. But notwithstanding this many warm men say, 'Nay, but you *do* separate from the Church.' Others are equally warm because, they say, I *do not.* I will nakedly declare the thing as it is.

I hold all the doctrines of the Church of England. I love her Liturgy. I approve her plan of discipline, and only wish it could be put in execution. I do not knowingly vary from any rule of the Church, unless in those few instances where I judge, and as far as I judge, there is an absolute necessity.

For instance: (1) As few clergymen open their churches to me, I am under the necessity of *preaching abroad.*

(2) As I know no forms that will suit all occasions, I am often under a necessity of *praying extempore.*

(3) In order to build up the flock of Christ in faith and love, I am under a necessity of uniting them together, and of dividing them into little companies, that they may provoke one another to love and good works.

(4) That my fellow-labourers and I may more effectually assist each other to save our own souls and those that hear us, I judge it necessary to meet the

preachers, or at least the greater part of them, once a year.

(5) In those Conferences we fix the stations of all the preachers for the ensuing year.

But all this is not separating from the Church. So far from it that whenever I have opportunity I attend the Church service myself, and advise all our societies so to do.

16. Nevertheless as [to] the generality even of religious people, who do not understand my motives of acting, and who on the one hand hear me profess that I will not separate from the Church, and on the other that I do vary from it in these instances, they will naturally think I am inconsistent with myself. And they cannot but think so, unless they observe my two principles: the one, that I dare not separate from the Church, that I believe it would be a sin so to do; the other, that I believe it would be a sin not to vary from it in the points above mentioned. I say, put these two principles together—first, I will not separate from the Church; yet, secondly, in cases of necessity I will vary from it (both of which I have constantly and openly avowed for upwards of fifty years)—and inconsistency vanishes away. I have been true to my profession from 1730 to this day.

17. 'But is it not contrary to your profession to permit service in Dublin at church hours? For what necessity is there for this? Or what good end does it answer?' I believe it answers several good ends, which could not so well be answered any other way. The first is (strange as it may sound) to *prevent a separation* from the Church. Many of our society were totally separated from the Church; they never attended it at all. But now they duly attend the Church every first Sunday in the month. 'But had they not better attend it every week?' Yes; but who can persuade them to it? I cannot. I have strove to do it twenty or thirty years; but in vain. The second is the weaning them from attending dissenting meetings, which many of them attended constantly, but have now wholly left. The third is, the constantly hearing that sound doctrine which is able to save their souls.

18. I wish all of you who are vulgarly termed Methodists would seriously consider what has been said. And particularly you whom God hath commissioned to call sinners to repentance. It does by no means follow from hence that ye are commissioned to baptize, or to administer the Lord's Supper. Ye never dreamed of this for ten or twenty years after ye began to preach. Ye did not then, like Korah, Dathan, and Abiram, 'seek the priesthood also'. Ye knew, 'No man taketh this honour unto himself, but he that is called of God, as was Aaron.' O contain yourselves within your own bounds. Be content with preaching the gospel. 'Do the work of evangelists.' Proclaim to all the world the loving-kindness of God our Saviour; declare to all: 'The kingdom of heaven is at hand; repent ye and believe the gospel.' I earnestly advise you, abide in your place; keep your own station. Ye were fifty years ago, those of you that

were then Methodist preachers, 'extraordinary messengers' of God, not going in your own will, but *thrust out*, not to supersede, but to 'provoke to jealousy' the 'ordinary messengers'. In God's name, stop there! Both by your preaching and example provoke them to love and to good works. Ye are a new phenomenon in the earth; a body of people who, being of no sect or party, are friends to all parties, and endeavour to forward all in heart religion, in the knowledge and love of God and man. Ye yourselves were at first called in the Church of England; and though ye have and will have a thousand temptations to leave it and set up for yourselves, regard them not. Be Church of England men still. Do not cast away the peculiar glory which God hath put upon you, and frustrate the design of Providence, the very end for which God raised you up.

19. I would add a few words to those serious people who are not connected with the Methodists, many of whom are of our own church, the Church of England. And why should *ye* be displeased with us? We do you no harm. We do not design or desire to offend you in anything. We hold your doctrines. We observe your rules, more than do most of the people in the kingdom. Some of you are clergymen. And why should *ye*, of all men, be displeased with us? We neither attack your character nor your revenue. We honour you for 'your work's sake'! If we see some things which we do not approve of, we do not publish them. We rather cast a mantle over them, and hide what we cannot commend. When ye treat us unkindly or unjustly, we suffer it. 'Being reviled, we bless.' We do not return railing for railing. O let not *your* hand be upon us!

20. Ye that are *rich* in this world, count us not your enemies because we tell you the truth; and it may be in a fuller and stronger manner than any others will or dare do. Ye have therefore need of us, inexpressible need. Ye cannot buy such friends at any price. All your gold and silver cannot purchase such. Make use of us while ye may. If it be possible, never be without some of those who will speak the truth from their heart. Otherwise ye may grow grey in your sins. Ye may say to your souls, 'Peace, peace!' while there is no peace! Ye may sleep on, and dream ye are in the way to heaven, till ye awake in everlasting fire.

21. But whether ye will hear, or whether ye will forbear, we, by the grace of God, hold on our way; being ourselves still members of the Church of England, as we were from the beginning, but receiving all that love God in every church as our brother, and sister, and mother. And in order to their union with us we require no unity in opinions, or in modes of worship, but barely that they 'fear God and work righteousness', as was observed. Now this is utterly a new thing, unheard of in any other Christian community. In what church or congregation beside, throughout the Christian world, can members be admitted upon these terms, without any other conditions? Point any such out,

whoever can. I know none in Europe, Asia, Africa, or America! This is the glory of the Methodists, and of them alone! They are themselves no particular sect or party; but they receive those of all parties who 'endeavour to do justly, and love mercy, and walk humbly with their God'.

CAUSES OF THE INEFFICACY OF CHRISTIANITY

Sermon 122 – 1789

AN INTRODUCTORY COMMENT

The problem represented in this sermon is the embarrassing disparity between Christianity's promise ('a universal remedy for a universal evil') and its actual performance. Wesley had reflected on this situation off and on for fifty years. Predestinarian explanations of this disparity had never persuaded him, and thus he had found himself, in characteristic candour, with a most unwelcome paradox: 'Does it not seem (and yet this cannot be) that Christianity, scriptural Christianity, has a tendency in process of time to undermine and destroy itself?' Why? Because 'wherever true Christianity spreads, it must cause diligence and frugality, which, in the natural course of things, must beget riches—and riches naturally beget pride, love of the world, and every temper that is destructive of Christianity.' Thus Wesley has brought us back around to a favourite cause: his denunciation of riches and his complaint against the stubborn refusal of the Methodist people to heed him on this pivotal point.

The reader should note the sermon's 'short summaries'. For instance, four lines in §6 list the 'first principles' of Christianity and thus define 'the analogy of faith' more compactly than anywhere else in the entire Wesley corpus. His cry, 'Where is Christian discipline!', hearkens back to an almost identical entry in his Georgia diary over fifty years earlier. Typical of the mature Wesley, he is not hesitant in this sermon to recall the disciplined praxis of the Oxford Methodists (woefully relaxed by the latter-day variety) as a model for authentic Christian living. What we have here, then, is an old man's sermon in which the flashes of his characteristic zeal and wisdom are still being struck off. Its organization is loose-jointed and its arguments more casual than usual, and yet Wesley's design is clear enough and the application is as trenchant as ever.

According to Wesley's postscript, this sermon was finished in 'Dublin, July 2, 1789'; it was then published without a title in the *Arminian Magazine* (1790). Joseph Benson gave it the present title (not at all typical of Wesley's terminology), which has been used since 1811.

Causes of the Inefficacy of Christianity

Is there no balm in Gilead? Is there no physician there?
Why then is not the health of the daughter of my people recovered?
Jeremiah 8:22

1. This question, as here proposed by the prophet, relates only to a particular people, the children of Israel. But I would here consider it in a general sense, with relation to all mankind. I would seriously inquire, Why has Christianity done so little good in the world? Is it not the balm, the outward means, which the Great Physician has given to men to restore their spiritual health? Why then is it not restored? You say, Because of the deep and the universal corruption of human nature. Most true. But here is the very difficulty. Was it not intended by our all-wise and almighty Creator to be the remedy for that corruption? An universal remedy for an universal evil? But it has not answered this intention. It never did. It does not answer it at this day. The disease still remains in its full strength: wickedness of every kind, vice inward and outward in all its forms, still overspread the face of the earth.

2. O Lord God, 'righteous art thou! Yet let us plead with thee!' How is this? Hast thou forgotten the world which thou hast made? Which thou hast created for thy own glory? Canst thou despise the work of thy own hands, the purchase of thy Son's blood? Thou hast given medicine to heal our sickness; yet our sickness is not healed. Yet darkness covers the earth, and thick darkness the people. Yea,

Darkness, such as devils feel,
Issuing from the pit of hell.

3. What a mystery is this! That Christianity should have done so little good in the world! Can any account of this be given? Can any reasons be assigned for it? Does it not seem that one reason it has done so little good is this: because it is so little known? Certainly it can do no good where it is not known. But it is not known at this day to the far greater part of the inhabitants of the earth. In the last century our ingenious and laborious countryman, Mr. Brerewood, travelled over great part of the known world on purpose to inquire, so far as was possible, what proportion the Christians bear to the heathens and Mahometans. And according to his computation (probably the most accurate which has yet been made) I suppose mankind to be divided into thirty parts; nineteen parts of these are still open heathens, having no more knowledge of

Christianity than the beasts that perish. And we may add to these the numerous nations which have been discovered in the present century. Add to these such as profess the Mahometan religion, and utterly scorn Christianity, and [twenty-]five parts out of thirty of mankind are not so much as nominally Christians. So then five parts of mankind out of six are totally ignorant of Christianity. It is therefore no wonder that five in six of mankind, perhaps nine in ten, have no advantage from it.

4. But why is it that so little advantage is derived from it to the Christian world? Are Christians any better than other men? Are they better than Mahometans or heathens? To say the truth, it is well if they are not worse, worse than either Mahometans or heathens. In many respects they are abundantly worse. But then they are not properly Christians. The generality of these, though they bear the Christian name, do not know what Christianity is. They no more understand it than they do Greek or Hebrew; therefore they can be no better for it. What do the Christians, so called, of the Eastern Church, dispersed throughout the Turkish dominions, know of genuine Christianity? Those of the Morea, of Circassia, Mingrelia, Georgia? Are they not the very dregs of mankind? And have we reason to think that those of the southern church, those inhabiting Abyssinia, have any more conception than them of 'worshipping God in spirit and in truth'? Look we nearer home. See the northern churches, those that are under the Patriarch of Moscow. How exceeding little do they know either of outward or inward Christianity! How many thousands, yea, myriads of those poor savages know nothing of Christianity but the name! How little more do they know than the heathen Tartars on the one hand, or the heathen Chinese on the other!

5. But is not Christianity well known at least to all the inhabitants of the western world? A great part of which is eminently termed Christendom, or the land of Christians. Part of these are still members of the Church of Rome; part are termed 'Protestants'. As to the former, Portuguese, Spaniards, Italians, French, Germans, what do the bulk of them know of scriptural Christianity? Having had frequent opportunity of conversing with many of these, both at home and abroad, I am bold to affirm that they are in general totally ignorant both as to the theory and practice of Christianity; so that they are *perishing* by thousands 'for lack of knowledge', for want of knowing the very first principles of Christianity.

6. 'But surely this cannot be the case of the Protestants in France, Switzerland, Germany, and Holland! Much less in Denmark and Sweden!' Indeed I hope it is not altogether. I am persuaded there are among them many knowing Christians. But I fear we must not think that one in ten, if one in fifty, is of this number; certainly not if we may form a judgment of them by those we find in Great Britain and Ireland. Let us see how matters stand at our own door. Do the people of England in general (not the highest or the

lowest, for these usually know nothing of the matter, but people of the middle rank) understand Christianity? Do they conceive what it is? Can they give an intelligible account either of the speculative or practical part of it? What know they of the very first principles of it? Of the natural and moral attributes of God? Of his particular providence? Of the redemption of man? Of the offices of Christ? Of the operations of the Holy Ghost? Of justification? Of the new birth? Of inward and outward sanctification? Speak of any of these things to the first ten persons you are in company with, and will you not find nine out of the ten ignorant of the whole affair? And are not most of the inhabitants of the Scotch highlands full as ignorant as these? Yea, and the common people in Ireland? (I mean the Protestants, of whom alone we are now speaking.) Make a fair inquiry, not only in the country cabins, but in the cities of Cork, Waterford, Limerick! Yea, in Dublin itself. How few know what Christianity means! How small a number will you find that have any conception of the analogy of faith! Of the connected chain of Scripture truths, and their relation to each other! Namely, the natural corruption of man, justification by faith, the new birth, inward and outward holiness. It must be acknowledged by all competent judges who converse freely with their neighbours in these kingdoms that a vast majority of them know no more of these things than they do of Hebrew or Arabic. And what good can Christianity do to these, who are so totally ignorant of it?

7. However, in some parts, both of England and Ireland, scriptural Christianity is well known; especially in London, Bristol, Dublin, and almost all the large and populous cities and towns of both kingdoms. In these every branch of Christianity is openly and largely declared, and thousands upon thousands continually hear and receive 'the truth as it is in Jesus'. Why is it then that even in these parts Christianity has had so little effect? Why are the generality of the people in all these places heathens still? No better than the heathens of Africa or America, either in their tempers or in their lives. Now how is this to be accounted for? I conceive thus. It was a common saying among the Christians in the primitive church, 'The soul and the body make a man; the spirit and discipline make a Christian'—implying that none could be real Christians without the help of Christian discipline. But if this be so, is it any wonder that we find so few Christians, for where is Christian discipline! In what part of England (to go no farther) is Christian discipline added to Christian doctrine? Now whatever doctrine is preached where there is not discipline, it cannot have its full effect upon the hearers.

8. To bring the matter closer still. Is not scriptural Christianity preached and generally known among the people commonly called Methodists? Impartial persons allow it is. And have they not Christian discipline, too, in all the essential branches of it regularly and constantly exercised? Let those who think any essential part of it is wanting point it out, and it shall not be wanting long.

Why then are not these altogether Christians? Who have both Christian doctrine and Christian discipline? Why is not the spiritual health of the people called Methodists recovered? Why is not all that 'mind in us which was also in Christ Jesus'? Why have we not learned of him our very first lesson, to be meek and lowly of heart? To say with him, in all circumstances of life, 'Not as I will, but as thou wilt'? 'I come not to do my own will, but the will of him that sent me'? Why are not we 'crucified to the world, and the world crucified to us'? Dead to 'the desire of the flesh, the desire of the eyes, and the pride of life'? Why do not all of us live 'the life that is hid with Christ in God'? O why do not we that have all possible helps 'walk as Christ also walked'? Hath he not 'left us an example, that we might tread in his steps'? But do we regard either his example or precept? To instance only in one point. Who regards those solemn words, 'Lay not up for yourselves treasures upon earth'? Of the three rules which are laid down on this head in the sermon on 'the mammon of unrighteousness' you may find many that observe the first rule, namely, 'Gain all you can.' You may find a few that observe the second, 'Save all you can.' But how many have you found that observe the third rule, 'Give all you can'? Have you reason to believe that five hundred of these are to be found among fifty thousand Methodists? And yet nothing can be more plain than that all who observe the two first rules without the third will be twofold more the children of hell than ever they were before.

9. O that God would enable me once more, before I go hence and am no more seen, to lift up my voice like a trumpet to those who *gain* and *save* all they can, but do not *give* all they can. Ye are the men, some of the chief men, who continually grieve the Holy Spirit of God, and in a great measure stop his gracious influence from descending on our assemblies. Many of your brethren, beloved of God, have not food to eat; they have not raiment to put on; they have not a place where to lay their head. And why are they thus distressed? Because *you* impiously, unjustly, and cruelly detain from them what your Master and theirs lodges in *your* hands on purpose to supply *their* wants! See that poor member of Christ pinched with hunger, shivering with cold, half naked! Meantime you have plenty of this world's goods, of meat, drink, and apparel. In the name of God, what are you doing? Do you neither fear God, nor regard man? Why do you not deal your bread to the hungry? And cover the naked with a garment? Have you laid out in your own costly apparel what would have answered both those intentions? Did God command you so to do? Does he commend you for so doing? Did he entrust you with *his* (not *your*) goods for this end? And does he now say, 'Servant of God, well done'? You well know he does not. This idle expense has no approbation, either from God or your own conscience. But, you say, you can 'afford' it! O be ashamed to take such miserable nonsense into your mouths. Never more utter such stupid cant, such palpable absurdity! Can any steward 'afford' to be an errant

knave? To waste his Lord's goods? Can any servant 'afford' to lay out his master's money any other wise than his master appoints him? So far from it that whoever does this ought to be excluded from a Christian society.

10. 'But is it possible to supply all the poor in our society with the necessaries of life?' It *was* possible once to do this, in a larger society than this. In the first church at Jerusalem 'there was not any among them that lacked, but distribution was made to everyone according as he had need.' And we have full proof that it may be so still. It is so among the people called Quakers. Yea, and among the Moravians, so called. And why should it not be so with *us*? 'Because they are ten times richer than us.' Perhaps fifty times. And yet we are able enough, if we were equally willing to do this.

A gentleman (a Methodist) told me some years since, 'I shall leave forty thousand pounds among my children.' Now suppose he had left them but twenty thousand, and given the other twenty thousand to God and the poor; would God have said to him, 'Thou fool'? And this would have set all the society far above want.

11. But I will not talk of giving to God, or leaving half your fortune. You might think this to be too high a price for heaven. I will come to lower terms. Are there not a few among you that could give a hundred pounds, perhaps some that could give a thousand, and yet leave your children as much as would help them to work out *their* own salvation? With two thousand pounds, and not much less, we could supply the present wants of all our poor, and put them in a way of supplying their own wants for the time to come. Now suppose this could be done, are we clear before God while it is not done? Is not the neglect of it one cause why so many are still sick and weak among you? And that both in soul and in body? That they still grieve the Holy Spirit by preferring the fashions of man to the commands of God? And I many times doubt whether we preachers are not in some measure partakers of their sin. I am in doubt whether it is not a kind of partiality. I doubt whether it is not a great mercy to keep them in our society. May it not hurt their souls by encouraging them to persevere in walking contrary to the Bible? And may it not in some measure intercept the salutary influences of the blessed Spirit upon the whole community?

12. I am distressed. I know not what to do. I see what I might have done once. I might have said peremptorily and expressly: 'Here I am: I and my Bible. I will not, I dare not vary from this book, either in great things or small. I have no power to dispense with one jot or tittle of what is contained therein. I am determined to be a Bible Christian, not almost but altogether. Who will meet me on this ground? Join me on this, or not at all.' With regard to dress in particular I might have been as firm (and I now see it would have been far better) as either the people called Quakers or the Moravian Brethren. I might have said: 'This is *our* manner of dress, which we know is both scriptural and

rational. If you join with us you are to dress as we do; but you need not join us unless you please.' But alas! the time is now past. And what I can do now I cannot tell.

13. But to return to the main question. Why has Christianity done so little good, even among us? Among the Methodists? Among them that hear and receive the whole Christian doctrine, and that have Christian discipline added thereto, in the most essential parts of it? Plainly because we have forgot, or at least not duly attended to those solemn words of our Lord, 'If any man will come after me, let him deny himself, and take up his cross daily and follow me.' It was the remark of a holy man several years ago, 'Never was there before a people in the Christian church who had so much of the power of God among them, with so little self-denial.' Indeed the work of God does go on, and in a surprising manner, notwithstanding this capital defect; but it cannot go on in the same degree as it otherwise would: neither can the word of God have its full effect unless the hearers of it 'deny themselves, and take up their cross daily'.

14. It would be easy to show in how many respects the Methodists in general are deplorably wanting in the practice of Christian self-denial; from which indeed they have been continually frighted by the silly outcries of the antinomians. To instance only in one. While we were at Oxford the rule of every Methodist was (unless in case of sickness) to *fast* every Wednesday and Friday in the year, in imitation of the primitive church, for which they had the highest reverence. Now this practice of the primitive church is universally allowed. 'Who does not know', says Epiphanius, an ancient writer, 'that the fasts of the fourth and sixth days of the week (Wednesday and Friday) are observed by the Christians throughout the whole world?' So they were by the Methodists for several years; by them all, without any exception. But afterwards some in London carried this to excess, and fasted so as to impair their health. It was not long before others made this a pretence for not fasting at all. And I fear there are now thousands of Methodists, so called, both in England and Ireland, who, following the same bad example, have entirely left off fasting; who are so far from fasting twice in the week (as all the stricter Pharisees did) that they do not fast twice in the month. Yea, are there not some of you who do not fast one day, from the beginning of the year to the end? But what excuse can there be for this? I do not say for those that call themselves members of the Church of England, but for any who profess to believe the Scripture to be the Word of God? Since, according to this, the man that never fasts is no more in the way to heaven than the man that never prays.

15. But can anyone deny that the members of the Church of Scotland fast constantly? Particularly on their sacramental occasions. In some parishes they return only once a year, but in others, suppose in large cities, they occur twice or even thrice a year. Now it is well known there is always a fast-day in the

week preceding the administration of the Lord's Supper. But occasionally looking into a book of accounts in one of their vestries I observed, 'So much set down *for the dinners* of the ministers on the fast-day!' And I am informed there is the same article in them all. And is there any doubt but the people fast just as their ministers do? But what a farce is this! What a miserable burlesque upon a plain Christian duty! O that the General Assembly would have regard to the honour of their nation! Let them roll away from it this shameful reproach, by either enforcing the duty, or removing that article from their books. Let it never appear there any more! Let it vanish away for ever!

16. But why is self-denial in general so little practised at present among the Methodists? Why is so exceeding little of it to be found even in the oldest and largest societies? The more I observe and consider things, the more clearly it appears what is the cause of this in London, in Bristol, in Birmingham, in Manchester, in Leeds, in Dublin, in Cork. The Methodists grow more and more self-indulgent, because they *grow rich*. Although many of them are still deplorably poor ('Tell it not in Gath; publish it not in the streets of Askelon!'), yet many others, in the space of twenty, thirty, or forty years, are twenty, thirty, yea, a hundred times richer than they were when they first entered the society. And it is an observation which admits of few exceptions, that nine in ten of these decreased in grace in the same proportion as they increased in wealth. Indeed, according to the natural tendency of riches, we cannot expect it to be otherwise.

17. But how astonishing a thing is this! How can we understand it? Does it not seem (and yet this cannot be!) that Christianity, true scriptural Christianity, has a tendency in process of time to undermine and destroy itself? For wherever true Christianity spreads it must cause diligence and frugality, which, in the natural course of things, must beget riches. And riches naturally beget pride, love of the world, and every temper that is destructive of Christianity. Now if there be no way to prevent this, Christianity is consistent with itself, and of consequence, cannot stand, cannot continue long among any people; since, wherever it generally prevails, it saps its own foundation.

18. But is there no way to prevent this? To continue Christianity among a people? Allowing that diligence and frugality must produce riches, is there no means to hinder riches from destroying the religion of those that possess them? I can see only one possible way—find out another who can. Do you gain all you can, and save all you can? Then you must in the nature of things grow rich. Then if you have any desire to escape the damnation of hell, *give* all you can. Otherwise I can have no more hope of your salvation than for that of Judas Iscariot.

19. I call God to record upon my soul, that I advise no more than I practise. I do, blessed be God, gain, and save, and give all I can. And so, I trust in God, I shall do, while the breath of God is in my nostrils. But what then? I count

all things but loss for the excellency of the knowledge of Jesus, my Lord! Still

> I give up every plea, beside
> 'Lord, I am damned–but thou hast died!'

ON THE WEDDING GARMENT

Sermon 127 – 1790

AN INTRODUCTORY COMMENT

This essay is the first (and easily the most important) in a group of six written sermons produced by Wesley in the last year of his life. In one sense, 'On the Wedding Garment' is a return full circle to the vision of salvation first delineated in 'The Circumcision of the Heart' fifty-seven years earlier. In another sense, it reflects an upward spiralling. On this account, the two sermons will repay careful comparison.

The Matthean parable of 'the wedding garment' had already had a long history of controverted interpretation. It had been taken by some as a metaphor for 'faith alone', by others as signifying 'charity implanted', by others as a veiled reference to the Lord's Supper. In his *Explanatory Notes*, Wesley had left open the question between 'faith' and 'charity', and had rejected only the third interpretation. As the Calvinists pressed him with their charges of 'works-righteousness', however, he seems to have felt it important to summarize his characteristic emphasis on the unity of faith and love in true holiness. His oral delivery of that distinctive message occurred on October 25, 1789, in London: 'Sunday, 25. In the morning I preached at West Street on Matt. 22:11 . . . and showed that this has no manner of respect either to the Lord's Supper or the righteousness of Christ, but that it means neither more nor less than holiness.'

Eight months later, he noted in his *Journal*: 'I finished my sermon on the Wedding Garment, perhaps the last that I shall write. My eyes are now waxed dim; my natural force is abated. However, while I can I would fain do a little for God before I drop into the dust.' It was not actually his last written sermon; it is, however, one of his most important. It is, in effect, his last word on 'impartation'. His postscript indicates that he finished the sermon in 'Madeley, March 26, 1790'. It was published a year later in the *Arminian Magazine* for March and April 1791 (he had died on March 2). George Story then included it in volume nine of the collected *Sermons* (1800). Joseph Benson, in his edition of 1812, supplied it with Wesley's title from the *Journal*; Thomas Jackson followed suit in 1825 and 1829.

On the Wedding Garment

How camest thou in hither, not having a wedding garment?
Matthew 22:12

1. In the verses preceding the text we read: 'After these things, Jesus spake to them again in parables, and said, A certain king made a supper for his son. And when the king came in to see the guests, he saw one who had not on a wedding garment. And he saith unto him, Friend, how camest thou in hither not having a wedding garment? And he was speechless. Then said the king to the servants, Bind him hand and foot, and cast him into outer darkness; there shall be weeping and gnashing of teeth.'

2. Upon this parable one of our most celebrated expositors comments in the following manner: 'The design of this parable is to set forth that gracious supply made by God to men in and by the preaching of the gospel. To invite them to this God sent forth his servants, the prophets and apostles.' And on these words, 'Why camest thou in hither, not having a wedding garment?' he proceeds thus: 'The punishment of which ought not to discourage us, or make us to turn our backs upon the holy ordinances.' Certainly it ought not; but nothing of this kind can be inferred from this parable, which has no reference to the ordinances, any more than to baptism and marriage. And probably we should never have imagined it, but that the word 'supper' occurred therein.

3. However, most of the English annotators have fallen into the same mistake with Mr. Burkitt. And so have thousands of their readers. Yet a mistake it certainly is. And such a mistake as has not any shadow of foundation in the text. It is true, indeed, that none ought to approach the Lord's table without habitual, at least (if not actual), preparation; that is, a firm purpose to keep all the commandments of God, and a sincere desire to receive all his promises. But that obligation cannot be inferred from this text, though it may from many other passages of Scripture. But there is no need of multiplying texts: one is as good as a thousand. There needs no more to induce any man of a tender conscience to communicate at all opportunities than that single commandment of our Lord, 'Do this in remembrance of me.'

4. But whatever preparation is necessary in order to our being worthy partakers of the Lord's Supper, it has no relation at all to the wedding garment mentioned in this parable. It cannot; for that commemoration of his death was not then ordained. It relates wholly to the proceedings of our Lord when he comes in the clouds of heaven to judge the quick and the dead; and to the

qualifications which will then be necessary to their 'inheriting the kingdom prepared for them from the foundation of the world'.

5. Many excellent men, who are thoroughly apprised of this, who are convinced the wedding garment here mentioned is not to be understood of any qualification for the Lord's Supper, but of the qualification for glory, interpret it of the righteousness of Christ, which (say they) is 'the sole qualification for heaven; this being the only righteousness wherein any man can stand in the day of the Lord'. For who, they ask, will then dare to appear before the great God, save in the righteousness of his well-beloved Son? 'Shall we not then at least, if not before, find the need of having a better righteousness than our own! And what other can that be than the righteousness of God our Saviour?' The late pious and ingenious Mr. Hervey descants largely upon this; particularly in his elaborate *Dialogues between Theron and Aspasio.*

6. Another elegant writer, now I trust with God, speaks strongly to the same effect in the preface to his comment on St. Paul's Epistle to the Romans. 'We certainly', says he, 'shall need a better righteousness than our own, wherein to stand at the bar of God in the day of judgment.' I do not understand the expression. Is it scriptural! Do we read it in the Bible? Either in the Old Testament or the New? I doubt, it is an unscriptural, awkward phrase, which has no determinate meaning. If you mean by that odd, uncouth question, 'In whose righteousness are you to stand at the last day?' for 'whose sake', or 'by whose merits' do you expect to enter into the glory of God, I answer, without the least hesitation, for the sake of Jesus Christ the righteous. It is through his merits alone that all believers are saved, that is, *justified,* saved from the guilt, *sanctified,* saved from the nature of sin, and *glorified,* taken into heaven.

7. It may be worth our while to spend a few more words on this important point. Is it possible to devise a more unintelligible expression than this? 'In what righteousness are we to stand before God at the last day?' Why do you not speak plain, and say, '*For whose sake* do you look to be saved?' Any plain peasant would then readily answer, 'For the sake of Jesus Christ.' But all those dark, ambiguous phrases tend only to puzzle the cause, and open a way for unwary hearers to slide into antinomianism.

8. Is there any expression similar to this of the wedding garment to be found in Holy Scripture? In the Revelation we find mention made of 'linen white and clean, which is the righteousness of the saints'. And this too many vehemently contend means the righteousness of Christ. But how then are we to reconcile this with that passage in the seventh chapter, 'They have washed their robes, and made them white in the blood of the Lamb'? Will they say, 'The righteousness of Christ was washed and made white in the blood of Christ?' Away with such antinomian jargon. Is not the plain meaning this?—it was from the atoning blood that the very righteousness of the saints derived its value and acceptableness to God.

9. In the nineteenth chapter of the Revelation, at the ninth verse, there is an expression which comes much nearer to this: 'The wedding supper of the Lamb'. There is a near resemblance between this and the supper mentioned in the parable. Yet they are not altogether the same: there is a clear difference between them. The supper mentioned in the parable belongs to the church militant, that mentioned in the Revelation to the church triumphant. The one to the kingdom of God on earth, the other to the kingdom of God in heaven. Accordingly in the former there may be found those who have not a wedding garment. But there will be none such to be found in the latter. No, not 'in that great multitude, which no man can number, out of every kindred, and tongue, and people, and nation'. They will all be 'kings and priests unto God', and 'shall reign with him for ever and ever'.

10. Does not that very expression, 'the righteousness of the saints', point out what is the wedding garment in the parable? It is the 'holiness without which no man shall see the Lord'. The righteousness of Christ is, doubtless, necessary for any soul that enters into glory. But so is personal holiness, too, for every child of man. But it is highly needful to be observed that they are necessary in different respects. The former is necessary to *entitle* us to heaven; the latter, to *qualify* us for it. Without the righteousness of Christ we could have no *claim* to glory; without holiness we could have no *fitness* for it. By the former we become members of Christ, children of God, and heirs of the kingdom of heaven. By the latter we are 'made meet to be partakers of the inheritance of the saints in light'.

11. From the very time that the Son of God delivered this weighty truth to the children of men, that all who had not the wedding garment would be cast into outward darkness, where are weeping and gnashing of teeth, the enemy of souls has been labouring to obscure it, that they might still seek death in the error of their life, and many ways has he tried to disguise the holiness without which we cannot be saved. How many things have been palmed, even upon the Christian world, in the place of this! Some of these are utterly contrary thereto, and subversive of it. Some were no ways connected with or related to it, but useless and insignificant trifles. Others might be deemed to be some part of it, but by no means the whole. It may be of use to enumerate some of them, lest ye should be ignorant of Satan's devices.

12. Of the first sort—things prescribed as Christian holiness, although flatly contrary thereto—is idolatry. How has this, in various shapes, been taught, and is to this day, as essential to holiness! How diligently is it now circulated, in a great part of the Christian church! Some of their idols are silver and gold, or wood and stone, 'graven by art and man's device'; some men of like passions with themselves, particularly the apostles of our Lord, and the Virgin Mary. To these they add numberless saints of their own creation, with no small company of angels.

13. Another thing, as directly contrary to the whole tenure of true religion, is what is diligently taught in many parts of the Christian church: I mean, the spirit of persecution; of persecuting their brethren even unto death. So that the earth has been often covered with blood by those who were called Christians, in order to 'make their calling and election sure'. It is true many, even in the Church of Rome, who were taught this horrid doctrine, now seem to be ashamed of it. But have the heads of that community as openly and explicitly renounced that capital doctrine of devils as they avowed it in the Council of Constance, and practised it for many ages? Till they have done this they will be chargeable with the blood of Jerome of Prague, basely murdered, and of many thousands, both in the sight of God and man.

14. Let it not be said: 'This does not concern us Protestants: we think and let think. We abhor the spirit of persecution, and maintain as an indisputable truth that every rational creature has a right to worship God as he is persuaded in his own mind.' But are we true to our *own* principles? So far, that we do not use fire and faggot. We do not persecute unto blood those that scruple to subscribe to our opinions. Blessed be God, the laws of our country do not allow of this. But is there no such thing to be found in England as domestic persecution? The saying or doing anything unkind to another for following his own conscience is a species of persecution. Now are we all clear of this? Is there no husband who in this sense persecutes his wife? Who uses her unkindly in word or deed for worshipping God after her own conscience? Do no parents thus persecute their children; no masters or mistresses their servants? If they do this, and think they do God service therein, they *must not cast the first stone at the Roman Catholics.*

15. When things of an *indifferent nature* are represented as necessary to salvation it is a folly of the same kind, though not of the same magnitude. Indeed it is not a little sin to represent trifles as necessary to salvation, such as going on pilgrimages, or anything that is not expressly enjoined in the Holy Scripture. Among these we may undoubtedly rank *orthodoxy*, or right opinions. We know indeed that wrong opinions in religion naturally lead to wrong tempers, or wrong practices; and that consequently it is our bounden duty to pray that we may have a right judgment in all things. But still a man may judge as accurately as the devil, and yet be as wicked as he.

16. Something more excusable are they who imagine holiness to consist in things that are only a part of it. (That is, when they are connected with the rest; otherwise they are no part of it at all.) Suppose, in doing no harm. And how exceeding common is this! How many take holiness and harmlessness to mean one and the same thing! Whereas were a man as harmless as a post he might be as far from holiness as heaven from earth. Suppose a man therefore to be exactly honest, to pay everyone his own, to cheat no man, to wrong no man, to hurt no man, to be just in all his dealings; suppose a woman to be

uniformly modest and virtuous in all her words and actions; suppose the one and the other to be steady practisers of morality, that is, of justice, mercy, and truth; yet all this, though it is good as far as it goes, is but a part of Christian holiness. Yea, suppose a person of this amiable character to do much good wherever he is, to feed the hungry, clothe the naked, relieve the stranger, the sick, the prisoner, yea, and to save many souls from death: it is possible he may still fall far short of that holiness without which he cannot see the Lord.

17. What then is that holiness which is the true wedding garment, the only qualification for glory? 'In Christ Jesus' (that is, according to the Christian institution, whatever be the case of the heathen world) 'neither circumcision availeth anything, nor uncircumcision, but a new creation,' the renewal of the soul 'in the image of God wherein it was created'. In 'Christ Jesus neither circumcision availeth anything nor uncircumcision', but 'faith which worketh by love'. It first, through the energy of God, worketh love to God and all mankind; and by this love every holy and heavenly temper. In particular, lowliness, meekness, gentleness, temperance, and long-suffering. 'It is neither circumcision', the attending on all the Christian ordinances, 'nor uncircumcision', the fulfilling of all heathen morality, but 'the keeping of the commandments of God'; particularly those, 'Thou shalt love the Lord thy God with all thy heart, and thy neighbour as thyself.' In a word, holiness is the having 'the mind that was in Christ', and the 'walking as Christ walked'.

18. Such has been my judgment for these threescore years, without any material alteration. Only about fifty years ago I had a clearer view than before of justification by faith: and in this from that very hour I never varied, no not an hair's breadth. Nevertheless an ingenious man has publicly accused me of a thousand variations. I pray God not to lay this to his charge! I am now on the borders of the grave, but by the grace of God I still witness the same confession. Indeed some have supposed that when I began to declare, 'By grace ye are saved through faith,' I retracted what I had before maintained, 'Without holiness no man shall see the Lord.' But it is an entire mistake; these Scriptures well consist with each other; the meaning of the former being plainly this, 'By faith we are saved from sin, made holy.' The imagination that faith *supersedes* holiness is the marrow of antinomianism.

19. The sum of all is this: the God of love is willing to save all the souls that he has made. This he has proclaimed to them in his Word, together with the terms of salvation revealed by the Son of his love, who gave his own life that they that believe in him might have everlasting life. And for these he has prepared a kingdom from the foundation of the world. But he will not force them to accept of it. He leaves them in the hands of their own counsel. He saith: 'Behold, I set before you life and death, blessing and cursing; choose life, that ye may live.' Choose holiness by my grace, which is the way, the only way, to everlasting life. He cries aloud, Be holy, and be happy; happy in this

world, and happy in the world to come. 'Holiness becometh his house for ever!' This is the wedding garment of all that are called to 'the marriage of the Lamb'. Clothed in this they will not be found naked: 'they have washed their robes and made them white in the blood of the Lamb.' But as to all those who appear in the last day without the wedding garment, the Judge will say: 'Cast them into outer darkness; there shall be weeping and gnashing of teeth.'

ON LIVING WITHOUT GOD

Sermon 130 – 1790

AN INTRODUCTORY COMMENT

This sermon amounts to a final reiteration of an old conviction: that the conventional disjunctions in religious epistemology, between empiricism and intuitionism, are superficial and misleading. What is distinctive here is the heightened emphasis upon intuition as a radical shift from spiritual darkness to spiritual 'sight' and, consequently, upon the importance of conversion as a prerequisite to an authentic vision of God. The anecdote of the toad with which he begins his argument sets the tone for what comes after. Wesley's source for the account was Oliver Goldsmith's *History of the Earth and Animated Nature* (1774). This story provides an alternative to the physical birth analogy for his discussion of the 'latent' spiritual senses that must be awakened in the regenerate. Wesley is here speaking to those he calls 'practical atheists', those who are 'living without God'—who have no more daily contact with God than the buried toad had with the world.

In the conclusion of his discussion, Wesley is also bold to reassert his by now familiar view of the primacy of holy living above orthodox opinions, claiming that God 'respects the goodness of the heart rather than the clearness of the head'. He is sure that holiness is a necessary prerequisite for salvation; he is not willing to make the same claim for 'clear ideas'.

The postscript indicates that this sermon was finished at 'Rotherham [Yorkshire], July 6, 1790'. The text of the sermon has no reference to events or issues that were taking up the bulk of his daily schedule at that time. Thus, we may conclude that it was still another item on Wesley's inventory of 'unfinished business'. His obvious concern was the rising influence of Enlightenment ideas about human autonomy, which he had come to regard as a mortal danger to evangelical Christianity.

No title was given this sermon when it appeared in the *Arminian Magazine* (1792). It was Joseph Benson who gave it its present title in 1812, and as usual he was followed by Thomas Jackson in 1825 and 1829.

On Living without God

Without God in the world.
Ephesians 2:12

1. Perhaps these words might be more properly translated 'atheists in the world'. This seems to be a little stronger expression than 'without God in the world', which sounds nearly negative, and does not necessarily imply any more than the having no fellowship or intercourse with God. On the contrary, the word 'atheist' is commonly understood to mean something *positive*, and not only disclaiming any intercourse with him, but denying his very being.

2. The case of these unhappy men may be much illustrated by a late incident, the truth of which cannot reasonably be doubted, there having been so large a number of eye-witnesses. An ancient oak being cut down, and split through the midst, out of the very heart of the tree crept a large toad, and walked away with all the speed he could. Now how long, may we probably imagine, had this creature continued there? It is not unlikely it might have remained in its nest above a hundred years. It is not improbable it was nearly, if not altogether, coeval with the oak; having been some way or other enclosed therein at the time that it was planted. It is not therefore unreasonable to suppose that it had lived that strange kind of life at least a century. We say, 'it had lived'! But what manner of life! How desirable! How enviable!

As Cowley says:

> O life, most precious and most dear!
> O life, that epicures would long to share!

Let us spend a few thoughts upon so uncommon a case, and make some improvement of it.

3. This poor animal had organs of sense; yet it had not any sensation. It had eyes, yet no ray of light ever entered its black abode. From the very first instant of its existence there, it was shut up in impenetrable darkness. It was shut up from the sun, moon, and stars, and from the beautiful face of nature; indeed from the whole visible world, as much as if it had no being.

4. As no air could penetrate its sable recess, it consequently could have no *hearing*. Whatever organs it was provided with, they could be of no use; seeing no undulating air could find a way through the walls that surrounded it. And there is no reason to believe that it had any sense analogous to those either of *smelling* or *tasting*. In a creature which did not need any food these could have

been of no possible use. Neither was there any way whereby the objects of smell or taste could make their approach to it. It must be very little, if at all, that it could be acquainted even with the general sense, that of *feeling*. As it always continued in one unvaried posture amidst the parts that surrounded it, all of these being immovably fixed could make no new impression upon it. So that it had only one feeling from hour to hour, and from day to day, during its whole duration.

5. And as this poor animal was destitute of *sensation*, it must have equally been destitute of *reflection*. Its head (of whatever sort it was), having no materials to work upon, no ideas of sensation of any kind, could not produce any degree of reflection. It scarce therefore could have any *memory*, or any *imagination*. Nor could it have any locative *power*, while it was so closely bound in on every side. If it had in itself some springs of motion, yet it was impossible that power should be exerted, because the narrowness of its cavern could not allow of any change of place.

6. How exact a parallel may be drawn between this creature (hardly to be called an animal) and a man that is 'without God in the world'—such as are a vast majority of even those that are called Christians! I do not mean that they are 'atheists' in the common sense of the word. I do not believe that these are so numerous as many have imagined. Making all the inquiry and observation I could for upwards of fifty years, I could not find twenty who seriously disbelieved the being of a God; nay, I have found only two of these (to the best of my judgment) in the British Islands: both of these then lived in London, and had been of this persuasion many years. But several years before they were called to appear before God, both John S— and John B— were fully convinced that there is a God, and what is more remarkable, they were first convinced that he is a terrible, and then that he is a merciful God. I mention these two accounts to show not only that there are real literal atheists in the world, but also that even then, if they will condescend to ask it, they may find 'grace to help in time of need'.

7. But I do not mean such as these when I speak of those who are 'atheists' or 'without God in the world', but of such as are only practical atheists, as have not God in all their thoughts; such as have not acquainted themselves with him, neither have any fellowship with him; such as have no more intercourse with God or the invisible world than this animal had with the visible. I will endeavour to draw the parallel between these. And may God apply it to their hearts!

8. Every one of these is in exactly such a situation with regard to the invisible as the toad was in respect to the visible world. That creature had undoubtedly a sort of life, such as it was. It certainly had all the internal and external parts that are essential to animal life. And without question it had suitable juices, which kept up a kind of circulation. This was a life indeed! And exactly such

a life is that of the atheist, the man without God in the world. What a thick veil is between him and the invisible world! Which with regard to him is as though it had no being. He has not the least perception of it; not the most distant idea. He has not the least sight of God, the intellectual Sun; nor any the least attraction toward him, or desire to have any knowledge of his ways. Although his light be gone forth into all lands, and his sound unto the end of the world, yet he *heareth* no more thereof than of the fabled music of the spheres. He *tastes* nothing of the goodness of God or the powers of the world to come. He does not *feel* (as our Church speaks) the working of the Holy Spirit in his heart. In a word, he has no more intercourse with a knowledge of the spiritual world than this poor creature had of the natural while shut up in its dark enclosure.

9. But the moment the Spirit of the Almighty strikes the heart of him that was till then without God in the world, it breaks the hardness of his heart, and creates all things new. The Sun of righteousness appears, and shines upon his soul, showing him the light of the glory of God in the face of Jesus Christ. He is in a new world. All things round him are become new. Such as it never before entered into his heart to conceive. He sees, so far as his newly opened eyes can bear the sight,

> The opening heavens around him shine,
> With beams of sacred bliss.

He sees that he has 'an advocate with the Father, Jesus Christ the righteous', and that he has 'redemption in his blood, the remission of his sins'. He sees a 'new way' that is 'opened into the holiest by the blood of Jesus'; and his 'light shineth more and more unto the perfect day'.

10. By the same gracious stroke, he that before had ears but heard not is now made capable of *hearing*. He hears the voice that raiseth the dead, the voice of him that is the resurrection and the life. He is no longer deaf to his invitations or commands, to his promises or threatenings, but gladly hears every word that proceeds out of his mouth; and governs thereby all his thoughts, words, and actions.

11. At the same time he receives other spiritual senses, capable of discerning spiritual good and evil. He is enabled to *taste*, as well as to see, how gracious the Lord is. He enters into the holiest by the blood of Jesus, and tastes of the powers of the world to come. He finds Jesus' love is far better than wine, yea sweeter than honey or the honeycomb. He knows what that meaneth, 'All thy garments smell of myrrh, aloes, and cassia.' He *feels* the love of God shed abroad in his heart by the Holy Ghost which is given unto him; or, as our Church expresses it, 'feels the workings of the Spirit of God in his heart'. Meantime it may easily be observed that the substance of all these figurative expressions is comprised in that one word 'faith', taken in its widest sense;

being enjoyed, more or less, by everyone that believes in the name of the Son of God. This change from spiritual death to spiritual life is properly the new birth; all the particulars whereof are admirably well expressed by Dr. Watts in one verse:

Renew my eyes, open my ears,
And form my soul afresh;
Give me new passions, joys and fears,
And turn the stone to flesh.

12. But before this universal change there may be many partial changes in a natural man, which are frequently mistaken for it, whereby many say, 'Peace, peace', to their soul, when there is no peace. There may be not only a considerable change in the life, so as to refrain from open sin, yea, the easily besetting sin; but also a considerable change of tempers, conviction of sin, strong desires, and good resolutions. And here we have need to take great care, not, on the one hand, to despise the day of small things, nor, on the other, to mistake any of these partial changes for that entire, general change, the new birth; that total change from the image of the earthly Adam into the image of the heavenly, from an earthly, sensual, devilish mind into the mind that was in Christ.

13. Settle it therefore in your hearts that however you may be changed in many other respects, yet in Christ Jesus, that is, according to the Christian institution, nothing will avail without the whole mind that was in Christ, enabling you to walk as Christ walked. Nothing is more sure than this: 'If any man be in Christ', a true believer in him, 'he is a new creature: old things' in him 'are passed away; all things are become new.'

14. From hence we may clearly perceive the wide difference there is between Christianity and morality. Indeed nothing can be more sure than that true Christianity cannot exist without both the inward experience and outward practice of justice, mercy, and truth; and this alone is given in morality. But it is equally certain that all morality, all the justice, mercy, and truth which can possibly exist without Christianity, profiteth nothing at all, is of no value in the sight of God, to those that are under the Christian dispensation. Let it be observed, I purposely add, 'to those that are under the Christian dispensation', because I have no authority from the Word of God 'to judge those that are without'. Nor do I conceive that any man living has a right to sentence all the heathen and Mahometan world to damnation. It is far better to leave them to him that made them, and who is 'the Father of the spirits of all flesh'; who is the God of the heathens as well as the Christians, and who hateth nothing that he hath made. But meantime this is nothing to those that name the name of Christ: all those being 'under the law', the Christian law, shall undoubtedly be judged thereby. And of consequence, unless those be so changed as was

the animal above mentioned, unless they have new senses, ideas, passions, tempers, they are no Christians! However just, true, or merciful they may be, they are but atheists still.

15. Perhaps there may be some well-meaning persons who carry this farther still; who aver that whatever change is wrought in men, whether in their hearts or lives, yet if they have not clear views of those capital doctrines, the fall of man, justification by faith, and of the atonement made by the death of Christ, and of his righteousness transferred to them, they can have no benefit from his death. I dare in no wise affirm this. Indeed I do not believe it. I believe the merciful God regards the lives and tempers of men more than their ideas. I believe he respects the goodness of the heart rather than the clearness of the head; and that if the heart of a man be filled (by the grace of God, and the power of his Spirit) with the humble, gentle, patient love of God and man, God will not cast him into everlasting fire prepared for the devil and his angels because his ideas are not clear, or because his conceptions are confused. Without holiness, I own, no man shall see the Lord; but I dare not add, or clear ideas.

16. But to return to the text. Let me entreat all of you who are still 'without God in the world' to consider with all your humanity, benevolence, virtue, you are still

Inclusi tenebris, et carcere caeco—

Enclosed in darkness and infernal shade.

My dear friends, you do not see God. You do not see the Sun of righteousness. You have no fellowship with the Father, or with his Son, Jesus Christ. You never heard the voice that raiseth the dead. Ye know not the voice of your Shepherd. Ye have not received the Holy Ghost. Ye have no spiritual senses. You have your old, natural ideas, passions, joys, and fears: you are not new creatures. O cry to God that he may rend the veil which is still upon your hearts! And which gives you occasion to complain:

O dark, dark, dark! I still must say,
Amidst the blaze of gospel day!

O that you may this day hear his voice, who speaketh as never man spake, saying, 'Arise, shine, for thy light is come, and the glory of the Lord is risen upon thee!' Is it not *his* voice that crieth aloud, 'Look unto me, and be thou saved!' He saith, Lo! I come! Even so, Lord Jesus! Come quickly!